T0178590

Lecture Notes in Computer Science 13017

More information about this subseries at http://www.springer.com/series/7412

George Bebis · Vassilis Athitsos ·
Tong Yan · Manfred Lau ·
Frederick Li · Conglei Shi ·
Xiaoru Yuan · Christos Mousas ·
Gerd Bruder (Eds.)

Advances in Visual Computing

16th International Symposium, ISVC 2021
Virtual Event, October 4–6, 2021
Proceedings, Part I

 Springer

Editors
George Bebis
University of Nevada
Reno, NV, USA

Vassilis Athitsos
University of Texas at Arlington
Arlington, TX, USA

Tong Yan
University of South Carolina
Columbia, SC, USA

Manfred Lau
City University of Hong Kong
Kowloon, Hong Kong

Frederick Li
School of Engineering and Computing
University of Durham
Durham, Durham, UK

Conglei Shi
Airbnb
New York, NY, USA

Xiaoru Yuan
Peking University
Beijing, China

Christos Mousas
Purdue University
West Lafayette, IN, USA

Gerd Bruder
IST, School of Modeling, Simulation,
and Training
Orlando, FL, USA

ISSN 0302-9743   ISSN 1611-3349 (electronic)
Lecture Notes in Computer Science
ISBN 978-3-030-90438-8   ISBN 978-3-030-90439-5 (eBook)
https://doi.org/10.1007/978-3-030-90439-5

LNCS Sublibrary: SL6 – Image Processing, Computer Vision, Pattern Recognition, and Graphics

This Springer imprint is published by the registered company Springer Nature Switzerland AG
The registered company address is: Gewerbestrasse 11, 6330 Cham, Switzerland

Preface

It is with great pleasure that we welcome you to the proceedings of the 16th International Symposium on Visual Computing (ISVC 2021), which was held virtually (October 4–6, 2021). ISVC provides a common umbrella for the four main areas of visual computing including vision, graphics, visualization, and virtual reality. The goal is to provide a forum for researchers, scientists, engineers, and practitioners throughout the world to present their latest research findings, ideas, developments, and applications in the broader area of visual computing.

This year, the program consisted of six keynote presentations, 11 oral sessions, two poster sessions, and three special tracks. We received close to 135 submissions for the main symposium from which we accepted 48 papers for oral presentation and 32 papers for poster presentation. A total of nine papers were accepted for oral presentation in the special tracks from 15 submissions.

All papers were reviewed with an emphasis on the potential to contribute to the state of the art in the field. Selection criteria included accuracy and originality of ideas, clarity and significance of results, and presentation quality. The review process was quite rigorous, involving three independent blind reviews followed by several days of discussion. During the discussion period we tried to correct anomalies and errors that might have existed in the initial reviews. Despite our efforts, we recognize that some papers worthy of inclusion may have not been included in the program. We offer our sincere apologies to authors whose contributions might have been overlooked.

We wish to thank everybody who submitted their work to ISVC 2021 for review. It was because of their contributions that we succeeded in having a technical program of high scientific quality. In particular, we would like to thank the keynote speakers, the program chairs, the steering committee, the international Program Committee, the special track organizers, the tutorial organizers, the reviewers, the sponsors, and especially, the authors who contributed their work to the symposium. We would like to express our appreciation to Springer for sponsoring the "best" paper award again this year and to Vzense for being a bronze sponsor.

Despite all the difficulties due to the pandemic, we sincerely hope that ISVC 2021 offered participants opportunities for professional growth.

September 2021

George Bebis
Vassilis Athitsos
Yan Tong
Manfred Lau
Frederick Li
Conglei Shi
Xiaoru Yuan
Christos Mousas
Gerd Bruder

Organization

Steering Committee Chair

George Bebis   University of Nevada, Reno, USA

Computer Vision Chairs

Vassilis Athitsos   University of Texas at Arlington, USA
Yan Tong   University of South Carolina, USA

Computer Graphics Chairs

Manfred Lau   City University of Hong Kong, Hong Kong
Frederick Li   Durham University, UK

Visualization Chairs

Conglei Shi   Airbnb, USA
Xiaoru Yuan   Peking University, China

Virtual Reality Chairs

Gerd Bruder   University of Central Florida, USA
Christos Mousas   Purdue University, USA

Program Committee

Emmanuel Agu   WPI, USA
Touqeer Ahmad   University of Colorado Colorado Springs, USA
Alfonso Alba   Universidad Autónoma de San Luis Potosí, Mexico
Usman Alim   University of Calgary, Canada
Amol Ambardekar   Microsoft, USA
Zahra Anvari   University of Texas at Arlington, USA
Mark Apperley   University of Waikato, New Zealand
Antonis Argyros   Foundation for Research and Technology - Hellas,
                              Greece
Vijayan K. Asari   University of Dayton, USA
Aishwarya Asesh   Adobe, USA
Vassilis Athitsos   University of Texas at Arlington, USA
Melinos Averkiou   University of Cyprus, Cyprus
George Baciu   Hong Kong Polytechnic University, Hong Kong
Abdul Bais   University of Regina, Canada

Abhishek Bajpayee   Massachusetts Institute of Technology, USA
Peter Balazs   University of Szeged, Hungary
Selim Balcisoy   Sabanci University, Turkey
Reneta Barneva   SUNY Fredonia, USA
Ronen Barzel   Independent, UK
Fereshteh S. Bashiri   University of Wisconsin-Madison, USA
Aryabrata Basu   Emory University, USA
Anil Ufuk Batmaz   Kadir Has University, Turkey
George Bebis   University of Nevada, Reno, USA
Jan Bender   RWTH Aachen University, Germany
Ayush Bhargava   Facebook, USA
Sanjiv Bhatia   University of Missouri at St. Louis, USA
Mark Billinghurst   University of South Australia, Australia
Ankur Bist   Govind Ballabh Pant University of Agriculture
                             and Technology, India
Ayan Biswas   Los Alamos National Laboratory, USA
Dibio Borges   Universidade de Braslia, Brazil
David Borland   University of North Carolina at Chapel Hill, USA
Nizar Bouguila   Concordia University, Canada
Jose Braz Pereira   EST Setúbal/IPS, Portugal
Wolfgang Broll   Ilmenau University of Technology, Germany
Gerd Bruder   University of Central Florida, USA
Tolga Capin   TED University, Turkey
Sek Chai   SRI International, USA
Jian Chang   Bournemouth University, UK
Sotirios Chatzis   Cyprus University of Technology, Cyprus
Rama Chellappa   University of Maryland, USA
Cunjian Chen   Michigan State University, USA
Yang Chen   HRL Laboratories, LLC, USA
Zhonggui Chen   Xiamen University, China
Yi-Jen Chiang   New York University, USA
Isaac Cho   Utah State University, USA
Amit Chourasia   University of California, San Diego, USA
Kichung Chung   SK Infosec, South Korea
Tommy Dang   Texas Tech University, USA
Aritra Dasgupta   New York University, USA
Jeremie Dequidt   University of Lille, France
Daljit Singh Dhillon   Clemson University, USA
Sotirios Diamantas   Tarleton State University, USA
Alexandra Diehl   University of Konstanz, Germany
John Dingliana   Trinity College Dublin, Ireland
Cosimo Distante   CNR, Italy
Ralf Doerner   RheinMain University of Applied Sciences, Germany
Anastasios Doulamis   Technical University of Crete, Greece
Shengzhi Du   Tshwane University of Technology, South Africa
Ye Duan   University of Missouri at Columbia, USA

Kresimir Matkovic	VRVis Research Center, Austria
Tim McGraw	Purdue University, USA
Tim McInerney	Ryerson University, Canada
Qurban Memon	UAE University, UAE
Daniel Mestre	Aix-Marseille University, France
Jean Meunier	University of Montreal, Canada
Xikui Miao	Brigham Young University, USA
Gabriel Mistelbauer	Otto-von-Guericke University Magdeburg, Germany
Kenneth Moreland	Oak Ridge National Laboratory, USA
Shigeo Morishima	Waseda University, Japan
Brendan Morris	University of Nevada, Las Vegas, USA
Chouaib Moujahdi	Mohammed V University in Rabat, Morocco
Christos Mousas	Purdue University, USA
Soraia Musse	Pontificia Universidade Catolica do Rio Grande do Sul, Brazil
Kawa Nazemi	Darmstadt University of Applied Sciences, Germany
Quang Vinh Nguyen	Western Sydney University, Australia
Mircea Nicolescu	University of Nevada, Reno, USA
Christophoros Nikou	University of Ioannina, Greece
Mark Nixon	University of Southampton, UK
Junyong Noh	Korea Advanced Institute of Science and Technology, South Korea
Klimis Ntalianis	University of West Attica, Greece
Scott Nykl	Air Force Institute of Technology, USA
Yoshihiro Okada	Kyushu University, Japan
Gustavo Olague	CICESE, Mexico
Masaki Oshita	Kyushu Institute of Technology, Japan
Volker Paelke	Hochschule Bremen, Germany
Kalman Palagyi	University of Szeged, Hungary
George Papagiannakis	University of Crete, Greece
George Papakostas	EMT Institute of Technology, Greece
Michael Papka	Argonne National Laboratory/Northern Illinois University, USA
Giuseppe Patanè	CNR-IMATI, Italy
Maurizio Patrignani	Roma Tre University, Italy
Shahram Payandeh	Simon Fraser University, Canada
Helio Pedrini	University of Campinas, Brazil
Jaakko Peltonen	Aalto University and University of Tampere, Finland
Euripides Petrakis	Technical University of Crete, Greece
Giuseppe Placidi	University of L'Aquila, Italy
Vijayakumar Ponnusamy	SRM Institute of Science and Technology, India
Kevin Ponto	University of Wisconsin-Madison, USA
Jiju Poovvancheri	University of Victoria, Canada
Nicolas Pronost	Université Claude Bernard Lyon 1, France
Hong Qin	Stony Brook University, Canada
Christopher Rasmussen	University of Delaware, Canada

Emma Regentova	University of Nevada, Las Vegas, USA
Guido Reina	University of Stuttgart, Germany
Erik Reinhard	InterDigitalm, France
Banafsheh Rekabdar	Southern Illinois University Carbondale, USA
Paolo Remagnino	Kingston University, UK
Hongliang Ren	National University of Singapore, Singapore
Theresa-Marie Rhyne	Independent Consultant, USA
Eraldo Ribeiro	Florida Institute of Technology, USA
Peter Rodgers	University of Kent, UK
Isaac Rudomin	BSC, Spain
Filip Sadlo	Heidelberg University, Germany
Punam Saha	University of Iowa, USA
Naohisa Sakamoto	Kobe University, Japan
Kristian Sandberg	Computational Solutions, Inc., USA
Alberto Santamaria Pang	Microsoft Health AI, USA
Nickolas S. Sapidis	University of Western Macedonia, Greece
Muhammad Sarfraz	Kuwait University. Kuwait
Fabien Scalzo	University of California, Los Angeles, USA
Jacob Scharcanski	Universidade Federal do Rio Grande do Sul, Brazil
Thomas Schultz	University of Bonn, Germany
Jurgen Schulze	University of California, San Diego, USA
Puneet Sharma	UiT-The Arctic University of Norway, Norway
Mohamed Shehata	Memorial University, Canada
Conglei Shi	Airbnb, USA
Gurjot Singh	Fairleigh Dickinson University, USA
Alexei Skurikhin	Los Alamos National Laboratory, USA
Pavel Slavik	Czech Technical University in Prague, Czech Republic
Jack Snoeyink	University of North Carolina at Chapel Hill, USA
Fabio Solari	University of Genoa, Italy
Paolo Spagnolo	CNR, Italy
Jaya Sreevalsan-Nair	IIIT Bangalore, India
Chung-Yen Su	National Taiwan Normal University, Taiwan
Changming Sun	CSIRO
Zehang Sun	Apple Inc., USA
Carlo H. Séquin	University of California, Berkeley, USA
Jules-Raymond Tapamo	Univesity of KwaZulu-Natal, South Africa
Alireza Tavakkoli	University of Nevada, Reno, USA
João Manuel R. S. Tavares	FEUP/INEGI, Portugal
Daniel Thalmann	Ecole Polytechnique Fédérale de Lausanne, Switzerland
Holger Theisel	Otto von Guericke University Magdeburg, Germany
Yuan Tian	Innopeak Tech Inc., USA
Yan Tong	University of South Carolina, USA
Thomas Torsney-Weir	VRVis, Austria
Mehmet Engin Tozal	University of Louisiana at Lafayette, USA
Stefano Tubaro	Politecnico di Milano, Italy

Georg Umlauf   Konstanz University of Applied Sciences, Germany
Daniela Ushizima   Lawrence Berkeley National Laboratory, USA
Serestina Viriri   University of KwaZulu-Natal, South Africa
Athanasios Voulodimos   University of West Attica, Greece
Chaoli Wang   University of Notre Dame, USA
Cuilan Wang   Georgia Gwinnett College, USA
Benjamin Weyers   Trier University, Germany
Thomas Wischgoll   Wright State University, USA
Kin Hong Wong   Chinese University of Hong Kong, Hong Kong
Wei Xu   Brookhaven National Laboratory, USA
Yasuyuki Yanagida   Meijo University, Japan
Fumeng Yang   Brown University, USA
Xiaosong Yang   Bournemouth University, UK
Hsu-Chun Yen   National Taiwan University, Taiwan
Lijun Yin   State University of New York at Binghamton, USA
Zeyun Yu   University of Wisconsin-Milwaukee, USA
Chunrong Yuan   Technische Hochschule Köln, Germany
Xiaoru Yuan   Peking University, China
Xenophon Zabulis   FORTH, Greece
Jiri Zara   Czech Technical University in Prague, Czech Republic
Wei Zeng   Florida International University, USA
Jian Zhao   University of Waterloo, Canada
Ying Zhu   Georgia State University, USA

Steering Committee

George Bebis   University of Nevada, Reno (chair)
Sabine Coquillart   Inria
James Klosowski   AT&T Labs Research
Yoshinori Kuno   Saitama University
Steve Lin   Microsoft
Peter Lindstrom   Lawrence Livermore National Laboratory
Kenneth Moreland   Sandia National Laboratories
Ara Nefian   NASA Ames Research Center
Ahmad P. Tafti   Mayo Clinic

Publicity

Ali Erol   Eksperta Software

Tutorials and Special Tracks

Emily Hand   University of Nevada, Reno
Alireza Tavakkoli   University of Nevada, Reno

Awards

Zehang Sun   Apple
Gholamreza Amayeh   Tesla

Web Master

Isayas Berhe Adhanom   University of Nevada, Reno

International Program Committee

Agu Emmanuel   WPI
Ahmad Touqeer   University of Colorado Colorado Springs
Alba Alfonso   Universidad Autónoma de San Luis Potosí
Alim Usman   University of Calgary
Ambardekar Amol   Microsoft
Anvari Zahra   University of Texas at Arlington
Apperley Mark   University of Waikato
Argyros Antonis   Foundation for Research and Technology - Hellas
Asari Vijayan K   University of Dayton
Asesh Aishwarya   Adobe
Averkiou Melinos   University of Cyprus
Baciu George   Hong Kong Polytechnic University
Bais Abdul   University of Regina
Bajpayee Abhishek   Massachusetts Institute of Technology
Balazs Peter   University of Szeged
Balcisoy Selim   Sabanci University
Barneva Reneta   SUNY Fredonia
Barzel Ronen   Independent
Bashiri Fereshteh S.   UW-Madison
Basu Aryabrata   Emory University
Batmaz Anil Ufuk   Kadir Has University
Bender Jan   RWTH Aachen University
Bhargava Ayush   Key Lime Interactive
Bhatia Sanjiv   University of Missouri at St. Louis
Billinghurst Mark   University of South Australia
Bist Ankur   Govind Ballabh Pant University of Agri. and Tech.
Biswas Ayan   Los Alamos National Laboratory
Borges Dibio   Universidade de Braslia
Borland David   University of North Carolina at Chapel Hill
Bouguila Nizar   Concordia University
Braz Pereira Jose   EST Setúbal/IPS
Broll Wolfgang   Ilmenau University of Technology
Capin Tolga   TED University
Chai Sek   SRI International
Chang Jian   Bournemouth University

Chatzis Sotirios	Cyprus University of Technology
Chellappa Rama	University of Maryland
Chen Yang	HRL Laboratories, LLC
Chen Cunjian	Michigan State University
Chen Zhonggui	Xiamen University
Chiang Yi-Jen	New York University
Cho Isaac	Utah State University
Chourasia Amit	San Diego Supercomputer Center, UCSD
Chung Kichung	SK Infosec
Dang Tommy	Texas Tech University
Dasgupta Aritra	NYU
Dequidt Jeremie	University of Lille
Dhillon Daljit Singh	Clemson University
Diamantas Sotirios	Tarleton State University, Texas A&M System
Diehl Alexandra	University of Konstanz
Dingliana John	Trinity College Dublin
Distante Cosimo	CNR
Doerner Ralf	RheinMain University of Applied Sciences
Doulamis Anastasios	Technical University of Crete
Du Shengzhi	Tshwane University of Technology
Duan Ye	University of Missouri at Columbia
Dutta Soumya	Los Alamos National Laboratory
Ebert Achim	University of Kaiserslautern
El Ansari Mohamed	University of Ibn Zohr
El-Alfy El-Sayed M.	King Fahd University of Petroleum and Minerals
Ens Barrett	Monash University
Entezari Alireza	University of Florida
Erol Ali	Sigun Information Technologies
Ertl Thomas	University of Stuttgart
Eslami Mohammad	Technical University of Munich
Fernandez Amanda	University of Texas at San Antonio
Ferrara Matteo	University of Bologna
Ferreira Nivan	Universidade Federal de Pernambuco
Ferrise Francesco	Politecnico di Milano
Fierrez Julian	Universidad Autonoma de Madrid
Fisher Robert	The University of Edinburgh
Foresti Gian Luca	University of Udine
Frey Steffen	University of Groningen
Fudos Ioannis	University of Ioannina
Fujishiro Issei	Keio University
Fusek Radovan	VŠB-Technical University of Ostrava
Ganovelli Fabio	ISTI-CNR
Gao Xifeng	Florida State University
Gavrilova M.	University of Calgary
Gdawiec Krzysztof	University of Silesia
Geist Robert	Clemson University

Giorgi Daniela	ISTI - CNR
Goh Wooi-Boon	Nanyang Technological University
Grosso Roberto	Friedrich-Alexander-Universität Erlangen-Nürnberg
Guo Hanqi	Argonne National Laboratory
Gustafson David	Kansas State University
Hamza-Lup Felix	Georgia Southern University
Hand Emily	University of Nevada, Reno
Hao Xuejun	Columbia University
Haworth Brandon	University of Victoria
Hazarika Subhashis	Los Alamos National Laboratory
Hodgson Eric	Miami University
Holmberg Bahnsen	ChrisAalborg University
Hua Jing	Wayne State University
Hussain Muhammad	King Saud University
Iglesias Guitián	José A.University of A Coruña
Imiya Atsushi	IMIT Chiba University
Iwasaki Kei	Wakayama University
Jang Yun	Sejong University
Jenkin Michael	York University
Jeschke Stefan	NVIDIA
Jiang Ming	LLNL
Jung Sungchul	HIT Lab NZ
Kam Ho Chuen	The Chinese University of Hong Kong
Kamberov George	University of Alaska Anchorage
Kamberova Gerda	Hofstra University
Kampel Martin	Vienna University of Technology
Kanai Takashi	The University of Tokyo
Khadka Rajiv	Idaho National Laboratory
Khan Waqar	Wellington Institute of Technology
Kim Edward	Drexel University
Kim Hyungseok	Konkuk University
Kim Min H.	Korea Advanced Inst of Science and Technology
Klosowski James	AT&T Labs Research
Kollias Stefanos	National Technical University of Athens
Komuro Takashi	Saitama University
Krueger Jens	University of Duisburg-Essen
Kuijper Arjan	TU Darmstadt
Kuno Yoshinori	Saitama University
La Hung	University of Nevada
Lai Yu-Kun	Cardiff University
Laramee Robert S.	University of Nottingham
Lee D. J.	Brigham Young University
Lewis Robert R.	Washington State University
Li Xin	Louisiana State University
Li Frederick	University of Durham
Lien Kuo-Chin	XMotors.ai

Lin Stephen	Microsoft
Lindstrom Peter	LLNL
Liu Zhanping	Old Dominion University
Liu Shiguang	Tianjin University
Loaiza Manuel	Universidad Católica San Pablo
Loss Leandro	QuantaVerse, ITU, ESSCA
Loviscach Joern	University of Applied Sciences
Lu Aidong	UNC Charlotte
Luo Xun	Tianjin University of Technology
Macdonald Brendan	NIOSH
Makrogiannis Sokratis	Delaware State University
Malomo Luigi	ISTI - CNR
Management Cultural	University of Patras
Mansoor Hamid	Worcester Polytechnic Institute
Martins Rafael M.	Linnaeus University, Växjö
Masutani Yoshitaka	Hiroshima City University
Mathews Sherin	University of Delaware
Matkovic Kresimir	VRVis Research Center
Mcgraw Tim	Purdue University
McInerney Tim	Ryerson University
Memon Qurban	UAE University
Mestre Daniel	Aix-Marseille University
Meunier Jean	University of Montreal
Miao Xikui	Brigham Young University
Mistelbauer Gabriel	Otto-von-Guericke University Magdeburg
Moreland Kenneth	Sandia National Laboratories
Morishima Shigeo	Waseda University
Morris Brendan	University of Nevada, Las Vegas
Moujahdi Chouaib	Mohammed V University in Rabat
Musse Soraia	Pontificia Univ Catolica do Roi Grande do Sul
Nazemi Kawa	Darmstadt University of Applied Sciences
Nguyen Quang Vinh	Western Sydney University
Nicolescu Mircea	University of Nevada, Reno
Nikou Christophoros	University of Ioannina, Ioannina
Nixon Mark	University of Southampton
Noh Junyong	Korea Advanced Inst of Science and Technology
Ntalianis Klimis	University of West Attica
Nykl Scott	Air Force Institute of Technology
Okada Yoshihiro	Kyushu University
Olague Gustavo	CICESE
Oshita Masaki	Kyushu Institute of Technology
Paelke Volker	Hochschule Bremen
Palagyi Kalman	University of Szeged
Papagiannakis George	University of Crete
Papakostas George	EMT Institute of Technology

Papka Michael	Argonne National Laboratory and Northern Illinois University
Patanè Giuseppe	CNR-IMATI
Patrignani Maurizio	Roma Tre University
Payandeh Shahram	Simon Fraser University
Pedrini Helio	University of Campinas
Peltonen Jaakko	Aalto University and University of Tampere
Petrakis Euripides	Technical University of Crete
Placidi Giuseppe	University of L'Aquila
Ponnusamy Vijayakumar	SRM university
Ponto Kevin	University of Wisconsin-Madison
Poovvancheri Jiju	University of Victoria
Pronost Nicolas	Université Claude Bernard Lyon 1
Qin Hong	Stony Brook University
Rasmussen Christopher	University of Delaware
Regentova Emma	UNLV
Reina Guido	University of Stuttgart
Reinhard Erik	InterDigital
Rekabdar Banafsheh	Southern Illinois University Carbondale
Remagnino Paolo	Kingston University
Ren Hongliang	National University of Singapore
Rhyne Theresa-Marie	Consultant
Ribeiro Eraldo	Florida Institute of Technology
Rodgers Peter	University of Kent
Rudomin Isaac	BSC
Sadlo Filip	Heidelberg University
Saha Punam	University of Iowa
Sakamoto Naohisa	Kobe University
Sandberg Kristian	Computational Solutions, Inc.
Santamaria Pang Alberto	General Electric Research
Sapidis Nickolas S.	University of Western Macedonia
Sarfraz Muhammad	Kuwait University
Scalzo Fabien	University of California, Los Angeles
Scharcanski Jacob	UFRGS
Schultz Thomas	University of Bonn
Schulze Jurgen	University of California San Diego
Séquin Carlo H.	University of California, Berkeley
Sharma Puneet	UiT-The Arctic University of Norway
Shehata Mohamed	Memorial University
Singh Gurjot	Fairleigh Dickinson University
Singh Gurjot	Fairleigh Dickinson University
Skurikhin Alexei	Los Alamos National Laboratory
Slavik Pavel	Czech Technical University
Snoeyink Jack	The University of North Carolina at Chapel Hill
Solari Fabio	University of Genoa - DIBRIS
Spagnolo Paolo	National Research Council

Sreevalsan-Nair Jaya	IIIT Bangalore
Su Chung-Yen	National Taiwan Normal University
Sun Zehang	Apple inc.
Sun Changming	CSIRO
Tapamo Jules-Raymond	Univesity of KwaZulu-Natal
Tavakkoli Alireza	University of Nevada, Reno
Tavares João Manuel R. S.	FEUP & INEGI
Thalmann Daniel	Ecole Polytechnique Fédérale de Lausanne
Theisel Holger	Otto-von-Guericke University
Tian Yuan	Innopeak Tech Inc
Torsney-Weir Thomas	VRVis
Tozal Mehmet Engin	University of Louisiana at Lafayette
Tubaro Stefano	Politecnico di Milano
Umlauf Georg	Universityof Applied Science Constance
Ushizima Daniela	Lawrence Berkeley National Laboratory
Viriri Serestina	University of KwaZulu-Natal
Voulodimos Athanasios	University of West Attica
Wang Cuilan	Georgia Gwinnett College
Wang Chaoli	University of Notre Dame
Weyers Benjamin	Trier University
Wischgoll Thomas	Wright State University
Wong Kin Hong	The Chinese University of Hong Kong
Xu Wei	Brookhaven National Lab
Yanagida Yasuyuki	Meijo University
Yang Xiaosong	Bournemouth University
Yang Fumeng	Brown University
Yen Hsu-Chun	National Taiwan University
Yin Lijun	State University of New York at Binghamton
Yu Zeyun	University of Wisconsin-Milwaukee
Yuan Chunrong	Technische Hochschule Köln
Zabulis Xenophon	FORTH
Zara Jiri	Czech Technical University in Prague
Zeng Wei	Florida International University
Zhao Jian	University of Waterloo
Zhu Ying	Georgia State University

Keynote Talks

Embodied Perception in-the-Wild

Deva Ramanan

Carnegie-Mellon University, USA

Abstract. Computer vision is undergoing a period of rapid progress, rekindling the relationship between perception, action, and cognition. Such connections may be best practically explored in the context of autonomous robotics. In this talk, I will discuss perceptual understanding tasks motivated by embodied "in-the-wild" autonomous robots, focusing on the illustrative case of autonomous vehicles. I will argue that many challenges that surface are not well-explored in contemporary computer vision. These include streaming perception with bounded resources, generalization via spatiotemporal grouping, rethinking the interface between perception and action, and robust processing that can recognize anomalous out-of-sample events. I will conclude with a description of open challenges for embodied perception in-the-wild.

Design Tools for Material Appearance

Holly Rushmeier

Yale University, USA

Abstract. The design of material appearance for both virtual and physical design remains a challenging problem. There aren't straightforward intuitive techniques as there are in geometric design where shapes can be sketched or assembled from geometric primitives. In this talk I will present a series of contributions to developing intuitive appearance design tools. This includes studies of material appearance perception which form the basis of the development of perceptual axes for reflectance distribution design. I will also present novel interfaces for design including hybrid slider/image navigation and augmented reality interfaces. I will discuss the unique problems involved in designing appearance for objects to be physically manufactured rather than simply displayed in virtual environments. Finally, I will show how exemplars of spatially varying materials can be inverted to produce procedural models.

Guidance-Enriched Visual Analytics: Challenges and Opportunities

Silvia Miksch

TU Wien, Austria

Abstract. On the one hand, we investigate appropriate, expressive, and effective Visual Analytics concepts and solutions for particular users, their data, and their tasks in mind. On the other hand, we explore the usage and potential of guidance. Guidance aims to support the user while working with Visual Analytics solutions. Guidance assists users with the selection of appropriate visual means and interaction techniques, the utilization of analytical methods, as well as the configuration instantiation of these algorithms with suitable parameter settings and the combinations thereof. After a visualization or Visual Analytics method and parameters are selected, guidance is also needed to explore the data, identify interesting data nuggets and findings, collect and group insights to explore high level hypotheses, and gain new insights and knowledge. In this talk, I will contextualize the different aspects of guidance-enriched Visual Analytics. I will present a framework for guidance designers which comprising requirements, a set of specific phases with quality criteria designers should go through when designing guidance-enriched Visual Analytics. Various examples will illustrate what has been achieved so far and show possible future directions and challenges.

Learning and Accruing Knowledge over Time Using Modular Architectures

Marc'Aurelio Ranzato

Facebook AI Research, USA

Abstract. A typical trait of any intelligent system is the ability to learn new skills quickly without too many interactions with a teacher. Over time we also would expect an intelligent system to become better at solving new tasks, coming up with a better solution in even less time if the new task relates to something already learned in the past. While nowadays machine learning methods excel at learning a single task from large amounts of labeled data, and more recently, even from little labeled data provided suitable pretraining on a vast amount of unlabeled data, knowledge is seldom accrued over time. Whenever more data and compute are available, bigger models are often retrained from scratch. In this talk, I argue that by considering the sequence of learning tasks, and more generally, the sequential nature of the data acquisition process, we may grant our artificial learners an unprecedented opportunity to transfer knowledge and even accrue knowledge over time, potentially leading to more efficient and effective learning of future tasks. From the modeling side, I will introduce a few variants of hierarchical mixtures of experts, which are deep modular networks. These architectures are appealing for a twofold reason. First, since they are modular it is natural to add modules over time to accommodate the acquisition of new knowledge. The modularity also leads to computational efficiency since run time can be made constant with respect to the number of modules. Second, by recombining modules in novel ways compositional generalization emerges, yielding learners that learn faster as time goes by. I will demonstrate these ideas on several learning settings applied to vision, namely compositional 0-shot learning, continual learning and anytime learning. Although these are admittedly baby steps towards our grand goal, I believe there is an untapped potential for more effective and efficient learning once we frame learning as a life-long learning experience.

Combining Brain-Computer Interfaces and Virtual Reality: Novel 3D Interactions and Promising Applications

Anatole Lécuyer

Inria, France

Abstract. In this talk I will present a research path on Brain-Computer Interfaces (BCI) aiming to establish a solid connection with Virtual Reality (VR) and Augmented Reality (AR). I will first evoke the great success of OpenViBE, an open-source software platform dedicated to BCI research used today all over the world, notably with VR systems. Then, I will illustrate how BCI and VR/AR technologies can be combined to design novel 3D interactions and effective applications, e.g. for health, sport, entertainment, or training.

Direct Estimation of Appearance Models for Image Segmentation

Pedro Felzenszwalb

Brown University, USA

Abstract. Image segmentation algorithms often depend on appearance models that characterize the distribution of pixel values in different image regions. We describe a novel approach for estimating appearance models directly from an image, without explicit consideration of the pixels that make up each region. Our approach is based on algebraic expressions that relate local image statistics to the appearance models of spatially coherent regions. The approach leads to two different algorithms for estimating appearance models. We present experimental results that demonstrate the proposed methods work well in practice and lead to effective image segmentation algorithms.

Contents – Part I

Applications

Deep Learning II

Computer Graphics II

3D Vision

Virtual Reality

Motion and Tracking

Object Detection and Recognition

Contents – Part II

Poster

Deep Learning I

Real-World Thermal Image Super-Resolution

Moaaz Allahham[1]([✉])[iD], Andreas Aakerberg[1][iD], Kamal Nasrollahi[1,2][iD], and Thomas B. Moeslund[1][iD]

[1] Visual Analysis and Perception Laboratory, Aalborg University, Aalborg, Denmark
[2] Research Department, Milestone Systems A/S, Milestone Systems, Brøndby, Denmark
{anaa,kn,tbm}@create.aau.dk

Abstract. Thermal cameras are used in various domains where the vision of RGB cameras is limited. Thermographic imaging enables the visualizations of objects beyond the visible range, which enables its use in many applications like autonomous cars, nightly footage, military, or surveillance. However, the high cost of manufacturing this type of camera limits the spatial resolution that it can provide. Real-World Super-Resolution (RWSR) is a topic that can be used to solve this problem by using image processing techniques that enhance the quality of a real-world image by reconstructing lost high-frequency information. This work adapts an existing RWSR framework that is designed to super-resolve real-world RGB images. This framework estimates the degradation parameters needed to generate realistic Low-resolution (LR) and High-resolution (HR) image pairs, then the SR model learns the mapping between the LR and HR domains using the constructed image pairs and applies this mapping to new LR thermal images. The experiments results show a clear improvement in the perceptual quality in terms of clarity and sharpness, which surpasses the performance of the current SotA method for thermal image SR.

Keywords: Thermal imaging · Super-resolution · Image registration

1 Introduction

In recent years, thermal imaging has grown considerably and is being used in various domains where a typical RGB camera can not get the job done, like nightly footage, surveillance, or in autonomous cars. However, thermal images generally have some shortcomings like insufficient details and blurred edges, and most importantly considerably low-resolution. This makes it too hard to observe the structure and recognize objects in an image. However, having a thermal camera that is capable of capturing high-resolution images is not as affordable as using RGB cameras. Even the most expensive thermal cameras, which can vary from US$200 to more than US$20,000 [20], still can not deliver sufficient resolutions. To the best of our knowledge, the highest resolution that a thermal camera can

G. Bebis et al. (Eds.): ISVC 2021, LNCS 13017, pp. 3–14, 2021.
https://doi.org/10.1007/978-3-030-90439-5_1

provide as for today is 1920 × 1200 pixels for the Vayu HD [24], thus enhancing real images captured by thermal cameras is therefore important. However, although increasing the resolution of a thermal image with an image processing algorithm would not compensate for the true information that is not captured by the camera's sensor, having an enhanced and higher resolution image makes it easier to recognize objects and structure in an image. The efficiency of this process can be improved by taking advantage of computer vision techniques that can assist in enhancing these images. Many methods were developed to perform image super-resolution, however, most of these methods perform poorly when used on real LR images. This is because they follow the approach of downsampling HR images to construct LR and HR pairs and then they super-resolve the LR image back to match the HR image quality. Such methods fail when given a real-world image as the degradation process is not entirely known. Therefore recent studies have been working on developing methods that would be more robust to previously unseen real-world images that are acquired directly from cameras with unknown degradation parameters. This RWSR issue also applies to the thermal imaging domain, making it an interesting area to investigate since it has not been widely explored. Hence, the goal of this project was to explore the state-of-the-Art (SotA) SR algorithms that deal with RGB images and investigate its usability in the thermal imaging domain, and explore the possibility of tuning these methods to fit the thermal domain. The main contributions of this work are:

- A comparison of the performance of existing RGB-based RWSR solutions in the thermal imaging domain.
- SotA results within the real-world thermal SR domain are achieved.

2   Related Work

2.1   RGB Image Super-Resolution

Zero-Shot Methods. In 2017, ZSSR [23] was introduced as the first blind SR algorithm (self-learning-based) that performed SR on LR real-world images without relying on any prior image examples or prior training. Instead, ZSSR trains an image-specific CNN using the recurrence of small patches across different scales within the same image at test time. This was done by downscaling the test image to smaller versions of itself, then applying data-augmentation to the smaller versions to fulfill the need of having multiple examples as a training dataset. The image-specific CNN learns to reconstruct the original LR image using the downscaled examples, then they finally apply the trained CNN to the original test image to construct the desired HR output. ZSSR outperformed external-based SotA methods in some regions when tested on images with salient recurrence of information. A drawback of ZSSR is the fact that the learning process fully depends on the internal information in the test image, which makes it require thousands of back-propagation gradient updates. This yields slow testing time as well as poor results in some regions compared to other external-based methods [26]. Inspired from ZSSR, Meta-Transfer Learning for Zero-Shot Super-Resolution (MZSR) [26] was introduced, where the authors of MZSR utilize the powerful parts of ZSSR and improve upon it by introducing the concept of Meta-Transfer learning. The idea behind how meta-learning works is to make the model adapt fast to new blur kernel scenarios by adding a meta-training step, then utilize transfer-learning by pre-training the SR network using a large-scale dataset DIV2K [1]. The combination of Meta-transfer learning and ZSSR exploits both the internal (the test image) and external (the DIV2k) information. The main advantage that was introduced in the MZSR work, was the flexibility and fast running time compared to the ZSSR method, as well as outperforming other supervised SotA algorithms such as CARN [2] and RCAN [28]. Different zero-shot methods were designed following the ZSSR principle, however the most recent study that was able to achieve competetive SotA results was Dual Super-resolution (DualSR) [8]. DualSR addresses the RWSR problem in a similar way to the way it was addressed in the ZSSR work, where they learn the image-specific LR-HR relations by training their proposed network at the test time using patches extracted from the test image. Their proposed network is split into mainly two parts, the downsampler which learns the degradation process using a generative adversarial network (GAN), and an upsampler that learns to super-resolve the LR image. Both the up-sampler and down-sampler are trained simultaneously by improving each other using the cycle-consistency loss, the masked interpolation loss, and the adversarial loss.

Learned Degradation Based Super-Resolution. Many supervised SR approaches make the assumption that LR images are a bicubicly downscaled version of their HR counterpart, and that Gaussian noise is usually used to simulate the sensor noise. However, these approaches fail when tested on real images because those images were not degraded using ideal degradation operation (bicubic kernel + Gaussian noise). For this reason, Fritsche et al. [9] introduced DSGAN (the winner of AIM2019 RWSR challenge [17]), which is a GAN network that learns to generate the appropriate LR images, which have the same corruptions as the original HR images. Bell-Kligler et al. [3] introduced another realistic degradation method KernelGAN, an image-specific Internal-GAN, which trains solely on the LR test image at test time and learns its internal distribution of patches. The generator of the network is trained to produce a lower resolution image such that the network's discriminator can not distinguish between the patch distribution of the generated image and the patch distribution of the original LR image. Ji et al. [11] proposed their method RealSR, which is divided into two stages. They first use KernelGAN to estimate the degradation from the real data and use it to construct the LR images, and then they train an SR model based on the constructed data. RealSR method was the winner of the NTIRE 2020 challenge [17], and by the time of doing this work, RealSR is considered to be the SotA in the real-world super-resolution field for RGB images.

2.2   Thermal Image Super-Resolution

All the methods mentioned in 2.1 are examples of super-resolution methods that deal with images in the RGB spectrum. However, there are only a few studies that developed methods for super-resolving LR thermal images. Cho et al. [4] conducted a study where they tried to enhance thermal images by training a CNN using different image spectrums aiming to find the best representation that would fit the thermal domain. They found that a grayscale trained network provided the best enhancement. Lee et al. [14] proposed a similar CNN-based on enhancement for thermal images, where they evaluated four RGB-based domains with a residual-learning technique. That improved the enhancement in comparison to the previous work by [4]. Rivadeneira et al. [5] was motivated by the two previously proposed methods, so he proposed the Thermal Enhancement Network (TEN), which was the first CNN-based method to be trained specifically using thermal dataset unlike the two previous proposals by [4,14]. TEN was based on the SRCNN model [7], which utilizes the residual net and dense connections technique. TEN was able to outperform the previously proposed methods, which was due to training the network using thermal images instead of RGB-based domains. Recently, Rivadeneira et al. [20] proposed another thermal SR method that is based on the well-known CycleGAN [29] architecture. Two-way Generative-Adversarial-network (CycleGAN) is a technique that is used to map information from one domain to another. So the authors of [20] used the CycleGAN network to map information from the LR domain to the HR domain. They trained their proposed network to perform x2 scale SR following two scenarios, LR to medium-resolution (MR) and MR to HR. Chudasama et al. [6] proposed TherISuRNet, which is another method to super-resolve thermal images by progressively upscaling the LR test image to obtain the final SR image. They achieve different upscaling factors (x2, x3, and x4) by applying residual learning. The TherISuRNet network consists of four main modules: low-frequency feature extraction modules, high-frequency feature extraction modules, second high-frequency feature extraction modules, and finally an image reconstruction module that is responsible for reconstructing the final SR image. They measured the performance of their proposed method by comparing its performance to the most common SotA methods [5,15,16,18,28] and bicubic interpolation, and they were able to surpass all the other methods when testing on thermal images. TherISuRNet was the winning method of the Thermal Image Super-Resolution Challenge PBVS 2020 [19], which makes the TherISuRNet the SotA method for the thermal image SR domain.

Constraints Noted from Related Works. Having reviewed the relevant literature on super-resolution applied to both RGB and thermal images, we witness that, to the best of our knowledge:

- None of the studies try to investigate the performance of RGB-based SR methods in the thermal domain.
- All the existing thermal SR methods were trained using synthetically constructed image pairs.

3   Dataset

One of the challenges when working with RWSR methods is the lack of ground truth data that could be used for supervised learning and to evaluate the performance of the SR methods leading to unreliable performance when testing on single real world images. For this work, the PBVS dataset [19,20] was used as it offers three subsets called *Domo, Axis* and *GT* with different native resolutions (160×120, 320×240, 640×512, respectively), which were acquired using three different cameras. For this work, the Domo and GT subsets are used as the source and target domains respectively. Each of these subsets includes a total of 951 training images and 50 images for validation. The Axis subset was discarded since the goal of this work was to super-resolve a given resolution with an upscaling factor of $s = 4$ and later evaluate the performance by comparing it to the ground-truth, which has a native resolution that matches the SR output images. Therefore, it was decided to super-resolve the input images (Domo validation subset) and compare the output with the ground truth (GT validation subset). However, one of the problems with the PBVS dataset is the limited number of images in each subset, which is considered too little to be used for training a neural network. Therefore, we used the augmented version of the PBVS dataset, which was provided by the authors of the TherISuRNet [6]. The augmentation operations they apply on the original dataset are horizontal flipping, 180° rotation, and two affine operations, resulting in a total of 4755 training images for each subset.

4   Thermal RealSR

This section describes the two-step pipeline that T-RealSR uses to achieve the final SR results. The first step aims to realistically degrade the HR from the target domain Y, such that the degraded images have the same image characteristics as the LR images in the source domain X. The second step is to use the LR-HR image pairs to train a SR model that can be used to super-resolve real-world thermal images.

4.1   Realistic Degradation Using KernelGAN and Noise Injection

To understand how we can construct a realistic LR image that does not have ideal blurring and noise characteristics, let's assume an LR image is obtained following the degradation operation [11]:

$$I_{LR} = (I_{HR} * k) \downarrow_s + n \tag{1}$$

Where k denotes the kernel used to blur the image, n denotes the noise added to the image, and s denotes the downscaling factor. Instead of using ideal kernels (e.g. Bicubic downscaling), T-RealSR explicitly utilizes KernelGAN to create a pool of kernels, and it extract noise patches from a real LR images to create a noise patches pool. Then both these pools are used to construct the realistic LR-HR image pairs.

Kernel Degradation. In general, KernelGAN is an image-specific Internal-GAN [22] that trains solely on a given LR image at test time and learns its internal distribution of patches. Its generator (G) is trained to generate a down-scaled version of the given image, such that its discriminator (D) can not distinguish between the patch-distribution of the generated image and the patch distribution of the original image. D is trained to output a heat map, referred to as *D-map*, indicating for each pixel how likely is its surrounding patch to be drawn from the original patch-distribution. The loss is the pixel-wise MSE difference between the output *D-map* and the label map. Where the label map is all the ones in the crops extracted from the original image, and all the zeros in the crops extracted from the downscaled image [3].

Noise Extraction. In addition to creating the kernel pool, T-RealSR introduces a simple filtering rule for extracting noise patches from source images. The idea behind extracting these noise patches is to inject them into the degraded images, so LR images from the two different domains (source LR and generated LR images) will have similar noise distribution. The filtering rule used to choose the relevant noise patch is as follows:

$$\sigma(n_i) < v \tag{2}$$

Where $\sigma(\cdot)$ denotes the function used to calculate the noise variance, and v is the max value of variance.

Having created a series of kernels $\{k1, k2, \ldots, kl\}$ and a series of noise patches $\{n1, n2 \cdots n_m\}$, the degradation process is performed as follows:

$$I_{LR} = (I_{HR} * k_i) \downarrow_s + n_j, i \in 1, 2, \ldots, l, j \in 1, 2, \ldots, m \tag{3}$$

Where s denotes the sampling stride.

4.2   Super-Resolution Model

As mentioned in Sect. 2.1, T-RealSR consists of two phases, the first is constructing the realistic image pairs using KernelGAN and the second phase is training the SR model, which is based on ESRGAN with some modification. To understand the T-RealSR SR backbone, we need to first understand how ESRGAN works and then understand how T-RealSR adjust the ESRGAN architecture to make it more flexible to different image sizes. ESRGAN [27] stands for Enhanced Super-Resolution Generative Adversarial Networks, which is a generative adversarial network that is based on SRGAN [13]. SRGAN is a GAN network that is capable of generating realistic textures during single-image SR, whose discriminator aims to base its prediction on perceptual quality. However, ESRGAN improves SRGAN by adjusting the SRGAN architecture where they introduce their Residual-in-Residual Dense Block (RRDB) without batch normalization, as well as improving the SRGAN discriminator by making it judge whether an image is more realistic than another rather than judging whether an image is real or fake. ESRGAN improvement over SRGAN resulted in sharper and more visually pleasing results [27].

From the name Enhanced Super-Resolution GAN, we can tell that the architecture should contain the two main modules, discriminator D and generator G networks. The G network takes a low-resolution image (LR) as input, and it passes it through a 2D convolutional layer (Conv1) with small 3×3 kernels and 64 feature maps. It is then passed through 23 Residual in Residual Dense Blocks (RRDB). The image is then passed through another convolutional layer (Conv2) in which its output is summed with the output of the first (Conv1). At this stage, the image gets upscaled with a factor of 4 by passing it through an upsampling block that consists of two convolutional layers for reconstruction, with LeakyReLU (LReLU) activation ($\alpha = 0.2$) on each layer. After upsampling, the image is passed through another convolutional layer (Conv3) with LReLU activation ($\alpha = 0.2$). Finally, the image is passed through the final convolutional layer (Conv4) that final super-resolved image. The other part of the network is the discriminator D, and to be more specific it is called the Relativistic Discriminator [12]. Following [27] this specific discriminator was used rather than using the standard discriminator used in SRGAN [13]. This is because the relativistic discriminator estimates the probability that a real image x_r is relatively more realistic than a fake one x_f. Where a standard discriminator estimates only whether an image x is natural enough to be real.

We adapted the ESRGAN structure and trained it using the constructed paired data $\{I_{LR}, I_{HR}\}$. Several losses were used during the training including:

- **Pixel loss L_1**: or so called Mean Absolute Error (MAE), which measures the mean absolute pixel difference of all pixels in two given images.
- **Perceptual loss L_{per}**: proposed to enhance the visual quality by minimizing the error in feature space instead of pixel space. It uses the inactive features of VGG-19 [25] and aims to enhance the visual quality of low-frequency information like edges.
- **Adversarial loss L_{adv}** This loss is used to enhance the texture details to make the image look more realistic.

The final loss function was the weighted sum of all the above losses as follows:

$$L_{total} = \lambda_1 L_1 + \lambda_{per} L_{per} + \lambda_{adv} L_{adv} \qquad (4)$$

where λ_1, λ_{per}, and λ_{adv} are constants used to specify the weight of each of the losses on the total loss.

PatchGAN Discriminator. The discriminator (VGG-128) used in the ESRGAN may introduce many artefacts, so PatchGAN [10] was used instead for two reasons: First is that VGG-128 used by ESRGAN limits the size of the generated image to 128, making multi-scaling training not as simple, Second is that the VGG-128 fixed fully connected layer makes the discriminator pays more attention to the global features and ignore the local ones. Where the PatchGAN has a fully convolutional structure that maintains a fixed receptive field that restricts the discriminator's attention to the local image patches. The structure of Patch-GAN only penalizes structure at the scale of patches, meaning that it tries to classify if each $N \times N$ patch in an image is real or fake. The responses of all patches get averaged afterward forming the final D output to guarantee global consistency, then gets fed back to the generator.

5   Experiments and Results

5.1   Evaluation Metrics

Usually, the most challenging part when dealing with RWSR images is the lack of GT reference images. However, despite having the GT images, which the PBVS dataset provides, the SR and GT images are not perfectly aligned together. Making it difficult to use reference-based IQA methods such as SSIM, PSNR, or LPIPS, however we still use them for reference purposes. Additionally, it was decided to take another evaluation approach by following the IQA evaluation protocol from the NTIRE2020 challenge, where they used non-reference-based IQA methods including PIQE, NIQE, and BRISQUE. In addition to that, the Mean Opinion Score (MOS) method was used to support the previously mentioned non-reference-based methods, which correlate poorly with human opinion. For the MOS, a total of 20 participants were given a set of 13 SR images that were generated using different methods. Then the participants were asked to give unique scores that range between 1 and 6 (best to worse respectively) to each individual images based on the perceived clarity and sharpness of the images. The results of 6 different SR methods were used, where the methods were shuffled randomly when presented to the participants to avoid bias. The scores were then averaged for the individual images for each method, and were then used to calculate the final MOS scores.

5.2   Comparison with the State of the Art

To the best of our knowledge, an evaluation of the adapted T-RealSR method as well as the other mentioned SotA SR rgb-methods within the thermal domain, in comparison to the SotA thermal SR method has not be done before. Therefore, we compare the adapted method to bicubic upscaling, as well as with a number of RWSR methods including two zero-shot SR methods (DualSR [8], Kernel-GAN+ZSSR [3,23]) and the ESRGAN [27] RWSR method, and for the thermal SotA SR method TherISuRNet [6]. To ensure a fair comparison, ESRGAN [27] was retrained using the same dataset used to train the adapted T-RealSR, and employing the settings suggested by the authors of the ESRGAN. For DualSR [8] and KernelGAN+ZSSR [3,23], a training is not needed, as it is a part of the inference phase; the settings suggested by the authors were used. For the TherISuRNet [6], the retraining was needed as pretrained weights were not provided by the authors, and the same settings were adapted because the method was designed specifically for the utilized PBVS dataset.

Image Registration. We explained in Sect. 3 how the PBVS subsets (Domo and GT) were acquired using different cameras. Despite the effort by the authors to acquire two identical pictures of the same scene using different cameras, the process was physically impossible. That introduced some challenges when having to evaluate the performance of the different SR methods. Besides the different light conditions and different sensors' noise that resulted in brightness and contrast differences, the images were not perfectly aligned together. The imperfect alignment of the images meant that reference-based IQA methods in general and PSNR in specific, will be inaccurate to be used on their own. Therefore, we decided to apply image registration between the SR images and the GT reference images prior to evaluating the images using the non-reference-based methods. To do so, the ORB detector [21] with a target number of features $N = 5000$ was used to align the images together as illustrated in Fig. 1. The central crop (50%) of both the SR and GT images was used for evaluation. This was done to discard the black areas around the registered images and to make the comparison as fair as possible, since lens distortion is at its minimum in the central part of the image.

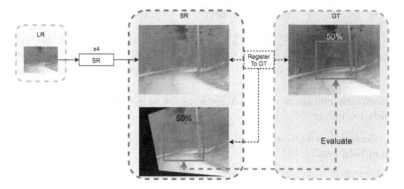

Fig. 1. The evaluation pipeline used to evaluate the super-resolved LR image in comparison to the GT.

Quantitative and Qualitative Evaluation. We evaluate the performance of the methods on the PBVS test dataset, where we show the quantitative results in Table 1. For the qualitative results a number of patches taken from some test images are shown in Fig. 2. The adapted T-RealSR method outperforms the other thermal and rgb-based SR methods by a large margin. Where it is possible to see that the traditional non-reference-based IQA methods (PIQE, NIQE, BRISQUE) correlate well with the human-opinion based MOS method. However, the reference-based IQA methods (SSIM and PSNR) correlate poorly with the other IQA methods. This is due to brightness and contrast differences. A method such as PSNR, will penalize the performance in case the registered image is shifted one pixel in any direction, and we know for sure that this is most likely the case with our test data.

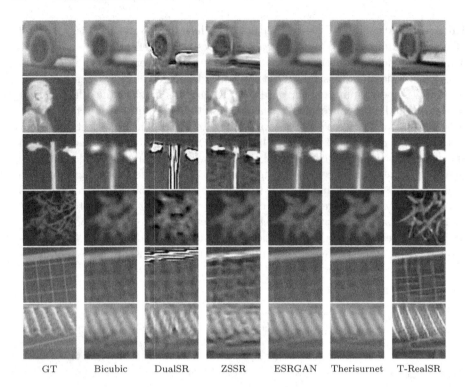

Fig. 2. Qualitative comparison of SotA methods for x4 SR of real LR images from the Domo validation subset.

Table 1. Comparison between the SotA methods that have been tested. The best values are in bold text.

Method	PSNR↑	SSIM↑	LPIPS↓	PIQE↓	NIQE↓	BRISQUE↓	MOS↓
Bicubic	20.11	0.70	0.46	67.39	5.55	57.20	4.10
DualSR [8]	18.77	0.59	0.43	56.48	4.18	43.03	4.74
ZSSR+KernelGAN [3]	19.01	0.57	0.44	60.79	5.71	46.14	4.15
ESRGAN [27]	18.37	0.65	0.43	76.77	5.72	53.74	2.98
TherISuRNet [6]	**20.10**	**0.71**	0.42	88.69	5.20	55.34	3.20
T-RealSR [11]	18.78	0.52	**0.37**	**36.33**	**3.31**	**34.31**	**1.45**

6   Conclusion

In this work we investigate the possibility of using rgb-based RWSR methods to super-resolve real-world thermal images. The images used for evaluation were upscaled with a factor of 4, and we found that tuning the T-RealSR by training it using thermal images is able to achieve SotA performance that surpasses the current SotA thermal-based SR method by a large margin in terms of perceived quality. This was proven by the different IQA methods, which showed results that correlate with the human-based MOS evaluation method. This work is, up to our knowledge, the first work that train on thermal images using realistically degraded image pairs, making it robust to real images that contain some of the most common degradation types (blurring and sensor noise).

References

1. Agustsson, E., Timofte, R.: NTIRE 2017 challenge on single image super-resolution: dataset and study. In: The IEEE Conference on Computer Vision and Pattern Recognition (CVPR) Workshops, July 2017
2. Ahn, N., Kang, B., Sohn, K.A.: Fast, accurate, and lightweight super-resolution with cascading residual network. In: Proceedings of the European Conference on Computer Vision (ECCV), pp. 252–268 (2018)
3. Bell-Kligler, S., Shocher, A., Irani, M.: Blind super-resolution kernel estimation using an internal-gan (2020)
4. Cho, Y., Bianchi-Berthouze, N., Marquardt, N., Julier, S.J.: Deep thermal imaging. In: Proceedings of the 2018 CHI Conference on Human Factors in Computing Systems, April 2018. https://doi.org/10.1145/3173574.3173576
5. Choi, Y., Kim, N., Hwang, S., Kweon, I.S.: Thermal image enhancement using convolutional neural network. In: 2016 IEEE/RSJ International Conference on Intelligent Robots and Systems (IROS), pp. 223–230. IEEE (2016)
6. Chudasama, V., et al.: Therisurnet - a computationally efficient thermal image super-resolution network. In: Proceedings of the IEEE/CVF Conference on Computer Vision and Pattern Recognition (CVPR) Workshops, June 2020
7. Dong, C., Loy, C.C., He, K., Tang, X.: Image super-resolution using deep convolutional networks. IEEE Trans. Pattern Anal. Mach. Intell. **38**(2), 295–307 (2015)
8. Emad, M., Peemen, M., Corporaal, H.: Dualsr: Zero-shot dual learning for real-world super-resolution. In: Proceedings of the IEEE/CVF Winter Conference on Applications of Computer Vision (WACV), pp. 1630–1639, January 2021
9. Fritsche, M., Gu, S., Timofte, R.: Frequency separation for real-world super-resolution. In: 2019 IEEE/CVF International Conference on Computer Vision Workshop (ICCVW), pp. 3599–3608 (2019)
10. Isola, P., Zhu, J.Y., Zhou, T., Efros, A.A.: Image-to-image translation with conditional adversarial networks. In: Proceedings of the IEEE Conference on Computer Vision and Pattern Recognition, pp. 1125–1134 (2018)
11. Ji, X., Cao, Y., Tai, Y., Wang, C., Li, J., Huang, F.: Real-world super-resolution via kernel estimation and noise injection. In: The IEEE/CVF Conference on Computer Vision and Pattern Recognition (CVPR) Workshops, June 2020
12. Jolicoeur-Martineau, A.: The relativistic discriminator: a key element missing from standard GAN (2018)
13. Ledig, C., et al.: Photo-realistic single image super-resolution using a generative adversarial network. In: Proceedings of the IEEE Conference on Computer Vision and Pattern Recognition, pp. 4681–4690 (2017)
14. Lee, K., Lee, J., Lee, J., Hwang, S., Lee, S.: Brightness-based convolutional neural network for thermal image enhancement. IEEE Access **5**, 26867–26879 (2017). https://doi.org/10.1109/ACCESS.2017.2769687
15. Li, J., Fang, F., Mei, K., Zhang, G.: Multi-scale residual network for image super-resolution. In: The European Conference on Computer Vision (ECCV), September 2018

16. Lim, B., Son, S., Kim, H., Nah, S., Lee, K.M.: Enhanced deep residual networks for single image super-resolution. In: Proceedings of the IEEE Conference on Computer Vision and Pattern Recognition Workshops, pp. 136–144 (2017)
17. Lugmayr, A., et al.: NTIRE 2020 challenge on real-world image super-resolution: Methods and results. In: Proceedings of the IEEE/CVF Conference on Computer Vision and Pattern Recognition Workshops, pp. 494–495 (2020)
18. Park, S.J., Son, H., Cho, S., Hong, K.S., Lee, S.: Srfeat: single image super-resolution with feature discrimination. In: Proceedings of the European Conference on Computer Vision (ECCV), September 2018
19. Rivadeneira, R.E.: Thermal image super-resolution challenge - PBVS 2020. In: 2020 IEEE/CVF Conference on Computer Vision and Pattern Recognition Workshops (CVPRW), pp. 432–439 (2020). https://doi.org/10.1109/CVPRW50498.2020.00056
20. Rivadeneira, R.E., Sappa, A.D., Vintimilla, B.X.: Thermal image super-resolution: a novel architecture and dataset. In: International Conference on Computer Vision Theory and Applications, pp. 1–2 (2020)
21. Rublee, E., Rabaud, V., Konolige, K., Bradski, G.: Orb: An efficient alternative to sift or surf. In: 2011 International Conference on Computer Vision, pp. 2564–2571 (2011). https://doi.org/10.1109/ICCV.2011.6126544
22. Shocher, A., Bagon, S., Isola, P., Irani, M.: Ingan: capturing and remapping the DNA of a natural image (2019)
23. Shocher, A., Cohen, N., Irani, M.: Zero-Shot super-resolution using deep internal learning (2017)
24. Sierra-Olympic: Vayu HD feature specification. https://sierraolympic.com/wp-content/uploads/2020/06/2020_VayuHD_Sell-Sheet_FINAL.pdf. Accessed 02 June 2021
25. Simonyan, K., Zisserman, A.: Very deep convolutional networks for large-scale image recognition. In: International Conference on Learning Representations (2015)
26. Soh, J.W., Cho, S., Cho, N.I.: Meta-transfer learning for zero-shot super-resolution. In: Proceedings of the IEEE/CVF Conference on Computer Vision and Pattern Recognition, pp. 3516–3525 (2020)
27. Wang, X., et al.: Esrgan: enhanced super-resolution generative adversarial networks. In: Proceedings of the European Conference on Computer Vision (ECCV) Workshops (2018)
28. Zhang, Y., Li, K., Li, K., Wang, L., Zhong, B., Fu, Y.: Image super-resolution using very deep residual channel attention networks. In: Proceedings of the European Conference on Computer Vision (ECCV), pp. 286–301 (2018)
29. Zhu, J.Y., Park, T., Isola, P., Efros, A.A.: Unpaired image-to-image translation using cycle-consistent adversarial networks. In: Proceedings of the IEEE International Conference on Computer Vision, pp. 2223–2232 (2017)

QR Code Style Transfer Method Based on Conditional Instance Regularization

Li Haisheng$^{(\boxtimes)}$, Huang Huafeng, and Xue Fan

Guangxi Normal University, Guilin, China

Abstract. We present a Quick Response (QR) code style transfer network based on conditional instance regularization to retain more QR code information and incorporate multiple styles into a single model. Firstly, we introduce conditional instance regularization into the QR code style transfer network and incorporate multiple styles into a single model. It improves the efficiency of multi-style transfer training. Secondly, the weighted fusion corrected method of the styled QR code is designed to repair the damage of positioning graphics and information modules in the QR code, enhance the styled QR code's identifiability and guarantee the integrity of information modules. Because of the shortcomings of the static QR code, a dynamic artistic style QR code is proposed. The experimental results show that the proposed QR code style transfer method is effective.

Keywords: Convolutional neural network · QR code · Style transfer

1 Introduction

Style transfer is a semantic representation of different styles images and a difficult image processing task [1]. The seminal work of Gatys et al. [2] showed the power of Convolutional Neural Networks (CNN) to create artistic images by encoding image content and image styles. Risser et al. [3] added gradient histogram loss to the model to enhance the texture features of the generated images to obtain better stylized images. The style transfer method of [2,3] is flexible enough to combine content and style of arbitrary images. However, itrelies on an optimization process that is prohibitively slow. Johnson et al. [4] and Ulyanov et al. [5] attempted to train feed-forward neural networks that perform stylization with a single forward pass. A major limitation of most feed-forward methods is that each network is restricted to a single style. Vincent et al. [6] and Zhang et al. [7] proposed a single model incorporating multiple styles, but the number of styles included is limited. More recently, Huang and Belongie et al. [8] designed a novel adaptive instance normalization layer that transfers the mean and variance statistics of the channels between style and content feature activation, enabling arbitrary style conversion.

Supported by the National Natural Science Foundation of China (No. 61762012) and the Natural Science Foundation of Guangxi (No. 2020GXNSFDA238023).

© Springer Nature Switzerland AG 2021
G. Bebis et al. (Eds.): ISVC 2021, LNCS 13017, pp. 15–26, 2021.
https://doi.org/10.1007/978-3-030-90439-5_2

QR codes [9] are widely used as information carriers in the world. The structure of the traditional QR code is shown in Fig. 1, which mainly consists of positioning graphics and information modules. The disadvantage of the traditional QR code is the single color and poor visual effect. Li et al. [10] implements style transfer for QR codes, but each model is restricted to a single style. When performing the transfer of a new style, the model must be trained from scratch, and thus is not conducive to practical applications. In terms of visual effect, their approach brings some unnatural style elements in the margins of the images.

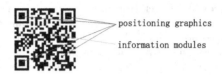

Fig. 1. Traditional QR code.

To solve the above problems we design a more efficient image style transfer method for transferring standard QR codes into QR codes with artistic style. The main contributions of our work are as follows:

(1) Our proposed style transfer network introduces conditional instance regularization [6], which incorporates multiple styles into a single mode, thus improving the network training efficiency and making it more practical. Moreover, our method does not bring unnatural style elements in the margins of the image.
(2) In order to ensure that the stylized QR codes can be recognized accurately and quickly, a weighted fusion correction method for styled QR codes is proposed, which can repair the damage of the positioning graphics and information modules.
(3) A dynamic stylized QR code generation method is introduced to incorporate multiple stylized QR codes in GIF image format into a dynamic stylized QR code, which is more eye-catching while increasing the information capacity of a single QR code.

2 Related Works

2.1 QR Code Style Transfer System

The traditional QR code is composed of two color modules in black and white, which lacks beauty and artistry. The QR code style transfer system in Fig. 2 has been implemented to generate stylized QR codes [10]. The core of the QR code style transfer system is a style transfer network that transforms a blended QR code into an artistic style QR code. The styled QR code produced by style transfer has a specified artistic style and still retains the original QR code information.

Fig. 2. QR code style transfer system.

2.2 Structure of the Style Transfer Network

Inspired by methods of Li et al. [10], we propose a network structure for QR code style transfer as shown in Fig. 3. The network consists of a style transfer network, which is a deep residual network, and a loss network, which is a pre-trained VGG19 network. We train the QR code style transfer network to transfer the content images into stylized images. The loss network is kept constant throughout the training period of the network. The content loss is computed at layer relu4-1, while the style loss is computed at layer relu1-1,relu2-1,relu3-1,relu4-1 of the VGG19 network.

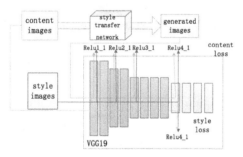

Fig. 3. Model architecture of the proposed style transfer system. The system consists of style transfer network and loss network.

3   Style Transfer Network Based on Conditional Instance Regularization

3.1   Conditional Instance Regularization

Conditional instance regularization [6] adds γ and β parameters to the instance regularization [11], which are N × C matrices, where N is the number of styles and C is the number of layers in the output feature map. The introduction of conditional instance regularization in the OR code transfer model of Li et al. [10] enables the incorporation of multiple styles into a single model and reduces the time when the model is trained for multiple style transfer. By selecting a content image and a group of style identifiers γ and β, an artistic image corresponding to that style can be generated. During training, all convolutional weights of the style transfer network can be shared among many styles, and incorporating new styles is sufficient to train only a set of parameters γ and β. The conditional instance regularization is defined by:

$$CIN\left(x\right) = \gamma_s \left(\frac{x - \mu\left(x\right)}{\sigma\left(x\right)} \right) + \beta_s \tag{1}$$

Where μ and σ are the mean and standard deviation of x on the spatial axis, respectively. γ_s and β_s are obtained by selecting the row corresponding to s in the γ and β matrices.

3.2   Residual Connected Module

Figure 4 shows the residual connected module [12] of our method, which consists of convolutional layer, conditional instance regularization layer, and activation function.

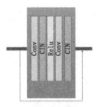

Fig. 4. Residual connected module.

3.3   Style Transfer Network Structure

Figure 5 shows the structure of our proposed style transfer network. As opposed to approach of Li et al. [10], we replace batch regularization with conditional instance regularization and introduce conditional instance regularization in the residual connected module. Our model can incorporate multiple styles into a single model while improving the quality of the generated images. The input image is first extracted with the main features of the image through convolutional layers. Then the image output from the convolutional layers is reconstructed by residual connected modules. Finally, the size of the input image is recovered by deconvolution layers.

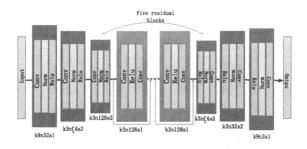

Fig. 5. The architecture of the style transfer network.

3.4 Weighted Fusion Correction for Styled QR Codes

We found that the stylized QR code positioning graphics and information modules are changed to some extent, causing the styled QR code to become undetectable for recognition or QR code information is lost.

To solve this problem we propose a correction method for weighted fusion of styled QR codes [13], and Fig. 6 shows the basic principle of the method. A blended QR code is passed through the style transfer network to generate a stylized QR code. The subsequent operation is the image fusion. The fusion weights W1 and W2 also represent the original QR code information weight and the style information weight of the stylized QR code. The values of the fusion weights determine the visual effect of the fused images.

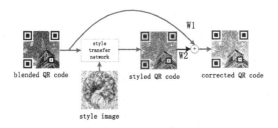

Fig. 6. Weighted fusion correction method.

Figure 7 shows the results of the exploration of fusion weights W1 and W2. When the fusion weights W1 and W2 take low values, the fused images are dark and their style information and content information are not well presented. When the fusion weights W1 and W2 take high values, the fused image is very bright, and some of the originally brighter information is lost, and the information of the style image is not well presented.

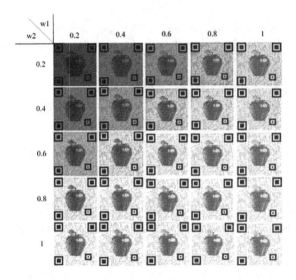

Fig. 7. Fusion weighting exploration.

3.5　Artistic Style QR Code Dynamics

With the development of LED electronic displays, electronic screens are gradually applied in more and more forms, so that the application of dynamic QR codes have a hardware basis. As Fig. 8 shows the principle of dynamic artistic style QR code, we use four different styles of artistic style QR codes and synthesize them into one dynamic artistic style QR code in GIF format [14], and GIF format images are widely used in social media and networks [15].

We propose two QR code dynamization methods:

Method 1, multiple QR codes carrying the same information are combined into one dynamic QR code, which greatly increases the error tolerance of styled QR codes. Each QR code is decorated with a different art style.

Method 2, multiple QR codes carrying different information are merged into one dynamic QR code. Each QR code uses a different art style. This allows a dynamic QR code to carry more information and can broaden the application scenarios of QR codes.

We use four QR codes combined into one dynamic QR code for investigation. The method 1 compared to the method 2, the amount of information carried is

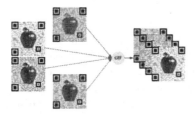

Fig. 8. Artistic style QR code dynamics.

increased four times. For the recognition correct rate, the analysis was performed using the minimum correct rate of 96% shown in Sect. 3. The total correct rate of method 1 is 96%, while the correct rate of method 2 will be greatly increased to 99.9%.

4   Experiment

4.1   Training

We trained our model using the Microsoft-COCO dataset [16], including 82,783 images. we use a scripting tool to remove the single-channel images from the dataset. The final dataset for our experiments is 82,396 three-channel images.

We use TensorFlow-GPU to call GTX-1660 6 GB graphics card to enhance the computing rate during model training. We resize the image size in the dataset to 128 × 128 resolution during training. We performed 40000 iterations using the method proposed by Adam [17] with the learning rate set to 0.001.

4.2   Single-Style Training

Figure 9 (left) shows the learning curves for content, and Fig. 9 (right) shows the learning curves for style. Model-1 is our model and model-2 is the model of Li et al. [10]. The model of Li et al. [10] and our model have the same convergence speed both in terms of style loss and content loss.

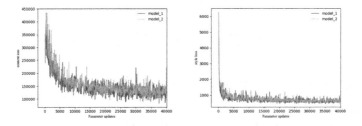

Fig. 9. Single-style learning curves.

4.3   Multi-style Training

Since all weights in the network are shared among all trained styles, the method of incorporating new styles into the training network is to keep the trained weights constant and learn a new set of γ and β parameters. To test the efficiency of this approach, we incorporate the new style into the network trained with 12 different styles. Figure 10 shows that this is much faster than training a new network from scratch, with both content loss and style loss converging at 10k iterations. Figure 11 (left) shows the results of training a new network from scratch for 10k iterations, and Fig. 11 (right) shows the results of fine-tuning the network for 10k iterations in a network that has completed training in 12 different styles. Even if the fine-tuned parameter updates are less than the retrained parameter updates, the fine-tuned model can also produce better results.

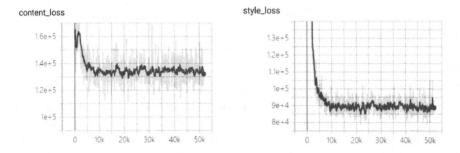

Fig. 10. Multi-style learning curves.

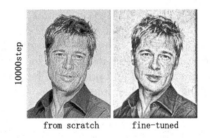

Fig. 11. From scratch and fine-tuned.

4.4   Comparison of Experiment Results

The experiment results are shown in Figs. 12, 13 and 14, (a) is the original image and its target style image, (b) is the experiment result of Li et al. [10], and (c) is the experiment result of our method. We zoom in on parts of the image to make it easier to see the details. For the method of Li et al. [10], the edges of the buildings can be distinguished, but the details of the buildings are blurred, and some unnatural style elements are introduced in some blank areas such as the sky. For the method of us, the edges of the buildings are clearly outlined, the details of each building are clear, and some blank areas such as the sky look very natural without introducing too many unnecessary stylistic elements.

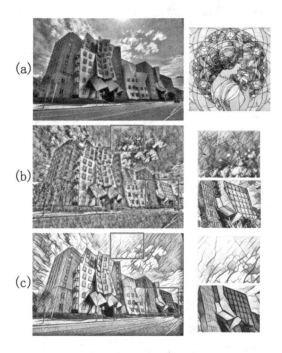

Fig. 12. The first building pictures.

In Fig. 14, the outline of the building is visible in the method of Li et al. [10], and the image detail information is also preserved to a certain extent, but the degree of completeness of the QR code information module, which is one of the most important keys for the application of artistic style QR codes, still cannot reach the practical needs. The outline of the background building is clearly visible in our method, and the image detail information is retained intact, and the QR code information module is also well preserved, which can meet the application requirements of QR code.

We used the structural similarity measure (SSIM) [18] to quantitatively assess the level of content information retention of the experimental results for the original images. Table 1 demonstrates that our method can produce better results for different types of images.

Through the intuitive visual judgment of the experimental results and the quantitative evaluation of SSIM, the effectiveness of our proposed QR style transfer method is fully demonstrated.

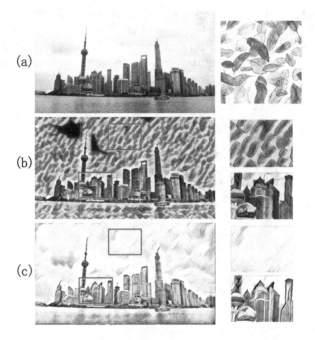

Fig. 13. The second building pictures.

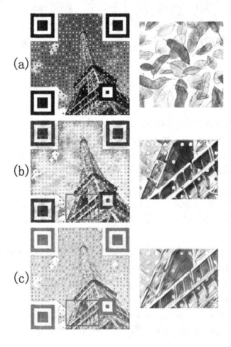

Fig. 14. Blended QR code.

Table 1. The SSIM values of the experimental results.

SSIM	Li et al. [10]	Ours
Figure 12	0.2342	**0.4294**
Figure 13	0.2963	**0.6845**
Figure 14	0.2641	**0.5423**

5 Conclusion

We propose a QR code style transfer method based on conditional instance regularization, which is centered on the introduction of a style transfer network with conditional instance regularization. We replace batch regularization with conditional instance regularization and introduce conditional instance regularization in the residual connection module to improve the quality of generated images while incorporate multiple styles into a single model, thus improving the efficiency and more practicality of the network for multiple styles transfer training.

The proposed artistic style QR code weighted fusion correction method can repair the damage of some specific styles to the QR code information module, ensure the integrity of the information module and enhance the recognizability of the styled QR code. The proposed dynamic artistic style QR code method increases the aesthetics of QR codes and broadens the application scenarios of artistic style QR codes. Experiments demonstrate the effectiveness of the proposed QR code style transfer method.

References

1. Gatys, L., Ecker, A., Bethge, M.: Image style transfer using convolutional neural networks. In: IEEE Conference on Computer Vision and Pattern Recognition, pp. 32414–2423 (2016)
2. Gatys, L., Ecker, A., Bethge, M.: A neural algorithm of artistic style. J. Vis. **111**(1), 98–136 (2016)
3. Risser, E., Wilmot, P., Barnes, C.: Stable and controllable neural texture synthesis and style transfer using histogram losses (2017). arXiv:1701.08893
4. Johnson, J., Alahi, A., Fei-Fei, L.: Perceptual losses for real-time style transfer and super-resolution. In: Leibe, B., Matas, J., Sebe, N., Welling, M. (eds.) ECCV 2016. LNCS, vol. 9906, pp. 694–711. Springer, Cham (2016). https://doi.org/10.1007/978-3-319-46475-6_43
5. Ulyanov, D., Lebedev, V., Vedaldi, A., Lempitsky, V.: Texture networks: feed-forward synthesis of textures and stylized images (2016). arXiv: 1603.03418
6. Dumoulin, V., Shlens, J., Kudlur, M.: A learned representation for artistic style (2016). arXiv:1610.07629
7. Zhang, H., Dana, K.: Multi-style generative network for real-time transfer (2017). arXiv:1703.06953

8. Huang, X., Belongie, S.: Arbitrary style transfer in real-time with adaptive instance normalization. In: International Conference on Computer Vision, pp. 1501–1510 (2016)
9. Yue, L., Ju, Y., Liu, M.: Recognition of QR code with mobile phones. In: Control and Decision Conference, pp. 203–206 (2008)
10. Li, H.S., Xue, F., Xia, H.Y.: Style transfer for QR code. Multimedia Tools Appl. **79**, 1–14 (2020)
11. Ulyanov, D., Vedaldi, A., Lempitsky, V.: Instance normalization: the missing ingredient for fast stylization (2016). arXiv:1607.08022
12. He, K., Zhang, X., Ren, S., Sun, J.: Deep residual learning for image recognition. In: Proceedings of the IEEE Conference on Computer Vision and Pattern Recognition, pp. 770–77. Las Vegas, Nevada, USA (2016)
13. Zhu, L., Sun, F., Xia, F.: Review on image fusion research. Transducer Microsyst. Technol. **2014**(2), 14–18 (2016)
14. Dai, S., Zhang, Y.: Image and graphic image filtering in GIF format on the Internet. Appl. Electron. Tech. **028**(001), 48–49 (2002)
15. Liu, Y.: GIF: an increasingly popular new media in the era of social media. Chin. J. **01**, 102–103 (2016)
16. Lin, T.-Y., et al.: Microsoft COCO: common objects in context. In: Fleet, D., Pajdla, T., Schiele, B., Tuytelaars, T. (eds.) ECCV 2014. LNCS, vol. 8693, pp. 740–755. Springer, Cham (2014). https://doi.org/10.1007/978-3-319-10602-1_48
17. Kingma, D., Ba, J.: Adam: a method for stochastic optimization. In: International Conference on Learning Representations (2014). arXiv:1412.6980
18. Wang, Z.: Image quality assessment: from error visibility to structural similarity. IEEE Trans. Image Process. **13**(4), 600–612 (2004)

Multimodal Multi-tasking for Skin Lesion Classification Using Deep Neural Networks

Rafaela Carvalho[1,2]($\boxtimes$) (iD), João Pedrosa[2,3] (iD), and Tudor Nedelcu[1] (iD)

[1] Fraunhofer Portugal AICOS, Rua Alfredo Allen 455, 4200-135 Porto, Portugal
`{rafaela.carvalho,tudor.nedelcu}@fraunhofer.pt`
[2] Faculty of Engineering of the University of Porto, Rua Dr. Roberto Frias,
4200-465 Porto, Portugal
[3] Institute for Systems and Computer Engineering, Technology and Science
(INESC TEC), Rua Dr. Roberto Frias, 4200-465 Porto, Portugal
`joao.m.pedrosa@inesctec.pt`

Abstract. Skin cancer is one of the most common types of cancer and, with its increasing incidence, accurate early diagnosis is crucial to improve prognosis of patients. In the process of visual inspection, dermatologists follow specific dermoscopic algorithms and identify important features to provide a diagnosis. This process can be automated as such characteristics can be extracted by computer vision techniques. Although deep neural networks can extract useful features from digital images for skin lesion classification, performance can be improved by providing additional information. The extracted pseudo-features can be used as input (multimodal) or output (multi-tasking) to train a robust deep learning model. This work investigates the multimodal and multi-tasking techniques for more efficient training, given the single optimization of several related tasks in the latter, and generation of better diagnosis predictions. Additionally, the role of lesion segmentation is also studied. Results show that multi-tasking improves learning of beneficial features which lead to better predictions, and pseudo-features inspired by the ABCD rule provide readily available helpful information about the skin lesion.

Keywords: Skin lesions · Multimodal learning · Multi-task learning

1 Introduction

Skin cancer refers to the abnormal growth of aberrant skin cells and is divided into two main types: malignant melanoma and non-melanoma skin cancer, which are ranked the 19th and 4th most common cancers in the world [16], respectively.

Early diagnosis improves prognosis of skin cancer. If it happens in a localized stage, patients have a 98% 5-year relative survival rate, whereas if diagnosed in a distant stage, it drops to 17% [14]. The lives of human beings highly depend on a timely diagnosis, however this process can be challenging due to the variability in the appearance of skin lesions. This has led to the development of a non-invasive

© The Author(s) 2021
G. Bebis et al. (Eds.): ISVC 2021, LNCS 13017, pp. 27–38, 2021.
https://doi.org/10.1007/978-3-030-90439-5_3

imaging technique: dermoscopy, which provides a higher diagnosis accuracy by revealing dimensions of skin morphological characteristics imperceptible to the naked eye. The most commonly employed algorithms for lesion inspection using dermoscopy are: ABCD rule of dermoscopy, Menzies scoring method, and seven-point checklist [7]. Such algorithms allow for an increased performance of the diagnosis process but the process remains highly dependent on the observer's experience and training. Moreover, as dermatology is suited for telemedicine and with the burden in healthcare systems at present, automated systems may be the answer towards diagnosis of malignant skin lesions at an early stage.

The emergence of deep learning has promoted the development of promising skin lesion analysis methodologies. The majority of the works found in the literature use transfer learning from well-established convolutional neural networks (CNNs) pre-trained on the ImageNet dataset [12].

One of the most important implementations of skin lesion classification with CNNs was achieved by Esteva et al. (2017) [4]. The authors adapted the pre-trained Inception v3 [17] network for skin lesion diagnosis and trained it on a large private dataset of 129.450 clinical images, consisting of 2032 different diseases. For data balancing, a hierarchical partitioning algorithm using a taxonomy tree was used. They reported performance results on par with 21 experts, indicating a solution with a level of competence comparable to dermatologists.

Multi-task learning (MTL) has been gaining traction and Liao et al. (2018) [10] built a deep MTL framework to exploit the correlation between skin lesions and their body site distributions. The dermatology images used in the study were collected from DermQuest (deactivated in 2019), an atlas with 25 types of skin lesions and 23 different body location labels.

Multimodal methods have also been proposed for skin lesion diagnosis. Yap et al. (2018) [19] investigated the combination of available data for classification. The ResNet-50 [5] with weights pre-trained on ImageNet was used to reduce the overfitting for a dataset of 2917 cases containing both clinical and dermoscopic images. When trained on dermoscopic images, it presented higher accuracy than on clinical images. Nonetheless, the combination of feature information from dermoscopic and clinical images outperformed single modal CNN, which indicates that both imaging modalities have dissimilar classification information.

Kawahara et al. (2019) [8] proposed a multimodal multi-task deep CNN with a base model Inception v3, pre-trained on ImageNet. The architecture was trained on multimodal data (clinical and dermoscopic images, as well as patient metadata), to classify the 7-point checklist criteria and perform skin lesion diagnosis. Their dataset containing the 2022 images and metadata has been made publicly available online. The network was trained using a combination of multimodal and multi-tasking losses, thus creating a robust model.

The focus of this work is to implement a system for skin lesion diagnosis using deep neural networks, while investigating the emerging multi-tasking and multimodal methods for more efficient training and an enhanced prediction. ABCD rule inspired pseudo-features are extracted through computer vision techniques and used as output (multi-tasking) or input (multimodal) to train a robust deep learning model.

2 Methodology

2.1 Dataset

The dataset employed in this work is from the ISIC 2017 challenge [3] and contains dermoscopic images which are labelled, according to expert consensus and pathology report information, as malignant melanocytic melanoma (MM), benign non-melanocytic seborrheic keratosis (SK) and benign melanocytic nevus (NV). Expert manual tracing of the lesion boundaries and superpixel-mapped annotations of the presence of dermoscopic criteria: pigment network (PN), negative network (NN), milia like cyst (MLC) and streaks (ST), are also provided.

We used the data split set by the challenge: a training set with 2000 images (1372 NV, 374 MM, 254 SK), 150 validation (78 NV, 30 MM, 42 SK) and 600 test samples (393 NV, 117 MM, 90 SK). By using the same distribution, this work's results can be compared with other methods from the literature, in particular the ISIC 2017 challenge submissions.

2.2 ABCD Rule Feature Extraction

Among the diagnosis algorithms of dermatology, the most popular and responsible for inspiring many CAD systems is the ABCD rule of dermoscopy [7]. According to this method, skin lesions can be characterized based on four criteria: asymmetry, border, color and number of dermoscopic structures.

As the dataset of this work does not contain expert annotations of ABCD criteria, extraction of those traits and subsequent data labelling is required for application of the multimodal and multi-tasking techniques. The framework for asymmetry and border extraction can be seen in Fig. 1. Color was not investigated in this paper and is under consideration for future work.

Asymmetry. A skin lesion is asymmetric when its two halves do not match. The asymmetry score (A_{score}) of a lesion is important when evaluating its malignant potential. This assessment will be concerning the shape: benign lesions are usually circular, whereas asymmetric lesions provide a warning sign of MM.

The major axis of the lesion is identified using the provided segmentation mask by calculating its orientation (θ), as described by Celebi et al. (2007) [2]. The lesion is rotated θ degrees clockwise to align its major and minor axes with the x and y axes of the image, and is centered. For each axis, the mirrored version of one half is overlapped with its correspondent and their exclusive OR area is computed. A non-overlapping area mask is obtained, allowing to estimate an asymmetry ratio between the preceding and the total lesion area.

According to the ABCD rule, skin lesions are divided in three levels: fully symmetric (0), asymmetric on one (1) and two axes (2). For the definition of such classes given the asymmetry ratio, a threshold is set in such a way that more than half of MMs have $A_{score} = 2$ and approximately 60% of benign lesions are scored 0 or 1 (please note that MMs are typically asymmetric whereas both halves of benign lesions usually match). Hence, if the non-overlapping area exceeds 6% of the lesion area, the lesion is considered asymmetric in that axis.

Border. MMs are usually associated with irregular and poorly defined borders, while NV's are even and smooth. In the clinical evaluation of the border, the sharpness of the transition from the lesion to the skin (B_{score}) is determined.

The gradient is computed along the border points, using the blue channel as skin lesions are usually more noticeable in this channel [1]. Firstly, the contour is characterized with 200 equidistant points and the normal direction of each point is found. The gradient in each border area is reduced to the mean difference of the pixel intensities along a line, whose length equals 30% of the lesion radius. The lesion is subsequently divided into 8 equi-angle slices, and, for each, an average value of the gradient is computed, as in Iyatomi et al. (2007) [6].

For definition of the B_{score}, we set an empiric threshold value of 50 for the average gradient which classifies the transition in each particular slice into either soft (0) or abrupt (1). This procedure is executed for all the divisions, resulting in a final B_{score} between 0 and 8.

Dermoscopic Structures. The superpixel annotations from the dataset are used to infer the existence of PN, NN, MLC and ST structures and, consequently, label the data according to their presence or absence.

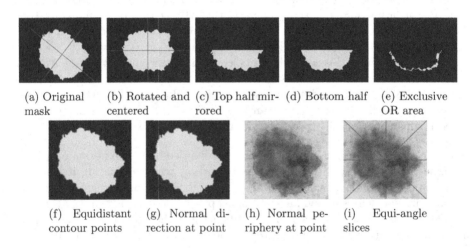

(a) Original mask   (b) Rotated and centered   (c) Top half mirrored   (d) Bottom half   (e) Exclusive OR area

(f) Equidistant contour points   (g) Normal direction at point   (h) Normal periphery at point   (i) Equi-angle slices

Fig. 1. Illustration of asymmetry (top row) and border (bottom row) extraction.

2.3   Proposed Model

EfficientNet [18] is a group of CNNs developed based on network scaling (depth, width and resolution), whose dimensions vary depending on the variant selected (B0 to B7). This architecture focuses on accuracy and efficiency, and is able to achieve state-of-the-art results while being multiple times smaller and faster [18].

An EfficientNet-B3 architecture, with weights and biases pre-trained on ImageNet, is used as the backbone of the experiments performed in this work. Variant

B3 is chosen because of the balance when comparing the number of parameters required and accuracy achieved with other CNNs.

Each dermoscopic image is resized to (300×300) pixels to make it compatible with the original dimensions of the network. Data augmentation transformations to simulate new samples and avoid overfitting are applied: rotations in the range of $[1, 5]$ degrees, zoom between 80% and 120%, horizontal flips and shifts up to 20% of the image size, and brightness adjustment in the range $[0.2, 0.8]$.

To accommodate the network for the desired tasks, a global average pooling layer is introduced on top of the frozen base network to reduce the number of parameters for the classifier, followed by batch normalization and dropout (rate of 0.2) layers as regularization to prevent overfitting. The original classifier is replaced by a softmax layer with 3 (skin lesion classes) neurons and parameters are updated using a learning rate of 1e–3. A frozen layer approach [8] is adopted to improve training by reducing the effect of transfer learning for the bottom layers, which are designed to extract more general features. The approach consists of unfreezing a EfficientNet-B3 block and fitting the model for 5 epochs using a lower learning rate (1e–6), repeating this until all blocks are unfrozen.

Each CNN model is compiled using the Adam optimization algorithm [9] and the loss function is specified to be categorical cross entropy (CCE).

2.4 Class Balancing Techniques

The skin lesion dataset of this work is imbalanced between classes. As a result, bias is introduced towards the most represented class, compromising the performance of the models.

A procedure which ensures data frequency [8] is carried out, i.e., each batch is verified to always hold at least 1 positive sample of every unique skin lesion and dermoscopic structure class, resulting in a batch size of 6. Since the category labels are not mutually exclusive, it is important that the same sample is not represented twice in the same batch; this is ensured by removing each case from the set after picking it. By guaranteeing one case of each unique label, model weights will be updated based on all the unique labels in each gradient descent step [8]. Nonetheless, while this improves class balance, there is still imbalance as including a case within one category will also include its labels in all other categories. To further address this issue, class weights are introduced. These are used to penalize the misclassification of samples from the minority classes. The weight W_i of each class i is given by $W_i = \frac{N}{C \cdot n_i}$, where N is the total number of samples, C is the number of classes, and n_i is the number of samples for class i.

By applying this modification (W_i) in the loss function employed in this work (CCE), a weighted loss function (Eq. 1) is obtained:

$$\text{Weighted Cross Entropy} = -\sum_{i=1}^{K} W_i \cdot y_i \cdot log(\hat{y}_i) \tag{1}$$

with K equaling to the number of scalar values in the model output, $\hat{y}_i$ being the i-th predicted value and y_i the corresponding true value.

3   Experiments

Hand-crafted features inspired by the ABCD rule are extracted and used as new auxiliary tasks to be predicted or as additional input merged with the embeddings extracted by the CNN. Additionally, since the ISIC 2017 dataset contains segmentation masks and extensive work was conducted regarding this aspect, the impact of segmentation maps is also investigated in this study.

3.1   ABCD Rule for Multimodal Multi-tasking

This dataset does not provide access to expert annotations of dermoscopic criteria (except dermoscopic structures), unlike the 7-point checklist dataset [8]. Thus, hand-crafted pseudo-features based on the ABCD rule are extracted by computer vision techniques, and are used as input (multimodal) or output (multi-tasking) to train a robust model.

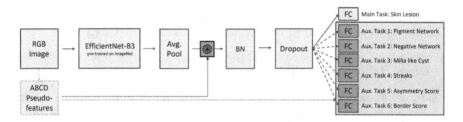

Fig. 2. Diagram of the models' structure. Baseline model is represented in grey ■; modifications regarding the multi-tasking and multimodal approaches are presented in green ■ and red ■, respectively. (Color figure online)

Multi-tasking. Multi-tasking is performed to guide the model to extract meaningful features for a specific task by predicting other closely related auxiliary tasks. The aim of this experiment is detecting ABCD traits to infer a skin lesion diagnosis. The motivation behind this design is to make use of the correlation between these criteria and lesion diagnosis: for example, MM has typically high A_{score} and B_{score}; in terms of dermoscopic structures, milia like cyst is usually indicative of SK [15] whereas negative network is a MM-specific structure [11].

The baseline model is adapted to a multi-task network with a hard parameter sharing approach, i.e., sharing the hidden layers between all tasks while keeping separate task-specific output softmax layers (Fig. 2). This model is able to simultaneously predict the skin lesion diagnosis and classify ABCD criteria. By predicting different characteristics of the lesion, these helpful representations are shared with the main task, thus improving diagnosis. All multi-task models studied focus on the classification of the presence of dermoscopic structures – ABC(D). However, prediction of A_{score} and B_{score} is tested concurrently – (AB)C(D) – or each separately – (A)BC(D) and A(B)C(D).

Multimodal Multi-tasking. Through this approach, the network is provided with readily available information tailored to what physicians use (ABCD rule) and which are thus characteristics proven to be relevant for malignancy classification. With these appropriate features, we aim to decrease the amount of overfitting, therefore enhancing the performance of CNN-based algorithms.

Late feature fusion is performed with the multi-task model set to receive two inputs, dermoscopic images and two characteristics of skin lesions that doctors look for when diagnosing MMs: asymmetry and border. Hence, the aforementioned hand-crafted ABCD features are directly concatenated with the feature vector obtained by the EfficientNet-B3, as observed in Fig. 2. Not all features might be beneficial to the classification task, some can possibly weaken the performance of the classifier. Consequently, different cases are tested: including only asymmetry or border information – (A)BC(D) and A(B)C(D) multimodal multi-task – or both simultaneously – (AB)C(D) multimodal multi-task.

3.2   Role of Segmentation in Lesion Classification

Artifacts such as hair, ruler markings, non-target lesions, and background noise in images can potentially deceive a model's classifier. A segmentation step is investigated to verify whether removing the pixel intensities outside the target lesion is advantageous for classification. Additionally, we test calculation of dynamic weights, i.e., weights based on the distribution of classes in each batch.

The performances of the ABC(D) multi-task model with dynamic weights receiving different inputs, observed in Fig. 3, are assessed.

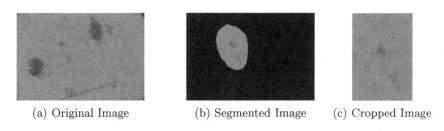

(a) Original Image   (b) Segmented Image   (c) Cropped Image

Fig. 3. Examples of the inputs for the multi-task model.

4   Results and Discussion

To evaluate the performance of the techniques tested in this work, the area under the curve (AUC), sensitivity (SE), specificity (SP), and balanced multi-class accuracy (BMA) are reported. Table 1 summarizes the overall diagnosis results and Table 2 presents the AUC for dermoscopic features classification. Bold values highlight the best result for each metric.

Table 1. Results of the models for the diagnosis task.

Model	AUC			SE (%)			SP (%)			BMA (%)
	NV	MM	SK	NV	MM	SK	NV	MM	SK	
Baseline model	**0,84**	**0,81**	**0,90**	**84**	42	68	65	**93**	**90**	65
ABC(D) multi-task	0,82	0,74	0,88	69	**50**	80	81	84	84	**66**
(A)BC(D) multi-task	0,82	0,71	0,89	58	46	87	90	84	73	64
A(B)C(D) multi-task	0,81	0,67	0,88	62	29	**90**	84	90	69	60
(AB)C(D) multi-task	0,81	0,69	0,87	57	32	88	84	88	67	59
(A)BC(D) multimodal multi-task	0,82	0,75	0,89	63	38	84	83	89	73	62
A(B)C(D) multimodal multi-task	0,83	0,73	**0,90**	66	36	87	84	91	72	63
(AB)C(D) multimodal multi-task	0,83	0,74	**0,90**	53	44	**90**	**91**	83	69	62

Table 2. Area under curve (AUC) values of the models for the auxiliary tasks. For asymmetry (Asym) and border (Bord), the average AUC is considered.

Model	AUC					
	PN	NN	MLC	ST	Asym	Bord
ABC(D) multi-task	0,76	0,61	0,61	0,77	–	–
(A)BC(D) multi-task	**0,79**	0,66	0,63	0,84	**0,567**	–
A(B)C(D) multi-task	**0,79**	0,67	0,59	0,81	–	0,822
(AB)C(D) multi-task	0,78	0,65	0,58	0,80	0,563	**0,824**
(A)BC(D) multimodal multi-task	**0,79**	0,69	0,63	0,84	–	–
A(B)C(D) multimodal multi-task	0,78	**0,70**	**0,64**	**0,87**	–	–
(AB)C(D) multimodal multi-task	**0,79**	**0,70**	0,61	0,83	–	–

The performances of the networks are similar regarding the BMA (Table 1). The strong correlation between dermoscopic features and MM is observed in this experiment, when dermatological attributes are used as auxiliary tasks (ABC(D) multi-task), as denoted by the 8% increase in MM SE and 7% decrease in SP. Other experiments regarding prediction of more tasks did not improve the BMA. With A_{score} prediction as an additional task, SP for NV is increased by 9% while SE is reduced by 11%. The opposite behaviour is observed for prediction of SK, where SE is increased by 10% while SP is reduced by 15%. When predicting all auxiliary tasks related to asymmetry, border and dermoscopic features, the model achieves the lowest performance regarding BMA. This reduction could be induced by the balancing techniques, which are difficult to perform for a small dataset with several outputs.

To investigate if a multimodal multi-tasking approach can boost the classifier performance, the combination of the ABCD rule inspired pseudo-features and CNN features was tested. No major improvement regarding the prediction of skin lesion diagnosis is observed, confirming that the network is able to automatically learn good image representations. However, AUC values of the multimodal multi-tasking models are slightly enhanced when compared to its corresponding backbone (ABC(D) multi-task): there is an improvement for NV and SK when using the border gradient and the addition of asymmetry benefits MM. Regarding dermoscopic structures, we noticed an improvement in their detection (Table 2), specifically with the introduction of the border gradient.

The GradCAM technique [13] was applied to have visual feedback on where the network's activations, previous to the softmax layer, were more predominant. Analyzing Fig. 4, the superiority of multi-tasking is confirmed, by showing that closely related auxiliary tasks help the network to focus on the lesion.

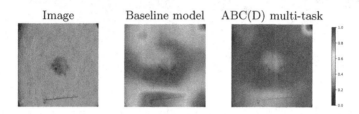

Fig. 4. GradCAM diagnosis heat maps from the baseline and multi-task models. Color represents the degree of activation from low (blue – 0) to high (red – 1). (Color figure online)

Table 3 depicts the role of lesion segmentation in the classifier's performance.

Using a segmentation mask to remove background information and pass only the lesion as input to the model considerably decreases performance, when comparing it with the unaltered input. Segmented images possibly removed contextual information which could be relevant for the classification task. Results of the original dataset and the bounding box images are extremely similar, with the original images providing advantage in the AUC of MM, but the cropped images achieving higher MM SE, which could be preferable in a clinical setting.

Table 3. Results of models with modified images as inputs.

Model input	AUC			SE (%)			SP (%)			BMA (%)
	NV	MM	SK	NV	MM	SK	NV	MM	SK	
Original images	**0,84**	**0,75**	0,89	**76**	45	**78**	80	**89**	84	**66**
Segmented images	0,75	0,69	0,82	75	44	50	62	82	**91**	56
Cropped images	**0,84**	0,73	**0,91**	67	**52**	**78**	**82**	78	88	**66**

GradCAM was once again employed to compare the impact of segmentation maps on the network's activations. The heat maps (Fig. 5) suggest the network learns to roughly detect the skin lesion. Artifacts such as ruler markings are also activated, which was expected. For the diagnosis task, it is noticeable that the network trained on segmented images considers a wider portion of the image than

Image	Diagnosis	Pigment Network	Negative Network	Milia like Cyst	Streaks	

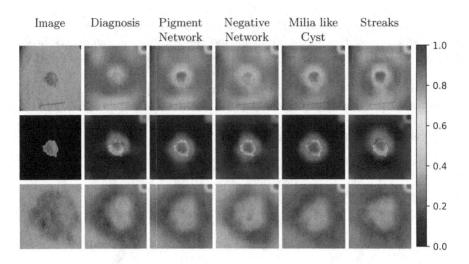

Fig. 5. Example of the different inputs for a skin lesion and respective GradCAM heat maps for each model task.

the original images, including parts for which there is no information, therefore leading to worse performance; activation on cropped images misses parts of the lesion which may contain important features to discriminate between classes. It is worth noting neighbor pixels surrounding the lesion are important as the difference between background (skin) and foreground (lesion) intensities provides relevant information regarding color and texture variations. The same behaviour is observed in the tasks related to dermoscopic criteria classification.

The leading approach of this work (ABC(D) multi-task) reached an average AUC of 87% for the diagnosis task, placing it among the top 35% of the ISIC 2017 challenge leaderboard[1]. The most successful challenge submissions implemented ensembles of DL networks and extended the dataset with additional data sources [3], whereas this work was limited to a single model and no external data.

5   Conclusion

This paper proposes multi-tasking and multimodal strategies to improve state-of-the-art automated systems for the problem of skin lesion diagnosis, while handling the imbalanced dataset. To the best of our knowledge, there is a small number of comprehensive studies in the literature related to this topic, therefore the aim of the work is to contribute to this line of research.

The yielded results show potential in the use of MTL, proving that it allows different tasks to share meaningful features and beneficial representations. This was corroborated by the heat maps obtained for the baseline and ABC(D) multi-task models. Auxiliary classification of ABCD rule criteria did not translate

---

[1] https://challenge.isic-archive.com/leaderboards/2017.

into enhanced performance, which can possibly be explained by the difficulty to train a model which predicts a large number of tasks on a small and imbalanced dataset. Plus, this information was manually extracted, divided in classes and labelled, thus being imperfect and introducing bias. The use of ABCD ratings annotated by experts has the potential to yield superior results. Even so, the multimodal technique with such descriptors increased AUCs.

Additionally, this work provided insight on the role of background information, through the comparison of the same model with different inputs: original dermoscopic view, images cropped around the lesion and images containing only lesion information. The analysis of the heat maps for diagnosis and dermoscopic criteria classification tasks in models with a segmentation step confirmed that all networks roughly detected the lesion, but the latter led to poor results, explained by the removal of contextual information.

The learning paradigms investigated in this work are active areas for improvement and can lead to reliable skin lesion classification systems. Multi-tasking models provide the advantage of running on inference without extracting ABCD features. Moreover, multimodal and multi-tasking can potentially enhance the possibility of explainability. Further future work considers developing the models presented to incorporate patient information and/or clinical images as additional inputs, since combining complementary information from multiple modalities has the potential to improve performance. Given the limitation of the small size of the dataset, these approaches must be tested on a larger one.

Acknowledgments. This work was done under the scope of project "DERM.AI: Usage of Artificial Intelligence to Power Teledermatological Screening", and supported by national funds through 'FCT–Foundation for Science and Technology, I.P.', with reference DSAIPA/AI/0031/2018.

References

1. Celebi, M.E., Iyatomi, H., Schaefer, G., Stoecker, W.V.: Lesion border detection in dermoscopy images. Comput. Med. Imaging Graph. **33**(2), 148–153 (2009)
2. Celebi, M.E., et al.: A methodological approach to the classification of dermoscopy images. Comput. Med. Imaging Graph. **31**(6), 362–373 (2007)
3. Codella, N.C., et al.: Skin lesion analysis toward melanoma detection: a challenge at the 2017 international symposium on biomedical imaging (isbi), hosted by the international skin imaging collaboration (isic). In: 2018 IEEE 15th International Symposium on Biomedical Imaging (ISBI 2018), pp. 168–172. IEEE (2018)
4. Esteva, A., et al.: Dermatologist-level classification of skin cancer with deep neural networks. Nature **542**(7639), 115–118 (2017)
5. He, K., Zhang, X., Ren, S., Sun, J.: Deep residual learning for image recognition. In: Proceedings of the IEEE Conference on Computer Vision and Pattern Recognition, pp. 770–778 (2016)
6. Iyatomi, H., Oka, H., Celebi, M.E., Tanaka, M., Ogawa, K.: Parameterization of dermoscopic findings for the internet-based melanoma screening system. In: 2007 IEEE Symposium on Computational Intelligence in Image and Signal Processing, pp. 189–193. IEEE (2007)

7. Johr, R.H.: Dermoscopy: alternative melanocytic algorithms–the abcd rule of dermatoscopy, menzies scoring method, and 7-point checklist. Clin. Dermatol. **20**(3), 240–247 (2002)
8. Kawahara, J., Daneshvar, S., Argenziano, G., Hamarneh, G.: Seven-point checklist and skin lesion classification using multitask multimodal neural nets. IEEE J. Biomed. Health Inform. **23**(2), 538–546 (2018)
9. Kingma, D.P., Ba, J.: Adam: A method for stochastic optimization. arXiv preprint arXiv:1412.6980 (2014)
10. Liao, H., Luo, J.: A deep multi-task learning approach to skin lesion classification. arXiv preprint arXiv:1812.03527 (2018)
11. Pizzichetta, M.A., et al.: Negative pigment network: an additional dermoscopic feature for the diagnosis of melanoma. J. Am. Acad. Dermatol. **68**(4), 552–559 (2013)
12. Russakovsky, O., et al.: Imagenet large scale visual recognition challenge. Int. J. Comput. Vis. **115**(3), 211–252 (2015)
13. Selvaraju, R.R., Cogswell, M., Das, A., Vedantam, R., Parikh, D., Batra, D.: Gradcam: Visual explanations from deep networks via gradient-based localization. In: Proceedings of the IEEE International Conference on Computer Vision, pp. 618–626 (2017)
14. Siegel, R.L., Miller, K.D., Jemal, A.: Cancer statistics, 2019. CA: Canc. J. Clin. **69**(1), 7–34 (2019)
15. Stricklin, S., Stoecker, W., Oliviero, M., Rabinovitz, H., Mahajan, S.: Cloudy and starry milia-like cysts: how well do they distinguish seborrheic keratoses from malignant melanomas? J. Euro. Acad. Dermatol. Venereology **25**(10), 1222–1224 (2011)
16. Sung, H., et al.: Global cancer statistics 2020: globocan estimates of incidence and mortality worldwide for 36 cancers in 185 countries. CA: Canc. J. Clin. **71**(3), 209–249 (2021)
17. Szegedy, C., et al.: Going deeper with convolutions. In: Proceedings of the IEEE Conference on Computer Vision and Pattern Recognition, pp. 1–9 (2015)
18. Tan, M., Le, Q.: Efficientnet: rethinking model scaling for convolutional neural networks. In: International Conference on Machine Learning, pp. 6105–6114. PMLR (2019)
19. Yap, J., Yolland, W., Tschandl, P.: Multimodal skin lesion classification using deep learning. Exp. Dermatol. **27**(11), 1261–1267 (2018)

DeepSolfège: Recognizing Solfège Hand Signs Using Convolutional Neural Networks

Dominic Ferreira$^{(\boxtimes)}$ ⓘ and Brandon Haworth ⓘ

University of Victoria, Victoria, Canada
{dominicf,bhaworth}@uvic.ca

Abstract. Hand signs have long been a part of elementary music theory education systems through the use of Kodály-Curwen Solfège hand signs. This paper discusses a deep learning convolutional neural network model that can identify 12 hand signs and the absences of a hand sign directly from pixels both quickly and effectively. Such a model would be useful for automated Solfège assessment in educational environments, as well as, providing a novel human computer interface for musical expression. A dataset was designed for this study containing 16,900 RGB images. Additional domain-specific image augmentation procedures were designed for this application. The proposed CNN achieves a precision, recall, and F1 score of 94%. We demonstrate the model's capabilities by simulating a real-time environment.

Keywords: CNN · Image classification · Solfège

1 Introduction

Solfège is a musical education method that makes use of static hand signs to represent musical notes. The hand signs correspond to the 12 tone equal temperament system, common in Western Music, and act as a kinesthetic aid for learning singing [10,17]. This elementary system's popularity, history, and formalized mapping of hand signs make it a good candidate to automate the identification process so that it can be deployed in learning applications.

This paper identifies an effective convolutional neural network for classifying Solfège hand signs. During each stage of development, careful consideration was made to make this network useful in a wide variety of applications. Particular emphasis was placed on ensuring real world performance was responsive, adaptable, and accurate. The target platform during experimentation was a mid-range consumer PC using a single webcam. The two proposed use cases that would benefit from the CNN identified in this paper are that of applications in the educational and artistic domains. Many education systems globally are increasing their use of online resources and automated evaluations which facilitate larger audiences as well as distance learning. These educational tools often require tailored solutions to provide the most effective experience for the users. Using our

ⓒ Springer Nature Switzerland AG 2021
G. Bebis et al. (Eds.): ISVC 2021, LNCS 13017, pp. 39–50, 2021.
https://doi.org/10.1007/978-3-030-90439-5_4

CNN, an educational application could be built which teaches these signs to students and validates that they are correctly learning the techniques. Any curriculum that utilizes Solfège could deploy this application as a convenient way to track a student's progress.

Additionally, this CNN could provide a system to be used as an input device to control an instrument. A common technical standard for controlling instruments is MIDI. The predicted labels could be output as MIDI signals, allowing for seamless integration into many synthesizers and digital audio workstations. This would allow for live performances using only the Solfège hand signs as an input.

In this paper, we propose a CNN for real-time Solfège hand sign classifications which was trained on our augmented dataset. Our contributions include the CNN architecture, dataset curation, augmentation methodology, and a real world simulation. We evaluate our method extensively by analyzing and presenting the precision, recall, F1 scores, and confusion matrix for our proposed architecture. Our model is cross-validated and subject to an ablation study. We also compare the effects that input resolution has on accuracy and computation time. Finally, we simulate real world accuracy by feeding a video through the network to validate usability in applications.

2   Related Work

Barehanded image recognition has a long history in human computer interaction applications [19]. In recent years, Convolutional Neural Networks (CNN) have been a boon for image classification, recognition, segmentation, but also barehanded human computer interaction [5]. CNNs are capable of learning and extracting features directly from pixels, recognizing patterns, classifying images, and have been used to solve similar problems to the domain presented here [8]. Advances in that field which focused on human computer interaction have created many educational and accessibility tools, such as sign language recognition [2]. Sign language recognition is an interdisciplinary topic combining elements of computer vision, natural language processing, and machine learning. While some problems in this field require temporal information or linguistic considerations, static image classification does not rely on context external to the current frame. Some work has been done specifically to solve the temporal aspect of recognizing hand gestures in sign language by implementing the use of 3D CNNs [4]. In this paper, we propose single frame predictions on static hand signs which is similar to other static sign language detection research [20]. We account for real-time use on video through careful dataset augmentation and include a real-time video based analysis for evaluation. A comparison of CNN models used for static image classification is found in Table 1.

Solfège as a whole encompasses several techniques and is often combined with other methods to aid in learning musicianship skills. For example, there are methods that use a set of syllables to help memorization and audiation of pitches, or assigning words and phrases to different rhythms. Other works have

Table 1. Related CNN models used for classification

Classification domain	Input dimensions	Convolution layers	Fully connected layers	Regularization	Accuracy
Poultry health [6]	150 × 300	3	1	Dropout	86%
Dentistry [3]	996 × 564	6	2	Dropout	87%
Sign language [12]	128 × 128	4	1	None	92%
Age and Gender [1]	227 × 227	4	2	Dropout and batch normalization	96%

automated the assessing of accuracy for singing pitch or gestural tempo [13,14]. Another work uses pitches played back to visually impaired users to help detect and analyze the position of objects in front of them [7]. While these works do use Solfège elements in unique applications, they do not contribute to the specific domain of hand sign classification.

Solfège hand sign recognition is an under-researched area with only a single work covering the topic. The only related work feeds an isolated hand silhouette into a random forest classifier running on a Google Glass device to make near real time predictions [15]. While the classification accuracy reported in this paper is high at 95%, it uses only seven Solfège hand signs, which significantly reduces the musical possibilities. The Google Glass device used captures images in an egocentric perspective, which is an uncommon perspective in consumer capture hardware like laptops, cell phones, and webcams.

3 Dataset

The dataset used in these experiments was built specifically for this application. No other dataset for this kind of application is publicly available to the best of the Authors' knowledge. It contains 16,900 photos evenly split across 13 different label classifications and with images captured from several different environments. All photos were captured in RGB format at a resolution of 640 × 480 pixels using a readily available consumer webcam. Several considerations went into the design of this dataset, most notably the label selection, collection hardware, and background environments.

3.1 Labels

There are several Solfège hand signs and variations, so we must specify which are included in the dataset. A subset of the possible Solfège signs were selected by balancing functionality and complexity. To represent the 12 tones found in the chromatic scale, at least 12 symbols are needed. Solfège includes several enharmonically equivalent notes, meaning that there are multiple hand signs that map to the same notes. To reduce the number of labels, we have not included any

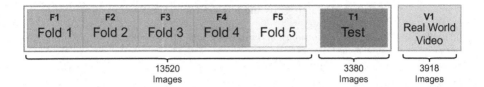

Fig. 1. Dataset and subsets breakdown

enharmonically equivalent symbols in our dataset. The 12 selected symbols used are the main seven Diatonic notes, as well as the five Flat notes, as seen in Fig. 2. Some methods of teaching Solfège add the additional element of assigning each symbol a location in vertical space. This potentially complicates the network used for identification and thus was omitted. In return, this grants the user freedom to show the sign anywhere within the frame and for the network to be able to recognize it. We discuss this further in our Sect. 6. Another necessary label in the dataset is a null symbol representing any frame that does not contain one of the 12 selected Solfège signs. This would be useful in both educational and artistic applications when a user does not want to play a note, as well as real time applications for disambiguation of hand movement between notes. A similar approach is used in the other work with their inclusion of a 'no gesture' class; however, they use another additional label for 'noisy' data, when no hand sign is present [15]. We combine the content of those two separate labels into a single one, which we call 'no symbol', since the functionality desired is the same in either case. The data collected for our null symbol include images with no hands visible, a hand that is visible but not showing any Solfège sign, and a hand that is showing a Solfège sign but is blurred or obscured beyond human recognition. The latter class of images was derived from empirical tests that showed this improved the misclassification of hand movements between symbols in the real-time case where motion blur may be extreme on consumer webcams. This brings the total number of labels to 13.

3.2   Preprocessing

The first stage of processing the dataset is to break it into three different subsets; training, validation, and test sets. Twenty percent of the dataset was reserved for testing, $T1$ as seen in Fig. 1. The remaining set is broken into five even pieces, $F1$ through $F5$, which will be used for cross-validation during training. All inputs into the network are scaled down to a resolution of 80×60 pixels for network input. This resolution allows our network to quickly process images, and we found that, below this threshold, important features for classification were being lost and accuracy significantly degraded.

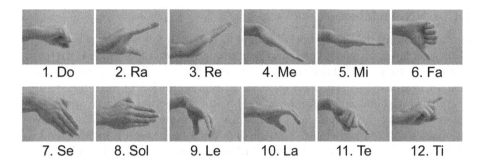

Fig. 2. Solfège hand signs samples from dataset, in ascending musical order. Typical samples from the dataset include noisy backgrounds, humans, and typical indoor background elements, the samples shown here have been cropped for symbol clarity.

There were several different augmentations applied to the dataset during training. The set of possible augmentations, S, correspond to seven unique parametric transformations, A_1 through A_7, such that S_n can be any combination of A_1 through A_7 within their respective ranges given in Table 2.

Table 2. Transformations used for dataset augmentation

Index	Transformation	Range
A_1	Rotation	$\pm 12°$
A_2	Zoom out	10–30%
A_3	Width shift	$\pm 15\%$
A_4	Height shift	$\pm 15\%$
A_5	Shear	$\pm 15\%$
A_6	Brightness reduction	30%
A_7	Horizontal flip	Binary

We constrain the range for A_1 such that it preserves the image's orientation, since some of the hand signs are rotationally variant, and we are designing for a landscape input. A_2 is used to ensure that after any combination of transformation, the hand sign is still within the input frame. After S_n is applied to an image, any part of the transformed image that does not fill the entire CNN input dimension is filled with black pixels.

4   Method

The proposed CNN architecture and variations were inspired by similar state-of-the-art designs. This section outlines an effective CNN, discusses our training procedures, and compares variations in an ablation study.

4.1 CNN Architecture

Our architecture uses three convolutional layers, each followed by a batch normalization layer, Maxpool layer, and then dropout layer, after which is flattened and passed to a single fully connected layer before the output layer with the final 13 neurons. Figure 3 provides a visual representation of our architecture. Every convolutional and dense layer used a ReLU function for activation, with the exception of the output layer, which used a Softmax function. Each convolution uses a 3 × 3 kernel size, a stride of two, 64 filters, and is zero padded to output the same height and width dimension as the input. The Maxpooling layer uses a 2 × 2 window and is used to downsample the feature maps. Each dropout layer randomly sets 30% of input units to zero. After being flattened, the input is passed into a fully connected layer with 1024 neurons. The last layer uses a Softmax activation to output a probability across our 13 classes. The input to the system is a 80 × 60 RGB image array.

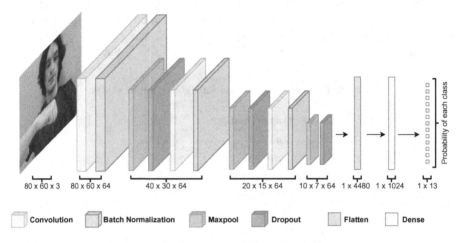

Fig. 3. Model architecture, from the input image on the left to the output probability on the right.

4.2 Training

Our proposed model, as well as all other models constructed for comparison, use the same training methods and parameters outlined in this section. We used Keras as our framework for all of our experiments, and trained the models using an AMD Ryzen 9 5900X CPU. We used the Adam optimization algorithm, with a learning rate of 0.001, beta 1 of 0.85, beta 2 of 0.999, and epsilon value of 1e−7. Each model was trained over 250 epochs with a batch size of 64. Each image used during learning was passed through S_n for augmentation at run-time. Checkpoints were saved as the model trains, and the checkpoint with the highest validation accuracy was selected.

4.3 Ablation Study

In this section we perform an ablation study on our proposed architecture. Four elements of our architecture were tested in isolation to validate the design. The components considered in this study are the pooling layer methods, normalization techniques used, convolution layer configuration as well as number of neurons in the fully connected layer.

We compare two different pooling methods in Table 3, where every pooling layer in the model is replaced with the corresponding method. Both batch normalization and dropout are techniques used to mitigate overfitting and reduce training time [11,16], and as seen in Table 1, are commonly used in similar applications. We compare the effects that a variety of configurations has on our model in Table 4. The batch normalization and dropout layers used in this experiment have been used between every convolution layer in the network. Table 5 shows the result of adding an additional duplicate convolution layer, as well as removing one. Table 6 compares a range of values for the number of neurons in the fully connected layer of the network. Each component of our proposed network utilizes the optimal solution within the range of tested configurations.

Table 3. Pooling method comparison

Pooling method	Accuracy
MaxPooling2D	**93.9%**
AvgPooling2D	91.6%

Table 4. Regularization comparison

Regularization method	Accuracy
None	89.9%
Dropout	88.6%
Batch normalization	90.4%
Both	**93.9%**

Table 5. Convolution layer comparison

Convolution layers	Accuracy
2	86.6%
3	**93.9%**
4	84.3%

Table 6. Fully connected layer comparison

Layer width	Accuracy
1024	**93.9%**
512	90.9%
256	90.5%

5 Evaluation

Our proposed model was five-fold cross-validated and achieved an average accuracy of 93.3%, with the best model having an F1 score of 93.9% on the $T1$ dataset. The best model was selected from the cross-validation and was used for the metrics in Table 7 and Fig. 4. The precision, recall and F1 scores are presented in Table 7. Figure 4 is a confusion matrix, which highlights a couple classes that perform poorly. The largest anomaly in the confusion matrix illustrates the class Le's poor recall performance, in particular that it misclassifies it as Te 5.4% of the time. This can be attributed to the nature of the hand symbols sharing similar features, as seen in Fig. 2.

Table 7. Model classification report. Each class has 260 samples of support.

	Precision	Recall	F1 score
Do	0.881	0.912	0.896
Fa	0.959	0.908	0.933
La	0.956	0.923	0.939
Le	0.940	0.896	0.917
Me	0.969	0.969	0.969
Mi	0.918	0.950	0.934
No symbol	0.936	0.954	0.945
Ra	0.961	0.958	0.960
Re	0.944	0.969	0.956
Se	0.946	0.942	0.944
Sol	0.945	0.985	0.964
Te	0.892	0.923	0.903
Ti	0.968	0.919	0.943
Average	0.940	0.939	0.939

5.1 Real World Application

Two experiments have been conducted to explore the real world performance of the proposed CNN.

The resolution comparison in Table 8 explores the relationship between accuracy and computational cost. The model was retrained using different input resolutions. The computational cost is calculated by averaging the time it takes to make a prediction using only a CPU, an Intel i7-6700HQ and an AMD Ryzen 9 5900X, in a Jupyter Notebook environment, across the 3380 samples in $T1$. To contextualize the requirements for computation time of a single frame in terms of music, a single 32nd note at 180 beats per minute lasts 42 ms. Another work studied how sensitive humans are to latency when using a gesture controlled instrument [9]. The work claims a 20 to 30 ms just noticeable difference, which means our proposed model is just within the acceptable tolerance. Using only the CPU for predictions increases accessibility since it does not rely on the user possessing a capable, discrete GPU. A GPU implementation may be preferable for optimal performance because of the classification speed benefits [18].

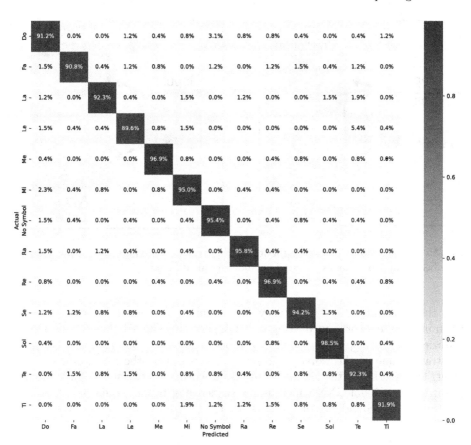

Fig. 4. Confusion matrix

Table 8. Resolution performance comparison

Resolution	Accuracy	Computation time i7-6700HQ	Computation time Ryzen 9 5900X
160 × 120	90.9%	51.3 ms	25.1 ms
80 × 60	**93.9%**	**42.5 ms**	**19.5 ms**
40 × 30	88.0%	38.6 ms	17.0 ms

To evaluate the model's accuracy on a real world incoming video feed, we created a separate dataset, $V1$, to simulate the environment. A continuous video was captured at 30 frames per second where all 13 classes were performed in sequential order with each appearing for approximately 10 s. The frames were then annotated by a human, and then compared against the model's offline predictions. The model achieved an accuracy of 89.3% over the 3918 frames. Another experiment is necessary to identify the other computational costs not factored

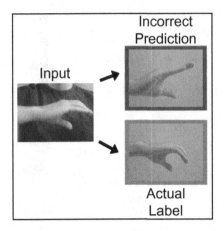 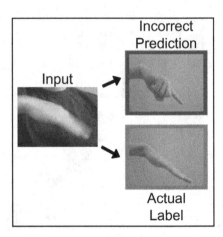

Fig. 5. The two most misclassified labels during real world experiment. Input images have been cropped to focus on hand symbol for this diagram.

into these calculations. The latency for capturing webcam frames, processing them into the network, outputting the class, creating the MIDI signal, and synthesizing the corresponding sound were not included in our analysis. Figure 5 illustrates some of the worst performing classes during the real world experiment, and highlights the similarity of visual features between certain symbols. A three-dimensional CNN which uses a sequence of frames could be a possible solution for low confidence predictions and the transitions interval between hand signs.

6   Conclusion

This work builds a foundation for future Solfège applications that require hand sign classification. Our proposed convolutional neural network achieves a 94% accuracy and is capable of real-time predictions. Our evaluations motivate further work into utilizing the model as a viable hand sign input method. In future work, we hope to further improve handling low confidence classifications, as well as, ensure the model's robustness in a variety of environments. This also includes the investigation of temporal methods and even sequence or Markov methods for future sign prediction and correction. The video and static image datasets are carefully varied to cross a broad range of environments and lighting conditions, however they include the same participant. Similarly, a broader range of camera sources and methodologies for normalizing sources for input should be investigated for Solfège specific applications. Thus further dataset development is needed to broaden the generalizability to arbitrary users. With the 13 classes used in our dataset, we are limited to represent a single musical octave. By having another input to represent octaves, one could combine such a method with our model to map the entire chromatic scale. This is advantageous for designing a fully featured MIDI input method. In fact, with the success of this method and the utility of Solfège, many human-computer interaction, usability, usefulness, education, and training opportunities arise. We look forward to expanding the dataset, exploring usability and use cases, and optimizing the network for specific applications.

References

1. Agbo-Ajala, O., Viriri, S., et al.: Age group and gender classification of unconstrained faces. In: Bebis, G. (ed.) ISVC 2019. LNCS, vol. 11844, pp. 418–429. Springer, Cham (2019). https://doi.org/10.1007/978-3-030-33720-9_32
2. Ardiansyah, A., Hitoyoshi, B., Halim, M., Hanafiah, N., Wibisurya, A.: Systematic literature review: American sign language translator. Proc. Comput. Sci. **179**, 541–549 (2021)
3. Campos, L.S., Salvadeo, D.H.P.: Multi-label classification of panoramic radiographic images using a convolutional neural network. In: ISVC 2020. LNCS, vol. 12509, pp. 346–358. Springer, Cham (2020). https://doi.org/10.1007/978-3-030-64556-4_27
4. Huang, J., Zhou, W., Li, H., Li, W.: Sign language recognition using 3D convolutional neural networks. In: 2015 IEEE International Conference on Multimedia and Expo (ICME), pp. 1–6. IEEE (2015)
5. Islam, M.M., Islam, M.R., Islam, M.S.: An efficient human computer interaction through hand gesture using deep convolutional neural network. SN Comput. Sci. **1**(4), 1–9 (2020)
6. Jørgensen, A., Fagertun, J., Moeslund, T.B., et al.: Classify broiler viscera using an iterative approach on noisy labeled training data. In: Bebis, G. (ed.) ISVC 2018. LNCS, vol. 11241, pp. 264–273. Springer, Cham (2018). https://doi.org/10.1007/978-3-030-03801-4_24
7. Kalra, S., Jain, S., Agarwal, A.: Fixed do solfège based object detection and positional analysis for the visually impaired. In: 2017 6th International Conference on Reliability, Infocom Technologies and Optimization (Trends and Future Directions)(ICRITO), pp. 594–598. IEEE (2017)
8. Khan, A., Sohail, A., Zahoora, U., Qureshi, A.S.: A survey of the recent architectures of deep convolutional neural networks. Artif. Intell. Rev. **53**(8), 5455–5516 (2020). https://doi.org/10.1007/s10462-020-09825-6
9. Mäki-Patola, T., Hämäläinen, P.: Latency tolerance for gesture controlled continuous sound instrument without tactile feedback. In: ICMC. Citeseer (2004)
10. McClung, A.C.: Sight-singing scores of high school choristers with extensive training in movable solfège syllables and curwen hand signs. J. Res. Music Educ. **56**(3), 255–266 (2008)
11. Park, S., Kwak, N.: Analysis on the dropout effect in convolutional neural networks. In: Lai, S.-H., Lepetit, V., Nishino, K., Sato, Y. (eds.) ACCV 2016. LNCS, vol. 10112, pp. 189–204. Springer, Cham (2017). https://doi.org/10.1007/978-3-319-54184-6_12
12. Rao, G.A., Syamala, K., Kishore, P., Sastry, A.: Deep convolutional neural networks for sign language recognition. In: 2018 Conference on Signal Processing And Communication Engineering Systems (SPACES), pp. 194–197. IEEE (2018)
13. Schramm, R., Nunes, H.D.S., Jung, C.R.: Audiovisual tool for solfège assessment. ACM Trans. Multi. Comput. Commun. Appl. (TOMM) **13**(1), 1–21 (2016)

14. Schramm, R., de Souza Nunes, H., Jung, C.R.: Automatic solfège assessment. In: ISMIR. pp. 183–189 (2015)
15. Sörös, G., Giger, J., Song, J.: Solfège hand sign recognition with smart glasses. In: First International Workshop on Egocentric Perception, Interaction, and Computing (EPIC 2016). First International Workshop on Egocentric Perception, Interaction, and ... (2016)
16. Srivastava, N., Hinton, G., Krizhevsky, A., Sutskever, I., Salakhutdinov, R.: Dropout: a simple way to prevent neural networks from overfitting. J. Mach. Learn. Res. **15**(1), 1929–1958 (2014)
17. Steeves, C.: The effect of Curwen-Kodaly hand signs on pitch and interval discrimination within a Kodaly curricular framework. University of Calgary (1984)
18. Strigl, D., Kofler, K., Podlipnig, S.: Performance and scalability of GPU-based convolutional neural networks. In: 2010 18th Euromicro Conference on Parallel, Distributed and Network-based Processing, pp. 317–324. IEEE (2010)
19. Von Hardenberg, C., Bérard, F.: Bare-hand human-computer interaction. In: Proceedings of the 2001 Workshop on Perceptive User Interfaces, pp. 1–8 (2001)
20. Wadhawan, A., Kumar, P.: Deep learning-based sign language recognition system for static signs. Neural Comput. Appl. **32**(12), 7957–7968 (2020). https://doi.org/10.1007/s00521-019-04691-y

Image Prior Transfer and Ensemble Architectures for Parkinson's Disease Detection

Tahjid Ashfaque Mostafa[✉] and Irene Cheng

Department of Computing Science, University of Alberta,
Edmonton, AB T6G 2E8, Canada
{tahjid,locheng}@ualberta.ca

Abstract. Neural networks have shown promising results in many applications including computer aided diagnosis systems. However, insufficient effort has been expended on model knowledge transfer combined with ensemble architecture structures. Here, our use case focuses on detecting Parkinson's Disease (PD) by automatic pattern recognition in brain magnetic resonance (MR) images. In order to train a robust neural network, sufficiently large amount of labeled MR image data is essential. However, this is challenging because ground truth data needs to be labeled by clinical experts, who often have busy daily schedules. Furthermore, brain MR images are not often captured for PD patients. Therefore, we explore the effectiveness of pre-training neural networks using natural images instead of brain MR images of PD patients. We also propose different ensemble architecture structures, and demonstrate that they outperform existing models on PD detection. Experimental results show that our detection performance is significantly better compared to models without prior training using natural images. This finding suggests a promising direction when no or insufficient MR image training data is available. Furthermore, we performed occlusion analysis to identify the brain regions that the models focused on to deliver higher performance on PD detection during the decision making process.

Keywords: Parkinson's disease detection · Model knowledge transfer · Ensemble learning · Deep learning · Magnetic resonance imaging

1 Introduction

Computer aided diagnosis systems based on brain imaging have shown merits in the diagnosis of Parkinson's Disease (PD) by automatic recognition of patterns that characterize symptoms. PD is the second most common neurodegenerative disorder and the most common movement disorder affecting the elderly next to the Alzheimer's disease [19]. PD is caused by the loss of neurons in the Substantia Nigra region of the brain, responsible for the production of Dopamine.

Supported by Multimedia Research Center (MRC), Department of Computing Science, University of Alberta, Edmonton, Canada.

G. Bebis et al. (Eds.): ISVC 2021, LNCS 13017, pp. 51–62, 2021.
https://doi.org/10.1007/978-3-030-90439-5_5

It facilitates the communication between neurons for body movement coordination, and a shortage of dopamine will lead to PD. PD has been associated with neurological symptoms like speech impediments, olfactory dysfunctions, sleep disorders, autonomic dysfunctions, fatigue and motor symptoms like tremors, Bradykinesia, postural instability, rigidity of the limbs, impaired gait etc. It has been clinically studied for a long time, but the exact causes leading to PD are still not properly identified [20]. PD is usually diagnosed with motor symptoms, which might not become apparent until 50%–70% of the neurons have been damaged [21], when it is too late for any effective preventive measures. A guaranteed cure for PD has not been discovered, but early detection might offer an opportunity for slowing or stopping the progression of the disease. New forms of treatment like Exenatide [22], show promising results with cases where PD was detected in the initial stages. One of the techniques that has been found to be successful in detecting neurodegenerative diseases with cognitive impairments is the analysis of the structural changes in the brain using Medical Imaging techniques, such as MR images, which provide high contrast and resolution within soft tissue. Inspired by the promising performance of machine learning in recent years, researchers attempted to apply neural networks in analyzing brain MR images to diagnose neurodegenerative diseases, including PD. The challenge lies in the lack of a sufficiently large amount of labeled data, which is critical in order to train a robust neural network. Note that MR images are seldom taken from PD patients, and even if they are available, they are not properly labeled. In this work, (1) we explore the feasibility of detecting PD by first pre-training neural networks using a large quantity of more widely available natural images, before training with a limited set of brain MR images of PD patients, (2) we propose different ensemble architecture structures and analyze which structures can deliver higher PD detection accuracy, (3) we compare the performances between models with and without being pre-trained on natural images and (4) we identify the key regions of the brain in the decision making process using occlusion analysis. In this context, the natural images are taken from the Imagenet [7] dataset. Experimental results show that we achieve over 90% detection accuracy for all our proposed architectures with the highest being 96.3%, which is significantly better than existing models. We also found that using models pre-trained on the Imagenet [7] dataset yields much better performance than just training the model with the limited set of PD MR images.

2   Background and Related Works

Many Machine Learning (ML) and Deep Learning (DL) based approaches have been introduced for the detection of Parkinson's Disease (PD). Babu et al. [2] achieved a 87.21% accuracy in classifying PD using Gray Matter (GM) with a Computer Aided Diagnosis (CAD) system. Rana et al. [3] used a Support Vector Machine (SVM) for classification with t-test feature selection on White Matter (WM) and GM, and also on Cerebrospinal Fluid (CSF). They achieved 86.67% accuracy for GM and WM, and 83.33% accuracy for CSF. In another work [4],

Table 1. Demographic data

	PD	HC	Average
Age (Years)	62.0 ± 9.54	49.2 ± 16.9	55.6 ± 15.1
Sex (Male/Female)	189/110	172/127	361/237

the authors used the relation between tissues instead of considering the tissues separately and achieved an accuracy of 89.67%. Radial Basis Function Neural Network (RBFNN) was used by Pazhanirajan et al. [23] for PD classification. Tahjid et al. [12], demonstrated that an ensemble architecture trained on only WM and GM data performed better than using the whole brain MR scan for detecting PD. In this work, we explore the feasibility of supplementing the training set with natural images (non-PD related) before using a limited set of PD MR images. We also explore 3 ensemble architectures with two model blocks to process WM and GM separately. The proposed architectures were first pre-trained using non-PD related ImageNet [7] (natural) images. We then further trained the architectures with MR images. We separated WM and GM from the MR scans of the brain, and passed them through our architectures separately.

3 Proposed Method

3.1 Dataset

For MR images, We used Parkinson Progression Markers Initiative (PPMI) dataset [5], which consists of T1-weighted sMRI scans for 568 PD and Healthy Control (HC) subjects. We only chose 445 subjects and discarded the rest due to structural anomalies during preprocessing steps. There was a class imbalance in the resulting data with 299 PD and 146 HC subjects. To balance the data, we collected 153 HC T1-weighted sMRI scans from the publicly available IXI dataset [6]. The final dataset was class balanced with 598 subjects. The demographic for the dataset is presented in Table 1. Note that the total of 598 subjects is still regarded as insufficient for learning-based model training. Thus, our strategy is to start from models pre-trained with natural images. The dataset was generated following the works of West et al. [24].

3.2 Preprocessing

The preprocessing pipeline from Tahjid et al. [12] was used for preprocessing the data, which gave us WM (with and without smoothing) and GM (with and without smoothing); 4 categories in total.

3.3 Models

We selected six existing models of the ImageNet Large Scale Visual Recognition Challenge (ILSVRC) [8] implemented in Pytorch [10], to form various model block combinations.

– ResNet 101 [13], SqueezeNet 1.1 [14], DenseNet 201 [15], VGG 19 [16], MobileNet V2 [17], ShuffleNet V2 [18]

The six ILSVRC models are available from Torchvision [11] in two versions: without any training (untrained) and trained on the ImageNet dataset. We trained and tested each model on the MRI data. We then chose the top performing model combinations to create ensemble architectures. The same model block design was used to process the WM, and GM input. We used both untrained and pre-trained models to construct our ensemble model blocks and compared the performances of the resultant architectures to examine if training on the non-PD related ImageNet dataset makes the architectures perform better in PD detection. Since the six models were originally designed to process the ImageNet dataset, we had to modify the input layers of all models to accommodate the format of our MRI input and the output layers were changed to predict between 2 classes (PD and HC) instead of the 1000 ImageNet classes. Based on the top performing model combinations, we propose different architectures described below.

3.4 Ensemble Architecture 1

For this architecture, all six models were stacked as shown in Fig. 1. This design was created with only one data modality in mind. Two versions (untrained and pre-trained) of this model was trained with GM and WM scans separately. The output from all six models was passed through a ReLU layer followed by a linear layer to predict the output.

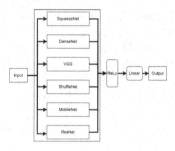

Fig. 1. Ensemble architecture 1

3.5 Ensemble Architecture 2

The extracted GM and WM scan dimension was $121 \times 145 \times 121$. We passed them in parallel through two model blocks, each of which was comprised of multiple ILSVRC models. We then concatenated the output from both blocks and passed them through a ReLU activation layer followed by a final linear layer, which predicted between the two output classes (PD and HC). Figure 2 shows a visual representation of this architecture. We used 3 different model block designs.

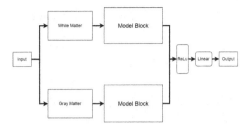

Fig. 2. Ensemble architecture 2

Design 1 - TriNet1. The model block was comprised of DenseNet, ShuffleNet and SqueezeNet in parallel. The input was passed through all three models simultaneously, as shown in Fig. 3a.

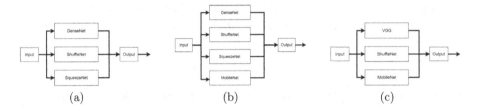

      (a)   (b)   (c)

Fig. 3. (a) Design 1 : TriNet1, (b) Design 2 : QuadNet, (c) Design 3 : TriNet2

Design 2 - QuadNet. The model block was created by adding MobileNet to Model Block 1, so it was comprised of DenseNet, ShuffleNet, SqueezeNet and MobileNet in parallel. The input was passed through all four models simultaneously, as shown in Fig. 3b.

Design 3 - TriNet2. The model block was created with ShuffleNet, VGG and MobileNet in parallel. The input was passed through all three models simultaneously, as shown in Fig. 3c

4   Experimental Results

We had two separate versions for each of our ensemble architectures: constituent models untrained and pre-trained with ImageNet data. The brain MR dataset was randomly split and 80% was selected for training and 20% for testing. At each epoch, the training set was further split randomly and 20% was selected for validation. The models were trained with various learning rates including **0.01**, **.001** and **.0001** and the process was repeated 5 times. For reference purpose, Table 2 presents the results of some existing approaches using similar data.

Table 2. Accuracy results of some related works analyzing WM and GM

Source	Accuracy
Focke et al. [1] [GM]	0.3953
Focke et al. [1] [WM]	0.4186
Babu et al. [2] [GM]	0.8721
Rana et al. [3] [GM & WM]	0.8667
Rana et al. [4]	0.8967

Table 3. Results for resnet with learning rate of 0.0001

Data type	Pre trained	Accuracy	MCC	Precision	Recall	F1 score
Gray matter	True	**0.948**	**0.895**	**0.948**	**0.948**	**0.948**
	False	0.522	0.064	0.751	0.522	0.363
White matter	True	**0.963**	**0.925**	**0.955**	**0.955**	**0.955**
	False	0.526	0.052	0.639	0.524	0.444

Table 4. Results for VGG with learning rate of 0.0001

Data type	Pre trained	Accuracy	MCC	Precision	Recall	F1 score
Gray matter	True	**0.925**	**0.848**	**0.926**	**0.925**	**0.926**
	False	0.545	0.139	0.584	0.545	0.535
White matter	True	**0.940**	**0.880**	**0.933**	**0.933**	**0.933**
	False	0.541	0.098	0.569	0.543	0.498

Table 5. Results for densenet with learning rate of 0.0001

Data type	Pre trained	Accuracy	MCC	Precision	Recall	F1 score
Gray matter	True	**0.918**	**0.838**	**0.921**	**0.918**	**0.918**
	False	0.854	0.716	0.862	0.854	0.855
White matter	True	**0.955**	**0.909**	**0.938**	**0.937**	**0.937**
	False	0.877	0.756	0.871	0.866	0.866

Table 6. Results for mobilenet with learning rate of 0.0001

Data type	Pre trained	Accuracy	MCC	Precision	Recall	F1 score
Gray matter	True	**0.925**	**0.852**	**0.927**	**0.925**	**0.925**
	False	0.534	0.041	0.526	0.534	0.496
White matter	True	**0.925**	**0.849**	**0.926**	**0.925**	**0.925**
	False	0.604	0.203	0.565	0.569	0.550

Table 7. Results for shufflenet with learning rate of 0.0001

Data type	Pre trained	Accuracy	MCC	Precision	Recall	F1 score
Gray matter	True	**0.918**	**0.836**	**0.920**	**0.918**	**0.918**
	False	0.534	0.042	0.533	0.534	0.453
White matter	True	**0.937**	**0.874**	**0.929**	**0.927**	**0.927**
	False	0.494	0.111	0.531	0.485	0.420

Table 8. Results for squeezenet with learning rate of 0.0001

Data type	Pre trained	Accuracy	MCC	Precision	Recall	F1 score
gray Matter	True	**0.873**	**0.747**	**0.874**	**0.873**	**0.873**
	False	0.757	0.542	0.790	0.757	0.748
White matter	True	**0.948**	**0.898**	**0.912**	**0.910**	**0.910**
	False	0.765	0.530	0.779	0.761	0.755

Table 9. Results for ensemble architecture 2 with pre trained constituent models for gray matter and white matter

Model block	LR	Accuracy	MCC	Precision	Recall	F1 score
TriNet1	0.0001	0.903	0.811	0.926	0.923	0.923
QuadNet	0.0001	**0.963**	**0.927**	**0.951**	**0.950**	**0.950**
TriNet2	0.0001	0.955	0.910	0.947	0.947	0.947

Table 10. Results for ensemble architecture 1 with pre trained constituent models for gray matter and white matter

Datatype	LR	Accuracy	MCC	Precision	Recall	F1 score
WM	0.0001	**0.963**	**0.928**	**0.944**	**0.943**	**0.943**
GM	0.0001	0.948	0.896	0.936	0.935	0.935

The tables report multiple evaluation metric scores including Accuracy, Precision, Recall, F_1 score and MCC score. All scores are reported in the range of $(0, 1)$, except MCC score, which is in the range of $(-1, 1)$. The scores are reported in $Mean \pm Standard\,Deviation$ format. The best scores for each model using the same modality of data but with different window sizes were reported in bold font. Tables 3, 4, 5, 6, 7 and 8 present the performance of Resnet [13], VGG [16], Densenet [15], MobileNet [17], ShuffleNet [18] and SqueezeNet [14], but we modified the input and output layers to handle GM and WM scans. The learning rate was 0.0001. Comparing the overall performance, we can conclude that WM achieved the best performance across all metrics for PD detection. GM also has high performance across all metrics, although the scores were lower than that of WM. Modified Resnet with WM achieved one of the best scores across all metrics among all of the tested models. Using smoothed scans did not improve the performance than using the original scans, probably due to losing fine details. But we notice that no matter testing with the original or smoothed scans, models pretrained with Imagenet data showed significantly better performances than models only trained with MRI data. Table 9 presents different results for Ensemble Architecture 2 using three different model block designs with a learning rate of 0.0001. We only included results using original WM and GM scans, as using smoothed scans gave inferior performance. We can see that QuadNet achieved the highest metric scores. Table 10 shows the results of Ensemble Architecture 1. This architecture was different in the sense that it was only trained for one data modality at a time. Two instances of the model were trained, with one for GM and one for WM. The learning rate was 0.0001. By using the same parameter setting, WM produced the superior scores. Based on our findings, we can say that our methods performed better than related work (Table 2) for analyzing WM and GM. WM provided better information for detecting PD, with the understanding that the smoothed scans might have lost details compared with the orignal scans. It is obvious that our proposed ensemble architectures generated better results than the individual models. Also, architectures pre-trained with the ImageNet database performed better than only trained with a limited set of MRI scans.

5   Occlusion Analysis to Locate Relevant Regions

To understand which regions of the brain are important for the models' decision making process, we performed a slightly modified version of occlusion analysis proposed by Rieke et al. [9]. In this analysis, usually a part of the scan is occluded with a gray or white patch. The occluded region is considered to be important if the probability of detecting the target class decreases compared to the original image. The heatmap of relevance is calculated by sliding the patch across the image and plotting the difference in the probability in red. The brightness of the red-shaded region indicates the importance of the region. In our experiment, the relevance was calculated such that the sum of relevance of all areas was 1. Our heatmaps contain slices taken from the original MRI scan at specific x, y and z coordinates and the difference in probability at that point. Occlusion analysis was performed on multiple models, but due to page limit, the results of two models that produced the best performance are presented in this section. The models were modified Resnet [13] and Ensemble Architecture 1 [3.4]. All models were pre-trained with the ImageNet [7] dataset, and they were trained with a learning rate of 0.0001. We found that analyzing the GM and WM regions separately produced better results than analyzing the whole brain scan Tahjid et al. [12]. Therefore, only models trained on GM or WM were selected for occlusion analysis. The relevance area was calculated from the generated occlusion heatmaps using methods provided by Rieke et al. [9].

5.1   Occlusion Analysis for Modified ResNet

Modified Resnet [13] produced the best results out of the 6 individual models as shown in Table 3. Two versions of the model were trained, with one on WM and the other on GM. Figure 4a shows that the Middle Temporal Gyrus and Superior Temporal Gyrus were significant in the decision making process when using WM, followed by the Postcentral Gyrus region. Figure 4b shows that when using GM, the relevance were more evenly distributed, but Middle Temporal Gyrus was once again vital in the decision making process, followed by Middle Frontal Gyrus, Frontal Superior Medial Gyrus, and Thalamus and Superior Temporal Gyrus.

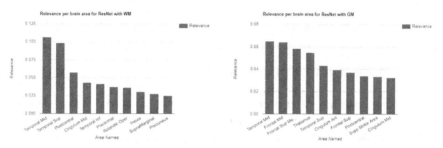

(a) Relevance per brain area for White Matter analysis based on Pretrained ResNet [16]

(b) Relevance per brain area for Gray Matter analysis based on Pretrained ResNet [16]

Fig. 4. Relevance per brain area for PD detection based on pretrained resnet

5.2   Occlusion Analysis for Ensemble Architecture - Model 1

Ensemble Architecture 1 [3.4] performed very well when trained on GM and WM as presented in Table 10. The relevance area was computed on 2 versions of the model: WM and GM separately. Figure 5a illustrates the relevance area while using only WM, showing the Middle Frontal, Middle Occipital and Middle Temporal Gyrus to be the three most relevant areas for decision making. However, the Thalamus, Superior Temporal and Middle Temporal Gyrus appear to be the most relevant when using GM as shown in Fig. 5b. Since analyzing WM delivers better detection performance, we believe that, based on our occlusion analysis, the Middle Temporal Gyrus and Middle Frontal should be focused on in future work.

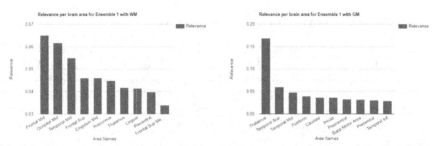

(a) Relevance per brain area for White (b) Relevance per brain area for Gray Mat-Matter using Ensemble Architecture 1 with ter using Ensemble Architecture 1 with pretrained constituent models   pretrained constituent models

Fig. 5. Relevance area based on ensemble architecture 1.

6   Conclusion and Future Works

We introduce 2 ensemble architecture structures and demonstrate that their performances outperform individual models for PD detection. By enhancing the concept of ensemble architectures [12], we also explored the performance of detecting PD symptoms in MR images by pre-training with a sufficiently larger number of non-PD related images before training the models with a limited set of PD related WM and GM scans. The learnt image prior significantly enhanced the performance compared to models only trained with the limited MRI scans. In addition, we propose new model block designs with new data modalities for PD Detection. Our results outperform related works in terms of accuracy using similar dataset. This finding suggests that training data unrelated to PD can be used to supplement insufficient PD training data. We also performed occlusion analysis to identify brain regions of high relevance in the decision making process for PD detection.

In future work, we plan to further analyze and understand the decision making process of a model, and focus on the relevant brain regions discovered using occlusion analysis in this paper. We were not able to consult experts and validate our findings regarding relevant areas from occlusion analysis in light of medical literature due to ongoing Covid-19 situation, however that is also in our future plans. Furthermore, we want to understand which features are better explained by which specific model, based on which we can structure a more efficient ensemble architecture.

Acknowledgment. Data used in the preparation of this article was obtained from the Parkinson's Progression Markers Initiative (PPMI) database (www.ppmi-info.org/data). For up-to-date information on the study, visit www.ppmi-info.org. PPMI is a public-private partnership funded by the Michael J. Fox Foundation for Parkinson's Research and other funding partners listed at www.ppmi-info.org/fundingpartners. Financial support from the Natural Sciences and Engineering Research Council of Canada (NSERC) is gratefully acknowledged.

References

1. Focke, N.K., et al.: Individual voxel-based subtype prediction can differentiate progressive supranuclear palsy from idiopathic parkinson syndrome and healthy controls. Hum. Brain Map. **32**(11), 1905–1915 (2011)
2. Babu, G.S., Suresh, S., Mahanand, B.S.: A novel PBL-McRBFN-RFE approach for identification of critical brain regions responsible for parkinson's 235 disease. Expert Syst. Appl. **41**(2), 478–488 (2014)
3. Rana, B., et al.: Graph-theory-based spectral feature selection for computer aided diagnosis of parkinson's disease using t1-weighted MRI. Int. J. Imaging Syst. Technol. **25**(3), 245–255 (2015)
4. Rana, B., et al.: Relevant 3D local binary pattern based features from fused feature descriptor for differential diagnosis of parkinsons disease using structural MRI. Biomed. Signal Process. Control **34**, 134–143 (2017)
5. Parkinsons Progression Markers Initiative (PPMI). https://www.260ppmi-info. org/. Accessed 30 Sept 2019
6. IXI Dataset. https://brain-development.org/ixi-dataset/. Accessed 30 Sept 2019
7. Deng, J., Dong, W., Socher, R., Li, L.-J., Li, K., Fei-Fei, L.: ImageNet: a large-scale hierarchical image database. In: CVPR09 (2009)
8. Russakovsky, O., et al.: ImageNet large scale visual recognition challenge. Int. J. Comput. Vis. 115(3), 211–252 (2015). https://doi.org/10.1007/s11263-015-0816-y
9. Rieke, J., Eitel, F., Weygandt, M., Haynes, J.-D., Ritter, K., et al.: Visualizing convolutional networks for MRI-based diagnosis of Alzheimer's disease. In: Stoyanov, D. (ed.) MLCN/DLF/IMIMIC -2018. LNCS, vol. 11038, pp. 24–31. Springer, Cham (2018). https://doi.org/10.1007/978-3-030-02628-8_3
10. Paszke, A., et al.: Pytorch: an imperative style, high-performance deep learning library. In: Wallach, H., Larochelle, H., Beygelzimer, A., dAlch e-Buc, F., Fox, E., Garnett, R. (eds): Advances in Neural Information Processing Systems 32, pp. 8024–8035. Curran Associates, Inc. (2019)
11. Marcel, S., Rodriguez, Y.: Torchvision the machine-vision package of torch. In: Proceedings of the 18th ACM International Conference on Multimedia, MM '10, New York, NY, USA, pp. 1485–1488. Association for Computing Machinery (2010)
12. Mostafa, T.A., Cheng, I.: Parkinson's Disease Detection Using Ensemble Architecture From MR Images (2020)
13. He, K., Zhang, X., Ren, S., Sun, J.: Deep residual learning for image recognition. arXiv preprint arXiv:1512.03385 (2015)
14. Iandola, F.N., Moskewicz, M.W., Ashraf, K., Han, S., Dally, W.J., Keutzer, K.: Squeezenet: Alexnet-level accuracy with 50x fewer parameters and <1mb model size. arXiv:1602.07360 (2016)
15. Huang, G., Liu, Z., van der Maaten, L., Weinberger, K.Q.: Densely Connected Convolutional Networks (2016)
16. Simonyan, K., Zisserman, A.: Very deep convolutional networks for large-scale image recognition (2014)
17. Sandler, M., Howard, A., Zhu, M., Zhmoginov, A., Chen, L.C.: Mobilenetv 2: Inverted residuals and linear bottlenecks (2018)
18. Ma, N., Zhang, X., Zheng, H.T., Sun, J.: Shufflenet v2: Practical guidelines for efficient CNN architecture design (2018)
19. Mhyre, T.R., Boyd, J.T., Hamill, R.W., Maguire-Zeiss, K.: Parkinson's disease. In: Harris, J. (ed.) Protein Aggregation and Fibrillogenesis in Cerebral and Systemic Amyloid Disease. Subcellular Biochemistry, vol. 65, pp. 389–455. Springer, Dordrecht (2012). https://doi.org/10.1007/978-94-007-5416-4_16

20. Peng, B., et al.: A multilevel-ROI-features-based machine learning method for detection of morphometric biomarkers in parkinson's disease. Neurosci. Lett. **651**, 88–94 (2017)
21. Cheng, H.-C., Ulane, C.M., Burke, R.E.: Clinical progression in Parkinson disease and the neurobiology of axons. Ann. Neurol. **67**(6), 715–725 (2010)
22. Athauda, D., et al.: Exenatide once weekly versus placebo in Parkinsons disease: a randomised, double-blind, placebo-controlled trial. Lancet **390**(10103), 16641675 (2017)
23. Pazhanirajan, S., Dhanalakshmi, P.: Classification of parkinson's disease using MRI images. Int. J. Comput. Sci. Soft. Eng. **5**(10), 233 (2016)
24. McDaniel, T., Berretti, S., Curcio, I.D.D., Basu, A. (eds.): ICSM 2019. LNCS, vol. 12015. Springer, Cham (2020). https://doi.org/10.1007/978-3-030-54407-2

Computer Graphics I

BRDF Measurement of Real Materials Using Handheld Cameras

Haru Otani and Takashi Komuro$^{(\boxtimes)}$

Saitama University, Saitama 338-8570, Japan
`komuro@mail.saitama-u.ac.jp`

Abstract. In this paper, we propose a method for measuring the Bidirectional Reflectance Distribution Function (BRDF) of real planar materials using a simple apparatus. Our proposed method uses two handheld cameras, a light source mounted on one of the cameras, and a box with markers attached to each face. A planar material is placed on the box and the user acquires video images of the material while moving the two cameras around the material. The system obtains a sampled BRDF using the light source and viewpoint positions and pixel values at a certain point on the material. Then, a dense BRDF is estimated by interpolating the sampled BRDF using the technique of compressed sensing. The experimental results showed that the proposed method can reproduce the reflectance properties of real materials. It was also shown that compressed sensing was more suitable than RBF interpolation for estimating dense BRDFs.

Keywords: Reflectance measurement · Compressed sensing · Data interpolation

1 Introduction

In recent years, there has been a growing demand for 3D computer graphics (CG) technology for video work. In order to create more realistic CG, many studies have been conducted to reproduce the appearance of real materials by measuring the reflectance properties of material surfaces. Reflectance properties are often represented by a function called the Bidirectional Reflectance Distribution Function (BRDF), which defines the ratio of the reflected radiance to the incident irradiance for given incoming and outgoing directions. In order to measure dense BRDFs, there are methods in which a light source and a camera are moved with a special device, and methods in which many light sources and cameras are placed around the material [2,3,14]. By observing the reflected light for any combination of incoming and outgoing light directions, it is possible to measure the dense BRDF of a real material. However, these methods have the problems that the measurement is time consuming and the equipment is expensive.

On the other hand, to reduce the number of samples required to measure the BRDF, there are methods that approximate an unknown BRDF using a linear combination of known BRDFs [7,9,10] or a parametric reflectance model

© Springer Nature Switzerland AG 2021
G. Bebis et al. (Eds.): ISVC 2021, LNCS 13017, pp. 65–77, 2021.
https://doi.org/10.1007/978-3-030-90439-5_6

[1,5,6,8,11,16]. These methods require a relatively small number of samples, which allows measurements to be performed in a short time or by using simple equipment. However, there are some problems; for example, the BRDFs that can be represented are limited by the known BRDF data or the reflectance models used, and BRDFs with local variations are difficult to recover.

There are also methods that estimate the dense BRDF by interpolating a sparsely sampled BRDF. Zickler et al. proposed a method to obtain the BRDF of an object with a known shape by interpolating the sampled BRDF using Radial Basis Functions (RBFs) [17]. Zupancic proposed a method to interpolate the sampled BRDF using compressed sensing [18], but they only applied their method to a synthetic image.

Based on these studies, we propose a method that can measure dense BRDFs of real materials using a simple apparatus. Our proposed method uses two hand-held cameras, one of which is equipped with a light source, and a box with markers (marker box). A planar material is placed in the center of the top surface of the marker box, and the two handheld cameras are moved around the material to observe the light coming from various directions and reflected in various directions. Part of the BRDF data is obtained using the light source and viewpoint positions, and pixel values at a certain point on the material. Since it is difficult to obtain samples for all combinations of light source and viewpoint positions, the dense BRDF is estimated by interpolating the sampled BRDF using the technique of compressed sensing.

2   BRDF Measurement Using Handheld Cameras

2.1   Use of Bivariate BRDF

The BRDF is a function that expresses the reflectance properties by the ratio of the radiance $L_r(\omega_r)$ (energy of reflected light) to the irradiance $E_i(\omega_i)$ (energy of incident light) of a surface, and is generally expressed by:

$$f_{\text{BRDF}}(\omega_i, \omega_r) = \frac{dL_r(\omega_r)}{dE_i(\omega_i)}, \qquad (1)$$

where ω_i and ω_r are vectors representing the incoming and outgoing light directions, respectively. Let the elevation angles of the vectors be θ_i and θ_r and the azimuth angles be ϕ_i and ϕ_r. The general BRDF is represented as shown in Fig. 1(a).

In this study, we use the bivariate BRDF proposed by Romeiro et al. [12]. The bivariate BRDF is defined as a function of the angles θ_h $(0 \leq \theta_h < \frac{\pi}{2})$ and θ_d $(0 \leq \theta_d < \frac{\pi}{2})$, as shown in Fig. 1(b). Here, θ_h is the angle between the halfway vector h (between ω_i and ω_r) and the normal n. θ_d is the angle between ω_i and h. We use this bivariate BRDF expression since compressed sensing is mainly applied to 1D or 2D data, and also it is easy to visualize.

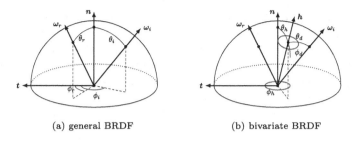

(a) general BRDF   (b) bivariate BRDF

Fig. 1. BRDF expressions.

2.2 BRDF Sampling

The measurement system is shown in Fig. 2. In order to measure the BRDF, we need to obtain the reflectances at various light source and viewpoint positions. Therefore, we use two handheld cameras, a light source mounted on one of the cameras, and a rectangular box with ChArUco markers [4,13] attached to each face. The user acquires video images of a planar material placed on the box while moving the two cameras around the material. Using the markers in the images, the poses of the two cameras in each frame are determined. If markers are put on a plane, the markers will not be recognized when they are seen from a nearly horizontal direction. The marker box makes it possible to recognize markers from any direction.

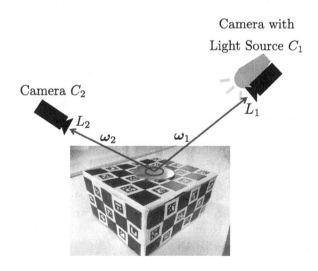

Fig. 2. Measurement system.

Using the poses of the cameras and the pixel values in the camera images that correspond to a certain point on the material surface, it is possible to obtain the light source position, viewpoint position, and radiance for each camera. The light source and viewpoint positions corresponding to the radiance L_1 acquired by the camera C_1 are both (ω_1, d_1), where ω indicates the direction, and d indicates the distance. The light source and viewpoint positions corresponding to the radiance L_2 acquired by the camera C_2 are (ω_1, d_1) and (ω_2, d_2), respectively.

Integrating both sides of Eq. (1) over the hemisphere Ω in the spherical coordinate system, the radiance L_r from the surface is expressed by:

$$L_r = \int_\Omega f_{\text{BRDF}}(\omega_i, \omega_r) dE_i. \tag{2}$$

Assuming that there is only one single point light source and that no light from other sources enters, L_r can be rewritten as follows using the radiant intensity I, incident angle θ_i, and distance d of the light source:

$$L_r = \frac{I \cos \theta_i}{d^2} f_{\text{BRDF}}(\omega_i, \omega_r). \tag{3}$$

Therefore, in a single light source measurement, if the light source position, viewpoint position, and the radiance are known, the corresponding BRDF value can be calculated using:

$$f_{\text{BRDF}}(\omega_i, \omega_r) = \frac{L_r d^2}{I \cos \theta_i}. \tag{4}$$

2.3   Dense BRDF Estimation

We can obtain sampled BRDF data using the method above. However, since it is difficult to measure the reflectances for all incoming and outgoing directions, a dense BRDF is estimated by interpolating the values in the missing directions.

BRDF Estimation Using Compressed Sensing. A dense BRDF is estimated from the sampled data using compressed sensing. Compressed sensing is a method of estimating the overall data from fewer observations than normally required when the unknown data can be assumed to be sparse, i.e., have few non-zero components, on a given representation space.

The bivariate BRDF $f(\theta_h, \theta_d)$ used in this study can be visualized as an image as shown in Fig. 3(a) by storing the corresponding RGB values in a 2D array with θ_h on the horizontal axis and θ_d on the vertical axis. As can be seen in Fig. 3(a), BRDFs are generally not sparse, but they can be sparsely represented by applying the Discrete Cosine Transform (DCT) to the 2D array that is divided into blocks, as shown in Fig. 3(b). Hereinafter, BRDFs on this sparse representation space are referred to as "sparse BRDFs".

The dense BRDF is reconstructed from the sampled BRDF in the following way. Assume that the possible values of θ_h and θ_d in ascending order can be written as

$$\theta_h = \theta_{h,1}, \ldots, \theta_{h,p}, \ldots, \theta_{h,N_h} \tag{5}$$

$$\theta_d = \theta_{d,1}, \ldots, \theta_{d,q}, \ldots, \theta_{d,N_d}. \tag{6}$$

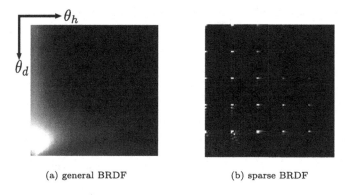

(a) general BRDF   (b) sparse BRDF

Fig. 3. Sparse BRDF representation using DCT.

The RGB values of the sampled BRDF are allocated in the vector $\boldsymbol{y} = (y_1, \ldots, y_m)^T$, and the RGB values of the dense BRDF to be estimated are allocated in the vector $\boldsymbol{x} = (x_1, \ldots, x_n)^T$, where $n = N_h N_d$. Defining the observation matrix $A = (a_{i,j})$ with m rows and n columns as:

$$a_{i,j} = \begin{cases} 1 & \begin{pmatrix} y_i = x_j = f(\theta_{h,p}, \theta_{d,q}), \\ j = N_h q + p \end{pmatrix} \\ 0 & \text{(other)} \end{cases} \tag{7}$$

gives

$$\boldsymbol{y} = A\boldsymbol{x}. \tag{8}$$

Letting the matrix that performs DCT on the dense BRDF be W, the sparse BRDF can be written as $W\boldsymbol{x}$, and the relationship between $\boldsymbol{y}$ and $W\boldsymbol{x}$ is represented as in Fig. 4.

Using Lasso regularization [15], which is a type of sparse vector estimation method used in compressed sensing, the sparse BRDF is estimated as a solution to the optimization problem shown in:

$$W\hat{\boldsymbol{x}} = \arg\min_{W\boldsymbol{x}} \frac{1}{2m} \|\boldsymbol{y} - A\boldsymbol{x}\|_2^2 + \lambda \|W\boldsymbol{x}\|_1, \tag{9}$$

where $\lambda > 0$ is a control parameter, and m is the number of samples. The dense BRDF is obtained by applying an inverse DCT to the estimated $W\hat{\boldsymbol{x}}$.

BRDF Estimation Using RBF Interpolation. Another method is to estimate the dense BRDF by RBF interpolation on the measured data.

The RBF is a function whose value depends only on the distance $r = \|\boldsymbol{x} - \boldsymbol{c}\|_2$ from the center point $\boldsymbol{c}$, and is expressed as $\phi(r)$. RBF interpolation of the function $f(\boldsymbol{x})$ is performed by using:

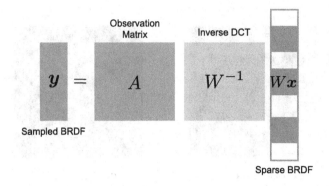

Fig. 4. Relationship between sampled BRDF and sparse BRDF

$$f(\boldsymbol{x}) = \sum_{i}^{N} w_i \phi(\|\boldsymbol{x} - \boldsymbol{x}_i\|_2). \tag{10}$$

In the case of the bivariate BRDF $f(\theta_h, \theta_d)$, $\boldsymbol{x} = (\theta_h, \theta_d)$ and $\boldsymbol{x}_i = (\theta_{h_i}, \theta_{d_i})$, which corresponds to a measured BRDF value $y_i = f(\theta_{h_i}, \theta_{d_i})$. The weights w_i are determined so that the interpolated function passes through all sample points, specifically by solving the following equation for the vector $\boldsymbol{w} = (w_1, \ldots, w_N)^T$:

$$\begin{pmatrix} y_1 \\ \vdots \\ y_N \end{pmatrix} = \begin{pmatrix} \phi(\|\boldsymbol{x}_1 - \boldsymbol{x}_1\|_2) & \cdots & \phi(\|\boldsymbol{x}_1 - \boldsymbol{x}_N\|_2) \\ \vdots & \ddots & \vdots \\ \phi(\|\boldsymbol{x}_N - \boldsymbol{x}_1\|_2) & \cdots & \phi(\|\boldsymbol{x}_N - \boldsymbol{x}_N\|_2) \end{pmatrix} \begin{pmatrix} w_1 \\ \vdots \\ w_N \end{pmatrix}. \tag{11}$$

From the obtained weights $\boldsymbol{w}$ and N sample points $(\boldsymbol{x}_i, y_i)\,(i = 1, \ldots, N)$, the dense BRDF is estimated using Eq. (10).

3 BRDF Measurement of Real Materials

3.1 Experimental Setup

We conducted an experiment to perform BRDF measurements of real materials using the proposed method. We used FLIR FL3-U3-120S3C cameras as handheld cameras and captured video images with an image size of 1440×1080, a frame rate of about 6 fps, and 16-bit resolution. We used 16-bit resolution images to avoid saturation in highlights, but we used only the lower 8 bits for detecting markers.

We set the angular resolution of the BRDF to $\pi/180$. The optimization problem of compressed sensing was solved using the Python optimization library CVXPY. The RBF interpolation was performed using SciPy, a Python library for scientific and technical computing. We used a Gaussian RBF $\phi(r) = e^{-(\varepsilon r)^2}$ for RBF interpolation.

Using the measurement system shown in Fig. 3, we captured video images of a color aluminum foil sheet with relatively strong specular reflection and a plastic case with relatively weak specular reflection. Some of the video images captured using the measurement system are shown in Fig. 5.

(a) color foil

(b) plastic

Fig. 5. Some of the video images captured using the measurement system.

The sampled BRDF was calculated from the captured images, and the dense BRDF was estimated using compressed sensing and RBF interpolation. There was a very bright part in the estimated BRDF, as shown in Fig. 6, but such parts are rarely used for rendering. Therefore, we cropped the ranges to $\theta_h < 2\pi/5$ and $\theta_d < 2\pi/5$, which is important for reproducing the appearance of objects and adjusted the brightness to make them clearer.

3.2   Estimation Results

The results of dense BRDF estimation from sampled BRDFs using compressed sensing and RBF interpolation for different numbers of samples m are shown in Fig. 7 and Fig. 8, respectively.

The estimation result using compressed sensing shows that the BRDF values that were not measured were smoothly interpolated. The rendering results show that the specular reflection of the color foil was reproduced, and detailed reflection was expressed as the number of samples increased.

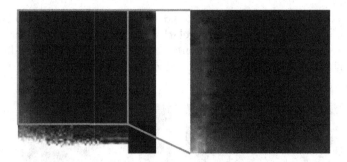

Fig. 6. An example of the estimated BRDF.

The RBF interpolation resulted in partial holes at all percentages of acquisition, and this effect was also observed in the rendering results. The holes in the rendered results became smaller as the percentage of acquisition increased, suggesting that more samples are needed when using RBF interpolation to estimate a dense BRDF.

Finally, the estimation results for the plastic material using compressed sensing are shown in Fig. 9. We can see that the specular reflection was weaker and the diffuse reflection was stronger than those of the colored foil, accurately reproducing the reflectance properties of the plastic material.

3.3   Measurement Time

The number of captured frames and measurement time until the BRDF acquisition rate reached 10%, 20%, 30%, and 40% in the color foil measurement are shown in Fig. 10. The number of captured frames and capturing time were not completely proportional since the frames in which no marker was detected were not recorded.

We can see that the slopes of the number of captured images and the measurement time became steeper as the acquisition rate increased. This is due to the fact that the amount of unacquired parts decreased as the measurement proceeded, making it difficult to acquire new data. Therefore, considering the balance between the quality of the estimated results and the measurement time, an acquisition rate of 30 to 40% is recommended.

Since we captured images at about 6 fps, and markers were successfully recognized only in about 30% of frames, it took about 40 min to achieve an acquisition rate of 30%. On the other hand, it took only about 2 min for estimation using compressed sensing when the acquisition rate was 30%, indicating that the time required for data acquisition is dominant. However, there is room for a further reduction in time by improving the frame rate and stabilizing the marker detection, which would further enhance the usefulness of the proposed method.

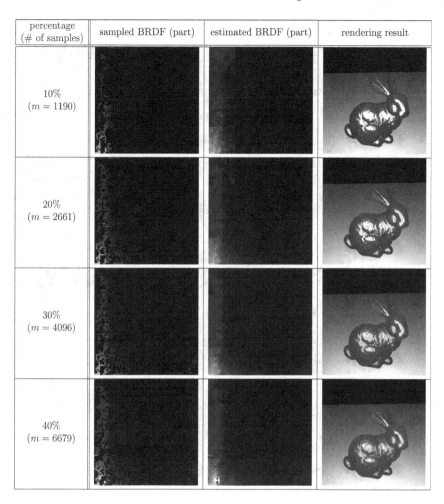

Fig. 7. Results of dense BRDF estimation using compressed sensing for different numbers of samples m (color foil, 5×5 blocks, $\lambda = 10^{-6}$).

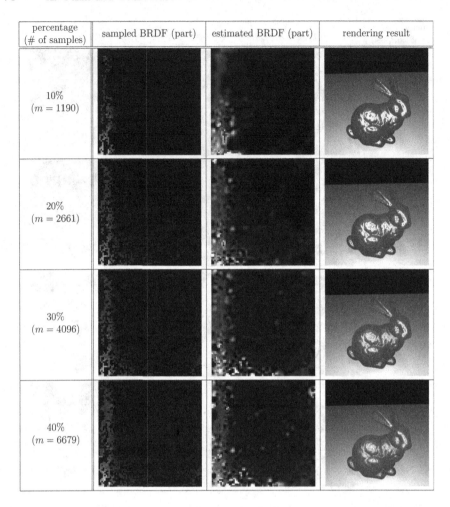

Fig. 8. Results of dense BRDF estimation using RBF interpolation for different numbers of samples m (color foil, $\phi(r) = e^{-(\varepsilon r)^2}$, $\varepsilon = 2.4$).

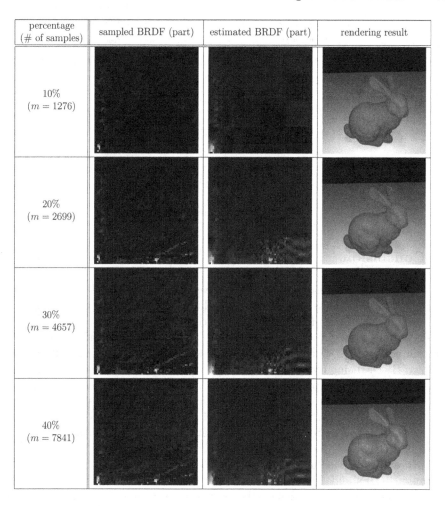

percentage (# of samples)	sampled BRDF (part)	estimated BRDF (part)	rendering result

Fig. 9. Results of dense BRDF estimation using compressed sensing for different numbers of samples m (plastic, 5×5 blocks, $\lambda = 10^{-6}$)).

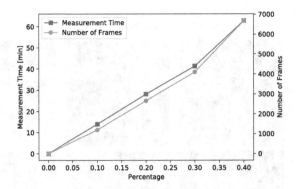

Fig. 10. Measurement time.

4   Conclusion

In this study, we proposed a system for measuring the BRDF of real materials using handheld cameras. By moving two handheld cameras around a planar material placed on top of a marker box, we could acquire images of the material under various combinations of light source and viewpoint positions to obtain the sampled BDRF. Then, a dense BRDF was estimated by interpolating the sampled BRDF using compressed sensing.

We conducted an experiment to measure the BRDFs using real planar materials. It was confirmed that dense BRDFs could be sufficiently reproduced when the acquisition rate of BRDF data was 30% or more. We also found that compressed sensing was more effective for estimating dense BRDFs than RBF interpolation was.

Future work will include the application of the proposed method to 3-variable isotropic BRDFs and 4-variable anisotropic BRDFs. By extending the DCT to 3 or 4 dimensions, and by using other sparse transformation methods suitable for these dimensions, it should be possible to perform 3- or 4-variable BRDF estimation. Another challenge is to apply the proposed method to non-planar objects. If we can measure the normals of the objects' surfaces, it will be possible to measure the BRDFs of non-planar objects.

References

1. Aittala, M., Weyrich, T., Lehtinen, J., et al.: Two-shot SVBRDF capture for stationary materials. ACM Trans. Graph. (TOG) **34**(4), 110:1-110:13 (2015)
2. Debevec, P., Hawkins, T., Tchou, C., Duiker, H.P., Sarokin, W., Sagar, M.: Acquiring the reflectance field of a human face. In: Proceedings of the 27th Annual Conference on Computer Graphics and Interactive Techniques, pp. 145–156 (2000)
3. Foo, S.C.: A Gonioreflectometer for Measuring the Bidirectional Reflectance of Material for Use in Illumination Computation. Ph.D. thesis, Cornell University (1997)

4. Garrido-Jurado, S., Munoz-Salinas, R., Madrid-Cuevas, F.J., Medina-Carnicer, R.: Generation of fiducial marker dictionaries using mixed integer linear programming. Pattern Recogn. **51**, 481–491 (2016)
5. Holzschuch, N., Pacanowski, R.: Identifying diffraction effects in measured reflectances. In: Proceedings of Eurographics Workshop on Material Appearance Modeling, pp. 31–34 (2015)
6. Hui, Z., Sunkavalli, K., Lee, J.Y., Hadap, S., Wang, J., Sankaranarayanan, A.C.: Reflectance capture using univariate sampling of BRDFS. In: Proceedings of the IEEE International Conference on Computer Vision, pp. 5362–5370 (2017)
7. Matusik, W., Pfister, H., Brand, M., McMillan, L.: A data-driven reflectance model. ACM Trans. Graph. (TOG) **22**(3), 759–769 (2003)
8. Nam, G., Lee, J.H., Gutierrez, D., Kim, M.H.: Practical SVBRDF acquisition of 3D objects with unstructured flash photography. ACM Trans. Graph. **37**(6), 267 (2018)
9. Nielsen, J.B., Jensen, H.W., Ramamoorthi, R.: On optimal, minimal BRDF sampling for reflectance acquisition. ACM Trans. Graph. (TOG) **34**(6), 1–11 (2015)
10. Ren, P., Wang, J., Snyder, J., Tong, X., Guo, B.: Pocket reflectometry. ACM Trans. Graph. (TOG) **30**(4), 1–10 (2011)
11. Riviere, J., Peers, P., Ghosh, A.: Mobile surface reflectometry. Comput. Graph. Forum **35**(1), 191–202 (2016)
12. Romeiro, F., Vasilyev, Y., Zickler, T.: Passive reflectometry. In: Forsyth, D., Torr, P., Zisserman, A. (eds.) ECCV 2008. LNCS, vol. 5305, pp. 859–872. Springer, Heidelberg (2008). https://doi.org/10.1007/978-3-540-88693-8_63
13. Romero-Ramirez, F.J., Muñoz-Salinas, R., Medina-Carnicer, R.: Speeded up detection of squared fiducial markers. Image Vis. Comput. **76**, 38–47 (2018)
14. Schwartz, C., Sarlette, R., Weinmann, M., Klein, R.: Dome II: a parallelized BTF acquisition system. In: Proceedings of Material Appearance Modeling, pp. 25–31 (2013)
15. Tibshirani, R.: Regression shrinkage and selection via the lasso. J. R. Stat. Soc. Ser. B (Methodol.) **58**(1), 267–288 (1996)
16. Wu, T.Y., Ma, W.C., Chuang, Y.Y., Chen, B.Y., Ouhyoung, M.: Image-based BRDF acquisition for non-spherical objects. In: Proceedings of Workshop on Computer Vision & Graphic Image Processing, vol. 5 (2005)
17. Zickler, T.E., Enrique, S., Ramamoorthi, R., Belhumeur, P.N.: Reflectance sharing: image-based rendering from a sparse set of images. In: Proceedings of Rendering Techniques, pp. 253–264 (2005)
18. Zupancic, B., Soler, C.: Sparse BRDF approximation using compressive sensing. In: Proceedings of ACM SIGGRAPH Conference and Exhibition on Computer Graphics and Interactive Techniques in Asia, p. 42 (2013)

SORGATE: Extracting Geometry and Texture from Images of Solids of Revolution

Antonio Ledesma and Robert R. Lewis$^{(\boxtimes)}$

Washington State University, Tri-Cities, Richland, USA
bobl@wsu.edu

Abstract. We describe SORGATE, a procedure for extracting geometry and texture from images of solids of revolution (SORs). It uses multivariate optimization to determine the parameters of the camera in order to build the viewing transform, as well as to reconstruct the geometry of the SOR using the silhouette. In addition to individual image analyses, it can use the data extracted from the same SOR viewed from different directions to produce a single, composite texture which can be combined with their blended geometries to produce a reconstructed 3D model. No prior knowledge other than the object's rotational symmetry is required. Camera viewing parameters are derived directly from the image.

SORGATE is useful when 3D modeling of SORs is needed yet direct measurement the physical objects is infeasible. As it does not require camera calibration, it is also fast, inexpensive, and practical. One use case might be for researchers and curators who wish to display and/or analyze the art on historical vases; metric reconstruction and proper texturing of the objects would allow this without requiring viewing in person.

Keywords: Image-based modeling and rendering · Solids of revolution · Geometry extraction · Texture extraction

1 Introduction

The task of extracting 3D information about objects appearing in 2D images and videos has wide application and is a fundamental research area in image-based modeling and rendering. To simplify the problem, methods often focus on certain classes of objects, such as those that exhibit symmetric properties. Accepting such properties as given makes it easier to extract the information. A common symmetry found in many everyday objects is rotational symmetry about an axis; objects with this symmetry are known as solids of revolution (SORs).

We present here a method which we refer to as "SORGATE" (Solid of Revolution Geometry And Texture Extraction) for doing this, as shown in Fig. 1. If we have multiple images of the same SOR from different viewpoints, we can create a single composite texture that applies to as much of the SOR as the individual images cover. We can then combine this with the merged geometry information to, for example, produce a textured model of the SOR. We have

© Springer Nature Switzerland AG 2021
G. Bebis et al. (Eds.): ISVC 2021, LNCS 13017, pp. 78–90, 2021.
https://doi.org/10.1007/978-3-030-90439-5_7

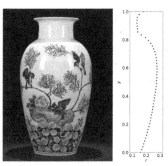

Fig. 1. Overview: Starting with one or more uncalibrated photographs (left) of an SOR, we can extract geometry and textures (center), and apply them to 3D models (right). (In this paper, pixels with no data (i.e. transparent) are coded in magenta.)

incorporated this procedure into an application that can be used by people who have minimal knowledge of it.

After this introduction, Sect. 2 highlights some similar work that has been done in the past using different approaches. Section 3 describes our overall design for the project, detailing how we apply the primary concepts and algorithms to the SOR reconstruction and texture extraction problem. Section 4 focuses on how the SORGATE application embodies the design and how a user should use the application. Section 5 describes how we evaluated each piece of the design separately, as well as discusses the results of the full process on real images. Finally, Section 6 contains concluding remarks and possible avenues of future work for the project.

This application is useful, for example, to analyze objects created on a pottery wheel or lathe which may not be viewable or measurable in person, perhaps because the object is inaccessible or no longer exists. It could also be used commercially to quickly and inexpensively generate 3D textured models of these objects for viewing on the web or for 3D printing duplicates to serve the purposes of education or advertisement.

2   Previous Work

Image-based modeling and rendering, the extraction of both geometric and texture information from images for the purpose of rendering, dates back to the work of Debevec, Taylor, and Malik [7]. Like texturing itself, its goal is to reduce the need for detailed modelling of both geometry and light interaction to improve realism.

A common first step is to determine the camera pose from the image [2,22]. Reducing the problem domain by assuming that the object is an SOR makes the problem more tractable. Several approaches make use of projective geometry. Chellali et al. use only object contours and projective geometry to build 3D geometric models from a single image [5]. They do, however, require a calibration object in image at the base of the SOR.

Circular cross sections of SORs project to ellipses with certain invariant properties and symmetries [17,23]. Many techniques use this and therefore require accurate fitting of ellipses to silhouette data. Liu and Hu use minimal contour data to model spacecraft that exhibit SOR properties through accurate ellipse fitting [14]. Their technique shows much improvement over older techniques [8] when applied to multiple ellipses that share the same central axis. Wong, et al. are also able to recover the geometry of an SOR from a single image by determining the surface normals from the its silhouette and use this to recover depth information [24]. Puech et al. explore a technique which extracts the three Eulerian angles relating the camera and object coordinate systems, though their technique requires two well-defined cross sections to be visible [18]. Zhang et al. propose a technique that does not require any explicit cross sections be visible, but rather a well-defined silhouette. This is useful for SORs with smooth surfaces or which lack defined tops and/or bases [26].

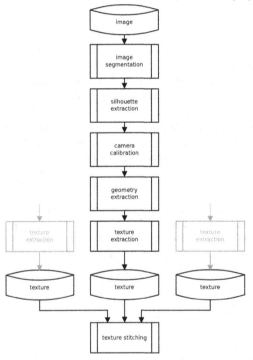

The work done by Columbo et al. perhaps most closely relates to ours differing in that it constructs the viewing matrix through projective geometry rather than parameterized viewing transforms [6,16]. This is a more elegant approach than ours, but our approach of finding the viewing parameters by optimization greatly simplifies the image stitching. Jain's work in [11] is also closely related, though the author imposes more constraints on the problem, such as assuming the camera is coplanar with the top cross section of the object.

Fig. 2. The SORGATE processing pipeline.

3   Design

There are six major steps (Fig. 2) in the processing pipeline for SORGATE. Starting with an image, we first segment the foreground (the SOR itself) from the background (any other objects/surfaces). By applying filtering and edge detection techniques and analyzing the curvature of the silhouette we then determine the circular planar base and top cross sections of the SOR. Then we find the viewing parameters of the camera that generated the image, as well as the radii of the base and top cross sections. Next, we determine the geometry of the SOR: a set of (y, r) pairs estimating the SOR's radius as a function of height. In the following texture

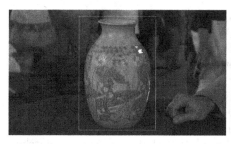 

Fig. 3. Image segmentation (left) and silhouette extraction (right). *(Image source:* [1]*)*

extraction step, we create a flattened version of as much of the SOR's texture as is visible in the image. Finally, if we have multiple images of the same SOR from differing viewpoints, we stitch them together to form a single texture, which we can then merge back with the geometry to create an interactive 3D representation of the SOR.

Space does not permit us to show how our initial design changed as a result of implementation, so we have incorporated those insights in this "design" section. Nor does it permit us to provide all of our formulae and algorithms and their derivations. We provide both of them in [13].

Image Segmentation. An important part of image analysis is segmentation: isolating the pixels describing the object of interest from those that are irrelevant [21].

As Fig. 2 shows, the image is the only data input to SORGATE. Segmentation is the first step. In our case, we use the very popular *GrabCut* algorithm [3, 19] to segment the image. We used *GrabCut* primarily because it allowed for adjustments to the segmentation at the pixel level, though one of the more recent deep learning techniques as described in [9] would allow greater automation.

GrabCut usually needs an initial hint (here, a bounding box) from the user about the location of the desired segment. Later, they may add additional "hints" for refinements on later iterations to improve the segmentation. We allow for these. Figure 3 (left) shows a typical result.

Silhouette Extraction. After segmentation, the SOR is the only object in the image. From this, we apply the commonly-used Canny edge detector [4] to extract the contours, of which there may be several. This does require some interactive and perhaps unintuitive adjustments to a set of parameters; thus, our method would once again benefit from using a more precise and automated technique here. Even so, using Canny's technique, we finally take the contour with the largest area to be the silhouette. Figure 3 (right) shows this.

We need to extract the *sub-silhouettes*, those parts of the silhouette that arise from the base and the top of the SOR. We assume that the SOR rests on the xz (i.e., $y = 0$) plane and that the camera is positioned above it (i.e., $o_y > 0$) defining the z axis. The base sub-silhouette, then, is the projection of the front part of the base.

If the camera height is less than the height of the SOR, the top sub-silhouette is the projection of the front part ($z > 0$) of the SOR. Otherwise, the top sub-silhouette is the projection of the back part ($z < 0$) of the sub-silhouette. We compute both possibilities and choose the solution that most closely matches that of the bottom sub-silhouette.

To extract the sub-silhouettes, we look for discontinuities in the curvature. Although we considered a number of methods for digital curvature estimation [25], in the end we chose our own approach. We first smooth the pixel coordinates with a Gaussian kernel, then compute the three-point curvature at each pixel. We then smooth the curvatures with another Gaussian kernel and, starting from the bottom or top extremum, find their left and right maxima. The sub-silhouettes, then, lie between these two maxima.

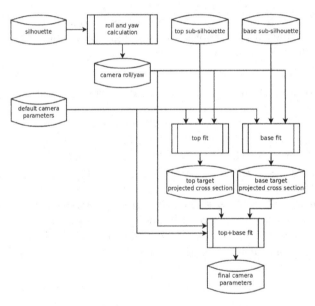

Fig. 4. Camera calibration

Camera Calibration. Our task is to map each pixel inside the silhouette to a 2D texture. This requires finding the transform from any point on the 3D surface of the SOR to the texture and its inverse.

Due to the nature of the SOR, the intrinsically circular base and top cross sections project to the elliptical sub-silhouettes. That projection, which determines both sub-silhouettes, depends on the camera's pose.

In general, a camera pose has six degrees of freedom: its 3D position ($\equiv \tilde{o}$) relative to the origin and its orientation (roll, pitch, and yaw). Due to the symmetry of the SOR, we can reduce this to five by requiring that the camera lie within the yz plane (i.e., o_x is 0).

A (homogeneous) point $\tilde{p}$ in the world frame of the SOR (typically, on its surface) maps to a point $\tilde{p}'$ on the image as

$$\begin{bmatrix} p'_x p'_w \\ p'_y p'_w \\ p'_z p'_w \\ p'_w \end{bmatrix} = \mathbf{M}_{vp}\mathbf{M}_{can}\mathbf{M}_{persp}\mathbf{M}_{cam}\tilde{\mathbf{p}} \qquad (1)$$

where the matrix product is a typical "modelview" transform [20]. $\mathbf{M}_{vp}$, the viewport transform, depends on the (known) image horizontal and vertical resolutions. $\mathbf{M}_{can}$, the canonical view transform, depends on the camera's (unknown) field of view and (known) image aspect ratio. $\mathbf{M}_{cam}$, the camera transform, depends on the (unknown) camera pose. $\mathbf{M}_{persp}$, the perspective transform, also depends on the camera pose.

As the base of the SOR is at the origin, a uniform scale of all coordinates produces no change in the image, so length units are arbitrary. We therefore choose our length unit to be the SOR's height. The top of the SOR is therefore at $y = 1$.

We can determine the camera's roll and yaw from the silhouette alone. In the case of roll, we use principal component analysis [12] to find the silhouette's major and minor axes. The departure of one of them (usually the major) from the vertical gives us the roll. Assuming that the center of the image corresponds to the optical axis, the yaw may then be computed trigonometrically.

We therefore have the following six unknown parameters: two components of the camera's position, o_y and o_z, the camera's vertical field of view, θ_y, the camera's pitch, β_{cam}, and the radii of the base and top cross sections, r_{base} and r_{top}.

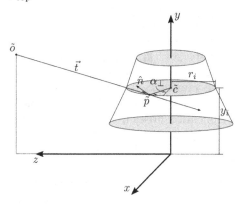

We initially tried to fit all parameters at once but this approach proved not to be robust. Instead, we determine their values using three multivariate "fits", as shown in Fig. 4. Each of them uses Nelder-Mead optimization [15] to yield all or a subset of the parameters. The first fit applies to the base sub-silhouette, yielding values for all parameters except r_{top}. The second fit applies to the top sub-silhouette, yielding values for all parameters except r_{base}. The third fit applies to

Fig. 5. Viewing Ray-Silhouette Intersection

whole ellipses based on values from the first two fits and robustly yields all parameters.

Geometry Extraction. We next extract the SOR's geometry. Due to its axial symmetry, this is simply the radius as function of height, i.e. $r = r(y)$. To derive this from the silhouette, we first treat it as a set of horizontal extrema $\{w_j\}$. For a given row of pixels j, w_j is the distance between the left and right extrema of the silhouette. We also start with a given N $\{y_i, r_i\}$ "cross section" samples of $r(y)$, $(0 \leq i < N)$. The y_i's are uniformly spaced. The (unknown) r_i's are initially zero.

It is important to keep in mind that not every row of the silhouette contributes to $r(y)$: The top or base may obstruct some part of the geometry. In an extreme case, imagine a conical SOR viewed from a great height $(o_y \gg 1)$. In that case, the silhouette would only show the elliptical base of the SOR and no radii could be extracted.

Looking at Fig. 5, valid w_j's that contribute to $r(y)$ arise in situations where a viewing ray is tangential to the normal $\hat{\mathbf{n}}$ at a "horizon point" $\tilde{\mathbf{p}}$ on the surface of the SOR. This corresponds to an angle $\alpha_\perp$, a particular value of the azimuthal angle α measured clockwise from $\hat{\mathbf{x}}$ in the xz plane. All pixels with $\alpha_\perp \leq \alpha \leq \pi - \alpha_\perp$ are visible.

In the orthographic view $(o_z \to \infty)$, $\alpha_\perp = 0$. Or if the SOR were a cylinder, $\alpha_\perp$ would be a constant for any camera position. But for a general SOR, $\alpha_\perp$ depends on $\hat{\mathbf{n}}$, which depends on $\hat{\mathbf{N}} = (N_x, N_y, 0)$, the "unrotated" normal of the SOR in the xy plane (for $x \geq 0$, the right side of the image). In [13], we derive

$$\alpha_\perp = \arcsin \left[\frac{r_i N_x + N_y(y_i - o_y)}{o_z N_x} \right] \tag{2}$$

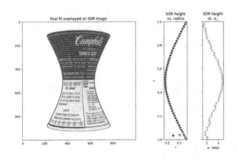

Fig. 6. Geometry extraction

There are two complications: First, $\hat{\mathbf{N}}$ depends on the derivative of $r(y)$, the quantity we're trying to solve for. To approximate $\hat{\mathbf{N}}$ at a cross-section i, we compute the normal to parametrically-fit parabolas based on previous estimates of (y_{i-1}, r_{i-1}), (y_i, r_i), and (y_{i+1}, r_{i+1}), so solving for r_i requires r_{i-1} and r_{i+1}. This requires the solution to be iterative. The second complication arises if the absolute value of the arcsin argument in Equation (2) exceeds 1. Then the camera cannot see that horizon point, so that value of r_i is invalid, at least on that iteration.

To solve for $\{r_i\}$, we developed the *scaled difference method*. Starting with an initial $\{r_i\}$, we project these to a set of silhouette widths $\{w'_i\}$ and use the departures of these from the known $\{w_i\}$s to produce a new $\{r_i\}$. When $\{w'_i\}$ falls within a given (RMSD) tolerance of the $\{w_i\}$, we have our $\{r_i\}$. It was necessary to incorporate an empirically-determined scaling factor which slows the rate of convergence in order to reduce the chance for the $\{r_i\}$'s to produce impossible $\alpha_\perp$ values. Figure 6 shows typical $\{r_i\}$ and $\{\alpha_{\perp,i}\}$ results.

Texture Extraction. The inputs to texture extraction are the camera calibration and the SOR geometry. The output is a texture of any desired resolution. Figure 7 shows a typical result.

Fig. 7. Texture Extraction

Rows correspond to varying α values, where $\pi \geq \alpha \geq 0$. Since we only have data for $\alpha_\perp \leq \alpha \leq \pi - \alpha_\perp$, we use the transparency channel to indicate valid pixels.

Figure 7 shows a typical result using a synthetic image of known geometry. Height corresponds to the vertical path length along the side of the SOR. We expect a certain amount of distortion at the edges and where the SOR is narrow. These correspond to regions in the original image where the details may be difficult to see.

Texture Stitching. We have shown that we can capture the geometry of an SOR from a single image, but that image can show at most half of the SOR's texture. It may be desirable to combine, or "stitch", texture data from multiple images into a single texture that can be used, for instance, to re-create a textured 3D model viewable from any direction, to 3D print a replica of the SOR, or to display the whole of the SOR's surface in 2D media (an archaeological research publication, say).

So far, we have assumed that each image has its own coordinate system: The SOR's base is at the origin, its axis of symmetry is the y axis, and the camera lies above the z axis. To stitch images together, we would further need to know the relative azimuthal (α) angular differences of the images, but these are not provided. Each texture being a parameterization of path length vs. α, there should ideally be an exact match of the region of the SOR visible in both textures when they are overlaid with the proper vertical[1] and horizontal offsets.

Goshtasyby's text [10] on image registration contains detailed descriptions of algorithms for this, some of which have implementations available in computer vision libraries. However, the type of registration we need to do is simplified by the fact that there should be no rotation, scaling, or any complex type of homology necessary. Alignment for stitching two textures can therefore be done simply by finding horizontal and vertical displacements that minimize differences (here, RMSD) between the overlapping regions. Figure 8 shows this.

---

[1] Due to variations in camera pitch (β_{cam}), textures need to be aligned vertically as well as horizontally, if only slightly. Figure 8 exaggerates this for illustration.

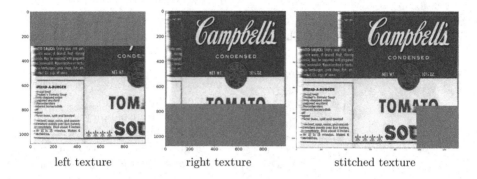

left texture   right texture   stitched texture

Fig. 8. Texture stitching

4 Implementation

We implemented SORGATE as an application program *sorgate* in the Python programming language, which supports a number of packages that were extremely useful. We used NumPy for array computations, SciPy for optimization, and OpenCV for image I/O, segmentation, filtering, edge detection, and contour extraction.

We built its user interface with tkinter and matplotlib. We rendered textures using OpenGL, PIL, and GLFW. Space does not allow us to describe it in detail, but Fig. 9 shows its general operation. We also used it to create many of the other images in this paper.

5 Evaluation

Synthetic Images. The images shown in Figs. 6 and 7 were created with a custom-built raytracer at a resolution of 1000×1000 pixels. This allowed us to compare the parameters and $\{r_i\}$ values *sorgate* extracted with the raytracer inputs and guaranteed that the object itself was a true SOR.

For these images we used a uniform background, so segmentation and silhouette extraction were trivially correct. Extracted and true camera parameters differed by no more than a fraction of a degree (for the angles) few percent (for the positions) in the worst cases. Figures 6 to 9 show typical results for geometry, texture extraction, and texture stitching. Figure 10 shows the quick convergence of the $\{r_i\}$ fit results.

Real Images. The goal of SORGATE is to extract data from real images, so those are a critical part of its evaluation. For segmentation and silhouette extraction, the *GrabCut* and Canny algorithms performed well on real images, as shown in Fig. 3. Extracted camera roll and yaw parameters were, again, within fractions of a degree.

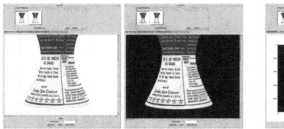

Segmentation   Silhouette Extraction

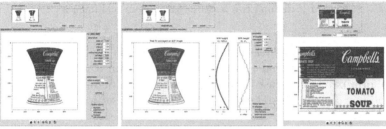

Camera Calibration   Geometry Extraction   Texture Stitching

Fig. 9. Overview of the *sorgate* application. This illustrates the data flow shown in Fig. 2.

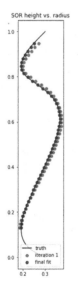

Fig. 10. $\{r_i\}$ Fit Results

More complicated images, such as those with SORs whose colors were similar to the background, or those with lighting that reduced the prominence of silhouette, required a lot more time spent making precise touch-ups and fine-tuning the Canny parameters to produce meaningful results; in these scenarios, the early stages of our method are quite cumbersome.

Figure 1 shows the result: We use stitched textures extracted from several real images used to create a 3D model of the original object. Although largely successful, certain images provided more of a challenge for the camera calibration parameters. SORs with rounded bases complicated sub-silhouette extraction, so it was necessary to adjust the base and top radii manually. Problems also arose with SORs where the viewing ray intersects both the stem and base, such as a goblet viewed from a high camera position. For this reason, we must, as we've done in Fig. 10, limit the range of $\{r_i\}$ values.

Before   After

Fig. 11. Stitching two textures taken from real images

Problems arose from stitching as well, as shown in Fig. 11 (the same vase shown in Fig. 1). Directional lighting and dealing with a glossy surface with large uniform patches confused the simple RMSD metric and we had to make several ad-hoc assumptions about the horizontal and vertical search ranges to make this work.

6   Conclusions and Future Work

We have shown that SORGATE is capable of extracting geometry and texture from a single SOR image and can combine multiple images of the same SOR into a single texture.

It worked well with synthetic images, but real images required more work. Segmentation, silhouette, and sub-silhouette extraction needed more user input, but the resulting camera calibration and geometry and texture extractions for individual images were satisfactory. Stitching multiple images together required more *ad hoc* adjustments to account for lighting and the SOR's material properties.

Future development of SORGATE should address these problems. We should be able to take better advantage of the SOR's symmetry and the smoothness of the silhouette (except at the sub-silhouette limits). Also, once we have an initial model of the SOR's geometry, we should be able to incorporate a lighting model to remove both diffuse and specular effects and retrieve the underlying material properties for use in rendering the SOR with arbitrary lighting.

The incorporation of the projective geometry approach (as in [6,16]) would also be likely to increase robustness and move us towards our goal of being able of extracting geometry and texture with a minimum of user intervention.

References

1. Overbeck Vase, ca 1920 — Antiques Roadshow — PBS (2017). https://image. pbs.org/video-assets/pbs/antiques-roadshow/256002/images/mezzanine_222.jpg. crop.379x212.jpg

2. Boyer, E., Berger, M.O.: 3D surface reconstruction using occluding contours. Int. J. Comput. Vis. **22**(3), 219–233 (1997)
3. Boykov, Y., Jolly, M.P.: Interactive graph cuts for optimal boundary & region segmentation of objects in N-D images. In: Proceedings Eighth IEEE International Conference on Computer Vision (ICCV 2001) 1, pp. 105–112 (2001)
4. Canny, J.: A computational approach to edge detection. IEEE Trans. Pattern Anal. Mach. Intell. PAMI **8**(6), 679–698 (1986)
5. Chellali, R., Fremont, V., Maaoui, C.: A new approach to 3-D modeling of objects with axial symmetry. IEEE Trans. Ind. Electron. **50**(4), 1–7 (2003)
6. Colombo, C., Del Bimbo, A., Pernici, F.: Uncalibrated 3D metric reconstruction and flattened texture acquisition from a single view of a surface of revolution. In: Proceedings - 1st International Symposium on 3D Data Processing Visualization and Transmission, 3DPVT 2002, vol. 27(1), pp. 277–284 (2002)
7. Debevec, P.E., Taylor, C.J., Malik, J.: Modeling and Rendering Architecture from Photographs: A hybrid geometry-and image-based approach. Technical report (1996)
8. Fitzgibbon, A., Pilu, M., Fisher, R.B.: Direct least square fitting of ellipses. IEEE Trans. Pattern Anal. Mach. Intell. **21**(5), 476–480 (1999)
9. Ghosh, S., Das, N., Das, I., Maulik, U.: Understanding deep learning techniques for image segmentation. ACM Comput. Surv. **52**, 1–35 (2019)
10. Goshtasby, A.A.: Image Registration: Principles, Tools and Methods. Springer, London (2012). https://doi.org/10.1007/978-1-4471-2458-0
11. Jain, A.: Automatic 3D Reconstruction for Symmetric Shapes (2016)
12. Jolliffe, I.: Principal Component Analysis. Springer, New York (1986). https://doi.org/10.1007/978-1-4757-1904-8
13. Ledesma, A.: SORGATE: Surface of Revolution Geometry and Texture Extraction. Master's thesis, May 2021
14. Liu, C., Hu, W.: Ellipse fitting for imaged cross sections of a surface of revolution. Pattern Recogn. **48**(4), 1440–1454 (2015). https://doi.org/10.1016/j.patcog.2014.09.028
15. Nelder, J.A., Mead, R.: A simplex method for function minimization. Comput. J. **7**(4), 308–313 (1965)
16. Pernici, F.: Two Results in Computer Vision using Projective Geometry. Ph.D. thesis, University of Florence (2005). https://www.micc.unifi.it/pernici/index_files/PhdThesis.pdf
17. Ponce, J., Chelberg, D., Mann, W.B.: Invariant properties of straight homogeneous generalized cylinders and their contours. IEEE Trans. Pattern Anal. Mach. Intell. **11**(9), 951–966 (1989)
18. Puech, W., Chassery, J.M., Pitas, I.: Cylindrical surface localization in monocular vision. Pattern Recogn. Lett. **18**(8), 711–722 (1997)
19. Rother, C., Kolmogorov, V., Blake, A.: GrabCut. ACM Trans. Graph. **23**(3), 309–314 (2004)
20. Shirley, P., Marschner, S.: Viewing. In: Fundamentals of Computer Graphics, 3rd edn. pp. 141–159. A K Peters/CRC Press, Boca Raton (2009). Chap. 7
21. Szeliski, R.: Computer Vision: Algorithms and Applications. Springer, London (2011). https://doi.org/10.1007/978-1-84882-935-0
22. Tsai, R.Y.: A versatile camera calibration techniaue for high-accuracy 3D machine vision metrology using off-the-shelf TV cameras and lenses ROGER. IEEE J. Robot. Autom. **3**(4), 323–344 (1987)

23. Ulupinar, F., Nevatia, R.: Shape from contour: straight homogeneous generalized cylinders and constant cross section generalized cylinders. IEEE Trans. Pattern Anal. Mach. Intell. **17**(2), 120–135 (1995)
24. Wong, K.Y.K., Mendonça, P.R., Cipolla, R.: Reconstruction of surfaces of revolution from single uncalibrated views. Image Vis. Comput. **22**(10 SPEC. ISS.), 829–836 (2004)
25. Worring, M., Smeulders, A.W.: Digital curvature estimation. Comput. Vis. Image Underst. **58**(3), 366–382 (1993)
26. Zhang, M., Zheng, Y., Liu, Y.: Using silhouette for pose estimation of object with surface of revolution. In: Proceedings - International Conference on Image Processing, ICIP, pp. 333–336 (2009)

Putting Table Cartograms into Practice

Mohammad Rakib Hasan, Debajyoti Mondal$^{(\boxtimes)}$, Jarin Tasnim,
and Kevin A. Schneider

Department of Computer Science, University of Saskatchewan, Saskatoon, Canada
{rakib.hasan,d.mondal,jarin.tasnim,kevin.schneider}@usask.ca

Abstract. Given an $m \times n$ table T of positive weights, and a rectangle R with an area equal to the sum of the weights, a table cartogram computes a partition of R into $m \times n$ convex quadrilateral faces such that each face has the same adjacencies as its corresponding cell in T, and has an area equal to the cell's weight. In this paper, we examine constraint optimization-based and physics-inspired cartographic transformation approaches to produce cartograms for large tables with thousands of cells. We show that large table cartograms may provide diagrammatic representations in various real-life scenarios, e.g., for analyzing correlations between geospatial variables and creating visual effects in images. Our experiments with real-life datasets provide insights into how one approach may outperform the other in various application contexts.

Keywords: Cartography · Algorithms · Optimization · Image processing

1 Introduction

A table cartogram is a cartographic representation for a two dimensional positive matrix or tabular data. Given a positive $m \times n$ matrix of weights, a table cartogram represents each cell as a distinct convex quadrilateral with an area proportional to the corresponding cell's weight such that the cell adjacencies are preserved, the quadrilaterals form a partition of a rectangle R, and the sum of all weights is equal to the area of R.

Evans et al. [6] showed that every $m \times n$ table admits a table cartogram. Their theoretical proof is based on first partitioning the table into weighted triangles, then computing cartograms for the triangles using the concept of barycentric coordinates, and finally, merging the triangles based on the necessity to obtain the final table cartogram. Although the proof guarantees to produce a table cartogram with zero cartographic error, the authors pointed out that the output may not be visually pleasing (also see Fig. 1(d)–(e)) and good heuristics are needed to improve the aesthetics. Since then a number of attempts [5,14,18,19] have been made to compute aesthetic table cartograms. Researchers have also looked at the scope for using table cartograms in practice, in particular, the

This research was undertaken thanks in part to funding from the Canada First Research Excellence Fund.

G. Bebis et al. (Eds.): ISVC 2021, LNCS 13017, pp. 91–102, 2021.
https://doi.org/10.1007/978-3-030-90439-5_8

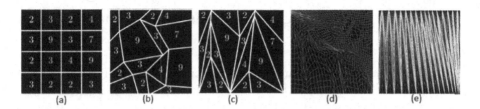

Fig. 1. (a) A table T. (b) A table cartogram of T using constraint optimization. (c) Evans et al.'s [6] output for T (based on a theoretical proof). (d) A cartogram for a large table based on constraint optimization, where (e) Evans et al.'s [6] approach produces skinny triangles.

Cartographic Transformation   Enhanced Illumination   Mosaic Art Effect

Fig. 2. Large table cartograms applied to different applications.

data and types of tasks that are well-suited for using a table cartogram [19]. However, all prior applications of table cartograms examined only various forms of small tabular data (e.g., periodic tables, temperature calendar, population demographics, line charts, etc.) with a few hundred cells.

Motivation: In this paper we examine cartograms for larger tables, i.e., with a thousands of cells. This opens up the possibility of applying the idea of table cartograms on images and geographic contour plots, and thus allows us to explore new application areas. However, when it comes to large tables, it is natural to ask whether it is important to keep the cells as convex polygons, which makes table cartograms unique from cartographic map transformations. Figure 2 illustrates some image-based applications that we will explore in this paper. While transforming images, concave cells may pose more challenges than the convex ones. An ideal situation would be that all the colors in the image maintain their pixel ratio even after the transformation, i.e., the area of the visual attributes will be scaled linearly based on the area transformation. However, for concave areas, the transformation often appears to be more distorted.

This motivated us to examine the following research questions:

RQ_1. What are the potential applications of large table cartograms to understand and interpret tabular data and beyond?

RQ_2. How crucial is it to maintain the convexity of the cells in such applications?

RQ_3. Can constraint optimization based approach be used to compute table cartograms for large tables with small cartographic error?

RQ_4. How constraint optimization based table cartogram compares to the cartographic map transformation algorithms in various quality metrics (e.g., number of convex cells, aspect ratio, etc.)?

Contribution: In this paper we propose TCarto, a constraint based optimization approach that leverages parallel computing to deform a table via local optimization using quadratic programming [7,12]. TCarto can handle tables over hundred thousands of cells (e.g., 512×512 tables in a few hours) and maintains convexity of each cell. We also adapt a physics-inspired cartographic transformation approach—FastFlow [9], which may produce concave cells.

We show that both TCarto and FastFlow (and thus large table cartograms) can potentially be useful in several real-life scenarios, e.g., for analyzing correlations between geospatial variables, and creating visual effects in images. We also compare the performances of TCarto and FastFlow empirically with two different real-life datasets: a meteorological dataset and a US State-to-State migration flow dataset. In particular, we examine well-known metrics for measuring cartographic errors, number of concave cells and mean aspect ratio of the cells. For meteorological dataset, where the data distribution does not contain high spikes and many local optima, both TCarto and FastFlow performed well, and Fast-Flow produced only a few concave cells. For the migration dataset with many sharp local optima, both TCarto and FastFlow produced low quality output, whereas for FastFlow we observed hundreds of concave cells. We also show how adding additional angle constraints can help mitigate this problem. The code and data is available at GitHub[1].

2 Related Work

Cartographic representation of maps is a classic area of research [20,22]. Early algorithms to compute cartograms were based on the metaphor that considers the original map as a rubber sheet, and defines forces on the points such that they move to realize the cartographic representation. A major challenge in such an approach is to ensure fast convergence, and preserve the shape of the regions on the map. Many algorithms [3,4,13] have been proposed to tackle these challenges, yet the slow convergence remained a problem.

The diffusion-based algorithm [8] is a popular method for drawing contiguous cartograms. This is inspired by the idea of diffusion in physics, where the points move from high density to the low-density regions. A diffusion-based algorithm often produces blob and spike like artifacts, and narrow corridors. Hence Cano et al. [2] proposed mosaic cartograms, where regions are represented as a set of regular tiles of the same size. The tiles help compare the regions via counting, better preserve the shape, but also have a cost of making winding region boundaries and tentacles like artifacts. There exist many approaches beyond rubber sheet or diffusion based algorithms. For example, medial-axis based cartogram [17] that transforms the regions based on the medial axis of the map polygon, neural network based approach inspired by self-organizing map [11], etc. In 2013, Sun [21] presented a rubber-sheet inspired algorithm (Carto3F) that significantly improves the computational efficiency by using a quadtree structure, and eliminates the topological error by adding appropriate conditions while computing

---

[1] https://github.com/rakib045/tcarto_applications.

forces. In addition, the implementation of Carto3F exploits parallel computation. Recently, Gastner et al. [9] proposed a flow-based technique (FastFlow), inspired by the way particles of varying density into the water diffuse across the water over time that also leverages parallelism for fast cartogram computation.

Table cartograms [6] were proposed to visualize tabular data, where cells are restricted to be convex and to form a tiling of a rectangle. However, if we relax table cartogram constraints, then it is possible to use existing physics-inspired cartogram algorithms to create cartograms for tables. Winter [24] used the diffusion-based cartographic representation to visualize periodic table of chemical elements. However, this deforms the outer boundary of the table, as well as produces non-convex cells. Cartogram algorithms (in particular Carto3F and flow-based approach) often use an underlying regular grid (sometimes of size 1024×1024, e.g., Carto3F allows using a quadtree of depth 10) to transform the map, but the number of map regions makes a major difference. The existing approaches for cartographic representation focus on transforming at most a few hundred regions, while a 1024×1024 table may contain over a million cells.

Since the introduction of table cartogram, there have been various attempts to produce aesthetic cartograms based on optimization. Inoue and Li [14] showed an optimization-based approach for the construction of table cartograms by changing the bearing angles on the edges of the polygons. McNutt and Kindlmann [18] proposed another approach that instead of convexity constraints, puts simpler restriction such as to preserve the x and y axis ordering of the grid points. They showed that one can construct multiple table cartograms that have the same cartographic error but visually look very different. Recently, McNutt [19] has further examined the data and tasks where table cartogram may be useful, and observed that table cartogram may be suited for various tasks such as understanding sorted order of cells or to find anomalies; especially when the table size is small.

3   TCarto: An Optimization Based Algorithm

TCarto is different than the known optimization based algorithms [14, 18, 19] in two ways. First, it contains explicit convexity constraints (instead of considering an under-constrained version). Second, it leverages parallel computing to handle large tables. TCarto is inspired by the classic Tutte's approach for drawing planar graphs [23]. At each iteration of the Tutte's algorithm, every vertex moves towards the barycenter of its neighbors, and hence over time, the algorithm attempts to minimize a global energy function defined on the layout. In TCarto, every vertex except four at the corner moves towards the locally optimum point. Let T be an $m \times n$ table. We normalize the cell weights $w_{i,j}$ to satisfy the following equality: $\sum W_{i,j} = m \times n$, where $W_{i,j}$ corresponds to the normalized value. We set the initial cartogram to be a regular $m \times n$ grid of area mn, where each cell area $A_{i,j}$ is one unit square. We can describe this with an undirected graph,

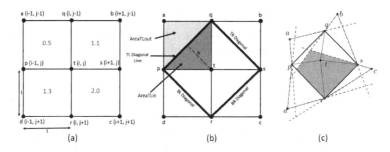

Fig. 3. (a) Initial setup. (b) Computation of the height, h'. (c) A feasible region for moving a point t.

$G = (V, E)$, where $V = V_{i,j}$ are the vertices ($i \in \{0, 1, ..., m\}$ and $j \in \{0, 1, ..., n\}$) and E are the edges connecting each vertex to its neighbouring vertices at its top, right, bottom and left side. We iteratively update the position of the vertices, $V_{i,j}$ to realize the cell areas.

We used quadratic programming for the local optimization, which depends on the neighborhood cells' vertices, weights and current areas. With several iterations, TCarto attempts to minimize the differences between the given weights and realized areas.

The inner vertices are moved based on local optimization. Let t be the current vertex to be moved (Fig. 3(c)), and consider the top left face $tpaq$ quadrangle of t. We now construct four constraints determined by the lines through pq, qs, sr, rp such that t must preserve its location relative to these lines even after the move. These four constraints alone cannot ensure that the four neighboring faces must remain convex after we move t. For example, moving t outside of the shaded region (but keeping it inside the quadrangle $pqsr$) would make one of the four faces non-convex. The reason is that for each face, the edges which are not incident to t also put constraints on where t can move. Hence, we need to add another set of eight constraints, two for each neighbor of t. Specifically, for a neighbor q, let qa and qb, where $t \notin \{a, b\}$, be the edges such that each lies on the boundary of one of the faces adjacent to the edge qt. Then the two constraints corresponding to q are determined by the lines corresponding to qa and qb. The twelve constraints together ensure that the neighboring faces of t remain convex even after the move. Since no other face is affected by the move of t, all the faces in the layout remain convex. The movement for boundary vertices are similar except that they can move either horizontally or vertically.

We now describe the optimization function. Let $h_{t,1}, h_{t,2}, h_{t,3}, h_{t,4}$ be the perpendicular distances (heights) of t from the lines pq, qs, sr, pr, respectively. Note that these heights relate to the errors of the corresponding faces, and moving t would change these heights (e.g., see Fig. 3(b)). We then define a set of required heights $h'_{t,i}$, where $1 \le i \le 4$. Here we only show how to compute $h'_{t,1}$. Denote by $W(tpaq)$ the target weight of a face $tpaq$, and let $A(tpaq)$ denote area of the face. Assume that $\gamma = W(tpaq) - A(tpaq) - \Delta tpq$. If $\gamma > 0$, i.e., we need to add more area by moving t, then the required height is determined by the equation $\frac{1}{2}|pq|h'_{t,1} = \gamma + \Delta tpq$, where $|pq|$ is the Euclidean distance between p, q. Otherwise, $\gamma \leq 0$, i.e., we already have more than the required area. In this case (for simplicity) we assume that $h'_{t,1} = h_{t,1}$. We then minimize the error $\sum_{w \in V} \sum_{1 \leq i \leq 4} (h'_{w,i} - h_{w,i})^2$, where V is the set of grid vertices.

Let $a_i x + b_i y = c_i$, where $1 \leq i \leq 4$, be the equation of four diagonal lines (pq, qs, sr, rp), and let h'_i be the required heights. We can thus model the movement of an inner vertex using a quadratic programming with the twelve constraints for convexity (Fig. 3(c)) and the following optimization function.

$$minimize \sum_{i=1}^{4} \left(\left(\frac{a_i^2 x^2}{a_i^2 + b_i^2} \right)^2 x^2 + \left(\frac{b_i^2 y^2}{a_i^2 + b_i^2} \right)^2 y^2 + \frac{a_i b_i xy}{\sqrt{a_i^2 + b_i^2}} + \frac{a_i(c_i - h'_i)x}{\sqrt{a_i^2 + b_i^2}} + \frac{b_i(c_i - h'_i)y}{\sqrt{a_i^2 + b_i^2}} \right)$$

Parallel Computing. To take advantage of parallel computing, we partition the vertices and distribute the load to different threads. At each iteration, we partition the columns into k regular intervals with one column gap in between. The iteration is completed in two phases. In the first phase, each thread moves their allocated points, and in the second phase the threads move the interleaved columns. We will refer to this procedure as PARALLEL-OPT.

The limitation of the PARALLEL-OPT is that if the data density is very high in a particular interval, then it would take many iterations until the points move towards a low density region. To cope with this challenge, we take a top-down approach, as follows. Let the input be a $2^j \times 2^j$ grid. For each i from 0 to j, in the ith level we group the cells into a $2^i \times 2^i$ grid and run the procedure PARALLEL-OPT for $j - \log(i) + 1$ iterations. Thus the major weight shift occurs early in the top levels and further refinement occurs at the bottom levels.

4   Potential Applications

Here we show some potential applications of large table cartograms (i.e., positive evidence towards **RQ$_1$**) and examine whether convexity of the cells is crucial for these applications (i.e., **RQ$_2$**).

Infographics to Reveal Spatial Relation. Consider two matrices representing two geospatial variables A and B. Let $Contour(B)$ be the contour plot of B. If we compute a table cartogram based on A and then apply piecewise affine transformation [10] on $Contour(B)$, then the resulting image can reveal potential spatial relation between A and B. Figure 4a (first column) illustrates how a contour plot of ALBEDO (the reflected solar energy by the surface) is transformed based on the table cartogram for soil liquid water (SH2O) values. The blue color in the contour plot indicates a low value (lakes and ocean) and yellow indicates a high value. Since the transformation grows the ocean, one can observe that SH2O is high in ocean (which is a low ALBEDO area).

Figure 4a shows the cartograms obtained using TCarto and FastFlow for various combinations of ALBEDO (Solar Energy Reflectance), TSK (Surface Skin Temperature), PBLH (Planetary Boundary Layer Height), SH2O (Soil Liquid

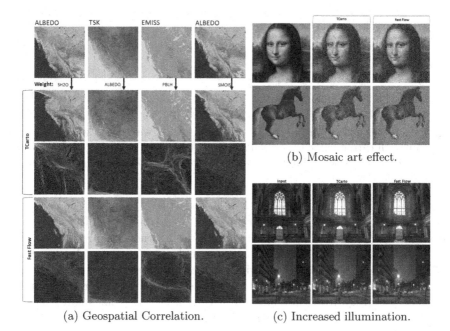

(a) Geospatial Correlation.

(b) Mosaic art effect.

(c) Increased illumination.

Fig. 4. Potential applications of large table cartograms.

Water), and EMISS (Surface Emissivity). In the contour plot, blue and yellow regions are the lowest and highest values consecutively. The expansion of yellow (high value) region or shrinkage of blue (low value) region indicates potential positive relation. For example, see Fig. 4a (third column) for shrinkage of blue. We can infer a negative relation if the opposite happens, e.g., see Fig. 4a (first, second and fourth columns) for expansion of blue.

Discussion: Both TCarto and FastFlow shows similar transformation in regions and reveals potential relation between geospatial variables ($\mathbf{RQ_1}$). The cell convexity does not appear to be a crucial phenomenon since the grid size is large ($\mathbf{RQ_2}$). However, a close inspection of the grid shows that there exist major differences that are not readily visible in the images, but in the transformed grid. Hence overlaying the grid on the image or placing them side-by-side may help guide the interpretation when creating infographic pictures. Note that two cartograms may look very different even when their cartographic error is small (Table 1). This has also been observed by McNutt [19], but for small tables. Hence such cartogram infographics are mostly useful to spark excitement among the viewers, or to convey a major concept.

Different Visual Effects in Images. Large table cartograms can potentially be used to create visual effects in images. Figure 4c illustrates examples where the lightness channel of HSL (Hue, Saturation and Lightness) has been transformed using table cartogram to expand the light illumination from the light sources.

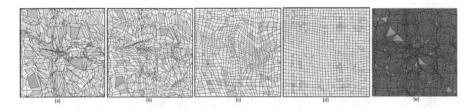

Fig. 5. (a-d) TCarto output for 2018 US migration data with 0, 25, 50 and 75 angle constraint with cartographic errors of 122.01, 174.65, 175.33 and 184.71, respectively. (e) FastFlow output after 3rd iteration with 152 concave (red) cells (it got stuck in an infinite loop afterwards).

This has been achieved by overlaying a 64×64 grid on the image and then creating a weighted table T by accumulating the lightness values for each grid cell. Next the lightness channel has been adapted based on the table cartogram of T, which enlarges the brighter regions and compresses the darker areas.

Another visual effect that we can create using large table cartograms is similar to mosaic arts (Fig. 4b). A mosaic art generates a picture using small stones or glass fragments. To generate the mosaic image effect, we produce a 64×64 table T with random weights. We then transform the image based on the table cartogram of T and then overlay the grid to create the mosaic effect.

Discussion: Both TCarto and FastFlow are able to create some mosaic effect ($\mathbf{RQ_1}$), where the cell sizes in the FastFlow cartogram appear to be more uniform compared to that of TCarto. While we only focus on potential application, it would be interesting to investigate whether one is more artistic than the other. Since the weights were chosen at random in a small interval, the cells were convex, with FastFlow cells having better average aspect ratio ($\mathbf{RQ_2}$).

Tabular Data with Angle Constraint. Here we examine large table cartograms for general tabular data. This is a challenging case because a general table may contain many sharp local maxima and minima compared to the ones we observed in image applications or weather dataset. In addition, the values between adjacent cells can be drastically different. In such scenario, the available implementation of FastFlow performed poorly, i.e., it generated many concave cells and also failed to converge.

Since the perception of rows and columns are important in interpreting a table, we augmented TCarto with angle constraints so that the corner of each cell is above a given angle threshold. Figure 5(a)–(d) illustrate TCarto outputs for US migration data on 2018, where rows and columns represent a subset of 32 states and each cell (i, j) corresponds to the quantity that migrated from i to j. The cells are color coded based on their weights, where higher values are represented in blue. The angle constraints that have been used from left is $0°, 25°, 50°, 75°$, respectively. The available implementation of FastFlow does not support any angle constraints. It fails to converge and the predictor-corrector method [9] that iteratively moves the points gets stuck after 3rd iteration. It produces 152 concave cells as shown in red in Fig. 5(e). To overcome this situation, we replaced the predictor-corrector method with uniform step size. Although it allowed us to run for more iterations, it created more concave cells and error.

Discussion: For large tabular data with many sharp local optima, TCarto performs better than FastFlow. The rows and columns are hard to follow in a TCarto output, but it improves with larger angle constraints. Larger angle constraints also contribute to larger cartographic errors, and hence for real-life use cases (**RQ₁**), it is important to choose an appropriate angle constraint that balances the trade-off between readability and cartographic error. This is where the convexity appears to be important than most other applications (**RQ₂**).

5 Experimental Results

In this section we compare the constraint based (TCarto) and physics-inspired (FastFlow) approaches under various quality metrics. We also report the performance of the theoretical algorithm of Evans et al. [6] (BaseCase). We used two datasets for our experiments: the Weather Research and Forecasting (WRF) model output for several weather parameters [25] (Table 1) and the United States (US) State-to-State Migration Flows from 2015 to 2019 published by the US Census Bureau [1] (Table 2) .

Quality Metrics: One standard quality metric is the *average cartographic error*, $\widetilde{e}_i$. If $A_i^{desired}$ is the desired area or the given weight of ith polygon (cell) and A_i^{actual} is the actual area after the cartographic transformation [15], then $\widetilde{e}_i$ is computed as follows: $\widetilde{e}_i = \frac{1}{N}\left[\sum_{i=1}^{N} e_i\right]$, $where\, e_i = \frac{\left|A_i^{desired} - A_i^{actual}\right|}{A_i^{desired}}$.

The mean quadratic error I_{MQE} is another commonly used quality metric used in the literature [16]: $I_{MQE} = \frac{1}{N}\sqrt{\sum_{i=1}^{N} e_i{}^2}$, where $e_i = \frac{\left|A_i^{desired} - A_i^{actual}\right|}{A_i^{desired} + A_i^{actual}}$. We also considered *mean aspect ratio* (average AR) and *concave count* to better compare TCarto and FastFlow with respect to the convexity constraints. The *concave count* (α) is simply the number of concave quadrilaterals in the output. The mean aspect ratio is defined as follows: $Mean\, AR = \frac{1}{N}\sum_{1 \leq i \leq N} \frac{\min(w_i, h_i)}{\max(w_i, h_i)}$, where w_i and h_i are the width and height of the ith cell, respectively.

Performance Comparison: From Tables 1 and 2, we can observe that the BaseCase (theoretical algorithm of Evans et al. [6]) had a very high accuracy but the average aspect ratio was too low to be used in the applications that we explored in Sect. 4.

Table 1 reports the results on weather datasets, where each cell reports a metric value averaged over 10 inputs (similar to Fig. 4a). Both TCarto and Fast-Flow had very small average cartographic error and mean quadratic error (**RQ₃**), with FastFlow having the smaller average among the two. The average cell aspect ratio was above 0.75 for both TCarto and FastFlow, where FastFlow had better aspect ratio compared to TCarto. Only a few concave cells appeared in Fast-Flow (even for large tables). This suggests FastFlow to be the preferred option for weather datasets (**RQ₄**).

Table 1. Cartographic error $(\widetilde{e}_i)$, mean quadratic error (I_{MQE}), mean aspect ratio (AR) and average concave count (α) for weather dataset.

Grid	Algorithm	$\widetilde{e}_i$	I_{MQE}	Mean AR	α
16 by 16	BaseCase	0.00007	0.0000026	0.21039	0
	TCarto	0.03421	0.00161	0.76672	0
	FastFlow	0.00763	0.00034	0.79762	0
32 by 32	BaseCase	0.0004	0.0000012	0.12073	0
	TCarto	0.02905	0.00076	0.82364	0
	FastFlow	0.00648	0.00014	0.85596	0.7
64 by 64	BaseCase	0.00007	0.0000009	0.11617	0
	TCarto	0.03632	0.00052	0.75623	0
	FastFlow	0.00817	0.000095	0.791	5

Table 2. Results on US State-to-State Migration Flows from 2015 to 2019 published by the US Census Bureau [1]. On each input, FastFlow was run on 15 iterations with our modification to tackle the convergence problem.

Year	Algorithm	$\widetilde{e}_i$	I_{MQE}	Mean AR	α
2019	BaseCase	0.0083	0.00170	0.12322	0
	TCarto	119.777	0.01297	0.563086	0
	FastFlow	5.9962	0.00813	0.539933	346
2017	BaseCase	0.0081	0.00086	0.125121	0
	TCarto	111.805	0.01261	0.568921	0
	FastFlow	2100.1133	0.02229	0.187013	766
2015	BaseCase	0.0086	0.00093	0.123013	0
	TCarto	131.5762	0.01229	0.571858	0
	FastFlow	2562.7078	0.02280	0.424352	752

Table 2 reports the results on US migration dataset, where we have many sharp maxima and minima and the values in adjacent cells may vary widely. Here we observed TCarto to have lower cartographic error, and better aspect ratio compared to FastFlow (**RQ$_4$**). Furthermore, FastFlow produced hundreds of concave cells. TCarto output further improved with angle constraints. Therefore, it would be interesting to investigate whether flow-based approach could be adapted to create better cartograms for such tabular datasets.

6   Limitations and Directions for Future Research

We observed that large table cartograms have potential to be used in various real-life applications. For example, in creating infographics of cartographic transformations that can reveal correlations among different geospatial variables, or to create various visual effects in images. In all these applications, the underlying data has the property that the neighbouring cells' values are similar and the number of local optima is small. We observed both TCarto and FastFlow to perform similarly in such scenarios. However, the cells in the FastFlow output appeared to be much more uniform compared to those of TCarto. Therefore, in the image-based applications, the images were less distorted in the FastFlow output. Since such visual observation is subject to human interpretation, it would thus be interesting to devise performance metrics that takes also the image distortion into account.

In general, for large tabular dataset with many local optima with large spikes and large value differences between adjacent cells, neither the TCarto nor FastFlow produced appealing output. However, TCarto with angle constraints improved the readability of the table with the expense of introducing cartographic error. This suggests the importance of choosing an appropriate angle constraint that allows users to follow the rows and columns, as well as to understand the relative cell areas, peaks and valley regions.

Since we invested our effort largely on exploring the scope of table cartograms, we did not focus on conducting controlled user studies or interviews with the domain experts (artists or photographers) to evaluate the artistic quality of the outputs generated by TCarto and FastFlow. For weather dataset, such interviews with meteorologists may potentially help understand which technique reveals the relation among various weather parameters better than the other. It would also be interesting to examine how cartogram based approach compares with today's artificial intelligence based approaches for creating digital arts. Both TCarto and FastFlow could handle large tables (128×128, Fig. 4b), but none of the current implementations leverages GPU computation. Thus it would be an interesting avenue to explore whether GPUs can be leveraged to compute table cartograms in interaction time.

Both the constraint-based and physics-inspired cartographic map transformations are effective in generating large scale cartograms (with low cartographic error, good cell aspect ratio and few concave cells) for image and weather datasets. However, for data tables with large number of local optima and high spikes, we observed constraint based optimization to work better than flow-based approach. We believe our investigation on the scope and opportunities with large table cartograms would inspire future research on cartogram based image transformation.

References

1. Bureau, U.C.: State-to-state migration flows. https://www.census.gov/data/tables/time-series/demo/geographic-mobility/state-to-state-migration.html. Accessed Nov 2020
2. Cano, R.G., Buchin, K., Castermans, T., Pieterse, A., Sonke, W., Speckmann, B.: Mosaic drawings and cartograms. In: Computer Graphics Forum, vol. 34, pp. 361–370. Wiley Online Library (2015)

3. Cauvin, C., Schneider, C.: Cartographic transformations and the Piezopleth maps method. Cartographic J. **26**(2), 96–104 (1989)
4. Dougenik, J.A., Chrisman, N.R., Niemeyer, D.R.: An algorithm to construct continuous area cartograms. Professional Geograph. **37**(1), 75–81 (1985)
5. Espenant, J., Mondal, D.: Streamtable: an area proportional visualization for tables with flowing streams. In: European Workshop on Computational Geometry, pp. 28:1–28:7 (2021). arXiv:https://arxiv.org/abs/2103.15037
6. Evans, W., et al.: Table cartogram. Comput. Geometry **68**, 174–185 (2018)
7. Fletcher, R.: A general quadratic programming algorithm. IMA J. Appl. Math. **7**(1), 76–91 (1971)
8. Gastner, M.T., Newman, M.E.: Diffusion-based method for producing density-equalizing maps. Proc. Nat. Acad. Sci. **101**(20), 7499–7504 (2004)
9. Gastner, M.T., Seguy, V., More, P.: Fast flow-based algorithm for creating density-equalizing map projections. Proc. Nat. Acad. Sci. **115**(10), E2156–E2164 (2018)
10. Hartley, R., Zisserman, A.: Multiple View Geometry in Computer Vision. Cambridge University Press, Cambridge (2003)
11. Henriques, R., Bação, F., Lobo, V.: Carto-SOM: cartogram creation using self-organizing maps. Int. J. Geograph. Inf. Sci. **23**(4), 483–511 (2009)
12. Hildreth, C., et al.: A quadratic programming procedure. Naval Res. Logist. Q. **4**(1), 79–85 (1957)
13. House, D.H., Kocmoud, C.J.: Continuous cartogram construction. In: Proceedings Visualization 1998, pp. 197–204. IEEE (1998)
14. Inoue, R., Li, M.: Optimization-based construction of quadrilateral table cartograms. ISPRS Int. J. Geo-Inf. **9**(1), 43 (2020)
15. Inoue, R., Shimizu, E.: A new algorithm for continuous area cartogram construction with triangulation of regions and restriction on bearing changes of edges. Cartogr. Geogr. Inf. Sci. **33**(2), 115–125 (2006)
16. Keim, D.A., North, S.C., Panse, C.: Cartodraw: a fast algorithm for generating contiguous cartograms. IEEE Trans. Visual Comput. Graphics **10**(1), 95–110 (2004)
17. Keim, D.A., Panse, C., North, S.C.: Medial-axis-based cartograms. IEEE Comput. Graphics Appl. **25**(3), 60–68 (2005)
18. McNutt, A., Kindlmann, G.: A minimally constrained optimization algorithm for table cartograms. IEEEVIS InfoVis Posters (2020), OSF Preprints. https://doi.org/10.31219/osf.io/kem6j
19. McNutt, A.: What are table cartograms good for anyway? an algebraic analysis. In: Eurographics Conference on Visualization (EuroVis), vol. 40 (2021, to appear)
20. Nusrat, S., Kobourov, S.: The state of the art in cartograms. In: Computer Graphics Forum, vol. 35, pp. 619–642. Wiley Online Library (2016)
21. Sun, S.: A fast, free-form rubber-sheet algorithm for contiguous area cartograms. Int. J. Geogr. Inf. Sci. **27**(3), 567–593 (2013)
22. Tobler, W.: Thirty five years of computer cartograms. Ann. Assoc. Am. Geogr. **94**(1), 58–73 (2004)
23. Tutte, W.T.: How to Draw a Graph, vol. 3, pp. 743–767. Wiley Online Library, Hoboken (1963)
24. Winter, M.J.: Diffusion cartograms for the display of periodic table data. J. Chem. Educ. **88**(11), 1507–1510 (2011)
25. Zahan, G.M.H., Mondal, D., Gutwin, C.: Contour line stylization to visualize multivariate information. In: Proceedings of Graphics Interface (GI). pp. 28:1–28:7 (2021)

Perceived Naturalness of Interpolation Methods for Character Upper Body Animation

Xingyu Lei[1]([⊠]), Nicoletta Adamo-Villani[1]([⊠]), Bedrich Benes[1]([⊠]),
Zhiquan Wang[1], Zachary Meyer[1], Richard Mayer[2], and Alyssa Lawson[2]

[1] Purdue University, West Lafayette, IN 47906, USA
{lei64,nadamovi,bbenes}@purdue.edu
[2] University of California, Santa Barbara, Santa Barbara, CA 93106, USA

Abstract. We compare the perceived naturalness of character animations generated using three interpolation methods: linear Euler, spherical linear quaternion, and spherical spline quaternion. While previous work focused on the mathematical description of these interpolation types, our work studies the perceptual evaluation of animated upper body character gestures generated using these interpolations. Ninety-seven participants watched 12 animation clips of a character performing four different upper body motions: a beat gesture, a deictic gesture, an iconic gesture, and a metaphoric gesture. Three animation clips were generated for each gesture using the three interpolation methods. The participants rated their naturalness on a 5-point Likert scale. The results showed that animations generated using spherical spline quaternion interpolation were perceived as significantly more natural than those generated using the other two interpolation methods. The findings held true for all subjects regardless of gender and animation experience and across all four gestures.

Keywords: Virtual characters · Procedural animation ·
Interpolation · Human motion · Gesture animation · Perception

Fig. 1. Examples of four types of gestures (from left to right: metaphoric, iconic, deictic, and beat)

© Springer Nature Switzerland AG 2021
G. Bebis et al. (Eds.): ISVC 2021, LNCS 13017, pp. 103–115, 2021.
https://doi.org/10.1007/978-3-030-90439-5_9

1   Introduction

The ability to express and react to emotions is an essential element of human social interaction, and virtual characters in human-computer interaction (HCI) scenarios can enhance user experience [18]. Therefore, virtual characters must express and respond to emotions.

Creating believable character animation in real-time remains challenging. Keyframe animation is a traditional way to generate animation by defining extreme poses at crucial moments. However, the creation, assembly, and control of the animation is time-consuming, requires great expertise [9]. Motion capture has become affordable and accurate, with improvements in optical hardware and motion sensors. However, all of the actor's movements need to be pre-defined and cannot reflect real-time interaction. Dynamic simulations generate physically correct body reactions, but full-body dynamics are still complex to handle [19].

Animation applications increasingly require on-the-fly adaption [10,28]. Pre-recorded animation sequences can be blended together and mixed by using interpolation [19]. Interpolation algorithms are well-studied in computation complexity, error of the approximation, and the amount of missing information. However, only a handful of studies have examined the human perception of different interpolation methods in character animation [19].

Our work, aiming to study the effects of different interpolations on perceived naturalness of animated characters' upper body movements, has important practical implications. First, game studios would benefit from using a procedural way of identifying motion segments and applying effective interpolation [13], as it is expensive to create transition animations using keyframe and motion-capture techniques [10]. Second, this technique could enable artists to create animation prototypes faster, make motion more natural for background characters with fewer keyframes, and allow more time for other creative decisions. Third, animation interpolation can be used in state-machine, a common game mechanism in many HCI applications.

2   Prior Work

Animation Interpolation Methods: Dam et al. [6] introduced rotation represented by Euler angles, rotation matrices and quaternions. Euler angles are used by artists and supported in common content creation software, but they can lead to gimbal lock. Quaternions provide natural spherical interpolation, but they have a complicated mathematical model that is not intuitive to everyday users and are computationally demanding.

Traditional pose-to-pose animation is based on keyframes drawn by experienced artists. In-between frames can be interpolated by computers [6]. It has excellent applications not only in traditional 2D animation but also in modern 3D animation [15]. Key pose represents a "signature" motion that is unique and extreme [26]. Algorithms are effective in extracting critical motions. So and Baciu [26] measured the difference of poses in directional movements. The poses were ranked, with key poses having a more considerable difference.

The interpolation algorithm defines the smoothness of the transition. In the context of 3D character animation, motion is created by animating a character's major skeletal joints, which drive the character's skinned mesh. The interpolation of translation has been well studied in flat 3D Euclidean space. Character animation, however, is primarily achieved through joint rotation, and rotation lies in non-Euclidean space [1].

The interpolation path on a unit sphere can be translated into the orientation of a joint rotating from its base. Bloom et al. [3] identified three properties of the mechanical analysis of interpolation: the path, angular velocity, and commutativity. Similarly, Wang et al. [30] suggested dividing breaking down animation interpolation into three parts: blending time, path, and angular velocity.

Perception of Naturalness in Animation: Mezger et al. [19] mentioned that the study of interpolation methods for character animation "needs to be addressed by combining computer graphics and perception research" [19, p.1]. Moreover, they suggested that "psychophysical measures seemed to be more sensitive and appropriate for quantifying slight quality differences between animation techniques than the tested physical criterion" [19, p.8].

Interpolation of rotation is often analyzed at isolated joints, but full-body involvement is crucial for the naturalness of motion [12]. Even though user studies are invaluable for measuring motion naturalness, most naturalness metrics do not take into account human observation [27].

According to Blake and Shiffrar [2], both the form and the motion greatly influence the perception of human action. Motor learning (viewers' actions and experiences), social constraints and neural mechanisms, also play an essential role. Respectfully, Etemad et al. [7] studied two sets of themes representing different features of human motion: primary themes specifying actions and secondary themes specifying styles or characteristics.

People tend to make accurate judgments of simple, one-dimensional motion and make inaccurate judgments of complex, multi-dimensional motions [22]. According to Vicovaro et al. [29], people tend to rely on heuristic strategies rather than perceptual judgment. However, if more perceptual information is given, viewers will evaluate perceptually rather than heuristically.

The visual representation of the character can affect how viewers perceive the animation. Studies have found that robots designed to be highly human-like give viewers an eerie feeling [21]. Human traits in non-human objects known as anthropomorphism have been studied using virtual characters [4]. The more anthropomorphic the characters are, the more likely viewers are to report their motion as artificial, supported by fMRI examination [23].

Another important factor is the viewer's level of experience with animation. Those familiar with animation are very likely to spot errors in human motion than those who are new to animation [19]. The gender of the viewer and of the character influence human-computer interaction. Krämer et al. [14] found a difference concerning learning when viewers interacted with animated pedagogical agents of the same or opposite sex. For neutral motions such as walking or conversational gestures, viewers' judgments of male or female characters were similar; when certain emotions were involved, however, such as sadness or anger, gender bias appeared more prominently [31]. Emotional state of the animated character affects the viewer as shown in recent works [5,16,17].

Jansen and Van Welbergen [12] proposed three evaluation methods for naturalness in human motion: Two-alternative forced-choice (2AFC), Yes/No and Rating. Rating method could provide more valuable information on the naturalness of individual motion; Yes/No method and 2AFC are suitable for discriminating clips [12]. Hyde et al. [11] used a similar rating method to evaluate the naturalness of a character's facial expressions.

3   Methods

3.1   Studied Interpolations

Linear Euler Interpolation (LinEuler) is an interpolation between two tuples of Euler angles. Let a point in 3D space be represented as $P = [x, y, z] \in \mathbb{R}^3$; and a vector from the world's origin to that point is $v = (x, y, z)$ in the associated vector space $\mathbb{V}^3$. Consider a unit sphere, where a vector from the center to one point on the surface is represented as $v_0 = (x_0, y_0, z_0) \in \mathbb{R}^3$ and another as $v_1 = (x_1, y_1, z_1) \in \mathbb{R}^3$. Linear Euler interpolation between v_1 and v_2 is written as follow where $h \in [0, 1]$ is a blending parameter:

$$LinEuler(v_0, v_1, h) = (1 - h)v_0 + hv_1, \tag{1}$$

Spherical Linear Quaternion Interpolation (Slerp). A quaternion q consists of a scalar and a vector part: $q = s, x, y, z$ where $s, x, y, z \in \mathbb{R}^3$, also written as $q = s + ix + jy + kz$ where $s, x, y, z \in \mathbb{R}^3$ and $i^2 = j^2 = k^2 = ijk = -1$.

Slerp [24] interpolates the rotation along the shortest path on a unit sphere at a constant velocity, which causes a sudden change of angular direction when performing a series of rotations, making keyframes visible. Let H be a set of quaternions, where $p, q \in H$, $\cos \Omega = pq$ and $h \in [0, 1]$ is the interpolation parameter. Slerp is:

$$Slerp(p, q, h) = \frac{p \sin((1 - h)\Omega) + q \sin(h\Omega)}{\sin(\Omega)} \tag{2}$$

Spherical Spline Quaternion Interpolation (Spherical and Quadrangle, or Squad) is the spherical cubic equivalent of the Bézier cubic curve in the quaternion space. Shoemake [25] presented Squad and then proved the continuous differentiability of Squad at control points. Where $h \in [0, 1]$ and $s_i = q_i exp(-(log(q_i^{-1}q_{i+1}) + log(q_i^{-1}q_{i-1}))/4)$.

$$Squad(q_i, q_{i+1}, s_i, s_{i+1}, h)$$
$$= Slerp(Slerp(q_i, q_{i+1}, h), Slerp(s_i, s_{i+1}, h), 2h(1 - h)) \tag{3}$$

The three algorithms generate different interpolation paths as shown in Example: Fig. 2. Although algorithms for more complex interpolations exists [1, 6,8], they also require more complex parameters and were not considered in our study.

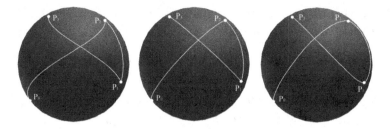

Fig. 2. Interpolation curve on a unit sphere using LinEuler (left), Slerp (middle), and Squad (right).

3.2   Study Design

This study aimed to examine the effects of the three interpolation methods: linear Euler (LinEuler; Eq. 1), spherical linear quaternion (Slerp; Eq. 2), and spherical spline quaternion (Squad; Eq. 3), on the perceived naturalness of four upper body character animations. The study included interpolation type, gesture type, participant's gender, and participant's level of animation experience as independent variables. The dependent variable of the experiment was the participant's perceived naturalness of each animation clip rated on a 5-point Likert scale (1 = not natural at all, 5 = very natural). Figure 1 shows the four gestures selected for this study: right arm throwing an object (metaphoric gesture); both arms moving outward, showing the size of an object (iconic gesture); right arm pointing to the sky (deictic gesture); both arms moving forwards in parallel (beat gesture).

The main null hypothesis of the study was that all the interpolation methods would be given the same naturalness ratings, meaning all three interpolation methods have equal effects on the viewer's perception of naturalness in character animation. The main alternative hypothesis was that at least one of the interpolation methods would be given a different rating; that is, the viewer would perceive some methods more or less natural than others.

Null Hypothesis 1 $(H1_0)$. *The three interpolation methods are given equal ratings by the participants (i.e. $r_{LinEuler} = r_{Slerp} = r_{Squad}$)*

Alterative Hypothesis 1 $(H1_a)$. *The three interpolations methods are given significantly different ratings by the participants*

The secondary hypotheses of the study were the following:

Null Hypothesis 2 $(H2_0)$. *The three interpolation methods are given equal ratings regardless of the participants' animation experience (experts vs. novices)*

Alterative Hypothesis 2 $(H2_a)$. *The three interpolations methods are given significantly different ratings based on the participants' animation experience*

Null Hypothesis 3 $(H3_0)$. *The three interpolation methods are given equal ratings regardless of character's gesture type (beat, deictic, iconic, or metaphoric)*

Alterative Hypothesis 3 ($H3_a$). *The three interpolations methods are given significantly different ratings based on character's gesture type*

Null Hypothesis 4 ($H4_0$). *The three interpolation methods are given equal ratings regardless of the participants' gender*

Alterative Hypothesis 4 ($H4_a$). *The three interpolations methods are given significantly different ratings based on the participants' gender*

3.3 Experiment Design

Surveys were designed and hosted on Qualtrics and distributed through Prolific and Purdue University Computer Graphics Department's (CGT) email list. Four motion-captured recordings (duration ranged from 1.6 to 2.4 s) corresponded to four types of gesture. Four frames were identified to generate 12 stimuli clips using different interpolation methods. Figure 3 shows frames from the three different interpolation clips of metaphoric gesture.

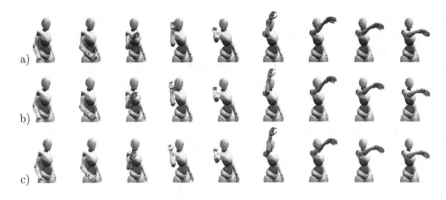

Fig. 3. Metaphoric gesture: LinEuler a), Slerp b), and Squad c).

Motion data (.fbx file) were obtained from Motion-capture system Xsens and Motion-capture library Mixamo. They were then remapped to the character X Bot [20] through MotionBuilder's retarget feature. Minimum adjustments were applied for the motion to look correct. Next, the data were imported into Maya for clipping, and a custom script identified four frames and extracted rotation values along the joint hierarchy. It output XML files and passed to Unity, which performed the interpolation of rotation on individual joints.

3.4   Study Procedure

The study is divided into the pilot study and the main study. During each study, participants were first presented with an overview of the survey and asked to provide their demographic information, including age, gender, race, highest completed education, and experience in animation.

Second, they were asked to watch and evaluate different animation clips. This part consisted of 12 animations divided into four gesture groups. The gesture groups were presented in counter-balanced random order. Three animation clips of that gesture using different interpolation methods were presented in random order within each group. Each clip was looped and was shown along with a descriptive text (e.g. "The character is throwing an object"). After viewing each clip, the participants were asked to rate the clip on a 5-point Likert scale. A hidden timer was used to track the time spent on each clip. Rules were used to filter out participants who were potentially rushing through the survey by giving patterned or random responses.

3.5   Data Collection and Analysis

The analysis followed a three-step procedure. In the first step, the mean rating for each interpolation method was calculated using linear regression, with LinEuler as the baseline. In the second step, a one-way analysis of variance (ANOVA) test was conducted. Its outcome p-value was used to either reject or fail to reject the null hypothesis using an alpha value of 0.05. Tukey's honest significant difference test (Tukey's HSD) was performed for post-comparison if the null hypothesis was rejected. The outcome adjusted p-value from Tukey's HSD identifies which pairs of groups are different. The result further indicates which method is different compared to the others in terms of perceived naturalness using a confidence level of 95%.

A power analysis was performed based on the data collected from the pilot study to determine the ideal sample size; the power level was set at 80%.

The Pilot Study: A total of 18 responses were used for analysis. The mean values are reported in Table 1. The p-value obtained from the one-way ANOVA was 1.99e-12, far less than the alpha value.

In the Tukey HSD post-ANOVA comparison, the Squad-LinEuler pair and Squad-Slerp pair had a p-value <0.05, rejecting the null hypothesis that the two groups had identical ratings. Slerp-LinEuler pair had p-values >0.05, which failed to reject the null hypothesis that the two groups had equal ratings.

Table 1. Mean table for the pilot study

	LinEuler	Slerp	Squad
Mean	2.2500	2.0694	3.3611

The Main Study: A total of 97 responses were used for the analysis. The number of participants was far greater than the minimum of 48 (obtained using power analysis for ANOVA in the pilot study), which gave this study a power level of approximately 98%.

The mean rating values are reported in Table 2. The one-way ANOVA test yielded a p-value equal to 2e-16, which is <0.05.

The adjusted p-value from the Tukey HSD matched the result from the pilot study, with the Squad-LinEuler pair and the Squad-Slerp pair's p-values <0.05; thus, the null hypothesis that the two groups had identical ratings was rejected. The Slerp-LinEuler pair had a p-value >0.05 which failed to reject the null hypothesis that the two groups had equal ratings.

Table 2. Mean table for the combined main study

	LinEuler	Slerp	Squad
Mean	2.6598	2.7010	3.4948

The main study combined results from two platforms: Prolific and CGT. The latter was biased toward animation-major students; therefore, the analysis was also conducted on data collected solely from Prolific, with a total of 42 subjects.

The means are reported in Table 3. And the one-way ANOVA test yielded a p-value of 1.1e-6, which was still significantly <0.05. Therefore, there was significant evidence to reject the null hypothesis $H1_0$.

In the Tukey HSD, Squad-LinEuler pair and Squad-Slerp pair yielded p-values <0.05, thus rejecting the null hypothesis that these two groups had identical ratings. As for the Slerp-LinEuler pair, the p-value was >0.05, which failed to reject the null hypothesis that the two groups had equal ratings.

Table 3. Mean table for Prolific subjects in the main study

	LinEuler	Slerp	Squad
Mean	2.8333	2.8929	3.3929

Analysis based on Animation Experience: Seventy-two subjects were novice, and 25 had some animation experience. The means for both groups are reported in Table 4. The p-values for both groups were 2e-16, which is significantly <0.05. Therefore, there was significant evidence for both groups to reject the null hypothesis $H2_0$.

The Tukey HSD test results for the two groups showed that the Squad-LinEuler pair and Squad-Slerp pair p-values were <0.05, rejecting the null hypothesis. As for the Slerp-LinEuler pair, both groups' p-values were >0.05, which failed to reject the null hypothesis that the two groups have equal ratings.

Table 4. Mean table for different animation experience level

	Novice	Experienced
LinEuler	2.7778	2.3200
Slerp	2.8125	2.3800
Squad	3.4688	3.5700

Analysis based on Gesture Type: Some gestures showed more differences in perceived naturalness compared to others. A sample size of 97 was used for this analysis. The mean values for the linear regression model are reported in Table 5. The one-way ANOVA tests yielded p-values that were all significantly <0.05 (Beat gesture 3.76e-09; Deictic gesture 4.78e-05; Iconic gesture 2.8e-16; Metaphoric gesture 6.82e-08). Therefore, there was significant evidence to reject the null hypothesis $H3_0$.

The Tukey HSD showed all Squad-LinEuler pair and Squad-Slerp pairs had p-values <0.05, rejecting the hypothesis that these two groups were identical in all gesture groups. As for the Slerp-LinEuler pair, all the p-values were >0.05, which failed to reject the hypothesis that the two groups had equal ratings in all gesture groups.

Table 5. Mean table for different gesture types

	Beat	Deictic	Iconic	Metaphoric
LinEuler	2.5464	3.0825	2.5155	2.4948
Slerp	2.5567	3.0412	2.6082	2.5979
Squad	3.3814	3.6289	3.6701	3.2989

Analysis based on Gender: The pool of subjects included self-identified 43 males and 49 females. The means for the two gender groups are reported in Table 6. Results of the one-way ANOVA test showed that the male group had a p-value of 2e-16 and the female group a p-value of 1.13e-11, which were both significantly <0.05. Therefore, for both male and female viewers, there was significant evidence to reject the null hypothesis $H4_0$.

The Tukey HSD test for the two groups showed that the Squad-LinEuler pair and Squad-Slerp pair's p-values were <0.05, rejecting the null hypothesis that there are no significant differences based on gender. As for the Slerp-LinEuler pair, both groups' p-values were > 0.05, which fails to reject the hypothesis that the two groups gave equal ratings.

Table 6. Mean table for different gender

	Male	Female
LinEuler	2.6512	2.6888
Slerp	2.5581	2.8414
Squad	3.5872	3.4082

4 Discussion

The findings from the data analysis provide sufficient evidence to reject the null hypothesis that LinEuler, Slerp, and Squad would be given the same naturalness ratings. It was found that upper body animation generated by Squad interpolation was perceived as significantly more natural than that generated by LinEuler or Slerp. This conclusion holds not only for audiences with different levels of expertise in animation and different gender groups, but also for different gesture types.

Although LinEuler and Slerp use entirely different rotation models and interpolation calculations, there was insufficient evidence to reject the hypothesis that LinEuler and Slerp interpolation would be given the same naturalness rating. These two interpolation methods, therefore, had the same effect on the viewer's perception of naturalness. This finding was consistent across all the data subsets.

We believe Squad interpolation is superior to the other two linear models due to its algorithm, which generates a smoother path and continuous angular velocity. Our perceptual experiment has shown it to produce the most natural animations. The average naturalness rating for animations generated using Squad interpolation was between 3 ("neutral") and 4 ("somewhat natural"). In contrast, animations generated using LinEuler and Slerp were rated between 2 ("somewhat unnatural") and 3 ("neutral").

Findings also suggest that experienced viewers can distinguish interpolation methods more clearly than inexperienced viewers. Results of our study also showed there were no significant differences based on participants' gender. In regard to the perceived naturalness of different gesture types, findings show that the iconic gesture was rated the most different between interpolations, and the deictic gesture showed the least difference.

5 Conclusion and Future Work

The experiment reported in the paper investigated the effect of different animation interpolation methods on perceived naturalness of four types of animated body gestures. Findings showed that animations generated with Squad interpolation were perceived as significantly more natural than animations generated with the other two methods (i.e. LinEuler and Slerp). Findings held true across the four gesture types, and there were no significant differences in ratings based on participants' gender and animation experience.

The experiment had a few limitations that could be overcome in future work. First, given the wide range of possible upper body motions, more gesture types could be tested in the future to further support these findings. Second, other test paradigms proposed by Jansen and Van Welbergen [12], could also be used in future work aside from subjective rating. Post-experiment qualitative questions could also help explain why Squad is perceived as more natural than the other two methods. Different camera views could be explored in future studies.

Third, one of the essential elements of interpolation algorithms is the control points (translated by extracting key poses). This work used the researcher's judgment to identify the key poses of motion-captured clips; in future work it is possible to algorithmically determine the key pose to interpolate. This method could potentially be used for other purposes such as keyframe reduction. Furthermore, the number of control points and the frame interval between each point also play a considerable part in the animation's smoothness. Although there are usually no limits to the number of keyframes that can be added, fewer and pre-planned control points saves memory. When the motion range exceeds $180°$ between two orientations, using quaternions will interpolate along the shortest path. Applying no-flip rules to the algorithm could avoid such an extreme case.

Lastly, the algorithms themselves have some limitations. All three methods interpolate along a perfectly planned path, but human motion is imperfect. Furthermore, the rotation starts and ends at the same time with no variation. Animation interpolation methods also fail to handle the collision of body parts, which could result in model clipping. Improvements could be implemented, such as adding random noise to avoid perfectly smooth curves. Interpolating with timed offsets based on joint hierarchy could add secondary motion and specifying rotation constraints for limbs could reduce the chance of model clipping.

Despite the limitations, our findings are important as they could benefit both real-time and non-real-time applications. The state-machine mechanism which utilizes interpolation is commonly used in games and other interactive applications. A more natural behavior of the virtual character enhances user experience. The implementation of a more natural animation can also reduce stress for developers: by saving time on repetitive tasks and allocating more resources for creative decisions. It also enables independent developers to create content more quickly, and larger studios to generate animation prototypes faster. Furthermore, this semi-procedural approach for creating human motion encourages people with little professional knowledge to take an interest in animation. Lastly, the work reported in the paper has created a basis for further research into the evaluation of animation techniques.

Acknowledgements. The work reported in the paper is supported in part by NSF–IIS-Cyberlearning & Future Learning Technologies, Award #1821894, Title: Multimodal Affective Pedagogical Agents for Different Types of Learners.

References

1. Barr, A.H., Currin, B., Gabriel, S., Hughes, J.F.: Smooth interpolation of orientations with angular velocity constraints using quaternions. Comput. Graph., 8 (1992)
2. Blake, R., Shiffrar, M.: Perception of human motion. Annual Rev. Psychol. **58**(1), 47–73 (2007)
3. Bloom, C., Blow, J., Muratori, C.: Errors and omissions in marc Alexa's "Linear Combination of Transformations", p. 5 (2004)
4. Chaminade, T., Hodgins, J., Kawato, M.: Anthropomorphism influences perception of computer-animated characters' actions. Soc. Cogn. Affect. Neurosci. **2**(3), 206–216 (2007)
5. Cheng, J., Zhou, W., Lei, X., Adamo, N., Benes, B.: The effects of body gestures and gender on viewer's perception of animated pedagogical agent's emotions. In: Kurosu, M. (ed.) HCII 2020. LNCS, vol. 12182, pp. 169–186. Springer, Cham (2020). https://doi.org/10.1007/978-3-030-49062-1_11
6. Dam, E.B., Koch, M., Lillholm, M.: Quaternions, interpolation and animation, p. 103 (1998)
7. Etemad, S.A., Arya, A., Parush, A., DiPaola, S.: Perceptual validity in animation of human motion: Perceptual validity in animation of human motion. Comp. Anim. Virt. Worlds **27**(1), 58–71 (2016)
8. Geier, M.: Quanterion-nursery (2020). https://github.com/mgeier/quaternion-nursery
9. Heloir, A., Kipp, M.: EMBR: a realtime animation engine for interactive embodied agents, p. 2 (2009)
10. Horswill, I.D.: Lightweight procedural animation with believable physical interactions. IEEE Trans. Comput. Intell. AI Games **1**(1), 39–49 (2009)
11. Hyde, J., Carter, E.J., Kiesler, S., Hodgins, J.K.: Assessing naturalness and emotional intensity: a perceptual study of animated facial motion, p. 8 (2014)
12. Jansen, S.E.M., van Welbergen, H.: Methodologies for the user evaluation of the motion of virtual humans. In: Ruttkay, Z., Kipp, M., Nijholt, A., Vilhjálmsson, H.H. (eds.) IVA 2009. LNCS (LNAI), vol. 5773, pp. 125–131. Springer, Heidelberg (2009). https://doi.org/10.1007/978-3-642-04380-2_16
13. Johansen, R.S.: Automated semi-procedural animation for character locomotion p. 114 (2009)
14. Krämer, N.C., Karacora, B., Lucas, G., Dehghani, M., Rüther, G., Gratch, J.: Closing the gender gap in STEM with friendly male instructors? On the effects of rapport behavior and gender of a virtual agent in an instructional interaction. Comput. Educat. **99**, 1–13 (2016)
15. Lasseter, J.: Principles of traditional animation applied to 3D computer animation. ACM Comput. Graph. **21**(4), 35–44 (1987)
16. Lawson, A.P., Mayer, R.E., Adamo-Villani, N., Benes, B., Lei, X., Cheng, J.: Do learners recognize and relate to the emotions displayed by virtual instructors? Int. J. Artif. Intell. Educ. **114**, 1560–4306 (2021)
17. Lawson, A.P., Mayer, R.E., Adamo-Villani, N., Benes, B., Lei, X., Cheng, J.: Recognizing the emotional state of human and virtual instructors. Comput. Hum. Behav. **114**, 106554 (2021)
18. Matsiola, M., Dimoulas, C., Veglis, A., Kalliris, G.: Augmenting user interaction experience through embedded multimodal media agents in social networking environments (2005)

19. Mezger, J., Ilg, W., Giese, M.A.: Trajectory synthesis by hierarchical spatio-temporal correspondence: comparison of different methods. In: Proceedings of the 2nd symposium on Appied perception in graphics and visualization - APGV 2005, p. 25. ACM Press (2005)
20. Mixamo: X Bot (2008). https://www.mixamo.com/#/?page=3&type=Character
21. Mori, M.: The Uncanny Valley. In: The uncanny valley, vol. 7(4), pp. 33–35, Energy (1970)
22. Proffitt, D.R., Gilden, D.L.: Understanding natural dynamics. J. Exp. Psychol. Hum. Percet. Perform. **15**(2), 384–393 (1989)
23. Reitsma, P.S.A., Andrews, J., Pollard, N.S.: Effect of character animacy and preparatory motion on perceptual magnitude of errors in ballistic motion. Comp. Graph. Forum **27**(2), 201–210 (2008)
24. Shoemake, K.: Animating rotation with quaternion curves. SIGGRAPH 1985 19(3) (1985)
25. Shoemake, K.: Quaternion calculus and fast animation (1987)
26. So, C.K.F., Baciu, G.: Entropy-based motion extraction for motion capture animation. Comp. Anim. Virt. Worlds **16**(3–4), 225–235 (2005)
27. Van Welbergen, H., Van Basten, B.J.H., Egges, A., Ruttkay, Z.M., Overmars, M.H.: Real time animation of virtual humans: a trade-off between naturalness and control. Comp. Graph. Forum **29**(8), 2530–2554 (2010)
28. van Welbergen, H., Yaghoubzadeh, R., Kopp, S.: AsapRealizer 2.0: the next steps in fluent behavior realization for ECAs. In: Bickmore, T., Marsella, S., Sidner, C. (eds.) IVA 2014. LNCS (LNAI), vol. 8637, pp. 449–462. Springer, Cham (2014). https://doi.org/10.1007/978-3-319-09767-1_56
29. Vicovaro, M., Hoyet, L., Burigana, L., O'sullivan, C.: Perceptual evaluation of motion editing for realistic throwing animations. ACM Trans. Appl. Percept. **11**(2), 1–23 (2014)
30. Wang, Y., Lang, F., Wang, Z., Xu, B.: Automatic variable-timing animation transition based on hierarchical interpolation method. In: Proceedings of the 10th International Conference on Computer Graphics Theory and Applications, pp. 309–316. SCITEPRESS - Science and and Technology Publications (2015)
31. Zibrek, K., Hoyet, L., Ruhland, K., McDonnell, R.: Exploring the effect of motion type and emotions on the perception of gender in virtual humans. ACM Trans. Appl. Percept. **12**(3), 1–20 (2015)

Neuromuscular Control of the Face-Head-Neck Biomechanical Complex with Learning-Based Expression Transfer from Images and Videos

Xiao S. Zeng[1(✉)], Surya Dwarakanath[1], Wuyue Lu[1], Masaki Nakada[2], and Demetri Terzopoulos[1]

[1] Computer Science Department, University of California, Los Angeles, CA, USA
stevennz@cs.ucla.edu
[2] NeuralX, Inc., Los Angeles, CA, USA

Abstract. The transfer of facial expressions from people to 3D face models is a classic computer graphics problem. In this paper, we present a novel, learning-based approach to transferring facial expressions and head movements from images and videos to a biomechanical model of the face-head-neck complex. Leveraging the Facial Action Coding System (FACS) as an intermediate representation of the expression space, we train a deep neural network to take in FACS Action Units (AUs) and output suitable facial muscle and jaw activation signals for the musculoskeletal model. Through biomechanical simulation, the activations deform the facial soft tissues, thereby transferring the expression to the model. Our approach has advantages over previous approaches. First, the facial expressions are anatomically consistent as our biomechanical model emulates the relevant anatomy of the face, head, and neck. Second, by training the neural network using data generated from the biomechanical model itself, we eliminate the manual effort of data collection for expression transfer. The success of our approach is demonstrated through experiments involving the transfer onto our face-head-neck model of facial expressions and head poses from a range of facial images and videos.

Keywords: Animation · Physical simulation · Computer vision · Deep learning

1 Introduction

The face, actuated by the muscles of facial expression, and head movements, actuated by the cervical muscles, are a powerful mode of nonverbal communication between humans. The simulation of the face-head-neck musculoskeletal complex is of importance in understanding how we convey thinking and feeling in fields from affective science to 3D computer animation. Biomechanical human musculoskeletal models realistically capture the anatomy and physics underlying human

---

X. S. Zeng and S. Dwarakanath—Co-first author.

© Springer Nature Switzerland AG 2021
G. Bebis et al. (Eds.): ISVC 2021, LNCS 13017, pp. 116–127, 2021.
https://doi.org/10.1007/978-3-030-90439-5_10

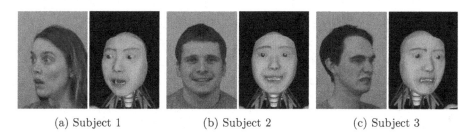

(a) Subject 1   (b) Subject 2   (c) Subject 3

Fig. 1. Our deep learning framework enables the transfer of facial expressions and head poses from images or videos to a biomechanical face-head-neck model.

motion generation. In particular, those pertaining to the simulation of the human face have succeeded in convincingly emulating facial expressiveness; however, they require significant effort in parameter tuning to produce realistic results.

In this paper, we show how to endow a biomechanical, musculoskeletal model of the human face with the ability to produce facial expressions via machine learning from real-world reference images and videos (Fig. 1). To this end, we introduce a deep neural-network-based method for learning the representation of human facial expressions through Ekman's Facial Action Coding System (FACS) [5] in the context of the muscle actuators that drive the musculoskeletal face model augmented with a musculoskeletal cervicocephalic (neck-head) system to animate head movement during facial expression synthesis.

The novelty of our framework lies in the following features: We propose the first biomechanical face-head-neck animation system that is capable of learning to reproduce expressions and head orientations through neuromuscular control. Our novel deep neuromuscular motor controller learns to map between FACS Action Units (AUs) extracted from human facial images and videos and the activations of the muscle actuators that drive the biomechanical system. As a proof of concept, we demonstrate an automated processing pipeline (Fig. 2) for animating expressions and head poses using an improved version of the physics-based neck-head-face animation system developed by Lee and Terzopoulos [10], but which can potentially be applied to any muscle-driven model.

2   Related Work

Muscle-based facial animation has been studied for decades [19]. A series of studies have endeavored to build increasingly anatomically accurate musculoskeletal face models. Using such models, Terzopoulos and Waters [17] and Sifakis et al. [15], among others, have addressed the automatic determination of facial muscle activations from videos, but these methods require nonrigid motion trackers or motion capture markers. We present a markerless, real-time biomechanical face-head-neck simulation system that can automatically learn muscle activation parameters for a variety of expressions from reference images and videos. Most relevant to our work in the present paper is an existing biomechanical model of the cervicocephalic complex [10], which incorporates an improved version of the face model developed by Lee et al. [11].

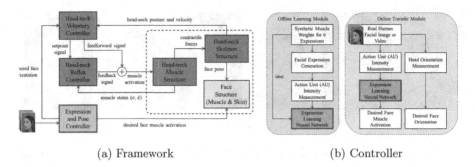

(a) Framework   (b) Controller

Fig. 2. The structure of our expression and head pose transfer framework (a) and the components of the facial expression and head pose controller (b). The expression learning neural network (yellow) is first trained offline. In a transfer task, an image or a video sequence of a real face is fed into the online transfer module of the expression and pose controller to output the desired facial muscle activations and head orientation information. The muscle activations are input to the biomechanical face model (orange) to perform the corresponding expression and the head orientation is provided to the head-neck biomechanical neuromuscular system (green) to produce the desired head pose. (Color figure online)

Many facial animation researchers have made use of the well-known FACS [8], a quantitative phenomenological abstraction that decomposes facial expressions into the intensity levels of Action Units (AUs), each of which corresponds to the actions of one or more facial muscles. An advantage of using the FACS is that it encodes anatomical and psychological semantics [5].

Expression transfer or retargeting is a trending topic and recent approaches often use FACS-based blendshapes as the basic parametric representation [18,20, 24]. Others have used techniques such as interactive mesh deformation control [22] and neural-network-based perceptual models [1] to represent expressions in blendshapes. However, transferring expressions using a musculoskeletal system is more natural since facial actions are the result of coordinated muscle contractions inducing soft tissue deformation. Despite the existing literature, there remains a deficiency of work in transferring expressions to musculoskeletal facial systems.

3   Musculoskeletal Model

Our real-time musculoskeletal model is based on the one of Lee and Terzopoulos [10], but both the underlying face-head-neck control system and the facial expression system are significantly improved. Its overall architecture is controlled in a hierarchical manner, as illustrated in Fig. 2a. Specifically, the skeletal structure is an articulated multibody dynamics system, with bones and joints consistent with human anatomy. The skeletal system is driven by a Hill-type muscle actuator model.

The biomechanical face component consists of a facial soft tissue model comprising epidermis, dermal-fatty, fascia, and muscle layers supported by an underlying skull, which is constructed based on the work of Lee et al. [11]. The soft tissue is a deformable model assembled from discrete uniaxial finite elements, which simulates dynamic facial deformation in an anatomically consistent yet simplified way compared to the models described in [15, 21], and [6], thus maintaining a low computational cost that affords real-time simulation performance on readily available hardware.

There are 26 pairs of primary facial muscles embedded in the biomechanical face, including the frontalis, corrugator, levator labii, orbicularis oculi, mentalis, and orbicularis oris muscle groups. The contractions of these muscles apply forces to the facial soft tissue layers, inducing deformations that produce meaningful facial expressions. We have augmented the expressive details, such as wrinkles on the face model, by applying multiple levels of subdivision to increase significantly the number of surface nodes that can be activated by muscle forces, and applied a high resolution texture map to the surface mesh for a natural appearance.

The appendix of reference [23] explains the biomechanical components of our model in greater detail.

3.1 Control

To control the face-head-neck system, our novel neural network-based expression and pose controller generates facial muscle activations that produce recognizable expressions. It concurrently outputs head pose estimates to the head-neck musculoskeletal complex, where voluntary and reflex neuromuscular control layers generate muscle activation signals to achieve the desired head orientations.

The higher-level voluntary controller receives the current head-neck posture and velocity information, as well as the desired adjustment of the posture, and generates a feedforward muscle activation signal and a setpoint control signal. The latter, which encodes the desired muscle strains and strain rates, is input to the reflex controller that then generates a feedback muscle activation signal and adds it to the feedforward signal generated by the voluntary controller. As a result, each cervical muscle receives an activation signal a and, through simulation, generates a contractile muscle force accordingly. Together with the external environmental forces and gravity, the whole system is simulated through time and rendered as a physics-based animation. The voluntary controller runs 25 Hz (in simulation time), while the reflex controller runs at 4KHz along with the physical simulation time steps.

4 Expression Learning

We next explain our machine learning approach of using a deep neural network to transfer facial expressions to our biomechanical face model. We leverage the FACS and synthesize the muscle activations for the model using the trained deep neural network. The following sections describe the architecture of the network,

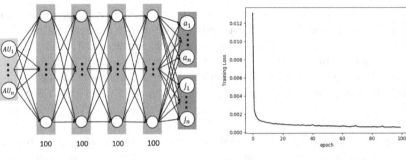

(a) Neural network architecture   (b) Convergence of the neural network

Fig. 3. The expression learning neural network.

the pipeline for using the biomechanical face model to generate training data, and the process of training the neural network.

4.1 Network Architecture

The function of the neural network is to generate activation signals for the muscles of the biomechanical face model such that they generate contractile forces that deform the synthetic facial tissues to produce facial expressions. We employ a fully connected deep neural network architecture for this purpose (Fig. 3a). The input layer consists of a total of 17 neurons representing the important AUs that are involved in the majority of facial movements, each neuron corresponding to a single normalized AU. We include 4 hidden layers with 100 neurons in each layer and ReLU activation.[1] The output layer consists of 56 neurons, 52 of which encode the activations a_i, with $1 \leq i \leq 52$, for each of the 26 pairs of facial muscles, and the remaining 4 encode the jaw rotation, jaw slide, jaw twist, and an auxiliary value. Given its architecture, the network has a total of 37,300 weights. It is implemented in Keras with a TensorFlow backend.

4.2 Training Data Generation

The training data generation process is divided into two steps:

1. generation of muscle activations, and
2. generation of AUs for the corresponding muscle activations.

Each basic expression requires a combination of muscles to be activated. Given n muscles, we define W_e as a set of weights w_i, with $1 \leq i \leq n$, which determine the effect each muscle will have on an expression e. The activation

---

[1] This choice was based on observed Mean Squared Errors (MSE) on test data of networks with different numbers of hidden layers and different numbers of neurons per hidden layer.

for each muscle a_i for an expression is then defined as $a_i = w_i s$, where $w_i \in W_e$ and s is a scale term. For a single expression, we determine the weights in a set W_e manually by visually analyzing the facial expressions formed by the face model. We repeat the process for all the basic expressions, namely (1) Joy, (2) Sadness, (3) Anger, (4) Fear, (5) Disgust, and (6) Surprise to generate the sets W_{Joy}, W_{Sadness}, W_{Anger}, W_{Fear}, W_{Disgust} and W_{Surprise}, respectively.

We then sample the value of s randomly in the range $[0.0, 1.0]$ to generate all the muscle activations a_i. We also assign a random value between 0 and 1 for the jaw rotation. For the purpose of our experiments, we maintain the jaw twist and jaw slide at a value of 0.5. We further form a set A consisting of all the muscle activations a_i, where $1 \leq i \leq n$, and the jaw activations including jaw rotation, jaw twist and jaw slide. We iterate the above process, generating the set A by repeatedly sampling the value of s for a single expression. We finally extend this to all basic expressions and obtain multiple sets A_{Joy}, A_{Sadness}, A_{Anger}, A_{Fear}, A_{Disgust} and A_{Surprise} for each expression.

We leverage the functionality of OpenFace 2.0 [2] for facial expression recognition and head pose estimation. OpenFace is a computer vision tool capable of facial landmark detection, head pose estimation, facial AU recognition, and eye-gaze estimation. OpenFace employs Convolutional Experts Constrained Local Models (CE-CLMs) for facial landmark detection and tracking. CE-CLMs use a 3D representation of the detected facial landmarks by which OpenFace estimates the head pose. Eye gaze estimation is done using a Constrained Local Neural Fields (CLNF) landmark detector. The final task, facial expression recognition, is performed using Support Vector Machines and Support Vector Regression.

We use a single set A formed by the above described procedure to activate the muscles and jaw of the biomechanical face model. We then render the model to form an image. The image is input to OpenFace, which performs facial expression recognition and head pose estimation, outputting the estimated AUs and head orientation associated with the input image. We repeat this process for each set A formed (as described previously) to obtain the corresponding AUs and head orientations.

Thus, we synthesize a large quantity of training data pairs each consisting of (i) muscle and jaw activations A and (ii) the associated AUs and head orientations.

4.3 Network Training

We use the aforementioned data to train our deep neural network to input AUs and output corresponding muscle and jaw activations.

The AUs from each training pair, generated as described in the previous section, are passed to the network as input. We then compare the corresponding muscle and jaw activations; i.e., the ground truth compared to the predictions of muscle and jaw activations given by the neural network. We use a Mean Square Error (MSE) training loss between the predictions and the ground truth, which is backpropagated to update the weights, thus training the neural network.

We normalize the intensity values of each AU class across all pairs to remove the disparity of intensity values between synthetic faces and real faces. We use a total of 6,000 pairs, with about 1,000 pairs for each basic expression.

To train the neural network, we use the ADAM stochastic gradient descent optimizer with an MSE loss, a batch size of 32, and a learning rate of 0.01. We train the network in a total of 100 epochs, running on an NVIDIA GeForce GTX 1650 GPU installed on a Windows 10 machine with a 2.6 GHz Intel Core i7-9750H CPU. Figure 3b shows the convergence of the training error.

4.4   Expression Transfer Pipeline

To transfer real facial expressions on the fly, we use a pipeline similar to the offline training module, again leveraging OpenFace for facial expression recognition and head pose estimation. We input an image of an expressive face into OpenFace to obtain all of the corresponding AUs and head orientations. The AUs are then passed into the trained neural network which outputs predictions of the muscle and jaw activations, driving the biomechanical face to deform the muscles and transfer the expressions onto it.

We transfer both image and video inputs. Each frame in a video is processed independently and a resulting video is created using the transferred frames. The intensity values for each AU class are normalized across all the images or frames as in the case of the training pipeline.

5   Experiments and Results

We next present the results of transferring facial expressions from the wild using our trained neural network. We evaluate our expression transfer pipeline on different expressions while using a variation of AUs and muscles in the biomechanical face model.

5.1   Facial Expression Datasets

Several facial expression datasets are available online. The datasets that we used in our experiments are as follows:

Karolinska Directed Emotional Faces (KDEF) [3]. The KDEF dataset consists of 4,900 pictures of human facial expressions. It covers 70 subjects (35 female and 35 male) enacting all the basic facial expressions, namely Neutral, Joy, Sadness, Anger, Fear, Disgust, and Surprise. Each expression performed by the subject is imaged from multiple directions. We use the dataset to transfer facial expressions onto the biomechanical face model and visually analyze the performance of our trained neural network in this paper.

Cohn Kanade Dataset (CK) and *Extended Cohn Kanade Dataset (CK+)* [9,13]. The CK and the CK+ dataset combined consist of 593 video sequences of 123 subjects. Each sequence consists of images from a neutral expression (first frame) to a peak expression (last frame). The peak expressions are FACS

Table 1. Comparison of the Mean Squared Errors for training individual neural networks for each expression and for training a single neural network for all.

MSE_{Joy}	$MSE_{Sadness}$	MSE_{Fear}	MSE_{Anger}	$MSE_{Surprise}$	$MSE_{Disgust}$	MSE_{All}
0.000591	0.002925	0.001611	0.009689	0.000266	0.002516	0.000729

coded for AUs. We use the sequences in the CK+ dataset to transfer videos of expression transitions onto the biomechanical face.

Ryerson Audio-Visual Database of Emotional Speech and Song (RAVDESS) [12]. The original RAVDESS dataset consists of 24 actors vocalizing two lexically-matched statements. An extension of the dataset, named *RAVDESS Facial Landmark Tracking*, contains tracked facial landmark movements from the original RAVDESS datasets [16]. Each actor performs 60 speech trials and about 44 song trials. This yields a total of 2,452 video files for the complete dataset. We leverage this dataset to test the transfer of actor faces in speech videos onto the biomechanical face.

5.2 Action Units and Muscle Activations

There exist a total of 30 Action Units (AUs) corresponding to facial expressions. OpenFace provides occurrence predictions for 18 out the 30 AUs and measures intensity values for 17 out of the 30 AUs. We consider the 17 AUs for which the intensity values are present as the super-set of the AUs for our use case.

Due to the correlation between the AUs and muscles in the face, there also exists a correlation between a basic facial expression and the AUs activated by it. Our initial experiments focused on training the neural network for each expression in an isolated manner. The neural network was trained to output muscle activation· for muscles corresponding to a single expression using AUs which pertained to the same expression. In further trials, we observed that usage of all 17 AUs and all facial muscles improved the performance and the scalability of the expression transfer pipeline.

Table 1 provides a comparison between training a single neural network for all expressions and training individual neural networks for each expression, where each network is trained only from the AUs and muscles relevant to its expression (using the mappings of expressions to AUs and AUs to muscles presented in [4,7] and [14]). We observe better performance when training a single neural network for all the expressions, suggesting that AUs not directly relevant to an expression also play a role in expression transfer.

Due to limitations in the biomechanical model, the range of each AU class differs from that of the real faces. Hence, we use normalization to overcome the bias and better transfer real facial expressions onto the biomechanical model. The expression intensities in transferred expressions with normalization better represent the real faces than those without normalization.

Table 2. Average MSE of selected AUs in the original data and transfer results using different settings. Note that we randomly select 8 out of 17 AUs output by OpenFace. The last column is the average MSE over all the AUs in each setting.

Dataset	MSE_{AU1}	MSE_{AU4}	MSE_{AU6}	MSE_{AU9}	MSE_{AU12}	MSE_{AU15}	MSE_{AU20}	MSE_{AU25}	Average
KDEF (unnormalized)	0.191	0.088	0.186	0.133	0.011	0.155	0.129	0.092	0.157
KDEF (normalized)	0.118	0.064	0.186	0.068	0.028	0.109	0.146	0.052	0.129
RAVDESS (video)	0.012	0.222	0.107	0.044	0.083	0.016	0.077	0.036	0.086
CK (video)	0.038	0.054	0.059	0.015	0.008	0.023	0.057	0.034	0.048

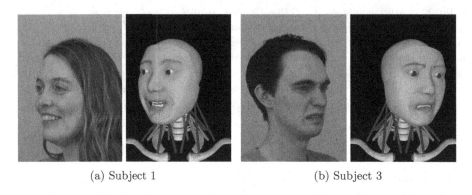

(a) Subject 1   (b) Subject 3

Fig. 4. Transfer of head orientation along with facial expression.

We choose to activate only jaw rotation so as to maintain the symmetry of the expression for our use case. We observe, that without jaw activations, expressions such as surprise are not well synthesized by the biomechanical face model.

5.3   Head Orientation

Leveraging OpenFace for head pose estimation, we pass the estimated orientation of the head into the trained neck controller to activate the neck muscles. This in turn actuates the neck to adjust the head orientation in accordance with the input image. Figure 4 presents sample transferred results including head orientations from the KDEF dataset.

5.4   Facial Expression Transfer

The results for the facial expression transfer for each of the expressions is shown in Fig. 5. We present transfer results of a small sample of the KDEF dataset, selecting two subjects (a female and a male) enacting all the basic expressions.

We also evaluate the transfer results by comparing the MSE of selected AUs in Table 2. We calculate the average MSE by AUs over all transferred expressions and their corresponding reference data, then compute the mean value of the average MSEs over all AUs in each experimental setting. We report such mean

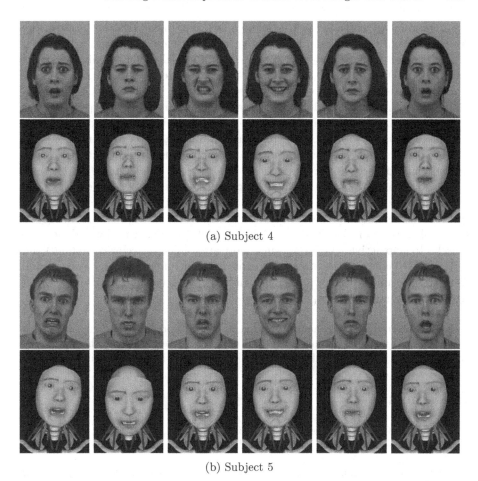

(a) Subject 4

(b) Subject 5

Fig. 5. Transfer of facial expressions (fear, anger, disgust, joy, sadness, surprise) and head poses from KDEF images to the biomechanical face-head-neck model.

values together with 8 randomly chosen AUs. The normalization step decreases the MSEs of most selected AUs and yields results with higher AU similarity. The more subtle expressions performed by subjects in the videos result in the lower average MSEs compared with those of the image dataset.

6   Conclusion and Future Work

Our expression transfer approach is uniquely advantageous. First, it is anatomically consistent as the biomechanical model emulates the human cervicocephalic musculoskeletal system. Further, our approach is based on the Facial Action Coding System, which is a widely adopted representation of facial expressions, including in the computer animation field. Finally, our approach is based on deep learning, which can capture the complex, non-linear relation between the Action Units of the FACS and associated facial muscle activations.

Additionally, our neural-network-based approach does not require any manual data collection as the training data is generated directly using the biomechanical model itself. This only needs to take place once, in advance. Once trained offline using the synthesized training data, the neural network can quickly transfer a large number of facial expressions. Unlike popular face tracking software such as Faceware, which requires manual calibration steps to transfer expressions of different subjects, our proposed approach needs no additional parameter adjustments to perform the same task.

Although we have achieved satisfactory transfer results for all the basic facial expressions, note that the simulation and transfer of complex mouth and eye movements lies outside the scope of our current work. To improve the fidelity of the results, we plan to extend our musculoskeletal model (e.g., by adding more muscles to help activate facial AUs in a more anatomically accurate manner) and its associated control system so as to explicitly control the lips and eyes, as well as to transfer mixtures of expressions, subtle expressions, and microexpressions, which the human face is capable of producing.

Acknowledgements. We thank CyberAgent, Inc., for providing the high resolution texture for the facial mesh that we used in our model. We also thank the curators of RAVDESS, CK/CK+, and KDEF for granting us permission to use their datasets.

References

1. Aneja, D., Colburn, A., Faigin, G., Shapiro, L., Mones, B.: Modeling stylized character expressions via deep learning. In: Proceedings Asian Conference on Computer Vision, pp. 136–153 (2016)
2. Baltrusaitis, T., Zadeh, A., Lim, Y.C., Morency, L.P.: OpenFace 2.0: facial behavior analysis toolkit. In: Proceedings IEEE Conference on Automatic Face and Gesture Recognition, pp. 59–66 (2018)
3. Calvo, M.G., Lundqvist, D.: Facial expressions of emotion (KDEF): identification under different display-duration conditions. Behav. Res. Methods **40**(1), 109–115 (2008)
4. Clark, E.A., et al.: The facial action coding system for characterization of human affective response to consumer product-based stimuli: a systematic review. Front. Psychol. **11**, 920 (2020)
5. Cohn, J.F., Ambadar, Z., Ekman, P.: Observer-based measurement of facial expression with the facial action coding system. Handbook Emotion Elicitat. Assessment **1**(3), 203–221 (2007)
6. Cong, M., Bao, M., E, J.L., Bhat, K.S., Fedkiw, R.: Fully automatic generation of anatomical face simulation models. In: Proceedings ACM SIGGRAPH/EG Symposium on Computer Animation, pp. 175–183 (2015)
7. Du, S., Tao, Y., Martinez, A.M.: Compound facial expressions of emotion. Proc. Natl. Acad. Sci. **111**(15), E1454–E1462 (2014)
8. Ekman, P., Friesen, W.V.: Manual for the Facial Action Coding System. Consulting Psychologists Press, Palo Alto (1978)

9. Kanade, T., Cohn, J., Tian, Y.: Comprehensive database for facial expression analysis. In: Proceedings of the Fourth IEEE International Conference on Automatic Face and Gesture Recognition, pp. 46–53 (2000)
10. Lee, S.H., Terzopoulos, D.: Heads up! Biomechanical modeling and neuromuscular control of the neck. ACM Trans. Graph. **25**(3), 1188–1198 (2006)
11. Lee, Y., Terzopoulos, D., Waters, K.: Realistic modeling for facial animation. In: Proceedings ACM SIGGRAPH 95 Conference, pp. 55–62 (1995)
12. Livingstone, S.R., Russo, F.A.: The Ryerson audio-visual database of emotional speech and song (RAVDESS): a dynamic, multimodal set of facial and vocal expressions in North American English. PLOS ONE **13**(5), 1–35 (2018)
13. Lucey, P., Cohn, J.F., Kanade, T., Saragih, J., Ambadar, Z., Matthews, I.: The extended Cohn-Kanade dataset (CK+): a complete dataset for action unit and emotion-specified expression. In: Proceedings IEEE CVPR Workshops, pp. 94–101 (2010)
14. Scherer, K.R., Ellgring, H., Dieckmann, A., Unfried, M., Mortillaro, M.: Dynamic facial expression of emotion and observer inference. Front. Psychol. **10**, 508 (2019)
15. Sifakis, E., Neverov, I., Fedkiw, R.: Automatic determination of facial muscle activations from sparse motion capture marker data. In: Proceedings ACM SIGGRAPH 2005 Conference, pp. 417–425 (2005)
16. Swanson, R., Livingstone, S., Russo, F.: RAVDESS facial landmark tracking (version 1.0.0) [dataset] (2019). http://doi.org/10.5281/zenodo.3255102
17. Terzopoulos, D., Waters, K.: Analysis and synthesis of facial image sequences using physical and anatomical models. IEEE Trans. Pattern Anal. Mach. Intell. **15**(6), 569–579 (1993)
18. Thies, J., Zollhofer, M., Stamminger, M., Theobalt, C., Nießner, M.: Face2face: real-time face capture and reenactment of RGB videos. In: Proceedings IEEE Conference on Computer Vision and Pattern Recognition, pp. 2387–2395 (2016)
19. Waters, K.: A muscle model for animation three-dimensional facial expression. In: Proceedings ACM SIGGRAPH 1987 Conference, vol. 21, no. 4, pp. 17–24 (1987)
20. Weise, T., Bouaziz, S., Li, H., Pauly, M.: Realtime performance-based facial animation. ACM Trans. Graph. **30**(4), 1–10 (2011)
21. Wu, T., Hung, A., Mithraratne, K.: Generating facial expressions using an anatomically accurate biomechanical model. IEEE Trans. Visual Comput. Graph. **20**(11), 1519–1529 (2014)
22. Xu, F., Chai, J., Liu, Y., Tong, X.: Controllable high-fidelity facial performance transfer. ACM Trans. Graph. **33**(4), 1–11 (2014)
23. Zeng, X., Dwarakanath, S., Lu, W., Nakada, M., Terzopoulos, D.: Neuromuscular control of the face-head-neck biomechanical complex with learning-based expression transfer from images and videos. arXiv Preprint (2021)
24. Zhang, J., Chen, K., Zheng, J.: Facial expression retargeting from human to avatar made easy. IEEE Tran. Visualizat. Comput. Graph. (2020)

Segmentation

Synthesized Image Datasets: Towards an Annotation-Free Instance Segmentation Strategy

Henry O. Velesaca[1], Patricia L. Suárez[1], Dario Carpio[1], and Angel D. Sappa[1,2(✉)]

[1] ESPOL Polytechnic University, FIEC, CIDIS, Guayaquil, Ecuador
{hvelesac,plsuarez,dncarpio,asappa}@espol.edu.ec
[2] Computer Vision Center, 08193 Bellaterra, Barcelona, Spain
asappa@cvc.uab.es

Abstract. This paper presents a complete pipeline to perform deep learning-based instance segmentation of different types of grains (e.g., corn, sunflower, soybeans, lentils, chickpeas, mote, and beans). The proposed approach consists of using synthesized image datasets for the training process, which are easily generated according to the category of the instance to be segmented. The synthesized imaging process allows generating a large set of well-annotated grain samples with high variability—as large and high as the user requires. Instance segmentation is performed through a popular deep learning based approach, the Mask R-CNN architecture, but any learning-based instance segmentation approach can be considered. Results obtained by the proposed pipeline show that the strategy of using synthesized image datasets for training instance segmentation helps to avoid the time-consuming image annotation stage, as well as to achieve higher intersection over union and average precision performances. Results obtained with different varieties of grains are shown, as well as comparisons with manually annotated images, showing both the simplicity of the process and the improvements in the performance.

Keywords: Instance segmentation · Food grains · Synthesized dataset generation

1 Introduction

Deep learning based approaches have shown to be the best option to tackle challenging computer vision problems such as segmentation [14], recognition [13,15], 3D estimation [21], scene understanding [23] just to mention a few. Actually, deep learning based solutions have become the facto approaches to tackle challenging tasks in computer vision, as well as in many fields. Although there are deep learning based models able to obtain good results with a few training samples, in most of the cases their performance depends on the amount of annotated data available during the training process.

Most of deep learning based models, for instance ResNet [8], VGG [16], AlexNet [10], Mask R-CNN [7], are able to reach very accurate results for different applications when trained on large and well-annotated datasets. Unfortunately, collecting annotations at scale is not feasible or it is prohibitively expensive. Actually, this expensive

© Springer Nature Switzerland AG 2021
G. Bebis et al. (Eds.): ISVC 2021, LNCS 13017, pp. 131–143, 2021.
https://doi.org/10.1007/978-3-030-90439-5_11

task has been tackled in recent year by different initiatives for a few number of categories (e.g., pedestrians, cars, dogs, trains, among others) resulting in the well known PASCAL VOC [5], COCO [12], ImageNet [4], SUN [22] datasets. These datasets contain hundred of thousand of images with millions of annotations (bounding boxes, used for recognition tasks), or thousands of well-annotated masks (instance's contour, used for segmentation applications).

The datasets mentioned above have been the starting point to develop interesting and useful applications for the video surveillance [6] or driving assistance [20] fields, where categories such as a person, car, bike, among others, are needed for training object detection algorithms, or regions correctly annotated in urban scenarios for semantic segmentation tasks. A bottleneck of most of deep learning based approaches lies is the need of having large and well-annotated instances. In the current work, the seed segmentation problem is tackled. In other words, given a cluster of crowded instances, the algorithm should return the boundary of every single instance in the scene. Although there are robust and efficient architectures to solve this problem (e.g., Mask R-CNN [7], YOLACT [2], Deep watershed transform [1]), their performance is highly affected by the dataset used for training; not only the quantity of instances in the given datasets is important, but also the quality of annotations (i.e., objects' boundary) is a key factor. Furthermore, it is not easy to find datasets that adapt to the requirements of different tasks.

Having in mind the limitations mentioned above, the current work proposes a novel strategy to generate annotated images to be used for training instance segmentation algorithms. Although the proposed strategy is evaluated on the well-known Mask R-CNN [7], it can be also applied with other instance segmentation models. The main contribution lies in the pipeline that allows to automatically generate annotated synthesized images that can be used for training or to extend manually annotated datasets. This mainly reduces time and annotation effort and allows the network to easily be trained for different scenarios and acquisition sensors. The segmentation of instances of different types of grains is approached, taking into consideration the corn grains as a case study to evaluate the effectiveness of the use of synthesized images comparing them with the results obtained using only real images.

The manuscript is organized as follows. Section 2 presents works related to the instance segmentation as well as recent approaches on grain segmentation. The approach proposed for generating synthesized datasets is introduced in Sect. 3. Experimental results with different categories and evaluations using ground truth images are depicted in Sect. 4. Finally, conclusions are presented in Sect. 5.

2   Related Work

As mentioned above, current work addresses the problem of kernel instance segmentation and the need for datasets of large size and variability. In other words, this work is focused on obtaining all the instances (i.e., grains) present in a cluster image with a random distribution. This section reviews the most relevant works on these topics, highlighting the main characteristics of each of the reviewed approaches.

Regarding instance segmentation, the Mask R-CNN architecture has become a referent in recent years in the area of object detection and instance segmentation; it extends

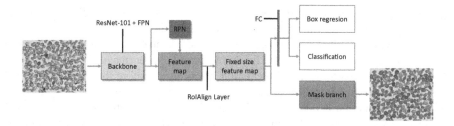

Fig. 1. Mask R-CNN architecture used for grain instance segmentation. Images of synthesized clusters of corn grains are shown as an example (classification module is not used).

the Faster R-CNN object detection framework by adding a branch for the generation of the masks at the end of the model, thus achieving the instances segmentation
for each output proposal box. In addition, the segmentation is executed in parallel to
the identification and location. The Mask R-CNN framework consists of three stages
(see Fig. 1). First, the backbone extracts feature maps from the input images. Second,
the feature maps generated by the backbone are sent to the Region Proposal Network
(RPN) to generate Regions of Interest (RoIs). Third, the ROIs generated by RPN are
assigned to extract the corresponding target features in the shared feature maps, and
subsequently mapping to a fully connected layer, for target classification and segmentation instances. The process generates the classification scores, bounding boxes, and
segmentation masks [7,24].

Recently, some works have been proposed for the instance segmentation of grains.
For instance, Toda et al. [17] present an instance segmentation neural network to determine the morphological phenotype of barley grains. The authors propose to use a synthetically generated dataset for the training stage, where the seeds are randomly oriented to give the corresponding variability. The model trained with synthesized images
has given better results compared to the training with real images. In addition, the
authors validate the strategy in other types of grains such as wheat, rice, oat, and let-
tuce grains. The proposed strategy allows generating appealing results. Similarly, our
approach tackles the generation of synthesized corn kernel clusters by randomly distributing kernels but in our case, the HSV color space is used to obtain the area of every
single instance (i.e., corn kernel). In this color space, more precise contours are obtained
and shadows are easily removed.

On the other hand, Kar et al. [9] present a system for automatically estimating the
quality of food grains in which wheat grains are presented as a case study. In this case,
grains are segmented and classified into eight categories to analyze their quality. To
carry out this objective, a convolutional network is trained with a dataset that consists
of around 5000 synthesized images, according to the authors this model presents good
results both at the time of instance segmentation and classification. One of the differences with the proposal in the current work is that the work presented by Kar et al. [9]
uses the U-Net network for segmenting single grains which are later on used to generating the synthesized images; in the current work single grains' mask are obtained
by simple thresholding in the HSV color space, which consumes much fewer resources

and processing time. Another difference from the approach proposed by Kar et al. [9] in which the input grains are randomly distributed concerning ours is that the distribution in grid format provides better robustness because there is no error when segmenting the instances that are used to generate the final synthesized cluster image.

Another works to carry out segmentation of instances before the classification of types and defects in corn grains is the one presented by Velesaca et al. [18]. In that work, the segmentation is performed using the Mask R-CNN network for subsequent classification with a lightweight convolutional network. The segmentation algorithm is trained using a real dataset manually annotated; a crowdsourcing platform, Labelbox[1], has been used to label every single element (e.g., impurities and grains) in the image. This annotation process requires a lot of time and resources.

In [3] the authors present an evaluation of the effectiveness of segmentation using images with uniform and textured regions in synthetically generated gray levels, using unsupervised evaluation criteria based on image regions. Another segmentation technique based on multichannel texture filtering, which according to the authors allows detecting similar regions and determining abrupt changes in patterns at the texture level of the images is presented in [11]. This method was tested using both real and synthetic images of simple patterns and wood grains, obtaining results similar in segmentation by regions. Following the segmentation line, Wang et al. [19] presents a technique that allows segmenting granular rock based on an extension of the skeleton of the image, differentially eroding it to detect the cores of the granular rock. The results show good effectiveness when compared to methods such as watershed.

3   Proposed Approach

This section first summarizes the Mask R-CNN instance segmentation network used in the current work. Then, the proposed strategy for the generation of synthesized images is presented. The proposed strategy has been evaluated through seven different categories of grains: corn, beans, lentils, mote, soybeans, chickpeas, and sunflower. The corn kernel is used as a case study to illustrate the performance of the proposed pipeline; in this case, study instances are manually annotated to be used as ground truth.

3.1   Segmentation Algorithm

This section introduces the instance segmentation algorithm used to validate the synthesized imaging strategy presented in the current work. Among the different approaches, the Mask R-CNN has been selected due to its great performance in the instances segmentation task for different categories. Another characteristic of the Mask R-CNN is that it uses the ResNet 101 architecture to extract features from the image and has a large number of parameters (i.e., 63738 K), which makes it a complex architecture that requires datasets with a lot of images for the training stage.

As mentioned above, the Mask R-CNN network is used for segmenting the given image in instances—i.e., grains present on it. Initially, the model trained with just the

---

[1] labelbox.com.

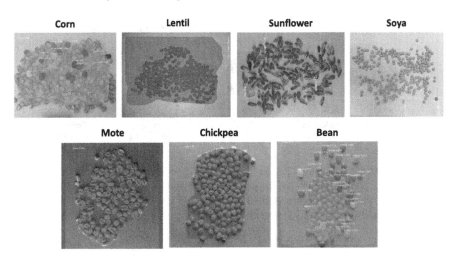

Fig. 2. Examples on different types of grains from the Mask R-CNN network pre-trained with COCO dataset.

COCO dataset is considered—in the 91 classes of COCO there are not seeds, grains, or cereals categories, hence the network is not able to correctly segment the given images. Figure 2 shows illustrations of the results obtained for seven different types of grains; as can be appreciated, inconsistent results are obtained both in the area of each segmented grain and in the number of predicted classes, in some cases (e.g., lentil) the result is just a single big patch. As a conclusion, it can be stated that it is necessary to apply a training process for this particular problem in order to achieve acceptable results in these scenarios. For the training process, a large dataset of annotated instances is required; the image annotation can be performed manually, as performed in [18], or by using the strategy proposed in the current work, which consists of generating synthesized images, which are directly annotated, from single real grains. The synthesized image generation process is presented in the next section.

3.2 Synthesized Image Generation

As mentioned above, training instance segmentation algorithms require a large and well-annotated dataset. This section presents a strategy for avoiding this time-consuming task, as well as for a cost-effective at scale dataset annotation. In this way, large datasets for different varieties of grains can be easily generated for the training process. The proposed approach consists of two tasks: firstly images of single grains are acquired from real scenes, and secondly, synthesized images of a cluster of grains are generated by using sets of single grains. The number of grains in the resulting cluster as well as their distribution can be set by the user as detailed below. Figure 3 shows the pipeline proposed to obtain the synthesized images of different types of grains that will be then applied to the case study of corn kernels.

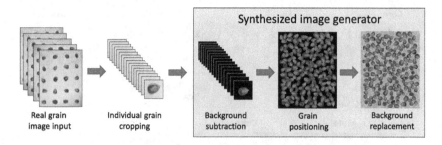

Fig. 3. Overall pipeline for synthesized clusters of grains generation. Firstly, each grain from the real images—i.e., grids of grains—is cropped. Then, the grain's area is extracted using background subtraction. Next, grains are inserted into an empty synthetic image by the positioning algorithm; and finally, a custom background is applied to the synthesized image.

The first task for the generation of a synthesized image dataset consists of acquiring images with samples of non-touching kernels—grids of kernels. The kernel sample acquisition process consists of taking images of an A4 sheet where grains are uniformly distributed. The amount of grains per sheet as well as the color of the sheet depends on the type of grain, for instance, a blue sheet has been used for the mote and chickpea grains, while other colors have been considered in lentil or sunflower to obtain a higher contrast between grains and background. In each case, a grid is drawn to split the image up into small regions containing a single grain in each cell. Images have been acquired with a mobile device (12MP images) orthogonal to the A4 sheet. The resulting ROI images are used in the next step to generate the synthesized images of a cluster of grains. Figure 3($left$) shows an illustration of an image with single kernels (i.e., corn grains) uniformly distributed on a light gray A4 sheet.

The next step after obtaining **single kernel crops** is to apply a **background subtraction** technique to extract the area corresponding to the grain in the image. The background subtraction is performed in the HSV color space to obtain a result robust to illumination changes—background threshold has been adjusted for each variety of grains considered in this work according to the background and illumination conditions. Finally, morphological operators are applied to refine and improve contours by eliminating shadows in the scene. The resulting mask is then used to extract the points that define the contour of a given grain. Figure 3($middle$) shows illustrations of the cropped regions as well as the results after background subtraction.

The generation of **synthesized images of a cluster of grains** is finally performed by distributing the number of single grains in an empty background image with a homogeneous color. This generation process allows to set different parameters according to the requirements of the final user: the number of grains, size of the resulting synthesized image, background color, percentage of grains in contact, percentage of grains on the image borders (i.e., cut grains) and the number of images to be generated. The algorithm receives as an input a set of images of individual grains randomly selected. Then, based on the number of grains previously defined by the user, and according to a scale factor that takes into account the size of the synthesized cluster image, kernels are randomly rotated and placed one by one in available spaces, ensuring that the grains do not overlap each other. This algorithm does not maximize the contact perimeter between elements, it only ensures that there is a contact according to the random rotation. Since the kernel selection is randomly performed, a grain sample could be considered twice, but by sure with a different orientation in the final image. Figure 3 shows an illustration of the whole pipeline.

4 Experimental Results

This section presents experimental results obtained by using the proposed synthesized image strategy to train instance segmentation approaches. First, the results of a case study that evaluates the performance of the proposed strategy are presented. This case study consists of a set of 23 manually annotated images of corn kernels, the obtained results are considered as a benchmark to compare them with the results obtained when using the synthesized images for training. Then, other categories of grains are included in the evaluation. In this second case, since there are no annotated instances (object's contour), the number of detected instances is considered as the evaluation criteria.

The Mask R-CNN network [7] was trained to generate a model that allows obtaining all the instances of grains present in a given image. The Mask R-CNN network implementation used in this work is based on ResNet-101 as the backbone and pretrained COCO weight. In addition, the images in the training dataset have been resized to 1024×1024, to reduce the computational cost of the entire process. The number of images used in the different datasets has the following distribution: 16 images for training, 4 images for validation, and 3 images for testing. Figure 1 shows the architecture of the Mask R-CNN network used in this work.

The results obtained by training the Mask R-CNN network using different datasets are evaluated in the Sect. 4.2. The metrics used to measure the performance of the trained networks are IoU, the number of grain instances correctly detected, average precision (AP) in IoU 50% (AP_{50}), 75% (AP_{75}), and the average value of IoU 50% to 95% with a step size of 5% (AP@[.5:.95]). Furthermore, the synthesized datasets generated for the different grain varieties have been considered in the training process by using two approaches: (i) first, the Mask R-CNN is individually trained for each grain variety—i.e., single-grain approach; and (ii) the Mask R-CNN is trained considering all the grain varieties at once—i.e., multi-category grain approach.

4.1   Case Study

The results obtained by training the Mask R-CNN network using a real and synthesized clusters of corn kernels datasets are evaluated in this section. The performance of the different schemes (single- and multi-grains) is evaluated as follows: i) by taking into account the number of grain instances correctly counted; ii) by means of the IoU; and iii) through the average precision metric. Table 1 shows experimental results

Table 1. Results on *testing images* (manually annotated ground truth) when the Mask R-CNN network is trained with: Real images (Re); Synthesized single category grain dataset (Sn); Synthesized multi-category grain dataset (Ml)—GT: Ground Truth.

Testing	# of instances				IoU		
images	GT	Re	Sn	Ml	Re	Sn	Ml
Image 1	200	199	198	198	0.901	0.914	0.905
Image 2	190	189	188	187	0.897	0.911	0.902
Image 3	223	215	215	212	0.898	0.900	0.895
Avg	613	**603**	601	593	0.899	**0.908**	0.901

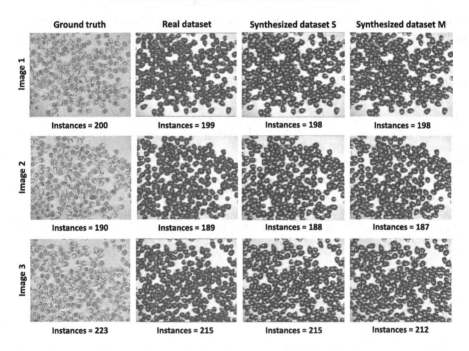

Fig. 4. Results obtained on *testing images* (manually annotated ground truth images) when Mask R-CNN is trained with real and synthesized datasets. (*1st col*) Ground truth labeled with Labelbox. (*2nd col*) Results obtained when training with the real image dataset. (*3rd col*) Results obtained when training is performed with the synthesized single category grain dataset. (*4th col*) Results obtained when training is performed with the synthesized multi-category grain dataset.

obtained with the proposed strategy. The obtained number of instances and the IoU metric computed on a set of testing image datasets (three manually annotated images considered as ground truth) are presented; GT column corresponds to the ground truth number of instances per image; Re columns show the number of predicted instances and IoU metric when the Mask R-CNN network is trained with the real image dataset (manually-annotated images). Sn columns show the number of instances predicted by the network, as well as the IoU metric when trained with the synthesized corn kernels dataset; just the corn category is considered. Finally, the Ml columns correspond to the results obtained when the Mask R-CNN is trained with all synthesized image datasets, in other words, when all grain categories are considered; both numbers of instances and IoU are depicted. Looking at the results depicted in the table, although the number of instances is slightly better when real images are used for training (just one instance error in the first and second testing images) it does not happen the same in the case of IoU metric. The results of the IoU metric show a better performance, in all the cases, when the synthesized dataset is considered (single category grain), an improvement of up to almost 1.4% can be observed in the first testing image. On the other hand, AP results for this case study are depicted in Table 2, where the AP@[.5:.95], AP_{75} and AP_{50} metric values are shown. It can be seen that the Mask R-CNN trained with synthesized images presents a better performance in the metrics AP@[.5:.95] and AP_{75} while the real dataset presents a better result in the metric AP_{50}. The results obtained in the IoU and AP metrics show that the use of synthesized datasets allows with a high percentage of accuracy to correctly delimit the area and contour of the corn kernels confirming the effectiveness and validity of the proposed approach.

Finally, qualitative results and ground truth annotations on the three testing images are shown in Fig. 4, where the number of instances predicted by Mask R-CNN and ground truth values is also depicted. In order to facilitate the qualitative evaluation, the area of each grain segmented by the Mask R-CNN is brown colored while manual annotations are shown in green. In addition, a blue circle has been used to highlight each individual instance together with the corresponding instance number, to check there are no duplicate or bad segmented grains.

Table 2. Results using the AP metric on *testing images* (manually annotated ground truth) when the Mask R-CNN network is trained with: Real images (Re); Synthesized single category grain dataset (Sn); Synthesized multi-category grain dataset (Ml).

Testing images	AP@[.5:.95]			AP_{75}			AP_{50}		
	Re	Sn	Ml	Re	Sn	Ml	Re	Sn	Ml
Image 1	0.790	0.830	0.790	0.964	0.980	0.957	0.989	0.980	0.974
Image 2	0.800	0.830	0.800	0.978	0.984	0.926	0.995	0.989	0.945
Image 3	0.780	0.790	0.750	0.950	0.945	0.884	0.964	0.964	0.903
Avg	0.793	**0.818**	0.781	0.958	**0.964**	0.922	**0.982**	0.978	0.9410

4.2 Free Annotation Results

In order to evaluate the usefulness of the proposed approach in other grain categories, the Mask R-CNN network has been trained with synthesized images generated with the grain types presented in Sect. 3.2. In all these cases, the performance of the network trained with different schemes (single- and multi-grains) is evaluated using the IoU and AP metrics together with the number of correctly detected instances. It should be mentioned that in all these categories of grains (except corn) there are not manually annotated ground truths, hence in the case of real images just qualitative illustrations are depicted together with the number of detected instances, which is used as a quantitative evaluation. Table 3 shows results (i.e., number of instances, IoU, and the AP metrics) obtained when the Mask R-CNN network is trained with the synthesized single category grain dataset (Sn) and with the synthesized multi-category grain dataset (Ml). The number of instances in the GT column corresponds to the total number of grains of the whole testing image sets, while IoU and AP metrics are average values for the whole testing image sets. Three testing images have been used per category; these images contain a random number of instances. It can be appreciated that in most of the cases the best results are obtained when the Mask R-CNN is trained with the synthesized single category grain dataset. Finally, in order to evaluate the performance on real images, Table 4 shows results on different grain categories, just the number of instances, when the Mask R-CNN is trained with synthesized single- and multi- categories schemes, is depicted since there are not manual annotations. Just as illustrations of the performance on real images, Fig. 5 shows segmentation results on real images, obtained by the Mask R-CNN trained with synthesized single category grain dataset for different types of grains.

Table 3. Evaluation results—IoU and AP metrics—of the Mask R-CNN network when trained with synthesized single- and multi- categories; just three testing images per category of synthesized grain clusters are considered. Testing images contain a random number of instances, the total number of instances per category, adding up the three testing images, is depicted in the second column. Ground truth (GT); Synthesized single category grain dataset (Sn); Synthesized multi-category grain dataset (Ml).

Type of grain	# of instances			IoU		AP@[.5:.95]		AP$_{75}$		AP$_{50}$	
	GT	Sn	Ml	Sn	Ml	Sn	Ml	Sn	Ml	Sn	Ml
Bean	973	973	973	0.943	0.937	0.918	0.884	0.999	0.998	0.999	0.999
Chickpea	903	903	903	0.936	0.928	0.928	0.643	0.999	0.998	0.999	0.981
Corn	598	598	598	0.942	0.934	0.929	0.886	0.998	0.997	0.997	0.988
Lentil	913	912	912	0.946	0.936	0.917	0.907	0.999	0.998	0.999	0.999
Mote	840	840	840	0.935	0.929	0.917	0.904	0.999	0.998	0.999	0.999
Soybean	1836	1835	1835	0.906	0.902	0.836	0.830	0.999	0.998	0.999	0.999
Sunflower	768	768	768	0.928	0.923	0.899	0.876	0.999	0.998	0.999	0.998

Table 4. Evaluation results on real-world grain cluster testing images: number of instances obtained by the Mask R-CNN network when trained with synthesized single- and multi- categories. Ground truth (GT); Synthesized single category grain dataset (Sn); Synthesized multi-category grain dataset (Ml).

Type of grain	Testing images	# of instances		
		GT	Sn	Ml
Bean	13	1890	1888	1887
Chickpea	23	2871	2864	2868
Corn	9	1388	1387	1387
Lentil	9	2142	2137	2140
Mote	23	2985	2973	2969
Soybean	11	2500	2494	2484
Sunflower	22	3000	2829	2751

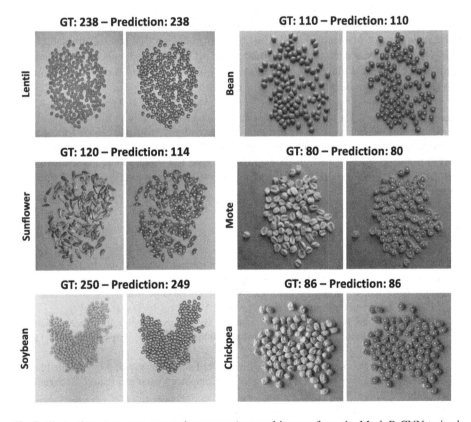

Fig. 5. Illustrations (one case per grain category) on real images from the Mask R-CNN trained with the corresponding synthesized single category grain dataset.

5   Conclusions

This paper proposes a simple but efficient strategy to automatically obtain annotations to be used in the grain segmentation problem. Although it has been evaluated with the Mask R-CNN architecture, it can be used in other deep learning based approaches. The corn kernel case study shows that the Mask R-CNN network trained with the proposed synthesized datasets achieves similar or better results, both IoU and AP, than when trained with manually annotated images. The simplicity of the proposed strategy allows generating ground truth information (annotated set of instances) just by taking a set of images with instances regularly distributed in a grid; in other words, the time-consuming annotation task is not required, speeding up the training process and at the same time reaching better results. It should be mentioned that the results obtained by the proposed strategy can be easily improved by just increasing the number of instances initially acquired (regular grid), or increasing the variability of considered grains. In other words, there is still space for improvement. In addition to the case study, the proposed strategy has been evaluated with other types of grains, which include different shapes, textures, and background colors (e.g., lentil, sunflower, bean, mote, chickpea, and soybean). In all the cases the proposed strategy shows its validity. Again, results can be improved by enlarging the synthesized images in the dataset used for training as well as the variability of instances. Finally, just to confirm the need of having annotation for each type of grains, a dataset with annotations of all the classes has been evaluated, in all the cases the single class case reaches better results—i.e., the Mask R-CNN trained with the grain type to be considered.

Acknowledgements. This work has been partially supported by the ESPOL Polytechnic University; the Spanish Government under Project TIN2017-89723-P; and the "CERCA Programme/Generalitat de Catalunya". The authors gratefully acknowledge the support of the CYTED Network: "Ibero-American Thematic Network on ICT Applications for Smart Cities" (REF-518RT0559) and the NVIDIA Corporation with the donation of the Titan Xp GPU used for this research.

References

1. Bai, M., Urtasun, R.: Deep watershed transform for instance segmentation. In: IEEE Conference on Computer Vision and Pattern Recognition, pp. 5221–5229 (2017)
2. Bolya, D., Zhou, C., Xiao, F., Lee, Y.J.: YOLACT: real-time instance segmentation. In: IEEE/CVF International Conference on Computer Vision, pp. 9157–9166 (2019)
3. Chabrier, S., Emile, B., Rosenberger, C., Laurent, H.: Unsupervised performance evaluation of image segmentation. J. Adv. Signal Process. **2006**, 1–12 (2006). https://doi.org/10.1155/ASP/2006/96306
4. Deng, J., Dong, W., Socher, R., Li, L.J., Li, K., Fei-Fei, L.: Imagenet: a large-scale hierarchical image database. In: IEEE Conference on Computer Vision and Pattern Recognition, pp. 248–255 (2009)
5. Everingham, M., Van Gool, L., Williams, C.K., Winn, J., Zisserman, A.: The PASCAL visual object classes (VOC) challenge. Int. J. Comput. Vis. **88**(2), 303–338 (2010). https://doi.org/10.1007/s11263-009-0275-4

6. Fedorov, A., Nikolskaia, K., Ivanov, S., Shepelev, V., Minbaleev, A.: Traffic flow estimation with data from a video surveillance camera. J. Big Data **6**(1), 1–15 (2019). https://doi.org/10.1186/s40537-019-0234-z
7. He, K., Gkioxari, G., Dollár, P., Girshick, R.: Mask R-CNN. In: IEEE International Conference on Computer Vision, pp. 2961–2969 (2017)
8. He, K., Zhang, X., Ren, S., Sun, J.: Deep residual learning for image recognition. In: Proceedings of the IEEE Conference on Computer Vision and Pattern Recognition, pp. 770–778 (2016)
9. Kar, A., Kulshreshtha, P., Agrawal, A., Palakkal, S., Boregowda, L.R.: Annotation-free quality estimation of food grains using deep neural network. In: 30th British Machine Vision Conference, pp. 1–12 (2019)
10. Krizhevsky, A., Sutskever, I., Hinton, G.E.: ImageNet classification with deep convolutional neural networks. In: Advances in Neural Information Processing Systems, pp. 1097–1105 (2012)
11. Levesque, V.: Texture segmentation using Gabor filters, pp. 1–8. Center for Intelligent Machines. McGill University (2000)
12. Lin, T.-Y., et al.: Microsoft COCO: common objects in context. In: Fleet, D., Pajdla, T., Schiele, B., Tuytelaars, T. (eds.) ECCV 2014, Part V. LNCS, vol. 8693, pp. 740–755. Springer, Cham (2014). https://doi.org/10.1007/978-3-319-10602-1_48
13. Mao, J., Xiao, T., Jiang, Y., Cao, Z.: What can help pedestrian detection? In: IEEE Conference on Computer Vision and Pattern Recognition, pp. 3127–3136 (2017)
14. Poma, X.S., Riba, E., Sappa, A.: Dense extreme inception network: towards a robust CNN model for edge detection. In: Proceedings of the IEEE/CVF Winter Conference on Applications of Computer Vision, pp. 1923–1932 (2020)
15. Radovic, M., Adarkwa, O., Wang, Q.: Object recognition in aerial images using convolutional neural networks. J. Imaging **3**(2), 1–21 (2017)
16. Simonyan, K., Zisserman, A.: Very deep convolutional networks for large-scale image recognition. In: International Conference on Learning Representations, pp. 1–14 (2015)
17. Toda, Y., Okura, F., Ito, J., Okada, S., Kinoshita, T., Tsuji, H., Saisho, D.: Training instance segmentation neural network with synthetic datasets for crop seed phenotyping. Commun. Biol. **3**(1), 1–12 (2020)
18. Velesaca, H.O., Mira, R., Suarez, P.L., Larrea, C.X., Sappa, A.D.: Deep learning based corn kernel classification. In: IEEE International Conference on Computer Vision and Pattern Recognition Workshops, pp. 294–302 (2020)
19. Wang, Y., Sun, S.: Image-based grain partitioning using skeleton extension erosion method. J. Pet. Sci. Eng. **205**, 1–11 (2021)
20. Wei, J., He, J., Zhou, Y., Chen, K., Tang, Z., Xiong, Z.: Enhanced object detection with deep convolutional neural networks for advanced driving assistance. IEEE Trans. Intell. Transp. Syst. **21**(4), 1572–1583 (2019)
21. Wofk, D., Ma, F., Yang, T.J., Karaman, S., Sze, V.: FastDepth: fast monocular depth estimation on embedded systems. In: IEEE International Conference on Robotics and Automation, pp. 6101–6108 (2019)
22. Xiao, J., Hays, J., Ehinger, K.A., Oliva, A., Torralba, A.: Sun database: large-scale scene recognition from abbey to zoo. In: IEEE Computer Society Conference on Computer Vision and Pattern Recognition, pp. 3485–3492 (2010)
23. Yang, S., Wang, W., Liu, C., Deng, W.: Scene understanding in deep learning-based end-to-end controllers for autonomous vehicles. IEEE Trans. Syst. Man Cybern. Syst. **49**(1), 53–63 (2018)
24. Yu, Y., Zhang, K., Yang, L., Zhang, D.: Fruit detection for strawberry harvesting robot in non-structural environment based on Mask R-CNN. Comput. Electron. Agric. **163**, 1–9 (2019)

Holistically-Nested Structure-Aware Graph Neural Network for Road Extraction

Tinghuai Wang[✉], Guangming Wang, and Kuan Eeik Tan

Huawei Helsinki Research Center, Helsinki, Finland
tinghuaiwang@huawei.com

Abstract. Convolutional neural networks (CNN) have made significant advances in detecting roads from satellite images. However, existing CNN approaches are generally repurposed semantic segmentation architectures and suffer from the poor delineation of long and curved regions. Lack of overall road topology and structure information further deteriorates their performance on challenging remote sensing images. This paper presents a novel multi-task graph neural network (GNN) which simultaneously detects both road regions and road borders; the inter-play between these two tasks unlocks superior performance from two perspectives: (1) the hierarchically detected road borders enable the network to capture and encode holistic road structure to enhance road connectivity (2) identifying the intrinsic correlation of semantic landcover regions mitigates the difficulty in recognizing roads cluttered by regions with similar appearance. Experiments on challenging dataset demonstrate that the proposed architecture can improve the road border delineation and road extraction accuracy compared with the existing methods.

1 Introduction

Accurate road extraction from high-resolution satellite images has become critical in various geospatial applications such as cartography, map updating, urban planning, and navigation. The high-resolution images have posed new challenges for road extraction methods by presenting more details, such as multiscale roads and complex background.

Recent years has witnessed the tremendous success of applying deep convolutional neural networks (CNNs) in tackling this challenge, by formulating road extraction as a binary segmentation problem. To this end, existing CNN based methods largely adopt semantic image segmentation neural architectures which are repurposed for road extraction task. None-the-less, these architectures normally suffer from two major drawbacks: (1) semantic segmentation architectures are not optimized to recognize thin, long and curved shapes which are frequently mis-segmented due to the nature of spatial downsampling operations of convolutional neural networks; this lack of contour modeling limits their ability to precisely localize road borders which however are the key information for generating map data (2) these architectures focus on per-pixel prediction gathering local context however road topology and holistic road structure information are

© Springer Nature Switzerland AG 2021
G. Bebis et al. (Eds.): ISVC 2021, LNCS 13017, pp. 144–156, 2021.
https://doi.org/10.1007/978-3-030-90439-5_12

not utilized; road regions are sparsely distributed over the broad spatial domain cluttered by trees, shadows and buildings etc. – in the representation of deep features, some road fragments might be easier to be detected than other road fragments, and thus road topology and holistic structure information should be incorporated to enhance road connectivity in designing deep neural networks.

In this paper, we present a novel multi-task graph neural network (GNN) which simultaneously detects both road regions and road borders; the inter-play between the two tasks unlocks superior performance from two perspectives: (1) the hierarchically detected road borders enable the network to capture and encode holistic road structure to enhance road connectivity (2) identifying the intrinsic correlation of landcover regions mitigates the difficulty in recognizing roads cluttered by regions with similar appearance, such as roads around parking area.

To this end, this paper makes the following novel contributions:

– We propose to hierarchically detect road borders in an end-to-end manner in order to emphasizes morphological feature learning and border localization
– We propose a novel architecture to reason the interplay between road regions and borders, which consists of a set of nested parallel graph convolutional networks with one branch harnessing morphological feature which inferences the connectivity of detected road regions, and the other branch capturing the correlation among border features represented in landcover feature space which in turn discriminates subtle borders which can only be inferred based on contextual information of landcover regions.

2 Related Work

A variety of methods for road extraction have been proposed in recent years. Road extraction is generally considered as a binary segmentation or pixel-level classification problem, and machine learning algorithms have been applied. For instance, support vector machines (SVMs) have been utilized to detect roads by classifying hand-crafted features *e.g.* shape index features [22] or salient features [4]; graph optimization approach has also been adopted *e.g.* [1] based on the hierarchical graph-based image segmentation work [5].

The past decade has witnessed the remarkable success of deep learning in various challenging computer vision [37] and remote sensing [8,9,23,29] tasks. One of the first deep learning based road extraction methods was developed by Mnih and Hinton [16], which proposed to adopt restricted Boltzmann machines (RBMs) to detect road from high resolution aerial images. Saito *et al.* [20] applied Convolutional Neural Network (CNN) to extract both buildings and roads from satellite images without pre-processing step required by [16]. A U-shaped fully convolutional network (FCN) [13] architecture was proposed by Ramesh *et al.* [10]. This architecture comprised a stack of convolutions followed by corresponding stack of mirrored deconvolutions with the usage of skip connections in between for preserving the local information. Zhang *et al.* [35] combined the strengths of U-Net [19] and residual learning [7] in training deep neural networks for road extraction. Methods in tackling the small receptive field issue have also been proposed. For instance, Zhou *et al.* [36] built upon the dilated convolution [3] layers to adjust receptive fields of feature points without decreasing the resolution of feature maps.

Multi-task learning has been adopted for improving the accuracy of road extractions. Liu *et al.* [12] developed multi-task learning network to extract road surfaces, centerlines, and edges simultaneously using FCN networks. Lu *et al.* [14] utilized U-Net with two prediction outputs to perform both road detection and centerline extraction tasks. Yang *et al.* [34] proposed a similar U-Net type network to perform simultaneous prediction of road detection and centerline extraction tasks. Shao *et al.* [21] proposed a two-task network which contains two joint U-Net type networks for both road detection and centerline extraction. The focus of these multi-task networks is to produce multiple predictions adapting U-Net type networks rather than exploring the intrinsic interplay among multiple predictions as in our work. The fact that existing methods utilize CNN architectures further limit their capability to embed topology information and reason over longer range connectivities.

The connectivity in road extraction has attracted considerable research efforts. Chen *et al.* [2] proposed a two-stage method which applied connection analysis on the discrete line features with directional consistency to extract potential road objects and evaluate potential road objects using shape features to refine the road extraction results. Gao *et al.* [6], another two-stage method, used semantic segmentation to obtain pixel-level road segmentation results, and then used tensor voting to connect broken roads. Oner *et al.* [17] proposed a differentiable loss function which enforced connectivity on the output of binary segmentation N-Net for the purpose of road network delineation.

3   Method

In this section, we present our holistically-nested structure-aware graph neural network architecture for road extraction. As illustrated in Fig. 1, our network consists of two streams of networks, *i.e.* encoder network and road structure inference network. The encoder comprises of four residual blocks according to the size of feature maps, whilst the rest of the blocks constitute the road structure inference network. Encoder extracts appearance and contextual information at various hierarchies, with decreasing spatial details and increasing semantic information from encoding block-1, -2, -3 to block-4. At the output of each encoding block, the encoder interfaces with the proposed road structure inference network by providing feature map as input. Road structure inference network mainly comprises of road border detection, road structure aware GNNs and element-wise attention modules.

3.1   Road Border Detection

Road border detection module takes feature map, *i.e.* road feature, as input at a certain hierarchy level and estimates road borders. As depicted in 3, border detection module consists of two convolutional layers and a softmax layer. Border detection is achieved through deep supervision. Specifically we generate ground-truth data by extracting borders from road masks in the training data, then we use supervised binary cross entropy loss on output borders to supervise the

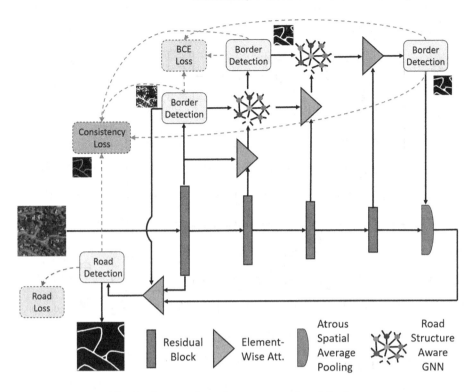

Fig. 1. An overview of our proposed architecture.

training of road border detection. The feature maps immediately before sigmoid layer are considered as border features which encode key information of road borders.

3.2 Road Structure Aware GNN

Road structure aware GNN is the core module of our network which inferences road regions by seamlessly fusing holistic road structure and appearance information via graph inference. Road structure aware GNN module comprises two streams of GNN architectures, as illustrated in Fig. 2. This module takes border feature and road feature as input. Road feature is the fusion of feature maps from adjacent encoding blocks via element-wise attention module described in later section, which contains the semantic representation of regions.

As shown in Fig. 2, the upper stream is utilizing a self-attention mechanism where a query and a set of key-value pairs are generated. Specifically, border feature, denoted as $\mathbf{X_b}$, is transformed into a query feature $\rho(\mathbf{X_b})$ and a key feature $\kappa(\mathbf{X_b})$, and road feature, denoted as $\mathbf{X_r}$, is transformed into a value feature $\upsilon(\mathbf{X_r})$, through learnable linear transformations ρ, κ and υ respectively. Following the scaled dot-product self-attention [31], we define a co-attention embedding operation as

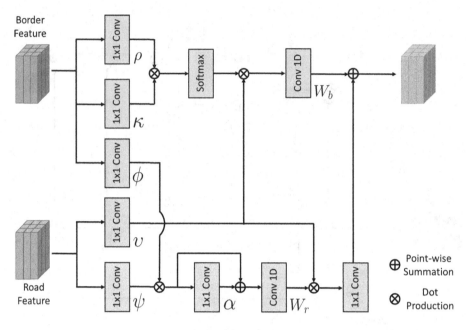

Road Structure Aware GNN

Fig. 2. Illustration of road structure aware GNN.

$$\text{softmax}(\frac{\rho(\mathbf{X_b})\kappa(\mathbf{X_b})^T}{\sqrt{d}})\upsilon(\mathbf{X_r}), \tag{1}$$

where d is dimension of query and key. The softmax dot-product operation scales to have unit norm which is equivalent to cosine similarity used as the adjacency matrix. The significance of this operation is that for each border feature in the query, the weighted sum of value features, *i.e.* semantic road features, is taken as its soft nearest neighbor in border space. Therefore, the output of this operation can be seen as feature in the semantic road feature space but the information of query, *i.e.* border feature, is embedded. This promotes the semantic road feature to flow with an awareness of the intrinsic structure of road borders.

The lower stream further takes two features as input, namely border feature $\phi(\mathbf{X_b}) \in \mathbb{R}^{N \times D_1}$ and semantic road feature $\psi(\mathbf{X_r}) \in \mathbb{R}^{N \times D_2}$ through learnable linear transformations ϕ and ψ respectively. Multiplying these two features

$$\mathbf{X_f} = \phi(\mathbf{X_b})^T \psi(\mathbf{X_r}) \tag{2}$$

results in a new feature $\mathbf{X_f} \in \mathbb{R}^{D_1 \times D_2}$, which consists of D_1 nodes, each of dimension D_2. This operation projects each border feature dimension in semantic road feature space.

After projection, a graph $\mathcal{G}$ with adjacency matrix $\mathbf{A}_{\mathcal{G}} \in \mathbb{R}^{D_1 \times D_1}$ in the road feature space, where each node contains the semantic road feature. Denoting the

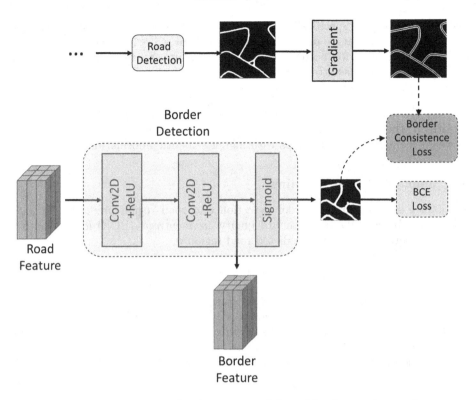

Fig. 3. Illustration of border detection module and border consistence loss.

trainable weights of convolutional layer as $\mathbf{W}_r \in \mathbb{R}^{D_2 \times D_2}$, the GNN convolution is defined as

$$\mathbf{X_l} = (\mathbf{I} - \mathbf{A}_\mathcal{G})\mathbf{X_f}\mathbf{W}_r \tag{3}$$

Laplacian smoothing [11, 24–27, 30] is adopted by updating the adjacency matrix to $\mathbf{I} - \mathbf{A}_\mathcal{G}$ to propagate the node features over the graph. Rather than estimating adjacency matrix in the upper stream, we randomly initialize and optimize $\mathbf{A}_\mathcal{G}$ by gradient descent in an end-to-end fashion. After the graph reasoning, feature $\mathbf{X_l}$ is projected back to the original road feature space by multiplying $\upsilon(\mathbf{X_r})$. After another convolutional layer, the new feature is fused with feature from upper stream by point-wise summation. Intuitively, the lower stream identifies the intrinsic correlation of semantic landcover regions which mitigates the difficulty in recognizing roads cluttered by regions with similar appearance, such as roads around parking area.

3.3 Element-Wise Attention

Element-wise attention module is used in multiple locations to fuse the features between neighboring encoding blocks or features from road structure aware GNN and encoding block. Specifically, an attention map $\alpha \in \mathbb{R}^{H \times W}$ is obtained by concatenating two feature maps which is followed by a 1×1 convolutional layer and a sigmoid layer for normalization. For a feature $\mathbf{X_e}$ from later encoding block, the element-wise attention is computed as

$$\hat{\mathbf{X}}_{\mathbf{e}} = (\mathbf{X_e} \odot \alpha + \mathbf{X_e})\mathbf{W}_e. \tag{4}$$

Intuitively, the attention map carries important lower level border information to weigh the area of feature maps with higher semantic information.

3.4 Joint Multi-task Training

We jointly supervise road border detection and road region prediction in an end-to-end fashion. We use standard binary cross-entropy (BCE) loss on both predicted border map b and predicted road region y,

$$\mathcal{L}_r = \mathcal{L}_{BCE}(b, \hat{b}) + \mathcal{L}_{BCE}(y, \hat{y}) \tag{5}$$

where $\hat{b})$ and $\hat{y})$ denote road border and road region ground-truth labels. The high imbalance between road and non-road, as well as border and non-border pixels is also properly compensated following [32].

We further define a border consistence loss by measuring the dependency between the predicted border and the border of predicted road region,

$$\mathcal{L}_c^i = \frac{1}{|\mathcal{N}^+|} \sum |\frac{1}{\sqrt{2}}|| \bigtriangledown \hat{y}|| - \hat{b}^i| \tag{6}$$

where $\mathcal{N}^+$ denotes the union of border pixels in both border maps, superscript i indicates the loss defined at layer i border prediction, $\bigtriangledown$ represents the spatial derivative operation.

4 Experimental Results

In this section, we conduct extensive experiments on a publicly available aerial imagery dataset for roads in Massachusetts, USA [15]. This dataset provides 1171 images including 1108 training images, 49 test images, and 14 validation images. The spatial resolution is 1.2 m for all images which are 1500×1500 pixels. This dataset is a challenging aerial image labeling dataset since the images cover an area of 2600 km^2 with a wide variety of geographic types including urban, suburban and rural regions.

Similar with previous work, e.g. [33] , we use random crops of size 256×256 pixels from training set for training the network whilst we directly test on the test images at 1500×1500 pixels without any processing. We train the network with a batch size of 20 for 50 epochs, using Adam optimizer with learning rate of 10^{-3}.

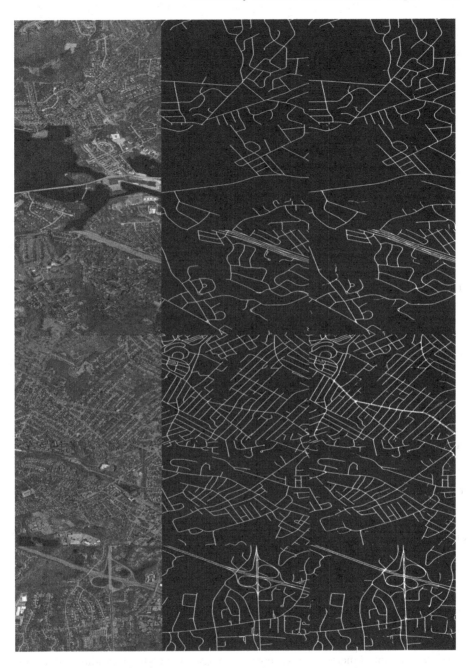

Fig. 4. Qualitative results of proposed architecture on Massachusetts road dataset. Left: source image; middle: ground-truth; right: road prediction results.

4.1   Evaluation Metrics

We used both IoU and F1-score to evaluate quantitative performance. The IoU metric measures the intersection of the prediction and ground truth regions over their union,

$$\mathrm{IoU} = \frac{TP}{TP+FP+FN},$$

where TP, FP and FN represent the number of true positives, false positives and false negatives respectively. F1-score is also used which is defined as

$$F1 = \frac{2 \cdot \text{precision} \cdot \text{recall}}{\text{precision} + \text{recall}} \tag{7}$$

$$\text{recall} = \frac{TP}{TP+FN}, \quad \text{precision} = \frac{TP}{TP+FP}.$$

In addition to the above region based metrics, we follow a boundary metric [18] to evaluate the quality of our road predictions. This metric computes the F-score along the boundary of the predicted mask, given a small relax in distance. In our experiments, we use thresholds 1, 2, 3, 4, 5 pixels respectively.

4.2   Results

We quantitatively and qualitatively evaluate our proposed method and compare with various recent deep learning based methods to demonstrate its effectiveness.

Table 1 presents the quantitative results obtained by different methods on the Massachusetts dataset. Our proposed approach outperforms all the competing state-of-the-art neural architectures. As opposed to the general convolutional neural architectures adopted by the compared methods, our method is the only graph neural network architecture for road extraction. We owe the superior performance of our method to the multiple graph reasoning across the information from multi-task learning. Specifically, we construct a set of nested parallel graph convolutional networks with one stream harnessing morphological feature which inferences the connectivity of detected road regions, and the other stream capturing the correlation among border features represented in semantic feature space which in turn discriminates subtle borders which can only be inferred based on contextual information of landcover regions.

Figure 4 shows visual results of our proposed architecture where superior border accuracy and road connectivity of predictions can be clearly observed. Such excellent border delineation is quantitatively confirmed by comparing with state-of-the-art architectures in terms of boundary F1-score as shown in Fig. 5, where our proposed method consistently demonstrates higher boundary accuracy regardless of varying thresholds and larger margin in the case of 1-pixel threshold.

We also conduct abalation study to investigate the contribution of each proposed modules. The first baseline network, *i.e.* HNS-GNN-BU, removes border detection and road structure aware GNN modules and only keeps element-wise attention based feature fusion, which attains F1-score of 74.95%. Comparing with

Table 1. Comparisons of the proposed and other deep learning based road extraction methods on Massachusetts road dataset test set.

Metric (%)	U-Net [19]	DeepLab v3 [3]	D-LinkNet [36]	GL-Dense-UNet [33]	CDG [28]	Ours
IoU	60.94	60.52	60.71	60.93	61.90	62.94
F1-Score	75.24	75.81	75.15	75.72	76.10	76.96

Table 2. Ablation studies of our proposed architecture on Massachusetts road dataset.

Metric	HNS-GNN-BU	HNS-GNN-SG	HNS-GNN-E1	HNS-GNN-E2	Ours
F1-Score (%)	74.95	75.67	75.78	76.89	76.96

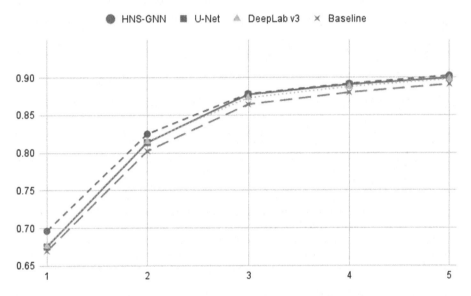

Fig. 5. Comparison vs baselines at different thresholds in terms of boundary F-score on Massachusetts road dataset test set.

our final architecture, *i.e.* HNS-GNN, our core contribution of multitask learning and graph reasoning increases the accuracy by 2.6%. The second baseline, *i.e.* HNS-GNN-SG, adds the upper stream GNN to HNS-GNN-BU which increases 0.96%. The third and fourth baseline, *i.e.* HNS-GNN-B1 and HNS-GNN-B2, corresponding to keeping one or two border detection and GNN modules respectively, give accuracy gains of 1.1% and 2.58% respectively (Table 2).

5   Conclusions

In this paper, we proposed a novel architecture for extracting road from satellite images. This multi-task graph neural network is able to hierarchically detect road borders which in turn enable the network to capture and encode holistic road structure to enhance road connectivity. Graph reasoning further identifies the intrinsic correlation of semantic landcover regions which mitigates the difficulty in recognizing roads cluttered by regions with similar appearance.

References

1. Alshehhi, R., Marpu, P.R.: Hierarchical graph-based segmentation for extracting road networks from high-resolution satellite images. ISPRS J. Photogram. Remote Sens. **126**, 245–260 (2017)
2. Chen, L., Zhu, Q., Xie, X., Hu, H., Zeng, H.: Road extraction from VHR remote-sensing imagery via object segmentation constrained by Gabor features. ISPRS Int. J. Geo-Information **7**(9), 362 (2018)
3. Chen, L.C., Papandreou, G., Schroff, F., Adam, H.: Rethinking atrous convolution for semantic image segmentation. arXiv preprint arXiv:1706.05587 (2017)
4. Das, S., Mirnalinee, T.T., Varghese, K.: Use of salient features for the design of a multistage framework to extract roads from high-resolution multispectral satellite images. IEEE TGRS **49**(10), 3906–3931 (2011). https://doi.org/10.1109/TGRS.2011.2136381
5. Felzenszwalb, P.F., Huttenlocher, D.P.: Efficient graph-based image segmentation. IJCV **59**(2), 167–181 (2004). https://doi.org/10.1023/B:VISI.0000022288.19776.77
6. Gao, L., Song, W., Dai, J., Chen, Y.: Road extraction from high-resolution remote sensing imagery using refined deep residual convolutional neural network. Remote Sens. **11**(5), 552 (2019)
7. He, K., Zhang, X., Ren, S., Sun, J.: Deep residual learning for image recognition. In: CVPR, pp. 770–778 (2016)
8. Jia, J., et al.: Tradeoffs in the spatial and spectral resolution of airborne hyperspectral imaging systems crop identification case study. IEEE TGRS 1–18 (2021)
9. Jia, J., et al.: Road extraction technology based on multi-source remote sensing data: Review and prospects. Opt. Precis. Eng. **29**
10. Kestur, R., Farooq, S., Abdal, R., Mehraj, E., Narasipura, O.S., Mudigere, M.: UFCN: a fully convolutional neural network for road extraction in RGB imagery acquired by remote sensing from an unmanned aerial vehicle. J. Appl. Remote Sens. **12**(1), 016020 (2018)
11. Li, Q., Han, Z., Wu, X.M.: Deeper insights into graph convolutional networks for semi-supervised learning. In: AAAI (2018)
12. Liu, Y., Yao, J., Lu, X., Xia, M., Wang, X., Liu, Y.: RoadNet: learning to comprehensively analyze road networks in complex urban scenes from high-resolution remotely sensed images. IEEE TGRS **57**(4), 2043–2056 (2018)
13. Long, J., Shelhamer, E., Darrell, T.: Fully convolutional networks for semantic segmentation. In: CVPR, pp. 3431–3440 (2015)
14. Lu, X., et al.: Multi-scale and multi-task deep learning framework for automatic road extraction. IEEE TGRS **57**(11), 9362–9377 (2019)
15. Mnih, V.: Machine learning for aerial image labeling. University of Toronto, Canada (2013)
16. Mnih, V., Hinton, G.E.: Learning to detect roads in high-resolution aerial images. In: Daniilidis, K., Maragos, P., Paragios, N. (eds.) ECCV 2010, Part VI. LNCS, vol. 6316, pp. 210–223. Springer, Heidelberg (2010). https://doi.org/10.1007/978-3-642-15567-3_16

17. Oner, D., Koziński, M., Citraro, L., Dadap, N.C., Konings, A.G., Fua, P.: Promoting connectivity of network-like structures by enforcing region separation. arXiv preprint arXiv:2009.07011 (2020)

18. Perazzi, F., Pont-Tuset, J., McWilliams, B., Van Gool, L., Gross, M., Sorkine-Hornung, A.: A benchmark dataset and evaluation methodology for video object segmentation. In: CVPR, pp. 724–732 (2016)

19. Ronneberger, O., Fischer, P., Brox, T.: U-Net: convolutional networks for biomedical image segmentation. In: Navab, N., Hornegger, J., Wells, W.M., Frangi, A.F. (eds.) MICCAI 2015, Part III. LNCS, vol. 9351, pp. 234–241. Springer, Cham (2015). https://doi.org/10.1007/978-3-319-24574-4_28

20. Saito, S., Yamashita, T., Aoki, Y.: Multiple object extraction from aerial imagery with convolutional neural networks. Electron. Imaging **2016**(10), 1–9 (2016)

21. Shao, Z., Zhou, Z., Huang, X., Zhang, Y.: MRENet: simultaneous extraction of road surface and road centerline in complex urban scenes from very high-resolution images. Remote Sens. **13**(2), 239 (2021)

22. Song, M., Civco, D.: Road extraction using SVM and image segmentation. Photogram. Eng. Remote Sens. **70**(12), 1365–1371 (2004)

23. Wang, H.: Spectral graph reasoning network for hyperspectral image classification. In: Farkaš, I., Masulli, P., Wermter, S. (eds.) ICANN 2020, Part I. LNCS, vol. 12396, pp. 711–723. Springer, Cham (2020). https://doi.org/10.1007/978-3-030-61609-0_56

24. Wang, H., Raiko, T., Lensu, L., Wang, T., Karhunen, J.: Semi-supervised domain adaptation for weakly labeled semantic video object segmentation. In: Lai, S.-H., Lepetit, V., Nishino, K., Sato, Y. (eds.) ACCV 2016, Part I. LNCS, vol. 10111, pp. 163–179. Springer, Cham (2017). https://doi.org/10.1007/978-3-319-54181-5_11

25. Wang, H., Wang, T.: Boosting objectness: semi-supervised learning for object detection and segmentation in multi-view images. In: ICASSP, pp. 1796–1800 (2016)

26. Wang, H., Wang, T.: Primary object discovery and segmentation in videos via graph-based transductive inference. Comput. Vis. Image Underst. **143**, 159–172 (2016)

27. Wang, H., Wang, T., Chen, K., Kämäräinen, J.K.: Cross-granularity graph inference for semantic video object segmentation. In: IJCAI, pp. 4544–4550 (2017)

28. Wang, S., Yang, H., Wu, Q., Zheng, Z., Wu, Y., Li, J.: An improved method for road extraction from high-resolution remote-sensing images that enhances boundary information. Sensors **20**(7), 2064 (2020)

29. Wang, T., Wang, G., Tan, K.E., Tan, D., et al.: Hyperspectral image classification via pyramid graph reasoning. In: Bebis, G. (ed.) ISVC 2020, Part I. LNCS, vol. 12509, pp. 707–718. Springer, Cham (2020). https://doi.org/10.1007/978-3-030-64556-4_55

30. Wang, T., Wang, H.: Graph transduction learning of object proposals for video object segmentation. In: Cremers, D., Reid, I., Saito, H., Yang, M.-H. (eds.) ACCV 2014, Part IV. LNCS, vol. 9006, pp. 553–568. Springer, Cham (2015). https://doi.org/10.1007/978-3-319-16817-3_36

31. Waswani, A., et al.: Attention is all you need. In: NIPS (2017)

32. Xie, S., Tu, Z.: Holistically-nested edge detection. In: ICCV,p. 1395–1403 (2015)

33. Xu, Y., Xie, Z., Feng, Y., Chen, Z.: Road extraction from high-resolution remote sensing imagery using deep learning. Remote Sens. **10**(9), 1461 (2018)

34. Yang, X., Li, X., Ye, Y., Lau, R.Y., Zhang, X., Huang, X.: Road detection and centerline extraction via deep recurrent convolutional neural network u-net. IEEE TGRS **57**(9), 7209–7220 (2019)

35. Zhang, Z., Liu, Q., Wang, Y.: Road extraction by deep residual U-Net. IEEE Geosci. Remote Sens. Lett. **15**(5), 749–753 (2018)
36. Zhou, L., Zhang, C., Wu, M.: D-LinkNet: LinkNet with pretrained encoder and dilated convolution for high resolution satellite imagery road extraction. In: CVPR Workshops, pp. 182–186 (2018)
37. Zhu, L., Wang, T., Aksu, E., Kamarainen, J.: Portrait instance segmentation for mobile devices. In: ICME, pp. 1630–1635 (2019)

Extraction and Merging of Stroke Structure of Chinese Characters

Jian Shu[1]($\boxtimes$), Yuehui Chen[2], Yi Cao[3], and Yaou Zhao[2]

[1] School of Information Science and Engineering, University of Jinan, Jinan, China
[2] Artificial Intelligence Institute (School of Information Science and Engineering),
University of Jinan, No. 336, Jinan, China
{yhchen,ise_zhaoyo}@ujn.edu.cn
[3] Shandong Provincial Key Laboratory of Network Based Intelligent Computing
(School of Information Science and Engineering), University of Jinan,
No. 336, Jinan, China
ise_caoy@ujn.edu.cn

Abstract. Chinese characters are complex graphics with strokes as the basic unit. In order to analyze their structure, stroke extraction is the first step. This paper presents an automatic extraction method of Chinese character strokes, which regards the extraction of Chinese character strokes as finding the optimal path and merging. Based on the superpixel network, the path network is applied to enumerate all possible stroke segments. Then, the repeated strokes are merged according to the Intersection over Union. Experimental results show that the method can effectively extract accurate strokes and obtain single strokes with high-level semantic features and complete information.

Keywords: Stroke extraction · Superpixel network · Intersection over union

1 Introduction

The structure of Chinese is relatively complex. Structure analysis is an essential method of Chinese character image processing. As the fundamental element of Chinese character structure, stroke is also a necessary feature of Chinese character image processing. Due to the cohesion of Chinese character strokes, Chinese character strokes cannot be calculated separately. Therefore, the automatic extraction of strokes is considered to be meaningful. To accomplish this task, a two-step strategy is appropriate. The first step is to extract the stroke path, and the second step is to deal with segmentation optimization and stroke combination.

In this field, there are many ways to extract strokes by morphological thinning. Although this is conducive to image data compression and reduces the time complexity, simple skeleton extraction [5] will lose the original stroke information of Chinese characters. It is also difficult to judge some complex stroke types. With the development of deep learning, stroke extraction has also been developed. Firstly, the method of semantic segmentation [1,10] is used to extract

© Springer Nature Switzerland AG 2021
G. Bebis et al. (Eds.): ISVC 2021, LNCS 13017, pp. 157–165, 2021.
https://doi.org/10.1007/978-3-030-90439-5_13

Chinese character strokes. The problem of stroke truncation and multiple labels due to intersection is challenging to solve with the experiment. Therefore, this paper proposes a path network based on a superpixel neural network to predict the stroke path of each pixel and deliberately blur the area around the intersection. Finally, the merging of stroke segments is realized, and the expected complete results are obtained.

2   Related Work

Stroke extraction of Chinese characters is a new word processing task, which aims at the follow-up evaluation function. Stroke extraction can be divided into two categories: one is based on traditional morphological operation methods, and the other is deep learning methods. The traditional stroke extraction method extracts strokes according to the morphological characteristics of Chinese characters through certain constraints.

Cheng et al. [11] proposed a stroke extraction model based on the PBOD curve peak algorithm. The algorithm is used to determine the type of intersection to obtain the segment type of the stroke. Then, the combination optimization is performed to get a complete stroke segment. Zhang et al. [14] used the crawler method to extract strokes. Select the correct path according to the intersection location, calculates the stroke segment type according to the 8-neighborhood process, assigns it to different kinds of meetings according to the intersection type of the intersection contour stroke, and finally completes the contour line to obtain the complete stroke segment. Zhu et al. [15] constructed the undirected graph of Chinese characters based on the PBOD algorithm to divide Stroke. Yang et al. [13] divide the strokes of the characters according to the vector information of the outline. Traditional methods have many disadvantages. If only using the thinning algorithm, there will be burr and distortion problems, causing the deformation of Chinese characters and the missing or redundant position of the intersection. Compared with the thinning algorithm, the contour algorithm avoids these problems, but the time cost is several times of thinning algorithm, so it is challenging to apply it in practice. With the continuous progress of deep learning, some scholars have explored the stroke structure of Chinese characters. Zhang. [17] used BP neural network to judge and optimize the intersection of Chinese characters. Finally, the corresponding corners are connected based on the CFER corner detection algorithm to segment and extract the Chinese strokes. Fukun Bi et al. [2] segmented strokes through conditional generation confrontation network, which can obtain local and overall visual results, and solve the problem that the traditional algorithm has high segmentation error rate and cannot extract high-level semantics. Moreover, from the perspective of application feasibility, this algorithm has more advantages than traditional ones.

3   Methodology

Our main work is to design a neural network to predict the meaningful segmentation path of each pixel. Specifically, given a Chinese character, each stroke should be precisely extracted without any duplication. To this end, all possible strokes are first enumerated by the path net, which extracts a single stroke based on a pixel in this stroke. Then, duplicated strokes are merged based on the IoU.

3.1   The Path Network

In order to calculate the path similarity between two pixels, the energy function is defined according to s/t-cut [3]. The process is as follows:

$$E(l) = \lambda \sum_{pq \in N} V_{pq}(l_p, l_q) \tag{1}$$

V_{pq} calculates the similarity of the path between two pixels, N represents the set of all pixels, λ represents the penalty term coefficient, and pq is the pixel in N respectively. If pq is two similar pixels but assigned to different labels, the value of V_{pq} It will be huge and incur huge costs, and vice versa. Path net is used to calculate V_{pq} to predict the probability that two pixels are on the same stroke path. Network structure (see Fig. 1). The input of the model adopts the tensor composed of Fig. 2(a) and takes the stroke where the green dot is located as the label. After calculation through multiple modules, the V_{pq} of the predicted point and the pixel of the original image is obtained, and the similar ones are classified into one category, that is, the output stroke segment.

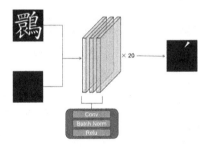

Fig. 1. Schematic diagram of the network structure, including input and output.

To calculate the value of V_{pq}, a path net based on the VDSR [8] neural network was developed. The network has a total of 20 modules. Each module contains a convolutional layer, a BN layer, and an activation layer, and the final output layer has only one channel output, which is the predicted value representing the similarity of V_{pq}.

Training provides a dual-channel input X_p for the network, including the original image I, and the second mask image, which is black everywhere except for a single indicator pixel p. The network is trained to output a single channel image Y_p, which measures path similarity from all pixels to the indicated pixel p. The L_2 loss function is used to train the entire network to the known path

Y, that is, the loss is $||Y - Y_p||_2$. The Adam [9] optimizer for the entire network can effectively reduce the degree of overfitting.

The model effect from training. It can be seen from Fig. 2(b) that when the movement reaches 1000 epochs, there are many noises in addition to the stroke segmentation at this point. When the number of training comes 50000 epochs, the best segmentation result is obtained, as shown in Fig. 2(c).

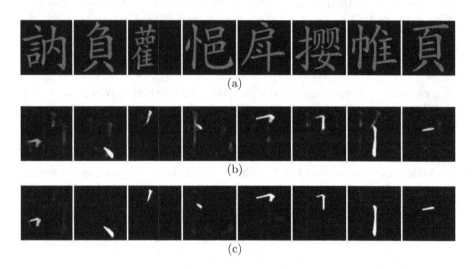

Fig. 2. (a) The input image contains the original image and a pixel. (b) Prediction effect of 1000 epochs of training. (c) Prediction effect of 50000 epochs of training.

3.2 Pixel Selection for Path Net

The thinning algorithm is mainly used to find the intersection information and avoid the multi-label problem caused by intersection prediction. The pixels obtained after using the thinning algorithm can be divided into three categories: endpoint, common point, and intersection. When predicting common points and endpoints, a typical unambiguous prediction can be generated in the path. However, when we use the intersection to expect, the expected path will produce multiple labels. Multiple stroke segments may occur at the same point.

In order to avoid the ambiguity caused by predicting the intersection, the thinning algorithm [4] is used to find out all the intersection pixel positions in the skeleton diagram. In Fig. 3(a)(b)(c), the results of the thinning algorithm. After removing the intersection of the Chinese character skeleton image, many incoherent stroke segments will be generated, and then we will find a few points from each connected domain. These points can ensure that all stroke paths in a picture can be extracted to a reasonable number of pixels. Last extracted point (see Fig. 3(d)(e)(f)).

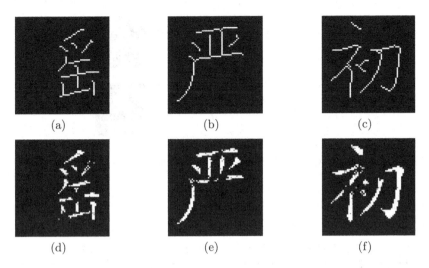

Fig. 3. Chinese character skeleton image obtained after thinning algorithm, where (a)-(c) is the character skeleton image generated by the thinning algorithm, and (d)-(f) is the result of blurring the original image after finding the intersection.

3.3   Stroke Merging Algorithm

IoU is an essential basis for rule merging. After obtaining multiple stroke segments, the information of some stroke segments is incomplete. Since each pixel will produce a predicted image, we can optimize the combination and merge the best stroke segments according to the degree of overlap of the contents in the picture.

After the point set is obtained and predicted by thinning the point finding method, the generated stroke segmentation needs to be processed to make the extracted stroke segmentation more obvious. The boundary information of stroke segments $(x_{min}, y_{min}, x_{max}, y_{max})$ is obtained by calculating the minimum surrounding matrix of stroke content in the image. Finally, the similarity between stroke segments is obtained by calculating the IoU between the boundary and the boundary. The formula is as follows:

$$IoU = \frac{A \cap B}{A \cup B} \tag{2}$$

The A in the formula represents the similarity between each image generated by traversing and the intersection and union of image B other than A. Set the threshold $= 0.3$ to merge eligible images. This is the most appropriate number selected from 0 to 1 through continuous experiments. At the same time, further restrictions, such as the coverage of pixels in the border, are needed to prevent some larger boundaries from forcing smaller boundaries to merge. (see Fig. 4).

Fig. 4. This is the merging effect of two stroke segments in a Chinese character

This is pseudo-code flow based on IOU merging algorithm, the algorithm process (shown in Algorithm 1).

Algorithm 1: The merging algorithm based on IOU.

Input: Multiple stroke segmented pictures: $(imgs)$;
Output: Generate a series of complete stroke segments: $(Strokenums)$.

1 **for** $i = 0$ to $len(imgs) > 0$ **do**
2 | Calculate the border coordinates of the largest
     | $biou(xmin, ymin, xmax, ymax)$ of each stroke;
3 **end**
4 Add all the obtained biou information to the array bious
5 **for** $i = 0$ to $len(bious)$ **do**
6 | **for** $j = i + 1$ to $len(bious)$ **do**
7 | $IoU = \frac{bious[i] \cap bious[j]}{bious[i] \cup bious[j]}$
8 | **if** $IOU > threshold$ **then**
9 | There is also a pixel level restriction;
10 | Gather the $Strokenums[i]$ within a given threshold;
11 | **end**
12 | **end**
13 **end**

---

4 Experiment Results

The open-source data set of Make Me a Hanzi is used [7], which contains two types of Chinese characters. One is the ordinary simplified Chinese characters, and the other is the more complex traditional Chinese characters. For SVG images, each image contains its stroke information, which can be converted into corresponding labels. The data set includes a total of 9507 Chinese characters.

The network model uses Adam as the optimizer because it makes the learning rate adaptive. It is not easy to produce overfitting in the training process, and the convergence speed is faster. When training the VDSR network, an adjustable gradient clipping is used to suppress the gradient explosion problem and maximize the training speed. The training process is carried out under fixed parameters. The training (64×64) image on an NVIDIA GeForce GTX 2080 Ti was carried out in 50,000 rounds of iterations, and the training was carried out for more than 1 h.

We processed the image sequences and got the information needed to train the image sequences. Since we consider the intersection problem, we select all pixels around the fuzzy intersection to avoid the multi-label problem caused by the intersection of predicted strokes, calculate the value of IoU, and set the $threshold = 0.3$ to gather the quality frames together. At the same time, the pixel level is limited to prevent the suppression of large frames from small frames. Finally, the collected images are merged to obtain the required complete stroke segmentation.

(In Fig. 5). It is the visualization of the training process of the entire network. As the iteration continued, the loss tended to be stable, and the maximum ACC was close to 0.99.

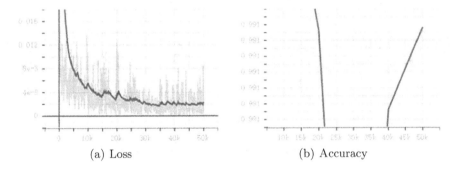

(a) Loss   (b) Accuracy

Fig. 5. In the VDSR network prediction process, (a) represents the change of the loss function during 50,000 iterations, and (b) represents the change of the test accuracy.

In our experiment, we selected 3000 commonly used Chinese characters as the predictive input. Since the extracted strokes have no semantic information, we cannot judge whether the classification is correct. We only use manual review and the number of extracted strokes as the criterion. The experimental results are shown in (Table 1). Under the same data set of 3000 characters, the accuracy of PBOD based algorithm [12] in completely dividing each Chinese character can only reach 48.3%, and the accuracy of Crawling algorithm [14] can reach 86.1%. Still, the quality of strokes generated is relatively poor. Our algorithm can achieve 93.2% accuracy in the same number of Chinese characters, and the stroke segments we get can be used as the data set of stroke segment recognition. It can be seen that the accuracy and quality of stroke segment extraction have significantly been improved.

Table 1. A rough comparison of the accuracy of stroke extraction algorithms.

Method	Number of words	Correct extraction	Accuracy
PBOD based algorithm	3000	1442	0.483
Crawling algorithm	3000	2584	0.861
Ours	3000	2797	0.932

After predicting the path, we generate the desired stroke segments through continuous iterative merging.(see Fig. 6)

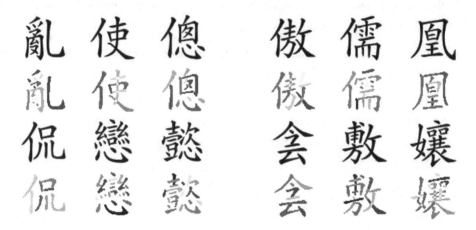

Fig. 6. The visual image after merging the whole stroke segments.

5   Conclusion

The extraction of Chinese character strokes is of great significance for Chinese character beautification, and style recognition [6,16,18]. This paper solves the high misjudgment rate of Chinese character extraction in traditional algorithms by predicting paths and merging strokes. At the same time, it also solves the problem of not extracting high-level semantic information, that is, preserving the original stroke, thickness, and other attributes of Chinese characters. From the feasibility perspective, the method proposed in this paper has more advantages than the traditional method.

At present, we are only doing experiments on the Kaiti dataset. In the later stage, we will achieve this effect on more fonts, improve the robustness of extraction, and finally achieve our expected results, and we can extract strokes of different fonts.

Acknowledgement. This work was supported in part by the University Innovation Team Project of Jinan (2019GXRC015), and in part by Key Science & Technology Innovation Project of Shandong Province (2019JZZY010324).

References

1. Badrinarayanan, V., Kendall, A., Cipolla, R.: SegNet: a deep convolutional encoder-decoder architecture for image segmentation. IEEE Trans. Pattern Anal. Mach. Intell. **39**(12), 2481–2495 (2017)
2. Bi, F., Han, J., Tian, Y., Wang, Y.: Ssgan: generative adversarial networks for the stroke segmentation of calligraphic characters. Vis. Comput. 1–10 (2021). https://doi.org/10.1007/s00371-021-02133-2
3. Boykov, Y., Funka-Lea, G.: Graph cuts and efficient nd image segmentation. Int. J. Comput. Vis. **70**(2), 109–131 (2006)
4. Chen, W., Sui, L., Xu, Z., Lang, Y.: Improved Zhang-Suen thinning algorithm in binary line drawing applications. In: 2012 International Conference on Systems and Informatics (ICSAI2012), pp. 1947–1950. IEEE (2012)
5. Fang, L., Yunyang, Z.: Research on a Tibetan image refinement algorithm based on adjacent pixel points information. Comput. Technol. Dev. **28**(4), 21–24 (2018)
6. Fucheng, Z.: Research on Calligraphy Style Recognition Based on Convolutional Neural Network. Master's thesis, Xi'an University of Technology (2018)
7. Kim, B., Wang, O., Öztireli, A.C., Gross, M.: Semantic segmentation for line drawing vectorization using neural networks. In: Computer Graphics Forum, vol. 37, pp. 329–338. Wiley Online Library (2018)
8. Kim, J., Lee, J.K., Lee, K.M.: Accurate image super-resolution using very deep convolutional networks. In: Proceedings of the IEEE Conference on Computer Vision and Pattern Recognition, pp. 1646–1654 (2016)
9. Lin, T.-Y., et al.: Microsoft COCO: common objects in context. In: Fleet, D., Pajdla, T., Schiele, B., Tuytelaars, T. (eds.) ECCV 2014, Part V. LNCS, vol. 8693, pp. 740–755. Springer, Cham (2014). https://doi.org/10.1007/978-3-319-10602-1_48
10. Ronneberger, O., Fischer, P., Brox, T.: U-Net: convolutional networks for biomedical image segmentation. In: Navab, N., Hornegger, J., Wells, W.M., Frangi, A.F. (eds.) MICCAI 2015. LNCS, vol. 9351, pp. 234–241. Springer, Cham (2015). https://doi.org/10.1007/978-3-319-24574-4_28
11. Rui, C., Yan, T.: An improved stroke extraction model for Chinese character and its implementation. Comput. Sci **31**(12) (2004)
12. Rui, C., Yan, T.: A stroke extraction model for Chinese character. Department of Computer Science **31**(12), 164 (2004)
13. Wenlu, Y., Yehao, W., Hong, X.: An algorithm of stroke separation based on TTF vector font outline. Comput. Sci. **29** (2019)
14. Xiafen, Z., Jiayan, L.: Extracting Chinese calligraphy strokes using stroke crawler. J. Comput. Aided Des. Graph. **2**, 301–309 (2016)
15. Xinwei, Z., Changqiang, Y.: Graph based stroke extraction for Chinese calligraphy. Softw. Guide **18**(4), 184–187 (2019)
16. Xu, S., Lau, F.C., Cheung, W.K., Pan, Y.: Automatic generation of artistic Chinese calligraphy. IEEE Intell. Syst. **20**(3), 32–39 (2005)
17. Yang, Z.: Brush stroke extraction based on BP neural network. Ph.D. thesis, Shandong University of science and technology (2018)
18. Zhang, J.S., Yu, J.H., Mao, G.H., Ye, X.Z.: Denoising of Chinese calligraphy tablet images based on run-length statistics and structure characteristic of character strokes. J. Zhejiang Univ. Sci. A **7**(7), 1178–1186 (2006). https://doi.org/10.1631/jzus.2006.A1178

Analysis of Multi-temporal Image Series for the Preventive Conservation of Varnished Wooden Surfaces

Alireza Rezaei[1] , Sylvie Le Hégarat-Mascle[1] , Emanuel Aldea[1(✉)] ,
Piercarlo Dondi[2,4] , and Marco Malagodi[3,4]

[1] SATIE Laboratory, University Paris Saclay, rue Noetzlin, Gif-sur-Yvette 91190, France
{alireza.rezaei,sylvie.le-hegarat,
emanuel.aldea}@universite-paris-saclay.fr
[2] Department of Electrical, Computer and Biomedical Engineering,
University of Pavia, Via Ferrata 5, 27100 Pavia, Italy
piercarlo.dondi@unipv.it
[3] Department of Musicology and Cultural Heritage, University of Pavia,
Corso Garibaldi 178, 26100 Cremona, Italy
marco.malagodi@unipv.it
[4] CISRiC - Arvedi Laboratory of Non-Invasive Diagnostics, University of Pavia,
Via Bell'Aspa 3, 26100 Cremona, Italy

Abstract. Preventive conservation is a vital practice in Cultural Heritage that consists in the constant monitoring of the state of conservation of an artwork, with the final goal of minimizing the risk of damages and thus, to reduce the need of restorations. In this work, we propose a probabilistic approach for analyzing alterations appearing on varnished wooden surfaces (such as those of historical violins) based on an a-contrario framework. Our method works on time series of images, it is robust to noise and avoids parameter tuning as well as any assumption about the quantity and the shape of the worn-out areas. Furthermore, the proposed algorithm is adapted to the context of preventive conservation, with few data samples and imprecise annotations. As test set, we used image sequences included in the "Violins UVIFL imagery" dataset. Results illustrate the capability of the proposed method to distinguish altered areas from the surrounding noise and artifacts.

Keywords: A-contrario methods · Cultural heritage · Preventive conservation

1 Introduction

In the Cultural Heritage field, preventive conservation, namely the constant monitoring of the state of conservation of artworks and monuments, is becoming a common practice, fundamental to reducing the risk of damages and the need of restorations [4,28]. Handling an effective preventive conservation is particularly complex and, generally, requires an interdisciplinary approach to properly interpret and manage the effects of chemical, physical, and biological alterations [19,33,34]. In this context, image processing can be helpful to simplify the overall procedure. Even if images alone are not enough to perfectly characterize the state of an artwork, they are ideal to provide a quick

© Springer Nature Switzerland AG 2021
G. Bebis et al. (Eds.): ISVC 2021, LNCS 13017, pp. 166–179, 2021.
https://doi.org/10.1007/978-3-030-90439-5_14

preliminary examination and to identify regions of interest on a surface. This paper addresses this specific problem, focusing in particular on varnished wooden surfaces.

The varnishes applied on wooden surfaces of historical relics are generally delicate and can be easily damaged if the artifact is not properly handled. Historical musical instruments, such as violins or violas, are a common example of artworks with a varnished wooden surface that can be subject to wear. In fact, differently from other artworks that are simply held in museums, historical musical instruments are occasionally played even today, leading to a clear risk of mechanical wear, especially in those areas in direct contact with the musician.

Varnished wooden surfaces present various complexities: firstly, they are generally highly reflective, thus, noisy reflections, that can be confused for alterations, are common during photo acquisition; secondly, varnish wear can evolve in different ways depending on both the initial conditions of the surface and the different substances present; finally, the surface can be very complex and stratified due to multiple restorations occurred during centuries (which is very common for historical violins).

The combined use of multiple analytical techniques has proved beneficial for handling these issues [15,40], however, as previously said, this "traditional" preventive conservation approach is very time consuming. A more efficient procedure should consist of regular but rapid optical analysis of the images to quickly identify *possible* altered areas. The result of this analysis will indicate where a more thorough multi-modal analysis is needed. Image acquisition is very fast compared to other chemical-physical examinations, thus, ideally, using image processing, it would be possible to frequently examine the state of conservation of one or more artworks in a limited amount of time.

In this work, we describe a probabilistic method for early detection and analysis of alterations through a multi-temporal image series. We specifically work with varnished wooden surfaces subjected to mechanical wear over time. Our proposition is based on the a-contrario framework [9,10] and it improves the method presented in [37] which deals with detection of changes between two single frames: a reference image and an up-to-date acquisition. In this study, we extend the detection framework in order to process a temporal sequence of changes and to account thus for their significance with respect to the spatial plus time dimensions. The main novelty of our work is that the analysis is focused on the evolution of the alterations in time, which in turn allows us to detect the wear earlier and more reliably. This way, we can successfully handle noise and artifacts that would have been detrimental in change detection between only two frames.

The remainder of the paper is structured as follows: Sect. 2 provides a brief overview of the state of art; Sect. 3 discusses the proposed approach; Sect. 4 discusses the experiments; and finally, Sect. 5 draws the conclusions.

2 Related Works

2.1 Change and Damage Detection

In recent years, change detection has been tackled with deep neural networks for a variety of applications, among which remote sensing, traffic and medical monitoring, or quality control in manufacturing [24,25,29,42,43,46]. Typically, the feature extraction modules of these architectures are fine-tuned on an appropriate quantity of samples of the target domain in order to reach high levels of task accuracy. In our considered application however, the relative scarcity of the data coupled with the high level of imprecision of the expert annotations favor statistical approaches in which prior information may be more readily integrated into the models. This is a common problem in the Cultural Heritage field. Even if machine and deep learning approaches are used, their adoption is not widespread as in other fields, mainly due to the limited availability of data [16].

In Cultural Heritage, methods for automatic wear and damage detection mainly rely on traditional computer vision techniques, but nevertheless they proved to be very useful and applicable in different scenarios. A widely studied topic is the detection of crack in paintings. Notable approaches in this field include the use of content-based analysis [1], the extension of morphological operations to hyper-spectral images [8] and the combination of elongated filters, multiscale morphology and K-SVD [7], subsequently improved using multimodal data [35].

Another related topic is the damage detection in stone artifacts. For example, Gelli et al. [18] used Shape from Shading for identifying degradation in historical buildings; Cerimele and Cossu [5] identified decay in ancient monuments using fast marching numerical method; while Manfredini et al. [30] used a combination of 2D and 3D segmentation to discriminate among different types of deterioration.

Image processing techniques are also used for monitoring the decay of frescoes [21] and even for detecting damaged archaeological sites from space [6].

Despite their wide applicability, computer vision methods are still rarely used for wear detection in varnished wooden surfaces, as those of historical musical instruments. Attempts have been made to detect areas with established wear, that had peculiar chromatic characteristics [13]. More recently, Rezaei et al. [36,37] proposed a method for detecting changed pixels between two multi-modal images and then grouping them together, while Dondi et al. [14] presented a segmentation approach based on histogram quantization and genetic algorithm. However, all these works study the evolution of alterations using no more than two frames at a time.

2.2 A-Contrario Framework

Since wear areas are highly variable, we look for some approaches which can handle the difficulties in wear detection (unknown shape, unknown distribution, high amount of noise) and at the same time can give us a criterion to judge how *surprising* a certain arrangement of points is. Both spatially and temporally extraordinary closeness of points could indicate a wear region. The a-contrario framework introduced by Desolneux et al. [10] has the potential to satisfy the mentioned requirements. Across the computer vision field, it has been used in variety of areas such as texture analysis [20], motion detection [44,45], edge and line detection [2,3,47], or reconstruction from motion [32]. At the same time, grouping principles have been used for tasks related to the higher-level perceptual organization of scenes as well [31,48], owing to their general nature.

In our case, we are interested in the applications dealing with the detection of changed areas across multi-temporal images. In early studies, Lisani and Morel [26] used a-contrario framework and spectral invariant features to detect meaningful changes between two satellite images of the same area taken in different times. In 2007, Rousseau et al. [39] proposed an a-contrario approach for change detection in three dimensional multi-modal medical images such as Magnetic Resonance sequences. In 2010, a similar approach was proposed by Robin et al. [38] for sub-pixel change detection in a time-series of satellite images. Flenner and Hewer [17] further investigated this approach by using exchangeable random variables instead of independent and identically distributed (IID) assumption. As a later example, Liu et al. [27] applied a-contrario framework for comparing very high-resolution images of urban areas.

In the field of preventive conservation, a-contrario framework has been used for comparison of two single images to detect candidate points (seed detection) and then group them together (clustering) [36]. Later, Rezaei et al. [37] introduced a noise model to detect in one step very unlikely (under noise model assumption) arrangements of pixels based both on their location and their gray-level value. They assume the gray-level values to be a third axis and introduce a custom 3D distance to relate all three axes together. While this approach handles some of the aforementioned problems; it still only works with two frames of the series at a time, missing some potentially very useful information present in the evolution of the clusters through time to make the distinction between wear and noise more evident. The current paper aims to introduce to notion of time into the a-contrario framework through the definition of the noise model and the computation of the number of false alarms.

3   Proposed Approach

Let $\{I_t\}_{t=0}^n$ be a series of n multi-temporal RGB images taken from a varnished wooden sample; I_0 being the reference image. The size of each I_t is $w \times h$. We perform the change detection in each $I_t(t > 0)$ image with respect to I_0 using the method described in [37]. This results in a set of binary images denoted $\{B_t\}_{t=1}^n$. It is important to note that this step is not part of the algorithm; therefore, it can be performed using any proper 2D change detection and clustering algorithm. If the 2D change detection method outputs a change map, it needs to be converted to a binary image prior to being used in the following steps. The proposed algorithm gets this series of binary images as input.

The following sections summarize each step of the algorithm that produces as output, three dimensional clusters ranked based on their significance.

3.1   Distance Matrix

Considering the whole series $\{B_t\}_{t=1}^n$, we create the $3D$ point cloud $\mathcal{P}$ with the two spatial lines and columns axes of each image alongside time as the third axis (Fig. 1):

$$\mathcal{P} = \{(x, y, z), x \in \{1, 2, \ldots, w\}, y \in \{1, 2, \ldots, h\}, z | z/c_t \in \{1, 2, \ldots, n\}\}, \quad (1)$$

where c_t is the time coefficient; a real valued constant that controls the importance of a distance in time compared to a distance in image space. If $c_t = 1$, then we give the same importance to both.

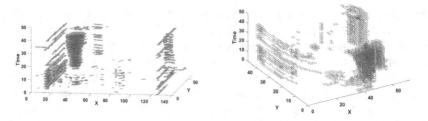

Fig. 1. Point cloud $\mathcal{P}$ derived from the sequence WS01 (left) and SV01 (right). X and Y axes are in pixels, while the time dimension (Z axis) depends on the factor c_t (in these experiments $c_t = 2$).

After constructing $\mathcal{P}$, we aim to segment it into 3D clusters and rank them based on their visual significance in the 3D (2D + time) space. The cluster detection using the a-contrario approach is based on point distance [11]. A Euclidean distance between the points of $\mathcal{P}$ automatically considers their spatial proximity as well as their closeness in time. The distance matrix D is constructed by computing the 3D distance between each pair $(x_a, y_a, z_a), (x_b, y_b, z_b) \in \mathcal{P}$:

$$D_{a,b} = \sqrt{(x_a - x_b)^2 + (y_a - y_b)^2 + (z_a - z_b)^2}. \tag{2}$$

3.2 Number of False Alarms

In order to define and evaluate the significance of the clusters formed by any subset of points in $\mathcal{P}$, we use an a-contrario criterion. Our naive model $\mathcal{M}$ represents spatial and temporal inconsistency for the points in $\mathcal{P}$. Specifically,

Definition 1 (Naive model $\mathcal{M}$). *The set of points $\mathcal{P}$ is a random set of $|\mathcal{P}|$ independent uniformly distributed variables over the 3D cube of the image series ($[1, w] \times [1, h] \times [1, n \times c_t]$).*

Let us consider a sub-volume O in the image cube; the probability that a point belongs to O, under the naive model $\mathcal{M}$, is given as:

$$p_O = \frac{V_O}{w \times h \times n \times c_t}, \tag{3}$$

where V_O is the volume of O. The probability $\mathbb{P}_{\mathcal{M}}(p_O, |\mathcal{P}|, \kappa)$ of observing κ points within O by chance, is given by the tail of the binomial distribution. The Number of False Alarms (NFA) can then be derived by extending the formulation proposed in [9] to 3D clusters.

$$NFA(p_O, |\mathcal{P}|, \kappa) = N_{test} \times \sum_{i=\kappa}^{|\mathcal{P}|} \binom{|\mathcal{P}|}{i} p_O^i (1 - p_O)^{|\mathcal{P}|-i}. \tag{4}$$

In practice, the volume V_O needed for the computation of the term p_O^i, is estimated as the *lower bound* of the volume of the points in O which can form any 3D shape. The term $(1 - p_O)$ on the other hand represents the relative volume of the region that is definitely outside the cluster i.e., outside the *upper bound* of the cluster. These two volumes are calculated by morphological operations extending the approach detailed in [9] to work with 3D data. It is worth noting that the distance between each two points indicated in D is defined as a 3D Euclidean distance; therefore, the morphological operations used here are usual dilation and erosion with a 3D kernel.

In Eq. (4), N_{test}, called the numbers of tests, controls the average number of false alarms [11]. In this work, we make this number constant for a given image cube (image series), i.e., independent of the considered cluster O, so that it is not involved in NFA minimization.

3.3 Maximal Clusters

Using Eq. (2) a minimum spanning tree is created for the points in $\mathcal{P}$. Using this tree, we group the points from smallest cluster(s) (nearest couple of points) to the biggest cluster (all points). For each cluster, we compute the NFA using Eq. (4). The used ranking criterion for clusters (O containing κ points) is their meaningfulness $\mathcal{S}$ defined as:

$$\mathcal{S}(O) = -\log(NFA(p_O, |\mathcal{P}|, \kappa)). \tag{5}$$

In our case, we want to partition $\mathcal{P}$; therefore, from all the possible clusters of points in $\mathcal{P}$, only the *maximal* clusters are considered, with *maximal* clusters defined according to [9]:

Definition 2. *A cluster $\mathcal{C} \subset \mathcal{P}$ is said maximal if $\forall \mathcal{L} \subsetneq \mathcal{C}, \mathcal{S}(\mathcal{L}) < \mathcal{S}(\mathcal{C})$ and $\forall \mathcal{L} \supsetneq \mathcal{C}, \mathcal{S}(\mathcal{L}) \leq \mathcal{S}(\mathcal{C})$.*

The list of maximal clusters sorted by their $\mathcal{S}$ value is the output of the algorithm. The cluster with the highest $\mathcal{S}$ is most significant cluster in the image series.

4 Experiments

4.1 Dataset

As test set, we used the "Violins UVIFL imagery" dataset[1] [14], a collection of multi-temporal UV induced fluorescence (UVF or UVIFL) images, referring to both real instruments and artificially altered samples created in laboratory.

UVIFL photography is a well-known non-invasive diagnostic technique that allows us to observe details not perceivable using visible light [23]. For example, in the case of historical violins, UVIFL images are commonly used to highlight possible restorations or regions of interest where it would be advisable to apply more precise but slower diagnostic techniques [12], such as X-Ray Fluorescence (XRF) [41] or Fourier Transform Infrared (FTIR) spectroscopy [22]. The capability to see "hidden" details of a surface is

---

[1] https://vision.unipv.it/research/UVIFL-Dataset/.

particularly valuable for our goal since it potentially allows for an early detection of new alterations. Please note that UV induced fluoresce is a phenomenon due to the specific properties of substances commonly used in the varnishes, that react to the light in the UV-A spectrum (315–400 nm) re-emitting radiations in the visible spectrum (400–700 nm), and thus, the image acquisition is performed with a standard RGB camera [12].

In our experiments we focused only on the artificially created sequences present in the dataset, since those referring to real historical violins contain only three sessions each, too few for performing a proper multi-temporal analysis. Each sequence consists in one to three images of the initial state of the sample and then a series of subsequent frames where the surface was altered, and the wear starts and grows. We use the following sequences from the dataset: WS01, a 20-frame sequence that displays the appearing and the growing of an alteration in an area with intact varnish; and SV01, a 20-frame sequence that shows the growing of an already worn-out region on a sample violin back plate.

4.2   Results

Using the sequences WS01 and SV01, for each frame, we generate binary change images respect to the reference frame, applying the method described in [37]. Figures 2 and 3 show, respectively for WS01 and SV01, four sample frames and their corresponding binary image.

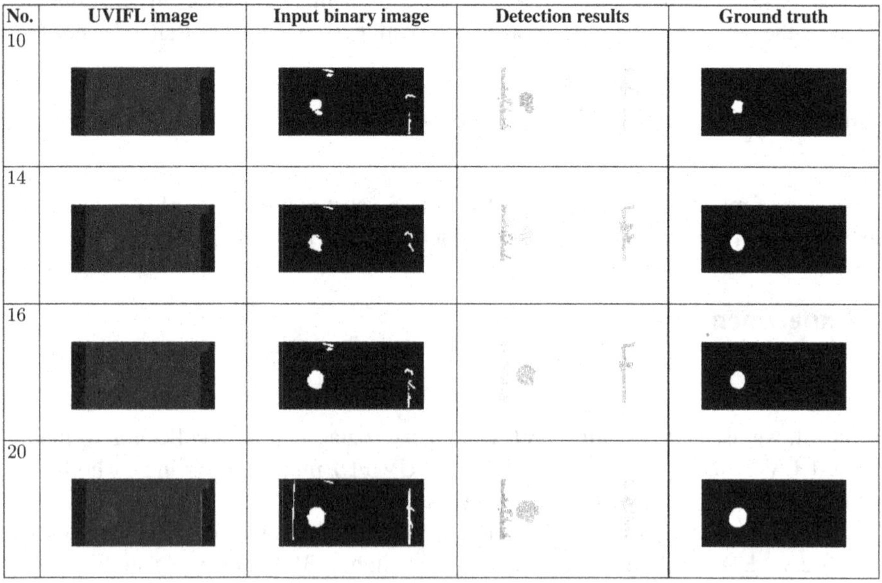

Fig. 2. Four sample frames from the sequence WS01 and their corresponding cluster detection results. At each frame, the first, second and third cluster according to decreasing order of meaningfulness are shown in red, green, and blue, respectively. (Color figure online)

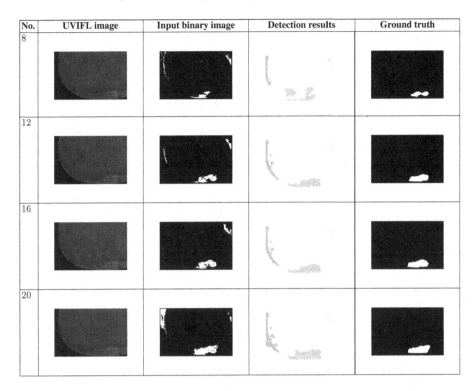

No.	UVIFL image	Input binary image	Detection results	Ground truth
8				
12				
16				
20				

Fig. 3. Four sample frames from the sequence SV01 and their corresponding cluster detection results. At each frame, the first, second and third cluster according to decreasing order of meaningfulness are shown in red, green, and blue, respectively. (Color figure online)

Figure 1 shows the point cloud created by accumulating the change detection results for each frame of both sequences. The coefficient c_t is set to 2 (this gives slightly more importance to spatial proximity over time proximity, penalizes the clusters which disappear in some frames and keeps the size of the representation domain small enough for a better performance). The time domain is the upward axis in all visualizations. As we can see, there is a considerable amount of noise present in both point clouds. In addition, there are two sets of artifacts in the left and right sides of both sequences, which are related to the UV reflections from the wooden sample.

In practice, the optical monitoring of a varnished wooden surface is an ongoing and never-ending process. This means that the number of available frames and the accuracy of the detection increases as the time goes on. Of course, if the sequence of available images becomes too large, we only keep the last n frames with n chosen as a compromise between computation resources and detection performance. In our case, we keep every frame available from the first until the last one.

To simulate a practical optical monitoring process and to analyze different detection results in any given point in time, we started the experiment with 10 frames for the sequence WS01 and 8 for the sequence SV01; then, we ran the algorithm repeatedly

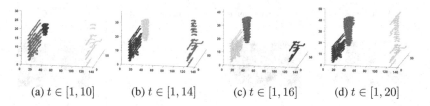

Fig. 4. Evolution of the detection by increasing the number of used time frames t in the sequence WS01. Color code gives the rank according to significance: red first, green second, blue third. The time domain is the upward axis in all visualizations. (Color figure online)

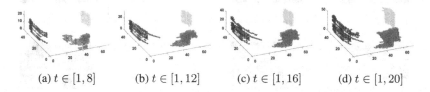

Fig. 5. Evolution of the detection by increasing the number of used time frames t in the sequence SV01. Same conventions of Fig. 4.

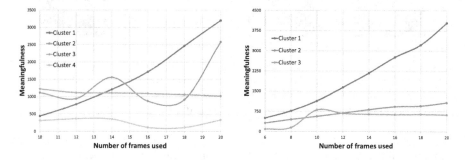

Fig. 6. The evolution of the meaningfulness value of sample clusters in different runs of the algorithm for sequence WS01 (left) and SV01 (right).

increasing the considered number of frames in each run until processing all frames. Each run gives us a list of clusters sorted by their meaningfulness value. The rank of each cluster among the whole set of clusters can change from one run to another. In general, assuming that the wear region expands over time, our expectation is that the wear starts in lower ranks and steadily rises to the first rank. We can also follow the evolution of the meaningfulness value from one run to the next. Again, we expect that the significance of the wear region increases as we get more frames. On the other hand, the meaningfulness value for the noise and artifact clusters should remain nearly unchanged or go up and down randomly. Another difference between the wear region and the rest is that it shall be present in every frame after its first appearance. Therefore, it is possible that a detected area is divided into two clusters along the time axis. In that case, we only take into account the one with the highest meaningfulness.

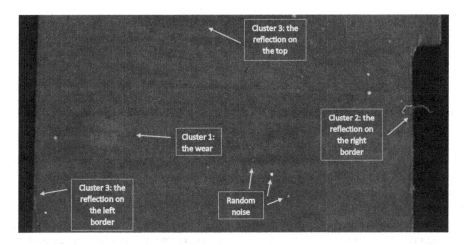

Fig. 7. Location of clusters 1 to 4 on a sample frame (frame 8) from the sequence WS01.

Figures 4 and 5 illustrate the detection results through time, i.e., based on the number of frames used as input. In each case, the top three clusters have been shown. As one may notice, firstly, only clusters which are consistent have been detected. Minor artifacts and small noises have been disregarded, a fact which is a very desirable behavior when multi-temporal information is available. Secondly, the region of interest which is the actual changed area has been chosen by the end of the sequence as the most significant cluster. The evolution of meaningfulness of each cluster for the two sequences is depicted in Fig. 6.

For a more in-depth analysis, we can consider the four main clusters present in the sequence WS01 (see Fig. 7 for their location on a sample frame) and as a result in $\mathcal{P}$:

- Cluster 1: the wear area.
- Cluster 2: the artifact related to the right border.
- Cluster 3: the artifact related to the left border.
- Cluster 4: the noise present in the upper part of some frames.

Considering the left chart in Fig. 6, which illustrates the meaningfulness values for these four clusters in each run of the algorithm, we can deduce the following:

- The values for both clusters 3 and 4 remain fairly constant in each run which indicates artifacts with the same size appearing consistently in all frames. On the other hand, the values for cluster 2 behave more erratically and go up and down. This is due to appearing and disappearing of the artifact in some frames. Therefore, the detection is divided in multiple clusters along the time axis.
- Only cluster 1, the wear region, has values that consistently increase over time. This is in line with our expectation about an "ideal" wear that keeps growing. In practice, the wear may not expand over multiple acquisitions which will show itself as a plateau. However, it will never shrink or disappear so the values should remain increasing overall. Moreover, even if the wear region becomes the most meaningful

cluster only at frame 16, we can notice that it is the only growing cluster already at frames 11–12, meaning that we can trigger a "possible alteration" alert at this early stage.

The same deductions for WS01 can be observed for SV01, as well. This time we have three main clusters (see Fig. 6, right): cluster 1, the wear, and clusters 2 and 3, which are reflections present on most of the samples. In this case the alteration is correctly detected early than in sequence WS01. In fact, at frames 7–8, cluster 1 is both the most meaningful cluster and the most rapidly growing. This is coherent with the type of input data. Sequence WS01 displays the growing of a completely new damaged area, which is initially small and slowly growing, while SVO1 shows the worsening of an already worn-out region, thus it is reasonable that the new alteration appears earlier and grows faster.

Overall, results clearly show that, with respect to previous works leveraging single change maps [37], this analysis based on the temporal dynamics of the changes is able to pinpoint at an earlier stage and more reliably the emergence of a wear, in full accord with the preventive conservation principle.

5   Conclusions

In this paper, we introduced a probabilistic method for detecting significant changes located in clusters within a noisy multi-temporal series of images. The proposed method can be used in preventive conservation, as a fast preliminary examination of a varnished wooden surface able to identify the most likely new altered areas. Thus, a verification using more precise but slower techniques (like spectroscopic analyses) will be done only on these detected areas, optimizing the monitoring procedure. This approach, rooted in the Gestalt theory, is particularly interesting for the task of historical violin analysis with respect to other statistical learning-based and deep learning methods, given the limited amount of available data and also the difficulty of performing reliable annotations.

Future works will involve more tests, to further validate our approach, as well as refinements in the clustering method to achieve an even earlier detection of wear (ideally, as close as possible to the beginning of the alteration, when only a few pixels change).

Acknowledgments. The authors gratefully acknowledge support from the French-Italian Galileo PHC partnership (project 44391VL/G20-160, *MUSical Instrument Conservation with Optical Monitoring (MUSICOM)*).

References

1. Abas, F.S., Martinez, K.: Classification of painting cracks for content-based analysis. In: Proceedings of SPIE 5011, Machine Vision Applications in Industrial Inspection XI, vol. 5011, pp. 149–161 (2003)

2. Akinlar, C., Topal, C.: EDLines: a real-time line segment detector with a false detection control. Pattern Recogn. Lett. **32**(13), 1633–1642 (2011). https://doi.org/10.1016/j.patrec. 2011.06.001
3. Aldea, E., Le Hégarat-Mascle, S.: Robust crack detection for unmanned aerial vehicles inspection in an a-contrario decision framework. J. Electron. Imaging **24**(6), 061119–061119 (2015)
4. Bradley, S.: Preventive conservation research and practice at the British museum. J. Am. Inst. Conserv. **44**(3), 159–173 (2005). https://doi.org/10.1179/019713605806082248
5. Cerimele, M.M., Cossu, R.: Decay regions segmentation from color images of ancient monuments using fast marching method. J. Cult. Herit. **8**(2), 170–175 (2007). https://doi.org/10.1016/j.culher.2007.01.006
6. Cerra, D., Plank, S., Lysandrou, V., Tian, J.: Cultural heritage sites in danger-towards automatic damage detection from space. Remote Sens. **8**(9), 781 (2016). https://doi.org/10.3390/rs8090781
7. Cornelis, B., et al.: Crack detection and inpainting for virtual restoration of paintings: the case of the Ghent altarpiece. Sig. Process. **93**(3), 605–619 (2013)
8. Deborah, H., Richard, N., Hardeberg, J.Y.: Hyperspectral crack detection in paintings. In: 2015 Colour and Visual Computing Symposium (CVCS), pp. 1–6 (2015). https://doi.org/10.1109/CVCS.2015.7274902
9. Desolneux, A., Moisan, L., Morel, J.M.: A grouping principle and four applications. IEEE Trans. Pattern Anal. Mach. Intell. **25**(4), 508–513 (2003)
10. Desolneux, A., Moisan, L., Morel, J.M.: Meaningful alignments. Int. J. Comput. Vis. **40**(1), 7–23 (2000)
11. Desolneux, A., Moisan, L., Morel, J.M.: From Gestalt Theory to Image Analysis: A Probabilistic Approach, vol. 34. Springer, New York (2007). https://doi.org/10.1007/978-0-387-74378-3
12. Dondi, P., Lombardi, L., Invernizzi, C., Rovetta, T., Malagodi, M., Licchelli, M.: Automatic analysis of UV-induced fluorescence imagery of historical violins. J. Comput. Cult. Herit. **10**(2), 12:1–12:13 (2017). https://doi.org/10.1145/3051472
13. Dondi, P., Lombardi, L., Malagodi, M., Licchelli, M.: Automatic identification of varnish wear on historical instruments: the case of Antonio Stradivari violins. J. Cult. Herit. **22**, 968–973 (2016)
14. Dondi, P., Lombardi, L., Malagodi, M., Licchelli, M.: Segmentation of multi-temporal UV-induced fluorescence images of historical violins. In: Cristani, M., Prati, A., Lanz, O., Messelodi, S., Sebe, N. (eds.) ICIAP 2019. LNCS, vol. 11808, pp. 81–91. Springer, Cham (2019). https://doi.org/10.1007/978-3-030-30754-7_9
15. Fichera, G.V., et al.: Innovative monitoring plan for the preventive conservation of historical musical instruments. Stud. Conserv. **63**(sup1), 351–354 (2018). https://doi.org/10.1080/00393630.2018.1499853
16. Fiorucci, M., Khoroshiltseva, M., Pontil, M., Traviglia, A., Del Bue, A., James, S.: Machine learning for cultural heritage: a survey. Pattern Recogn. Lett. **133**, 102–108 (2020). https://doi.org/10.1016/j.patrec.2020.02.017
17. Flenner, A., Hewer, G.: A Helmholtz principle approach to parameter free change detection and coherent motion using exchangeable random variables. SIAM J. Imaging Sci. **4**(1), 243–276 (2011)
18. Gelli, D., March, R., Salonia, P., Vitulano, D.: Surface analysis of stone materials integrating spatial data and computer vision techniques. J. Cult. Herit. **4**(2), 117–125 (2003)
19. Ghedini, N., Ozga, I., Bonazza, A., Dilillo, M., Cachier, H., Sabbioni, C.: Atmospheric aerosol monitoring as a strategy for the preventive conservation of urban monumental heritage: the florence baptistery. Atmos. Environ. **45**(33), 5979–5987 (2011). https://doi.org/10.1016/j.atmosenv.2011.08.001

20. Grosjean, B., Moisan, L.: A-contrario detectability of spots in textured backgrounds. J. Math. Imaging Vis. **33**(3), 313 (2009)
21. Guarneri, M., Danielis, A., Francucci, M., Collibus, M.F.D., Fornetti, G., Mencattini, A.: 3D remote colorimetry and watershed segmentation techniques for fresco and artwork decay monitoring and preservation. J. Archaeol. Sci. **46**, 182–190 (2014)
22. Invernizzi, C., Fichera, G.V., Licchelli, M., Malagodi, M.: A non-invasive stratigraphic study by reflection FT-IR spectroscopy and UV-induced fluorescence technique: the case of historical violins. Microchem. J. **138**, 273–281 (2018). https://doi.org/10.1016/j.microc.2018.01.021
23. Janssens, K., Van Grieken, R.: Non-Destructive Micro Analysis of Cultural Heritage Materials, vol. 42. Elsevier, Amsterdam (2004)
24. Khelifi, L., Mignotte, M.: Deep learning for change detection in remote sensing images: comprehensive review and meta-analysis. IEEE Access **8**, 126385–126400 (2020)
25. Li, M.D., et al.: Siamese neural networks for continuous disease severity evaluation and change detection in medical imaging. NPJ Digit. Med. **3**(1), 1–9 (2020)
26. Lisani, J.L., Morel, J.M.: Detection of major changes in satellite images. In: Proceedings 2003 International Conference on Image Processing (Cat. No. 03CH37429), vol. 1, pp. I-941. IEEE (2003)
27. Liu, G., Gousseau, Y., Tupin, F.: A contrario comparison of local descriptors for change detection in very high spatial resolution satellite images of urban areas. IEEE Trans. Geosci. Remote Sens. **57**(6), 3904–3918 (2019)
28. Lucchi, E.: Review of preventive conservation in museum buildings. J. Cult. Herit. **29**, 180–193 (2018). https://doi.org/10.1016/j.culher.2017.09.003
29. Mandal, M., Vipparthi, S.K.: An empirical review of deep learning frameworks for change detection: model design, experimental frameworks, challenges and research needs. IEEE Trans. Intell. Transp. Syst. (2021)
30. Manferdini, A.M., Baroncini, V., Corsi, C.: An integrated and automated segmentation approach to deteriorated regions recognition on 3D reality-based models of cultural heritage artifacts. J. Cult. Herit. **13**(4), 371–378 (2012). https://doi.org/10.1016/j.culher.2012.01.014
31. Michaelsen, E.: Self-organizing maps and gestalt organization as components of an advanced system for remotely sensed data: An example with thermal hyper-spectra. Pattern Recogn. Lett. **83**, 169 – 177 (2016). https://doi.org/10.1016/j.patrec.2016.06.004. Advances in Pattern Recognition in Remote Sensing
32. Moulon, P., Monasse, P., Marlet, R.: Adaptive structure from motion with *a contrario* model estimation. In: Lee, K.M., Matsushita, Y., Rehg, J.M., Hu, Z. (eds.) ACCV 2012. LNCS, vol. 7727, pp. 257–270. Springer, Heidelberg (2013). https://doi.org/10.1007/978-3-642-37447-0_20
33. Ortiz, R., Ortiz, P.: Vulnerability index: a new approach for preventive conservation of monuments. Int. J. Architect. Herit. **10**(8), 1078–1100 (2016). https://doi.org/10.1080/15583058.2016.1186758
34. Perles, A., et al.: An energy-efficient internet of things (IoT) architecture for preventive conservation of cultural heritage. Future Gener. Comput. Syst. **81**, 566–581 (2018). https://doi.org/10.1016/j.future.2017.06.030
35. Pizurica, A., et al.: Digital image processing of the Ghent altarpiece: supporting the painting's study and conservation treatment. IEEE Sig. Process. Mag. **32**(4), 112–122 (2015). https://doi.org/10.1109/MSP.2015.2411753
36. Rezaei, A., Aldea, E., Dondi, P., Malagodi, M., Le Hégarat-Mascle, S.: Detecting alterations in historical violins with optical monitoring. In: Proceedings of the 14th International Conference on Quality Control by Artificial Vision (QCAV), vol. 11172, pp. 1117210-1–1117210-8 (2019). https://doi.org/10.1117/12.2521702

37. Rezaei, A., Le Hégarat-Mascle, S., Aldea, E., Dondi, P., Malagodi, M.: One step clustering based on a-contrario framework for detection of alterations in historical violins. In: 25th International Conference on Pattern Recognition (ICPR2020), pp. 9348–9355 (2021)

38. Robin, A., Moisan, L., Le Hégarat-Mascle, S.: An a-contrario approach for subpixel change detection in satellite imagery. IEEE Trans. Pattern Anal. Mach. Intell. **32**(11), 1977–1993 (2010)

39. Rousseau, F., et al.: An a contrario approach for change detection in 3D multimodal images: application to multiple sclerosis in MRI. In: 2007 29th Annual International Conference of the IEEE Engineering in Medicine and Biology Society, pp. 2069–2072. IEEE (2007)

40. Rovetta, T., et al.: The case of Antonio Stradivari 1718 ex-San Lorenzo violin: history, restorations and conservation perspectives. J. Archaeol. Sci.: Rep. **23**, 443–450 (2019). https://doi.org/10.1016/j.jasrep.2018.11.010

41. Rovetta, T., Invernizzi, C., Licchelli, M., Cacciatori, F., Malagodi, M.: The elemental composition of Stradivari's musical instruments: new results through non-invasive EDXRF analysis. X-Ray Spectrom. **47**(2), 159–170 (2018). https://doi.org/10.1002/xrs.2825

42. Sturari, M., Paolanti, M., Frontoni, E., Mancini, A., Zingaretti, P.: Robotic platform for deep change detection for rail safety and security. In: 2017 European Conference on Mobile Robots (ECMR), pp. 1–6. IEEE (2017)

43. Varghese, A., Gubbi, J., Ramaswamy, A., Balamuralidhar, P.: ChangeNet: a deep learning architecture for visual change detection. In: Leal-Taixé, L., Roth, S. (eds.) ECCV 2018. LNCS, vol. 11130, pp. 129–145. Springer, Cham (2019). https://doi.org/10.1007/978-3-030-11012-3_10

44. Veit, T., Cao, F., Bouthemy, P.: An a contrario decision framework for region-based motion detection. Int. J. Comput. Vis. **68**(2), 163–178 (2006)

45. Veit, T., Cao, F., Bouthemy, P.: Space-time a contrario clustering for detecting coherent motions. In: Proceedings 2007 IEEE International Conference on Robotics and Automation, pp. 33–39. IEEE (2007)

46. Verma, S., Panigrahi, A., Gupta, S.: QFabric: multi-task change detection dataset. In: Proceedings of the IEEE/CVF Conference on Computer Vision and Pattern Recognition, pp. 1052–1061 (2021)

47. Widynski, N., Mignotte, M.: A contrario edge detection with edgelets. In: 2011 IEEE International Conference on Signal and Image Processing Applications (ICSIPA), pp. 421–426. IEEE (2011)

48. Yan, Y., et al.: Unsupervised image saliency detection with gestalt-laws guided optimization and visual attention based refinement. Pattern Recogn. **79**, 65–78 (2018). https://doi.org/10.1016/j.patcog.2018.02.004

Visualization

Evaluating User Interfaces for a Driver Guidance System to Support Stationary Wireless Charging of Electric Vehicles

Bijan Shahbaz Nejad$^{(\boxtimes)}$, Peter Roch, Marcus Handte, and Pedro José Marrón

University of Duisburg-Essen, Essen, Germany
bijan.shahbaz-nejad@uni-due.de

Abstract. Stationary wireless charging could be a convenient alternative to wired charging of electric vehicles. The prerequisite for efficient wireless charging is that the charging components located under the car are precisely aligned. Drivers cannot observe the state of alignment from their perspective, which makes it challenging to identify whether the vehicle's position is accurate enough. In this paper, we present user interfaces that can support the driver in achieving the technically required precision. We provide three visualizations with different abstraction levels displayed on two screen types, which we evaluate experimentally in a user study. As part of the user study, we create a positioning scenario as it might occur with wireless charging. Participants must try to achieve the required precision by being guided by the user interfaces. The results of the user study indicate that, regardless of the visualization and screen type, drivers can position the vehicle within the defined tolerance range of 10 cm. However, the user experience differs significantly. In terms of usability and workload, drivers prefer a visualization that presents the positioning scenario from a bird's eye view. Moreover, the time to complete the task using the bird's eye view visualization took less than 44 s on average, which is probably shorter than parking and plugging in a charging cable. In contrast, an arrow-based visualization took in average up to 1.5 times longer than bird's eye view visualization to complete the task and was the most criticized by the participants.

Keywords: Visualization · Evaluation · Driver guidance · Wireless charging · User study · User experience · Precision · Pose estimation · Computer vision

1 Introduction

Electric vehicles are an interesting topic of our time because of a multitude of technological and ecological challenges associated with them. Since the air in many cities is contaminated by vehicle exhaust fumes [16], electric vehicles offer local air quality benefits due to zero exhaust emissions [7].

Although there are valid reasons for driving electric vehicles, initializing a wired charging process can be inconvenient. For example, drivers might need to

© Springer Nature Switzerland AG 2021
G. Bebis et al. (Eds.): ISVC 2021, LNCS 13017, pp. 183–196, 2021.
https://doi.org/10.1007/978-3-030-90439-5_15

leave the vehicle to establish a physical connection between the charging station and the car while risking exposure to severe weather conditions. In contrast, wireless charging could be a convenient alternative to wired charging as drivers can stay in the vehicle. Accordingly, Andersson et al. [1] indicate that there are benefits of inductive charging which might increase the attractiveness of electric vehicles.

Technically, wireless charging is enabled by a transmitter coil integrated into the floor, which transmits the energy through the air without contact to a receiver coil installed at the vehicle's underbody [25]. A constraint of wireless charging is that precise alignment of the charging components is required within a tolerance range that is defined by the technical properties of the charging system. Otherwise, the charging process cannot proceed efficiently [8]. Accordingly, the driver has to position the vehicle so that the charging components overlap as precisely as possible. A problem that arises is that many drivers are not used to precisely positioning their vehicle, such as observed in the studies from [3] where only 5% of the vehicles reached a position that could enable efficient wireless charging. Furthermore, the charging components are located under the vehicle and therefore outside of the driver's field of view. Various approaches could be applied to facilitate the positioning process. For instance, markings could be made on the ground, which can serve as an orientation during the positioning. Besides, parking stoppers that protrude from the ground can serve as a physical restriction. The limitation of these approaches is that they cannot be utilized universally for all vehicle types, since vehicle dimensions differ. Alternatively, mechanical systems can be utilized that align the charging components by moving them towards one another. The advantage of a mechanical system is that it might be used for different types of vehicles, for example by using multiple configurations. However, buying and installing a mechanical system is expensive. Besides, complicated maintenance work may be required since vandalism or street cleaning can cause damage if, for example, parts protrude from the floor.

As part of the research presented in this paper, we want to make efficient wireless charging of electric cars accessible in everyday use. There are already approaches that include concepts for positioning [5,12,15,18], however, the focus is often on the technical components. In this paper, we focus on the user's perspective. We aim to find a usable user interface for a positioning system that will help the driver to achieve the precision required for efficient wireless charging while ensuring a low workload. For this reason, we conduct a user study under realistic conditions in which participants have to position their vehicle as accurately as possible on a target point. To support the drivers, we provide various user interfaces composed of two screen and three visualization types.

The structure of this paper is as follows: In the following section we present related work. Subsequently, in Sect. 3 we define the goals for the user interface and our system design. The user study is presented in Sect. 4. In Sect. 5 we discuss the results and observations. Finally, in Sect. 6 we present our conclusions.

2   Related Work

In contrast to other positioning contexts such as automotive navigation and parking, accurate positioning is crucial for efficient wireless charging, since the charging components must be aligned precisely. Depending on the restrictions that result from the charging hardware, a maximum deviation between the charging components can be defined for energy transmission. A deviation in the range of a few centimeters can already lead to inefficient charging. As a result, the vehicle must be positioned an order of magnitude more accurate than it is required in the aforementioned contexts. Accordingly, different approaches attempt to solve the positioning from a technical perspective. For example, in [5,15] approaches are presented which utilize RFID for the positioning of the vehicle. There are also approaches in which the positioning is supported by mechanical concepts. In [12], an approach is presented in which the distance between the charging components is mechanically adjusted for dynamic charging. Also in [18] the charging components' misalignment is determined using wireless sensors, whereupon an electromechanical system automatically adjusts the position of the coil which is integrated into the floor.

In addition to the approaches that deal with technical positioning concepts, some authors present supporting user interfaces. Hudecek et al. [11] provide an assistance system for stationary wireless charging, which gives the driver visual feedback on positioning in three stages. The first stage illustrates the vehicle interior from the driver's perspective. This visualization should not distract the driver from driving and symbolizes the readiness of the system. As soon as the charging station is recognized by the positioning system, a path visualization takes place, which specifies a lane to the target position. If the distance to the target position is reduced to less than 10 m, the positioning scene is shown from the third perspective for a better overview. From the point where the distance to the target position is less than 3 m, the visualization changes the perspective to the bird's eye view with a high zoom level. The vehicle is displayed transparently so that the alignment of the charging components can be observed. An alternative to stationary charging is dynamic charging, in which the vehicle can be charged while it is in motion. Similar to stationary charging, deviations between the charging components can lead to inefficient energy transmission. A driver guidance system has been developed which can support to reduce the lateral deviation of the charging components [13]. The user interface developed for this purpose presents the current deviation in centimeters on a linear gauge, which encodes certain distance intervals with different colors. Besides, the authors of [14] present a lane-keeping assistant, which displays the misalignment in real-time on a colored linear scale. Also in [2] a user interface is presented, which is designed to guide the driver on a route where the charging power is high. A visualization of a green line is used for this, which is placed vertically in the middle of the screen. As soon as the position of the vehicle deviates laterally, a red arrow is drawn which points orthogonally to the center line in the compensation direction and has a length that is proportional to the degree of lateral deviation.

Although the presented works show various user interfaces, they are not evaluated in terms of user experience, precision and time in the context of stationary wireless charging. In order to find a usable user interface that can support drivers to reach the required precision in a reasonable time, we introduce a system with different visual user interfaces that we compare in a user study.

3   System

Driven by the motivation to find a suitable user interface for efficient wireless charging, we propose goals, followed by a solution system setup with various visual modalities.

3.1   Goals

In order to realize efficient wireless charging the user interface must achieve three goals which we roughly summarize in the following:

Precision. Accurate alignment of the charging components is an essential prerequisite for efficient wireless charging. The range of accepted misalignment is limited by the technical characteristics of the charging hardware. In contrast to vehicle navigation and parking, the precision required for positioning is an order of magnitude higher and is in the range of a few centimeters. Although the air gap between the charging components can also be a problem, in this paper we focus on the lateral and longitudinal offset, as these misalignment can be regulated by driving without hardware adjustment. Based on the misalignment tolerances of current inductive charging systems [3], we define a maximum distance of 10 cm in a radial area around the optimal position, without taking the air gap into account.

User Experience. The possible lack of attractiveness in the required vehicle positioning should not be the reason for drivers to reject the concept of wireless charging. Therefore, the user interface should be a valid and accepted tool to assist the driver with accurate positioning. The user interface should be intuitive to use. Ambiguity and confusion should be avoided so that no new problems arise that could make positioning even more difficult. Accordingly, the user interface must have a high degree of usability. In addition to positioning the vehicle for wireless charging, the driver has additional tasks in parallel, such as avoiding dangerous situations in traffic. In order to not distract the driver from the other tasks, the workload that arises when being guided by the user interface must be as low as possible. Moreover, when interacting with the user interface the driver must not be frustrated so that the positioning process is not perceived as unattractive.

Time. Drivers should be able to achieve precise positioning within a reasonable time frame. We define around 2 min as a reference value, as we estimate that parking and plugging in the charging cable could each take up to a minute. The suitability of wireless charging for everyday use depends on the time required for positioning the vehicle. Wireless charging may be convenient, but if positioning takes significantly longer than connecting the car by wire, drivers may prefer wired charging.

3.2 Overview

Figure 1 depicts an overview of the components of the system. For driver guidance the spatial relationship between the charging components must be tracked from a technical point of view. Accordingly, we utilize the approach from [19] in which the relative position of the primary coil is configured manually and the relative position of the secondary coil is derived from the position and rotation of the vehicle. In order to determine the position and rotation of the vehicle, the authors of [19] apply computer vision algorithms. Instead of the proposed camera, we utilize a lidar to acquire raw sensor data due to fewer configuration steps and increased accuracy. Furthermore, a backend computer processes the raw data and estimates the vehicle's pose, which is composed of the position and the rotation relative to the sensor device. A visualization software consumes the vehicle's last estimated pose via a REST interface to generate visualizations. There are two screen variants that present the visual information. A smartphone is used within the cockpit for visualization, which retrieves the positioning data via WiFi from the REST interface. Alternatively, outside the cockpit, the visualization is displayed on a stationary monitor, which is connected to the backend computer.

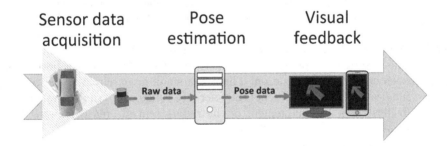

Fig. 1. Overview of the system components and processing pipeline.

3.3 Visualization Types

This section presents the visualization types provided by our system. We present three visualizations with ascending levels of abstraction. The first visualization renders a spatial overview of the positioning situation. The second reduces the presented information to the two-dimensional relative distances to reach the target. Finally, the third prescribes the direction to be driven. To avoid visual over-stimulation and to compactly communicate the positioning information, we choose minimalistic visualization designs. Figure 2 gives an overview of all visualization types.

Bird's Eye View. We aim to realistically reflect the current positioning situation, for the first type of visualization. Numerous parking assistance systems utilize cameras installed around the vehicle to give an overview of the surroundings such as presented in [9,22] to support the driver in the parking process. Inspired by this concept, we provide a visualization that supports the driver with an overview, that presents the spatial relationship between the vehicle and the target position from a bird's eye view. Based on the given overview, the driver can freely reason about the next vehicle maneuver in order to reach the target position. Figure 2a presents an exemplary state of the visualization during a positioning process. The yellow rectangle represents the vehicle and its position and the blue rectangle symbolizes the target position as a parking lot metaphor. Driver's task is to move the rectangle of the vehicle as precisely as possible into the rectangle of the target position by positioning the vehicle. The more the two rectangles overlap, the closer the vehicle approaches the ideal position.

Radar. For the second visualization, we increase the abstraction level by only showing the distance to the target. A linear gauge [13] or horizontal arrows [2] can communicate the lateral deviation from a target position in the context of dynamic wireless charging. Our application context is stationary wireless charging requiring the vehicle to be aligned longitudinally as well. Accordingly, we provide a visualization that presents the longitudinal and lateral offset between the charging components. Figure 2b illustrates the second visualization type, which is inspired by the aircraft's primary flight display such as illustrated in [6,17]. A round radar-like surface is utilized, on which two red bars move horizontally and vertically from the driver's perspective. The horizontal bar moves vertically and indicates the relative longitudinal offset between the charging components. The vertical bar moves horizontally and shows the lateral offset. An optimal alignment of the charging components is reached when the intersection of both bars is in the center of the visualization. There is a small green circle in the center of the visualization which represents the tolerance range of 10 cm. The rectangle in Fig. 2b illustrates an enlargement of the radars central area containing the tolerance range.

Arrow. The third type of visualization has a higher level of abstraction, since only the information of driving direction is given. For this purpose, a path visualization can be used, as shown in [11]. If the driver is too far from the screen, parts of the path may no longer be visible. An alternative is to visualize an arrow. Since numerous traffic signs display arrows, many people are likely to recognize them from a great distance. Furthermore, they are utilized in various navigation contexts to metaphorically indicate the relative location of a object such as in [20,23]. This is why our third type of visualization presents the driving direction from the driver's perspective using an arrow as depicted in Fig. 2c. By following the direction which is indicated by the arrow, the driver can reach a target location which enables efficient wireless charging. Since the direction is given, the driver is not required to extract the driving direction from the visualization himself, as it is required by the other visualization types.

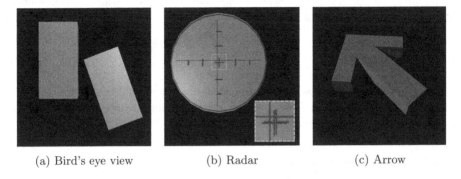

(a) Bird's eye view   (b) Radar   (c) Arrow

Fig. 2. Overview of the visualization types of the proposed system.

3.4   Information Output Setup

In addition to the visualization itself, an essential part of the user interface is the screen modality. Drivers receive information concerning the current traffic situation from various sources. Within the cockpit, different parameters are presented that might be needed while driving, for example, via the speedometer, the navigation device, or a head-up display. Outside the cockpit, for example, traffic signs or lights communicate traffic information. Based on this assumption, the visualization is alternatively displayed inside the cockpit and outside of the cockpit.

Inside the Cockpit. An advantage of utilizing screens within the cockpit for driver guidance is that many drivers are used to getting information from monitors in the vehicle from other contexts while driving. Another advantage is that they are protected against environmental influences such as rain, and it is probable that the illumination conditions inside the vehicle do not severely restrict the readability of information. In the context of our application, the monitor must be integrable with little effort and low cost and be applicable regardless of the vehicle type. Since smartphones can be used with negligible effort regardless of the vehicle type, we decide to utilize one as a displaying device. The visualizations are implemented for Android devices using OpenGL ES [21].

Outside the Cockpit. While driving, drivers receive traffic information outside of the vehicle, for example via traffic signs. As an alternative to the screen inside the vehicle, we also install a stationary screen outside the vehicle, similar to a traffic sign. The advantage of a screen outside the vehicle is that the focus can remain outside the cockpit during positioning and does not require to look inside the vehicle as with other devices. This means that the traffic situation can still be kept in view and possible risky situations can be prevented. The visualization is rendered using software that was implemented using the Unity Engine [24] and running at the backend server. To protect the screen from environmental influences, we optionally use a waterproof casing.

4   User Study

In order to analyze to what extent the visualization modalities of the system can meet the requirements, we conduct an experimental user study, which is described in the following sections.

4.1   Test Environment

We set up a test environment, which we depict in Fig. 3. We visually mark the target position with a red adhesive point having a radius of approximately 1.5 cm. Furthermore, we utilize a lidar since lidars typically enable precise measurements. We adjust the lidar to face towards the defined target area to record it. By directly aiming to a target position in a distance of 3 m and a configured field of view of 90° the lidar can perceive the vehicle in about 3 m to the left and right of the target position. With an offset of 1 m in $+z$ and 11 ms in the $-x$ direction, we select the starting position in a parking lot so that the driver has to make a slight curve while driving forward to reach the target position. We select a Dell P2311Hb with 23″ of screen size and install it at a height of about 1.4 m. We set up the device 1 m in the $+x$ direction so that the driver can observe it while positioning. Moreover, we provide each participant with a Samsung Galaxy S7 Edge, which can be freely placed in the cockpit of their personal vehicle, depending on their preference.

4.2   Task

The task of the participants is to move their own vehicle, guided by each visualization in combination with each screen modality, three times from the starting position to the target position within a radius of 10 cm. As soon as the condition is fulfilled, the background of the visualization turns green and the driver can end the positioning process. The vehicle's reference point is located in the center of the side directed towards the lidar. Since the vehicle type can differ among the participants, the length of each vehicle is configured in the system. Visualization and screen modality is being assigned in a random order. However, after utilizing all user interfaces, the driver must repeat the task without any user interface.

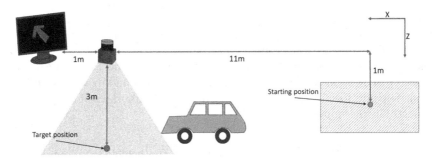

Fig. 3. Overview of the experimental setup with lines symbolizing the distances in the setup. The orange area represents a parking lot containing the starting position. The purple region symbolizes the lidar's tracking area containing the target position.

4.3   Data Acquisition

We provide digital questionnaires to each participant, which should be filled out on their smartphone, to obtain various information. The participants specify their gender, age and the number of years they own a driving license. Besides, the participants should rate their parking skills and IT skills on a scale from 1 for poor to 10 for very good. After every third repetition of using a visualization modality, feedback about the usability and workload is requested. To get a deeper insight into usability, the participants fill out a SUS (System Usability Scale [4]). We also provide a questionnaire that we derived from NASA-TLX [10] to measure the workload in our context. Since the user should fill out the questionnaire on their smartphone, we use a scale with a maximum of 5 points, whereby we equate the weighting of all questions. During the entire user study, each participant is motivated to express their experiences to evaluate the visualization modalities besides the questionnaires. Furthermore, we measure the end position when using each visualization modality to determine the resulting positioning error. The positioning error results from the distance between the vehicle's reference point and the target position. In addition, the time is measured during positioning to determine whether the required duration is within a reasonable time frame.

4.4   Results

In this section we introduce the set of participants and the collected measurement results of the user study.

Participants. A total of 12 people took part in the user study, of which 7 are male and 5 female. The participants' age covers a wide range on the scale from 20 to 57 years with an average being around 37 years. Driving license ownership also spans a wide range from 0 to 38 years, with an average of 17 years. On the one hand, there are participants in the group who are novice drivers and on the other hand, there are participants who have been driving for decades.

Most drivers rated their parking skills with 5 or better, several with 10 and one with 2, resulting in an average of 7.3. Comparable with the parking skills, the IT skills were rated with an average of around 6.4. In contrast to the parking skills, more participants rated themselves with a value below 5, which leads to a balanced distribution within the range. In terms of age and driving experience, the participants form a relatively balanced group, while the self-assessed skills are mostly in the upper range.

Measurements. Based on the end position of the vehicle, we determine the average positioning error for each combination of visualization and screen. We calculate the average Euclidean distance symbolized by σ using Eq. 1:

$$\sigma = \frac{\sum_{i=1}^{n} \sqrt{(target_x - x_i)^2 + (target_z - z_i)^2}}{n} \tag{1}$$

The constants $target_x$ and $target_z$ represent the coordinates of the target position. The variables x and z represent the coordinates of the end position. Figure 4 illustrates the data which was actively collected during the study. For a shorter notation we define the following: (Screen)&(Visualization) with Screen = [S = Smartphone or M = Monitor] and Visualization = [B = Birds eye view or A = Arrow or R = Radar].

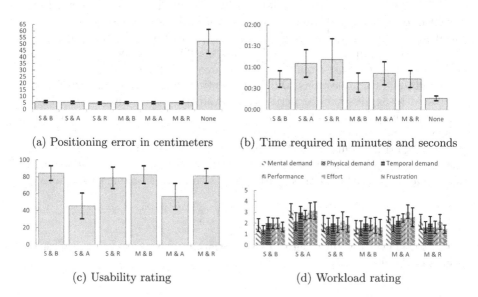

(a) Positioning error in centimeters   (b) Time required in minutes and seconds

(c) Usability rating   (d) Workload rating

Fig. 4. A visualization of the study results using bar charts for mean values and error bars representing the 95% confidence intervals.

5 Discussion

This section provides a discussion of the findings and observations made in the context of the user study.

5.1 Precision

Without utilizing a user interface for positioning, the error lies in a wide range around 50 cm. In contrast, the use of one of the user interfaces leads to a significantly higher precision with each having a similar positioning error of approximately 5 cm. Accordingly, positioning procedures assisted by the user interfaces are about a factor of 10 more precise than without assistance, while the precision requirement is fulfilled at the same time. In terms of precision, significant differences between the user interfaces were not discovered.

5.2 User Experience

In contrast to the findings made in the context of precision, differences arise in terms of user experience. Figure 4c indicates a high rating in terms of usability for bird's eye view visualization followed by radar visualization. In contrast, the arrow based visualization, was rated significantly less usable in comparison to the others. As observed with the usability rating, Fig. 4d indicates a comparable ranking in the context of workload. Especially arrow based visualization was rated with a higher workload than with the other modalities. During the study, participants should report their personal experiences and impressions. Most of the participants prefer to be supported by a bird's eye view visualization, since decisions on next positioning step can be reasoned freely based on the overview provided. As the results in Fig. 4c and 4d indicate, the arrow-based user interfaces are the most criticized. The problem arising from this representation is that exclusively the driving direction is provided and no information about the relative offset to the target is communicated. Many participants were unable to estimate the distance to the target and drove past it, causing the arrow to rotate in the opposite direction, which was perceived as confusing. Furthermore, the radar visualization was rated in a comparable way as the bird's eye view visualization, however some users required a period of time for familiarization to understand how the visualization works.

5.3 Time

Regarding the time required for positioning, Fig. 4b indicates that a time of less than 2 min can be achieved, which we consider to be suitable for every day use. However, the time required in the case of not utilizing a user interface for support is significantly less than in the other cases. This is caused by aborting positioning after a short period of time due to a lack of orientation. Without the support of a user interface, the participants were able to complete the positioning in just 1 out of 36 cases. Regardless of the visualization type, the average time required is consistently lower when utilizing a monitor. One reason for this result could be that we provided the participants with a smartphone, but no holder. Accordingly, most of the participants were not able to put the smartphones in a suitable location. However, three drivers were able to complete the task faster using the smartphone in at least 55% of their positioning attempts. These cases could indicate that the smartphone was in a suitable position in the vehicle. Comparing all visualization conditions, bird's eye view is the fastest regardless of the screen type.

5.4   Observations

At the beginning of the positioning task, some participants felt unsure, as this was the first time they had to position their vehicle with high accuracy. The average time required for each iteration indicates that uncertainty decreased when repeating the positioning since a learning and familiarization effect occurred. The first iteration took the participants an average of approximately 1 min, the second 50 s, and the third 40 s. Due to the measurement of time, some drivers felt compelled to perform well, but the measurement also unsettled others. In contrast to the smartphone screen, the stationary monitor is exposed to environmental conditions. Due to the problem that visualizations might be poorly visible caused by light reflections, we had to examine multiple angles for a suitable screen setup. To enable continuous operation of the outdoor screen setup, other influences such as rain and vandalism should be taken into account. In order to mitigate these environmental impacts, we have purchased a robust screen housing. Based on the experience gained in the user study, we conclude that a stationary monitor can only be used under certain conditions. Although the smartphone variant was rated to be more convenient, it was criticized for the fact that the device cannot be conveniently stored in every vehicle type. Such problems would not arise when displaying the visualization on screens that are integrated into the vehicle's dashboard. In order to improve the system, participants suggested that a combination of different visualizations could be helpful to benefit from the advantages of several visualization types. In addition, many participants mentioned that further information such as a numerical representation of the distance to the target should also be displayed. With regard to the sensing device, it was observed that the lidar occasionally produced inaccurate measurements. This effect occurred when the vehicle had reflective components such as chrome strips.

6   Conclusions

Wireless energy transfer for electric vehicles is conceived as a more convenient alternative to wired charging. For efficient wireless charging, the transmitter and receiver coil must be accurately aligned. Since charging components are often located under the vehicle, they are not visible to the driver, which makes precise alignment challenging. As part of our research, we provide a driver guidance system that supports the driver in fulfilling this task. Since in many cases the necessary positioning can only be carried out manually by the driver, a suitable user interface is required. Due to the novelty of this application context, there is a lack of experience in the design of such a user interface. In this paper, we try to identify a user interface for a driver guiding system that can support the driver to reach the required precision when positioning. Our system provides various visualization modalities, which we evaluated within a user study. A positioning scenario was simulated in which the study's participants should try to achieve a target precision using the system. The required precision could be achieved with all visualization modalities. However, the user experience differs significantly. The participants prefer a visualization from a bird's eye view, which gives an overview of the overall situation. In contrast, the participants were dissatisfied by using a visualization that presents an arrow pointing in the direction of the target position. The participants criticize that the spatial relationship between the current vehicle position and the target position is difficult to deduce. Moreover, the time to complete the task using the bird's eye view visualization took less than 44 s on average, which is probably shorter than parking and plugging in a charging cable. In contrast, an arrow-based visualization took in average up to 1.5 times longer than bird's eye view visualization to complete the task.

Although this paper focuses on stationary wireless charging, the user interfaces provided could be explored in the context of dynamic wireless charging. In addition to the driver guidance, the user interface could also send warning signals to the driver, to avoid collisions with objects in the surrounding.

Acknowledgment. This research was funded by the Bundesministerium für Wirtschaft und Energie as part of the TALAKO project (grant number 01MZ19002A).

References

1. Andersson, J., Nilsson, M., Pettersson, S.: Introducing wireless charging for drivers of electrical vehicles in Sweden-effects on charging behaviour and attitudes. In: Stanton, N., Landry, S., Di Bucchianico, G., Vallicelli, A. (eds.) Advances in Human Aspects of Transportation. Springer, Cham (2017). https://doi.org/10.1007/978-3-319-41682-3_78
2. Azad, A.N., Echols, A., Kulyukin, V.A., Zane, R., Pantic, Z.: Analysis, optimization, and demonstration of a vehicular detection system intended for dynamic wireless charging applications. IEEE Trans. Transp. Electrification 5(1), 147–161 (2019)
3. Birrell, S.A., Wilson, D., Yang, C.P., Dhadyalla, G., Jennings, P.: How driver behaviour and parking alignment affects inductive charging systems for electric vehicles. Transp. Res. Part C Emerg. Technol. 58, 721–731 (2015)
4. Brooke, J.: SUS: a 'quick and dirty' usability scale. Usability Eval. Ind. 189(194), 4–7 (1996)
5. Chen, S., Liao, C., Wang, L.: Research on positioning technique of wireless power transfer system for electric vehicles. In: ITEC Asia-Pacific (2014)

6. Doyon-Poulin, P., Ouellette, B., Robert, J.M.: Effects of visual clutter on pilot workload, flight performance and gaze pattern. In: Proceedings of the International Conference on Human-Computer Interaction in Aerospace (2014)
7. European Environment Agency: Electric vehicles from life cycle and circular economy perspectives no. 13/2018 (2018)
8. Gao, Y., Ginart, A., Farley, K.B., Tse, Z.T.H.: Misalignment effect on efficiency of wireless power transfer for electric vehicles. In: IEEE APEC (2016)
9. Gojak, V., Janjatovic, J., Vukota, N., Milosevic, M., Bjelica, M.Z.: Informational bird's eye view system for parking assistance. In: IEEE ICCE-Berlin (2017)
10. Hart, S.G.: Nasa-task load index (NASA-TLX); 20 years later. In: Proceedings of the Human Factors and Ergonomics Society Annual Meeting (2006)
11. Hudecek, J., Kufen, J., Langen, O., Dankert, J., Eckstein, L.: A system for precise positioning of vehicles aiming at increased inductive charging efficiency. In: IET Conference Proceedings (2014)
12. Karakitsios, I., et al.: An integrated approach for dynamic charging of electric vehicles by wireless power transfer - lessons learned from real-life implementation. SAE Int. J. Altern. Powertrains 6(1), 15–24 (2017)
13. Kobeissi, A.H., Bellotti, F., Berta, R., De Gloria, A.: IoT grid alignment assistant system for dynamic wireless charging of electric vehicles. In: IOTSMS (2018)
14. Laporte, S., Coquery, G., Deniau, V., De Bernardinis, A., Hautière, N.: Dynamic wireless power transfer charging infrastructure for future EVS: from experimental track to real circulated roads demonstrations. World Electric Vehicle J. 10(4), 84 (2019)
15. Loewel, T., Lange, C., Noack, F.: Identification and positioning system for inductive charging systems. In: EDPC (2013)
16. Mayer, H., Haustein, C., Matzarakis, A.: Urban air pollution caused by motor-traffic. Adv. Air Pollut. (1999)
17. Moacdieh, N., Prinet, J., Sarter, N.: Effects of modern primary flight display clutter. In: Proceedings of the Human Factors and Ergonomics Society Annual Meeting (2013)
18. Ni, W., et al.: Radio alignment for inductive charging of electric vehicles. IEEE Trans. Industr. Inform. 11(2), 427–440 (2015)
19. Shahbaz Nejad, B., Roch, P., Handte, M., Marrón, P.J.: A driver guidance system to support the stationary wireless charging of electric vehicles. In: Bebis, G., et al. (eds.) ISVC 2020. LNCS, vol. 12510, pp. 319–331. Springer, Cham (2020). https://doi.org/10.1007/978-3-030-64559-5_25
20. Tangmanee, K., Teeravarunyou, S.: Effects of guided arrows on head-up display towards the vehicle windshield. In: SEANES (2012)
21. The Khronos Group Inc.: OpenGL ES. www.khronos.org/opengles/. Accessed 13 Sept 2021
22. Thomas, B., Chithambaran, R., Picard, Y., Cougnard, C.: Development of a cost effective bird's eye view parking assistance system. In: IEEE Recent Advances in Intelligent Computational Systems (2011)
23. Tonnis, M., Sandor, C., Klinker, G., Lange, C., Bubb, H.: Experimental evaluation of an augmented reality visualization for directing a car driver's attention. In: IEEE ISMAR (2005)
24. Unity Technologies: Unity Engine. https://unity.com/. Accessed 12 Jan 2021
25. Wu, H.H., Gilchrist, A., Sealy, K., Israelsen, P., Muhs, J.: A review on inductive charging for electric vehicles. In: IEEE IEMDC (2011)

MOBA Coach: Exploring and Analyzing Multiplayer Online Battle Arena Data

Robin Horst[✉], Micha Lanvers, László von Kacsoh, and Ralf Dörner

RheinMain University of Applied Sciences, Wiesbaden, Germany
{Robin.Horst,Ralf.Doerner}@hs-rm.de
{Micha.Lanvers,Laszlo.Kacsoh}@student.hs-rm.de

Abstract. Multiplayer online battle arena (MOBA) games such as League of Legends (LoL) belong to the most played competitive game genres. This genre also represents a significant part of the electronic sports (e-sports) domain. MOBA e-sports events enjoy growing popularity in recent years, for example, concerning the number of spectating fans and cash prizes for e-sports teams within the range of several million dollars for single tournaments. This is also a reason for the growing demand for professional training methodologies in this developing area. In this paper, we introduce *MOBA Coach*, an information visualization tool that enables e-sports coaches to analyze past matches and includes functionality for performing coaching activities, such as discussing tactics with a team. We describe the concepts of MOBA Coach and demonstrate its advantages implementing it in the example of LoL data. We conducted an expert user study with eight professional coaches and players among the top 10.632% of the world's competitive LoL players to evaluate our tool. Based on statistically significant measures, we conclude that our participants could use MOBA Coach successfully to analyze MOBA matches and we elaborate on the suitability of different views we provide on the match data. Furthermore, we could point out that MOBA Coach has the potential to add value to the MOBA coaching toolchain.

Keywords: Data visualization · Multiplayer online battle arena · League of legends · E-Sports

1 Introduction

Compared to traditional competitive sports such as soccer, electronic sports (e-sports) is a relatively young but yet rapidly growing field [22]. One of the most popular e-sports genres are multiplayer online battle arena (MOBA) games [20], with League of Legends (LoL) as one of its most successful representatives measured by its number of players and highly remunerated tournaments.

The work is supported by the Federal Ministry of Education and Research of Germany in the project Innovative Hochschule (funding number: 03IHS071).

G. Bebis et al. (Eds.): ISVC 2021, LNCS 13017, pp. 197–209, 2021.
https://doi.org/10.1007/978-3-030-90439-5_16

Overall, MOBA games include a vast amount of variables and complex game mechanics to consider when developing novel tactics to outplay the opposing team. Hence, like in traditional competitive team sports, professional e-sports teams also have coaches [10] who plan training activities for the e-sports athletes (e-athletes). These training sessions include tactics discussions and match preparations and constitutes a significant part of the e-athletes' training [8,10]. E-sports data is similar to traditional tempo-spatial sports data, but can contain very different variables, for example, character skill trees, bought items, class distinction etc.

In this paper, we make the following contributions:

- We investigate the interactive information visualization of MOBA match data and propose *MOBA Coach* – a software tool that provides different views on MOBA match data as well as functionalities to be used during coaching activities with the team. We describe its design and introduce different concepts and views on the data in the example of LoL match data.
- Based on the results of an expert user study with eight professional coaches and players among the 10.632% best competitive LoL players of the current Season 11, we evaluate our tool, state lessons learned that should be incorporated in the future design of MOBA match analysis tools, and draw conclusions based on a statistical analysis.

The paper is organized as follows. We briefly review related work in the next section. Then, we present MOBA Coach's design and analysis concepts. In Sect. 4, we report our tool's evaluation and discuss the findings from our user study. Finally, we conclude our work and point out future directions.

2   Related Work

E-sports coaches, similar to traditional sports coaches, analyse past matches of their own and opposing teams on aspects such as individual abilities of players and the players' habits (e.g., positioning, communication, etc.) [21]. A study by Deja and Mateusz [3] emphasizes the impact of coaching methodologies within e-sports and describes it as crucial for the outcome of a match. Concerning the training of e-athletes, various methodologies and types of training are involved. Besides practical training targeting the game mechanics (e.g., actually playing the game), e-sports training also includes theory sessions where mentioned tactics discussions are performed [8] but also sessions that target the physical [12] and mental health of the e-athletes [19]. Within theory sessions, a common task is reviewing matches together with the e-athletes and drawing onto a mini-map visualization [6] illustrate ideas.

Regarding the analysis of e-sports and particularly MOBA matches, there exists various work that deals with the identification of indicators that are essential for winning a match. Work by Nascimento Junior et al. [15] analyzed LoL team behaviors based on data provided by the Riot Games API. They used machine learning and statistical analysis for clustering match data of different teams and examining features with a particularly high impact on a team's win or loss. Features they classified as highly influential on the outcome of a match were the number of champion deaths of a team, the number of killing sprees, and how many neutral monsters were killed in the enemy jungle area. Furthermore, aspects such as how many minions and neutral minions were killed, how many wards were placed, and the total amount of healing provided by the players were considered influential as well. Consequently, we derive the recommendation that a tool for match analysts should make these aspects easily accessible.

Work by Novak et al. [16] also investigates variables with a statistical impact on a team's victory. Their work relies on a performance analysis, in which three professional LoL coaches made pre-selections of variables using a Likert scale based on their experience. Then, the observed 14 variables were tested using a generalized linear mixed model with a binomial logit link function. Novak et al. [16] indicated that the percentage of towers that were destroyed during the game and the number of inhibitors taken have a high impact on a match's outcome. This information should also be easy to discover in an analysis tool.

Eaton et al. [5] investigate the effect of *critical team members* on a LoL team's match performance. They define a critical team member as a member of a team 'whose presence (or absence) can have a dramatic impact' on the team's performance in a match and consequently on the team's chances to win. The work particularly explored the importance of the *carry* role of a team. Eaton et al. [5] conclude that while one team's carry is dead, statistically critical game events such as tower kills and elite monster kills accumulate in favor of the other team, giving them a considerable advantage. This suggests that coaches are interested in quickly figuring out these moments of a game and then explaining to their team how the death of a critical team member might have been prevented. Another study investigating in the individual players' contribution to a team's performance was conducted by Maymin [13]. The study concluded that it is not possible to generalize which individual actions of players are directly related to their team's victory. These must be considered in the specific context they were performed, for example, to determine meaningful kills and meaningless deaths, which then can be discussed by a coach.

There also exists work about MOBA match analysis tools. Afonso, Carmo, and Moucho [1] present *VisuaLeague II* – a tool that supports coaches in analyzing LoL match data using animated maps. In a comparative user study, they compared VisuaLeague II to the in-game replay viewer and *OP.GG* [17]. The in-game viewer enables users to watch past matches and also visualizes different match events. However, performing analyses with this tool can be time-consuming, and users can only review their own matches. OP.GG is an online tool representing various statistical match data from different e-sports games in charts or tabular forms. Previous studies did emphasize that generic chart representation provided by such online tools do not exploit the full potential of the match data and should be aligned with the needs of target audiences such as coaches [2,11]. The study of Afonso, Carmo, and Moucho [1] indicated that the participants liked the overall spatio-temporal data presentation on a visual map, however, the participants also noted the absence of further statistical data representation that OP.GG provides. This indicates that a LoL match analysis tool should include both traditional information visualization techniques, for example, for gold, items, and kills, as well as map visualization techniques for the spatio-temporal data of a LoL match, such as a player's positioning.

Finally, our literature research shows that some of the mentioned work [1,9] and also further applications and approaches [2,4,24] already provide analysis tools that include map- or graph-based visualizations. However, most are not intended to be used by coaches and thus do not consider specific needs of coaches that may arise when using such tools in tactics discussions with the team after initial analysis approaches (e.g., drawing on the mini-map during discussions [6], or adjusting a player's or a ward's current position to a different and hypothetical one). Furthermore, most studies we mentioned lack evaluations involving experts such as coaches or e-athletes to investigate how such a MOBA analysis tool for coaches should be designed. Previous work suggests that such tools for coaches need interactive map-based visualizations (for both analysis and discussion purposes), chart visualizations, as well as access to tabular data representations to analyze the specific aspects we identified (e.g., percentage of towers [16], number of inhibitors taken [16], number of champion deaths of a team [15], the number of killing sprees [15], how many neutral monsters were killed in the enemy jungle area [15], etc.).

3   MOBA Coach Tool

The user interface (UI) of our tool consists of six views.

View 1 – Overview: After selecting the desired game (in our case LoL) and match to be analyzed, users find themselves in the *overview*. This view gives users some high-level information about the match at a glance and gives a rough overview to start the analysis. For example, it is shown which team has won, the total number of a team's gold, and kills, as well as the number of minions and champions killed for each player.

View 2 – Tactics View: The *tactics view* (Fig. 1) offers users both analysis- and coaching-relevant functionalities. Overall, the tactics view provides a view on the match data at one specific point in time. It shows a mini-map in the center, illustrating icons of champions, towers, elite monsters, etc., on it in the state it had at the selected time of the match. The towers and the borders of the champions visualize the team affiliation either in red or blue. If a character or elite monster is currently dead or a tower is destroyed, the icon is shown semi-transparently. The slider below the mini-map is used to select the desired time of the match. However, we utilized the official Riot API to obtain the match data, which only provides one-minute intervals. Upon switching the time on the slider, the icons on the mini-map are positioned accordingly.

The buttons above the mini-map allow users that are not only interested in the analysis but also in coaching a team functionalities to support such tasks. The

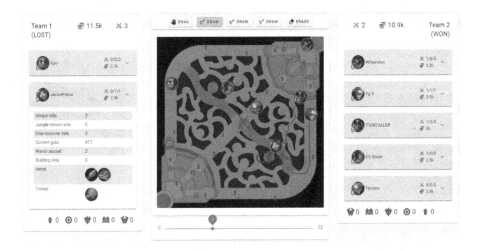

Fig. 1. A screenshot of MOBA Coach's tactics view. A tactics discussion is currently prepared/conducted using drawing and player repositioning.

first button activates the *move mode*, allowing users to reposition icons on the map, such as the champions or elite monsters. This feature can be used to better explain certain contexts to the team. The next three buttons switch modes to the *drawing mode* – each allowing to draw on the map in a different color indicating the team affiliation: red (opponents), green (neutrals), or blue (own team). The drawing functionality allows coaches to visualize alternative movement routes, highlight certain positions, and visualize tactics decisions during discussions.

Finally, information on the sides of the mini-map shows information about the individual champions at the chosen time and allows getting an overview of the data at a glance. For example, this includes the current level, kills, deaths, assists, and gold. Additional information can be obtained on demand by clicking on a champion and unfolding the panel (Fig. 1 left). The view can be adjusted by deselecting certain champions, whose information then is displayed transparently on the mini-map and whose panels are hidden until reselected again.

View 3 – Statistics View: The *statistics view* (Fig. 2) provides users with both underlying tabular data and visualizations concerning 13 relevant aspects such as how many neutral monsters were killed in the enemy jungle area [15], or the number of inhibitors taken over the match's course [16]. Again, champions can be deselected to hide their data in the tables and graphs. Furthermore, brushing and linking is utilized when users select more than one aspect they want to analyze. Multiple graphs are displayed highlighting the selected data. Besides brushing and linking graphs on the statistics view, we also use the currently selected information to choose corresponding data within the tactics page so that users may switch back and forth between the views without interrupting the analysis flow due to synchronizing selected information manually.

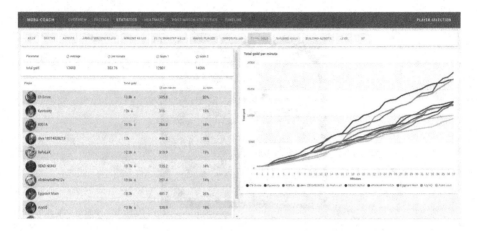

Fig. 2. A screenshot of MOBA Coach's statistics view.

View 4 – Post-match Statistics View: Within the *post-match statistics view*, detailed statistics about the outcome of a match are presented. Tabular data is initially ordered using a prioritization based on our findings from Sect. 2, however, it might be reordered during analysis based on the analysis goal. Salient information such as the highest and lowest values in each row are highlighted. Besides comparing data of single champions, users can choose to compare the entire teams instead, showing aggregated data.

View 5 – Heat Map View: The *heat map view* (Fig. 3) offers users heat map visualizations based on three different tempo-spatial aspects – the movement of selected champions, kills, and death. For example, this visualization can help analyzing in which area of the map a team or an individual player was most active, such as in which area a jungle champion type was performing throughout the match. In the example of kills and death, users can investigate which lane a team or certain champions died particularly often or in which areas a champion was particularly strong.

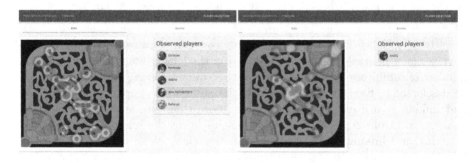

Fig. 3. A screenshot of MOBA Coach's heat map view with an entire team selected (left) and a single champion (right).

View 6 – Timeline View: Finally, the *timeline view* provides users with an overview of specific match events that are displayed in chronological order. The data can be filtered by event types, for example, when users have gotten some assumptions during the analysis process they want to consolidate. We also provide different types of filter groups that combine multiple events. For example, the *wards* filter we provide includes both the events for wards being placed and wards being destroyed. Furthermore, information such as the first kill of the match, elite monsters slain, or the first tower kill are displayed additionally at the specific events to support users in finding particular important key moments of the match and related them to the events. Again, linking and brushing is used across the views so that an event selected in the timeline view will also be shown within the other views if applicable.

4   Evaluation

We evaluated MOBA Coach within an expert user study that involved eight unpaid and voluntary participants between 19 and 27 years with Ø 22.63 and SD 3.42. We classify them as expert users for our tool by means of their official LoL competitive rank (platinum or higher, belonging at least to the top ~10% of the world's LoL players) or currently coaching professionally (six coaches). The user study was conducted as a moderated remote study.

We introduced them to the UI of the tool and the process of the evaluation. Then our participants were asked to perform eight tasks with the tool, such as familiarizing with the tool for some minutes, searching for a LoL replay through the interface of our tool, loading and analyzing it, drawing conclusions on tactical aspects that could be derived with the tool, and preparing a tactics discussion for a team session. Finally, we asked our participants to fill out a questionnaire. We evaluated four aspects with this questionnaire:

[A1] *Effectiveness:* How well could the participants solve analysis tasks with our tool?

[A2] *Analysis ability:* How well does our tool support analysts to conduct analyses based on the provided functionalities and information scope?

[A3] *Coaching specifics:* How well does our tool comply with requirements concerning a team's coaching, such as tactics development and discussions?

[A4] *Product character:* The product character [7] is a measure incorporating both pragmatic and hedonic qualities.

Relating to the product character (A4), we utilized the AttrakDiff questionnaire items [23] as an established tool for measuring it. Aspects 1–3 were captured with 14 questions Q1–Q14, based on a 7-point semantic differential scale. Finally, open questions and free space for suggestions such as written comments and demographic questions concluded the questionnaire. A single session of the study was performed within a roughly one hour timeframe.

4.1   Analysis of the Results

Figure 4 represents the value distributions of the single items and aspects that were answered on the 7-point scale. The box-whisker plots show that all mean values lie above the scale's neutral value (3) except Q10. We conducted Wilcoxon signed-rank tests on the individual items to analyze how MOBA Coach was rated by our participants compared to a neutral rating. With a threshold for statistical significance of 5%, the tests for Q1, Q2, Q3, Q4, Q5, Q6, Q7, Q12, Q13, Q14, A1, A2, and A3 did confirm significant differences (Table 1).

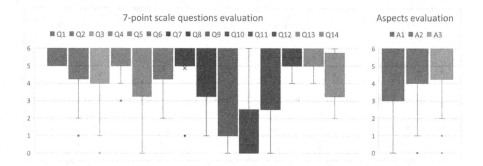

Fig. 4. Descriptive statistics of our study results.

Our participants' written comments, their oral statements during the study, and our observations were used to capture additional information and were clustered and assigned to A1–A3. Concerning A1, we noticed some suggestions regarding the usability of our tool. For example, multiple participants mentioned that the graphs and charts displayed in the statistics view were unclear due to the line coloring and size. Two third of the participants had problems selecting single champions filter the graphs' data. Furthermore, one participant noted that he has dyslexia and would prefer a graphical display of all information instead of textual table representations of raw data such as the listing of events in the timeline view. Overall, we noticed that our participants could successfully fulfill all tasks, and they stated that finding the requested information was easy.

Concerning A2, four participants were enthusiastic about the usefulness of the heat maps view and stated they found it helpful. The remaining four (all coaches) mentioned the heat map view critically, particularly due to the one-minute interval that was chosen due to the Riot API data restrictions. They noted that one-minute intervals might not be meaningful enough. Furthermore, our participants suggested providing a slider to select a limited time interval instead of using the entire match data for generating heat maps. A minimum interval of five to ten seconds between data points was suggested, but an interval of one second would be even better. All participants indicated that the ability to take into account the team roles (e.g., supporter, damage-dealer, and tank) within the table representation of player-specific data. For example, a supporter

Table 1. Mean values, SD, and output of the Wilcoxon signed-rank tests.

Questions/aspects	Associated aspect	Ø-values	SD	P-values
Q1	Effectiveness (A1)	5.3750	0.5175	$p = 0.0078$
Q2	Coaching (A3)	4.6563	1.4943	$p \leq 0.0001$
Q3	Analysis ability (A2)	4.5000	1.5027	$p = 0.0002$
Q4	Analysis ability (A2)	5.2188	0.8322	$p \leq 0.0001$
Q5	Analysis ability (A2)	4.0938	1.7845	$p = 0.0048$
Q6	Analysis ability (A2)	4.8125	1.2297	$p \leq 0.0001$
Q7	Coaching (A3)	4.8750	1.6421	$p = 0.0391$
Q8	Effectiveness (A1)	4.5000	1.7728	$p = 0.0781$
Q9	Effectiveness (A1)	3.7500	2.6592	$p = 0.3828$
Q10	Effectiveness (A1)	1.3750	2.1339	$p = 0.1563$
Q11	Coaching (A3)	4.3750	2.2638	$p = 0.1484$
Q12	Analysis ability (A2)	5.3750	0.7440	$p = 0.0078$
Q13	Effectiveness (A1)	5.5000	0.7559	$p = 0.0078$
Q14	Effectiveness (A1)	4.5000	1.4142	$p = 0.0313$
A1	Effectiveness	4.1667	2.1371	$p = 0.0019$
A2	Analysis ability	4.6985	1.4054	$p \leq 0.0001$
A3	Coaching	4.6458	1.6307	$p \leq 0.0001$

having only a few or no kills is not necessarily bad since it is in the spirit of this role to leave kills to the damage-dealers. It was also suggested that not only data from one match but cross-match data for roles, champions, and specific players could be used as reference values to put the current match data into perspective. Finally, highlighting the highest and lowest entries in our tabular representations were mentioned positively.

Concerning A3, the coaching suitability, all of our participants indicated that they would use MOBA coach for coaching activities. However, only half of them stated to be willing to use our tool exclusively. These four participants also listed tools they would use in the same coaching toolchain with our tool, which were METAscrc [14] (for data aggregation), OP.GG [17] (for player and team scouting), PentaQ BP [18] (for drafting analysis), in-game replay and statistics functionality (for video replay and ad-hoc analysis with the team), and a more sophisticated drawing tool (for scribbling on the map indicating alternative movements and pathways). One of the participants noted that MOBA coach would fit in well in his current coaching toolchain and could use MOBA coach auxiliary to his current tools, not for the analysis functionalities but specifically for filling gaps concerning teaching purposes, for example, within tactics discussions with the team.

We analyzed the items from the AttrakDiff questionnaire concerning the product character of MOBA Coach (A4). The aspects constituting the product character [7] (pragmatic quality, hedonic quality, and attractiveness) are visualized in Fig. 5. It shows that MOBA Coach was awarded higher values than the AttrkDiff's neutral value in the mean. The attractiveness was rated most optimistic of the three aspects, whereas the practical quality of MOBA coach was rated lowest.

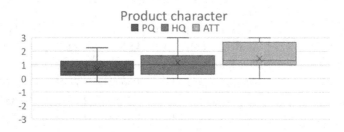

Fig. 5. Box-whisker plots depicting the AttrakDiff item results aggregated to the three aspects that the product character [7] consists of (pragmatic qualities (PQ), hedonic qualities (HQ), and overall attractiveness (ATT)).

4.2 Discussion of the Results

The evaluation results show that professional e-sports coaches and players could successfully use MOBA Coach to analyze LoL matches and prepare tactics discussions. The effectiveness (A1) was rated generally very positive, and by means of statistical significance, also more effective than the average MOBA match analysis tool. However, the mixed ratings regarding Q9 and Q10 that asked the participants about the usefulness of brushing and linking techniques and the one-minute time interval indicate that some adjustments for these aspects could be improved. Brushing and linking across the different views were criticized and should be visualized more clearly within the MOBA Coach's UI. However, supplemental temporal data points cannot easily be interpolated. Still, alternative data sources could be incorporated, or novel data generation techniques for MOBA matches, for example, data generated by the combination of computer vision, dynamic client hooks, machine learning, and cloud computing techniques as proposed by Maymin [13], might improve the tool and solve this issue partially.

The mentioned one-minute restriction was also mentioned concerning the analysis ability (A2). However, the results show that this aspect was attributed with a significantly higher analysis ability than average MOBA analysis tools. The significantly positive results for each of the respective questions support this claim. Still, specific aspects of improvement were pointed out as well. For example, the results emphasize that our tool is rather used as one particular tool within the analysis toolchain that fills the gap preparing and conducting tactics sessions than as an all-encompassing one.

Similar conclusions are also supported by our study results concerning the coaching specifics (A3). Our participants suggested that the coaching functionalities provided on the tactics view are well suitable for preparing and supporting tactics discussions with the team, however, that auxiliary tools might be needed. The significantly positive results support the overall suitability to aid coaching activities. One particular aspect that might be improved is the ability to replay matches from a player's view, as provided by the in-game replay tool.

The results also show that the aspects concerning the product character (A4) were rated positively by our participants. However, several minor improvements of the UI's usability that we pointed out are also reflected in the comparably low pragmatic qualities. The product character-related results also suggest improving the visual attractiveness of the UI.

5   Conclusion and Future Work

In this paper, we investigated in an information visualization tool that enables e-sports coaches to analyze past MOBA matches and includes aspects intended for coaching activities such as preparing and conducting tactics discussions with a team. We described the concepts including tactics preparations and the implementation of our tool in the example of LoL data. The tool was evaluated within user study with professional coaches and highly renowned players. A general finding of our work that should be considered in future research is that coaching functionalities can and should be included within eSports analysis tools, and that professional coaches assessed such a combination particularly useful.

Future work should consider the lessons learned presented within the implementation and evaluation section to design future MOBA analysis and particularly coaching tools. In the related work section, we already mentioned work (e.g., [13]) that investigates different techniques to generate data based on recorded videos or in-game replays. Based on our work's conclusions, this is considered a valuable effort and would make e-sports analysis and coaching tools less dependent on the official APIs and contributes to self-contained software design of such tools and processes.

References

1. Afonso, A.P., Carmo, M.B., Moucho, T.: Comparison of visualization tools for matches analysis of a MOBA game. In: 2019 23rd International Conference Information Visualisation (IV), pp. 118–126. IEEE (2019)
2. Bowman, B., Elmqvist, N., Jankun-Kelly, T.: Toward visualization for games: theory, design space, and patterns. IEEE Trans. Vis. Comput. Graph. **18**(11), 1956–1968 (2012)
3. Deja, D., Myślak, M.: Topological clues for predicting outcomes of multiplayer online battle arena games. In: IADIS International Conference Interfaces and Human Computer Interaction (2015)

4. Drachen, A., Schubert, M.: Spatial game analytics. In: Seif El-Nasr, M., Drachen, A., Canossa, A. (eds.) Game Analytics, pp. 365–402. Springer, London (2013). https://doi.org/10.1007/978-1-4471-4769-5_17

5. Eaton, J.A., Sangster, M.D.D., Renaud, M., Mendonca, D.J., Gray, W.D.: Carrying the team: the importance of one player's survival for team success in league of legends. In: Proceedings of the Human Factors and Ergonomics Society Annual Meeting, vol. 61, pp. 272–276. SAGE Publications Sage CA: Los Angeles (2017)

6. Fanfarelli, J.R.: Expertise in professional overwatch play. Int. J. Gaming Comput.-Mediated Simul. (IJGCMS) 10(1), 1–22 (2018)

7. Hassenzahl, M.: The thing and I: understanding the relationship between user and product. In: Blythe, M., Monk, A. (eds.) Funology 2. HIS, pp. 301–313. Springer, Cham (2018). https://doi.org/10.1007/978-3-319-68213-6_19

8. Kari, T., Karhulahti, V.M.: Do e-athletes move?: a study on training and physical exercise in elite e-sports. Int. J. Gaming Comput.-Mediated Simul. (IJGCMS) 8(4), 53–66 (2016)

9. Li, Q., et al.: A visual analytics approach for understanding reasons behind snowballing and comeback in MOBA games. IEEE Trans. Vis. Comput. Graph. 23(1), 211–220 (2016)

10. Lipovaya, V., Lima, Y., Grillo, P., Barbosa, C.E., de Souza, J.M., Duarte, F.J.d.C.M.: Coordination, communication, and competition in eSports: a comparative analysis of teams in two action games. In: Proceedings of 16th European Conference on Computer-Supported Cooperative Work-Exploratory Papers. European Society for Socially Embedded Technologies (EUSSET) (2018)

11. Loh, C.S., Sheng, Y., Ifenthaler, D.: Serious games analytics: theoretical framework. In: Loh, C.S., Sheng, Y., Ifenthaler, D. (eds.) Serious Games Analytics. AGL, pp. 3–29. Springer, Cham (2015). https://doi.org/10.1007/978-3-319-05834-4_1

12. Martin-Niedecken, A.L., Schättin, A.: Let the body'n'brain games begin: toward innovative training approaches in eSports athletes. Front. Psychol. 11, 138 (2020)

13. Maymin, P.Z.: Smart kills and worthless deaths: eSports analytics for league of legends. J. Quant. Anal. Sports 1(ahead-of-print), 11–27 (2020)

14. METAsrc: Metasrc (2021). https://www.metasrc.com/5v5. Accessed 28 Oct 2021. 18:17:02

15. Nascimento Junior, F.F.d., Melo, A.S.d.C., da Costa, I.B., Marinho, L.B.: Profiling successful team behaviors in league of legends. In: Proceedings of the 23rd Brazillian Symposium on Multimedia and the Web, pp. 261–268 (2017)

16. Novak, A.R., Bennett, K.J., Pluss, M.A., Fransen, J.: Performance analysis in eSports: modelling performance at the 2018 league of legends world championship. Int. J. Sports Sci. Coaching 15(5–6), 809–817 (2020)

17. OP.GG: Op.gg online e-sports analysis (2021). https://euw.op.gg/. Accessed 28 Oct 2021. 18:17:02

18. PentaQ BP: Pentaq BP (2021). https://data.pentaq.com/BP. Accessed 28 Oct 2021. 18:17:02

19. Reer, F., Krämer, N.C.: Psychological need satisfaction and well-being in first-person shooter clans: Investigating underlying factors. Comput. Hum. Behav. 84, 383–391 (2018)

20. Smithies, T.D., Toth, A.J., Conroy, E., Ramsbottom, N., Kowal, M., Campbell, M.J.: Life after eSports: a grand field challenge. Front. Psychol. 11, 883 (2020)

21. Snavely, T.L.: History and analysis of eSport systems. Ph.D. thesis, University of Texas at Austin (2014)

22. Sylvester, R., Rennie, P.: The world's fastest-growing sport: maximizing the economic success of esports whilst balancing regulatory concerns and ensuring the protection of those involved. Gaming Law Rev. **21**(8), 625–629 (2017)
23. User Interface Design GmbH: Attrakdiff questionnaire (2021). http://attrakdiff. de/index-en.html. Accessed 28 Oct 2021. 18:17:02
24. Wallner, G., Kriglstein, S.: Visualization-based analysis of gameplay data-a review of literature. Entertainment Comput. **4**(3), 143–155 (2013)

JobNet: 2D and 3D Visualization for Temporal and Structural Association in High-Performance Computing System

Ngan V. T. Nguyen[1]([⊠]) [iD], Huyen N. Nguyen[1] [iD], Jon Hass[2],
and Tommy Dang[1] [iD]

[1] Texas Tech University, Lubbock, TX, USA
Ngan.V.T.Nguyen@ttu.edu
[2] Dell Inc., Austin, TX, USA

Abstract. Performance monitoring in a High-Performance Computing (HPC) system is an essential and challenging task. With a large number of system components, coupled with health metrics that need to be reported, visualizing the system's internal structure over time will uncover patterns and enable insights, empowering analysis from monitoring. This paper presents a visualization tool that visualizes the temporal and structural association of HPC system components using a force-directed graph layout algorithm. The visualization contains 2D and 3D representation, supporting a complete analysis of the compute usage, how users and job submission are interconnected throughout the observational interval. Design alternatives for time representation are discussed and depicted in 2D and 3D visualization encodings, with animation and exclusive presentation. The interaction capabilities of the tool assist visual exploration of health metrics and changes in system status over time. The tool's usefulness and effectiveness in the monitoring task are demonstrated by a case study on a real-world HPC dataset.

Keywords: HPC monitoring · Force-directed layout · 2D and 3D visualization

1 Introduction

High-Performance Computing (HPC) supercharges innovative technologies to empower complex computation and deliver data insights with quick and accurate results. The innovations in the HPC system encompass the advancement in system components and simultaneously increases the complexity, making the monitoring task of such elements more demanding and challenging. It is important for the system administrators to inspect the system components and their structural association with their corresponding elements for the purpose of monitoring and analysis. For example, to examine the performance of a job running on a compute server, there needs to be put in the context of who is the user submitting that job, the status of health metric indicators at the time, what

© Springer Nature Switzerland AG 2021
G. Bebis et al. (Eds.): ISVC 2021, LNCS 13017, pp. 210–221, 2021.
https://doi.org/10.1007/978-3-030-90439-5_17

kind of job that node is running, whether it is data-intensive, memory-intensive or other usage behavior category.

Graph visualizations are commonly used to present the complex relationship structure between internal components inside a system. One of the most well-known visualization techniques for visualizing node-link-based structure is force-directed layout [4]. The principle behind force-directed approaches lies in node positioning so that all edges are of approximately equal length and maintain minimum edge crossings as possible [7]. The equilibrium state is achieved by considering forces within the layout simulated as a physical system such that the edges are springs and the nodes are electrically charged particles.

Our objective is to show how interactive visualization can demonstrate the dynamic characteristic of temporal and structural association within the HPC system. We propose a new visualization metaphor in 2D and 3D for monitoring HPC system components. Our method is based on force-directed layout, applied for both the 2D and 3D views, which allows the representation of multiple servers, jobs, and users in the same view. In the 2D visualization, the animation is incorporated to foster an interactive interface, showing the temporal shifts in server usages. The new visualization metaphor in the 3D interface depicts the evolution over time for the entire observation period, accompanied by efficient use of screen space without cluttering the view. Finally, we validate this approach and demonstrate its usefulness by conducting a case study on a real-world HPC monitoring dataset. The contribution of this work can be laid out as follows:

- An interactive visualization for monitoring the temporal and structural association of HPC system components, called *JobNet*, which:
  - employs force-directed layout for visualizing multiple compute servers, jobs, and users in the same view
  - provides a 2D visualization showing dynamic characteristics of the network made of servers over time
  - presents a 3D representation of the entire observation period with emphasis on the temporal evolution
- Demonstration of the approach by applying it to a dataset acquired from a real-world HPC center. The tool is also applied to a movie dataset to examine its applicability.

The rest of this paper is organized as follows: Sect. 2 summarizes existing work that is close to our paper. Section 3 describes the domain problem leading to design rationale and decisions. Section 4 shows the findings through case studies with the real HPC data for the 2D and 3D visualization, along with a movie dataset. Section 5 concludes our paper with outlook for future work direction.

2   Related Work

In HPC monitoring, visualization has presented as an intuitive approach for the representation of vast volumes of data, seeking to analyze and explore it for insights. In a vision for next-generation monitoring infrastructure, Sanchez et al. [17] presents that visualization helps to monitor computing nodes to support a variety of tasks with parallel log and data collection, assisting multiple sources for data correlation and management, conducting analysis over time. Grafana [5] is an open-source analytics and monitoring solution commonly used for HPC systems. Built upon Grafana, Schwaller et al. [18] incorporate analysis-driven visualizations in an HPC system data pipeline, where the results of analyses and HPC-oriented summaries are presented in the Grafana front-end interface.

Regarding monitoring tools, Ganglia [10] is a scalable, distributed monitoring tool for high-performance computing systems and compute grids, such as the cluster of web servers. RRDtool [14] serves as a back-end database to Ganglia, which can be applied for off-system analysis and visualization. Nguyen and Dang [13] propose an interactive visual interface for real-time monitoring the health status of HPC systems, emphasizing on detection of abnormal events and their temporal and spatial correlations. Visualization can serve as the fourth and final stage, along with Collection, Storage and Analysis in PIKA, monitoring infrastructure proposed by Dietrich et al. [3], where recorded metadata and time-series data can be visualized at runtime or post-mortem, and data can then be stored for further long-term analysis.

Graph-based approaches in visualization have been used in monitoring HPC performance in previous literature. Haridasan and Pfitscher [6] propose an approach for cluster monitoring with graphical visualization for performance analysis of MPI applications, where the edition of vertices and edges represents tasks and communication. The tasks contain information associated such as rank, execution time, a path of the corresponding executable file, and the machine responsible for the execution, which is relatively similar to our approach. Event flow graphs are proved by Aguilar et al. [1] to use less storage reduction than regular event traces and allows the full ordered sequence of events performed by the application to be recovered. When the demands of monitoring require multiple monitors in a single virtual display, a graph-based approach is adapted [8] where graph viewers can be easily enhanced so that they can operate on virtual reality-enabled multi-monitor environments.

The principle of node positioning and the resulting flexibility in force-directed layout lead to its application in monitoring. Mansman et al. [9] present a visual analytics tool that visualizes network host behavior through positional changes in a two-dimensional space for a large dataset, using a force-directed graph layout algorithm. Upon the infrastructure of the cloud computing platform CLAVIRE, Zagarskikh et al. [23] presents a visualization provision tool for resource visualization, based on a modified force-directed layout to produce new force balance and geographical coordinates. Also incorporated with geo-location, this layout algorithm is used for community detection for situational analytics [12]. Cryptocurrency system is one of the emerging fields recently, resulting in the surveillance of the mining pools playing an essential role in such system. Xia et al. [22] incorporate the force-directed algorithm in providing interactions in a dynamic network for cross-view analysis and identity marking in mining pool surveillance. In recent research, TRACER, a tool for visual exploration of network topology with 3D force-directed layout proposed by Tretyakov et al. [20], is applied to CERN computing infrastructure and can be deployed in near real-time network monitoring.

While graphs have previously been applied to monitoring tasks, the force-directed layout has limited use and has been unexplored in HPC monitoring. The novelty of our approach lies in its objective to make use of the flexibility of the force-directed algorithm in demonstrating the dynamic characteristics in the temporal and structural association among HPC system components. In this paper, we develop 2D and 3D visualization to better depict the internal structure and changes in topology over time. At the same time, user interaction facilitates in-depth analysis and supports details-on-demand through visual exploration.

3   Design and Implementation

3.1   Terms and Definitions

In this section, we define terms that are related to the structural components inside the HPC system [2]. These components and their associations, reflecting the data structure, are presented as visual elements in the visualization of *Job-Net*.

Cluster: The top-level organizational unit of an HPC cluster, comprising a set of nodes, a queue, and jobs.

Node: A single, named host (compute server) in the cluster.

Task: The execution of a user application.

Job: A resource request that is submitted for execution that contains one or more tasks. One job can run on one or more nodes.

Queue: A list of jobs that have been submitted to the service to be run by the cluster. A set of scheduling policies determines the order in which to run jobs from the queue.

User: An entity that submits a job for execution. A user is associated with a set of a running job at a particular time point.

3.2   Design Rationale

Visualizing Structural Association. Monitoring the HPC system can be formulated as observational tasks and ultimately decision making on the temporal changes on the HPC system components. The dynamic nature of such structures as a network of users, jobs, compute nodes, and their associations can make the monitoring task more complex.

The basic building blocks, represented by the leaves in the graph, are the compute servers, also known as computing nodes. Each of these nodes is associated with the job that executes on it, where one job can have multiple nodes running simultaneously, and one compute server can run one or more jobs simultaneously. In a similar idea, each job is associated with the user submitting it; while one user can submit multiple jobs, each job only belongs to one user. At a particular time point, a job can release the node after finishing, start or continue using a node.

Our design decisions are based on the visual information mantra by Shneiderman [19]: Overview first, zoom and filter, then details-on-demand. *JobNet* applies force-directed layout to demonstrate the aforementioned structural association between compute servers, jobs, and users. This design concept is applied for both 2D and 3D versions. The dynamic characteristics of this structure, or the network topology changes over time, are described in the next section.

To assist the task of performance monitoring, *JobNet* users can investigate every indicator within the health metrics, including CPU temperatures (of main processing unit CPU1 and supporting unit CPU2), Inlet temperature, Fan speed (per each of four fans for dissipating heated air away from the components), and Power consumption. The color scale is consistent across all health metrics, ranging from the corresponding minimum to maximum value.

Time Representation. There are various ways to incorporate time into the visualization. One common approach is to have the timeline as an axis and represent dependent visual elements along the timeline. However, with a large number of visual elements of the graph at a time point, visualizing all elements along the timeline would make the view cluttered and difficult to understand. This issue is addressed in 2D and 3D visualization as follows.

Incorporating Animation. In the 2D visualization, the timeline is combined with the time slider and a play/pause button. The changes in graph topology over time are made visible by the transition in animation. As default, the clock on the time slider runs automatically, and the corresponding topology will be updated accordingly on the graph. The view is coupled with a narration of the changes in nodes usage. Details-on-demand is provided upon mouse-click to support in-depth analysis into computing usage for the entire time.

Visualizing Changes Exclusively. For the 3D visualization, we utilize the added dimension for time representation. Taking into account the issue of view cluttering, *JobNet* only visualizes the changes of node releasing or node starting to be used in the whole structure. This 3D representation allows 360-degree rotation so that the user can examine the entire graph from the beginning until the end of the observation period from a different angle for the complete view. For this 3D interface, we use canvas [11] to present the visual elements. Canvas is suitable for fast rendering when there are a large number of visual elements involved, as all elements drawn on a canvas element do not manifest in the DOM and save a substantial amount of work for the browser [21].

4 Case Study

4.1 JobNet2D

The 2D visualization of *JobNet* is demonstrated in Fig. 1. First, the user can have an overview of the current snapshot at the particular time point determined at

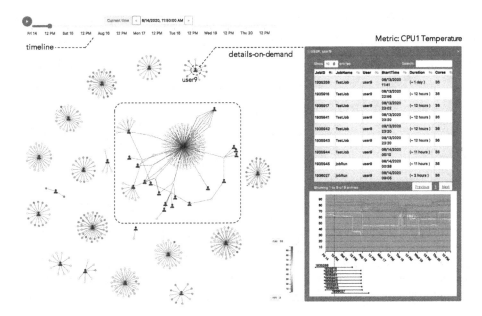

Fig. 1. 2D interface of JobNet. Details-on-demand is available upon mouse click.

the time slider incorporated with the timeline at the top. From the overview, we can see that the force-directed layout algorithm clearly presents the users with their corresponding compute nodes, including the cases where one compute is used by multiple users, which is emphasized in the dashed-line box in the middle of the graph in Fig. 1. The current metric on displaying is CPU1 temperature.

The interface provides details-on-demand upon mouse clicking on the user. As the selection of *user9* is specified, the details of running jobs and their executing computes are shown on the pop-up panel in Fig. 1. The details show that the compute nodes for *user9* have high indicators for CPU1 *JobNet* users can also zoom in the network for a close-up view at the graph vertices. On mouse hovering, the selection of the user or node will be displayed; other visual elements will be filtered. Upon drag and drop, the *JobNet* user can filter the nodes based on the corresponding thresholds set on health metrics, as depicted in Fig. 3. The nodes whose value is greater than the threshold will be pulled closer to the metric box; otherwise, the nodes will be pushed away from the box.

For simplicity, the default presentation shows users and their running compute servers. *JobNet* user can also enable the visibility of jobs to show the order of association of the user-job-compute server. Figure 2 shows the difference between visualizing users and compute servers alone, with the same network, but with the addition of jobs as the middle level, *user10* and its set of the same compute servers are highlighted in two cases. Without the visibility of jobs, we cannot see that there are actually two jobs running on that group of nodes. This detail comes with a trade-off of network complexity and legibility.

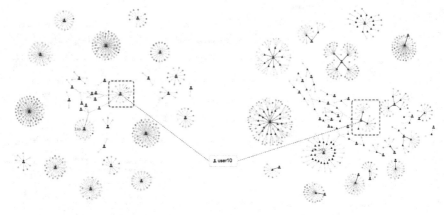

Visualizing users and compute servers   The same network with **jobs** as the middle level

Fig. 2. The default option for visualizing users and compute servers (left), and the detailed option having jobs added as the middle level for the order of association of user-job-compute server.

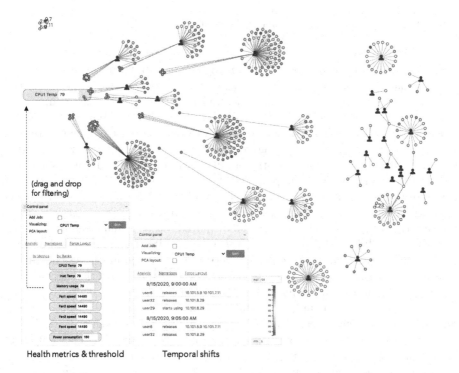

Health metrics & threshold   Temporal shifts

Fig. 3. Interactions: Drag and drop health metrics boxes with their threshold into the graph area for intuitive filtering: The nodes whose value greater than the threshold will be pulled closer to the metric box, otherwise the nodes will be pushed away from the box.

4.2   JobNet3D

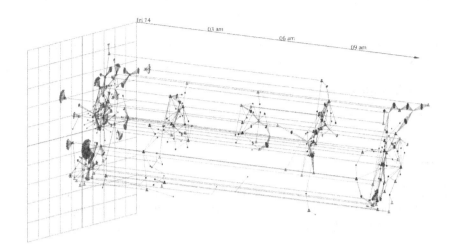

Fig. 4. 3D interface of JobNet. (Color figure online)

Figure 4 demonstrate the 3D interface of *JobNet*. Instead of repeating the complete network topology in every time step, *JobNet* presents the visual elements carrying changes in status: a red line represents a node being released (job finished), whereas a green line corresponds to a node started to be put in execution. The spatial locations of the nodes and users remain consistent along the timeline. Compared to the 2D version, the 3D interface shows all changes that occur in the entire observational interval at once, instead of relying on *JobNet* user's eyes activity and mental memory upon transition. In other words, the view provided by the 3D visualization indicates global evolution without cluttering the view, also helps users spot changes without spending too much mental energy on remembering the preceding state.

The visualization allows adjusting the time resolution (time compressing) for showing data for single time steps (every 5 min) or aggregation at 30 min, or 1, 2, or 3 h for simplicity and demonstration purpose. The time resolution for the visualization in Fig. 4 is 3 h. The smaller window for aggregation results in more discrete data points along the timeline, leading to more precise positions but also a more cluttered view.

Outlier Detection. *JobNet* in 3D provides users with interactive filtering through specifying a range on the parallel coordinates in the control panel. Figure 5 shows *JobNet* visualization with an outlier highlighted upon mouse hovering. The outlier implementation for 3D representation is based on the work of Pham and Dang [16]. The said outlier, *user74* only has green links connected to it, meaning that the user executes on more and more compute nodes but never releases one.

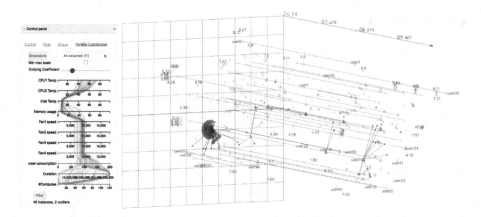

Fig. 5. Filtering options with *JobNet*. The filtering panel shows the parallel coordinates where outlier users is indicated. *JobNet* 3D interface is highlighted with mouse hovering interaction over an outlier. (Color figure online)

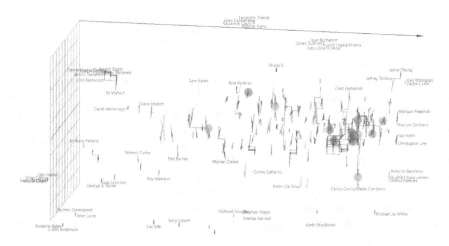

Fig. 6. 3D visualization of *JobNet* applied on the PopCha! dataset.

Applying on a Different Domain. This case study applies on PopCha! [15], an Android application that allows its users to follow their movies, discover movies with the recommendation and sharing feature. The dataset that we use in this work is a subset of the movie network produced from data in the PopCha! application. Movies related to each other as they get picked by PopCha! users. The dataset contains records for 51 years. Figure 6 demonstrates the use of *Job-Net* on the PopCha! dataset. In terms of visual encodings, nodes in the graph are actors or actresses (1,113 elements), a link between two nodes shows that the two people are co-stars in a movie (6,200 links), while the color of a link indicates the genre of the movie they appear together.

Figure 7 depicts the pattern upon zooming for a close-up view. Within the captured time period, there are one-time patterns in two movies, *Apocalypse Now* and *Blade Runner* as circled in black and blue. There is also a repeated pattern, including actor Harrison Ford in all occurrences, which signifies the three sequels of the movie Star Wars.

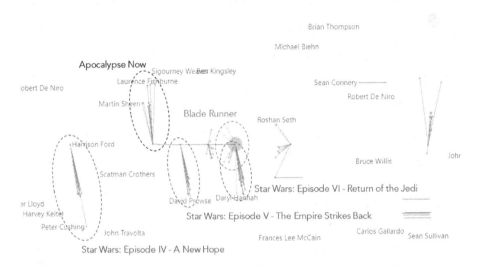

Fig. 7. Close-up view on the 3D visualization of *JobNet*. The repeated pattern is highlighted in red: A similar cast (inferred from the similar structures of the subnetworks) appear three times, indicating the three sequels of the movie Star Wars. (Color figure online)

5   Conclusion

In the scope of this paper, we discussed a novel visualization tool to monitor the temporal and structural association of HPC system components. The tool applies a force-directed layout algorithm on the 2D and 3D visualizations to represent the system users, jobs submitted, and compute servers for execution. Interactions on zooming, filtering, and detail-on-demand offer means for visual exploratory and support analysis. The usefulness of the tool is demonstrated by the case study on a real-world HPC job accounting dataset. Besides the HPC dataset, the 3D version of the tool shows its applicability to other domains and datasets having time constraints and mutual references among elements.

References

1. Aguilar, X., Fürlinger, K., Laure, E.: Visual MPI performance analysis using event flow graphs. Procedia Comput. Sci. **51**, 1353–1362 (2015)

2. Dan Lepow, J.L.: Overview of HPC job manager (2016). https://docs.microsoft.com/en-us/powershell/high-performance-computing/overview-of-hpc-job-manager?view=hpc19-ps

3. Dietrich, R., Winkler, F., Knüpfer, A., Nagel, W.: PIKA: center-wide and job-aware cluster monitoring. In: 2020 IEEE International Conference on Cluster Computing (CLUSTER), pp. 424–432. IEEE (2020)

4. Fruchterman, T.M., Reingold, E.M.: Graph drawing by force-directed placement. Softw. Pract. Exp. **21**(11), 1129–1164 (1991)

5. Grafana: The open platform for beautiful analytics and monitoring (2019). https://grafana.com/

6. Haridasan, M., Pfitscher, G.H.: PM/sup 2/P: a tool for performance monitoring of message passing applications in COTS PC clusters. In: Proceedings. 15th Symposium on Computer Architecture and High Performance Computing, pp. 218–225. IEEE (2003)

7. Holten, D., Van Wijk, J.J.: Force-directed edge bundling for graph visualization. In: Computer Graphics Forum, vol. 28, pp. 983–990. Wiley Online Library (2009)

8. Jingai, R., Kido, Y., Date, S., Shimojo, S.: Research note: a high resolution graph viewer for multi-monitor visualization environment. Rev. Socionetwork Strateg. **9**(1), 19–27 (2015)

9. Mansman, F., Meier, L., Keim, D.A.: Visualization of host behavior for network security. In: Goodall, J.R., Conti, G., Ma, K.L. (eds.) VizSEC 2007. MATHVISUAL, pp. 187–202. Springer, Heidelberg (2008). https://doi.org/10.1007/978-3-540-78243-8_13

10. Massie, M.L., Chun, B.N., Culler, D.E.: The ganglia distributed monitoring system: design, implementation, and experience. Parallel Comput. **30**(7), 817–840 (2004)

11. Network, M.D.: Canvas tutorial (2021). https://developer.mozilla.org/en-US/docs/Web/API/Canvas_API/Tutorial

12. Nguyen, H.N., Dang, T.: EQSA: earthquake situational analytics from social media. In: 2019 IEEE Conference on Visual Analytics Science and Technology (VAST), pp. 142–143 (2019). https://doi.org/10.1109/VAST47406.2019.8986947

13. Nguyen, N., Dang, T.: HiperViz: interactive visualization of CPU temperatures in high performance computing centers. In: Proceedings of the Practice and Experience in Advanced Research Computing on Rise of the Machines (Learning). PEARC 2019, Association for Computing Machinery, New York (2019). https://doi.org/10.1145/3332186.3337959

14. Oetiker, T.: Rrdtool (2014). http://rrdtool.org

15. PDI, T.: Popcha! movies, tv & theaters (2013). https://popcha-movies-tv-amp-theaters.soft112.com/

16. Pham, V., Dang, T., Wilkie, A., Banterle, F.: ScagnosticsJS: extended scatterplot visual features for the web. In: Eurographics (Short Papers), pp. 77–80 (2020)

17. Sanchez, S., et al.: Design and implementation of a scalable HPC monitoring system. In: 2016 IEEE International Parallel and Distributed Processing Symposium Workshops (IPDPSW), pp. 1721–1725. IEEE (2016)

18. Schwaller, B., Tucker, N., Tucker, T., Allan, B., Brandt, J.: HPC system data pipeline to enable meaningful insights through analysis-driven visualizations. In: 2020 IEEE International Conference on Cluster Computing (CLUSTER), pp. 433–441. IEEE (2020)

19. Shneiderman, B.: The eyes have it: a task by data type taxonomy for information visualizations. In: Proceedings 1996 IEEE Symposium on Visual Languages, pp. 336–343 (1996). https://doi.org/10.1109/VL.1996.545307

20. Tretyakov, E., Artamonov, A., Grigorieva, M., Klimentov, A., McKee, S., Vukotic, I.: TRACER (TRACe route ExploRer): a tool to explore OSG/WLCG network route topologies. Int. J. Mod. Phys. A **36**(5), 2130005-10 (2021)
21. Verspohl, L.: D3 and canvas in 3 steps (2017). https://www.freecodecamp.org/news/d3-and-canvas-in-3-steps-8505c8b27444/
22. Xia, J., et al.: SuPoolVisor: a visual analytics system for mining pool surveillance. Front. Inf. Technol. Electron. Eng. **21**(4), 507–523 (2020). https://doi.org/10.1631/FITEE.1900532
23. Zagarskikh, A., Karsakov, A., Mukhina, K., Nasonov, D., Bezgodov, A.: An efficient approach of infrastructure processing visualization within cloud computing platform. Procedia Comput. Sci. **66**, 705–710 (2015)

Evaluation and Selection of Autoencoders for Expressive Dimensionality Reduction of Spatial Ensembles

Hamid Gadirov[1]([✉])[iD], Gleb Tkachev[2][iD], Thomas Ertl[2][iD], and Steffen Frey[1,2][iD]

[1] University of Groningen, Bernoulli Institute, Nijenborgh 9,
9712 AG Groningen, The Netherlands
{h.gadirov,s.d.frey}@rug.nl
[2] Universität Stuttgart, Visualization Research Center, Allmandring 19,
70569 Stuttgart, Germany
{gleb.tkachev,thomas.ertl}@vis.uni-stuttgart.de

Abstract. This paper evaluates how autoencoder variants with different architectures and parameter settings affect the quality of 2D projections for spatial ensembles, and proposes a guided selection approach based on partially labeled data. Extracting features with autoencoders prior to applying techniques like UMAP substantially enhances the projection results and better conveys spatial structures and spatio-temporal behavior. Our comprehensive study demonstrates substantial impact of different variants, and shows that it is highly data-dependent which ones yield the best possible projection results. We propose to guide the selection of an autoencoder configuration for a specific ensemble based on projection metrics. These metrics are based on labels, which are however prohibitively time-consuming to obtain for the full ensemble. Addressing this, we demonstrate that a small subset of labeled members suffices for choosing an autoencoder configuration. We discuss results featuring various types of autoencoders applied to two fundamentally different ensembles featuring thousands of members: channel structures in soil from Markov chain Monte Carlo and time-dependent experimental data on droplet-film interaction.

Keywords: Feature learning · Machine learning · Dimensionality reduction · Clustering · Ensemble visualization

1 Introduction

Driven by technological advances, scientific ensembles of increasing size are obtained from simulations and experiments. They offer significant potential for new insights in various domains across engineering and natural sciences, but their analysis induces many challenges [35]. Dimensionality reduction (DR) techniques

Supplementary Information The online version contains supplementary material available at https://doi.org/10.1007/978-3-030-90439-5_18.

© Springer Nature Switzerland AG 2021
G. Bebis et al. (Eds.): ISVC 2021, LNCS 13017, pp. 222–234, 2021.
https://doi.org/10.1007/978-3-030-90439-5_18

have been successfully applied for analyzing large sample collections (e.g., [16]), and especially 2D projections widely used to provide a visual impression of the data distribution [22]. However, when applied directly to spatial data, the expressiveness of projection techniques like Uniform Manifold Approximation and Projection (UMAP) [23] is generally negatively impacted by the high dimensionality and hence sparsity of the data.

This work explores the usage of unsupervised feature learning techniques to produce more suitable data representations for DR of spatial data, and specifically, for 2D projections. We investigate standard and sparse *autoencoders* (AE), as well as more advanced versions such as *Sliced-Wasserstein* and *β-Variational* autoencoders (SWAE and β-VAE). Our study with two different scientific ensembles demonstrates that they improve expressiveness in comparison to directly projecting the spatial data via UMAP. However, it also shows that the performance of autoencoder variants is highly data-dependant, i.e., it is not clear a priori which one to choose to adequately capture what is of interest in the data. To address this, we propose to employ complementary metrics quantifying the quality of a projection and selecting a specific autoencoder variant based on Pareto efficiency. These metrics assess the quality of the projection based on labels (generally provided by an expert). While labels can be prohibitively expensive to obtain for the full ensemble, we demonstrate that a small subset of labeled members is already sufficient to yield expressive results.

We consider (1) the study of several autoencoder variants for dimensionality reduction with diverse scientific ensembles, (2) the evaluation of projection metric stability for small partial labelings, and (3) the Pareto-efficient selection of a variant on this basis to be the main contributions of this work.

2   Related Work

Ensemble Visualization. The analysis of ensemble data generally is a challenging visualization task [24]. Potter et al. [27] as well as Sanyal et al. [31] proposed early approaches to study climate ensembles, while Waser et al. [36] described a system for the interactive steering of simulation ensembles. Kehrer et al. [16], Sedlmair et al. [32], and Wang et al. [35] provided detailed surveys of techniques in the area. Bruckner and Möller [2] employ squared differences to explore the visual effects simulation space, Hummel et al. [14] compute region similarity via joint variance, and Kumpf et al. [20] track statistically-coherent regions using optical flow. Hao et al. [9] calculate shape similarities for particle data using an octree structure, while He et al. [10] employ surface density estimates for distances between surfaces. Fofonov et al. [3] propose fast isocontour calculation for visual representation of ensembles.

For projection of high-dimensional data, Vernier et al. [34] propose spatial and temporal stability metrics to evaluate the quality of PCA, t-SNE, UMAP, and Autoencoders. Bertini et al. [1] presented a systematic analysis of quality metrics supporting exploration. We, however, study how autoencoders impact the 2D projection quality when combined with traditional DR techniques.

Autoencoder-Based Feature Extraction. Several works confirm the ability of autoencoders to extract expressive features for ensemble data. Hinton et al. [13] first demonstrated that autoencoders can be utilized for DR and can be applied to large datasets. Plaut [26] performed principal component analysis using a linear autoencoder. Han et al. [8] developed an autoencoder-based framework *FlowNet* to extract such features as streamlines and stream surfaces. Jain et al. [15] utilized deep convolutional autoencoder to obtain a compact representation of multivariate time-varying volumes by learning high-level features. Lekschas et al. [21] developed a convolutional autoencoder-based technique *PEAX* for interactive visual pattern search. Guo et al. [7] developed a deep convolutional autoencoder minimizing the reconstruction and clustering losses for end-to-end learning of embedded features for clustering. Ge et al. [4] achieved state-of-the-art clustering performance on MNIST via dual adversarial autoencoders. He et al. [11] proposed a deep learning approach for comparison of multiple ensembles. Guo et al. [6] developed a visual analytics system based on autoencoders for medical records. Way et al. [37] utilize variational autoencoders to extract biologically relevant features from gene expression data. We also employ deep convolutional autoencoders to enable visual exploration of scientific data, but focus on a study of autoencoder variants and model selection in a partially labeled scenario.

3   Study Setup, Metrics and Selection

Standard DR techniques, such as PCA, t-SNE, and UMAP, lose efficiency when applied directly to high dimensional (ensemble) data (e.g. [13,37]). To address this, we first reduce the dimensionality of ensemble data with autoencoders and then construct a 2D projection. An autoencoder is a neural network for unsupervised learning of efficient data encodings. It consists of an encoder followed by a decoder, with the former compressing the input and the latter trying to reconstruct it as accurately as possible. Different architectures are employed below, and evaluated both visually and quantitatively with metrics. These metrics also provide the basis for Pareto efficient selection.

Scientific Ensemble Datasets. We consider two ensemble datasets in our study. The first dataset depicts channel structures in soil from Markov chain Monte Carlo, consisting of independent members generated during simulation [29]. The images are monochrome and have a resolution of 50×50. In total, there are 95K images. The second dataset Drop Dynamics stems from a physical experiment to study the impact of a droplet with a film [5]. The captured experiment images, similarly to the previous dataset, are monochrome and in this case have a resolution of 160×224. In total, there are 135K images from 1K members. Subsets of the members of both ensembles are exemplified in the grid views in Fig. 2. A subset from both datasets was manually labeled, as required by the metrics that we use to evaluate the projections. Labeling is based on different behavior types observed in ensembles and was performed by marking groups of images with similar behavior types as one class label. In the labeling process a number of

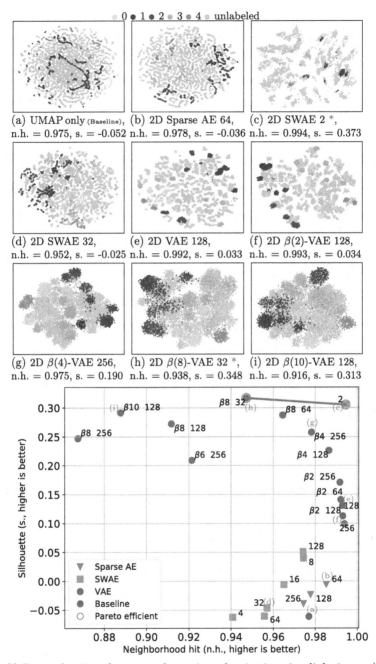

(j) Pareto frontier of autoencoder variants (projection view links in gray)

Fig. 1. (a–i) Autoencoders for feature learning prior to 2D projection improves the result for spatial ensembles (here: channel structures in soil from MCMC, Fig. 2a and Fig. 2c), but the outcome highly depends on architectures, parameters and underlying data. A partial labeling of 1% suffices to yield expressive quality metrics, and (j) allows to explore suitable variants on the Pareto frontier.

randomly selected members was considered. MCMC consists of five categorical classes (● ● ● ●) which depict qualitatively different types of channel structures. For Drop Dynamics, there are eight classes in total: "bubble", "bubble-splash", "column", "crown", "crown-splash", "splash", "drop", and "none" (not fitting any other category). 2.5K labeled images are available in total for MCMC and 7.2K for Drop Dynamics. On both projection views (Figs. 1 and 3) gray points (●) indicate unlabeled images.

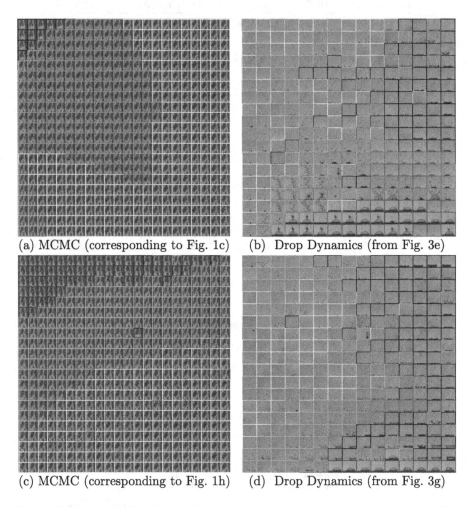

(a) MCMC (corresponding to Fig. 1c)   (b) Drop Dynamics (from Fig. 3e)

(c) MCMC (corresponding to Fig. 1h)   (d) Drop Dynamics (from Fig. 3g)

Fig. 2. Grid views with coloured frames around each image representing labels. The new position in the grid was found via linear assignment from a 2D projection to the grid [28].

Autoencoder-Based Feature Extraction. Besides standard and sparse autoencoders (AE), we utilize variational autoencoders (VAE) [18], based on a variational inference and learning algorithm, as well as its constrained version (β-VAE) [12]. VAE is scalable for large datasets and its inherent regularization brings latent vectors closer together. SWAE [19] is based on Wasserstein Autoencoders [33], which share properties of VAE while achieving better reconstruction. All types of considered autoencoders (AE, SWAE, VAE and β-VAE) have a symmetric structure - the decoder is reversed to the encoder. Both parts of autoencoders are represented via deep neural networks, containing several hidden *convolutional* and *fully connected* layers. The objective function used for training varies depending on the autoencoder type (see supplemental material for details). In our implementation of AEs and (β)-VAEs, we reduce the resolution of input images by half after each convolutional layer by using a *stride* of 2 in each dimension of spatial (2D) convolutions. For the spatio-temporal (3D) convolutions, a stride of 3 was used. The *kernel size* for convolution was set to 3 for each dimension, the *number of filters* of 64 in each hidden convolutional layer was used with zero *padding*. As an optimizer, *Adam* [17] with learning rate 0.0005 was employed throughout. The "ReLU" activation function was used in combination with random uniform weight initialization. We utilize L1 and L2 regularization for *Sparse Autoencoders*. We follow the implementation of SWAE from [19] utilizing "LReLU" activation and *average pooling*.

For MCMC dataset with no temporal information only 2D convolutional models were used, trained and validated on 20K unlabeled images. For the (spatio-temporal) Drop Dynamics, both 2D and 3D autoencoders were used, trained and validated on 15K unlabeled images. Note that we utilize unsupervised machine learning and projection techniques, labels are solely employed for the purpose of evaluation in this work (also see the discussion of metrics below).

Projection to 2D Space. After transforming the ensemble data from physical to feature space, we obtain a latent vector for each data sample. These feature vectors are subsequently projected to a 2D space using DR techniques. In general, we find that directly reducing the dimensionality of ensembles to 2D using autoencoders is inefficient for most of the models since the autoencoder cannot reasonably reconstruct the input which is an indication of poorly learned features (although there are exceptions, see discussion below). In the following, we restrict ourselves to UMAP projection, which outperformed other DR techniques such as t-SNE and PCA in preliminary experiments with the same subset of labels. UMAP is a non-linear technique and uses a smoothed version of k-nearest neighbors distance. We utilize UMAP with *min. distance = 1.0* parameter, deviating from the default. This value controls how close points are located on the newly created 2D map and produces visually less overlapping projections.

Metrics (and Partially Labeled Data). We use two commonly used complementary metrics to capture the projection quality: *neighborhood hit* and *silhouette*. While neighborhood hit measures how well the clusters are separated, silhouette additionally provides the measure of tightness. The *neighborhood hit* metric [34] is based on k-nearest neighbors [25] ($k = 17$ in our setting, values ranging from 7 to 27 yield similar results), and since it computes the fraction of neighbors belonging to the same class for each labeled data point, it provides an accurate measure of the separation and was preferred to other similar metrics. The output is in the range of [0, 1], where *higher values* represent a better separation of the clusters. The *silhouette* metric [30] is based on (Euclidean) distance and computes the distances between a data point and all data points in the same cluster. Since it takes into account distances to all data points in the nearest neighboring cluster as well, it still reaches a high score in the case of well separated friend-of-friends clusters and therefore was preferred to other similar metrics. The output is in the range of [−1, 1], where *higher values* represent a better matching of a data point to its own cluster rather than to neighboring clusters. Note that we also considered other metrics (Calinski-Harabasz and Davies-Bouldin) which, however, yielded similar results to the silhouette metric (see supplemental material).

Pareto Efficient Selection. We identify the best performing feature extraction models based on multi-objective optimality criteria (Pareto frontier). For this, from our two considered metrics we construct a 2D plot, demonstrating the results of evaluating the clustering quality of final projections, with the axes of neighborhood hit and silhouette (maximum is better) metrics. After obtaining the Pareto frontier, it is possible to select one of the best shown models, check its corresponding visualization, and investigate the projection of ensemble data.

4   Evaluation

We now discuss 2D projection results of our ensembles, demonstrate Pareto-efficient selection, and evaluate metric stability with labeled subsets (see supplemental material for 2D projections of all variants).

MCMC (Fig. 1). In the baseline method that uses UMAP directly (a), we can observe well separated but dispersed clusters of each class (reflected by high neighborhood hit but low silhouette). The projection results improved for all classes with the 2D sparse autoencoder (b). Note that the number after the autoencoder type indicates the dimensionality of the latent space. However, classes partitioned into different clusters and yielding highly irregular shapes can still be observed. This is reflected by low values in the silhouette which position AE results between the baseline and β-VAEs in Fig. 1j. For SWAE results (c and d), we observe an improvement with all classes being more tightly clustered. Both metrics are improved because of the influence of the SWAE objective function. Interestingly, SWAE with direct projection to 2D (not using UMAP) also yields a good projection (c). 2D VAE (e) and 2D $\beta(2)$-VAE (f) further improve the results. We see well-separated clusters and even higher neighborhood hit and silhouette values. Models like 2D $\beta(4)$-, $\beta(8)$-, and $\beta(10)$-VAE (g, h, and i) create clusters in a shape of a Gaussian distributions, further improving metric scores. These are also on the Pareto frontier (Fig. 1j). Interestingly, $\beta(8)$-VAE with a comparably low latent space dimensionality of 32 is able to extract features properly. Overall, we observe a significant benefit in performing feature extraction on the MCMC ensemble. Visualizations show that AE, SWAE, and

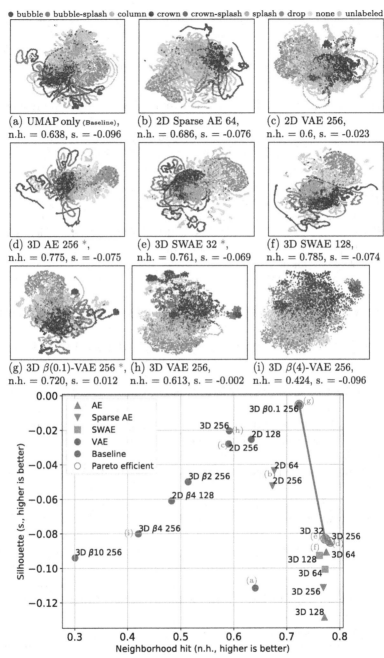

(j) Pareto frontier of autoencoder variants (projection view links in gray)

Fig. 3. (a–i) Projection views of the Drop Dynamics ensemble (* indicates the projection belonging to a set of Pareto efficient models in (j), see discussion in Sect. 4). (j) Metric values of projection and respective Pareto frontier (marked in green, links to projections in gray). (Color figure online)

(β-)VAE with different β values all outperform the baseline. In the final projection of almost all models, we see data points belonging to the same class located close to each other, forming clusters of the same classes. In the case of β-VAE, properly selected values of β (not too high) can improve the results and lead to visually pleasing projections.

Drop Dynamics (Fig. 3). The baseline result (a) successfully produces clusters of similar samples and thus achieves a relatively high neighborhood hit. This is clearly noticeable in the case of classes "bubble", "bubble-splash", "splash", and time steps without any behavior category ("none"). However, it scatters the samples of the same type across many small clusters, which is highlighted by the poor silhouette values. In the case of simple 2D Sparse AE with latent dimensionality 64 (b), the model also cannot group all data points belonging to the same class into one cluster. We can see the "bubble", "bubble-splash", and "splash" type time steps present in different parts of the final projection, which is based on the latent space learned by the autoencoder. In (c), clusters start to appear in the form of Gaussian distributions ("bubble"), due to the KL divergence regularization term in the VAE loss calculation, improving the silhouette score. In (d), corresponding to the 3D AE, we can notice better connected clusters in the case of "crown" and "drop" classes, which is reflected in the neighborhood hit score. Elongated clusters still persist, since there is no KL regularization applied in this case. In (e) and (f) corresponding to the SWAEs, most clusters are separated from each other, but still have multiple subclusters. This is related to WAE loss calculation: different latent codes remain far away from each other. In (g) corresponding to the $\beta(0.1)$-VAE with latent dimensionality of 256, we can notice better connected clusters in the case of "crown". In the case of "bubble", clusters are starting to appear in the form of a Gaussian distribution. This is reflected in the higher neighborhood hit and silhouette scores. In (h) corresponding to the VAE ($\beta = 1$), likewise decent projections can also be observed. Due to the KL divergence term in the VAE loss calculation, the 3D VAE model created clusters in the form of Gaussian distributions. It can be noticed e.g. in the case of "bubble" type time steps, no elongated clusters can be observed. In models with higher β values greater effect of KL loss can be observed. The influence of β trades off neighborhood hit for silhouette metric, helping to bring points of the same class closer, but also mixing some clusters. Such trade-offs are why we use Pareto optimality for our model selection (Fig. 3j). However, too high values of β (e.g. $\beta >= 4$) mix the data points in the final visualization because the input has only a minor impact on the latent vector, which leads to poorly learned features (Fig. 3i).

Overall, we see that the autoencoder-based feature extraction can improve the baseline results regarding the metrics, which capture important characteristics under the presence of a large chunk of unlabeled (previously unseen) data in particular. We also note that most 3D convolutional models outperform models with 2D convolutions. 3D models were able to learn better features by using three time steps in the input instead of one, without the need to increase the dimension of the latent space.

Pareto Efficient Selection (Fig. 3j and Fig. 1j). As can be seen in Fig. 1j, corresponding to MCMC, a significant improvement was achieved with $(\beta\text{-})$VAEs and SWAE over the baseline ($\bullet$). The most efficient are β-VAE models with the values of β ranging from two to eight and SWAE with direct 2D projection. As can be seen in Fig. 3j, corresponding to Drop Dynamics, an improvement was achieved with 2D/3D AEs, 3D SWAEs, 3D VAE. The Pareto efficient models, connected with green line, are 3D AE, 3D SWAE, and 3D $\beta(0.1)$-VAE.

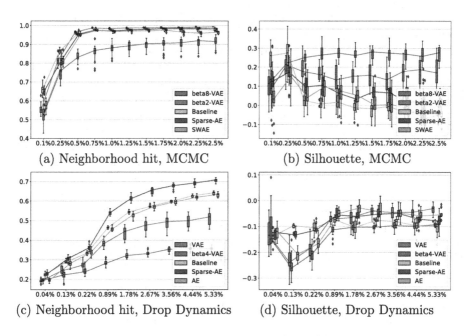

(a) Neighborhood hit, MCMC   (b) Silhouette, MCMC

(c) Neighborhood hit, Drop Dynamics   (d) Silhouette, Drop Dynamics

Fig. 4. Stability of metrics using labeled subsets, replicated on 20 runs.

Stability of Metrics Using Labeled Subsets (Fig. 4). Since we utilize only a small subset of the labeled data which supports the selection of autoencoder variants, it is crucial to test the stability of the results. In Fig. 4, we demonstrate that the considered models produce stable metric scores for different numbers of labels. We use random label subsets of different sizes, ranging from 0.1% to 2.5% for MCMC and from 0.04% to 5.33% for Drop Dynamics. We can see that as we increase the amount of labels for both datasets, the metric values are converging with low uncertainty. In contrast, a small amount of labels leads to a high uncertainty in metric values. When the number of labels is critically small, (c), the neighborhood hit metrics breaks down and produces low values and very low uncertainty because of the label sparsity. In this case, the neighborhood includes points from far away and the metric converges to the value of *1/number-of-classes* because it encounters points from all the classes. Overall, this stability study suggests that it is possible to achieve representative results utilizing a comparably small percentage of labeled data points.

5 Discussion and Outlook

The premise of this work is that unsupervised feature learning prior to dimensionality reduction with techniques like UMAP improves the results for spatial and spatiotemporal ensembles. The rationale is that higher-level features extracted via autoencoders from the field data yields a representation that better conveys characteristic differences between them, which are relevant for analyzing the ensemble. We demonstrate this by showing that all autoencoder variants yield superior results when considering the manually assigned labels that correspond to the characteristic cases.

The properties of the autoencoders are directly reflected in the projection. Most prominently, the Kullback-Leibler divergence term of (β)-VAE causes the clusters to have a Gaussian distribution, with the influence depending on the Lagrangian multiplier β. We initially aimed to provide general suggestions on which autoencoder architecture is the most suitable, but our experiments showed that the results are highly data-dependent. While not evaluated in this paper, we also found that simple modifications of the datasets, such as normalization and cropping can have a significant influence. This is due to the fact that especially methods with an MSE reconstruction objective encode noisy, randomly varying, and unimportant features presented in the input. To distinguish which differences are meaningful, one requires human input, which we took in the form of labels. In this work, we propose to use suitable projection metrics and a Pareto optimality to guide the selection. Crucially, as scientific datasets typically come without labeling and manual annotation is time-intensive, we were able to show that basing the decision on a small subset already suffices for an informed selection. However, for a practical application to a novel ensemble without labeling, we still consider our analysis provided in this work useful to serve as an initial basis for model selection. According to our observations, if the images do not contain a high proportion of useful information (i.e., a large portion of the pixels relevant for feature extraction), models like AEs, SWAEs, or VAEs with small values of β (< 1) are beneficial. Otherwise, VAEs with higher values of β (> 1) can achieve a better clustering results.

For MCMC with a high proportion of relevant elements in the data, autoencoders achieve a more significant improvement over the baseline in comparison to the Drop Dynamics ensemble (where the majority of pixels just represent background). To further improve such cases in particular, in future work, we aim to investigate other unsupervised learning approaches besides autoencoders or generative models with a semi-supervised setup. The robustness and general performance of the proposed pipeline could further benefit from adequate prior preparation of the data, e.g., via noise reduction or segmentation. For β-VAEs it was challenging to find the best Lagrangian multiplier β, rather than to employ a fixed value, and so it might be better to gradually increase the β-weighted KL term during training in order to achieve both disentangled representation and high reconstruction quality. Finally, 2D projection is just one prominent example where prior feature learning is beneficial for visual analysis, and we aim to explore further scenarios in future work like clustering and search.

References

1. Bertini, E., Tatu, A., Keim, D.: Quality metrics in high-dimensional data visualization: an overview and systematization. IEEE Trans. Visual Comput. Graphics **17**(12), 2203–2212 (2011)
2. Bruckner, S., Möller, T.: Result-driven exploration of simulation parameter spaces for visual effects design. IEEE Trans. Visual Comput. Graphics **16**(6), 1468–1476 (2010)
3. Fofonov, A., Molchanov, V., Linsen, L.: Visual analysis of multi-run spatiotemporal simulations using isocontour similarity for projected views. IEEE Trans. Visual Comput. Graphics **22**(8), 2037–2050 (2015)
4. Ge, P., Ren, C.X., Dai, D.Q., Feng, J., Yan, S.: Dual adversarial autoencoders for clustering. IEEE Trans. Neural Networks Learn. Syst. **31**(4), 1417–1424 (2019)
5. Geppert, A., Chatzianagnostou, D., Meister, C., Gomaa, H., Lamanna, G., Weigand, B.: Classification of impact morphology and splashing/deposition limit for n-hexadecane. Atomization Sprays **26**(10), 983–1007 (2016)
6. Guo, R., et al.: Comparative visual analytics for assessing medical records with sequence embedding. Visual Informatics **4**(2), 72–85 (2020)
7. Guo, X., Liu, X., Zhu, E., Yin, J.: Deep clustering with convolutional autoencoders. In: Liu, D., Xie, S., Li, Y., Zhao, D., El-Alfy, E.S. (eds.) ICONIP 2017. LNCS, vol. 10635, pp. 373–382. Springer, Cham (2017). https://doi.org/10.1007/978-3-319-70096-0_39
8. Han, J., Tao, J., Wang, C.: Flownet: a deep learning framework for clustering and selection of streamlines and stream surfaces. IEEE Trans. Visualization Comput. Graph. **26**, 1732–1744 (2018)
9. Hao, L., Healey, C.G., Bass, S.A.: Effective visualization of temporal ensembles. IEEE Trans. Visual Comput. Graphics **22**(1), 787–796 (2016). https://doi.org/10.1109/TVCG.2015.2468093
10. He, W., Guo, H., Shen, H.W., Peterka, T.: efesta: ensemble feature exploration with surface density estimates. IEEE Trans. Visual Comput. Graphics **26**(4), 1716–1731 (2018)
11. He, W., Wang, J., Guo, H., Shen, H.W., Peterka, T.: Cecav-dnn: collective ensemble comparison and visualization using deep neural networks. Visual Inf. **4**(2), 109–121 (2020)
12. Higgins, I., et al.: beta-vae: learning basic visual concepts with a constrained variational framework. Iclr **2**(5), 6 (2017)
13. Hinton, G.E., Salakhutdinov, R.R.: Reducing the dimensionality of data with neural networks. Science **313**(5786), 504–507 (2006)
14. Hummel, M., Obermaier, H., Garth, C., Joy, K.I.: Comparative visual analysis of lagrangian transport in CFD ensembles. IEEE Trans. Visual Comput. Graphics **19**(12), 2743–2752 (2013)
15. Jain, S., Griffin, W., Godil, A., Bullard, J.W., Terrill, J., Varshney, A.: Compressed volume rendering using deep learning (2017)
16. Kehrer, J., Hauser, H.: Visualization and visual analysis of multifaceted scientific data: a survey. IEEE Trans. Visual Comput. Graphics **19**(3), 495–513 (2013). https://doi.org/10.1109/TVCG.2012.110
17. Kingma, D.P., Ba, J.: Adam: a method for stochastic optimization. arXiv preprint arXiv:1412.6980 (2014)
18. Kingma, D.P., Welling, M.: Auto-encoding variational bayes. arXiv preprint arXiv:1312.6114 (2013)

19. Kolouri, S., Pope, P.E., Martin, C.E., Rohde, G.K.: Sliced-wasserstein autoencoder: An embarrassingly simple generative model. arXiv:1804.01947 (2018)
20. Kumpf, A., Rautenhaus, M., Riemer, M., Westermann, R.: Visual analysis of the temporal evolution of ensemble forecast sensitivities. IEEE Trans. Visual Comput. Graphics **25**(1), 98–108 (2018)
21. Lekschas, F., Peterson, B., Haehn, D., Ma, E., Gehlenborg, N., Pfister, H.: Peax: interactive visual pattern search in sequential data using unsupervised deep representation learning. Comput. Graph. Forum **39**, 167–179 (2020)
22. Liu, S., Maljovec, D., Wang, B., Bremer, P.T., Pascucci, V.: Visualizing high-dimensional data: advances in the past decade. IEEE Trans. Visual Comput. Graphics **23**(3), 1249–1268 (2016)
23. McInnes, L., Healy, J., Melville, J.: Umap: uniform manifold approximation and projection for dimension reduction. arXiv preprint arXiv:1802.03426 (2018)
24. Obermaier, H., Joy, K.I.: Future challenges for ensemble visualization. IEEE Comput. Graphics Appl. **34**(3), 8–11 (2014)
25. Peterson, L.E.: K-nearest neighbor. Scholarpedia **4**(2), 1883 (2009)
26. Plaut, E.: From principal subspaces to principal components with linear autoencoders. arXiv preprint arXiv:1804.10253 (2018)
27. Potter, K., et al.: Ensemble-Vis: a framework for the statistical visualization of ensemble data. In: Proceedings of the 2009 IEEE International Conference on Data Mining Workshops, pp. 233–240 (2009). https://doi.org/10.1109/ICDMW.2009.55
28. Quadrianto, N., Song, L., Smola, A.J.: Kernelized sorting. In: Advances in Neural Information Processing Systems, pp. 1289–1296 (2009)
29. Reuschen, S., Xu, T., Nowak, W.: Bayesian inversion of hierarchical geostatistical models using a parallel-tempering sequential gibbs mcmc. Adv. Water Resour. **141**, 103614 (2020)
30. Rousseeuw, P.J.: Silhouettes: a graphical aid to the interpretation and validation of cluster analysis. J. Comput. Appl. Math. **20**, 53–65 (1987)
31. Sanyal, J., Zhang, S., Dyer, J., Mercer, A., Amburn, P., Moorhead, R.: Noodles: a tool for visualization of numerical weather model ensemble uncertainty. IEEE Trans. Visual Comput. Graphics **16**(6), 1421–1430 (2010). https://doi.org/10.1109/TVCG.2010.181
32. Sedlmair, M., Heinzl, C., Bruckner, S., Piringer, H., Möller, T.: Visual parameter space analysis: a conceptual framework. IEEE Trans. Visual Comput. Graphics **20**(12), 2161–2170 (2014)
33. Tolstikhin, I., Bousquet, O., Gelly, S., Schoelkopf, B.: Wasserstein auto-encoders. arXiv preprint arXiv:1711.01558 (2017)
34. Vernier, E.F., Garcia, R., da Silva, I., Comba, J.L.D., Telea, A.C.: Quantitative evaluation of time-dependent multidimensional projection techniques. arXiv preprint arXiv:2002.07481 (2020)
35. Wang, J., Hazarika, S., Li, C., Shen, H.W.: Visualization and visual analysis of ensemble data: A survey. IEEE Trans. Visual Comput. Graphics **25**(9), 2853–2872 (2018)
36. Waser, J., Fuchs, R., Ribicic, H., Schindler, B., Bloschl, G., Groller, E.: World Lines. IEEE Trans. Visual Comput. Graphics **16**(6), 1458–1467 (2010). https://doi.org/10.1109/TVCG.2010.223
37. Way, G.P., Greene, C.S.: Extracting a biologically relevant latent space from cancer transcriptomes with variational autoencoders. BioRxiv, p. 174474 (2017)

Data-Driven Estimation
of Temporal-Sampling Errors
in Unsteady Flows

Harsh Bhatia[1]([⊠]), Steve N. Petruzza[2], Rushil Anirudh[1], Attila G. Gyulassy[3], Robert M. Kirby[3], Valerio Pascucci[3], and Peer-Timo Bremer[1]

[1] Center for Applied Scientific Computing, Lawrence Livermore National Laboratory,
Livermore, CA 94551, USA
{hbhatia,anirudh1,ptbremer}@llnl.gov
[2] Department of Computer Science, Utah State University, Logan, UT 84322, USA
steve.petruzza@usu.edu
[3] Scientific Computing and Imaging Institute, University of Utah,
Salt Lake City, UT 84112, USA
{jediati,kirby,pascucci}@sci.utah.edu

Abstract. While computer simulations typically store data at the highest available spatial resolution, it is often infeasible to do so for the temporal dimension. Instead, the common practice is to store data at regular intervals, the frequency of which is strictly limited by the available storage and I/O bandwidth. However, this manner of temporal subsampling can cause significant errors in subsequent analysis steps. More importantly, since the intermediate data is lost, there is no direct way of measuring this error after the fact. One particularly important use case that is affected is the analysis of unsteady flows using pathlines, as it depends on an accurate interpolation across time. Although the potential problem with temporal undersampling is widely acknowledged, there currently does not exist a practical way to estimate the potential impact. This paper presents a simple-to-implement yet powerful technique to estimate the error in pathlines due to temporal subsampling. Given an unsteady flow, we compute pathlines at the given temporal resolution as well as subsamples thereof. We then compute the error induced due to various levels of subsampling and use it to estimate the error between the given resolution and the unknown ground truth. Using two turbulent flows, we demonstrate that our approach, for the first time, provides an accurate, *a posteriori* error estimate for pathline computations. This estimate will enable scientists to better understand the uncertainties involved in pathline-based analysis techniques and can lead to new uncertainty visualization approaches using the predicted errors.

Keywords: Unsteady flow · Sampling errors · Temporal resolution · Uncertainty visualization

1 Introduction

Unsteady flows describe many natural and artificial phenomena and form the core of a large number of science and engineering applications [6,23,34]. In many

© Springer Nature Switzerland AG 2021
G. Bebis et al. (Eds.): ISVC 2021, LNCS 13017, pp. 235–248, 2021.
https://doi.org/10.1007/978-3-030-90439-5_19

cases, the primary focus is on understanding the transport of material in the flow, typically represented using *pathlines*—paths of massless particles advected by the time-varying flow (see Eq. 1). However, as pathlines are typically computed using iterative, numerical integration, they are susceptible to errors due to a number of sources.

In practice, errors due to insufficient temporal sampling of data are often considered to be most challenging for two main reasons: (1) the lack of data can be severe, and (2) the corresponding error cannot be easily computed. Virtually no large-scale simulation can afford to also store all available time-steps as this would increase simulation time by orders of magnitude and create unmanageable amounts of data. Instead, the data is subsampled in time, and often only every 500th or 1000th snapshot is saved and hence is available for analysis [12]. Since all intermediate data is lost, the error resulting from the subsampling cannot be directly computed and is often accepted as an inevitable consequence of the storage and I/O limitations. However, especially for the large-scale, turbulent simulations of greatest interest, the unknown error may dramatically impact computed pathlines.

Motivating Case Study. We consider a large-scale combustion simulation of a lifted jet flame [34,35] performed using S3D [13]. Such flows are used to study direct-injection spark ignition engines for commercial boilers as well as fundamental combustion phenomena. The simulation uses a $2025 \times 1600 \times 400$ rectilinear grid and captures several observables, such as velocities and temperature, resulting in about 280 GB of data per time-step. S3D uses an explicit Runge-Kutta (RK) integration scheme with a step size of 4×10^{-9} units. However, due to large I/O overheads and storage limitations, only every 500th snapshot is stored. It is important to note that the scientists consider this temporal resolution, *i.e.*, 2×10^{-6} units, *exceptionally high* for this type of study.

What make this simulation of particular interest for this paper is that it also includes a set of tracer particles computed *in situ*, which offers an opportunity to study errors introduced through temporal subsampling. Specifically, a total of 54,935 particles were tagged and traced alongside the simulation and stored at a step size of 2×10^{-7}. Particles are available for a total of 299 time-steps uniformly distributed in the time-range $[1.7, 1.7598] \times 10^{-3}$, effectively defining a set of highly-accurate pathlines. To compare these *in situ* pathlines with the ones computed in post-processing, we consider pathlines computed from the saved data covering the same range with the identical starting position. Since the data is spatially over-resolved, we use trilinear interpolation in space and the traditional linear interpolation in time with a conservative step-size of 2×10^{-8}.

Figure 1 provides a visual comparison between the *in situ* (particles) and the *post hoc* pathlines to highlight the differences, *e.g.*, how the pathlines on the right fail to capture the clear separation of the flow between the top and bottom layers in the flame. Figure 2 shows the distribution of point-wise errors between the two sets of pathlines (computed using Eq. 2) in spherical coordinates and conveys that most pathlines differ from the corresponding *in situ* particle paths by about 16 grid cells, and a substantial number of pathlines deviate by up to 50 grid cells. Similarly, the distribution of the azimuthal angle, φ, also has high

Fig. 1. A visual comparison of *in situ* (left) and *post hoc* (right) pathlines illustrates that the latter can misrepresent flow behavior, as they are affected by temporal sub-sampling errors. Pathlines are colored blue-to-red on time $[1.7, 1.7598] \times 10^{-3}$. (Color figure online)

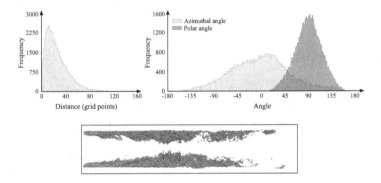

Fig. 2. Top: distributions of point-wise differences between the two set of pathlines indicate high variance in error. Bottom: spatial mapping of the polar angles of the difference to the corresponding seed points highlights that the errors appear to be distributed randomly, which may cause substantial artifacts in subsequent analysis.

variance and highlights that the computed pathlines are almost equally likely to be "ahead of" (faster than) the *in situ* particles ($|\varphi| < 90°$) or "behind" (slower than) them ($|\varphi| > 90°$). Figure 2 also maps the polar angle of the differences to the seed points of corresponding pathlines showing that they appear to be randomly distributed in space. This error behavior is of concern as one of the main uses of pathlines is the computation of derived quantities, such as the finite-time Lyapunov exponent (FTLE) [19]. The FTLE is defined through a spatial derivative of the particle positions and the random errors shown in Fig. 2 would cause substantial artifacts in the results. Nevertheless, without the *in situ* particles for verification, which only a few simulations provide, it is challenging to determine the expected accuracy of *post hoc* pathlines and conveying the resulting uncertainty.

Given that the sampling rate for this flow is considered exceptionally high, *post hoc* pathlines would likely have been accepted as a reliable approximation of the ground truth. However, the comparatively large and random errors discussed above raise significant concerns on the reliability of any pathline-based analysis. Although one would expect similar problems in other types of large-scale simulations of unsteady flows as well, without an understanding of the extent of inherent errors, scientists must currently choose between disregarding interesting results, because they cannot be validated, or accepting *post hoc* pathlines as best available information, potentially arriving at incorrect conclusions.

Contributions. To address this challenge, we present a data-driven approach to model subsampling errors in pathlines. Our *a posteriori* error estimate provides users with insights into the likely effects of temporal subsampling *without* access to the ground truth data. In particular, we compute pathlines at the given resolution as well as at successively coarser subsampled resolutions. Using two turbulent flows, we show that, in general, the differences between pathlines of successively-coarser resolutions can be modeled using a simple, supervised regression model that allows predicting the differences between the finest available resolution and the unknown ground truth. Our approach requires no additional implementation beyond the existing pathline computation and comparison, yet provides a reliable *a posteriori* error estimate for pathlines.

2   Related Work

Analyzing pathlines of unsteady flows is among the most fundamental ways of understanding its dynamic behavior [24]. *Pathlines* represent the path taken by a massless particle as it is advected by the flow. They have been used to compute the topological segmentation of 2D flows [30]; constructs similar to streak surfaces have been used for the topological analysis of 3D flows [15,22,31]. The notion of pathlines has also been extended to inertial particles to address more realistic physical phenomena [9,18]. Pathlines are often used to compute the FTLE [19] or the finite-space Lyapunov exponent (FSLE) [28], which are defined using the spatial derivative of the positions of neighboring seed particles after a given amount of time or distance, respectively. The FTLE and FSLE are believed to highlight the Lagrangian coherent structures (LCS) in the flow [20], such as material boundaries. However, dependent upon derivatives, the FTLE, the FSLE, and, hence, the LCS are highly sensitive to the errors in pathlines.

To date, the potential problems regarding uncertainty in pathlines remain largely unaddressed, despite their importance in the analysis of unsteady flows. In practice, pathlines are computed through numerical schemes, such as RK integration [7] with a high-order interpolation in space and a linear interpolation in time. It is well known that numerical integration is prone to compounding errors [14], especially if the source data is noisy or under-sampled. Almost all error studies in this context have focused on either the steady (time-independent) case or the analysis of uncertain data or errors in the integration. For example, there exist uncertainty visualization techniques for enhanced glyphs [27,33] to represent fields, and thick tubes [21,32] or streamwaves [3,4] to represent uncertainty in streamlines. Otto *et al.* [25,26] simulate uncertainty in data stochastically, but disregard uncertainty due to the computation of streamlines. For pathlines, Teitzel *et al.* [29] study the error resulting from numerical integration and compare different RK techniques with an additional focus on performance, and Darmofal and Haimes [14] provide detailed analysis of different integration schemes. Chen *et al.* [11] addressed the problem of integration uncertainty in sampled data by modeling the errors with Gaussian distributions. Nevertheless, no techniques exist that estimate and visualize subsampling uncertainty in unsteady flows, and the potential errors from a lack of temporal resolution have largely been ignored.

Recently, new Lagrangian representations have been proposed to alleviate the dependence of conventional representations on temporal resolution. Specifically, Agranovsky et al. [1] propose to compute and save a set of basis pathlines *in situ* with high accuracy and use those to compute any pathline in the post-processing. Along the same lines, Chandler et al. [10] utilize densely sampled in-situ particles to compute pathlines, thus reducing the numerical integration of pathlines to geometric interpolation. These representations alleviate some of the challenges of low temporal resolution at the cost of new errors when remapping particles between *in situ* pathlines. Nevertheless, assuming a sufficiently dense set of *in situ* pathlines, the remapping errors appear significantly smaller than the errors due to temporal subsampling. Unfortunately, very few simulations will natively compute *in situ* particles, and there exist a number of related challenges, such as, automatically computing good seed points. As a result, the applicability of these ideas is currently limited, and it remains important to find better ways to understand temporal subsampling errors in the current analysis pipeline.

3 Temporal Subsampling Errors in Pathlines

We consider the flow computed at the time-step of the simulation to be the ground truth and denote it as $\vec{V}_1(\mathbf{x}, t)$. Although $\vec{V}_1(\mathbf{x}, t)$ typically contains modeling and simulation errors and, therefore, in principle, may not be "correct" compared to the physical phenomenon under consideration, the analysis cannot be more accurate than the initial simulation itself, making this a reasonable assumption. The question we aim to answer is: *given a (temporally) subsampled flow $\vec{V}_k(\mathbf{x}, t)$, which contains timesteps only at some (temporal) resolution $k > 1$, and an algorithm to compute pathlines, how much is a pathline computed in $\vec{V}_k(\mathbf{x}, t)$ expected to differ from its counterpart computed for $\vec{V}_1(\mathbf{x}, t)$?*

Computing Pathlines and Measuring Errors. Pathlines represent paths of massless particles advected in the flow, given by the solution of the following integration of an ordinary differential equation.

$$\mathbf{p}(t) = \mathbf{p}_0 + \int_{t_0}^{t} \vec{V}(\mathbf{p}(\tau), \tau) \, d\tau, \tag{1}$$

with $\mathbf{p}_0 = \mathbf{p}(t_0)$. To explore sampling errors in pathlines, we use standard ways to interpolate flows and compute pathlines, keeping all parameters constant, varying only the temporal resolution. Specifically, we use a RK 4-5 integrator [7] with trilinear interpolation in space and linear interpolation in time.

Given two pathlines $\mathbf{p}(t)$ and $\mathbf{q}(t)$ with the same seed position $\mathbf{p}_0 = \mathbf{q}_0$, but computed at different temporal resolutions, we measure the error between them in terms of their maximal pointwise distances, *i.e.*,

$$\varepsilon(\mathbf{p}, \mathbf{q}) = \max_{0 \leq \tau \leq t} \|\mathbf{p}(\tau) - \mathbf{q}(\tau)\|. \tag{2}$$

We choose the maximal error as one typically wants to understand the worst case impact on any downstream analysis. Note that since $\mathbf{p}(t)$ and $\mathbf{q}(t)$ are computed using different temporal resolutions, care must be taken that the points corresponding to the same value of time are compared.

3.1   Temporal Subsampling of Simulated Unsteady Flows

Let $\vec{V}_\Delta(\mathbf{x}, t)$ represent a flow sampled at temporal resolution $\Delta \geq 1$. As discussed above, $\Delta = 1$ denotes the simulation time-step (the ground truth) and $\Delta = k$ the given sampling rate, $i.e.$, the flow stored at every k^{th} timestep. For a pathline computed at $\Delta = k$, the goal is to estimate the error introduced by temporal subsampling with respect to the ground truth. We denote this error as $\varepsilon_{(k,1)}$.

In order to estimate this error without requiring the ground truth, we further subsample the given data to resolutions $2k$, $3k$, ..., nk, and study the resulting errors between the corresponding pathlines at successive levels of subsampling, $i.e.$, $\varepsilon_{(2k,k)}$, $\varepsilon_{(3k,2k)}$, ..., $\varepsilon_{(nk,(n-1)k)}$. Specifically, we compute pathlines at these resolutions and analyze how coarser resolutions are related to the finer ones. Each successive subsampling is likely to introduce additional errors, and we expect them to be proportional to their magnitude, $i.e.$, pathlines with high $\varepsilon_{(2k,k)}$ are expected to show high $\varepsilon_{(3k,2k)}$. Therefore, we assume that the relationship between errors introduced at every level of subsampling can be modeled as

$$\varepsilon_{((n+1)k,nk)} = m_{nk}\ \varepsilon_{(nk,(n-1)k)}, \tag{3}$$

where m_{nk} is a resolution-dependent constant that quantifies the loss of information between the two subsampling steps.

We note that m_{nk} is not just influenced by the effective resolution nk but also by the "type" of pathline under consideration. A low m_{nk} indicates that the additional subsampling did not cause any significant increase in error. Typically, we expect a low m_{nk} for (1) pathlines that are mostly laminar and, hence, can be accurately computed at lower resolutions, or (2) pathlines that at nk already contain such a large error that further subsampling does not have a significant effect. On the other hand, for turbulent pathlines still containing meaningful information, one would expect m_{nk} to change significantly for different n, as a substantial amount of information may be lost at each level of subsampling. Furthermore, for most turbulent flows, we expect the value of m_{nk} to decay with subsampling, as most of the information is lost during the initial subsampling, whereas a relatively-smaller loss of information is incurred at later stages.

A similar technique to estimate sampling errors by upsampling and downsampling in the context of high-definition images was described by Berger et $al.$ [2]. Whereas they used a spine-tube interpolant to predict error for spatial subsampling, our goal is to estimate errors due to temporal subsampling.

3.2   Data-Driven Modeling of Errors

Consider the generalization of Eq. 3 as

$$\varepsilon_{(k,1)} = f\big(\varepsilon_{(2k,k)},\ \varepsilon_{(3k,2k)},\ \ldots,\ \varepsilon_{(nk,(n-1)k)}\big), \tag{4}$$

which parameterizes the error $\varepsilon_{(k,1)}$ as a function of errors occuring at lower sampling resolutions. If $f(\cdot)$ is linear, Eq. 4 generalizes Eq. 3 by including more than a single error with a nonzero weight. Recall that given $n-1$ subsampling errors for a pathline, $\varepsilon_{(2k,k)}$, $\varepsilon_{(3k,2k)}$, $\ldots$, $\varepsilon_{(nk,(n-1)k)}$, the goal is to predict $\varepsilon_{(k,1)}$. However, in most practical cases, the ground truth data is not available to validate our prediction; instead, we validate our model by predicting $\varepsilon_{(2k,k)}$ having observed the errors for subsequent resolutions.

The function $f(\cdot)$ can be estimated on a per pathline basis; however, it is conceivable that such an approach may fail due to a few reasons: (1) learning a unique $f(\cdot)$ for each pathline can easily result in over-fitting due to the small number of features available, and (2) such an approach fails to take into account any inherent spatial similarity in the error behavior, which can be useful information. Therefore, we train a single model for all pathlines in the flow and exploit a larger set of statistics for a better-fitting error model.

Error Prediction Using Supervised Linear Regression. The data can be represented as a $p \times (n-1)$ matrix, where errors for $n-1$ successive resolutions are given for p pathlines: each row in the matrix represents errors for a single pathline, and the column j represents the error $\varepsilon_{(j+1,j)}$. The goal is to predict the first column, $\varepsilon_{(2k,k)}$. Since we cannot use the same data for training and validation, and since availing additional data, either in terms of more pathlines or errors at more resolutions, is not possible, we instead train the model on columns $[3, 4, \ldots, n-1]$ to predict column two ($\varepsilon_{(3k,2k)}$). Next, we use the trained model, and predict on columns $[2, 3, \ldots, n-2]$, which we validate against the first column, $\varepsilon_{(2k,k)}$. The underlying hypothesis is that the regression model is able to capture the functional relationship between errors across temporal resolutions, which generalizes well to unseen data. In a realistic scenario, one would train the model using columns $[2, 3, \ldots, n-2]$ and predict the error $\varepsilon_{(k,1)}$

As argued already, we expect the errors for successive sampling to follow an exponential-decay trend. This intuition is supported by our observation that the model gives a better fit in $\log_{10}$ space. Nevertheless, after the first few subsampling steps, (especially the turbulent) pathlines may become significantly erroneous, and a low signal-to-noise ratio may preclude any information from being meaningful. Therefore, we are restricted to a small number of columns (in our experiments, we used $n \leq 10$). In order to improve the (linear) model, we increase the number of features (columns) by including polynomial combinations of existing features, up to degree 2. For example, if $[a, b]$ was the original set of features, we transform them to $[1, a, b, a^2, b^2, ab]$. This standard pre-processing step tends to improve regression performance for machine learning algorithms, as the non-linearity enables the algorithm to approximate more complex relationships similar to the kernel trick [5]. As a result, the size of the feature set becomes 36 (for n $= 7$), upon which we perform training and testing.

Furthermore, since we are changing the columns for testing, we control the difference on the value ranges between the training and test data by normalizing them to $[0, 1]$ through min/max scaling. This scaling controls the variance of the data, and allows the model to be applied to a different set of columns. The dependent variables for training ($\varepsilon_{(3,2)}$) and testing ($\varepsilon_{(2,1)}$) are not scaled.

Finally, we fit a linear regression model to the training data, and predict with the test data. The linear model is chosen for its ease of interpretation, and scalability for large-scale data.

Model Evaluation. To evaluate the performance of the model, we use two metrics: (1) the Spearman correlation, which describes how strongly two series of values are correlated, (≈ 1.0 indicates strong correlation), and (2) the R^2 statistic, or the coefficient of determination, which is the proportion of variance in the predicted value that can be explained from the true value, and takes a maximum value of 1.0 to indicate reliable prediction.

4   Validation and Results

Here we use two turbulent flows, one 2D and one 3D, to validate the error estimates discussed above. Using especially-high resolutions, or in the case of the lifted flame, *in situ* pathlines, we demonstrate that our model is able to predict the error due to temporal subsampling reasonably well.

4.1   2D Flow Past a Cylinder

Our first test data is a 2D flow past a cylinder, which was simulated using Nektar++ [8] on a 1300×600 regular grid, with a simulation time-step 0.01 ($\Delta = 1$) and Reynolds number 300. To obtain accurate data for experimentation and validation, snapshots of the flow were saved at an unusually-high frequency: every 10th simulation time-step, *i.e.*, $\Delta = k = 10$. Even for this moderately-sized data, the total size of storing only 600 snapshots of the simulated flow at the chosen resolution amounts to about 3.5 GB, highlighting the challenges in storing finer resolutions. To model subsampling errors, we compute a dense set of pathlines, seeded at every grid point and integrated until they exit the domain. Pathlines with same seed points are computed for subsampled flows, $\vec{V}_{nk}(\mathbf{x}, t)$, for $1 \leq n \leq 10$, and errors between pairs of pathlines are computed at successive resolutions.

Model Validation. Since true pathlines ($\Delta = 1$) are not known, we consider $\Delta = k$ as ground truth, and use the model described in the previous section to estimate $\varepsilon_{(2k,k)}$, using data of resolutions $2k$ and coarser only. Figure 3 shows the density scatter plot of the predicted $\varepsilon_{(2k,k)}$ plotted against the true $\varepsilon_{(2k,k)}$. It indicates a good fit around the ideal 45° line with a slight trend to over-predict for larger errors, as also determined by high values of R2 and Spearman coefficients. Note that the figure uses a logarithmic color map and highlights that the vast majority of pathlines are predicted well and contain errors less than 5 grid cells. Note that this figure provides a zoomed-in view to highlight the details and capture $\approx 99.2\%$ samples.

Error Prediction for the Given Resolution, $\Delta = k$. Finally, we use the model as we would in practice, *i.e.*, to predict the unknown error $\varepsilon_{(k,1)}$, and

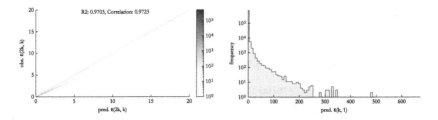

Fig. 3. Left: validation of our error model for the 2D flow past a cylinder. The model produces good prediction of subsampling errors as shown by the density visualization of correlation between predicted and observed errors. Right: predicted errors for the 2D flow past a cylinder sampled at the given resolution every 10th time-step. The distribution of predicted error shows that a non-negligible number of pathlines contain large errors, even at this unusually-high sampling.

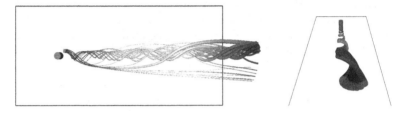

Fig. 4. Uncertainty visualization for the pathlines in the 2D flow past a cylinder. The figures show pathlines as thick tubes by mapping the point-wise error as radii, and time as color. The visualization in (a) shows intersections in these tubes, implying that subsequent FTLE-based analysis may contain arbitrary errors. (b) shows fewer pathlines from a different view point.

show the resulting histogram in Fig. 3. As seen in the figure, for the vast majority of pathlines, the predicted error is clustered around 0 (note the spike even on a logarithmic scale) as we would expect from the comparatively high temporal resolution. Nevertheless, there exist a relatively-small but not negligible set of pathlines with a predicted error of about 100 grid cells. Even considering the tendency to over-predict, this indicates that despite the high temporal resolution, the stored data contains regions of concern. Imagine, *e.g.*, FTLE computation using these pathlines with random pathline errors at the scale of multiple grid cells. These types of errors in hundreds of pathlines could create noticeable artifacts.

Uncertainty Visualization. We can use these estimations to visualize uncertainty in pathlines. By mapping point-wise errors to radii, we can display pathlines as thick tubes to understand the spatial manifestation of errors in the vicinity of other pathlines. Figure 4 show such visualizations for selected pathlines, where color represents time and thickness represents estimated error. In particular, the figure shows pathlines seeded from adjacent grid points in a 5×5 neighborhood, which show tubes corresponding to neighboring seed points intersecting. Here, we use the predicted error for a pathline to indicate the final thickness and vary it linearly along the pathline.

4.2 3D Lifted Ethylene Jet Flame

We next study the data presented in Sect. 1 to evaluate the given sampling rate. As discussed earlier, for the lifted flame, true particle paths are available at a 10× higher frequency than the velocity fields, providing a rare opportunity to validate our technique with highly-accurate simulation data. Nevertheless, since the pathlines errors are already large (see Fig. 2), and the given temporal resolution is already substantially lower, we subsample the data only upto $n = 3$. While this provides much-fewer data for the model, any further subsampling led to substantial artifacts and no longer reasonably approximated the flow.

Comparing the predicted errors for the pathlines at $\Delta = k$, with the computed errors (with respect to the *in situ* particles) leads to the scatter plot in Fig. 5, which shows that the densest parts of the scatterplot lie on the 45° line corroborating that, on an average, our metric estimates the error reasonably well. While the differences between our estimation and the true error has a high variance, as one would expect in such a complex flow, errors in most pathlines are estimated within about 100 grid points at an average error of around 20 grid cells. Even conservatively, one would, therefore, expect a random error in pathlines of about 20 grid cells which would raise significant concerns about the reliability of the underlying pathlines. Figure 5 shows the residual plot and highlights, once again, that whereas our model relatively over-predicts the error, most pathlines lie near the origin suggesting a good prediction overall.

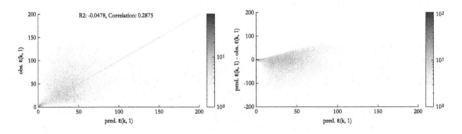

Fig. 5. Prediction of error in the pathlines of lifted flame. The figures correlate the predicted error with the computed error (using insitu-particles) as scatter and residual plots, showing that the prediction has low bias suggesting a good model fit, but contains high variance due to fewer available pathlines and resolutions.

By mapping the point-wise errors to radii, we show pathlines as thick tubes to visualize how the error evolves along the length of the pathline. As before, the final width of the tubes are as large as the predicted per-pathline error with the width scaled linearly along the length. Figure 6 shows large errors accumulated near the end of pathlines highlighting the potentially substantial errors in the given resolution and its implication on any subsequent analysis.

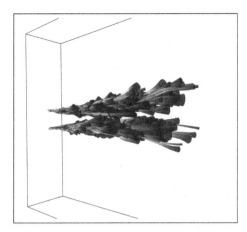

Fig. 6. Visualization of pathlines as tubes with radii mapped to point-wise error describes the evolution of error along the pathline, as well has enables understanding the sources of incorrect analysis in nearby pathlines.

5   Conclusion

This paper presents a new *a posteriori* estimate for errors in computation of pathlines due to temporal subsampling of unsteady flows. Whereas the existing error studies for pathline tracing either address other more-amenable sources of errors or require the knowledge of the ground truth and/or the expected time-scales of features in the flow, our technique estimates the error without requiring any prior knowledge about a given flow. Instead, our model directly analyzes relationships between error and temporal resolution for artificially subsampled data to derive error estimates.

Although we do not make any assumptions about the underlying flow and expect this technique to be generally applicable, it is important to better understand how other factors, such as other classes of flow and different integrators, would impact the model. We also assume that the given data is reasonably sampled and, therefore, expect that further subsampling creates a tractable loss of information. In cases where the initial data is already too sparse for meaningful results, further subsampling may not provide useful insights.

For the lifted flame data, only a small number of pathlines (54,935) are available, *all* of which are turbulent, and the errors are distributed rather randomly (see Fig. 2). As a result, the relationship between the errors at successive resolutions and the relationship between errors of different pathlines are difficult to capture and the model shows high variance, resulting in suboptimal predictions. In comparison, a much-larger set of pathlines is available for training the model for the 2D flow past a cylinder (780,000). Furthermore, many of these pathlines show coherent behavior, *e.g.*, many pathlines are laminar in a similar way, whereas, others produce similar turbulence. Therefore, we see low variance in the prediction. Unsurprisingly, the model produces more-accurate predictions when the training data set is large and coherent, whereas, in other cases, the predictions are less accurate. Moreover, since a majority of the pathlines are relatively simple and, therefore, show less error, the regression model is biased towards seeing such samples. With less training on complex pathlines, the model tends to over-predict. On the other hand, almost all pathlines are turbulent and contain large errors in which case the model provides unbiased results. The problems with creating biased prediction is a known limitations of such a simple model and more advanced regression techniques could likely improve the predictions. However, the results would be less interpretable and more challenging to reproduce. Furthermore, the goal is not necessarily to develop an accurate per-pathline prediction, which, given the chaotic nature of turbulence, is likely an unrealistic goal. Instead, our approach aims to highlight the overall trends to allow a qualitative assessment on which pathlines are likely to reliably represent an underlying flow. The overarching challenge remains in obtaining data that is sampled sufficiently finely, such that, a meaningful model can be constructed through temporal subsampling. Another potential direction of future work could be to reformulate the model as a classification task, where one could predict the error as being one of three classes—low, medium or high. This makes the learning problem more regularized, especially with respect to the extremely-turbulent pathlines. In addition, an added constraint could be to employ a loss function such as the Wasserstein loss [17], or use an ordinal classification framework [16], which enforces the natural ordering of classes (low error < medium error < high error) into the loss.

Discussion and Outlook. The analysis presented above raises serious concerns about the reliability of post-hoc pathlines and their subsequent analysis. Notice that even at impractically high temporal resolutions, the cylinder model suggests that there exist hundreds to thousands of pathlines with errors beyond five grid cells. Considering that one of the primary reason to compute pathlines is to derive FTLE fields, unstructured errors of this magnitude and beyond are likely to cause severe artifacts. Clearly, the exact impact of such artifacts will depend on the specific uses case, the nature of the flow, as well as a host of other factors. However, this study suggests that evaluating the impact of temporal subsampling should be an integral part of any pathline-based analysis to better understand the inherent uncertainties and potential errors.

Approaches like the one presented here open a number of interesting research directions and provide opportunities to re-engage the broader scientific community with new explicitly validated approaches and reliable error predictions. Furthermore, this work highlights the need to develop better interpolation schemes to reduce the errors or new representations like the Lagrangian one [1] to completely avoid temporal subsampling. In this context, the simple model proposed above represents only a first step in developing more general diagnostics for pathline-based analysis approaches.

Acknowledgements. This work was performed under the auspices of the U.S. Department of Energy by Lawrence Livermore National Laboratory under Contract

DE-AC52-07NA27344. This work was funded in part by NSF OAC awards 2127548, 1941085, NSF CMMI awards 1629660, DoE award DE-FE0031880, and the Intel Graphics and Visualization Institute of XeLLENCE. RMK acknowledges support from ARO W911NF-15-1-0222 (Program Manager Dr. Mike Coyle). Release number: LLNL-CONF-826636.

References

1. Agranovsky, A., Camp, D., Garth, C., Bethel, E.W., Joy, K.I., Childs, H.: Improved post hoc flow analysis via Lagrangian representations. In: Proceedings of IEEE Symposium on Large Data Analysis and Visualization (LDAV), pp. 67–75 (2014)
2. Berger, K., Berger, K., Callet, P.L.: UHD image reconstruction by estimating interpolation error. In: 2015 IEEE International Conference on Image Processing (ICIP), pp. 4743–4747 (September 2015)
3. Bhatia, H., et al.: Edge maps: representing flow with bounded error. In: Proceedings of 2011 IEEE Pacific Visualization Symposium, pp. 75–82 (March 2011)
4. Bhatia, H., et al.: Flow visualization with quantified spatial and temporal errors using edge maps. IEEE Trans. Vis. Comput. Graph. **18**(9), 1383–1396 (2012)
5. Bishop, C.M. (ed.): Mixture models and EM. In: Pattern Recognition and Machine Learning. ISS, pp. 423–459. Springer, New York (2006). https://doi.org/10.1007/978-0-387-45528-0_9
6. Braun, S.A., Montgomery, M.T., Pu, Z.: High-resolution simulation of hurricane bonnie (1998). Part I. J. Atmos. Sci. **63**(1), 19–42 (2006)
7. Butcher, J.C.: A history of Runge-Kutta methods. Appl. Numer. Math. **20**(3), 247–260 (1996)
8. Cantwell, C., et al.: Nektar++: an open-source spectral/element framework. Comput. Phys. Commun. **192**, 205–219 (2015)
9. Cartwright, J.H.E., Feudel, U., Károlyi, G., de Moura, A., Piro, O., Tél, T.: Dynamics of finite-size particles in chaotic fluid flows. In: Thiel, M., Kurths, J., Romano, M., Károlyi, G., Moura, A. (eds.) Nonlinear Dynamics and Chaos: Advances and Perspectives. Understanding Complex Systems. Springer, Heidelberg (2010). https://doi.org/10.1007/978-3-642-04629-2_4
10. Chandler, J., Obermaier, H., Joy, K.I.: Interpolation-based pathline tracing in particle-based flow visualization. IEEE Trans. Vis. Comput. Graph. **21**(1), 68–80 (2015)
11. Chen, C.M., Biswas, A., Shen, H.W.: Uncertainty modeling and error reduction for pathline computation in time-varying flow fields. In: Proceedings of 2015 IEEE Pacific Visualization Symposium, pp. 215–222 (April 2015)
12. Chen, J., et al.: Synergistic Challenges in Data-Intensive Science and Exascale Computing: DOE ASCAC Data Subcommittee Report. Department of Energy Office of Science (March 2013). Type: Report
13. Chen, J.H., et al.: Terascale direct numerical simulations of turbulent combustion using S3D. Comput. Sci. Discov. **2**(1), 015001 (2009)
14. Darmofal, D.L., Haimes, R.: An analysis of 3D particle path integration algorithms. J. Comput. Phys. **123**(1), 182–195 (1996)
15. Ferstl, F., Bürger, K., Theisel, H., Westermann, R.: Interactive separating streak surfaces. IEEE Trans. Vis. Comput. Graph. **16**(6), 1569–1577 (2010)
16. Frank, E., Hall, M.: A simple approach to ordinal classification. In: De Raedt, L., Flach, P. (eds.) ECML 2001. LNCS (LNAI), vol. 2167, pp. 145–156. Springer, Heidelberg (2001). https://doi.org/10.1007/3-540-44795-4_13

17. Frogner, C., Zhang, C., Mobahi, H., Araya, M., Poggio, T.A.: Learning with a Wasserstein loss. In: Advances in Neural Information Processing Systems, pp. 2053–2061 (2015)
18. Günther, T., Kuhn, A., Kutz, B., Theisel, H.: Mass-dependent integral curves in unsteady vector fields. Comput. Graph. Forum **32**(3pt2), 211–220 (2013)
19. Haller, G.: Finding finite-time invariant manifolds in two-dimensional velocity fields. Chaos **10**(1), 99–108 (2000)
20. Haller, G.: Lagrangian coherent structures and the rate of strain in two-dimensional turbulence. Phys. Fluids A **13**, 3365–3385 (2001)
21. Johnson, C.R., Sanderson, A.R.: A next step: visualizing errors and uncertainty. IEEE Comput. Graph. Appl. **23**(5), 6–10 (2003)
22. Krishnan, H., Garth, C., Joy, K.I.: Time and streak surfaces for flow visualization in large time-varying data sets. IEEE Trans. Vis. Comput. Graph. **15**(6), 1267–1274 (2009)
23. Maltrud, M., Bryan, F., Peacock, S.: Boundary impulse response functions in a century-long eddying global ocean simulation. Environ. Fluid Mech. **10**, 275–295 (2010)
24. McLoughlin, T., Laramee, R.S., Peikert, R., Post, F.H., Chen, M.: Over two decades of integration-based, geometric flow visualization. Comput. Graph. Forum **29**(6), 1807–1829 (2010)
25. Otto, M., Germer, T., Theisel, H.: Uncertain topology of 3D vector fields. In: 2011 IEEE Pacific Visualization Symposium, pp. 65–74 (2011)
26. Otto, M., Germer, T., Hege, H.C., Theisel, H.: Uncertain 2D vector field topology. Comput. Graph. Forum **29**(2), 347–356 (2010)
27. Pang, A.T., Wittenbrink, C.M., Lodha, S.K.: Approaches to uncertainty visualization. Vis. Comput. **13**(8), 370–390 (1996)
28. Peikert, R., Pobitzer, A., Sadlo, F., Schindler, B.: A comparison of finite-time and finite-size Lyapunov exponents. In: Bremer, P.-T., Hotz, I., Pascucci, V., Peikert, R. (eds.) Topological Methods in Data Analysis and Visualization III. MV, pp. 187–200. Springer, Cham (2014). https://doi.org/10.1007/978-3-319-04099-8_12
29. Teitzel, C., Grosso, R., Ertl, T.: Efficient and reliable integration methods for particle tracing in unsteady flows on discrete fneshes. In: Lefer, W., Grave, M. (eds.) Visualization in Scientific Computing 1997. Eurographics. Springer, Vienna (1997). https://doi.org/10.1007/978-3-7091-6876-9_4
30. Theisel, H., Weinkauf, T., Hege, H.C., Seidel, H.P.: Topological methods for 2D time-dependent vector fields based on stream lines and path lines. IEEE Trans. Vis. Comput. Graph. **11**(4), 383–394 (2005)
31. Üffinger, M., Sadlo, F., Ertl, T.: A time-dependent vector field topology based on streak surfaces. IEEE Trans. Vis. Comput. Graph. **19**(3), 379–392 (2013)
32. Verma, V., Pang, A.T.: Comparative flow visualization. IEEE Trans. Vis. Comput. Graph. **10**(6), 609–624 (2004)
33. Wittenbrink, C.M., Pang, A.T., Lodha, S.K.: Glyphs for visualizing uncertainty in vector fields. IEEE Trans. Vis. Comput. Graph. **2**(3), 266–279 (1996)
34. Yoo, C.S., Richardson, E.S., Sankaran, R., Chen, J.H.: A DNS study on the stabilization mechanism of a turbulent lifted ethylene jet flame in highly-heated coflow. Proc. Combust. Inst. **33**(1), 1619–1627 (2011)
35. Yoo, C.S., Sankaran, R., Chen, J.H.: Three-dimensional direct numerical simulation of a turbulent lifted hydrogen jet flame in heated coflow: flame stabilization and structure. J. Fluid Mech. **640**, 453–481 (2009)

Applications

ReGenMorph: Visibly Realistic GAN Generated Face Morphing Attacks by Attack Re-generation

Naser Damer[1,2](✉), Kiran Raja[3], Marius Süßmilch[1], Sushma Venkatesh[3],
Fadi Boutros[1,2], Meiling Fang[1,2], Florian Kirchbuchner[1], Raghavendra Ramachandra[3],
and Arjan Kuijper[1,2]

[1] Fraunhofer Institute for Computer Graphics Research IGD, Darmstadt, Germany
naser.damer@igd.fraunhofer.de
[2] Department of Computer Science, TU Darmstadt, Darmstadt, Germany
[3] Norwegian University of Science and Technology, Gjøvik, Norway

Abstract. Face morphing attacks aim at creating face images that are verifiable to be the face of multiple identities, which can lead to building faulty identity links in operations like border checks. While creating a morphed face detector (MFD), training on all possible attack types is essential to achieve good detection performance. Therefore, investigating new methods of creating morphing attacks drives the generalizability of MADs. Creating morphing attacks was performed on the image level, by landmark interpolation, or on the latent-space level, by manipulating latent vectors in a generative adversarial network. The earlier results in varying blending artifacts and the latter results in synthetic-like striping artifacts. This work presents the novel morphing pipeline, ReGenMorph, to eliminate the LMA blending artifacts by using a GAN-based generation, as well as, eliminate the manipulation in the latent space, resulting in visibly realistic morphed images compared to previous works. The generated ReGenMorph appearance is compared to recent morphing approaches and evaluated for face recognition vulnerability and attack detectability, whether as known or unknown attacks.

Keywords: Face recognition · Face morphing · Morphing attacks

1 Introduction

The deep-learning driven performance advances in face recognition [10], along with the relatively high social acceptance [2], have brought automatic face recognition to be a key technology in security sensitive applications of identity management (e.g. travel documents) [23]. However, face recognition systems are vulnerable to many attacks, one of these is face morphing attacks. Ferrara et al. [11] discussed the face morphing attack by showing that one face reference attack image can be, automatically and by human experts, successfully matched to more than one person. If such morphing attacks are used in travel or identity documents, it would allow multiple subjects to verify their identity to the one associated with the document. This faulty subject link to the document identity can lead to a wide range of illegal activities, including financial transactions, illegal immigration, human trafficking, and circumventing criminal identity lists.

© Springer Nature Switzerland AG 2021
G. Bebis et al. (Eds.): ISVC 2021, LNCS 13017, pp. 251–264, 2021.
https://doi.org/10.1007/978-3-030-90439-5_20

The first proposed morphing attacks were morphed on the image level. These are commonly created by interpolating facial landmarks in the morphed images and blending the texture information [12, 28], i.e. landmark-based attacks (LMA). However, this image-level interpolation commonly causes blending image artifacts. Knowing (during training) possible novel approaches of creating morphing attacks is essential to create generalizable morphing attack detectors (MAD) [8]. Motivated by that, several researchers proposed to take advantage of the ever-increasing capabilities of the generative adversarial networks (GAN) to generate face morphing attacks [5, 7, 34, 35]. These works performed the identity interpolation on the latent vector level, rather than the image-level in the LMA approaches. However, manipulating the latent vector resulted in generated images with slight synthetic-like striping artifacts, even in the most recent methods [35].

In this work, we propose a novel face morphing concept, the ReGenMorphand, to avoid both, the blending artifacts in LMA and the synthetic striping artifacts in GAN-based morphs. The proposed ReGenMorph approach achieves that by using a GAN-based generation, as well as, eliminate the manipulation in the latent space. This is done by performing the identity interpolation on the image level (just as LMA) but passing the image into a fine-tuned StylGAN encoder and generator, without latent space manipulation. This results in a generated morphed image of high quality and low visible artifacts, that also holds the identity information of the blended LMA image. This paper presents our ReGenMorph approach in detail. We present a face recognition vulnerability study in comparison to LMA and the latest GAN-based attacks. We also study the detectability of the ReGenMorph attacks as known and unknown attacks using two of the top-performing MAD. Samples of the ReGenMorph images are presented, along with LMA and recent GAN-based attacks, for visual comparison. In details, our experiments compare our ReGenMorphs to 3 morphing approached from [28] (IJCB2017), [34] (IWBF2020), and [35] (T-BIOM2021). We studied the vulnerability of all the considered attack types on both, top academic solution (ArcFace [10]) and one of the top COTS available [14]. We evaluated the detectability of the presented morphs in known and unknown settings using two detection methods [29] (ISBA2019) and [33] (FUSION2020) that achieved top performances in the morphing detection NIST challenge [25].

2   Related Works

Morphing face images was initially performed by detecting facial landmarks in the source image to be morphed. These landmarks are later interpolated and the texture is blended to produce the morphed face image (LMA morphs). Slightly different versions of this process were used in different work, such as the work of Ferrera et al. [12] and Ramachandra et al. [28]. A comparison [30] of these methods have shown that the approach used in [28] and [4] achieved the strongest face morphing attacks, i.e. highest identity preservation of the morphed identities. A more sophisticated variation of this process applied the interpolation on partial parts of the face [27], resulting in attacks that are harder to detect when they are not known to the morphing attack detector (MAD). The listed LMA morphs have various degrees of image artifacts introduced by the fact that the identity interpolation is performed on the image-level [35].

Taking advantage of the advanced GAN architectures and their ability to produce synthetic images, and to avoid the image-level interpolation, Damer et al. proposed the MorGAN GAN-based morphing approach [7]. The MorGAN transferred the original images to be morphed into the latent space of the GAN and performed a latent-level interpolation. The interpolated latent vector is then used by the GAN generator to generate the morphed face image. These MorGAN images preserved the identities moderately and had low resolution. The MorGAN attacks have proven to be hard to detect if they were unknown to the MAD [6,9]. A follow-up work added a post-generation cascaded enhancement step on the MorGAN network to increase the image quality, however, with the same identity preservation qualities [5]. Based on the idea of latent vector interpolation introduced in [7], Venkatesh et al. created much more realistic and higher quality morphed images with better identity preservation qualities [34]. This advancement in [34] was mainly due to the use of an advanced GAN architecture, namely the StyleGAN by Karras et al. [21]. Also based on the StyleGAN architecture [21], the MIPGAN-II generative morphing approach was introduced to generate images with higher identity preservation [35]. This was achieved in [35] by introducing a loss to optimize the identity preservation in the latent vector.

Although the existing LMA morphs have strong identity preservation capabilities, the fact that they build their identity blend on the image level makes them prone to image artifacts. The GAN-based morphs do generally preserve the identity to a lower degree [35], however, this is less relevant in such a scenario where the worst-case attack scenario needs to be considered. Despite the enhanced quality of the GAN-based morphed images, the manipulation in the latent space still produce synthetic-like generation artifacts [7,34,35]. This work aims to eliminate the LMA blending artifacts by using a GAN-based generation, as well as, eliminate the manipulation in the latent space, resulting in visibly realistic morphed images compared to previous works.

3 Methodology

This section introduces our novel face image morphing pipeline and the technical details of our adaption to this pipeline.

3.1 The ReGenMorph Face Morphing Pipeline

So far, the creation of face morphing attacks has focused on the interpolation of identity information in one of two spaces. The first is on the image space, where the detected facial landmarks in both images are interpolated, and the texture information is blended [28], as demonstrated in Fig. 1a. The second is based on utilizing GAN structures by encoding two original images into the latent space, where the two latent vectors are interpolated (and possibly optimized [35]), then the GAN generator would process the interpolated latent vector into the morphed image [5,7,34,35]. The pipeline of creating the morphed images using GAN structures with the interpolation on the latent space is demonstrated in Fig. 1b, where the first approach provides very high identity preservation, the interpolation, and blending commonly results in artifacts such as shadowing

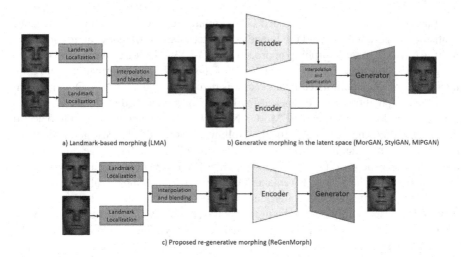

a) Landmark-based morphing (LMA)   b) Generative morphing in the latent space (MorGAN, StyIGAN, MIPGAN)

c) Proposed re-generative morphing (ReGenMorph)

Fig. 1. The face morphing pipelines using (a) facial landmarks - LMA [12,28], (b) conventional GAN-based morphing [5,7,34,35], and (c) the proposed ReGenMorph pipeline.

(see Fig. 2a). These artifacts can vary between different automatic and manual morphing processes. However, they are a common feature of such morphing techniques. The second approach requires latent space manipulation that introduces irregularities in the latent vector distribution, resulting in generative artifacts in the morphed image. Such artifacts are commonly seen as striping effect and overall synthetic appearance of the image, however, with no shadowing and blending artifacts. It must be noted that existing GAN-based morphs tend to have lower identity preservation in comparison to LMA morphs. Examples of such morphs can be seen in Figs. 2b and 2c.

To (a) take advantage of the lower blending artifacts in the LMA morphs, (b) avoid latent space manipulation and consequent GAN artifacts in GAN morphs, and (c) make full use of the GAN capabilities in producing realistic images, we propose our ReGen-Morph face morphing pipeline.

The proposed ReGenMorph pipeline is demonstrated in Fig. 1c, where the morphed images are first morphed identically to LMA morphs, resulting in a high-quality identity blend with blending effects. Then, the morphed image is processed into the latent space of a GAN structure, and simply re-generated by the GAN generator. This allows to take the identity blend of the LMA morph and allows the generator to create a realistic face image with minimum artifacts. This is motivated by a fact that the latent vector in this case is not manipulated and possesses distribution properties suitable for the generator (produced by its own encoder). In the following sub-section, the detailed implementation of the ReGenMorph pipeline is discussed.

3.2   Creating ReGenMorph Morphing Attacks

Creating the ReGenMorph morphing attacks starts with the LMA morphing of face image pairs as described in [28]. The LMA morph creation and database is described in more detail in Sect. 4.1. We use the StyleGAN architecture [21] as the backbone of our regeneration process. StyleGAN [21] is an extension to the typical GAN architecture with significant modifications to the generator model. These changes include the deployment of a mapping network to map points in latent space to an intermediate latent space, the utilization of intermediate latent space to control style at different stages in the generator model, and the introduction of noise as a variation at various stages in the generator model. This allows generating faces with varying levels of style manipulation, as well as high-quality Face images, the latter of which is interesting for the ReGenMorph pipeline.

We fine-tune the StyleGAN encoder to adapt the nature of the used images. The fine-tuned StyleGAN encoder is used to transfer the LMA morph, following face alignment and localization, into the latent space. The resulting latent vector is processed by the pre-trained StyleGAN generator to create our ReGenMorph morphing attack. This process and its technical details are presented in the following.

As a first step, the LMA morphed images are pre-processed by aligned and resized using the widely-used Multi-task Cascaded Convolutional Networks (MTCNN) [36]. The images are resized to 1024×1024 pixels to match the StyleGAN encoder input. The training split of the data will be used to finetune the encoder of the StyleGAN.

We fine-tune the encoder of the StyleGAN to adapt to the special distribution of the LMA morphs. This is done by freezing the Generator parameters and optimizing the loss between the features extracted from the input image and the output (from the generator) image. These features are embeddings extracted using a VGG16 [32] network as described in [21]. The used loss is the mean squared error. We used L-BFGS [3] as optimizer with a learning rate of 0.25, decay rate of 0.9, early stopping with a threshold of 0.5, and patience of 10. The input image size of the StyleGAN encoder is 1024×1024 pixels, the latent vector resulting of the encoder is of the size 512×1, and the output image of the generator is a 3 channel color image of the size 1024×1024 pixels.

The process of optimizing the latent space is described in detail in [1]. The source code of the used StyleGAN along with the used pre-trained models are available[1] as open-source. The pre-trained StyleGAN was trained on the FFHQ [21] and CelebA-HQ databases [20], while the pre-training hyperparameters are listed in [21].

To generate a ReGenMorph attack image, we create the LMA attack, detect, align, and resize the face as mentioned earlier. This attack is passed to the encoder and then the generator of the fine-tuned StyleGAN. The resulting image is our ReGenMorph. We generate a complete set of the training and testing data splits (described in Sect. 4.1). The training set is the same as the one used for fine-tuning and will only be used to train the MAD. All the examples, vulnerability analyses, and detectability results in this work are performed on the testing set. More details on the data structure are presented in Sect. 4.1.

---

[1] https://github.com/Puzer/stylegan-encoder.

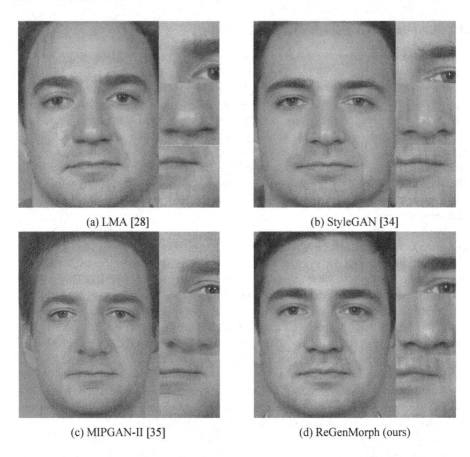

(a) LMA [28]   (b) StyleGAN [34]

(c) MIPGAN-II [35]   (d) ReGenMorph (ours)

Fig. 2. A large scale examples of a morphed image using LMA [28], StyleGAN [34], MIPGAN-II [35], and our ReGenMorph. The blending artifacts in the LMA and the striping artifacts in MIPGAN-II and StyleGAN are significantly more apparent than in our proposed ReGenMorph.

4   Experimental Setup

This section presents the database used for the training and testing phase of the various investigation in this work.

4.1   Database

As there are no publically available morphing databases (to the best of our knowledge), and there are minimum private ones that adhere to ICAO standard [18]. To enhance comparison to state-of-the-art, we chose the largest ICAO compliant database in the literature, requested the database pairs details from the authors of the first published version [34], and regenerated the images from the latest works [28, 34, 35]. We were not able to get access to the pairs and source image information of any other ICAO compliant [18] morphing data. However, we stress that the generalization is more important

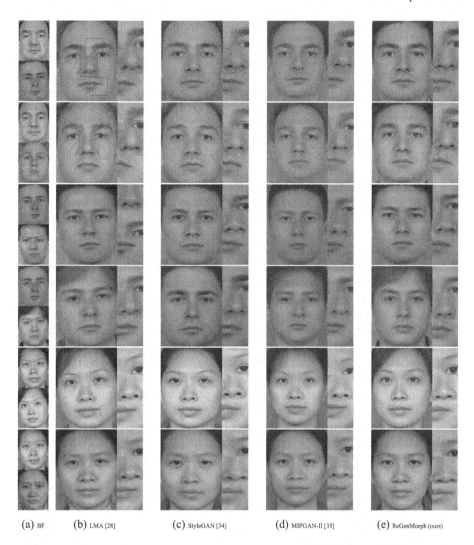

(a) BF   (b) LMA [28]   (c) StyleGAN [34]   (d) MIPGAN-II [35]   (e) ReGenMorph (ours)

Fig. 3. Samples of the morphed images using the LMA [28], StylGAN [34], MIPGAN-II [35], and the proposed ReGenMorph approaches. The source image pairs that are used to create the morphs are on the far left. The zoomed areas on the right of each morphed image are indicated in the top LMA morphed image with red squares. One can notice the relatively more realistic nature of the ReGenMorphs. full scale examples are presented in Fig. 2.

when presenting a morphing attack detector, while we present a novel attack generation protocol. Therefore one ICAO compliant database that enables a larger comparison with morphing approaches was our drive behind the database choice. The used data is part of the FRGC-V2 face database [26]. Based on this data, we generate morphing attacks using the proposed ReGenMorph approach, as well as the LMA approach defined in [28], the StyleGAN approach defined in [34], and the MIPGAN-II approach defined in [35]. For the sake of comparability, the generated database is based on the same database protocol and design (image pairs) as defined in, and provided by the authors of, [35]. The database consists of 2500 morphed images of each of the four kinds (LMA, StyleGAN, MIPGAN-II, ReGenMorph) and 1270 bona fide images. These morphing attacks are split into identity-disjoint training and testing sets. The training set contains 1190 morphed images of each kind and 690 bona fide images. The testing set contains 1310 morphed images of each kind and 580 bona fide images. The training set is used to fine-tune the StyleGAN encoder as discussed in Sect. 3.2 and to train the MADs presented in Sect. 4.3. The testing set is used to show visual genera-tion examples (Sect. 5.1), study face recognition vulnerability to the considered attacks (Sect. 5.2), and evaluate the attack detectability (Sect. 5.3). Other GAN-based morphing techniques, such as the MorGAN [7] and EMorGAN [5], were not considered, as their quality and identity preservation ability is far inferior to recent GAN-based approaches (like StyleGAN [34] and MIPGAN [35]). An LMA morphing tool from the University of Bologna [12] is widely used, however, it is not considered here as it proved [30] to be inferior (in identity preservation) to the LMA approach used in this work [28]. We con-sidered the option of measuring the statistical and perceptual image quality of the used morphs and found that previous works have shown no clear correlation between the image quality and the realistic appearance when dealing with Morphing attacks (typi-cally of ICAO standard [18] with not large quality variation) [35]. Therefore we decided that such investigation have proven to lead to misleading conclusions, and thus opted out of such investigation. The value of PSNR and SSIM, on the same morphing pairs used in this work, in [35] showed insignificant difference between the different attacks and the little difference was inconsistent with the perceived visual quality. The work in [5] showed that the clearly visibly unrealistic images of MorGAN [7] achieve higher statistical quality metrics (6 different metrics). In a recent study, researchers have shown that operations that apparent morphing artifacts do not consistently effect the estimated quality across a large number of quality estimation strategies [13]. Additionally, in a clearer study, Debiasi et al. have shown that even though MorGAN attacks have clearly low realistic appearance, they show closer perceptual quality distributions to bona fide images than attacks of the more realistic appearance.

4.2   Vulnerability Analyses

We evaluated the vulnerability of two face recognition systems to the morphing attacks created by our ReGenMorph pipeline in comparison to the three baseline attacks. In addition, we opted to evaluate one academic face recognition system and one com-mercial off-the-shelf (COTS) system. The following face recognition solutions were investigated:

ArcFace: ArcFace [10] scored state-of-the-art performance on several face recognition evaluation benchmarks such as LFW 99.83% and YTF 98.02%. ArcFace introduced Additive Angular Margin loss (ArcFace) to improve the discriminative ability of the face recognition model. We deployed ArcFace based on ReseNet-100 [17] architec-ture pre-trained on a refined version of the MS-Celeb-1M dataset [16] (MS1MV2). The MTCNN [36] solution is used, as recommended in [22], to detect (crop) and align (affine transformation) the face before passing into the network. To perform a comparison, an Euclidean distance, as recommended in [10], is calculated between two feature vectors produced from the network.

COTS: We used the Cognitec FaceVACS SDK version 9.4.2 [14]. We chose this COTS as the SDK achieved one of the best performances in the recent NIST report addressing the performance of vendor face verification products [15]. The face quality threshold was set to zero for probes and references to minimize the impact of inherent quality metrics. The full process containing face detection, alignment, feature extraction, and matching is part of the COTS and thus we are not able to provide details of its algorithm. Comparing two faces by the COTS produces a similarity score.

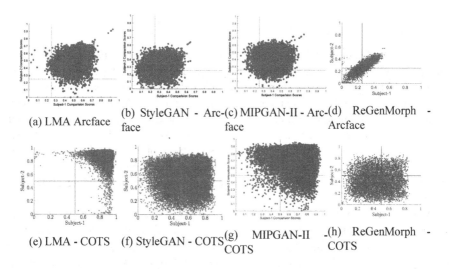

(a) LMA Arcface   (b) StyleGAN - Arc- (c) MIPGAN-II - Arc- (d) ReGenMorph - face   face   Arcface

(e) LMA - COTS   (f) StyleGAN - COTS (g) MIPGAN-II COTS   (h) ReGenMorph - COTS

Fig. 4. Vulnerability analysis using COTS and ArcFace. The scatter plots represents the comparison scores of morphed face image against two contributing subjects. The red lines represent decision threshold at 0.1% FMR. The more diagonal and the more towards the top right corner the distribution is, the more vulnerable is the face recognition system to the attack.

We present the vulnerability study results in the visual form as scatter plots depicting the similarity score of each morphing attack image to reference images (not used to create the morphing image) of the target identities. Ideally, a strong morphing attack will have a similar, and high similarity score to the target identities. We also present the vulnerability results in a quantifiable manner by giving the Mated Morphed Presentation Match Rate (MMPMR) [31] and the Fully Mated Morphed Presentation Match Rate (FMMPMR) [31] based on the decision threshold at the false match rate of (FMR) 0.1%. It must be noted that all the vulnerability results are presented on the testing data.

Table 1. Quantitative evaluation of vulnerability of COTS and ArcFace to various morph generation approaches. All values are in percentage (%). All value from our presented data, except for MorGAN, reported from the same database protocol in [34].

Generation	COTS		ArcFace	
	MMPMR(%)	FMMPMR(%)	MMPMR(%)	FMMPMR(%)
LMA [28]	100.00	98.84	99.68	98.00
StyleGAN [34]	64.68	41.49	72.80	56.95
MIPGAN-II [35]	92.93	81.59	94.21	86.94
MorGAN [7,34]	0.00	0.00	0.00	0.00
ReGenMorph	42.24	34.47	33.98	14.05

4.3 Detectability Analyses

To measure the detectability of the ReGenMorph attacks, we deploy two best-performing MADs. These two approaches are chosen by considering two different properties. One is based on Hybrid features [29] and the other based on Ensemble features [33].

The Hybrid features [29] extracts features using both scale space and color space combined with multiple classifiers, while the Ensemble features [33] deploys different textural features in conjunction with a set of classifiers. Both approaches proved to detect variations of morphing attacks holistically as previously shown in [29,33]. In addition, the Hybrid features [29] is submitted to the ongoing NIST FRVT morph challenge dataset [25] where it scored the best performance in detecting printed and scanned morph attacks.

We evaluate the detectability of our ReGenMorph attacks when they are already known to the detector developer, i.e. the training attack data is also ReGenAttack. More importantly, we evaluate the detectability of our ReGenMorph attacks as unknown attacks, i.e. novel attacks unknown to the detection algorithm. In the latter case, we evaluate the cases where the detectors are trained using LMA, StyleGAN, or MIPGAN-II attacks.

The morphing attack performance (detectability) is presented by the Attack Presentation Classification Error Rate (APCER), i.e. the proportion of attack images incorrectly classified as bona fide samples, and the Bona fide Presentation Classification Error Rate (BPCER), i.e. the proportion of bona fide images incorrectly classified as attack samples, as defined in the ISO/IEC 30107-3 [19]. Additionally, the Detection Equal Error Rate (D-EER), i.e. the value of APCER or BPCER at the decision threshold where they are equal, is reported. It must be noted that the training used only the training data while the detectability evaluation was performed only on the disjoint test data as described in Sect. 4.1.

5   Results

This section presents a visible representation of the ReGenMorph, a face recognition vulnerability analysis of the presented attacks, and detectability analyses of the ReGenMorph.

Table 2. The Detectability of the ReGenMorph attacks when they are used for training the MAD (known) and when LMA or MIPGAN-II attacks are used for training the MAD. One can notice the more challenging unknown ReGenMorph attack scenario. All BPCER and EER values are in percentage (%).

Approach	EER (%)	BPCER (%) @ APCER	
		=5%	=10%
Hybrid features [29]	2.48	4.97	4.97
Ensemble features [33]	0.00	0.00	0.00
Cross-set - Trained on LMA			
Hybrid features [29]	0.08	0.17	0.27
Ensemble features [33]	0.16	0.17	0.17
Cross-set - Trained on MIPGAN-II			
Hybrid features [29]	50.00	100.00	100.00
Ensemble features [33]	33.34	70.33	82.68

5.1 ReGenMorph Image Appearance

The visual appearance of morphed images is important because in the cases of 1) manual identity verification (e.g. border check) and 2) applying for an identity document with printed photo and no automatic attack detection, the only morphing detection possible is by the human operator. This human operator can commonly only identify visible image artifacts. Figure 3 presents several morphed images created by the proposed ReGenMorph and the baselines LMA [28], StyleGAN Fig. 4, and MIPGAN-II [35]. On the far left, the source images used to create the morphs are illustrated. It can be seen that the visible identity similarity of all morphed images to the source identities. LMA morphs show blending artifacts, especially in the nose and eye regions. The StyleGAN and MIPGAN-II morphs look slightly more synthetic and contain striping artifacts, especially in the flat skin areas. These artifacts are more visible in the MIPGAN-II, in comparison to StyleGAN morphs. There are significantly fewer artifacts in the proposed ReGenMorph morphs, with no clear consistent pattern of artifacts. To take a clearer look, three areas of each morphed image are zoomed in, as clarified in the top LMA morphed image in Fig. 3. To take a holistic clear look at the generated images, a morphing example from all the 4 morphing methods is presented in Fig. 2. The figure shows the realistic and low-artifact appearance of the ReGenMorph compared with baselines.

5.2 Vulnerability of Face Recognition to ReGenMorph

As detailed in Sect. 4.2, we measure the vulnerability of one COTS and the ArcFace [10]. The MMPMR and FMMPMR at 0.1% FMR are presented in Table 1. Both face recognition systems are less vulnerable to the ReGenMorph than to LMA, StyleGAN, or MIPGAN-II. However, many of the samples can cross the 0.1% FMR. This makes the ReGenMorph attacks of interest, given the worst-case attack scenario, and the realistic visible appearance of the attacks. A similar conclusion can be made from the scatter plots in Fig. 4. Where despite samples of ReGenMorph falling below the 0.1% FMR similarity threshold, those who don't can be considered a serious threat, especially given the realistic image appearance. In a conclusion, the ReGenMorphs can be considered a serious threat to face recognition systems with MMPMR and FMMPMR over 30% on top-performing COTS and at 0.1% FMR. Generally, as an attack, the system operators should not only be considering the strongest attack but should foresee all plausible attacks that can generate a serious threat. This is said, keeping in mind the importance of the realistic appearance as stated in Sect. 5.1.

5.3 Detectability of ReGenMorph

As detailed in Sect. 4.3, We measure the detectability of the ReGenMorph attacks under the know and unknown attack scenarios by using two state-of-the-art MAD methods [29,33]. Table 2 presents the BPCER values at different APCER thresholds. It should be noticed that the ReGenMorph attacks can be efficiently detected when the MAD is trained on the ReGenMorph or the LMA attacks. The fact that the ReGenMorph attacks can be detected by MAD trained on LMA attack does not mean that both attacks have the same appearance artifacts, as this is shown not to be the case (see Fig. 3). Detection algorithm can build their decisions on deeper statistical co-relations in the image that may not reflect the appearance, an example of that are the numerous studies on adversarial attacks [24]. On the other hand, the MAD performance is significantly worse when trained on the MIPGAN-II attacks. Both investigated MAD methods tend to have the same behavior pattern, however with varying performances (see Table 2). Beyond the automatic detectability, we stress that the realistic visual appearance is a serious threat to manual identity inspection as mentioned in Sect. 5.1. Therefore, it is essential to foresee new morphing concepts as the one presented in this work.

6   Conclusion

We propose in this work the novel ReGenMorph morphing pipeline to avoid blending artifacts caused by image-level morphing in LMA and synthetic-like striping artifacts caused by latent vector manipulation in GAN-based morphs. ReGenMorph exploits the GAN capabilities of creating realistic images without manipulating the latent vector, by feeding the encoder with an image that is morphed on the image level. The generated morph images exhibit high appearance quality in comparison to the latest morphing approaches. The identity preservation of the ReGenMorph is lower than the top morphing methods, however, given the security nature of the attack, worse-case scenarios should be considered. The detectability of the ReGenMorphs is low when they are not considered in the training, especially when the MAD is trained on the recent MIPGAN-II attacks.

Acknowledgment. This research work has been funded by the German Federal Ministry of Education and Research and the Hessian Ministry of Higher Education, Research, Science and the Arts within their joint support of the National Research Center for Applied Cybersecurity ATHENE.

References

1. Bojanowski, P., Joulin, A., Lopez-Paz, D., Szlam, A.: Optimizing the latent space of generative networks. In: ICML. Proceedings of Machine Learning Research, vol. 80, pp. 599–608. PMLR (2018)
2. Bolle, R., Pankanti, S.: Biometrics, Personal Identification in Networked Society: Personal Identification in Networked Society. Kluwer Academic Publishers, Norwell (1998)
3. Byrd, R., Lu, P., Nocedal, J., Zhu, C.: A limited memory algorithm for bound constrained optimization. SIAM J. Sci. Comput. **16**, 1190–1208 (1995). https://doi.org/10.1137/0916069
4. Damer, N., et al.: Detecting face morphing attacks by analyzing the directed distances of facial landmarks shifts. In: Brox, T., Bruhn, A., Fritz, M. (eds.) GCPR 2018. LNCS, vol. 11269, pp. 518–534. Springer, Cham (2019). https://doi.org/10.1007/978-3-030-12939-2_36
5. Damer, N., Boutros, F., Saladie, A.M., Kirchbuchner, F., Kuijper, A.: Realistic dreams: cascaded enhancement of GAN-generated images with an example in face morphing attacks. In: BTAS, pp. 1–10. IEEE (2019)
6. Damer, N., Grebe, J.H., Zienert, S., Kirchbuchner, F., Kuijper, A.: On the generalization of detecting face morphing attacks as anomalies: novelty vs. outlier detection. In: BTAS, pp. 1–5. IEEE (2019)
7. Damer, N., Saladie, A.M., Braun, A., Kuijper, A.: MorGAN: recognition vulnerability and attack detectability of face morphing attacks created by generative adversarial network. In: BTAS, pp. 1–10. IEEE (2018)
8. Damer, N., et al.: To detect or not to detect: the right faces to morph. In: ICB, pp. 1–8. IEEE (2019)
9. Damer, N., Zienert, S., Wainakh, Y., Saladie, A.M., Kirchbuchner, F., Kuijper, A.: A multi-detector solution towards an accurate and generalized detection of face morphing attacks. In: FUSION, pp. 1–8. IEEE (2019)
10. Deng, J., Guo, J., Xue, N., Zafeiriou, S.: Arcface: additive angular margin loss for deep face recognition. In: CVPR, pp. 4690–4699. Computer Vision Foundation/IEEE (2019)
11. Ferrara, M., Franco, A., Maltoni, D.: The magic passport. In: IJCB, pp. 1–7. IEEE (2014)
12. Ferrara, M., Franco, A., Maltoni, D.: Face demorphing. IEEE Trans. Inf. Forensics Secur. **13**(4), 1008–1017 (2018)
13. Fu, B., Spiller, N., Chen, C., Damer, N.: The effect of face morphing on face image quality. In: BIOSIG. LNI, Gesellschaft für Informatik e.V. (2021)
14. GmbH, C.S.: Facevacs technology - version 9.4.2 (2020). https://www.cognitec.com/facevacs-technology.html
15. Patrick, G., Mei, N., Kayee, H.: Ongoing face recognition vendor test (FRVT). NIST Interagency Report (2020)
16. Guo, Y., Zhang, L., Hu, Y., He, X., Gao, J.: MS-Celeb-1M: a dataset and benchmark for large-scale face recognition. In: Leibe, B., Matas, J., Sebe, N., Welling, M. (eds.) ECCV 2016. LNCS, vol. 9907, pp. 87–102. Springer, Cham (2016). https://doi.org/10.1007/978-3-319-46487-9_6
17. He, K., Zhang, X., Ren, S., Sun, J.: Deep residual learning for image recognition. In: CVPR, pp. 770–778. IEEE Computer Society (2016)
18. International Civil Aviation Organization, ICAO: Machine readable passports - part 9 - deployment of biometric identification and electronic storage of data in eMRTDs. Civil Aviation Organization (ICAO) (2015)
19. International Organization for Standardization: ISO/IEC DIS 30107-3:2016: Information Technology - Biometric presentation attack detection - P. 3: Testing and reporting (2017)
20. Karras, T., Aila, T., Laine, S., Lehtinen, J.: Progressive growing of GANs for improved quality, stability, and variation. In: ICLR. OpenReview.net (2018)

21. Karras, T., Laine, S., Aila, T.: A style-based generator architecture for generative adversarial networks. In: CVPR, pp. 4401–4410. Computer Vision Foundation/IEEE (2019)
22. Liu, W., Wen, Y., Yu, Z., Li, M., Raj, B., Song, L.: Sphereface: deep hypersphere embedding for face recognition. In: CVPR, pp. 6738–6746. IEEE Computer Society (2017)
23. Markets and Markets: Facial Recognition Market by Component (Software Tools and Services), Technology, Use Case (Emotion Recognition, Attendance Tracking and Monitoring, Access Control, Law Enforcement), End-User, and Region - Global Forecast to 2022. Report, November 2017
24. Massoli, F.V., Carrara, F., Amato, G., Falchi, F.: Detection of face recognition adversarial attacks. Comput. Vis. Image Underst. **202**, 103103 (2021)
25. NIST: FRVT morph web site. NIST Interagency Report (2020)
26. Phillips, P.J., et al.: Overview of the face recognition grand challenge. In: CVPR (1), pp. 947–954. IEEE Computer Society (2005)
27. Qin, L., Peng, F., Venkatesh, S., Ramachandra, R., Long, M., Busch, C.: Low visual distortion and robust morphing attacks based on partial face image manipulation. IEEE Trans. Biom. Behav. Identity Sci. **3**(1), 72–88 (2021)
28. Raghavendra, R., Raja, K.B., Venkatesh, S., Busch, C.: Face morphing versus face averaging: vulnerability and detection. In: IJCB, pp. 555–563. IEEE (2017)
29. Ramachandra, R., Venkatesh, S., Raja, K.B., Busch, C.: Towards making morphing attack detection robust using hybrid scale-space colour texture features. In: ISBA, pp. 1–8. IEEE (2019)
30. Scherhag, U., Kunze, J., Rathgeb, C., Busch, C.: Face morph detection for unknown morphing algorithms and image sources: a multi-scale block local binary pattern fusion approach. IET Biom. **9**(6), 278–289 (2020)
31. Scherhag, U., et al.: Biometric systems under morphing attacks: assessment of morphing techniques and vulnerability reporting. In: BIOSIG. LNI, vol. P-270, pp. 149–159. GI/IEEE (2017)
32. Simonyan, K., Zisserman, A.: Very deep convolutional networks for large-scale image recognition. In: ICLR (2015)
33. Venkatesh, S., Ramachandra, R., Raja, K.B., Busch, C.: Single image face morphing attack detection using ensemble of features. In: FUSION, pp. 1–6. IEEE (2020)
34. Venkatesh, S., Zhang, H., Ramachandra, R., Raja, K.B., Damer, N., Busch, C.: Can GAN generated morphs threaten face recognition systems equally as landmark based morphs? - vulnerability and detection. In: IWBF, pp. 1–6. IEEE (2020)
35. Zhang, H., Venkatesh, S., Ramachandra, R., Raja, K.B., Damer, N., Busch, C.: MIPGAN - generating robust and high quality morph attacks using identity prior driven GAN. CoRR abs/2009.01729 (2020)
36. Zhang, K., Zhang, Z., Li, Z., Qiao, Y.: Joint face detection and alignment using multitask cascaded convolutional networks. IEEE Signal Process. Lett. **23**(10), 1499–1503 (2016)

Car Pose Estimation Through Wheel Detection

Peter Roch[(✉)], Bijan Shahbaz Nejad, Marcus Handte, and Pedro José Marrón

University of Duisburg-Essen, Essen, Germany
peter.roch@uni-due.de

Abstract. Car pose estimation is an essential part of different applications, including traffic surveillance, Augmented Reality (AR) guides or inductive charging assistance systems. For many systems, the accuracy of the determined pose is important. When displaying AR guides, a small estimation error can result in a different visualization, which will be directly visible to the user. Inductive charging assistance systems have to guide the driver as precise as possible, as small deviations in the alignment of the charging coils can decrease charging efficiency significantly. For accurate pose estimation, matches between image coordinates and 3d real-world points have to be determined. Since wheels are a common feature of cars, we use the wheelbase and rim radius to compute those real-world points. The matching image coordinates are obtained by three different approaches, namely the circular Hough-Transform, ellipse-detection and a neural network. To evaluate the presented algorithms, we perform different experiments: First, we compare their accuracy and time performance regarding wheel-detection in a subset of the images of *The Comprehensive Cars (Comp-Cars) dataset* [37]. Second, we capture images of a car at known positions, and run the algorithms on these images to estimate the pose of the car. Our experiments show that the neural network based approach is the best in terms of accuracy and speed. However, if training of a neural network is not feasible, both other approaches are accurate alternatives.

Keywords: Computer vision · Pose estimation · Wheel detection · Applications

1   Introduction

Car pose estimation is an important task for different applications. These include automatically analyzing traffic scenes [17] or creating AR guides for automatic photo capture [21]. Using Occlusion-Net [28], Zensors utilizes car pose estimation to detect invalid turns, double parking or speeding [39].

Another use case for car pose estimation is inductive charging of electric vehicles [31]. While other applications may not need to estimate the pose accurately, charging efficiency is mainly determined by an accurate alignment of both inductive charging coils. To enable drivers of electric vehicles to position their car within a tolerance range of 10 cm, pose estimation has to be as accurate as possible. Shahbaz Nejad et al. [31] present an interesting use case, but only use the circular Hough-Transform to detect the wheels and estimate the pose. We extend that by comparing their work to other wheel detection techniques to improve pose estimation.

© Springer Nature Switzerland AG 2021
G. Bebis et al. (Eds.): ISVC 2021, LNCS 13017, pp. 265–277, 2021.
https://doi.org/10.1007/978-3-030-90439-5_21

Pose estimation usually requires matching 2D image coordinates with 3D real-world points. Shape, color or other visual features of cars may differ, therefore one cannot rely on such features to be present if the car is not known beforehand. In contrast, wheels are a common feature across cars independent of brand or model, which was used for pose estimation in previous research [16,31]. To match the wheels' image coordinates and real-world points, they must be detected as precisely as possible. Wheel detection was applied to different scenarios, including axle counting for classification of vehicles [12] or detecting other vehicles in images of an omnidirectional camera mounted on a moving car [2].

Wheel detection algorithms include circle detection, ellipse detection, feature extraction, and neural networks. Since accurate wheel detection is an integral part needed for pose estimation, we first compare different wheel-detection algorithms in terms of accuracy and time performance. Further, we evaluate their applicability to pose estimation. To evaluate computer vision algorithms, usually a large set of diverse images is required. Hence, we use a subset of *The Comprehensive Cars (CompCars) dataset* [37], featuring side-view images of cars of various models seen from different angles. Since the exact pose of the car is unknown in those images, we use this dataset only for evaluation of accuracy and time performance. To evaluate pose estimation, we manually collect images of a car at known distances and angles.

To summarize, this paper combines existing work to solve the application problem of guiding a driver to an inductive charging spot which requires a high accuracy (few cm) and low delay (multiple estimates per second), as explained in [31]. To achieve that, we make the following contributions:

1. We measure each algorithm's wheel detection accuracy and computation time.
2. We manually collect images of a car with a known ground truth pose.
3. We evaluate the accuracy of pose estimation using the detected wheels.

2   Related Work

Car pose estimation is useful for a broad spectrum of application scenarios, and as such was investigated in previous research. Hödlmoser et al. [17] present a framework for classification and pose estimation of vehicles by matching corresponding 3D models. Poses are further refined using consecutive images in videos. Another vehicle pose estimator utilizing a static stereo camera system is presented in [3]. Occlusion-Net [28] is a neural network, which is able to detect occluded keypoints in images of cars. Using this neural network, Zensors is able to estimate poses of multiple vehicles in order to detect invalid turns, speeding cars or other surveillance related statistics [39].

Apart from static camera systems mostly used for surveillance tasks, pose estimation can also be done on smartphones to assist the user in taking photos [21]. Driver assistance systems can make use of on board cameras to estimate the car's pose in relation to its environment [26] or to detect cars delimiting parking lots [19].

Most of these systems do not need to determine the exact pose of the car and can handle inaccurate measurements. However, in the case of a driver guidance system used for wireless charging of electric vehicles, the measured pose has to be as precise as possible, as explained in [31]. The authors estimate the vehicle's pose using the circular

Hough-transform to first detect the wheels, combined with background subtraction to filter out false positives. As wheels are a prominent feature in side-images of cars, wheel detection was already applied in previous research. Approaches to detect wheels in such images include using the circular Hough-transform combined with a SURF [4] feature detector [33] or using a difference of gaussian filterbank combined with a gaussian mixture model of wheels and non-wheels [1,2].

Since circles in 3d space are projected to ellipses in 2d images, ellipse detection methods can also be used to detect wheels. Both Xu et al. [36] and Hutter and Brewer [16] present ellipse-based wheel rim detectors. A more general ellipse detection algorithm is presented by Lu et al. [25]. Neural networks can be trained to detect custom objects. For instance, YOLOv4 [5] supports real-time detection and classification for arbitrary objects and improves both precision and speed of its predecessor YOLOv3 [29]. Neural network based pose estimators [15,27,38] have been evaluated using the LINEMOD [14] dataset. This dataset contains 3D models of all objects, which are used for training or during prediction. However, 3D models of vehicles may not be available. Moreover, they evaluate pose estimation accuracy in terms of correct/incorrect predictions and do not report the accuracy in real-world units.

Some of the aforementioned papers already present algorithms related to pose estimation and wheel detection. However, the presented pose estimation algorithms do not need to be as accurate as possible. Most of the papers on wheel detection only use these algorithms to perform simple tasks directly related to the detected wheels. In contrast to that, Shahbaz Nejad et al. [31] use the detected wheels to estimate the pose of the car. The pose is further used to assist the driver in positioning their car above the inductive charging coil. Hutter and Brewer [16] also use wheels to estimate a car's pose. However, they evaluate their algorithm using only synthetically generated images. For real images, they rely on visual inspection of the results, since the exact pose is unknown.

3   Wheel Detection Techniques

To detect wheels in images, we apply three different approaches, namely the Hough-Circle-Transform, Ellipse-Detection and a Neural Network.

Feature Detection & Matching: One possible solution to detect wheels is taking reference images and use a feature detector such as ORB [30] to match image regions to known features of wheels. A common downside of such feature detectors is that they rely on the features staying constant. They may be robust against most image transformations such as scale, rotation, and translation, but if features themselves change due to e.g. changing lighting conditions or reflections, they cannot be matched anymore.

Hough-Circle-Transform: In side-view images of cars, the wheels usually form a circle independent of the surrounding lighting conditions. The wheel's rubber usually is black, while most rims are in a lighter color. This difference can be used to detect the wheels. Hence, our first implementation is similar to the implementations presented in [31] and [33] and uses the circular Hough-transform [8,18] to detect the wheels.

First, we preprocess the image by grayscaling it and applying a Gaussian filter to smooth the image and filter out noise. After that, we apply the circular Hough-Transform and find circles in the image. This can be parameterized by several values.

First, the accumulator array size S_{aa} can be set in relation to the image resolution. Second, the accumulator threshold is defined by T_a. Internally, the Hough-Transform uses the Canny edge detector [6] to only retain edges in the image. This step uses two parameters (T_{low}, T_{high}). Additionally, constraints to the extracted circles can be configured. This includes the circles minimum and maximum radius r_{min} and r_{max}, as well as the minimum distance between two circles d_{min}. Appropriate choice of parameters already prevents many false positives at the detection stage. We assume that only one car is visible in the image. If more than two circles are found, we only retain the lowest two circles, since others are most likely false positives.

Ellipse-Detection: Since the circular form of the wheels can only be seen in a nearly perpendicular view of the car, the Hough-Circle-Transform has a limited range where wheels can be detected. If the car is rotated, the wheels will be distorted and projected as ellipses in the image, which makes them not detectable by the Hough-Circle-Transform. To address this limitation, our second implementation uses the method described in [25] to detect ellipses instead of circles. The authors define two parameters, T_r and T_{ac}, which control the number of detected ellipses. T_r describes the ratio of support inliers on an ellipse, with an expected minimum of $T_r \cdot \mathcal{B}$. Here, $\mathcal{B}$ is the corresponding perimeter, approximated as shown in Eq. 1 with a and b denoting the semi-major and semi-minor axis, respectively. The parameter T_{ac} describes the minimum angular coverage of the ellipse. Additionally, the algorithm can be configured to find only ellipses with positive or negative polarity.

Detected ellipses are filtered afterwards with Algorithm 1, which can be broken down into three steps: First, we discard all ellipses which cannot be wheels using constant thresholds. We define a range of (A_{min}, A_{max}) as the accepted size of ellipses. We further define R_{max} as the maximum ratio between semi-major and semi-minor axis to be considered circular and θ_{min} as the minimum angle for an ellipse to be considered vertical.

The base algorithm tends to detect multiple ellipses per wheel. Hence, our second step groups overlapping ellipses and selects only the best ellipse per group representing a wheel. The score of each ellipse is determined by Eq. 1:

$$\mathcal{B} \approx \pi \left[1.5 \, (a + b) - \sqrt{ab} \right] \quad \text{score} \, (e) = \sqrt{ \frac{ \# \{ p_i : p_i \in SI(e) \} }{ \mathcal{B} } \cdot \frac{\mathcal{C}}{360°} } \quad (1)$$

In this equation, $\mathcal{B}$ denotes the perimeter as described above, $\mathcal{C}$ is the angular coverage of the elliptic connected component of support inliers and $SI(e)$ denotes the support inliers of ellipse e. At this point, exactly one ellipse per detected wheel is left. As was done for the Hough-Circle-Transform, we only retain the lowest two ellipses and discard other ellipses, as they are most likely false positives.

Neural Network: Our third approach uses a neural network, namely YOLOv4 [5], specifically trained to detect wheels. For each input image, YOLO predicts multiple bounding boxes along with a confidence value between 0 and 1 describing how certain the network is in predicting the respective class. Similar to ellipse-detection, YOLOv4 detects bounding boxes for non-wheels, as well as multiple bounding boxes per wheel. The former can be filtered by using a confidence threshold T_c, the latter by applying Non-Maximum-Suppression (NMS). Both steps are described in Algorithm 2.

Algorithm 1. Ellipse filtering

1: **procedure** FILTERELLIPSES(E)
   Input: $E \leftarrow$ list of found ellipses
   Output: $W \leftarrow$ list of wheels
2:     Initialize filtered ellipses $E_f = \emptyset$
3:     **for all** $e \in E$ **do**
4:         **if** threshold e **then** $E_f = E_f \cup \{e\}$
5:         **end if**
6:     **end for**
7:     Initialize ellipse-groups $G_e =$
          overlapping ellipses from E_f
8:     Initialize wheels $W = \emptyset$
9:     **for all** $g \in G_e$ **do**
10:        $e \leftarrow$ best ellipse from g
11:        $W = W \cup \{e\}$
12:    **end for**
13:    filter W
14:    **return** W
15: **end procedure**

Algorithm 2. YOLO bounding box filtering

1: **procedure** FILTERBOUNDINGBOXES(B)
   Input: $B \leftarrow$ bounding boxes
   Output: $W \leftarrow$ wheels
2:     sort B by confidence
3:     **for all** $b \in B$ **do**
4:         $b_c \leftarrow$ confidence of b
5:         **if** $b_c < T_c$ **then** $B = B \setminus \{b\}$
6:         **end if**
7:     **end for**
8:     Initialize $B_f = \emptyset$
9:     **while** $B \neq \emptyset$ **do**
10:        $b_1 \leftarrow$ first element of B
11:        $B_f = B_f \cup \{b_1\}$
12:        $B = B \setminus \{b_1\}$
13:        **for all** $b_2 \in B$ **do**
14:            **if** $b_1 \equiv b_2$ **then** $B = B \setminus \{b_2\}$
15:            **end if**
16:        **end for**
17:    **end while**
18:    $W \leftarrow B_f$
19:    **return** W
20: **end procedure**

Filtering algorithms for ellipses and YOLO bounding boxes

4 Pose Estimation

To estimate the pose of the car, we need to find matches of 2d image coordinates and 3d real-world coordinates of corresponding points. Since the wheels can be described by wheelbase wb and rim radius r_r, we use these to compute eight 3d points $[p_1, \ldots, p_8]$ as the top, left, right and bottom point of each wheel. Naturally, the corresponding image points can be computed as the center of each edge of the detected bounding boxes.

In our test scenario, we know the exact real-world dimensions of the car. In a realistic scenario, the dimensions have to be configured beforehand if the application is limited to only one car. If multiple cars have to be positioned, the application first has to determine the type of the car and load its dimensions from a database.

Using the matched image points and real-world coordinates, we need to solve the *Perspective-n-Point (PnP)* problem. Different techniques to solve this problem were presented in previous research, either for the special case that $n = 3$ [20,35] or for the general case with $n \geq 3$ [13] or $n \geq 4$ [23]. Another method makes optimizations by constraining the points to be coplanar [7]. A much more recent PnP solver is SQPnP [32]. This algorithm has no constraints to the input points, yet it achieves accurate results at low computational cost.

The aforementioned PnP-algorithms are able to compute translation and rotation of objects in all three dimensions. Normally, a car can only be moved in the x/z-plane and rotated around the y-axis. Hence, we can correct the detected y-translation as well as rotations around x- and z-axes. The computed values could further be used for error estimation. While all PnP-algorithms are able to compute the pose for arbitrary objects in a noise-free environment, based on our experiments, SQPnP was the most robust among the tested algorithms for our scenario.

Fig. 1. Our system setup. The camera has a perpendicular view of the parking lot, showing the car from its side. (Color figure online)

Figure 1 describes the complete setup. The camera has a perpendicular view to the parking lot. If the car is visible in the camera's image, wheels are detected by previously described algorithms. Using the bounding box of each wheel, the corresponding image points are computed, which are shown in red. These points are matched to the measured real-world coordinates $[p_1, \ldots, p_8]$ to estimate the pose of the car.

5   Evaluation

In this chapter, we evaluate previously presented algorithms. First, we introduce the datasets we use for our evaluation. Afterwards, we explain parameterization of the used algorithms. The next section describes the evaluation metrics we use for comparing accuracy and time performance in wheel-detection, followed by the comparison itself. The last section covers an evaluation on each algorithm's pose estimation accuracy. All tests were carried out using a laptop with an Intel® Core™ i7-9750H CPU and an NVIDIA GeForce RTX 2070 with Max-Q Design GPU.

5.1   Evaluation Datasets

To overcome the problem of an unknown ground truth pose as described in [16], we searched for existing datasets such as CARLA [9] and KITTI [11]. Unfortunately, these were not suitable for our scenario. CARLA is not a dataset itself, but a simulator for autonomous driving. While it could be used to generate images with a known ground truth pose, the images would be synthetic. KITTI is a dataset containing images and lidar scans obtained from vehicle-mounted equipment. Using the provided lidar scans, the ground truth pose of other road users can be computed. However, since images were

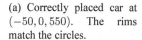

(a) Correctly placed car at $(-50, 0, 550)$. The rims match the circles.

(b) Correctly placed car at $(50, 0, 600)$. The rims match the circles.

(c) Incorrectly placed car at $(50, 0, 500)$. The car needs to be moved to the right / the camera needs to be moved to the left.

Fig. 2. Screenshots of the image recording application. Green circles indicate the expected final location of the wheels, assisting in placement of the camera. (Color figure online)

recorded by a vehicle-mounted camera, most other vehicles are shown from behind. Cars shown from the side are mostly too far away for accurate positioning.

To acquire realistic images closely reflecting the scenario of an inductive charging spot, we record new images of a car at predefined, and hence exactly known, positions. Our image acquisition is assisted by an application showing the expected location of both wheels. Using that information, we place the camera, a Logitech C270 HD WEB-CAM with a resolution of 1280×720 pixels, at the correct position in relation to the car. Example screenshots are shown in Fig. 2. Figures 2a and 2b show the car in the correct position. The green circles match the rim of each wheel. In contrast to that, Fig. 2c shows the car at a wrong position. The green circles indicate that the car has to be moved to the right in order to be correctly placed.

We record the car at 10 different positions. These include a placement of the car at 450 cm, 500 cm, 550 cm and 600 cm distance, as well as a horizontal translation of 50 cm to the left and right of the camera. At 450 cm distance, the car is too close for the wheels to both be visible when moved by 50 cm, hence we only include images with no horizontal translation for this distance. To account for slightly differing lighting conditions and other nondeterministic noise, we take multiple images of each recorded pose, and randomly select 25 images for evaluation. That means, we have 250 images in total, where we know the exact offset of the camera in relation to the car. To enable other researchers to make use of our data, we make our dataset available at https://www.nes.uni-due.de/research/data/.

Our pose estimation step relies on accuracy in wheel detection. Therefore, we first evaluate each algorithm's ability to accurately detect wheels. Furthermore, we measure the computation time in milliseconds. For this evaluation, we use a subset of the images from *The Comprehensive Cars (CompCars) dataset* [37]. This dataset contains many synthetic and real images of different cars in different environments. Since we are interested in detecting wheels, we filter out unsuited images to only take into account such images where the car can be seen from the side and both wheels are clearly visible. We split the images randomly into a training and testing set, containing 2000 and 300 images, respectively. Some parameters of the circular Hough-transform and also the ellipse detection algorithm depend on the image size. To reduce false positives and negatives due to a bad parameter choice, we resize all images to have a resolution of 1280×720 pixels, keeping the original aspect ratio and adding bars as necessary.

5.2 Algorithm Parameterization

Hough-Circle-Transform: Our first wheel detector will use the circular Hough-Transform and is abbreviated as HCT in the following sections. As explained in Sect. 3, we need to configure multiple parameters. First, the image is smoothed by a Gaussian filter using a kernel of size 9×9 and standard deviation of 1.5. Afterwards, we set the accumulator array size S_{aa} to equal the image size. Further, we set T_a to 35. The Canny edge detection thresholds are set to $(65, 130)$. Further, we specifiy the minimum distance between wheels to be 144 pixels, and the minimum and maximum radius to be 30 and 60 pixels, respectively. These parameters were chosen to reflect the parameterization in [31] to make results comparable.

Ellipse Detection: We use the algorithm explained in [25] to detect ellipses in the image. We do not change the default parameters of $T_r = 0.6$ and $T_{ac} = 165°$. Since rims are usually lighter colored than the wheels' rubber, we expect that only detecting ellipses with positive polarity increases accuracy by detecting less false positives. Less ellipses also improve the speed of the filtering algorithm afterwards. Hence, we distinguish between positive polarity as opposed to positive and negative polarity. We abbreviate both implementations as Ell_{pol} and Ell_{def}, respectively.

Neural Network: YOLO has plenty of configuration options and offers the possibility, to train a custom collection of images, as well as to use pre-trained weights. In this paper, we train YOLO using 2000 manually labeled images. For evaluating accuracy and time performance, we distinguish between two different configurations. First, we use the full model with an input resolution of 608×608 pixels, as described by Bochkovskiy et al. [5]. Second, we use a tiny model with reduced layers and reduced input resolution of 256×256 pixels and thus requiring fewer resources, leading to reduced accuracy but faster computation time. Additionally, we run the prediction on the CPU and on the GPU. To distinguish between these variations, we abbreviate them as $\text{YOLO}_{\text{Full}}^{\text{CPU}}$, $\text{YOLO}_{\text{Full}}^{\text{GPU}}$, $\text{YOLO}_{\text{Tiny}}^{\text{CPU}}$ and $\text{YOLO}_{\text{Tiny}}^{\text{GPU}}$.

5.3 Evaluation Metrics

After training both YOLO models, we run each algorithm on our testing images. For further computation, we first need to find the bounding box of the detected wheels. We use the notation of $[x_r, y_r, w_r, h_r]$ to describe a bounding box with its top left corner at (x_r, y_r), a width of w_r pixels and a height of h_r pixels. A circle is described by three parameters $[x_c, y_c, r_c]$, with its center at (x_c, y_c) and a radius of r_c. To compute the bounding box, we use Eq. 2:

$$x_r = x_c - r_c \quad y_r = y_c - r_c \quad w_r = 2r_c \quad h_r = 2r_c \tag{2}$$

An ellipse is described by five parameters $[x_e, y_e, a_e, b_e, \varphi_e]$. Here, (x_e, y_e) describes its center point, while a_e, b_e and φ_e are its semi-major axis, semi-minor axis

and rotation angle, respectively. To compute the bounding box of an ellipse, we use
Eq. 3 and 4:

$$u_x = a_e * \cos\left(\varphi_e\right) \qquad u_y = a_e * \sin\left(\varphi_e\right)$$
$$v_x = b_e * \cos\left(\varphi_e + \tfrac{\pi}{2}\right) \quad v_y = b_e * \sin\left(\varphi_e + \tfrac{\pi}{2}\right) \tag{3}$$

$$w_r = 2 * \sqrt{u_x{}^2 + v_x{}^2} \quad h_r = 2 * \sqrt{u_y{}^2 + v_y{}^2}$$
$$x_r = x_e - \tfrac{w_r}{2} \qquad y_r = y_e - \tfrac{h_r}{2} \tag{4}$$

Detected wheels are considered true positives if their *Intersection over Union (IoU)*
exceeds a threshold of 50%. This classification process was described in the *PASCAL
Visual Object Classes (VOC) Challenge* [10], as shown in Eq. 5:

$$\text{IoU} = \frac{\text{area}\left(B_p \cap B_{gt}\right)}{\text{area}\left(B_p \cup B_{gt}\right)} \tag{5}$$

Here, B_p denotes the predicted bounding box of the wheel, whereas B_{gt} denotes the
ground truth bounding box. $B_p \cap B_{gt}$ and $B_p \cup B_{gt}$ denote the intersection and union
of these two, respectively.

We use the *Average Precision (AP)* metric, which is also described in the PAS-
CAL VOC Challenge, as well as the *mean Average Precision (mAP)* metric, which is
described in the *Microsoft COCO* [24] dataset, to compute scores for each algorithm.
Both metrics are defined as follows: First, precision and recall are computed as defined
in Eq. 6:

$$\text{precision} = \frac{\text{correct predictions}}{\text{number of predictions}} \quad \text{recall} = \frac{\text{correct predictions}}{\text{number of elements}} \tag{6}$$

The interpolated precision p_{int} at a recall level r is defined as the maximum precision for which the corresponding recall exceeds r, while the Average Precision (AP) is
computed as the arithmetic mean of p_{int} at eleven equally spaced recall levels:

$$p_{int} = \max_{\tilde{r}:\tilde{r}\geq r}\left(p\left(\tilde{r}\right)\right) \quad \text{AP}^{\text{IoU}=0.50} = \frac{1}{11} \sum_{r\in\{0,0.1,\ldots,1\}} p_{int}\left(r\right) \tag{7}$$

Here, $\text{AP}^{\text{IoU}=0.50}$ indicates the IoU threshold of 50%. The mean Average Precision
(mAP) is computed as the arithmetic mean of the AP at ten different IoU thresholds, as
shown in Eq. 8:

$$\text{mAP} = \frac{1}{10} \sum_{t\in\{0.50,0.55,\ldots,0.95\}} \text{AP}^{\text{IoU}=t} \tag{8}$$

Both AP and mAP metrics focus only on the ratio between correct predictions, false
positives and false negatives. For pose estimation, the accuracy of found wheels is of
special interest, while wrong or missed wheels can be filtered by other means. In videos,
a background subtractor [40,41] or Kalman filter [34] can be used. Therefore, we also
include the *mean IoU (mIoU)* of all correctly identified wheels as an additional metric.
For most applications, there is a trade-off between accuracy and time performance.
Hence, we also measure the computation time of each algorithm in milliseconds.

5.4   Wheel Detection Accuracy and Time Performance

Table 1 shows the accuracy of previously described wheel detection algorithms, measured in AP ($AP^{IoU=0.50}$), mAP and mIoU, as defined above, as well as the time in milliseconds needed to detect wheels in one image. Figure 3 also visualizes the relation between detection time and AP-score of each detector.

As can be seen, the Hough-Circle-Transform and Tiny-YOLO are nearly equally fast, while Tiny-YOLO is much more accurate. The full network is even more accurate with a perfect AP-score of 1.0, but is substantially slower. That means, the full YOLO model is able to detect every wheel, while detecting no false positives. When ignoring AP and mAP and focusing on the accuracy of only correctly identified wheels, represented by mIoU, all detectors score reasonably well. Both YOLO models as well as the ellipse-detection algorithm have a mIoU of 0.9 or higher.

Table 1. Accuracy (measured in AP, mAP and mIoU as described in Sect. 5.3) and detection time (measured in ms) of each algorithm

Detector	AP	mAP	mIoU	Time
HCT	0.40	0.27	0.83	14.99 ms
Ell_{def}	0.69	0.61	0.92	1662.52 ms
Ell_{pol}	0.71	0.63	0.93	1041.18 ms
$YOLO_{Tiny}^{CPU}$	0.91	0.79	0.91	14.03 ms
$YOLO_{Tiny}^{GPU}$	0.91	0.79	0.91	13.63 ms
$YOLO_{Full}^{CPU}$	1.00	0.95	0.96	595.26 ms
$YOLO_{Full}^{GPU}$	1.00	0.95	0.96	350.99 ms

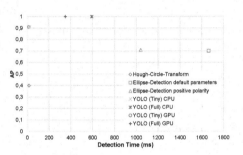

Fig. 3. Detection time in ms and corresponding accuracy in AP

5.5   Pose Estimation Accuracy

As mentioned in Sect. 5.1, we estimate the pose of a car recorded at 10 different positions, ranging from 4.50 m to 6.00 m distance between camera and car and 0.50 m translation on either side. We evaluate each algorithm's pose estimation accuracy by first detecting the wheels, extracting four keypoints per wheel (top, bottom, left and right) and using the SQPnP [32] algorithm to compute the vehicle's pose. Table 2 shows the average translation and rotation error for each axis. In a real application, y-translation and x-/z-rotation can safely assumed to be zero, since all wheels of the car must be standing on the ground. Hence, we also include the x/z translation error as a combined metric reflecting the accuracy of pose estimation on the x/z-plane. This is computed as the euclidean distance between the expected and the detected position, as shown in Eq. 9:

$$x/z = \sqrt{\left(x_e - x_d\right)^2 + \left(z_e - z_d\right)^2} \tag{9}$$

As can be seen, all algorithms have an x/z translation error of 4–7 cm. That is more accurate than the measurements taken in [31] and also lies within the tolerance range of

10 cm for inductive charging defined therein. A rotation error on the y-axis of 3.2 and less is also acceptable for inductive charging.

While the ellipse-detector was overall slightly more accurate than YOLO$_{Full}$, it did not detect both wheels in all images. YOLO$_{Full}$ was able to detect the car at all tested positions. YOLO$_{Tiny}$ was even more accurate with a x/z translation error of 4.31 cm.

Interestingly, the y-axis translation error was the lowest error for all algorithms, while the z-axis translation error was the highest. That means, the car was accurately located on the ground, while the detected distance to the camera was wrong by approximately 5 cm. The rotation error is of similar nature. Rotation around the z-axis was detected quite well with an average error of less than 1°. However, the rotation around the x-axis was comparatively high. That means, the car was detected as if it was slightly tilted towards or away from the camera.

Table 2. Average translation and rotation error in x-, y-, z-direction of each algorithm.

Detector	Translation error				Rotation error		
	x	y	z	x/z	x	y	z
HCT	2.50 cm	1.04 cm	5.59 cm	6.65 cm	5.93°	3.20°	0.55°
Ell$_{def}$	1.62 cm	0.87 cm	5.09 cm	5.56 cm	2.56°	3.09°	0.38°
Ell$_{pol}$	1.38 cm	0.79 cm	5.03 cm	5.34 cm	2.52°	2.89°	0.33°
YOLO$_{Tiny}$	1.38 cm	0.78 cm	3.89 cm	4.31 cm	2.72°	1.69°	0.43°
YOLO$_{Full}$	0.96 cm	0.71 cm	5.55 cm	5.70 cm	3.00°	1.67°	0.30°

6   Conclusion and Future Work

In this paper, we compared three different algorithms in regards to their suitability for pose estimation. We first evaluated accuracy and time performance in wheel detection, as that is the first step in our pose estimation pipeline. As shown, YOLO outperformed both other wheel detectors in terms of accuracy. Tiny-YOLO is the fastest detector, while only being slightly less accurate than the full YOLO-model. Training of a neural network needs a vast number of labeled images and a powerful computer. If one or both are not available, the presented Hough-Circle-Transform and Ellipse-Detection techniques represent good alternatives. The Hough-Circle-Transform is nearly equally fast as Tiny-YOLO and therefore is useful for real-time applications, while Ellipse-Detection is more accurate, but much slower.

When applied to pose estimation, all algorithms have an accuracy between 4 cm and 7 cm. Here, Tiny-YOLO is the most accurate detector. Ellipse-Detection is also able to accurately determine the pose in most cases, however, this algorithm did not detect both wheels in all tested images and hence was not able to determine the pose for 2 positions. We conclude that Tiny-YOLO is the best algorithm for pose estimation among the tested, since it offers high accuracy while being computationally efficient.

To further evaluate the usefulness of our pose estimation pipeline, we deployed the YOLO-based approach at a local taxi company. There we can gather more images at different angles and distances, as well as improve parameters of YOLO and Tiny-YOLO.

The images used for training and evaluation were all resized to have the same resolution in order to focus on the difference between the presented algorithms. Some parameters are resolution-dependent. To allow the input images to have different resolutions, an automatic parameter finding technique could be developed.

Another part that can be improved is the automatic generation of the training dataset. There are many image datasets already available, of which some are also labeled. But if custom labels or only a specific subset of images are needed, images need to be filtered and labeled manually, as was done for this paper. This process is very time-consuming and error-prone. If photo-realistic images can be generated randomly by using 3d-models of real objects, only those models need to be annotated. Properties of the resulting dataset, such as the number of objects per image, how the objects are labeled, etc. can be configured beforehand instead of adjusted retrospectively.

Acknowledgment. This research is funded by the Bundesministerium für Wirtschaft und Energie as part of the TALAKO project [22] (grant number 01MZ19002A).

References

1. Achler, O., Trivedi, M.M.: Camera based vehicle detection, tracking, and wheel baseline estimation approach. In: ITSC (2004)
2. Achler, O., Trivedi, M.M.: Vehicle wheel detector using 2d filter banks. In: IV (2004)
3. Barrois, B., Hristova, S., Wohler, C., Kummert, F., Hermes, C.: 3d pose estimation of vehicles using a stereo camera. In: IV (2009)
4. Bay, H., Tuytelaars, T., Van Gool, L.: Surf: Speeded up robust features. In: ECCV (2006)
5. Bochkovskiy, A., Wang, C.Y., Liao, H.Y.M.: YOLOv4: optimal speed and accuracy of object detection (2020)
6. Canny, J.: A Computational Approach to Edge Detection. TPAMI (1986)
7. Collins, T., Bartoli, A.: Infinitesimal plane-based pose estimation. IJCV (2014)
8. Davies, E.: A modified hough scheme for general circle location. Pattern Recogn. Lett. **7**, 37–43 (1988)
9. Dosovitskiy, A., Ros, G., Codevilla, F., Lopez, A., Koltun, V.: CARLA: an open urban driving simulator. In: CoRL (2017)
10. Everingham, M., Van Gool, L., Williams, C.K.I., Winn, J., Zisserman, A.: The pascal visual object classes (voc) challenge. IJCV (2010)
11. Geiger, A., Lenz, P., Urtasun, R.: Are we ready for autonomous driving? the kitti vision benchmark suite. In: CVPR (2012)
12. Grigoryev, A., Bocharov, D., Terekhin, A., Nikolaev, D.: Vision-based vehicle wheel detector and axle counter. In: ECMS (2015)
13. Hesch, J.A., Roumeliotis, S.I.: A direct least-squares (dls) method for pnp. In: ICCV (2011)
14. Hinterstoisser, S., et al.: Model based training, detection and pose estimation of texture-less 3d objects in heavily cluttered scenes. In: ACCV (2013)
15. Hu, Y., Hugonot, J., Fua, P., Salzmann, M.: Segmentation-driven 6d object pose estimation. In: CVPR (2019)

16. Hutter, M., Brewer, N.: Matching 2-d ellipses to 3-d circles with application to vehicle pose identification. In: IVCNZ (2009)
17. Hödlmoser, M., Micusik, B., Liu, M., Pollefeys, M., Kampel, M.: Classification and pose estimation of vehicles in videos by 3d modeling within discrete-continuous optimization. In: 3DIMPVT (2012)
18. Illingworth, J., Kittler, J.: The adaptive hough transform. TPAMI (1987)
19. Kaempchen, N., Franke, U., Ott, R.: Stereo vision based pose estimation of parking lots using 3d vehicle models. In: IV (2002)
20. Ke, T., Roumeliotis, S.I.: An efficient algebraic solution to the perspective-three-point problem. In: CVPR (2017)
21. Laan, C.: Real-time 3D car pose estimation trained on synthetic data (2019). https://labs.laan.com/blog/real-time-3d-car-pose-estimation-trained-on-synthetic-data.html. Accessed 16 Feb 2021
22. Lehrstuhl für Internationales Automobilmanagement, Universität Duisburg-Essen: Taxiladekonzept für Elektrotaxis im öffentlichen Raum. https://talako.uni-due.de/. Accessed 25 Jan 2021
23. Lepetit, V., Moreno-Noguer, F., Fua, P.: Epnp: an accurate o(n) solution to the PNP problem. IJCV (2009)
24. Lin, T.Y., et al.: Microsoft coco: common objects in context. In: ECCV (2014)
25. Lu, C., Xia, S., Shao, M., Fu, Y.: Arc-support line segments revisited: an efficient high-quality ellipse detection. IEEE Trans. Image Process. **29**, 768–781 (2020)
26. Nilsson, J., Fredriksson, J., Ödblom, A.C.E.: Reliable vehicle pose estimation using vision and a single-track model. T-ITS (2014)
27. Peng, S., Liu, Y., Huang, Q., Zhou, X., Bao, H.: Pvnet: pixel-wise voting network for 6dof pose estimation. In: CVPR (2019)
28. Reddy, N.D., Vo, M., Narasimhan, S.G.: Occlusion-net: 2d/3d occluded keypoint localization using graph networks. In: CVPR (2019)
29. Redmon, J., Farhadi, A.: YOLOv3: an incremental improvement (2018)
30. Rublee, E., Rabaud, V., Konolige, K., Bradski, G.: Orb: an efficient alternative to sift or surf. In: ICCV (2011)
31. Shahbaz Nejad, B., Roch, P., Handte, M., Marrón, P.J.: A driver guidance system to support the stationary wireless charging of electric vehicles. In: Advances in Visual Computing (2020)
32. Terzakis, G., Lourakis, M.: A consistently fast and globally optimal solution to the perspective-n-point problem. In: ECCV (2020)
33. Vinoharan, V., Ramanan, A., Kodituwakku, S.R.: A wheel-based side-view car detection using snake algorithm. In: ICIAfS (2012)
34. Welch, G., Bishop, G.: An introduction to the kalman filter (1997)
35. Gao, X.-S., Hou, X.-R., Tang, J.: Complete solution classification for the perspective-three-point problem. TPAMI, Hang-Fei Cheng (2003)
36. Xu, G., Su, J., Pan, H., Zhang, D.: A novel method for wheel rim recognition. In: ISECS (2008)
37. Yang, L., Luo, P., Loy, C.C., Tang, X.: A large-scale car dataset for fine-grained categorization and verification. In: CVPR (2015)
38. Zakharov, S., Shugurov, I., Ilic, S.: Dpod: 6d pose object detector and refiner. In: ICCV (2019)
39. Zensors: Car Pose Net (2019). https://www.zensors.com/car-pose/. Accessed 16 Feb 2021
40. Zivkovic, Z.: Improved adaptive gaussian mixture model for background subtraction. In: CVPR (2004)
41. Zivkovic, Z., van der Heijden, F.: Efficient adaptive density estimation per image pixel for the task of background subtraction. Pattern Recognition Letters (2006)

Improving Automatic Quality Inspection in the Automotive Industry by Combining Simulated and Real Data

Pedro Pinho[1]([✉]), Isabel Rio-Torto[1,2]([✉]) [iD], and Luís Filipe Teixeira[1,2] [iD]

[1] Department of Informatics and Computing Engineering, Faculty of Engineering, University of Porto, 4200-465 Porto, Portugal
up201605166@fe.up.pt
[2] INESC TEC - INESC Technology and Science, 4200-465 Porto, Portugal
{luisft,icrto}@fe.up.pt

Abstract. Considerable amounts of data are required for a deep learning model to generalize to unseen cases successfully. Furthermore, such data is often manually labeled, making its annotation process costly and time-consuming. We propose using unlabeled real-world data in conjunction with automatically labeled synthetic data, obtained from simulators, to surpass the increasing need for annotated data. By obtaining real counterparts of simulated samples using CycleGAN and subsequently performing fine-tuning with such samples, we manage to improve a vehicle part's detection system performance by 2.5%, compared to the baseline exclusively trained on simulated images. We explore adding a semantic consistency loss to CycleGAN by re-utilizing previous work's trained networks to regularize the conversion process. Moreover, the addition of a post-processing step, which we denominate global NMS, highlights our approach's effectiveness by better utilizing our detection model's predictions and ultimately improving the system's performance by 14.7%.

Keywords: Transfer learning · Domain adaptation · Deep learning · Simulated data · Quality inspection · Object detection

1 Introduction

One of the main particularities that make deep learning (DL) methods so distinguishable from others is the need for very large amounts of data to successfully build a well-performing model. Unfortunately, gathering and labelling the necessary data is costly and extremely labour-intensive since the annotations must be done manually by humans. To surpass the difficulties associated with data collection, synthetic images produced by simulators can be a cost-effective and reliable alternative [1,5,11,12] since they can automatically generate annotated data on-demand.

We improve upon a previous project, aimed to automate quality control at the end of a vehicle's production line. Previously, a hierarchical DL architecture that identified vehicle parts was trained solely on data obtained through

© Springer Nature Switzerland AG 2021
G. Bebis et al. (Eds.): ISVC 2021, LNCS 13017, pp. 278–290, 2021.
https://doi.org/10.1007/978-3-030-90439-5_22

a simulator. As annotations for real-world vehicles are not at our disposal we approached this scenario as a domain adaptation (DA) problem, where simulated and real images must be combined to retrieve useful information from both data sources and increase the detection system's overall performance. By performing domain mapping we convert simulated images to real counterparts while preserving their bounding box annotations and create a new dataset which we use to fine-tune the previously developed detector model. We use CycleGAN [15] as our domain mapping method as it does not require image pairs to perform image-to-image translation. Furthermore, we introduce a semantic consistency loss for our domain mapping task and a post-processing step to our vehicle parts detection model. The former helps regularize the translation process of our specific scenario of converting vehicles from the simulated to the real domain. The latter prunes specific vehicle parts detected instances to increase overall system performance.

2 Related Work

Domain Mapping. This is the task of converting images from a source domain to a target domain. The models that accomplish this task commonly use a cycle-consistency loss, usually the L1 or L2 distance, between the original and the reconverted images to force feature preservation during the cross-domain conversion. Some GAN-based models were concurrently released that used a cycle-consistency loss [3,7,8,15], the most notable being CycleGAN [15]. CycleGAN tackles the unpaired image-to-image translation problem, where an image from the source domain X is mapped to a target domain Y without the need for paired samples. While aiming to learn mapping in both directions $G : X \to Y$, $F : Y \to X$ a cycle-consistency loss is in place $F(G(X)) \approx X$, and vice-versa, to appropriately pair both domains. Cycle-consistent adversarial domain adaptation (CyCADA) [2] adds pixel, feature, and semantic losses on top of the cycle-consistency constraint. The authors applied this method to synthetic to real DA tasks. They concluded that adding these losses to enforce local and global feature preservation helps to recover information lost while bridging the domain gap.

Differentiable Augmentation (DiffAugment). DiffAugment [14] is a method that lessens the need for large datasets to train a GAN model successfully. The authors demonstrate their technique applied to StyleGAN2 [6]. DiffAugment can prevent mode collapse, when using limited amounts of data [14], and achieve a near-identical FID score with only 20% of training data compared to the standard StyleGAN2 with 100% training data. The authors apply differentiable image augmentations to both real and generator-made images propagating gradients through those augmentations for both generator and discriminator parameters update cycles. In this manner, the discriminator training is improved while the generator does not suffer from the different augmented distribution since the received gradients also flow through the applied augmentations.

Da and Object Detection. Inoue et al. [4] applied DA to the task of weakly-supervised object detection. The authors used CycleGAN [15] and pseudo-labeling to progressively fine-tune an already existent object detector model. By taking advantage of the CycleGAN, domain-translated images from the source to the target domain are produced, which serve as additional data for the fine-tuning process. This step helps to increase the available labeled data, and the converted images can be reused and applied to other tasks, as a new converted dataset with the same features as the original one is essentially being built, albeit with a different style.

3 Methods

3.1 Baseline

Rio-Torto et al. [10] proposed a system with the final goal of automating quality control at the end of a vehicle's production line. The core module of the system is its detection module, responsible for analyzing vehicle images and outputting a list of parts that compose the corresponding vehicle. This module is divided into two stages: an object detection and segmentation stage followed by a content-based image retrieval (CBIR) stage. The former performs a macro detection of vehicle parts in a given image. By macro detection we mean that only the location and part codes of each instance are inferred, leaving the task of determining the model, brand, and material codes to the CBIR stage. Using pre-trained weights of a ResNet-101 Feature Pyramid Network (FPN) backbone trained on the COCO dataset, a Detectron2 [13] model was fine-tuned on the simulated dataset. For the CBIR stage, multiple search indexes, one for each macro class detected by the Detectron2 model, are in place to facilitate the adjustment of vehicle parts during the manufacturing process. When receiving the macro codes from Detectron2, each detected instance is directed to the index of the corresponding class. According to its bounding box, a cropped image is produced, and an embedding vector is obtained from the feature extractor network. Afterward, the embedding's nearest neighbor is voted using the L2 Euclidean distance, obtaining the final code.

We propose fine-tuning the Detectron2 model with a converted dataset closer to the real-world distribution. To generate this novel dataset, we perform domain mapping using CycleGAN combined with DiffAugment and a semantic consistency loss to bridge the gap between simulated and real domains more adequately. As such, we obtain fully annotated realistic images from our existing simulated dataset, which are used for the fine-tuning process.

3.2 CycleGAN with Semantic Consistency

The main challenge of domain translation is to retain the original images' features when performing said translation. CycleGAN is known for preserving structural information during the domain translation, mostly adapting textures and

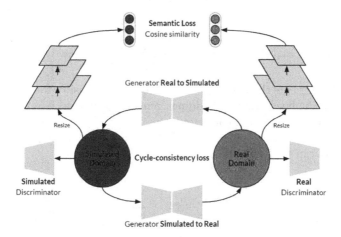

Fig. 1. Diagram of the modified CycleGAN with semantic consistency. In addition to the standard CycleGAN's generators and discriminators, we introduce a semantic consistency loss using Detectron2's FPN backbone.

colors in the resulting images [4,15]. However, in some cases, the model may revamp most of the simulated image, which would lead to severe information loss. To accommodate for these cases and to further improve other instances, a semantic loss is implemented. Based on CyCADA [2], its objective is to guide the generator training into preserving the embeddings of the original image during conversion.

In practice, this is achieved by re-utilizing the pre-trained Detectron2's backbone on simulated images. The generator's inputs are passed through the pre-trained backbone, obtaining the input embeddings. Afterward, the corresponding converted images' embeddings are obtained in the same fashion, and we compute the cosine similarity between both embeddings (Fig. 1). The pre-trained backbone is expecting 512 by 512 pixels images, while CycleGAN uses 256 by 256 pixels images. Therefore, all generator's inputs and outputs were properly converted to the expected backbone format during the training process. The backbone's parameters were not optimized during CycleGAN's training; it simply serves to regularize the generator's outputs.

The Detectron2's backbone is a FPN, meaning it has several output layers L from which regions of interest are extracted. We experimented with which layers to use to apply the semantic consistency loss: only on the last layer or on all layers. More precisely, the backbone has 5 output layers (p2, p3, p4, p5 and p6). From p2 to p6 the embeddings are iteratively encoded, diminishing in size, meaning layer p2 holds more detailed lower-level information while layer p6 has a higher-level image representation.

Formally, the new semantic consistency loss for a single input image x being converted by the generator G is as follows:

$$\ell_{sem}(G, B, l, x) = \frac{B_l(x) \cdot B_l(G(x))}{\|B_l(x))\|_2 \times \|B_l(G(x))\|_2} \tag{1}$$

where B represents the Detectron2's backbone, responsible for embedding the input at a specific layer l. All embeddings generated by Detectron2 are flattened before applying the semantic consistency loss.

The semantic loss was applied to both domains expecting helpful embeddings to be generated in both directions:

$$\mathcal{L}_{sem}(G_1, G_2, B) = \mathbb{E}_{x \sim P_{data}(x)} \sum_{l \in L} \ell_{sem}(G_1, B, l, x) \tag{2}$$

$$+ \mathbb{E}_{y \sim P_{data}(y)} \sum_{l \in L} \ell_{sem}(G_2, B, l, y) \tag{3}$$

where G_1 and G_2 represent the CycleGAN's generators, one for each domain conversion, x being the simulated domain samples and y the real domain samples. The new global loss can be formulated as such (all our experiments had $\lambda_{sem} = 1.0$, the same weight as the cycle-consistency and identity losses):

$$\mathcal{L}_{CycleGAN-Semantic}(G_1, G_2, D_X, D_Y, B) = \mathcal{L}_{CycleGAN}(G_1, G_2, D_X, D_Y) \tag{4}$$

$$+ \lambda_{sem} \mathcal{L}_{sem}(G_1, G_2, B) \tag{5}$$

3.3   Detection System's Improvements

Detector Fine-Tuning. When analyzing the previous work's findings [10] we reach the conclusion that the major bottleneck in the detection module is the object detection stage, performed by Detectron2. When evaluating the CBIR stage independently from the detection system the authors obtain very good results. This shows Detectron2 is at fault for the system's relatively poor performance on real data compared to simulated data. To choose the CycleGAN variant to use for the Detectron2's fine-tuning process we decided to convert a subset of the simulated dataset and determine the original Detectron2's performance on it. This subset was composed of 1134 images and had the same class distribution as the complete simulated dataset. Since Detectron2 was previously trained only on simulated data, it is expected not to generalize well to translated images. Nevertheless, considering that the translation models managed to preserve the original annotations, we argue that the model should be able to extract useful information to some extent and produce a few valid predictions. We perform domain mapping and subsequent fine-tuning using the translation model that provided us with the best validation accuracy.

Global Non-maximum Supression (NMS). This post-processing step prunes Detectron2's overlapping bounding boxes, which have an IoU value above 50%, independent of their classes. By default Detectron2 applies intra-class NMS, eliminating overlapping bounding boxes only if they belong to the same class. In our scenario, this poses an issue since it allows multiple predictions to be focused on a single location. As such, we also evaluate and compare the system's performance with and without applying global NMS.

4 Experiments

Datasets. For the simulated domain, we used the same 3D vehicle generator used for the original inspection system [10], and maintained the same 512 by 512 pixels RGB format. The simulated training and validation sets are composed of 3184 and 762 images, respectively. Ultimately, 6855 training and 762 validation real-world images were collected. These datasets are solely used for the training of the CycleGAN models. For the fine-tuning process we make use of the previous work's datasets [10], by converting them using the selected CycleGAN variant. Furthermore, the real dataset used for this portion only has image-level annotations, meaning that we have access to a list of the vehicle parts present in each image but not their bounding-boxes. In contrast, the simulated dataset is fully annotated with the parts' bounding boxes.

CycleGAN Architecture. We used the original CycleGAN code publicly available at GitHub. In the original implementation the decoding portion is composed of deconvolution operations, which were found to produce checkerboard artifacts [9]. To discourage such high-frequency artifacts, all generator deconvolutional layers with kernel size 3×3, stride 2, padding 1, and output padding 1 were replaced by a bi-linear upsample layer that increases the input's size by a factor of 2, followed by a convolutional layer with kernel size 3×3, stride 1 and padding 1.

Training Details. All CycleGAN experiments were run for 100 epochs and with an identity loss weight of 1.0 instead of the default 0.5. This change prevents unnecessary changes in the cars' color. The remaining hyperparameters were unaltered according to the original paper [15]. All datasets were resized to 256 by 256 pixels, the default input size of CycleGAN. For the fine-tuning process, the Detectron2 was fine-tuned on the converted images for 10 epochs with the same hyperparameters as in Detectron2's initial training on the simulated domain. The epoch with the lowest validation loss was used to verify its performance on real data. All the experiments were run on an RTX 2080 Ti graphics card.

System Evaluation. As we do not have bounding boxes for the real dataset and a single vehicle is composed of multiple parts, we consider this a multi-label multi-class classification problem. In our scenario, the accuracy metric does

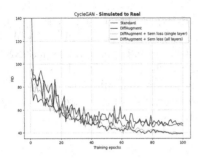 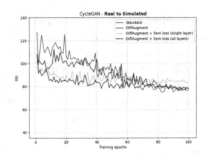

Fig. 2. FID score during training for all CycleGAN's variants for both translation directions.

not correctly measure our model's performance since it takes into account true negative predictions. As a vehicle incorporates only a few of all the parts, true negatives can have a strong influence on the model's accuracy. This implies that, compared to the baseline, a model may have a lower F1-score with higher accuracy, meaning that among the different model predictions, it managed to increase the true negatives at the cost of some true positives. We do not want to reward these occurrences; hence, we focus on the F1-score since it is based on the precision and recall metrics.

5   Results and Discussion

5.1   Domain Mapping

Since CycleGAN depends on a cycle-consistency loss, domain mapping is made in both directions. However, our goal is to obtain more realistic translations of the simulated images; therefore, we will focus on the simulated to real domain conversion. We adopted an iterative approach to decide the best combination of possible modifications. Thus, we assessed DiffAugment's influence in the training process, followed by applying the semantic consistency loss using the previous Detectron2 model.

DiffAugment. DiffAugment did not drastically affect CycleGAN's performance as the authors demonstrated with StyleGAN2 [14]. In fact, there was almost no difference between the FID scores obtained with and without the differential augmentations (Fig. 2). However, it did make an impact on the discriminators, generators, and respective cycle-consistency losses. Now, with augmented images, the discriminators' task of distinguishing between real and fake instances was more difficult to solve, as can be seen by their losses (Fig. 3). This, in theory, should provide the generators with more helpful gradients, which would help stabilize training and promote better image quality. Even though the FID score does not corroborate better image quality, cycle-consistency losses were lower in both translation directions compared to the standard CycleGAN.

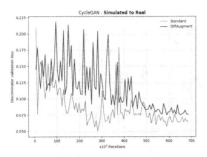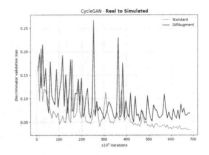

Fig. 3. CycleGAN discriminator validation losses for both domain conversions.

Ultimately, even though DiffAugment did not provide the same boost in performance as it did for StyleGAN2, it regularized training and lowered GAN's losses without increasing FID scores. Hence, we decided to maintain it for future experiments.

Semantic Consistency. Applying the proposed semantic loss to CycleGAN yields better results, further improving the FID score for the simulated to real conversion, as shown in Fig. 2, with noticeable image improvements. One failure case was with black vehicles where the model would produce a side view of a vehicle's door. The simulated images' black vehicle's chassis was converted into a glass-like surface, while the white floor would be the door where the corresponding glass window rested. The semantic loss lessened this effect drastically and protected the vehicle's composition, as can be seen in Fig. 4.

When analyzing in more detail the semantic loss values, we can see that they start at their lowest value and steadily rise throughout the training process (Fig. 5). This makes sense since the generator does not yet apply significant modifications to the input image in the early training stages, making the corresponding embeddings not that distinct. As the training progresses, the semantic loss in all layers reacts to the more significant adjustments made by the generator, reaching its highest value at the end of training. At first glance, one could think of this as unusual behavior since model losses are expected to decrease during training. However, the backbone's parameters are not being optimized during training, meaning that the generator must produce the exact original image for the semantic loss to be zero. Since the other losses (GAN losses and cycle-consistency loss) guide the training process by introducing changes to obtain an image that more adequately belongs to the target distribution, it becomes apparent why the semantic loss would increase during training.

When using all the backbone layers to apply the semantic loss, we can observe that the upper FPN layers, with larger sizes, produce a higher semantic loss compared to the lower layers. This is due to the fact that the overall image features to not fluctuate much during conversion. For example, layer p6 obtains the lowest loss of all layers since it encodes global image information. In contrast, layer p2 yields the highest loss due to image details being changed the most during

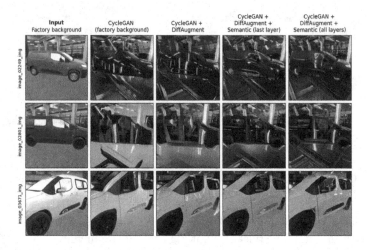

Fig. 4. Translation comparison given the same input on the 100th (final) epoch of each CycleGAN variation. Applying a semantic loss helps to prevent hallucinations and preserve the vehicle's format. Furthermore, the use of DiffAugment, compared to the standard CycleGAN, slightly improves vehicle clarity despite not being as noticeable as in the semantic loss outputs.

translation (Fig. 5a). Moreover, when layer p6 is backed up by additional layers to enforce the semantic loss, its individual loss is lower. This can be explained by the fact that the incoming features have already been influenced by the previous backbone layers whose embeddings are also being incorporated into the final semantic loss (Fig. 5b). Overall, this loss behaved exceptionally well for its purpose, which was to regularize training and not to fully guide it.

5.2   Detector Fine-Tuning

Domain Mapping Model Selection. To perform this selection, in addition to the last epoch, the epoch with the lowest FID score, as well as the epoch with the best compromise between FID score and semantic loss for each run were also considered. From Table 1 we can see that the model obtained from the epoch with best FID score on the default experiment retains more image information during conversion, therefore yielding better mAP than using the model from the last training epoch. Furthermore, the usage of DiffAugment also increases Detectron2's performance, proving that it helps to regularize the conversion process. Ultimately, CycleGAN with DiffAugment and semantic loss on all layers was chosen to convert the entire simulated dataset since it provided us with the best preliminary results.

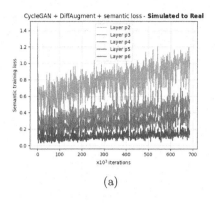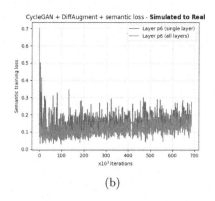

(a)   (b)

Fig. 5. Semantic consistency losses, during simulated to real translation; (a) Semantic consistency on all layers with each layer's individual loss; (b) Comparison between the same p6 layer when applying the semantic loss on all layers and when only applying it on the last (p6) layer.

Table 1. Detectron2 preliminary validation results on converted images for each method's last and best FID epoch. "Sem" is an abbreviation for semantic loss.

Method	Run	Detection			Segmentation		
		mAP	mAP@50	mAP@75	mAP	mAP@50	mAP@75
No conversion	—	87.052	98.598	96.643	71.707	87.490	79.098
CycleGAN	Default (last epoch)	4.192	5.925	4.817	2.918	5.126	2.922
	Default (best FID)	4.861	7.004	5.543	3.571	5.659	3.661
	DiffAugment (last epoch)	6.437	9.453	7.170	4.385	7.231	4.457
	DiffAugment (best FID)	9.172	12.887	10.565	6.747	10.839	7.012
	DiffAugment + Sem last layer (best FID)	36.965	51.395	42.844	21.967	38.940	21.760
	DiffAugment + Sem last layer (best FID + Sem loss)	39.753	54.697	45.813	24.358	42.933	23.816
	DiffAugment + Sem all layers (last epoch)	43.850	58.142	51.454	28.285	46.597	29.242
	DiffAugment + Sem all layers (best FID)	46.569	61.039	54.944	30.493	49.086	32.832
	DiffAugment + Sem all layers (best FID + Sem loss)	**48.748**	**63.433**	**57.412**	**32.964**	**52.885**	**34.961**

Fine-Tuning with Converted Images. Table 2 shows the Detectron2's performance on real images, with example-based metrics obtaining a 2.5% F1-score improvement using CycleGAN converted images compared to the baseline [10].

Among the Detectron2's predictions, multiple object instances overlapped to a much higher degree than expected. This should not happen since it introduces false positives and hinders the performance of the overall module. With the addition of global NMS, we managed to reduce false positives and make use of the obtained predictions more efficiently, which ultimately leads to better performance in the real domain. The effect this new post-processing step has on the complete detection module can also be seen in Table 2.

Table 2. Results on real data, reported as a multi-class multi-label classification problem, for the detection module using the Detectron2 fine-tuned on simulated images converted by the proposed CycleGAN. For the label-based results, the macro value followed by the micro value for each metric. In parenthesis are the relative percentage differences concerning the respective baselines.

	Metrics	Baseline [10]	CycleGAN	Baseline [10]	CycleGAN
				Applying global NMS	
Example based	Accuracy	0.280	0.294	0.244	0.289
	Precision	0.386	0.357 (-7.5%)	0.426	0.403 (-5.4%)
	Recall	0.517	0.621 (+20.1%)	0.356	0.497 (+39.6%)
	F1-score	0.442	0.453 (+2.5%)	0.388	0.445 (+14.7%)
	Hamming loss	0.343	0.396	0.291	0.329
Label based	Accuracy	0.657	0.604	0.709	0.671
	Precision	0.292 / 0.390	0.302 / 0.357 (+3.4%/-8.5%)	0.295 / 0.438	0.284 / 0.401 (-3.7%/-8.4%)
	Recall	0.438 / 0.521	0.513 / 0.622 (+17.1%/+19.4%)	0.322 / 0.359	0.428 / 0.498 (+32.9%/+38.7%)
	F1-score	0.307 / 0.446	0.323 / 0.454 (+5.2%/+1.8%)	0.264 / 0.395	0.293 / 0.444 (+11%/+12.4%)
	Jaccard index	0.221 / 0.287	0.228 / 0.293	0.199 / 0.246	0.213 / 0.286
	MCC	0.134 / 0.210	0.113 / 0.194	0.154 / 0.207	0.140 / 0.217

The use of global NMS decreases the baseline's overall performance but improves the fine-tuned variant. With this supplementary step, example-based metrics achieve an F1-score increase of 14.7% compared to the new global NMS baseline. Since global NMS removes the overlapping bounding boxes with the least probability associated with them, it could mean that the baseline was benefiting from other less confident auxiliary predictions. One could argue that applying this post-processing step demonstrates the module's performance more accurately since only the predictions which Detectron2 finds more probable are used for evaluation, not tainting the subsequently collected metrics with less meaningful predictions. With this in mind, the obtained performance numbers further highlight the improvement offered by fine-tuning as the gap between the baseline and the fine-tuned Detectron2 widens compared to not using global NMS.

6   Conclusion and Future Work

As the absence of fully annotated real-world data prevents us from further improving the previous vehicle parts detection system's ability to generalize to real samples with standard methods, we used domain translated images to fine-tune an object detection model (Detectron2) and bridge the gap between simulated and real domains. By doing so, we improved the system's example-based F1-score on real data by 2.5% without global NMS, and by 14.7% improvement when applying global NMS, compared to the baseline results [10]. In conclusion, this approach's success in improving the previous work's system, without the need for fully annotated real images in any step of the pipeline, demonstrates that DA techniques are exceptionally useful at improving previous applications and extending the use of DL to novel areas where data requirements are a nuisance. For future improvements we could analyze other domain mapping methods or improve the CBIR stage since it was not this work's focus. The use of other DA techniques to diminish the distance to the real domain could also be explored.

Acknowledgements. This work was funded by Project "INDTECH 4.0 – New technologies for smart manufacturing", n.º POCI- 01-0247-FEDER-026653, financed by the European Regional Development Fund (ERDF), through the COMPETE 2020 - Competitiveness and Internationalization Operational Program (POCI).

References

1. Bousmalis, K., Silberman, N., Dohan, D., Erhan, D., Krishnan, D.: Unsupervised pixel-level domain adaptation with generative adversarial networks. In: Proceedings of the IEEE Conference on Computer Vision and Pattern Recognition, pp. 3722–3731 (2017)
2. Hoffman, J., et al.: CyCADA: cycle-consistent adversarial domain adaptation. In: International Conference on Machine Learning, pp. 1989–1998. PMLR (2018)
3. Huang, X., Liu, M.-Y., Belongie, S., Kautz, J.: Multimodal unsupervised image-to-image translation. In: Ferrari, V., Hebert, M., Sminchisescu, C., Weiss, Y. (eds.) ECCV 2018. LNCS, vol. 11207, pp. 179–196. Springer, Cham (2018). https://doi.org/10.1007/978-3-030-01219-9_11
4. Inoue, N., Furuta, R., Yamasaki, T., Aizawa, K.: Cross-domain weakly-supervised object detection through progressive domain adaptation. In: Proceedings of the IEEE Conference on Computer Vision and Pattern Recognition, pp. 5001–5009 (2018)
5. James, S., et al.: Sim-to-real via sim-to-sim: data-efficient robotic grasping via randomized-to-canonical adaptation networks. In: Proceedings of the IEEE Conference on Computer Vision and Pattern Recognition, pp. 12627–12637 (2019)
6. Karras, T., Laine, S., Aittala, M., Hellsten, J., Lehtinen, J., Aila, T.: Analyzing and improving the image quality of StyleGAN. In: Proceedings of the IEEE/CVF Conference on Computer Vision and Pattern Recognition, pp. 8110–8119 (2020)
7. Kim, T., Cha, M., Kim, H., Lee, J.K., Kim, J.: Learning to discover cross-domain relations with generative adversarial networks. In: International Conference on Machine Learning, pp. 1857–1865. PMLR (2017)
8. Liu, M.Y., Breuel, T., Kautz, J.: Unsupervised image-to-image translation networks. In: Advances in Neural Information Processing Systems, pp. 700–708 (2017)
9. Odena, A., Dumoulin, V., Olah, C.: Deconvolution and checkerboard artifacts. Distill (2016). https://doi.org/10.23915/distill.00003
10. Rio-Torto, I., Campaniço, A.T., Pereira, A., Teixeira, L.F., Filipe, V.: Automatic quality inspection in the automotive industry: a hierarchical approach using simulated data. In: 2021 IEEE 8th International Conference on Industrial Engineering and Applications (ICIEA), pp. 342–347. IEEE (2021)
11. Shrivastava, A., Pfister, T., Tuzel, O., Susskind, J., Wang, W., Webb, R.: Learning from simulated and unsupervised images through adversarial training. In: Proceedings of the IEEE Conference on Computer Vision and Pattern Recognition, pp. 2107–2116 (2017)

12. Tremblay, J., et al.: Training deep networks with synthetic data: bridging the reality gap by domain randomization. In: Proceedings of the IEEE Conference on Computer Vision and Pattern Recognition Workshops, pp. 969–977 (2018)
13. Wu, Y., Kirillov, A., Massa, F., Lo, W.Y., Girshick, R.: Detectron2 (2019). https://github.com/facebookresearch/detectron2
14. Zhao, S., Liu, Z., Lin, J., Zhu, J.Y., Han, S.: Differentiable augmentation for data-efficient GAN training. In: Advances in Neural Information Processing Systems 33 (2020)
15. Zhu, J.Y., Park, T., Isola, P., Efros, A.A.: Unpaired image-to-image translation using cycle-consistent adversarial networks. In: Proceedings of the IEEE International Conference on Computer Vision, pp. 2223–2232 (2017)

PW-MAD: Pixel-Wise Supervision for Generalized Face Morphing Attack Detection

Naser Damer[1,2(✉)], Noémie Spiller[1], Meiling Fang[1,2], Fadi Boutros[1,2], Florian Kirchbuchner[1], and Arjan Kuijper[1,2]

[1] Fraunhofer Institute for Computer Graphics Research IGD, Darmstadt, Germany
naser.damer@igd.fraunhofer.de
[2] Department of Computer Science, TU Darmstadt, Darmstadt, Germany

Abstract. A face morphing attack image can be verified to multiple identities, making this attack a major vulnerability to processes based on identity verification, such as border checks. Various methods have been proposed to detect face morphing attacks, however, with low generalizability to unexpected post-morphing processes. A major post-morphing process is the print and scan operation performed in many countries when issuing a passport or identity document. In this work, we address this generalization problem by adapting a pixel-wise supervision approach where we train a network to classify each pixel of the image into an attack or not, rather than only having one label for the whole image. Our pixel-wise morphing attack detection (PW-MAD) solution proved to perform more accurately than a set of established baselines. More importantly, PW-MAD shows high generalizability in comparison to related works, when evaluated on unknown re-digitized attacks. Additionally to our PW-MAD approach, we create a new face morphing attack dataset with digital and re-digitized samples, namely the LMA-DRD dataset that is publicly available for research purposes upon request.

Keywords: Face recognition · Face morphing · Morphing attack detection

1 Introduction

The face recognition performance advances driven by deep-learning [4,17], along with the relatively high social acceptance [3], have introduced face recognition technologies to security sensitive applications (e.g. ID/travel documents) [28]. However, face recognition systems are vulnerable to many attacks [8,13,29], one of these is face morphing attack. Ferrara et al. [19] analyzed face morphing attacks early on by showing that one attack face image can be, automatically and by human experts, matched to more than one person. When morphing attacks are used in travel or identity documents, they allow multiple subjects to be verified to one document. This faulty subject link to the document identity can lead to a wide range of illegal activities, including financial transactions, illegal immigration, human trafficking, and circumventing criminal identity lists.

© Springer Nature Switzerland AG 2021
G. Bebis et al. (Eds.): ISVC 2021, LNCS 13017, pp. 291–304, 2021.
https://doi.org/10.1007/978-3-030-90439-5_23

Morphing attack detection solutions (MAD) are developed to classify an investigated face image into an attack or a bona fide (no attack). The performance of MAD solutions has been shown to drop substantially when facing unknown (not used in the training) variations in the investigated images. Such variations include the morphing technique [44,45], image compression [27], and re-digitization (print and scan) [20] among others. The re-digitization is one of the most studied of these variations as it represents the scenario where a printed image is presented when applying for an ID/travel document. This image is then scanned to be included on the document and possibly go through MAD. MAD solutions aiming at generalizability utilised handcrafted [30,32] and deep learning features [20,32], however, while using single binary target per image in the training.

This work aims at providing a generalizable MAD by proposing the adaption of pixel-wise supervision in the training process, giving the network the chance to distribute its focus on more evident manipulation effects, rather than, general image artifacts. This resulted in our pixel-wise supervised MAD (PW-MAD). To develop and evaluate our proposed solution, we additionally presented a publicly available morphing dataset that includes digital and re-digitized attacks and bona fide samples. Our solution proved to outperform a set of widely used baselines, especially when faced with unknown re-digitized images. Our PW-MAD has also shown better performance generalization over related works investigating the issue of re-digitized morphing attacks.

2   Related Work

MAD methods can be separated into two main categories, single image and differential MAD [43]. Single image MAD only analyses the investigated image to build a decision of attack or bona fide [1,14,31,32]. The differential MAD uses the investigated image and a live image (assuming that the process allows for that). Differential MAD analyses the relation between both images to build a decision of attack or bona fide [6,12,38,40]. This work focuses on single image MAD as it demands fewer requirements on the use-case.

Single image MAD solutions can be roughly categorized into ones using handcrafted features and ones using deep learning features. Such handcrafted features included Binarized Statistical Image Features (BSIF) [30,36], Local Binary Patterns (LBP) [11], Local Phase Quantization (LPQ) [31], or features established in the image forensic analyses such as the photo response non-uniformity (PRNU) [15]. The MAD solutions based on deep learning commonly used pre-trained networks with or without fine-tuning, such as versions of VGG [20], AlexNet [32], or networks trained for face recognition purposes such as OpenFace [14]. However, all these works, used a single binary label as the target of their training.

Many of these works have raised the issue of the generalizability of the MAD decisions when facing variabilities in the face morphing or image handling process. Such variabilities included the synthetic image generation processes [7,9,10,45], different data sources [37], morphing pair selection [12], image compression [27], and re-digitization [20,30,32]. These variabilities have been shown to cause a drop in the MAD performance when they were unknown in the MAD training phase. The most practically relevant of these is the re-digitization, as it reflects the practice of requiring a printed image for travel/identity document issuance, where the authorities would scan this printed image. For this case, a number of private databases were created along with the analyses of the generalization of different MAD solutions such as different versions of VGG [20], AlexNet [20], the fusion of different pre-trained networks [32], and the BSIF features with an SVM classifier [30,32]. All these works have shown a substantial drop in the MAD performance on the re-digitized attacks when they were not used in the training process, which is the research gap addressed in this paper.

3   Methodology

This section presents our proposed PW-MAD approach along with a set of baseline approaches.

3.1   The Proposed PW-MAD

Our proposed PW-MAD solution takes advantage of pixel-level supervision, i.e. a label of attack or bona fide for each image pixel, rather than being only supervised by one label for the whole image. This enhances the ability of the algorithm to distribute (spatially) its focus on areas with more evident manipulation. This is performed with the aim of bringing less focus on non-attack-related artifacts, and thus enhance the generalizability of the MAD decision. Such a supervision approach has been shown to gain these benefits when dealing with the generalizability of detecting iris and face spoofing attacks [18,22], however, it was never applied to the generalizability sensitive MAD.

Our PW-MAD utilizes a densely connected network framework for MAD with binary and deep pixel-wise supervision. This framework is based on the DenseNet [23] architecture, as motivated in [22]. Specifically, we use the DenseNet-121 architecture [23]. The use of this architecture is motivated by the high performances achieved in detecting iris and face spoofing attacks [18,22]. The architecture is modified to be simpler with only two dense blocks and two transition blocks with a fully connected layer with sigmoid activation to produce the binary output. In addition, a convolution layer with a kernel size of 1×1 is added before this fully connected layer, to generate the feature map for pixel-wise supervision. The feature map (size of 14 in our case) generated from this convolution layer is used to supervise the training of the network in a pixel-wise manner. Finally, the network is trained under pixel-wise and binary supervision. For the loss function, Binary Cross-Entropy (BCE) is used for both pixel-wise and binary supervision. The equation of BCE is:

$$\mathcal{L}_{BCE} = -[y \cdot \log x + (1 - y) \cdot \log(1 - x)]$$

where y presents the ground truth label. x is predicted probability. We use the $\mathcal{L}_{BCE}^{PW}$ to indicate the loss computed based on pixel-wise feature map and $\mathcal{L}_{BCE}^{B}$ is the loss computed based on binary output. Thus, an overall loss $\mathcal{L}_{overall}$ is formulated as

$$\mathcal{L}_{overall} = \lambda \cdot \mathcal{L}_{BCE}^{PW} + (1 - \lambda) \cdot \mathcal{L}_{BCE}^{B},$$

where λ is set to 0.5 in the experiments.

Furthermore, we use the hyper-parameters (Adam optimizer with a learning rate of 10^{-4} and weight decay of 10^{-5}) as motivated in [22] for the training. Additionally, we apply class weight and early stopping techniques to avoid overfitting. The final score for each test image is computed by binary output.

3.2   Baselines

LBP: The local binary patterns (LBP) are used extensively in MAD solutions with satisfactory results [11,41]. The face in a frame is first detected, cropped, and normalized into a size of 64×64 pixels. Then, an RGB face is converted into HSV and YCbCr color spaces. Third, the LBP features are extracted from each channel. The multi-channel extraction of LBP features has been shown to enhance the performance of MAD in a number of previous works [31,34]. The obtained six LBP feature vectors are then concatenated into one feature vector to feed into a Softmax classifier, resulting in a decision score.

VGG16: The VGG16 architecture [39] is used extensively in MAD solutions with very competitive results [20,32]. The used network is pretrained on large-scale ImageNet dataset [16] and provided as a pretrained network in [39]. Before processing the image, it is normalized to 224×224 pixels, then extracts the output of an intermediate layer of VGG16 which is used as a feature. The features are scaled before they are fed to a linear SVM classifier.

Inception$_{FT}$ and Inception$_{TFS}$: This baseline uses the Inception-v3 [42] network architecture as the cornerstone. This architecture has been used successfully for MAD [33] and fake face detection approaches [26]. We report the results of a fine-tuned version of the pre-trained Inception-v3, this will be referred to as Inception$_{FT}$ (the pre-trained network is trained on ImageNet dataset [16] and made available by [42]). The last classification layer of Inception-v3 is modified to fit our two classes case where an input image is either bona fide or attack. Only the weight of this classification layer is fine-tuned, while the weights of other layers are fixed. We also report the results of a trained from scratch Inception-v3 model, named Inception$_{TFS}$. In the training phase, the binary cross-entropy loss function and Adam optimizer with a learning rate of 10^{-4} and a weight decay of 10^{-5} are used. Moreover, the early stopping techniques used in our PW-MAD method are also applied for training of Inception$_{FT}$ and Inception$_{TFS}$ to avoid overfitting and for a fair comparison.

It must be noted that our PW-MAD and all the baseline solutions used only the training part of the data for training (and the development split for validation when training a neural network). All the three splits, train, development, and test, are identity-disjoint.

4 Experimental Setup

This section presents our newly created morphing attack dataset (with vulnerability analyses) along with the experimental settings and evaluation metrics.

4.1 The Dataset

As there is no suitable publicly available morphing dataset, we opted to create a carefully designed morphing dataset that is described in this section. This dataset will be referred to as the digital and re-digitized landmark-based morph dataset (LMA-DRD). The dataset is built on the VGGFace-2 dataset [5], which is composed of 3.31 million images of 9131 identities. This basic dataset was chosen as it has a large number of images per subject, which allows the choice of high-quality samples as will be explained in this section. The images are not scaled and therefore have different resolutions, however as will be clarified, we chose high-resolution images. To cover the frontal image condition in the International Civil Aviation Organisation (ICAO) travel document requirements [24], all non-frontal images are filtered out by detecting the central coordinate of the eyes and the upper coordinate of the nose. The two distances between each of the two eyes and the nose landmarks are calculated, and if the ratio of the difference between these distances to any of them was more than 0.05, the image is neglected. The detected landmarks were used to ensure that all the considered images had an eye-to-eye distance of at least 90 pixels as defined in [24]. Based on these criteria, the total number of images after filtering was 54010 images. This cleaned version of the data is the one that all the samples in our LMA-DRD dataset originate from.

Fig. 1. Face Morphing pipeline followed in this work and described in [31]. The pipeline starts with detecting landmarks in the original (to be morphed) images, and ends up with the blended morphed image.

From the filtered data, and as a starting point, 197 images of 197 identities were manually chosen so that they are split evenly between males and females, frontal faces, with a neutral expression, have no glasses, good illumination quality, and no occlusion. Each of these images is was paired with the two most similar faces of two different images of different identities. This is the typically recommended protocol, which makes sense if the goal is to create a confident attack [12]. This pairing depended on the similarity between the key image and the selected paired images. The similarity was measured by the Euclidean distance between the OpenFace representations [2]. The 197 key images were paired twice, resulting in 394 morphing pairs. The paired images (besides the key ones) were not paired with more than one key image. For each of these pairs, a morphed image has been created using the landmark-based approach and parameters presented in [31], the morphing pipeline is illustrated in Fig. 1. The 394 morphed images were manually inspected and any image with strong artifacts was removed, this resulted in a final 276 morphing attack images. From the same identities involved in the attacks, a second bona fide image was chosen (total 591 images), these were manually filtered for quality as described above to comply with ICAO standards. After filtering, the remaining images were 364 images. These 364 images are considered bona fide samples. In total, the created morphing LMA-DRD dataset contains 364 digital Bona fide (D-BF) images and 276 digital morphing attacks (D-M). These images were printed on 11,5cm × 9cm glossy photo paper in a professional studio and scanned with 600dpi scanner. They resulted in the same number of re-digitized bona fide (PS-BF) and attacks (PS-M). The resulted LMA-DRD dataset is split into three identity-disjoint parts, train, development, and test, splits. The splits are done so that they are identity-disjoint, have a similar number of samples, and are equally distributed over males and females to the best possible extend. In our experiments, the training uses only the training data split, the validation during the training (when training a neural network) uses only the development set, and the evaluation is performed only on the test set. The vulnerability analyses in the next paragraph are performed on the three data splits (train, develop, and test) as the analyses do not include any training. Table 1 present an overview of our LMA-DRD dataset and its splits. Samples of the images included in the dataset and morphing results are shown in Fig. 2.

Table 1. A detailed view of the presented LMA-DRD database. The numbers indicate the number of images in each data type and data split. Note that the training, development, and testing splits of the data are all identity-disjoint.

	Attacks		Bona fide	
	Digital (D-M)	Re-digitized (PS-M)	Digital (D-BF)	Re-digitized (PS-BF)
Train	96	96	121	121
Development	92	92	120	120
Test	88	88	123	123
Total	276	276	364	364

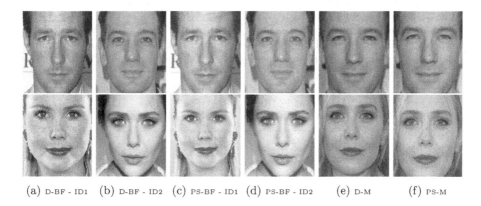

(a) D-BF - ID1   (b) D-BF - ID2   (c) PS-BF - ID1   (d) PS-BF - ID2   (e) D-M   (f) PS-M

Fig. 2. Samples of our LMA-DRD database with the digital bona fide samples ((a) and (b)), re-digitized bona fide ((c) and (d)), digital morphing attacks (e), and re-digitized morphing attacks (f).

A ResNet-100 ArcFace [17] pre-trained face recognition model is used to analyse the vulnerability of face recognition to the presented attacks, as it is one of the most widely used and best performing academic face recognition models with a publicly available pre-trained network. The vulnerability is measured as the Mated Morph Presentation Match Rate (MMPMR) (as defined in [35]) and is presented in Table 2 for a false match rate (FMR) of 0.1% (as recommended for border check operations by Frontex [21]) and 1.0%, which proves the validity of the considered attacks. An MMPMR of 91.30% at FMR of 1.0% means that 91.30% of the attacks will be matched to both contributing identities if the considered face recognition solution uses the decision threshold at 1.0% FMR. We notice, in Table 2, that the vulnerability to re-digitized attacks is slightly less than it is to digital attacks. This might be due to the image artifacts introduced in the re-digitization process. We additionally provide a visual illustration of the face recognition vulnerability to the attacks in Fig. 3. The figures plot the similarity score between the attacks (M-D in Fig. 3a and M-PS in Fig. 3b) and the first involved identity (x-axis) vs. the one with the second identity (y-axis). The red lines in these plots represent the threshold value that achieves FMR of 0.1%. This helps to put the plotted scores in perspective knowing that any attack represented by a dot in the figure successfully match both identities at this threshold (FMR = 0.1%) if it is above and to the right of the red lines. The plots in Fig. 3, confirm the MMPMR values in Table 2 by showing the high vulnerability of the face recognition system to the presented attacks and the slight drop in this vulnerability after the re-digitization process. The LMA-DRD data is publicly available to researchers upon request.

Table 2. The vulnerability to the LMA-DRD dataset attacks, both the digital (D-M) and the re-digitized (PS-M) represented by the MMPMR(%) at two different decision thresholds (FMR=0.1% and 1.0%) of the investigated ResNet-100 Arcface pre-trained model. Note the slight decrease in vulnerability to the re-digitized attacks when compared to the digital ones.

Attack	at FMR = 0.1%	at FMR = 1%
	MMPMR(%)	MMPMR(%)
D-M	80.07	91.30
PS-M	77.17	88.41

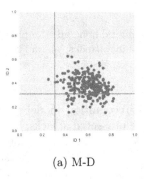   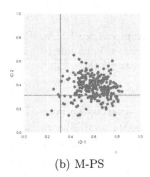

(a) M-D   (b) M-PS

Fig. 3. The vulnerability of face recognition to the attacks in the LMA-DRD dataset attacks is represented by the similarity of the attack to the two identities used to create the attack (ID1 on the X-axis and ID2 on the y-axis). The red lines represent the similarity threshold for the FMR of 0.1%, which indicates that all the attacks on the top and to the right of the red lines do match the targeted identities at this FMR setting. Plot (a) represents the digital attacks, and (b) represents the re-digitized attacks.

4.2   Experiments and Evaluation Metrics

Our experiments aim at evaluating the generalizability of our proposed PW-MAD and the other baseline MADs. As baseline experiments, we evaluate the different MADs on the same type of data (digital or re-digitized). This results in two baseline experimental settings, one uses the digital data for training and testing (Train-D Test-D) and one uses the re-digitized data for training and testing (Train-PS Test-PS). Two additional experimental setups measure the generalizability on data of an unknown type. One uses the digital data for training and re-digitized data for testing (Train-D Test-PS) and one uses the re-digitized data for training and digital data for testing (Train-PS Test-D). It must be noted that the "Train-D Test-PS" reflects the most application-relevant use-case and thus the most commonly reported case on MAD generalization in the literature [20,30,32]. In our experiments, the training uses only the training data split, the validation during the training (when training a neural network) uses only the development set, and the evaluation is performed only on the test set. The three sets are identity-disjoint to prevent biases in the evaluation.

The MAD performance is presented by the Attack Presentation Classification Error Rate (APCER), i.e. the proportion of attack images incorrectly classified as bona fide samples, and the Bona fide Presentation Classification Error Rate (BPCER), i.e. the proportion of bona fide images incorrectly classified as attack samples, as defined in the ISO/IEC 30107-3 [25]. To cover different operation points, and to present the comparative results, we report the BPCER at three different fixed APCER values (0.1%, 1.0%, and 10.0%). To provide a visual evaluation on a wider operation range, we plot receiver operating characteristic (ROC) curves by plotting the APCER on the x-axis and 1-BPCER on the y-axis at different operational points. It must be noted again that the MAD evaluation was performed only on the identity-disjoint test data as described in Sect. 4.1.

5   Results and Discussion

Table 3 lists the BPCER rates achieved at different APCER thresholds for the PW-MAD and the baseline MADs. On the intra-data type settings (Train D Test D) the PW-MAD solution outperforms all baselines at the lowest APCER operation point (0.1%) by scoring a BPCER of 17.74% in comparison to 34.67% for the next best MAD. For higher APCER values, the PW-MAD scores the second-best BPCER. Also for the intra-data type settings (Train PS Test PS), the PW-MAD scores the lowest BPCER (best) on all operational points (APCER thresholds). This is supported by the ROC curves in Figs. 4a and 4b.

In the more challenging inter-data type settings, the proposed PW-MAD outperformed all the baselines at all the APCER thresholds. For the "Train-D Test-PS" setting, the BPCER (at APCER of 1.0%) scored by our PW-MAD is 32.52% in comparison to 49.59% for the next best MAD. This constitutes a 34.4% drop in the BPCER value. For the "Train-PS Test-D" setting, the BPCER (at APCER of 1.0%) scored by our PW-MAD is 19.35% in comparison to 51.61% for the next best MAD. This constitutes a 62.5% drop in the BPCER value. These inter-data type evaluation results demonstrate the superior generalizability of our proposed PW-MAD in comparison to the baselines. These inter-data type conclusions are supported by the ROC curves in Figs. 4d and 4e, where the better maintenance of the performance (in comparison to the baselines) is apparent when comparing these curves to the ones in Figs. 4a and 4b.

To put the generalizability of the proposed approach in perspective, we compare our PW-MAD with the previously published approaches that targeted the detection of re-digitized morphing attacks [20,31,32]. As these works reported their results on private datasets, we are not able to build a direct performance comparison. We rather present the reported results when the MAD is trained and tested on digital morphs, along with the performance of the MAD trained on digital morphs and tested on re-digitized morphs, see Table 4 where the performances are reported in BPCER at APCER of 10% as it is the common reported measure between the relevant previous works. We also list the BPCER error

Table 3. The BPCER at different APCER values (the lower BPCER, the better the MAD performance) achieved by our PW-MAD and the different considered baselines. One can note the better performance of the proposed PW-MAD on most experimental settings, especially when considering the realistic cross-attack scenario on the bottom two tables. Train and Test indicate the data type used for training and testing (digital (D) or re-digitized (PS)). The lowest BPCER for each train/test setup is in bold for each APCER threshold.

Approach	Train	Test	BPCER (%) @ APCER =			Approach	Train	Test	BPCER (%) @ APCER =		
			0.1%	1.0%	10.0%				0.1%	1%	10%
LBP	D	D	51.61	51.61	25.80	LBP	PS	PS	98.37	95.93	57.72
VGG16	D	D	67.74	50.00	32.25	VGG16	PS	PS	63.41	54.47	39.83
Incep.$_{FT}$	D	D	98.38	97.58	81.45	Incep.$_{FT}$	PS	PS	97.56	97.56	91.05
Incep.$_{TFS}$	D	D	34.67	**12.09**	**4.83**	Incep.$_{TFS}$	PS	PS	71.54	48.78	13.00
PW-MAD	D	D	**17.74**	16.12	6.45	PW-MAD	PS	PS	**31.70**	**31.70**	**8.13**
LBP	D	PS	96.74	80.48	51.21	LBP	PS	D	75.80	75.00	46.77
VGG16	D	PS	80.48	74.79	40.65	VGG16	PS	D	70.96	51.61	33.06
Incep.$_{FT}$	D	PS	95.93	94.30	62.60	Incep.$_{FT}$	PS	D	95.16	86.29	79.03
Incep.$_{TFS}$	D	PS	69.91	49.59	28.45	Incep.$_{TFS}$	PS	D	81.45	62.09	25.80
PW-MAD	D	PS	**40.65**	**32.52**	**12.19**	PW-MAD	PS	D	**66.12**	**19.35**	**6.45**

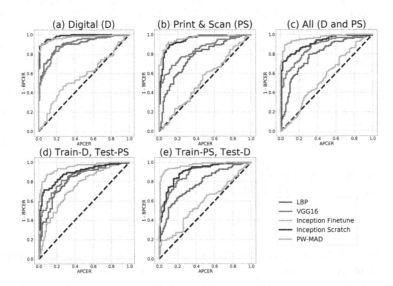

Fig. 4. ROC curves achieved by our PW-MAD solution along with the other baselines. The considered experimental settings are Train-D Test-D in (a), Train-PS Test-PS in (b), Train-D and PS, Test-D and PS in (c), Train-D Test-P in (d), and Train-PS Test-D in (e). Note the superior performance of the PW-MAD, especially in the inter-data type settings in (d) and (e).

increase (in percentage points) when moving from testing on the known digital morphs to the unknown re-digitized. This performance drop might not be an optimal measure of the performance, as it neglects the absolute performance, but it rather gives a clear indication of the generalization. It is noted in Table 4 that our proposed PW-MAD results in the lowest performance drop between previously reported results, indicating the relatively high generalizability of its decisions. When it comes to training on re-digitized attacks and testing on digital attacks, our PW-MAD actually gains performance, BPCER at 10% APCER moves from 8.13% to 6.45% as in Table 3. This training/testing protocol was only reported in previous literature in [32], where their transfer learning approach reported in the best-case scenario, a BPCER at 10% APCER of 16.43% on known re-digitized attacks and dropping to 30.13% when testing on the unknown digital attacks. This again points out the relative generalizability of our proposed PW-MAD approach.

Table 4. A comparison on the results presented in the state-of-the-art works reporting on experimental settings where the MAD is trained and tested on digital attacks (Train-D, Test-D) and when trained on digital attacks and tested on re-digitized attacks (Train-D, Test-PS). The BPCER values are not directly comparable, as each of the works considered a different (private) database. The increase in BPCER percentage points represents the generalizability of the MAD to unknown variations in the attack and it shows that our proposed PW-MAD achieves the lowest drop in the performance, and thus relatively high generalizability. The lowest increase (percentage points) in BPCER error between the two experimental setups is in bold. P1 and P2 indicate using different printers in the respective papers.

Approach	BPCER (%) @ APCER = 10%		BPCER increase in percentage points
	Train-D, Test-D	Train-D, Test-PS	
BSIF-SVM (P1) [30,32]	38.25	48.63	10.38
BSIF-SVM (P2) [30,32]	38.25	57.53	19.28
Transferable D-CNN (P1) [32]	7.53	24.65	17.12
Transferable D-CNN (P2) [32]	7.53	17.8	10.27
Fine-tune AlexNet [20]	0.8	50.8	50
Fine-tune VGG19 [20]	0.8	32.7	31.9
Fine-tune VGG-Face16 [20]	0.8	13.8	13
Fine-tune VGG-Face2 [20]	0.0	20	20
PW-MAD (ours)	6.45	12.19	**5.74**

6   Conclusion

This work targeted the enhancement of the generalizability of MAD performance. This is achieved by proposing the PW-MAD solution that leverages the adaption of pixel-wise supervision into the training process to produce a stable performance, even when facing unknown variations like re-digitized images. We presented a new dataset that included digital and re-digitized samples, allowing the development and evaluation of the proposed PW-MAD. The PW-MAD proved to provide a superior MAD generalizability over a set of widely used baselines and previously reported results in state-of-the-art.

Acknowledgment. This research work has been funded by the German Federal Ministry of Education and Research and the Hessian Ministry of Higher Education, Research, Science and the Arts within their joint support of the National Research Center for Applied Cybersecurity ATHENE.

References

1. Aghdaie, P., Chaudhary, B., Soleymani, S., Dawson, J.M., Nasrabadi, N.M.: Detection of morphed face images using discriminative wavelet sub-bands. In: IWBF, pp. 1–6. IEEE (2021)
2. Amos, B., Ludwiczuk, B., Satyanarayanan, M.: Openface: a general-purpose face recognition library with mobile applications. Technical report, CMU-CS-16-118, CMU School of Computer Science (2016)
3. Bolle, R., Pankanti, S.: Biometrics, Personal Identification in Networked Society: Personal Identification in Networked Society. Kluwer Academic Publishers, Norwell (1998)
4. Boutros, F., Damer, N., Kirchbuchner, F., Kuijper, A.: Elasticface: elastic margin loss for deep face recognition (2021)
5. Cao, Q., Shen, L., Xie, W., Parkhi, O.M., Zisserman, A.: Vggface2: a dataset for recognising faces across pose and age. In: FG, pp. 67–74. IEEE CS (2018)
6. Damer, N., et al.: Detecting face morphing attacks by analyzing the directed distances of facial landmarks shifts. In: Brox, T., Bruhn, A., Fritz, M. (eds.) GCPR 2018. LNCS, vol. 11269, pp. 518–534. Springer, Cham (2019). https://doi.org/10.1007/978-3-030-12939-2_36
7. Damer, N., Boutros, F., Saladie, A.M., Kirchbuchner, F., Kuijper, A.: Realistic dreams: Cascaded enhancement of GAN-generated images with an example in face morphing attacks. In: BTAS, pp. 1–10. IEEE (2019)
8. Damer, N., Dimitrov, K.: Practical view on face presentation attack detection. In: BMVC. BMVA Press (2016)
9. Damer, N., Grebe, J.H., Zienert, S., Kirchbuchner, F., Kuijper, A.: On the generalization of detecting face morphing attacks as anomalies: novelty vs. outlier detection. In: BTAS, pp. 1–5. IEEE (2019)
10. Damer, N., et al.: Regenmorph: visibly realistic GAN generated face morphing attacks by attack re-generation. CoRR abs/2108.09130 (2021)
11. Damer, N., Saladie, A.M., Braun, A., Kuijper, A.: MorGAN: recognition vulnerability and attack detectability of face morphing attacks created by generative adversarial network. In: BTAS, pp. 1–10. IEEE (2018)
12. Damer, N., et al.: To detect or not to detect: the right faces to morph. In: ICB, pp. 1–8. IEEE (2019)
13. Damer, N., et al.: Crazyfaces: unassisted circumvention of watchlist face identification. In: BTAS, pp. 1–9. IEEE (2018)
14. Damer, N., Zienert, S., Wainakh, Y., Saladie, A.M., Kirchbuchner, F., Kuijper, A.: A multi-detector solution towards an accurate and generalized detection of face morphing attacks. In: FUSION, pp. 1–8. IEEE (2019)

15. Debiasi, L., et al.: On the detection of GAN-based face morphs using established morph detectors. In: Ricci, E., Rota Bulò, S., Snoek, C., Lanz, O., Messelodi, S., Sebe, N. (eds.) ICIAP 2019. LNCS, vol. 11752, pp. 345–356. Springer, Cham (2019). https://doi.org/10.1007/978-3-030-30645-8_32

16. Deng, J., Dong, W., Socher, R., Li, L., Li, K., Li, F.: Imagenet: a large-scale hierarchical image database. In: CVPR, pp. 248–255. IEEE Computer Society (2009)

17. Deng, J., Guo, J., Xue, N., Zafeiriou, S.: Arcface: additive angular margin loss for deep face recognition. In: CVPR, pp. 4690–4699. Computer Vision Foundation/IEEE (2019)

18. Fang, M., Damer, N., Boutros, F., Kirchbuchner, F., Kuijper, A.: Iris presentation attack detection by attention-based and deep pixel-wise binary supervision network. In: IJCB, pp. 1–8. IEEE (2021)

19. Ferrara, M., Franco, A., Maltoni, D.: The magic passport. In: IJCB. IEEE (2014)

20. Ferrara, M., Franco, A., Maltoni, D.: Face morphing detection in the presence of printing/scanning and heterogeneous image sources. IET Biometrics **10**(3), 290–303 (2021)

21. Frontex: Best practice technical guidelines for automated border control (ABC) systems (2015)

22. George, A., Marcel, S.: Deep pixel-wise binary supervision for face presentation attack detection. In: 2019 International Conference on Biometrics, ICB 2019, Crete, Greece, 4–7 June 2019, pp. 1–8. IEEE (2019)

23. Huang, G., Liu, Z., van der Maaten, L., Weinberger, K.Q.: Densely connected convolutional networks. In: 2017 IEEE Conference on Computer Vision and Pattern Recognition, CVPR 2017, Honolulu, HI, USA, 21–26 July 2017, pp. 2261–2269. IEEE Computer Society (2017)

24. International Civil Aviation Organization, ICAO: Machine readable passports - part 9 - deployment of biometric identification and electronic storage of data in eMRTDs. Civil Aviation Organization (ICAO) (2015)

25. International Organization for Standardization: ISO/IEC DIS 30107–3:2016: Information Technology - Biometric presentation attack detection - P. 3: Testing and reporting (2017)

26. Khodabakhsh, A., Raghavendra, R., Raja, K.B., Wasnik, P.S., Busch, C.: Fake face detection methods: can they be generalized? In: BIOSIG. LNI, vol. P-282, pp. 1–6. GI/IEEE (2018)

27. Makrushin, A., Neubert, T., Dittmann, J.: Automatic generation and detection of visually faultless facial morphs. In: VISIGRAPP (6: VISAPP), pp. 39–50. SciTePress (2017)

28. Markets and Markets: Facial Recognition Market by Component (Software Tools and Services), Technology, Use Case (Emotion Recognition, Attendance Tracking and Monitoring, Access Control, Law Enforcement), End-User, and Region - Global Forecast to 2022. Report, November 2017

29. Massoli, F.V., Carrara, F., Amato, G., Falchi, F.: Detection of face recognition adversarial attacks. Comput. Vis. Image Underst. **202**, 103103 (2021)

30. Raghavendra, R., Raja, K.B., Busch, C.: Detecting morphed face images. In: BTAS, pp. 1–7. IEEE (2016)

31. Raghavendra, R., Raja, K.B., Venkatesh, S., Busch, C.: Face morphing versus face averaging: vulnerability and detection. In: IJCB, pp. 555–563. IEEE (2017)

32. Raghavendra, R., Raja, K.B., Venkatesh, S., Busch, C.: Transferable deep-CNN features for detecting digital and print-scanned morphed face images. In: CVPR Workshops, pp. 1822–1830. IEEE Computer Society (2017)

33. Ramachandra, R., Venkatesh, S., Raja, K., Busch, C.: Detecting face morphing attacks with collaborative representation of steerable features. In: Chaudhuri, B.B., Nakagawa, M., Khanna, P., Kumar, S. (eds.) Proceedings of 3rd International Conference on Computer Vision and Image Processing. AISC, vol. 1022, pp. 255–265. Springer, Singapore (2020). https://doi.org/10.1007/978-981-32-9088-4_22

34. Ramachandra, R., Venkatesh, S., Raja, K.B., Busch, C.: Towards making morphing attack detection robust using hybrid scale-space colour texture features. In: ISBA, pp. 1–8. IEEE (2019)

35. Scherhag, U., et al.: Biometric systems under morphing attacks: assessment of morphing techniques and vulnerability reporting. In: BIOSIG. LNI, vol. P-270, pp. 149–159. GI/IEEE (2017)

36. Scherhag, U., Raghavendra, R., Raja, K.B., Gomez-Barrero, M., Rathgeb, C., Busch, C.: On the vulnerability of face recognition systems towards morphed face attacks. In: IWBF, pp. 1–6. IEEE (2017)

37. Scherhag, U., Rathgeb, C., Busch, C.: Performance variation of morphed face image detection algorithms across different datasets. In: IWBF, pp. 1–6. IEEE (2018)

38. Scherhag, U., Rathgeb, C., Merkle, J., Busch, C.: Deep face representations for differential morphing attack detection. IEEE TIFS **15**, 3625–3639 (2020)

39. Simonyan, K., Zisserman, A.: Very deep convolutional networks for large-scale image recognition. In: ICLR (2015)

40. Soleymani, S., Chaudhary, B., Dabouei, A., Dawson, J., Nasrabadi, N.M., et al.: Differential morphed face detection using deep siamese networks. In: Del Bimbo, A. (ed.) ICPR 2021. LNCS, vol. 12666, pp. 560–572. Springer, Cham (2021). https://doi.org/10.1007/978-3-030-68780-9_44

41. Spreeuwers, L.J., Schils, M., Veldhuis, R.N.J.: Towards robust evaluation of face morphing detection. In: EUSIPCO, pp. 1027–1031. IEEE (2018)

42. Szegedy, C., Vanhoucke, V., Ioffe, S., Shlens, J., Wojna, Z.: Rethinking the inception architecture for computer vision. In: 2016 IEEE Conference on Computer Vision and Pattern Recognition, CVPR 2016, Las Vegas, NV, USA, 27–30 June 2016, pp. 2818–2826. IEEE Computer Society (2016)

43. Venkatesh, S., Ramachandra, R., Raja, K., Busch, C.: Face morphing attack generation and detection: a comprehensive survey. IEEE Trans. Technol. Soc. **2**(3), 128–145 (2021). https://doi.org/10.1109/TTS.2021.3066254

44. Venkatesh, S., Zhang, H., Ramachandra, R., Raja, K.B., Damer, N., Busch, C.: Can GAN generated morphs threaten face recognition systems equally as landmark based morphs? - vulnerability and detection. In: IWBF, pp. 1–6. IEEE (2020)

45. Zhang, H., Venkatesh, S., Ramachandra, R., Raja, K.B., Damer, N., Busch, C.: MIPGAN - generating strong and high quality morphing attacks using identity prior driven GAN. IEEE Trans. Biom. Behav. Identity Sci. **3**(3), 365–383 (2021)

Integration of a BCI with a Hand Tracking System and a Motorized Robotic Arm to Improve Decoding of Brain Signals Related to Hand and Finger Movements

Giuseppe Placidi[1]([✉]) [ID], Giovanni De Gasperis[2] [ID], Filippo Mignosi[2] [ID],
Matteo Polsinelli[1] [ID], and Matteo Spezialetti[2] [ID]

[1] A2VI-Lab, c/o Department of MeSVA, University of L'Aquila,
Via Vetoio Coppito, 67100 L'Aquila, Italy
`giuseppe.placidi@univaq.it`
[2] Department of DISIM, University of L'Aquila,
Via Vetoio Coppito, 67100 L'Aquila, Italy
`http://www.giuseppeplacidi.org`

Abstract. Nowadays, most of the functional relationships between brain signals and the corresponding complex hand/fingers movements (cause, effect, feedback) are not yet completely understood. In the last years it has been assisted to important advances in Brain Computer Interfaces (BCI), computer vision (CV)-based tracking systems and Robots, especially due to: hardware improvements and miniaturization; increasing pursuit of intelligent and real time tracking systems; fast design, prototyping and production of consumer robots facilitated by 3D printing technologies.

We present an integrated system composed by a BCI, a CV-based hand tracking system and a motorized robotic arm reproducing the hand and the forearm of a person (scale 1:1). The proposal is to synchronize and to monitor the brain activity during complex hand and fingers movements (interpreted and reproduced in real time on a numerical hand model by the tracking system). Further, we aim at recognizing the brain signals which give rise to specific movements and, finally, at using them for producing the corresponding movements on the robotic arm. Different scenarios and potential use-cases are reported and their usefulness discussed.

Keywords: Sensory-motor BCI · Computer vision · Virtual glove ·
Hand tracking · Robots · Neuroscience · Brain signal decoding

1 Introduction

In the field of neuroscience it is of paramount importance to completely understand the functional relationships (cause/effect/feedback) between a complex

© Springer Nature Switzerland AG 2021
G. Bebis et al. (Eds.): ISVC 2021, LNCS 13017, pp. 305–315, 2021.
https://doi.org/10.1007/978-3-030-90439-5_24

movement and the underlying brain signals [11,12,36]. In particular for the hand movements, despite the recent important progresses, the study is still far to be completed. A brief review significantly describes the complexity of the process of motor actuation and control [36]. Motor controls in the human body begins at the frontal and posterior parietal cortex (PPC) where high-level, abstract thinking on what actions undertake in a given situation are decided. The PPC receives input from the somatosensory cortex that encodes information on the current state of the body. It also has extensive inter-connection with the prefrontal cortex, which is responsible for abstract strategic thoughts. Besides sensory information, the prefrontal cortex may need to consider other factors regarding the environment. The combination of sensory information, past experience and strategic decision in the frontal and posterior parietal cortex determines what sequences of action to take.

The planning of the sequence of actions is then carried out by the pre-motor area (PMA) and the supplementary motor area (SMA), both located in the cortex. Stimulation of these areas is known to elicit complex a sequence of actions and intra-cortical recording in the PMA shows that it is activated about 1 s before movement and stops shortly after the movement is initiated. Some neurons in the PMA also appear to be tuned to the direction of movement, with some of them only be activated when the hand move in one direction but not in the other. After a sequence of actions is planned in PMA or SMA, input from the basal ganglia is required to actually start the movement. The basal ganglia contains the direct and indirect pathways: the first helps to select a particular action to initiate, while the second filters out inappropriate motor programs. Indirect and direct pathways activate different brain regions by using also different modalities.

After the basal ganglia has helped to filter out unwanted motor programs and to focus on the selected programs, the primary motor cortex (M1) is activated, being this responsible for their low-level execution.

The signal is transmitted from M1 to motor neurons in the spinal cord, through axons, to activate muscles and fibers. One motor neuron may supply multiple muscle fibers, collectively known as one motor unit. In smaller muscles, such as those in the fingers, one motor neuron may only supply 2 or 3 muscle fibers, enabling fine movement control: the hand and fingers movements are complex because several motor-neurons have to be activated by a complex brain synchronized activity. Moreover, the movement is controlled by a complex feedback, necessary to modulate and filter gestures, forces, haptic feedback and to finalize the action.

The motor control pathway, the systematic regulation of the movements of the human body, goes from the high level associative area of the brain, mediated by the motor cortex, through the spinal cord to the individual muscle fibers. Each of the stages plays a different role and uses different mechanisms to ensure that the movement is carried out in a coordinated and smooth manner. Each of these stages also offers different signal modalities and features that can be exploited for motor decoding.

In summary, the signals generated in the brain either both for preparation or for actuation/control are several and in several pathways and involve different areas.

Research on how to decode the neuro-physiological signals from the human brain is finalized to translate them into control signals for external devices. We are interested in hand and fingers movements which are very complex and highly synchronized movements. An ideal BCI would accurately interpret hand movement intents, and output smooth, accurate control toward external hand prosthesis. As describe before, this process requires cooperative interaction between the central nervous system and the musculo-skeletal system.

Brain signals measured and interpreted in BCI are collected through electrocorticography (ECoG) [20], electroencephalography (EEG) [14,39], functional magnetic resonance imaging (fMRI) [41], magneto-encephalography (MEG) [2], combined fMRI and MEG [3] and near-infrared spectroscopy (NIRS) [4,6,21, 23]. Each of these methodology has its own strengths and limitations but, for noninvasive applications, EEG offers a good trade off between sensitivity and spatial-temporal resolution [16,17].

EEG is a non invasive technique for recording, from the scalp, signals generated by the neuro-electrical activity which is practically usable, especially in applications where the biases introduced by the measuring device could be very high [8,35].

EEG-based BCI has been developed to decode a user's movement intention based on the markers of active brain involvement in the preparation of the desired movement [16]. However, the low sensitivity, the artifacts produced by surface muscles, heart and eyes, the reduced bandwidth and the incomplete collected information, make unclear whether EEG has sufficient elements to extract all the detailed information for decoding the brain signals about natural, voluntary, multi-joint movements of the upper limb [17]. Therefore, to hope in a complete decoding of brain signals deputy to hand/fingers movements is essential to: increase EEG precision, resolution and capability of signal decoding in BCI [13,14,27,32,33]; improve brain signal feature extraction/selection for creating "fingerprints" of specific hand/fingers movements through the synchronization of the brain signals with the upper limb movements captured by a CV-based hand tracking system [1,5,9,10,15,18,24–26,30,34,40]; check the defined brain "fingerprints" capability to drive upper limb robots [7,19] in as similar way to the human limb (with a sufficiently good temporal resolution).

The remainder of the paper is structured as follows: Sect. 2 describes the proposed system assembly; Sect. 3 illustrates some use-cases; Sect. 4 concludes the paper and defines future developments.

2   System Assembly

The logical scheme of the proposed system is reported in Fig. 1.

It consists of: a sensory-motor BCI of the type described in [22], whose signals are collected by a 32-channels WI-FI EEG system (Enobio 32, Neuroelectric Inc., https://www.neuroelectrics.com), equipped with advanced pre-processing methods for artefacts reductions [29], signal processing and interpretation strategies derived by [13,14,31–33]; a compact, low cost and accurate hand tracking

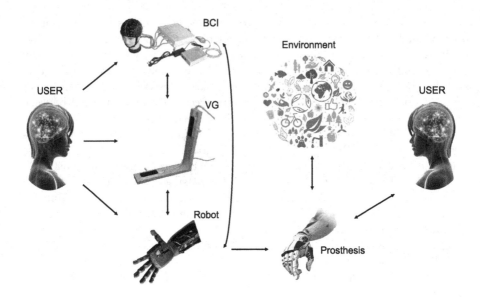

Fig. 1. Logic integration between a sensory-motor BCI, a VG hand tracking system and a motorized robotic arm. The prosthesis is represented to show an example of application: from the healthy users to a user with a prosthesis. One of the applications is to transfer the results obtained for the motorized robot to a hand prosthesis by which a disabled user can recover some of the capabilities to interact with the external environment.

system, called virtual glove (VG), based on two orthogonal LEAP sensors that merges data from both sensors to reduce occlusions[28, 30], and effective methods to improve tracking accuracy, efficiency and precision of the reconstructed numerical hand model in real-time [25]; a robot actuator reproducing a human arm, based on an available online model (https://www.thingiverse.com/thing: 2269115). The robotic arm is composed by 18 movable parts, 3D printed in rigid plastic material, driven by 6 servo-motors: 4 servo-motors are used for flexion and extension of the fingers (3 for thumb, index and medium and the last for the pair ring/little); the last 2 servo-motors are used for thumb opposition and wrist rotation, respectively. The flexion is performed by tending, through the motors, a fishing line attached to the tip of the fingers and passing through each of them; the extension is realized passively by releasing the line, while elastic rubber bands move the fingers backward. An Arduino board (https://store. arduino.cc) controls the servo-motors and interfaces the other devices.

The system is designed to let each subsystem behave separately, in couples or as a whole. The BCI behaves also as a recording EEG system. A PC server hosts the BCI, drives the experimental sessions through a clock which is used to synchronize the equipment and furnishes the commands for the servo-motors to move, stop and release the fingers of the robotic hand; a client PC drives the hand tracking system, reconstructs the numerical hand model in real-time (at least at 35 fps) and provides the storage of the whole experimental session (synchronized numerical hand model, EEG signals, robot and prosthesis movements) in the local memory. In this way, it is possible to track the synchronized sequence of all the actors of the system.

3   Use-Cases

Since the proposed system is modular, it is greatly flexible and adaptable to several situations. In what follows, some of the possible scenarios requiring the use of at least two of its subsystems (the usage of the subsystems, taken individually, are described in the literature cited above), are reported and discussed (see also Fig. 2). The order of presentation roughly resembles the steps necessary for decoding the hand movements in final applications:

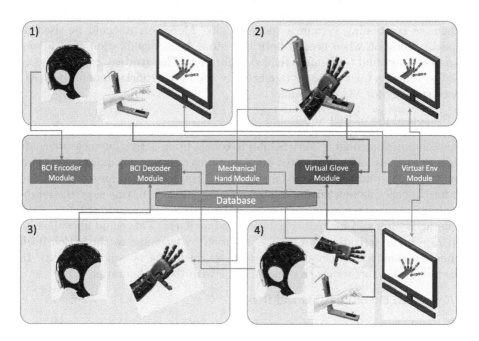

Fig. 2. The 4 Use Cases represented graphically. In particular: 1 combines BCI with VG; 2 Combines VG and Robot; 3 Combines BCI and Robot; 4 Combines BCI, VG and Robot.

1) Combined use of BCI and VG

The combination BCI-VG is necessary to collect synchronized data both from hand movements, through the numerical hand model at 35 fps, and the 32 channels EEG signals collected 1000 Hz. In this way, we could define a data set recording data from a series of hand and fingers motion exercises, both repetitive and in single-shot. The exercises could consist of free hand movements driven by the VG graphic interface, in a virtual reality scenario [23,38]. The data set could consist of repeated experimental sessions, performed both with left and right hand (one at a time), from a set of healthy human subjects of different age, gender and hand prevalence. In this way, we could have the possibility of studying: a) the general relationships between specific motions and the corresponding brain signals; b) generality and specificity (with respect to subjects) of the movements; c) the reduction of biases and artifacts; d) the comparison with counter-lateral activation, both in left-handed and in right-handed subjects; f) the calibration of the BCI to a specific subject.

2) Combined use of VG and Robot

The combined use of VG and robotic hand could allow the collection of data of reproducible hand/joints poses. This could be very helpful for implementing a data/driven calibration strategy for the VG without using an external and expensive positioning system as done in [30]. Moreover, it could be used to repeat calibration when needed both to restore perfect calibration after a long period of usage and to obtain a refined calibration. This strategy could be easily used to collect a huge data set to efficiently train an Artificial Intelligence (AI) based strategy for VG calibration.

3) Combined use of BCI and Robot

This combination could be very helpful to collect brain activation measurements while the user is looking repeated hand and fingers poses and movements. This could allow to study the effects on the brain when looking at an external hand performing specific movements (motor imagery [37,38]). In this case, the reproducibility of the experiment is fundamental for testing the reproducibility of the brain activation and for reducing biases and artifacts. This could also allow to separate brain activation due to the intention by that due to the action itself (intention could be common to several tasks, including non-motion tasks). In this last case, a further check could be done with the configuration n.1.

4) Combined use of BCI, VG and Robot

This configuration is particularly useful for testing the sensory-motor BCI after it has been trained on the features collected from the signals allowing to specific hand movements and to define the "fingerprints" of various movements. Moreover, it could be useful to translate "fingerprints" into commands for the robot's motors in order to attempt to reproduce the corresponding real hand movements. In this case, a huge help could be obtained by the numerical hand model position/silhouette for understanding potentialities and limits of the EEG to measure brain signals underlying to such fine hand movements and, in the affirmative case, to confirm fingerprints. Finally, this configuration could strongly contribute to study brain activation for a patient without an arm who has to wear a motor-guided prosthesis. In this case, it could be useful to characterize the prosthesis movements as a function of brain activation by using data from: healthy subjects while moving their hands; the same patient while moving his healthy arm (by performing counter-lateral studies and comparisons); the same patient while imagining to move the missing hand (with experiments performed while watching the robotic hand moving).

Figure 3 shows a picture in which the three subsystems are placed together, as they are currently still behaving separated, thought the integration has been started through the implementation of the synchronizing software and of the database for hosting measurements.

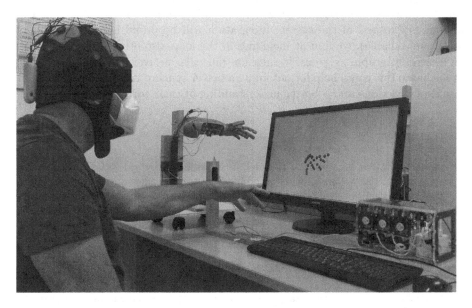

Fig. 3. The proposed system as a results of integration of the three devices: BCI, VG and arm robot. At present, the design of the integrated system has been made, its implementation has been started but not yet completed.

4 Conclusion

We have proposed a combined system between a sensory-motor BCI, a CV-based hand tracking system, VG, and a motorized robotic arm to study in deep and complex relationships between brain activation and the produced hand/fingers movements. This could greatly contribute to understand potentialities and limits of EEG in terms of resolution, sensitivity and robustness to biases and artifacts, in describing and decode the brain signals behind the intention to perform a movement and the movement itself. Moreover, it could also contribute to allow patients without an arm to recover, at least partially, the capabilities to move an artificial prosthetic arm. Finally, this could also contribute to improve BCI, VG and motorized prosthetic arms themselves by improving accuracy, sensitivity and operation.

We remark that, though each single component of the proposed system is robust and actually usable, the combined use in a single system has not been completed and it is greatly exposed to failure because: 1) it is still unclear if EEG is adapted to catch the dynamics of fine movements of hand and fingers; 2) signal processing/interpretation procedures could fail to find the fingerprints of these fine movements; 3) the reproducibility of the movements could fail: when operating with a movement, it is necessary also to reproduce its modulation, smoothness, to stop when the action is finished and to go back, if necessary.

However, we think that with the proposed integration project, a step further can be done toward the comprehension of the complex mechanisms of interaction between brain signals and the corresponding actions. In the future, if the preliminary results of the system integration will be promising (they are currently unavailable), we aim at including in the loop also other devices, such as an electromyographic system, to measure muscular activation in the proximity of the hand: this could help for obtaining a better synchronization between brain signals and actions and a better understanding of their correspondence.

References

1. Ameur, S., Ben Khalifa, A., Bouhlel, M.S.: A novel hybrid bidirectional unidirectional LSTM network for dynamic hand gesture recognition with leap motion. Entertain. Comput. **35**, 1–10 (2020)
2. Boostani, R., Moradi, M.H.: Evaluation of the forearm EMG signal features for the control of a prosthetic hand. Physiol. Meas. **24**(2), 309–319 (2003). https://doi.org/10.1088/0967-3334/24/2/307
3. Breitwieser, C., Kreilinger, A., Neuper, C., Müller-Putz, G.: The TOBI hybrid BCI-the data acquisition module. In: Proceedings of the First TOBI Workshop, vol. 58 (2010)
4. Carrieri, M., et al.: Prefrontal cortex activation upon a demanding virtual hand-controlled task: a new frontier for neuroergonomics. Front. Hum. Neurosci. **10**(53), 1–13 (2016)
5. Chatzis, T., Stergioulas, A., Konstantinidis, D., Dimitropoulos, K., Daras, P.: A comprehensive study on deep learning-based 3D hand pose estimation methods. Appl. Sci. **10**(19), 6850 (2020). https://doi.org/10.3390/app10196850
6. Coyle, S.M., Ward, T.E., Markham, C.M.: Brain-computer interface using a simplified functional near-infrared spectroscopy system. J. Neural Eng. **4**(3), 219–226 (2007). https://doi.org/10.1088/1741-2560/4/3/007
7. Devaraja, R.R., Maskeliūnas, R., Damaševičius, R.: Design and evaluation of anthropomorphic robotic hand for object grasping and shape recognition. Computers **10**(1), 1 (2020). https://doi.org/10.3390/computers10010001
8. Di Giamberardino, P., Iacoviello, D., Placidi, G., Polsinelli, M., Spezialetti, M.: A brain computer interface by EEG signals from self-induced emotions. In: Tavares, J.M.R.S., Natal Jorge, R.M. (eds.) ECCOMAS 2017. LNCVB, vol. 27, pp. 713–721. Springer, Cham (2018). https://doi.org/10.1007/978-3-319-68195-5_77
9. Erden, F., Çetin, A.E.: Hand gesture based remote control system using infrared sensors and a camera. IEEE Trans. Consum. Electron. **60**(4), 675–680 (2014)

10. Franchi, D., Maurizi, A., Placidi, G.: Characterization of a SimMechanics model for a virtual glove rehabilitation system. In: Barneva, R.P., Brimkov, V.E., Hauptman, H.A., Natal Jorge, R.M., Tavares, J.M.R.S. (eds.) CompIMAGE 2010. LNCS, vol. 6026, pp. 141–150. Springer, Heidelberg (2010). https://doi.org/10.1007/978-3-642-12712-0_13

11. Halsband, U., Lange, R.K.: Motor learning in man: a review of functional and clinical studies. J. Physiol.-Paris **99**(4–6), 414–424 (2006). https://doi.org/10.1016/j.jphysparis.2006.03.007

12. Hoshi, E.: Cortico-basal ganglia networks subserving goal-directed behavior mediated by conditional visuo-goal association. Front. Neural Circ. **7**, 158 (2013). https://doi.org/10.3389/fncir.2013.00158

13. Iacoviello, D., Pagnani, N., Petracca, A., Spezialetti, M., Placidi, G.: A poll oriented classifier for affective brain computer interfaces. In: Proceedings of the 3rd International Congress on Neurotechnology, Electronics and Informatics - Volume 1: NEUROTECHNIX, pp. 41–48 (2015)

14. Iacoviello, D., Petracca, A., Spezialetti, M., Placidi, G.: A classification algorithm for electroencephalography signals by self-induced emotional stimuli. IEEE Trans. Cybern. **46**(12), 3171–3180 (2016)

15. Kiselev, V., Khlamov, M., Chuvilin, K.: Hand gesture recognition with multiple leap motion devices. In: 2019 24th Conference of Open Innovations Association (FRUCT), pp. 163–169. IEEE (2019)

16. Li, T., Xue, T., Wang, B., Zhang, J.: Decoding voluntary movement of single hand based on analysis of brain connectivity by using EEG signals. Front. Hum. Neurosci. **12**, 381 (2018). https://doi.org/10.3389/fnhum.2018.00381

17. Liao, K., Xiao, R., Gonzalez, J., Ding, L.: Decoding individual finger movements from one hand using human EEG signals. PLoS ONE **9**(1), e85192 (2014). https://doi.org/10.1371/journal.pone.0085192

18. Marin, G., Dominio, F., Zanuttigh, P.: Hand gesture recognition with jointly calibrated leap motion and depth sensor. Multimedia Tools Appl. **75**(22), 14991–15015 (2016)

19. Mick, S., et al.: Reachy, a 3D-printed human-like robotic arm as a testbed for human-robot control strategies. Front. Neurorobotics **13**, 65 (2019). https://doi.org/10.3389/fnbot.2019.00065

20. Miller, K.J., Schalk, G., Fetz, E.E., den Nijs, M., Ojemann, J.G., Rao, R.P.: Cortical activity during motor execution, motor imagery, and imagery-based online feedback. Proc. Natl. Acad. Sci. **107**(9), 4430–4435 (2010). https://doi.org/10.1073/pnas.0913697107

21. Moro, S.B., et al.: A novel semi-immersive virtual reality visuo-motor task activates ventrolateral prefrontal cortex: a functional near-infrared spectroscopy study. J. Neural Eng. **13**(3), 1–14 (2016)

22. Müller-Putz, G.R., Schwarz, A., Pereira, J., Ofner, P.: From classic motor imagery to complex movement intention decoding. In: Progress in Brain Research, pp. 39–70. Elsevier (2016). https://doi.org/10.1016/bs.pbr.2016.04.017

23. Petracca, A., et al.: A virtual ball task driven by forearm movements for neuro-rehabilitation. In: 2015 International Conference on Virtual Rehabilitation (ICVR). pp. 162–163 (2015). https://doi.org/10.1109/ICVR.2015.7358600

24. Placidi, G.: A smart virtual glove for the hand telerehabilitation. Comput. Biol. Med. **37**(8), 1100–1107 (2007)

25. Placidi, G., Avola, D., Cinque, L., Polsinelli, M., Theodoridou, E., Tavares, J.M.R.S.: Data integration by two-sensors in a LEAP-based virtual glove for human-system interaction. Multimedia Tools Appl. **80**(12), 18263–18277 (2021). https://doi.org/10.1007/s11042-020-10296-8
26. Placidi, G., Avola, D., Iacoviello, D., Cinque, L.: Overall design and implementation of the virtual glove. Comput. Biol. Med. **43**(11), 1927–1940 (2013)
27. Placidi, G., Avola, D., Petracca, A., Sgallari, F., Spezialetti, M.: Basis for the implementation of an EEG-based single-trial binary brain computer interface through the disgust produced by remembering unpleasant odors. Neurocomputing **160**((C)), 308–318 (2015)
28. Placidi, G., Cinque, L., Petracca, A., Polsinelli, M., Spezialetti, M.: A virtual glove system for the hand rehabilitation based on two orthogonal leap motion controllers. In: Proceedings of the 6th International Conference on Pattern Recognition Applications and Methods - Volume 1: ICPRAM, pp. 184–192. INSTICC, SciTePress (2017)
29. Placidi, G., Cinque, L., Polsinelli, M.: A fast and scalable framework for automated artifact recognition from EEG signals represented in scalp topographies of independent components. Comput. Biol. Med. **132**, 104347 (2021). https://doi.org/10.1016/j.compbiomed.2021.104347
30. Placidi, G., Cinque, L., Polsinelli, M., Spezialetti, M.: Measurements by a leap-based virtual glove for the hand rehabilitation. Sensors **18**(3), 1–13 (2018)
31. Placidi, G., Giamberardino, P.D., Petracca, A., Spezialetti, M., Iacoviello, D.: Classification of emotional signals from the DEAP dataset. In: Proceedings of the 4th International Congress on Neurotechnology, Electronics and Informatics. SCITEPRESS - Science and Technology Publications (2016). https://doi.org/10.5220/0006043400150021
32. Placidi, G., Petracca, A., Spezialetti, M., Iacoviello, D.: Classification strategies for a single-trial binary brain computer interface based on remembering unpleasant odors. In: 2015 37th Annual International Conference of the IEEE Engineering in Medicine and Biology Society (EMBC), pp. 7019–7022 (2015)
33. Placidi, G., Petracca, A., Spezialetti, M., Iacoviello, D.: A modular framework for EEG web based binary brain computer interfaces to recover communication abilities in impaired people. J. Med. Syst. **40**(1), 34 (2016)
34. Shen, H., Yang, X., Hu, H., Mou, Q., Lou, Y.: Hand trajectory extraction of human assembly based on multi-leap motions. In: 2019 IEEE/ASME International Conference on Advanced Intelligent Mechatronics (AIM), pp. 193–198 (2019)
35. Spezialetti, M., Cinque, L., Tavares, J.M.R., Placidi, G.: Towards EEG-based BCI driven by emotions for addressing BCI-illiteracy: a meta-analytic review. Behav. Inf. Technol. **37**(8), 855–871 (2018). https://doi.org/10.1080/0144929x.2018.1485745
36. Kin Tam, W., Wu, T., Zhao, Q., Keefer, E., Yang, Z.: Human motor decoding from neural signals a review. BMC Biomed. Eng. **1**(1), 22 (2019). https://doi.org/10.1186/s42490-019-0022-z
37. Townsend, G., Graimann, B., Pfurtscheller, G.: Continuous EEG classification during motor imagery–simulation of an asynchronous BCI. IEEE Trans. Neural Syst. Rehabil. Eng. **12**(2), 258–265 (2004). https://doi.org/10.1109/tnsre.2004.827220
38. Vourvopoulos, A., Bermúdez i Badia, S.: Motor priming in virtual reality can augment motor-imagery training efficacy in restorative brain-computer interaction: a within-subject analysis. J. NeuroEngineering Rehabil. **13**(1), 69 (2016). https://doi.org/10.1186/s12984-016-0173-2

39. Wolpaw, J.R., McFarland, D.J.: Control of a two-dimensional movement signal by a noninvasive brain-computer interface in humans. Proc. Natl. Acad. Sci. **101**(51), 17849–17854 (2004). https://doi.org/10.1073/pnas.0403504101
40. Yang, L., Chen, J., Zhu, W.: Dynamic hand gesture recognition based on a leap motion controller and two-layer bidirectional recurrent neural network. Sensors **20**, 2106–2123 (2020)
41. Yoo, S.S., et al.: Brain-computer interface using fMRI: spatial navigation by thoughts. NeuroReport **15**(10), 1591–1595 (2004). https://doi.org/10.1097/01.wnr.0000133296.39160.fe

Deep Learning II

Fast Point Voxel Convolution Neural Network with Selective Feature Fusion for Point Cloud Semantic Segmentation

Xu Wang, Yuyan Li$^{(\boxtimes)}$, and Ye Duan

University of Missouri, Columbia, USA
{xwf32,yl235,duanye}@umsystem.edu

Abstract. We present a novel lightweight convolutional neural network for point cloud analysis. In contrast to many current CNNs which increase receptive field by downsampling point cloud, our method directly operates on the entire point sets without sampling and achieves good performances efficiently. Our network consists of point voxel convolution (PVC) layer as building block. Each layer has two parallel branches, namely the voxel branch and the point branch. For the voxel branch specifically, we aggregate local features on non-empty voxel centers to reduce geometric information loss caused by voxelization, then apply volumetric convolutions to enhance local neighborhood geometry encoding. For the point branch, we use Multi-Layer Perceptron (MLP) to extract fine-detailed point-wise features. Outputs from these two branches are adaptively fused via a feature selection module. Moreover, we supervise the output from every PVC layer to learn different levels of semantic information. The final prediction is made by averaging all intermediate predictions. We demonstrate empirically that our method is able to achieve comparable results while being fast and memory efficient. We evaluate our method on popular point cloud datasets for object classification and semantic segmentation tasks.

Keywords: Point cloud · Semantic segmentation · Deep learning

1 Introduction

Deep learning in 3D point cloud analysis has received increasing attention with the rising trend of Virtual Reality and 3D scene understanding applications, etc. Existing approaches have made great progresses in tasks such as point cloud classification [28] and point cloud semantic segmentation [1,3]. One fundamental issue to be tackled with in point cloud analysis is the representation of unstructured point clouds. Some early methods discretize point clouds into regular volumetric grids which can be directly fed into standard 3D CNNs. However, two main problems coupled with this volumetric representation are information loss and huge memory consumption. A high resolution voxel grid leads to expensive computation cost, while a low resolution inevitably suffers from information loss during voxelization procedure.

X. Wang and Y. Li—Equal contribution.

© Springer Nature Switzerland AG 2021
G. Bebis et al. (Eds.): ISVC 2021, LNCS 13017, pp. 319–330, 2021.
https://doi.org/10.1007/978-3-030-90439-5_25

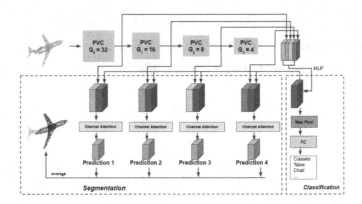

Fig. 1. Illustration of our proposed network. For an input 3D data, we pass it through a sequence of point-voxel convolution layers (PVC). G denotes grid resolution. Outputs from each PVC layer are concatenated together to form a global feature. MLP is used for feature dimension reduction. This global feature is concatenated with output from each PVC layer and passed through a channel attention module, which re-weights the features of all channels and increases feature discriminability. The final prediction is the average of all auxiliary predictions.

To address the problems mentioned above, another big stream is to directly consume sparse point clouds. The pioneer work is PointNet proposed by Qi et al. [17]. PointNet is able to process unordered point cloud inputs with permutation invariance using a sequence of multi-layer perceptron (MLP). The subsequent work PointNet++ [18] achieves better performance by proposing a hierarchical network that encodes local neighborhood information. Based on PointNet++ [18], a great number of networks [25,31,32] with more advanced local feature aggregation techniques are introduced. Apart from MLP-based methods, some recent works propose kernel-based approaches to mimic standard convolution [2,24,26,30]. In general, point-based approaches suffer from point sampling scalability, neighbor point searching efficiency, point density inconsistency issues. Most recently, Liu et al. [13] attempt to design a point-voxel CNN that represents 3D data as points to reduce memory footprint, and leverages voxel-based convolution to capture neighborhood features. This network is able to achieve reasonable performance with low memory usage and fast training/inference speed.

In this paper, we propose a novel CNN architecture that is well-balanced between efficiency and accuracy. Inspired by point-voxel CNN [13], we construct our network using point-voxel layer that takes advantages of both sparse point representation and volumetric convolution. Our point-voxel layer consists of two parallel branches, a voxel-based branch which aggregates local neighboring features, and a point-based branch which maintains fine-grained point-wise features. During discretization in voxel branch, we aggregate neighboring features on non-empty voxel centers and use standard 3D convolutions to enhance local feature encoding. Voxel features are propagated back to point domain through devox-elization. Outputs from point and voxel branches are fused self-adaptively via a feature selection module (FSM), which learns channel-wise attention for both branches.

Most of the existing studies rely heavily on point sampling strategy to avoid expensive computation cost as network goes deeper. However, point sampling cannot always retain the fine-detailed features for every point. Details of points are discarded as a trade-off for larger receptive field and processing speed. In our network, we only use a small number of point-voxel layers (default is 4 layers) that are carefully designed with effective feature encoding modules to facilitate processing efficiency. Supervision is applied on outputs from all layers to enforce semantic information learning. Though no point sampling is conducted, our network is able to remain lightweight, and effective to process large-scale point clouds. A visualization of our proposed network is shown in Fig. 1. We evaluate the performance and efficiency of our proposed model for object classification, object part segmentation and indoor scene semantic segmentation tasks (see Sect. 4).

2   Related Work

2.1   Volumentric Representation

Some early deep learning approaches transformed point clouds into 3D voxel struc-ture and convolve it with standard 3D kernels. VoxNet [15] and subsequent works [14,23,28] discretized point cloud into a 3D binary occupancy grid. The occu-pancy grid is fed to a CNN for object proposal and classification. These voxel-based methods suffered from high memory consumption due to the waste of com-putation on empty spaces. OctNet [19,22] proposed adaptive representation using octree structure to reduce memory consumption. Recent researches [4,8] intro-duced approaches to process high dimensional data and apply sparse convolution only on non-empty voxels. In general, volumetric methods preserve neighborhood information of point clouds, enable regular 3D CNN applications, but suffer from significant discretization artifacts.

2.2   Point-Based Representation

Point-wise models such as PointNet [17] and PointNet++ [18] directly oper-ates on point clouds. The former used MLPs to extract point-wise features and permutation- invariant max pooling operation to obtain a global feature. The latter built a hierarchical architecture that incorporates point downsampling and local structure aggregation strategies. Inspired by PointNet [17] and PointNet++ [18], many recent works propose advanced local feature learning modules. For example, PointWeb [32] built a dense fully connected web to explore local con-text, and used an Adaptive Feature Adjustment module for feature refinement. GACNet [25] proposed to selectively learn distinctive features by dynamically assigning attention weights to neighbouring points based on spatial positions and feature differences. ShellNet [31] built a model with several layers of ShellConv, and solved point ambiguity by constructing concentric shells and applying 1D convolution on ordered shells. Derived from point-based methods, some recent works define explicit kernels for point convolution. KCNet [20] developed a kernel correlation layer to compute affinities between each point's K nearest neighbors and a predefined set of kernel points. Local features are acquired by graph pooling layers. SpiderCNN [30] designed a family of Taylor polynomial kernels to aggregate neighbor features. PointCNN [12] introduced χ-transformation to exploit the canonical order of points. PCNN [26] built a network using parametric continuous convolutional layers. SPH3D [11] used spherical harmonic kernels during convolution on quantized space to identify distinctive geometric features. KPConv [24] defined rigid and deformable kernel points for local geometry encoding based on the Euclidean space relations between kernel point and neighborhood supporting points.

2.3 Efficiency of Current Models

When processing large-scale point clouds, efficiency is one of the fundamental measurements to evaluate models. Most of the point-based methods utilized point sampling to improve efficiency. However, it is non-trivial to choose an effective point sampling method. For example, Farthest Point Sampling (FPS) which is widely adopted in [18,31,32], has $O(NlogN)$ computation complexity, meaning it does not have good scalability. Random point sampling as used in RandLA-Net [9], has $O(1)$ time complexity, but random point sampling cannot be invariant to point densities and key information might be discarded. Other approaches manage to incorporate hybrid representations to avoid the redundant computing and storing of more useful spatial information. A recent work Grid-GCN [29] proposed a novel method which facilitates grid space structuring and provides more complete coverage of the point cloud. This method is able to handle massive points with fast speed and good scalability. Point-Voxel CNN [13] is most related to our method. This work combines fine-grained point features with coarse-grained voxel features with speedup and low memory consumption. Compared to their work, our method builds PVC layers with multi-resolution voxels, and incorporates more accurate local feature aggregation which reduce information loss artifacts.

3   Method

We build a deep architecture with a sequence of point-voxel convolution (PVC) layers. In this section, we introduce the details of our PVC layer, including voxelization, local feature aggregation, devoxelization, selective feature fusion, and deep supervision.

3.1   Point Voxel Convolution

Voxelization and Local Aggregation. The purpose of voxel branch is to encode contextual information through volumetric convolution. As aforementioned, information loss from the process of discretization is inevitable. Introducing large voxel grids reduces the loss, but burdens the network with huge computation overhead. In our design, we opt to use low-resolution volumetric grid, and mitigate information loss by effective local feature aggregation.

As the scale of point clouds varies, we first normalize the input data into a bounding box. For voxelization, we quantize point cloud by calculating voxel coordinates $(u, v, w) \in \mathbb{N}$ from point coordinates $(x, y, z) \in \mathbb{R}$.

$$u = floor((x - x_{min})/g_x), \ v = floor((y - y_{min})/g_y), \ w = floor((z - z_{min})/g_z) \tag{1}$$

where g_x, g_y, g_z is the grid length of x, y, z axis respectively:

$$g_x = (x_{max} - x_{min})/G, \ g_y = (y_{max} - y_{min})/G, \ g_z = (z_{max} - z_{min})/G \tag{2}$$

where $G \in \mathbb{N}$ is the grid resolution of this PVC layer.

Given the voxelized point cloud, we calculate the center location P_c of every voxel. To accelerate processing speed, we locate non-empty voxels and aggregates local features only on these voxels. For a non-empty voxel (u, v, w), we use the cell center as query position and gather K neighbors through K-nearest-neighbor (KNN). We adopt the dilated point convolution strategy as proposed in [6], in which $K \cdot n$ nearest neighbors and every $n - th$ neighbor is selected. The feature f for voxel (u, v, w) is the weighted summation of all K neighbors.

$$f_{u,v,w} = \sum_{k}^{K} l_k * f_k \tag{3}$$

where $l_k \in \mathbb{R}^{1 \times C}$ is the weight, $f_k \in \mathbb{R}^{1 \times C}$ is the feature of k-th neighbor. Inspired by [25,26], we use self-attention mechanism to learn weight of different neighboring points:

$$l_k = \sigma(\mathcal{G}(\Delta_{P_k}, f_k)) \tag{4}$$

where Δ_{P_k} is the normalized neighbor point coordinates, $\Delta_{P_k} = P_k - P_c$. $\mathcal{G}(*)$ takes the concatenation of Δ_{P_k} and f_k as input and models the attention weight. σ represents ReLU activation function. Through neighbor feature aggregation, we collect useful information and store it in the voxels. Next, we apply 3D convolutions on the voxel grid, as an enhancement of local neighborhood learning.

Devoxelization. To allow feature fusion from two branches, we propagate voxel features back to point domain based on their voxel coordinates. Taking efficiency into account, we assign voxel feature $f_{(u, v, w)}$ to all points that fall into this voxel. We observe that in our experiment since point-wise features are carried all along by point branch, fusing voxel feature with point feature would be effective to discriminate individual point.

Point and Voxel Feature Fusion. As illustrated in Fig. 2, for point branch, we use MLPs to extract point-wise features. While voxel features encode local neighborhood, point branch is able to carry fine-detailed per-point features. Next, we incorporate a feature selection module to correlate features. First, we use element-wise summation to fuse features from point and voxel branches:

$$f' = f_p + f_v \qquad (5)$$

where $f_p \in \mathbb{R}^{N \times C}$ and $f_v \in \mathbb{R}^{N \times C}$ are features from point and voxel branch respectively. Then a global average pooling is applied to squeeze N point to one compact point feature. Fully connected layer with non-linearity is used to provide guidance for feature selection:

$$S = \sigma(\mathcal{F}_{gp}(f') \cdot W_{fc}) \qquad (6)$$

where σ is the ReLU activation function, $\mathcal{F}_{gp}$ is the global average pooling, $W_{fc} \in \mathbb{R}^{C \times d}(d = C/4)$ is the learnable weight for fully connected layer. Two separate fully connected layers are applied to increase channel dimensions for S and produce soft attention vector $S_p \in \mathbb{R}^{1 \times C}$ and $S_v \in \mathbb{R}^{1 \times C}$.

$$S_p = S \cdot W_1, \quad S_v = S \cdot W_2 \qquad (7)$$

where $W_1 \in \mathbb{R}^{d \times C}$ and $W_2 \in \mathbb{R}^{d \times C}$ are learnable weights. We adopt the softmax mechanism on S_p and S_v to adaptively select features.

$$S_{p,c} = \frac{e^{S_{p,c}}}{e^{S_{p,c}} + e^{S_{v,c}}}, \quad S_{v,c} = \frac{e^{S_{v,c}}}{e^{S_{p,c}} + e^{S_{v,c}}} \qquad (8)$$

where $S_{p,c}$ and $S_{v,c}$ are soft attention vector for point and voxel feature at c^{th} channel. The fused feature at c^{th} channel can be calculated as follows:

$$F_{fused,c} = S_{p,c} \odot F_{p,c} + S_{v,c} \odot F_{v,c} \qquad (9)$$

Therefore, FSM adjusts channel-wise weight for different branches, and outputs the fused feature adaptively.

3.2 Deep Supervision

As shown in Fig. 1, we build our network with several PVC layers sequentially. Grid resolution decreases while output feature channel increases from shallow to deep. Different PVC layers extract different levels of semantic information. We add supervision on each PVC layer output to enforce different levels of semantic feature learning. Similar strategy is adopted by [21] for multi-scale medical image segmentation. In detail, we concatenate outputs from all PVC layers and use MLPs to produce a compact feature. Serving as a global guidance, this feature map is concatenated with the output of each PVC layer, then pass through a channel attention module to enhance feature representation of specific semantics. This attention module, inspired by [7], aggregates weighted features of all the

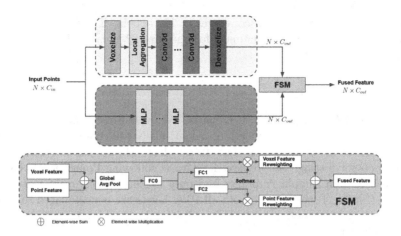

Fig. 2. Illustration of our PVC layer (top) and Feature Selection Module (bottom).

channels into the original features, and models discriminability between channels. The output from channel attention module produce an auxiliary loss. We add up all the losses and average the prediction probabilities for the final prediction. We show that incorporating channel attention module in our network boosts performances and not necessarily slow down inference speed (see Sect. 4.4).

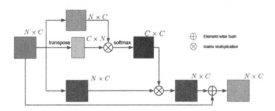

Fig. 3. Channel attention module

4   Experiment

In this section, we evaluate the performance of our method in point cloud learning tasks including object classification, object part segmentation, and indoor scene segmentation. For parameter settings, our network has a total of four PVC layers. From the first to the last layer, grid size is set to $G_0 = 32, G_1 = 16, G_2 = 8, G_3 = 4$ respectively. Number of neighbors for KNN search is 32. Dilation step is $n_0 = 1, n_1 = 2, n_2 = 4, n_3 = 8$. Our method is implemented with PyTorch [16] and run on a Nvidia TitanXP GPU. Batch size for training is set to be 16. We use the Adam optimizer [10] with default settings. The learning rate is initialized as 0.001 and decays by a rate of 0.5 every 20 epochs. Object classification converges around 100 epochs, part segmentation converges at 80 epochs, and indoor scene segmentation converges at 120 epochs. The full version of our network has $C = 64$ feature channels for the first PVC layer. Feature channel for l-th layer is $C \times 2^{l-1}$.

4.1 Object Classification

Datasets and Implementation Details. We evaluate our network on Model-Net40 [28] for 3D object classification task. ModelNet40 contains 12311 meshed CAD models from 40 categories. The dataset has 9843 objects for training and 2468 objects for testing. We prepare the dataset following PointNet [17] conventions. We random sample N points and only use normal as input feature. As illustrated in Fig. 1, the output from all PVC layers are concatenated to form a global feature. Max pooling followed by a fully connected layer are then used to produce a classification score.

Evaluation. We train three versions of classification network with variance on number of points and number of feature channels. Shown in Table 1, our method has a good balance between performance and efficiency.

Table 1. Results of ModelNet40 [28] classification. $1 \times C$ represents our full size model.

Method	Input data	OA	Latency (ms)
PointNet [17]	8×1024	89.2	**15**
Ours $(0.5 \times C)$	8×1024	**91.7**	20
PointNet++ [18]	8×1024	91.9	27
DGCNN [27]	8×1024	91.9	27
Ours $(0.75 \times C)$	8×1024	**92.3**	**26**
Grid-GCN (full) [29]	16×1024	**93.1**	42
Ours $(1 \times C)$	8×2048	92.5	**35**

4.2 Shape Segmentation

Data and Implementation Details. We conduct experiment on ShapeNet-Part [3] for shape segmentation. ShapeNetPart is a collection of 16681 point clouds (14006 for training, 2874 for testing) from 16 categories, each annotated with 2–6 labels. Input features are normals only, while point coordinates (x, y, z) are incorporated in the network for voxelization and local aggregation. We random sample 2048 points for training and use the original points for testing.

Evaluation. A comparison of our method and previous approaches is listed in Table 2. We report our result with mean instance IoU. We train three versions of our method, a compact network with $0.5 \times C$ feature channels, a medium size network with $0.75 \times C$ feature channels, and a full size network. Our compact network is able to achieve the same results as PointNet++ [18], with 2× speedup, and 0.7G less memory consumption. Comparing with DGCNN our compact method is 2× faster and only half of its memory usage. Comparing with PV CNN [13], our method achieves comparable results.

Table 2. Results of object part segmentation on ShapeNetPart [3]. Our method achieves comparable performance with fast inference speed, and low GPU consumption.

Method	Input data	InstanceIoU	Latency (ms)	GPU usage (G)
PointNet [17]	8 × 2048	83.7	**22**	1.5
3D-Unet [5]	Volume (8 × 96³)	84.6	682	8.8
PointNet++ [18]	8 × 2048	85.1	78	2.0
DGCNN [27]	8 × 2048	85.1	88	2.4
PV CNN (0.5 × C) [13]	8 × 2048	**85.5**	22	**1.0**
Ours (0.5 × C)	8 × 2048	**85.5**	32	1.3
PointCNN [12]	8 × 2048	86.1	136	2.5
PV CNN (1 × C) [13]	8 × 2048	86.2	**51**	**1.6**
Ours (1 × C)	8 × 2048	**86.3**	68	2.3

4.3 Indoor Scene Segmentation

Data and Implementation Details. We conduct experiments on S3DIS [1] for large-scale indoor scene segmentation. S3DIS [1] is a challenging dataset which consists of point clouds collected from six areas. Following the convention [12,17], we leave out area 5 for testing purpose. For data preparation, we split rooms into 2 m × 2 m blocks, with 0.5 m padding along each side (x, y). These context points do not involve in neither loss computation nor prediction during testing. We use color as input feature, point coordinates are incorporated in the network for voxelization and local aggregation. At training time, we random sample 8192 points from block data, and use original points at testing time.

To demonstrate the great potential of our proposed network, we also design experiments which replace regular 3D convolution layers with sparse 3D convolutions. We adopt Minkowski [4] sparse convolution in our experiment. Sparse convolution enables our network to process high-dimensional data with further speedup and reduce computation load on GPU.

Evaluation. A list of comparison of our method and previous approaches is shown in Table 3. We also train three versions for indoor scene segmentation. Compared with PV-CNN++ [13], our method is faster while able to achieve 2.9% higher mIoU score.

4.4 Ablation Study

To show the effectiveness of our proposed method, we gradually add a component while keeping the rest unchanged. To see the gain of each component, we train a

Table 3. Results of indoor scene segmentation on S3DIS [1], evaluated on Area 5. We report the result using mean Intersection-Over-Union (mIoU) metric. Compared with previous methods, our method is able to achieve top-ranking results while being lightweight and fast.

Method	Input data	mIoU	Latency (ms)	GPU usage (G)
PointNet [17]	8 × 4096	43.0	**21**	1.0
PointNet++ [18]	8 × 4096	52.3	–	–
3D-Unet [5]	Volume (8 × 96³)	55.0	575	6.8
DGCNN [27]	8 × 4096	48.0	178	2.4
PointCNN [12]	16 × 2048	57.3	282	4.6
PV CNN++ $(0.5 \times C)$ [13]	4 × 8192	57.6	41	**0.7**
PV CNN++ $(1 \times C)$ [13]	4 × 8192	59.0	70	0.8
Grid-GCN (full) [29]	8 × 4096	57.8	26	–
Ours $(0.5 \times C)$	4 × 8192	60.2	34	1.4
Ours $(0.75 \times C)$	4 × 8192	60.8	51	1.8
Ours $(1 \times C)$	4 × 8192	**61.7**	71	2.0
Ours $(1 \times C$, sparse$)$	4 × 8192	61.4	42	0.9

baseline network consists of four PVC layers. The baseline does not use local feature aggregation, instead an averaged feature of all points fall into the same voxel is taken. Fusion method is summation only. And no channel attention module (CAM) is used for prediction. Final prediction is directly produced from global feature without deep supervision. Experiments are conducted on ShapeNetPart [3]. The baseline model is the compact version $(0.5 \times C)$. From Table 4, we can see that each component is able to boost baseline method without necessarily increase latency too much.

Table 4. Ablation studies on ShapeNetPart[3].

	mIoU	Gain	Latency (ms)
Baseline	84.6	–	26
w/Local aggregation	84.8	+0.2	26
w/FSM	85.2	+0.6	28
w/CAM	84.9	+0.3	30
Full (Local aggregation + FSM + CAM)	85.5	+0.9	32

5   Conclusion

In this work, we propose a novel approach for fast and effective 3D point cloud learning. We designed a lightweight network that can incorporate both fine-grained point features and multi-scale local neighborhood information. We introduce feature selection module and deep supervision into our network for performance improvement. Experimental results on several point cloud datsets demonstrate that our method achieves comparable results while being fast and memory efficient.

References

1. Armeni, I., Sax, S., Zamir, A.R., Savarese, S.: Joint 2D–3D-semantic data for indoor scene understanding. arXiv preprint arXiv:1702.01105 (2017)
2. Boulch, A.: ConvPoint: continuous convolutions for point cloud processing. Computer. Graph. **88**, 24–34 (2020)
3. Chang, A.X., et al.: Shapenet: An information-rich 3D model repository. arXiv preprint arXiv:1512.03012 (2015)
4. Choy, C., Gwak, J., Savarese, S.: 4D spatio-temporal ConvNets: Minkowski convolutional neural networks. In: Proceedings of the IEEE Conference on Computer Vision and Pattern Recognition, pp. 3075–3084 (2019)
5. Çiçek, Ö., Abdulkadir, A., Lienkamp, S.S., Brox, T., Ronneberger, O.: 3D U-Net: learning dense volumetric segmentation from sparse annotation. In: Ourselin, S., Joskowicz, L., Sabuncu, M.R., Unal, G., Wells, W. (eds.) MICCAI 2016, Part II. LNCS, vol. 9901, pp. 424–432. Springer, Cham (2016). https://doi.org/10.1007/978-3-319-46723-8_49
6. Engelmann, F., Kontogianni, T., Leibe, B.: Dilated point convolutions: On the receptive field of point convolutions. arXiv preprint arXiv:1907.12046 (2019)
7. Fu, J., et al.: Dual attention network for scene segmentation. In: Proceedings of the IEEE Conference on Computer Vision and Pattern Recognition, pp. 3146–3154 (2019)
8. Graham, B., Engelcke, M., van der Maaten, L.: 3D semantic segmentation with submanifold sparse convolutional networks. In: Proceedings of the IEEE conference on computer vision and pattern recognition, pp. 9224–9232 (2018)
9. Hu, Q., et al.: RandLA-Net: Efficient semantic segmentation of large-scale point clouds. arXiv preprint arXiv:1911.11236 (2019)
10. Kingma, D.P., Ba, J.: Adam: A method for stochastic optimization. arXiv preprint arXiv:1412.6980 (2014)
11. Lei, H., Akhtar, N., Mian, A.: Spherical kernel for efficient graph convolution on 3D point clouds. arXiv preprint arXiv:1909.09287 (2019)
12. Li, Y., Bu, R., Sun, M., Wu, W., Di, X., Chen, B.: PointCNN: Convolution on x-transformed points. In: Advances in neural information processing systems. pp. 820–830 (2018)
13. Liu, Z., Tang, H., Lin, Y., Han, S.: Point-voxel CNN for efficient 3D deep learning. In: Advances in Neural Information Processing Systems, pp. 963–973 (2019)
14. Maturana, D., Scherer, S.: 3D convolutional neural networks for landing zone detection from lidar. In: 2015 IEEE International Conference on Robotics and Automation (ICRA), pp. 3471–3478. IEEE (2015)
15. Maturana, D., Scherer, S.: VoxNet: a 3D convolutional neural network for real-time object recognition. In: 2015 IEEE/RSJ International Conference on Intelligent Robots and Systems (IROS), pp. 922–928. IEEE (2015)
16. Paszke, A., et al.: Automatic differentiation in PyTorch (2017)
17. Qi, C.R., Su, H., Mo, K., Guibas, L.J.: Pointnet: deep learning on point sets for 3D classification and segmentation. In: Proceedings of the IEEE Conference on Computer Vision And Pattern Recognition, pp. 652–660 (2017)

18. Qi, C.R., Yi, L., Su, H., Guibas, L.J.: PointNet++: deep hierarchical feature learning on point sets in a metric space. In: Advances in Neural Information Processing Systems, pp. 5099–5108 (2017)
19. Riegler, G., Osman Ulusoy, A., Geiger, A.: OctNet: learning deep 3D representations at high resolutions. In: Proceedings of the IEEE Conference on Computer Vision and Pattern Recognition, pp. 3577–3586 (2017)
20. Shen, Y., Feng, C., Yang, Y., Tian, D.: Mining point cloud local structures by kernel correlation and graph pooling. In: Proceedings of the IEEE Conference on Computer Vision and Pattern Recognition, pp. 4548–4557 (2018)
21. Sinha, A., Dolz, J.: Multi-scale guided attention for medical image segmentation. arXiv preprint arXiv:1906.02849 (2019)
22. Tatarchenko, M., Dosovitskiy, A., Brox, T.: Octree generating networks: efficient convolutional architectures for high-resolution 3D outputs. In: Proceedings of the IEEE International Conference on Computer Vision, pp. 2088–2096 (2017)
23. Tchapmi, L., Choy, C., Armeni, I., Gwak, J., Savarese, S.: SEGCloud: semantic segmentation of 3D point clouds. In: 2017 International Conference on 3D Vision (3DV), pp. 537–547. IEEE (2017)
24. Thomas, H., Qi, C.R., Deschaud, J.E., Marcotegui, B., Goulette, F., Guibas, L.J.: KPConv: flexible and deformable convolution for point clouds. In: Proceedings of the IEEE International Conference on Computer Vision, pp. 6411–6420 (2019)
25. Wang, L., Huang, Y., Hou, Y., Zhang, S., Shan, J.: Graph attention convolution for point cloud semantic segmentation. In: Proceedings of the IEEE Conference on Computer Vision and Pattern Recognition, pp. 10296–10305 (2019)
26. Wang, S., Suo, S., Ma, W.C., Pokrovsky, A., Urtasun, R.: Deep parametric continuous convolutional neural networks. In: Proceedings of the IEEE Conference on Computer Vision and Pattern Recognition, pp. 2589–2597 (2018)
27. Wang, Y., Sun, Y., Liu, Z., Sarma, S.E., Bronstein, M.M., Solomon, J.M.: Dynamic graph CNN for learning on point clouds. ACM Trans. Graph. (TOG)D **38**(5), 1–12 (2019)
28. Wu, Z., et al.: 3D ShapeNets: a deep representation for volumetric shapes. In: Proceedings of the IEEE Conference on Computer Vision and Pattern Recognition, pp. 1912–1920 (2015)
29. Xu, Q.: Grid-GCN for fast and scalable point cloud learning. arXiv preprint arXiv:1912.02984 (2019)
30. Xu, Y., Fan, T., Xu, M., Zeng, L., Qiao, Yu.: SpiderCNN: deep learning on point sets with parameterized convolutional filters. In: Ferrari, V., Hebert, M., Sminchisescu, C., Weiss, Y. (eds.) ECCV 2018, Part VIII. LNCS, vol. 11212, pp. 90–105. Springer, Cham (2018). https://doi.org/10.1007/978-3-030-01237-3_6
31. Zhang, Z., Hua, B.S., Yeung, S.K.: ShellNet: efficient point cloud convolutional neural networks using concentric shells statistics. In: Proceedings of the IEEE International Conference on Computer Vision, pp. 1607–1616 (2019)
32. Zhao, H., Jiang, L., Fu, C.W., Jia, J.: PointWeb: enhancing local neighborhood features for point cloud processing. In: Proceedings of the IEEE Conference on Computer Vision and Pattern Recognition, pp. 5565–5573 (2019)

Behaviour of Sample Selection Techniques Under Explicit Regularization

Lakshya$^{(\boxtimes)}$

Samsung R&D Institute India - Bangalore, Bangalore, India
`lakshya.01@samsung.com`

Abstract. There is a multitude of sample selection-based learning strategies that have been developed for learning with noisy labels. However, It has also been indicated in the literature that perhaps early stopping is better than fully training the model for getting better performance. It leads us to wonder about the behavior of the sample selection strategies under explicit regularization. To this end, we considered four of the most fundamental sample selection-based models MentorNet, Coteaching, Coteaching-plus and JoCor. We provide empirical results of applying explicit L2 regularization to the above-mentioned approaches. We also compared the results with a baseline - a vanilla CNN model trained with just regularization. We show that under explicit regularization, the preconceived ranking of the approaches might change. We also show several instances where the baseline was able to outperform some or all of the existing approaches. Moreover, we show that under explicit regularization, the performance gap between the approaches can also reduce.

1   Introduction

Humans tend to learn much better and more quickly when presented with harder and harder concepts gradually. Yoshua Bengio formalized this notion as Curriculum learning [2]. Not only does Curriculum learning make the training process faster, but it also reaches superior quality minima in the case of non-convex optimization. Building on Curriculum Learning, Kumar [9] proposed Self-Paced Learning (SPL) for learning a latent variable model. Based on the findings of [1], according to which a neural network learns easy patterns first, MentorNet [8] made further progress along this line by using SPL for training with noisy labels.

Noisy labels are ubiquitous in practice. For example, noise may appear due to annotations carried out by computer programs on web crawled images [7,22] or annotations based on crowdsourcing [27]. Consequently, it is necessary to research techniques that are robust to noisy labeling.

Since MentorNet, a multitude of sample selection-based techniques has emerged. Coteaching [5] upgraded the MentorNet by utilizing two Networks. The mini-batch used for training one network was decided by the loss obtained on the samples using the second network. Coteaching-plus [36], further argued that the

© Springer Nature Switzerland AG 2021
G. Bebis et al. (Eds.): ISVC 2021, LNCS 13017, pp. 331–340, 2021.
https://doi.org/10.1007/978-3-030-90439-5_26

two networks should be kept diverged by disagreement in predictions, which can further benefit the training. JoCoR [30] aimed to reduce the diversity of the two models as opposed to Coteaching-plus. Recently DivideMix [11], EvidentialMix [25] were proposed, which try to incorporate semi-supervised learning on noisy classified labels as opposed to leaving them out of training. Another interesting approach is presented in [35], where a single model has been proposed for doing sample selection by relying on the consistency of predictions.

Meanwhile, it has also been argued that early-stopping might be a better strategy than fully training a network. Thus, in the presence of early stopping regularization, the benefits of MentorNet and other approaches remain unrealized. Although, finding the instance for early stopping or utilizing early stopping is an active area of research itself [14,31]. This compelled us to wonder about the behavior of the sample selection strategies under explicit regularization. Since, for most of the approaches, either the original results have been provided without explicit regularization or even if regularization was present, less attention was paid to regularization while comparing results.

To provide more insights on these matters, we make the following contributions through this paper.

- We provide empirical results of applying explicit L2 regularization to the sample selection based approaches. We also compared the results with a baseline - a vanilla CNN model trained with just regularization.
- We show that under explicit regularization, the pre-conceived ranking of the approaches might change.
- We also show several instances where the baseline was able to outperform some or all of the existing approaches.
- Moreover, we show that under explicit regularization, the performance gap between the approaches can also reduce.

2   Related Works

Various methodologies have been developed to learn with noisy labels. There are invested efforts in exploiting a noise transition matrix [6,12,15,32], using graph models [13,33]. Progress has also been made using meta-learning [23,26,29,34]. In [4], authors utilized different pseudo-labeling and sample selection strategies for Contrastive pre-training. In separate work, authors of [10] argue that even with overfitting to noise, good hidden representations are learned, which can be used to train a separate classifier with known correct labels. Authors of [19] learned a joint probability distribution for noisy and clean labels under the class-conditional noise process to identify the label errors in the dataset. Meanwhile, SELF [18] performs self ensembling to filter out the noisy label samples from the dataset, which are further used for unsupervised loss.

Authors have also tried developing robust surrogate loss functions that can help to learn in noisy labels setting [3,17,20,37]. In particular, in [16], authors proposed a curriculum loss (CL) which is a tight upper bound on the 0–1 loss and can also be used to adaptively select samples. Whereas authors of [28] added a reverse cross-entropy element with classical cross-entropy to create metric cross-entropy loss.

3   Experimentation

We considered four different sample selection algorithms and analyzed their results under explicit L2 regularization. We first conducted experiments to find the optimal weight decay value for each combination of algorithm, dataset, noise type, and noise rate. Next, we compared the results of the algorithms with their optimal weight decay values, which are provided in this section.

Existing Approaches. We used four different approaches for these experiments, Self-paced MentorNet, Coteaching, Coteaching-plus, and JoCor. We also considered a Baseline approach - a vanilla model trained only with weight decay.

Datasets. We used four different simulated noisy datasets for benchmarking, three vision-based datasets, MNIST, CIFAR-10, CIFAR-100, and one text-based dataset, NEWS. Although, we could only do the testing with JoCor on the CIFAR-10 and CIFAR-100 datasets, since we also had to find the optimal co-lambda [30] value for the experiments. We used three different simulated noise settings for our experiments. Namely, Symmetric noise [24] with 0.2 noise rate, Symmetric noise with 0.5 noise rate, and Pair-flipping [5] Noise with 0.45 noise rate.

Hyperparameters. Experiments were run for 200 epochs with three different seeds. All the other Hyperparameters, including warm-up schedule, were kept same as the original algorithm.

Network Architecture. For all our experiments, we used the following models (similar to Coteaching-plus).

- MNIST-MLP for MNIST: a 2 layer MLP with ReLU activation
- CNN-small for CIFAR-10: A CNN model with 2 convolutional layers and 3 Dense layers with ReLU activation.
- CNN-large for CIFAR-100: A CNN model with 6 convolutional layers and 1 Dense layer with ReLU activation.
- NEWS-MLP for NEWS: a 3 layer MLP with Softsign activation function on top of pre-trained word embeddings from GloVe [21].

Table 1 shows the details of these networks (This table is motivated by Coteaching-plus [36]).

Table 1. Different architectures used.

MNIST-MLP	CNN-small	CNN-large	NEWS-MLP
Dense 28 × 28 -> 256	5 × 5 Conv 6 2 × 2 Max-pool	3 × 3 Conv 64, BN, 3 × 3 Conv 64, BN 2 × 2 Max-Pool	300-D Embedding Flatten => 1000 × 300 Adaptive avg-pool -> 16 × 300
	5 × 5 Conv 16 2 × 2 Max-pool	3 × 3 Conv 128, BN 3 × 3 Conv 128, BN 2 × 2 Max-Pool	Dense 16 × 300 -> 4 × 300 BN, Softsign
	Dense 16 × 5 × 5 -> 120 Dense 120 ->84	3 × 3 Conv 196, BN 3 × 3 Conv 196, BN 2 × 2 Max-Pool	Dense 4 × 300 -> 300 BN, SoftSign
Dense 256 -> 10	Dense84 -> 10/100	Dense 256->10/100	Dense 300 -> 7

Table 2. Average last ten epoch accuracy for different Models at their optimal weight decay values on the CIFAR-10

Dataset	Type	Rate	Model	Test accuracy	Error (±)
CIFAR-10	Sym	0.2	JoCor	62.544	0.986
			Coteaching	60.364	3.317
			Baseline	59.187	4.667
			Mentornet	58.392	4.107
			Coteaching-plus	58.35	0.946
	Pairflip	0.45	Baseline	48.221	1.083
			Coteaching-plus	39.766	0.356
			Mentornet	39.666	1.137
			Coteaching	38.753	3.941
			JoCor	38.733	0.396
	Sym	0.5	JoCor	51.688	1.36
			Coteaching-plus	49.881	0.789
			Baseline	49.2	1.144
			Coteaching	48.589	4.684
			Mentornet	45.423	2.498

3.1 Observations

Tables 2, 3, 4, and 5 show the results of experimentation's on the CIFAR-10, CIFAR-100, MNIST and NEWS datasets, resp. Test accuracy's mentioned are average over last ten epoch across all the seeds. 'type' column refers to the noise type and 'rate' represents the noise rate. In these tables, for ease of analyzing, entries for a particular combination of dataset, noise type and noise rate are sorted by the Test Accuracy. Meanwhile, Figs. 1, 2, 3, and 4 show the test accuracy vs epoch plots during the training.

Table 3. Average last ten epoch accuracy for different Models at their optimal weight decay values on the CIFAR-100 dataset.

Dataset	Type	Rate	Model	Test accuracy	Error (±)
CIFAR-100	Sym	0.2	JoCor	53.626	0.212
			Coteaching-plus	49.332	0.32
			Coteaching	47.812	0.537
			Mentornet	47.437	0.527
			Baseline	37.561	0.434
	Pairflip	0.45	Coteaching-plus	30.116	0.374
			JoCor	29.562	0.351
			Coteaching	28.811	0.155
			Mentornet	27.333	0.42
			Baseline	25.119	0.478
	Sym	0.5	JoCor	43.41	0.401
			Coteaching-plus	40.445	0.429
			Coteaching	38.384	0.271
			Mentornet	37.507	0.485
			Baseline	22.872	0.472

Table 4. Average last ten epoch accuracy for different Models at their optimal weight decay values on the MNIST dataset.

Dataset	Type	Rate	Model	Test accuracy	Error (±)
MNIST	Sym	0.2	Coteaching-plus	97.776	0.111
			Baseline	97.52	0.119
			Mentornet	97.496	0.062
			Coteaching	97.49	0.062
	Pairflip	0.45	Coteaching	91.894	0.41
			Mentornet	91.852	0.538
			Coteaching-plus	86.403	4.367
			Baseline	77.084	0.29
	Sym	0.5	Coteaching	96.311	0.104
			Mentornet	96.265	0.098
			Coteaching-plus	95.995	0.113
			Baseline	95.799	0.062

Table 5. Average last ten epoch accuracy for different Models at their optimal weight decay values on the NEWS dataset.

Dataset	Type	Rate	Model	Test Accuracy	Error (±)
NEWS	Sym	0.2	Coteaching-plus	42.266	0.2
			Coteaching	38.768	0.21
			Mentornet	38.596	0.73
			Baseline	36.558	0.383
	Pairflip	0.45	Coteaching-plus	30.195	0.611
			Mentornet	29.669	0.322
			Coteaching	29.054	0.425
			Baseline	27.356	0.4
	Sym	0.5	Coteaching-plus	34.916	0.436
			Coteaching	33.919	0.562
			Mentornet	32.857	0.226
			Baseline	26.217	0.521

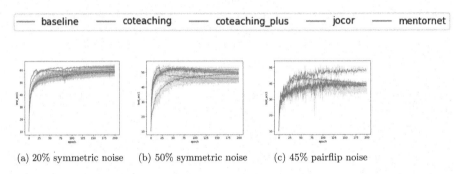

(a) 20% symmetric noise   (b) 50% symmetric noise   (c) 45% pairflip noise

Fig. 1. Results on the CIFAR-10 dataset for different Models at their optimal weight decay values

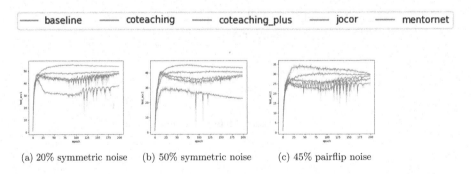

(a) 20% symmetric noise   (b) 50% symmetric noise   (c) 45% pairflip noise

Fig. 2. Results on the CIFAR-100 dataset for different Models at their optimal weight decay values

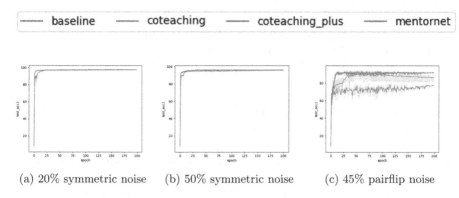

Fig. 3. Results on the MNIST dataset for different Models at their optimal weight decay values

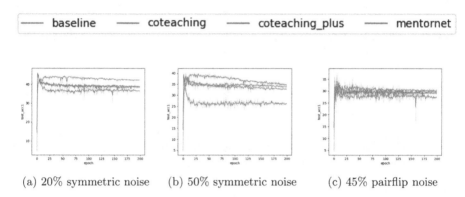

Fig. 4. Results on the NEWS dataset for different Models at their optimal weight decay values

Before we analyze the results, we present a ranking order for existing approaches and the baseline. Based on the existing claims in the literature, we can assume the following ranking order, JoCor (1st) > Coteaching-plus (2nd) > Coteaching (3rd) > MentorNet (4th) > Baseline (5th), where '>' implies better in terms of test-accuracy. Moreover, it is expected that if explicit regularization doesn't have any relative effect on the approaches, then this pre-defined rank order should be maintained in our experiments as well.

Please note that there are 12 different groups of experiments, corresponding to the twelve different combinations of the dataset, noise type, and noise rate. Moreover, in each of these groups, a ranking order of the approaches can be observed (Each Table 2, 3, 4, and 5 show 3 groups based on noise-type and noise-rate for a particular dataset.) We have made the following observations by comparing these ranking orders with the pre-defined ranking order.

- In 8 out of the 12 groups, the ranking order was different than the pre-defined ranking order. This gives a clear indication that explicit regularization can indeed change the relative ranking of the approaches.
- Among all the combinations, Pairflip-0.45 proved to get most affected by regularization, where ranking order broke for every dataset value. Pairflip-0.45 is the toughest noise category as can be seen by lowest test accuracy for any approach-dataset pair. Thus, higher amount of overfitting to noisy labels happens in Pairflip-0.45 case, thus, the effect of L2-regularization is more profound.
- There were 4 different groups in which Baseline wasn't at the bottom of the ranking order. This includes the group CIFAR-10-Pairflip-0.45, where Baseline ranked 1st with a difference of 8.455% between Baseline and the 2nd ranked approach.
- We also observed that the performance gap between the MentorNet and the Coteaching was reduced significantly (please check the plots). On 3 different groups, MentorNet was even able to outperform Coteaching. Moreover, on the remaining 9 groups, the average performance difference between the Coteaching and the MentorNet was only 1.0212%.
- Following observations were made regarding the individual performance of each approach. (We denote the group as a failure if the ranking of the approach in the group was lower than the pre-defined ranking. Similarly, a win if it was higher than the pre-defined ranking.)
  - JoCor failed on 2 (33.33%) groups out of 6 (since we only experimented with JoCor on the CIFAR-10 and the CIFAR-100).
  - Coteaching-plus failed 3 times and won once, which implies the ranking order was changed 4 (33.33%) times for it.
  - Coteaching failed 4 times and won 3 times i.e. 7 (58.33%) times the ranking order was changed.
  - MentorNet failed once and won 4 times.
  - Baseline won 4 times as well.

Based on this data, we can say that while the domination of one approach over the other might not be altered with explicit regularization (for instance, JoCor still ranks 1st in 4 out of 6 groups), in many instances, it can alter the outcome of the experiments and change the believed ranking of the approaches. Moreover, it can also reduce the performance gap between the algorithms as observed in the case of MentorNet and Coteaching.

4   Conclusion

In this paper, we showed that under explicit regularization, the pre-conceived ranking of the approaches might change. We also showed several instances where a vanilla CNN trained with just L2 regularization was able to outperform some or all of the existing approaches. Moreover, under explicit regularization, the performance gap between the approaches can also reduce. All these points suggest that special attention should be given to explicit regularization. Since explicit regularization can significantly alter the outcome, we suggest that it should be made sure that the comparison between the two approaches is done with their optimal regularization values.

References

1. Arpit, D., et al.: A closer look at memorization in deep networks (2017)
2. Bengio, Y., Louradour, J., Collobert, R., Weston, J.: Curriculum learning. In: Proceedings of the 26th Annual International Conference on Machine Learning, ICML 2009, pp. 41–48. Association for Computing Machinery, New York (2009). https://doi.org/10.1145/1553374.1553380
3. Cheng, H., Zhu, Z., Li, X., Gong, Y., Sun, X., Liu, Y.: Learning with instance-dependent label noise: a sample sieve approach (2021)
4. Ciortan, M., Dupuis, R., Peel, T.: A framework using contrastive learning for classification with noisy labels (2021)
5. Han, B., et al.: Co-teaching: robust training of deep neural networks with extremely noisy labels (2018)
6. Hendrycks, D., Mazeika, M., Wilson, D., Gimpel, K.: Using trusted data to train deep networks on labels corrupted by severe noise (2019)
7. Hu, M., Yang, Y., Shen, F., Zhang, L., Shen, H.T., Li, X.: Robust web image annotation via exploring multi-facet and structural knowledge. IEEE Trans. Image Process. **26**(10), 4871–4884 (2017). https://doi.org/10.1109/TIP.2017.2717185
8. Jiang, L., Zhou, Z., Leung, T., Li, L.J., Fei-Fei, L.: MentorNet: learning data-driven curriculum for very deep neural networks on corrupted labels (2018)
9. Kumar, M., Packer, B., Koller, D.: Self-paced learning for latent variable models. In: Lafferty, J., Williams, C., Shawe-Taylor, J., Zemel, R., Culotta, A. (eds.) Advances in Neural Information Processing Systems, vol. 23. Curran Associates, Inc. (2010). https://proceedings.neurips.cc/paper/2010/file/e57c6b956a6521b28495f2886ca0977a-Paper.pdf
10. Li, J., Zhang, M., Xu, K., Dickerson, J.P., Ba, J.: Noisy labels can induce good representations (2020)
11. Li, J., Socher, R., Hoi, S.C.H.: DivideMix: learning with noisy labels as semi-supervised learning (2020)
12. Li, X., Liu, T., Han, B., Niu, G., Sugiyama, M.: Provably end-to-end label-noise learning without anchor points (2021)
13. Li, Y., Yang, J., Song, Y., Cao, L., Luo, J., Li, L.J.: Learning from noisy labels with distillation (2017)
14. Liu, S., Niles-Weed, J., Razavian, N., Fernandez-Granda, C.: Early-learning regularization prevents memorization of noisy labels (2020)
15. Liu, T., Tao, D.: Classification with noisy labels by importance reweighting. IEEE Trans. Pattern Anal. Mach. Intell. **38**(3), 447–461 (2016). https://doi.org/10.1109/tpami.2015.2456899
16. Lyu, Y., Tsang, I.W.: Curriculum loss: robust learning and generalization against label corruption (2020)
17. Ma, X., et al.: Dimensionality-driven learning with noisy labels (2018)
18. Nguyen, D.T., Mummadi, C.K., Ngo, T.P.N., Nguyen, T.H.P., Beggel, L., Brox, T.: SELF: learning to filter noisy labels with self-ensembling (2019)
19. Northcutt, C.G., Jiang, L., Chuang, I.L.: Confident learning: estimating uncertainty in dataset labels (2021)

20. Patrini, G., Rozza, A., Menon, A., Nock, R., Qu, L.: Making deep neural networks robust to label noise: a loss correction approach (2017)
21. Pennington, J., Socher, R., Manning, C.: GloVe: global vectors for word representation. In: Proceedings of the 2014 Conference on Empirical Methods in Natural Language Processing (EMNLP), Doha, Qatar, pp. 1532–1543. Association for Computational Linguistics (October 2014). https://doi.org/10.3115/v1/D14-1162. https://www.aclweb.org/anthology/D14-1162
22. Ratner, A., Sa, C.D., Wu, S., Selsam, D., Ré, C.: Data programming: creating large training sets, quickly (2017)
23. Ren, M., Zeng, W., Yang, B., Urtasun, R.: Learning to reweight examples for robust deep learning (2019)
24. van Rooyen, B., Menon, A.K., Williamson, R.C.: Learning with symmetric label noise: the importance of being unhinged (2015)
25. Sachdeva, R., Cordeiro, F.R., Belagiannis, V., Reid, I., Carneiro, G.: Evidentialmix: learning with combined open-set and closed-set noisy labels. In: Proceedings of the IEEE/CVF Winter Conference on Applications of Computer Vision (WACV), pp. 3607–3615 (January 2021)
26. Shu, J., Xie, Q., Yi, L., Zhao, Q., Zhou, S., Xu, Z., Meng, D.: Meta-weight-net: Learning an explicit mapping for sample weighting (2019)
27. Su, H., Deng, J., Fei-Fei, L.: Crowdsourcing annotations for visual object detection, pp. 40–46 (January 2012)
28. Wang, Y., Ma, X., Chen, Z., Luo, Y., Yi, J., Bailey, J.: Symmetric cross entropy for robust learning with noisy labels. In: Proceedings of the IEEE/CVF International Conference on Computer Vision (ICCV) (October 2019)
29. Wang, Z., Hu, G., Hu, Q.: Training noise-robust deep neural networks via meta-learning. In: 2020 IEEE/CVF Conference on Computer Vision and Pattern Recognition (CVPR), pp. 4523–4532 (2020). https://doi.org/10.1109/CVPR42600.2020.00458
30. Wei, H., Feng, L., Chen, X., An, B.: Combating noisy labels by agreement: a joint training method with co-regularization (2020)
31. Xia, X., et al.: Robust early-learning: Hindering the memorization of noisy labels. In: International Conference on Learning Representations (2021). https://openreview.net/forum?id=Eql5b1_hTE4
32. Xia, X., et al.: Extended T: learning with mixed closed-set and open-set noisy labels (2020)
33. Xiao, T., Xia, T., Yang, Y., Huang, C., Wang, X.: Learning from massive noisy labeled data for image classification. In: 2015 IEEE Conference on Computer Vision and Pattern Recognition (CVPR), pp. 2691–2699 (2015). https://doi.org/10.1109/CVPR.2015.7298885
34. Xu, Y., Zhu, L., Jiang, L., Yang, Y.: Faster meta update strategy for noise-robust deep learning (2021)
35. Yi, R., Huang, Y.: Transform consistency for learning with noisy labels (2021)
36. Yu, X., Han, B., Yao, J., Niu, G., Tsang, I.W., Sugiyama, M.: How does disagreement help generalization against label corruption? (2019)
37. Ziyin, L., et al.: Learning not to learn in the presence of noisy labels (2020)

Adaptive Feature Norm for Unsupervised Subdomain Adaptation

Ashiq Imran$^{(\boxtimes)}$ and Vassilis Athitsos

Department of Computer Science and Engineering, University of Texas at Arlington,
Arlington, TX, USA
ashiq.imran@mavs.uta.edu, athitsos@uta.edu

Abstract. In many real-world problems, obtaining labeled data for a
specific machine learning task is expensive. Unsupervised Domain Adaptation (UDA) aims at learning a good predictive model for the target
domain using labeled information from the source but only unlabeled
samples from the target domain. Most of the previous methods tackle
this issue with adversarial methods that contain several loss functions
and converge slowly. Recently, subdomain adaptation, which focuses on
nuances of the distribution of the relevant subdomains, is getting more
and more attention in the UDA field. This paper proposes a technique
that uses the adaptive feature norm with subdomain adaptation to boost
the transfer gains. Subdomain adaptation can enhance the ability of deep
adaptation networks by capturing the fine-grained features from each
category. Additionally, we have incorporated an adaptive feature norm
approach to increase transfer gains. Our method shows state-of-the-art
results on the popular visual classification datasets, including Office-31,
Office Home, and Image-CLEF datasets.

Keywords: Domain adaptation · Transfer learning · Object
recognition

1 Introduction

Deep Neural Networks have shown remarkable performance in various domains in
the field of computer vision. To achieve good performance, they typically require a
vast amount of labeled data. Training larger and deeper networks is complicated if
the size of a dataset is small. Additionally, collecting well-annotated data is costly
and time-consuming. A popular way to regularize these networks is to simply use
a pre-trained model trained on a different dataset and use the model for the target
dataset. However, if the data distribution between source and target domains is
different, it may lead to adverse effects and hamper the generalization ability of
the models [3]. Unsupervised Domain Adaptation (UDA) focuses on transferring
knowledge from a labeled source domain to an unlabeled target domain, and a large
amount of research tries to achieve this by exploring domain-invariant representations to bridge the gap. Traditional machine-learning paradigms, like supervised

© Springer Nature Switzerland AG 2021
G. Bebis et al. (Eds.): ISVC 2021, LNCS 13017, pp. 341–352, 2021.
https://doi.org/10.1007/978-3-030-90439-5_27

learning, tend to train models to predict the outcome for unseen data. These models do not necessarily optimize performance if there is enough difference between the test and training data [21]. According to Tzeng *et al.* [23], while generically trained deep networks have a reduced dataset bias, there still exists a domain shift between different datasets, and it is required to adapt the features appropriately. [1] suggests that a fair domain adaptation method should be based on features that are near similar for the source and target domains while reducing the prediction error in the source domain as much as possible. However, domain adaptation can have a domain shift problem. For example, the target domain may contain images from different imaging device (e.g. webcam vs. dslr camera), resulting in different styles in photos. This means the object recognition model trained from the source domain requires to be adapted to the target domain. Therefore, to reduce the domain shift problem, the two domains marginal distributions need to be as similar as possible. The primary goal of UDA is to learn domain-invariant feature representations that can reduce the domain shift. According to existing studies, domain-invariant representations can be captured through several methods, e.g., Maximum Mean Discrepancy [10,14,30], divergence-based methods [1,18], correlation distance [20], etc. Addtionally, several adversarial based methods have been applied [5,8,19,22,25] to minimize an approximate domain discrepancy.

Recent studies have shown that, compared to shallow networks, deep networks can learn more transferable features for domain adaptation by extracting domain-invariant features [10,11,20,28]. The main observation from the previous domain adaptation methods is that the domain classifier should be confused maximally so that the source classifier treats the samples from the target domain in a similar fashion. Additionally, most successful methods have come up with such ways that can make the domain classifier more confused. Most of the previous domain adaptation methods consider aligning the source and target distributions globally. We adapt a subdomain based approach to learn the domain transfer. A subdomain consists of samples within the same class. This method will lead to a scenario where all the data from different domains will be confused, and discriminative structures can be mixed up [31]. The main advantage of the subdomains over domains is the local domain shift instead of the global domain shift. Because of the local domain shift, the learners precisely may align the distribution of relevant subdomains within the same category in the source and target domains. An illustrative example of the difference between Domain Adaptation and Subdomain adaptation is depicted in Fig. 1(a). After global domain adaptation, the resulting distributions of the two domains are quite similar, but the data in different subdomains are too adjacent to be correctly classified. The distributions of relevant subdomains can be aligned properly, hence the nuances of the information can be exploited for domain adaptation.

According to [26], larger norms enable more informative trasferability. Recent studies on the compression technique [27] support the above claim and suggest smaller norms contain less information during the inference. Inspired from the two studies as mentioned above, we incorporate the step-wise adaptive feature norm approach in subdomain space.

Xu *et al.* [26] demonstrates that progressively adapting the feature norms of two domains to a broad range of values can boost domain transfer. We present the local maximum mean discrepancy based method with adaptive progressively feature norm on subdomain space. For effective UDA, our goal is to endorse positive transfer and circumvent negative transfer.

In summary, the main contributions of our work are:

1. We propose an innovative stepwise adaptive feature norm-based approach for unsupervised subdomain adaptation. This approach employs to learn task-specific features in a progressive manner, which assists in aligning relevant subdomains in unsupervised scenarios.
2. We demonstrate a local MMD [31] based method with stepwise adaptive feature norm to achieve state-of-the-art results on Office-31, Office-Home, and ImageCLEF datasets.
3. We comapare our results with both adversarial and non-adversarial methods to show the efficacy of our work.

2   Related Work

Domain adaptation problem has been widely studied in the computer vision research community. Various methods have been employed to generalize the model across different domains by mitigating the domain shift problem. This section will discuss the relevant work in domain adaptation, subdomain adaptation, and maximum mean discrepancy.

2.1   Domain Adaptation

Domain adaptation can be a way to mitigate domain shift issues and reduce the effort of recollecting and retraining a model by transferring knowledge between tasks and domains. Domain adaptation can be defined as the task of training a model on labeled data from a source domain while minimizing test error on a target domain, where no labels for the target domain are available at training time. Several types of methods have been employed for unsupervised domain adaptation. Discrepancy based methods explore domain-invariant structures by reducing some specific statistic distances between the two domains. Maximum Mean Discrepancy (MMD) [2] has been adopted in many approaches [10,30] for domain adaptation. It enables the model to learn transferable features by reducing the MMD of their kernel embedding. Some other methods extended MMD [12,13] to measure the source and target data's joint distributions. In our case, we consider local MMD measures discrepancy of relevant subdomains between source and target domains. Adversarial DAs [5,19,22] are widely applied in this field. They involve a sub-network as the domain discriminator to distinguish features of alternate domains, whereas learners try to generate features that confuse the domain classifier.

2.2 Subdomain Adaptation

A significant amount of research for subdomain adaptation has been published recently. Multiadversarial domain adaptation (MADA) captures the multimode structures to enable fine-grained alignment of various data distributions [16]. CDAN [11] captures the adversarial domain adaptation on discriminative information to enable alignment of multimodal distributions. Moving the semantic transfer network (MSTN) [25] captures the semantic representation for unlabeled target samples by aligning the source and target centroid. Another method [9] creates multiple diverse feature spaces and aligns the source and target distributions in each of them separately while encouraging that alignments agree with each other with regard to the class predictions on the unlabeled target samples. All these methods have adopted adversarial loss. Compared to our work, we have adopted a discrepancy based strategy with stepwise adaptive feature norm approach which is more straightforward and can perform better than these previous methods.

2.3 Maximum Mean Discrepancy

Among discrepancy based methods, MMD is one of the most popular metrics of training for domain invariant features. In Deep Adaptation Network (DAN) architecture [10], the authors train the first layers of the model commonly with the source and target domains; after that, they train individual task-specific layers while minimizing MMD between layers. Additionally, MMD has been extended by [12,13]. However, most previous work considers global MMD measures to reduce discrepancies between the source and target samples. Our work is based on local MMD [31], which measures the discrepancy in relevant subdomains between the source and target domains.

Compared to the previous technique, we use a non-adversarial based subdomain adaptation method and incorporate adaptive feature norms within the subdomains to perform domain transfer. So, instead of just relying on a particular discrepancy metric, we take an additional approach as an adaptive feature norm. In our framework (Fig. 1(b)), we have shown that a progressive feature-norm-based loss function in a shared subdomain space can boost the domain adaptation performance.

3 Method

In unsupervised domain adaptation, we are given a source domain $D_s = \{(x_i^s, y_i^s)\}_{i=1}^{n_s}$ of n_s labeled examples and a target domain $D_t = \{x_j^t\}_{j=1}^{n_t}$ of unlabeled examples. The source domain and target domain are sampled from joint distributions $P(X^s, Y^s)$ and $Q(X^t, Y^t)$ respectively, where $P \neq Q$. The goal of our method is to develop a deep network architecture, that contains transfer features $f = G_f(x)$ and adaptive classifier $y = G_c(f)$. This model will minimize the shift in joint distribution across relevant subdomains and learns transferable representations simultaneously.

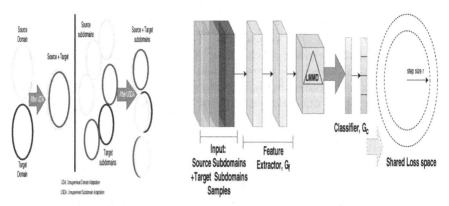

(a) Illustrative example of Subdomain Adaptation

(b) Architecture of Adaptive feature norm on unsupervised subdomain adapatation

Fig. 1. Domain adaptation vs subdomain adaptation and architecture of our proposed method.

The formal representation for unsupervised domain adaptation is as follows.

$$\min_f \frac{1}{n_s} \sum_{i=1}^{n_s} J(f(X_i^s), y_i^s) + \lambda \hat{d}(p, q) \tag{1}$$

where $J()$ is the cross-entropy loss function (classification loss) and $\hat{d}()$ is domain adaptation loss. $\lambda > 0$ is the trade-off parameter of the domain adaptation loss and the classification loss.

This representation covers the global source and target domain without taking into account the relevant information between subdomains within the same category between the source and target domains. Nevertheless, the global alignment may not capture the nuances among subdomains. This may lead to domain shift issue as well. The subdomain information can exploit the relationship between different domains. The formal representation of the loss of subdomain adaptation can be

$$\min_f \frac{1}{n_s} \sum_{i=1}^{n_s} J(f(X_i^s), y_i^s) + \lambda \mathbf{E}_c[\hat{d}(p^{(c)}, q^{(c)})] \tag{2}$$

where $\mathbf{E}_c[.]$ is a mathematical expectation of the class.

3.1 Local Maximum Mean Discrepancy

We have used local MMD as the baseline architecture. It was proposed by [31] to align distributions of the relevant subdomains.

$$d_H(p, q) = \mathbf{E}_c||\mathbf{E}_{p^{(c)}}[\phi(x^s)] - \mathbf{E}_{q^{(c)}}[\phi(x^t)]||_H^2 \tag{3}$$

where x^s and x^t are the instances in D_s and D_t, and $p^{(c)}$ and $q^{(c)}$ are the distributions of $D_s^{(c)}$ and $D_t^{(c)}$, respectively. The Eq. (3) can measure class by class difference of the relevant subdomains. Additionally, this can be used to align the subdomains within the target domain with those in the source domain. Since we have an assumption that each sample belongs to each class according to weight w^c, we use an unbiased estimator of Eq. (3) as

$$d_H(p,q) = \frac{1}{C} \sum_{c=1}^{C} || \sum_{x_i^s \in D_s} w_i^{sc} \phi(x_i^s) - \sum_{x_j^t \in D_t} w_j^{tc} \phi(x_j^t)||_H^2 \qquad (4)$$

where w_i^{sc} and w_j^{tc} represent the weight of x_i^s and x_j^t belonging to class c, respectively. The sum of weights are both equal to one. We can formulate w_i^c for the sample x_i as

$$w_i^c = \frac{y_{ic}}{\sum_{(x_j, y_j \in D)} y_{jc}} \qquad (5)$$

where y_{ic} is the cth entry of vector y_i. For source domain, we use the ground truth y_i^s as a one-hot vector to calculate w_i^c for each sample. But, for target domain, we use the probability of assigning x_i^t to each of the classes. we can not use the formula of Eq. (4) directly. The output of the deep neural network is a probability distribution. We use that probability distribution which characterizes the probability of assigning samples to the classes for each target sample. Then, we can calculate w_j^{tc}. Finally, we can calculate Eq. (4).

3.2   Architecture

Standard domain adaptation considers two domains to share a similar label space. In our framework, the input consists of subdomains from the source and target domains. We have a backbone network G_f, which denotes the feature extraction module. Classifier G_c is the task-specific classifier. We apply the feature norm adaptation along with the local MMD based method to optimize the source classification loss during each iteration.

In each iteration, each individual sample's feature norm is getting added a small but progressive step size of r. This way, if any target samples are far way from the small norm region, after the domain adaptation step, it could be classified correctly in an automatic manner. Figure 1(b) demonstrates the architecture of our approach.

3.3   Adaptive Feature Norm Loss

One of the major bottlenecks that we observe is smaller feature norm of the source and target samples that can lead to poor transfer gains [26]. Inspired from them, we extend the idea into subdomain spaces. We keep a parameter r, which progressively modifies the mean feature norm in each iteration. Instead of having a fixed feature norm, we consider a moving parameter which changes the mean feature norm. This method has been unexplored for the subdomain adaptation case. This loss value impacts the target samples to be correctly classified without additional supervision. This variant impacts positively towards learning task-specific features in a continuous manner. We propose

$$\hat{d}_H(p,q) = \mathbf{E}_c||\mathbf{E}_{p(c)}[\phi(x^s)] - \mathbf{E}_{q(c)}[\phi(x^t)]||_H^2 \\ + \mathbf{E}_c||\mathbf{E}_{p(c)}[(h(x_i;\theta_0) + \Delta r), h(x_i;\theta)]|| \tag{6}$$

where $h(x) = ||.||_2 \cdot G_f \cdot G_c(x)$, where θ_0 and θ are model parameters of last and current iterations. The effectiveness of this model parameter enables the optimization process fetching more informative features with larger norms.

4   Experiment

We evaluate our technique on three popular object recognition datasets, including Office-31, Office-Home, and ImageCLEF-DA. The code will be published in future.

4.1   Dataset

We present a detailed overview of the datasets that we use for our experiments.

Office-31 [17] is a very popular dataset for benchmarking domain adaptation. This dataset contains more than 4000 images in 31 classes collected from three different domains: Amazon (A), which consists of images downloaded from amazon.com, and Webcam (W), and DSLR (D), which comprises of images taken by web camera and digital SLR camera with various photographic settings, respectively. Table 1 reports the performance of our method compared with other works on Office-31 dataset.

Office-Home [24] is another challenging dataset for unsupervised domain adaptation. This dataset contains four domains: Art(Ar), Clipart(CI), Product(Pr), and Real-World(Rw). Each domain has common 65 categories. The Art domain contains the artistic description of objects including painting, sketches etc. The Clipart are the collection of clipart images. In the Product, domain images have no background. The Real-Work domain contains an object taken from a regular camera. In Table 2, we compare our result with previous methods on Office-Home dataset.

ImageCLEF-DA[1] contains three domains: Caltech-256(C), ILSVRC 2012 (I), and Pascal-VOC 2012 (P). Each domain has 12 common classes, and each class has 50 samples. In total, there are 600 images in each domain. Table 3 reports the performance of our method with previous methods on ImageCLEF dataset.

---

[1] http://imageclef.org/2014/adaptation.

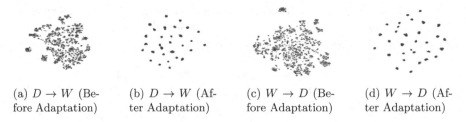

(a) $D \to W$ (Before Adaptation)   (b) $D \to W$ (After Adaptation)   (c) $W \to D$ (Before Adaptation)   (d) $W \to D$ (After Adaptation)

Fig. 2. t-SNE feature visualization from DSLR (Red) to webcam (Blue) ((a) & (b)) and from webcam (Red) to DSLR (Blue) ((c) & (d)) on office-31 dataset. (Color figure online)

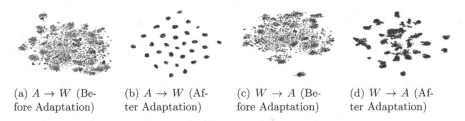

(a) $A \to D$ (Before Adaptation)   (b) $A \to D$ (After Adaptation)   (c) $D \to A$ (Before Adaptation)   (d) $D \to A$ (After Adaptation)

Fig. 3. t-SNE feature visualization from amazon (Red) to DSLR (Blue) ((a) & (b)) and from DSLR (Red) to amazon (Blue) ((c) & (d)) on office-31 dataset. (Color figure online)

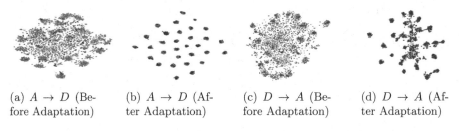

(a) $A \to W$ (Before Adaptation)   (b) $A \to W$ (After Adaptation)   (c) $W \to A$ (Before Adaptation)   (d) $W \to A$ (After Adaptation)

Fig. 4. t-SNE feature visualization from amazon (Red) to webcam (Blue) ((a) & (b)) and from webcam (Red) to amazon (Blue) ((c) & (d)) on office-31 dataset. (Color figure online)

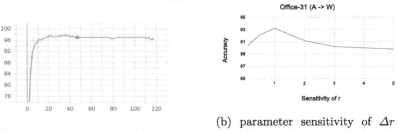

(a) Convergence Test on Webcam to DSLR on Office-31 dataset.

(b) parameter sensitivity of Δr on Office-31 (Amazon→Webcam) dataset.

Fig. 5. Convergence test on task webcam to DSLR and parameter sensitivity test on webcam to amazon on office-31 dataset.

4.2   Setup

In our experiment, we used the open-source implementation of a popular deep learning framework, Pytorch [15], to train the models on multiple Nvidia Geforce GTX 1080Ti GPUs. The machine has Intel Core-i7-5930k CPU@ 3.50 GHz x 12 processors with 64 GB of memory. For the visual classification task, we applied ResNet50 [7] as the backbone network. For comparison, all the baseline models use identical architecture. We fine-tune all the layers except classifier layers from ImageNet [4] pre-trained models and train the fully connected layers for classification through backward-propagation. We set the learning rate to 0.01, batch size to 32, we use stochastic gradient descent (SGD) with a momentum of 0.9, the learning rate is getting changed during SGD using the formula: $lr_{new} = lr_{old}/(1 + \alpha(epoch - 1)/epoch)^{\beta}$, where $\alpha = 10$, and $\beta = 0.75$. For the adaptation feature norm loss, we observe the embedding size of task-specific features played a major role in norm computation. We found $r = 1$ and $\lambda = 0.05$ provide the best result. The highest value of r is to $R = 5$, so it progresses each step r incrementally. The average classification accuracy and error are reported over three random repeats.

5   Results and Discussion

We use our proposed approach for unsupervised subdomain adaptation. We use the protocol to utilize source data with labels and target data without labels. The visual classification results of Office-31, Office-Home, and ImageCLEF-DA are promising. Our method outperforms previous methods on these datasets. Some of the observations from our experiments are:

– Comparing our proposed approach with the global domain adaptation methods and several adversarial subdomain adaptation methods [11,16,25], these methods are more complex compared to our approach. The reason is most of the methods use the adversarial loss function, and don't consider the kernel mean embeddings between source and target subdomains, and has more number of parameters. Moreover, our method achieves better accuracy compared with other methods in all three datasets.
– The t-SNE feature visualization on the transfer task between DSLR and Webcam, Amazon and DSLR, Webcam and Amazon is presented in Fig. 2, Fig. 3, Fig. 4 respectively. Source samples are colored as red and target samples are colored as blue in each figure from 2 to 4. This visualization shows the effectiveness of subdomain adaptation.
– We conducted convergence test (Fig. 5(a)) on task webcam to dslr and further case studies to investigate the sensitivity (on task Amazon to Webcam) of parameter Δr in Fig. 5(b). The accuracy increases upto $\Delta r = 1$ than gradually decreases.

Most of these methods do not consider the subdomain relationship, which effectively captures nuances for each class. Additionally, we incorporate adaptive feature norm loss inside of subdomain distributions. It contributes to apprehend more fine-grained information. The results validate the efficacy of our approach.

Table 1. Accuracy comparison of unsupervised domain adaptation on office-31 dataset

Method	A→W	D→W	W→D	A→D	D→A	W→A	Avg
ResNet [7]	68.4 ± 0.5	96.7 ± 0.5	99.3 ± 0.1	68.9 ± 0.2	62.5 ± 0.3	60.7 ± 0.3	76.1
DDC [23]	75.8 ± 0.2	95.0 ± 0.2	98.2 ± 0.1	77.5 ± 0.3	67.4 ± 0.3	64.0 ± 0.5	79.7
D-CORAL [20]	77.7 ± 0.3	97.6 ± 0.2	99.5 ± 0.1	81.1 ± 0.4	64.6 ± 0.3	64.0 ± 0.4	80.8
DAN [10]	83.8 ± 0.4	96.8 ± 0.2	99.5 ± 0.1	78.4 ± 0.2	66.7 ± 0.3	62.7 ± 0.2	81.3
DANN [6]	82.0 ± 0.4	96.8 ± 0.2	99.1 ± 0.1	79.7 ± 0.4	68.2 ± 0.4	67.4 ± 0.5	82.2
ADDA [22]	86.2 ± 0.5	96.2 ± 0.3	98.4 ± 0.3	77.8 ± 0.3	69.5 ± 0.4	68.9 ± 0.5	82.9
JAN [13]	85.4 ± 0.3	97.4 ± 0.2	99.8 ± 0.2	84.7 ± 0.3	68.6 ± 0.3	70.0 ± 0.4	84.3
MADA [16]	90.0 ± 0.1	97.4 ± 0.1	99.6 ± 0.1	87.8 ± 0.2	70.3 ± 0.3	66.4 ± 0.3	85.2
CDAN [11]	93.1 ± 0.2	98.2 ± 0.2	100 ± 0	89.8 ± 0.3	70.1 ± 0.4	68.0 ± 0.4	86.6
iCAN [29]	92.5 ± 0.2	98.8 ± 0.1	100 ± 0	90.1 ± 0.1	72.1 ± 0.2	69.9 ± 0.1	87.2
CDAN + E [11]	94.1 ± 0.1	98.6 ± 0.1	100 ± 0	92.9 ± 0.2	73.5 ± 0.5	69.3 ± 0.3	87.7
DSAN [31]	93.4 ± 0.2	98.3 ± 0.1	100 ± 0	90.2 ± 0.7	73.5 ± 0.5	74.8 ± 0.4	88.2
Ours	93.2 ± 0.2	98.7 ± 0.2	100 ± 0	90.1 ± 0.2	75.1 ± 0.3	72.8 ± 0.4	**88.5**

Table 2. Accuracy comparison of unsupservised domain adaptation on office-home dataset

Method	A→C	A→P	A→R	C→A	C→P	C→R	P→A	P→C	P→R	R→A	R→C	R→P	Avg
ResNet [7]	34.9	50.0	58.0	37.4	41.9	46.2	38.5	31.2	60.4	53.9	41.2	59.9	46.1
DAN [10]	43.6	57.0	67.9	45.8	56.5	60.4	44.0	43.6	67.7	63.1	51.5	74.3	56.3
DANN [6]	45.6	59.3	70.1	47.0	58.5	60.9	46.1	43.7	68.5	63.2	51.8	76.8	57.6
JAN [13]	45.9	61.2	68.9	50.4	59.7	61.0	45.8	43.4	70.3	63.9	52.4	76.8	58.3
CDAN [11]	49.0	69.3	74.5	54.4	66.0	68.4	55.6	48.3	75.9	68.4	55.4	80.5	63.8
CDAN + E [11]	50.7	70.8	76.0	57.6	70.0	70.0	57.4	50.9	77.3	70.9	56.7	81.6	65.8
DSAN [31]	54.4	70.8	75.4	60.4	67.8	68.0	62.6	55.9	78.5	73.8	60.6	83.1	67.5
Ours	55.0	71.0	75.3	61.1	69.4	68.0	61.4	55	78	72.9	60.0	83.6	**67.7**

Table 3. Accuracy comparison of unsupervised domain adaptation on ImageCLEF dataset

Method	I→P	P→I	I→C	C→I	C→P	P→C	Avg
ResNet [7]	74.8 ± 0.3	83.9 ± 0.1	91.5 ± 0.3	78.0 ± 0.2	65.5 ± 0.3	91.2 ± 0.3	80.7
DDC [23]	74.6 ± 0.3	85.7 ± 0.8	91.1 ± 0.3	82.3 ± 0.7	68.3 ± 0.4	88.8 ± 0.2	81.8
DAN [10]	75.0 ± 0.4	86.2 ± 0.2	93.3 ± 0.2	84.1 ± 0.4	69.8 ± 0.4	91.3 ± 0.4	83.3
DANN [6]	75.0 ± 0.4	86.0 ± 0.3	96.2 ± 0.4	87.0 ± 0.5	74.3 ± 0.5	91.5 ± 0.6	85.0
D-CORAL [20]	76.9 ± 0.2	88.5 ± 0.3	93.6 ± 0.3	86.8 ± 0.6	74.0 ± 0.3	91.6 ± 0.3	85.2
JAN [13]	76.8 ± 0.4	88.0 ± 0.2	94.7 ± 0.2	89.5 ± 0.3	74.2 ± 0.3	91.7 ± 0.3	85.8
MADA [16]	75.0 ± 0.3	87.9 ± 0.2	96.0 ± 0.3	88.8 ± 0.3	75.2 ± 0.2	92.2 ± 0.3	85.8
CDAN [11]	76.7 ± 0.3	90.6 ± 0.3	97.0 ± 0.4	90.5.8 ± 0.4	74.5 ± 0.3	93.5 ± 0.4	87.1
iCAN [29]	79.5 ± 0.1	89.7 ± 0.1	94.6 ± 0.2	89.9 ± 0.4	78.5 ± 0.1	92.0 ± 0.1	87.4
DSAN [31]	80.2 ± 0.2	93.3 ± 0.4	97.2 ± 0.3	93.8 ± 0.2	80.8 ± 0.4	95.9 ± 0.4	90.1
Ours	79.8 ± 0.2	93.5 ± 0.2	98.1 ± 0.2	94.4 ± 0.2	79.8 ± 0.1	96.3 ± 0.2	**90.4**

6   Conclusion

In this work, we have proposed an innovative UDA approach, which incorporates local mean distributed discrepancy measure(LMMD) with adaptive feature norm on subdomain adaptation. Our method can boost the transfer gains more and precisely align the distributions of related subdomains within the source and target domains' relevant category. Extensive experiments are performed on three of the most popular datasets for domain adaptation. Our results show the method's effectiveness, implying that task-specific features with larger norms are more transferable on subdomain adaptation.

References

1. Ben-David, S., Blitzer, J., Crammer, K., Kulesza, A., Pereira, F., Vaughan, J.W.: A theory of learning from different domains. Mach. learn. **79**(1–2), 151–175 (2010)
2. Borgwardt, K.M., Gretton, A., Rasch, M.J., Kriegel, H.P., Schölkopf, B., Smola, A.J.: Integrating structured biological data by kernel maximum mean discrepancy. Bioinformatics **22**(14), e49–e57 (2006)
3. Candela, J.Q., Sugiyama, M., Schwaighofer, A., Lawrence, N.D.: Dataset shift in machine learning. The MIT Press **1**, 5 (2009)
4. Deng, J., et al.: ImageNet: a large-scale hierarchical image database. In: CVPR09 (2009)
5. Ganin, Y., Lempitsky, V.: Unsupervised domain adaptation by backpropagation. In: International conference on machine learning, pp. 1180–1189. PMLR (2015)
6. Ganin, Y., Ustinova, E., Ajakan, H., Germain, P., Larochelle, H., Laviolette, F., Marchand, M., Lempitsky, V.: Domain-adversarial training of neural networks. J. Mach. Learn. Res. **17**(1), 2030–2096 (2016)
7. He, K., Zhang, X., Ren, S., Sun, J.: Deep residual learning for image recognition. In: Proceedings of the IEEE Conference on Computer Vision and Pattern Recognition, pp. 770–778 (2016)
8. Hoffman, J., et al.: Cycada: cycle-consistent adversarial domain adaptation. In: International Conference on Machine Learning, pp. 1989–1998. PMLR (2018)
9. Kumar, A., et al.: Co-regularized alignment for unsupervised domain adaptation. arXiv preprint arXiv:1811.05443 (2018)
10. Long, M., Cao, Y., Wang, J., Jordan, M.: Learning transferable features with deep adaptation networks. In: International Conference on Machine Learning. pp. 97–105. PMLR (2015)
11. Long, M., Cao, Z., Wang, J., Jordan, M.I.: Conditional adversarial domain adaptation. In: Advances in Neural Information Processing Systems, pp. 1640–1650 (2018)
12. Long, M., Wang, J., Ding, G., Sun, J., Yu, P.S.: Transfer feature learning with joint distribution adaptation. In: Proceedings of the IEEE International Conference on Computer Vision, pp. 2200–2207 (2013)
13. Long, M., Zhu, H., Wang, J., Jordan, M.I.: Deep transfer learning with joint adaptation networks. In: International Conference on Machine Learning, pp. 2208–2217. PMLR (2017)
14. Pan, S.J., Tsang, I.W., Kwok, J.T., Yang, Q.: Domain adaptation via transfer component analysis. IEEE Trans. Neural Netw. **22**(2), 199–210 (2010)

15. Paszke, A., et al.: Automatic differentiation in pytorch (2017)
16. Pei, Z., Cao, Z., Long, M., Wang, J.: Multi-adversarial domain adaptation. In: Proceedings of the IEEE Conference on AAAI, pp. 3934–3941 (2018)
17. Saenko, K., Kulis, B., Fritz, M., Darrell, T.: Adapting visual category models to new domains. In: Daniilidis, K., Maragos, P., Paragios, N. (eds.) ECCV 2010. LNCS, vol. 6314, pp. 213–226. Springer, Heidelberg (2010). https://doi.org/10.1007/978-3-642-15561-1_16
18. Saito, K., Watanabe, K., Ushiku, Y., Harada, T.: Maximum classifier discrepancy for unsupervised domain adaptation. In: Proceedings of the IEEE Conference on Computer Vision and Pattern Recognition, pp. 3723–3732 (2018)
19. Sankaranarayanan, S., Balaji, Y., Castillo, C.D., Chellappa, R.: Generate to adapt: aligning domains using generative adversarial networks. In: Proceedings of the IEEE Conference on Computer Vision and Pattern Recognition, pp. 8503–8512 (2018)
20. Sun, B., Saenko, K.: Deep CORAL: correlation alignment for deep domain adaptation. In: Hua, G., Jégou, H. (eds.) ECCV 2016. LNCS, vol. 9915, pp. 443–450. Springer, Cham (2016). https://doi.org/10.1007/978-3-319-49409-8_35
21. Torralba, A., Efros, A.A.: Unbiased look at dataset bias. In: CVPR 2011, pp. 1521–1528. IEEE (2011)
22. Tzeng, E., Hoffman, J., Saenko, K., Darrell, T.: Adversarial discriminative domain adaptation. In: Proceedings of the IEEE Conference on Computer Vision and Pattern Recognition, pp. 7167–7176 (2017)
23. Tzeng, E., Hoffman, J., Zhang, N., Saenko, K., Darrell, T.: Deep domain confusion: maximizing for domain invariance. arXiv preprint arXiv:1412.3474 (2014)
24. Venkateswara, H., Eusebio, J., Chakraborty, S., Panchanathan, S.: Deep hashing network for unsupervised domain adaptation. In: Proceedings of the IEEE Conference on Computer Vision and Pattern Recognition, pp. 5018–5027 (2017)
25. Xie, S., Zheng, Z., Chen, L., Chen, C.: Learning semantic representations for unsupervised domain adaptation. In: International Conference on Machine Learning, pp. 5423–5432 (2018)
26. Xu, R., Li, G., Yang, J., Lin, L.: Larger norm more transferable: an adaptive feature norm approach for unsupervised domain adaptation. In: Proceedings of the IEEE International Conference on Computer Vision, pp. 1426–1435 (2019)
27. Ye, J., Lu, X., Lin, Z., Wang, J.Z.: Rethinking the smaller-norm-less-informative assumption in channel pruning of convolution layers. arXiv preprint arXiv:1802.00124 (2018)
28. Yosinski, J., Clune, J., Bengio, Y., Lipson, H.: How transferable are features in deep neural networks? In: Advances in Neural Information Processing Systems, pp. 3320–3328 (2014)
29. Zhang, W., Ouyang, W., Li, W., Xu, D.: Collaborative and adversarial network for unsupervised domain adaptation. In: Proceedings of the IEEE Conference on Computer Vision and Pattern Recognition, pp. 3801–3809 (2018)
30. Zhu, Y., Zhuang, F., Wang, D.: Aligning domain-specific distribution and classifier for cross-domain classification from multiple sources. In: Proceedings of the AAAI Conference on Artificial Intelligence, vol. 33, pp. 5989–5996 (2019)
31. Zhu, Y., et al.: Deep subdomain adaptation network for image classification. IEEE Transactions on Neural Networks and Learning Systems (2020)

Normal Image Generation-Based Defect Detection by Generative Adversarial Network with Chaotic Random Images

Hiroki Kobayashi$^{(\boxtimes)}$, Ryo Miyoshi, and Manabu Hashimoto

Graduate School of Engineering, Chukyo University, Nagoya, Japan
{kobayashi,miyoshi,mana}@isl.sist.chukyo-u.ac.jp

Abstract. We propose a defect detection method called ChaosGAN (Generative Adversarial Network with Chaotic Random Images) for image generation that can output a normal image with high reconstruction performance regardless of whether the input image is normal or anomaly. A defect detection method based on image generation should be able to (i) convert from a normal image to the same normal image as input and (ii) convert from an anomaly image to normal image with the defective parts removed. ChaosGAN is a combination of Skip-GANomaly, which performs well at identity mapping of a normal image, and AnoGAN, which reconstructs a normal image by regarding a random image as an input latent space. We conducted an experiment to evaluate ChaosGAN using the area under the curve of receiver operating characteristic (AUROC). The AUROC was 0.76 with ChaosGAN (AnoGAN was 0.49, and Skip-GANomaly was 0.67), indicating that it performs better than other defect detection methods.

Keywords: Random image · Image generation · Uniformly distributed random number · Visual inspection · Defect detection

1 Introduction

Automation of visual inspection is necessary to reduce the burden on workers at manufacturing sites. This is being challenged by automatically determining the label (normal/anomaly) of an inspection image using Machine Learning-based methods. However, anomaly images for training cannot be sufficiently obtained since the probability of defect occurrence is extremely low at such sites.

There are generally two types of methods for solving this problem: data augmentation by generating anomaly images [1] and training using only normal images [2]. With the former, a large number of anomaly images are generated on the basis of prior knowledge about defects. However, the performance of such methods cannot be improved unless normal/anomaly teacher signals are correctly applied to the generated image. It is extremely difficult to automatically and correctly annotate images near the boundary of the normal/anomaly area.

© Springer Nature Switzerland AG 2021
G. Bebis et al. (Eds.): ISVC 2021, LNCS 13017, pp. 353–365, 2021.
https://doi.org/10.1007/978-3-030-90439-5_28

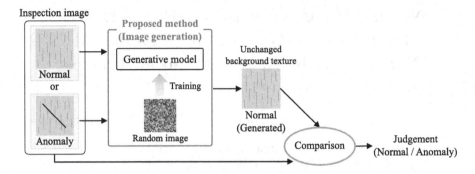

Fig. 1. Normal image generation-based defect detection. ChaosGAN generates normal image with same background texture as input. Input and output images are then compared and defects are detected.

The latter methods model the distribution of normal images used for training and label all images outside its distribution as "anomaly". These methods are superior in that they do not require annotation of anomalies and can detect unknown anomaly images.

Various defect detection methods based on training only normal images have been proposed such as statistical model-based methods [3,4], discriminative model-based methods [5,6], and generative model-based methods [2,7]. We use Deep Neural Network-based generative model that makes it easy to locate defects during visual inspection. It is necessary to construct a neural network that can generate a realistic normal image no matter what type of image (normal/anomaly) is input. This means that normal/anomaly can be easily determined by comparing inspection and normal images generated with such a model (Fig. 1).

Such a model should be able to (i) convert from a normal image to the same normal image as input and (ii) convert from an anomaly image to normal image with defective parts removed. Requirement (i) can be easily satisfied through training using normal images. However, satisfying (ii) is generally impossible because there are no anomaly images for training.

We propose a method of generating high-quality images and satisfying (i) and (ii) at the same time by combining a random number input-type GAN and image input-type GAN. The proposed method is called ChaosGAN (Generative Adversarial Network with Chaotic Random Images) because it trains GANs using chaotic random images for input. We first use Skip-GANomaly [8], which has high precision identity mapping to satisfy (i). We then use AnoGAN [2] with its input latent space formed by random numbers (i.e., noise) extended to a two-dimensional (2D) spatial shape from a one-dimensional (1D) dense shape to satisfy (ii). The main advantage of ChaosGAN is that translation from a random image (2D shape image by random numbers) to a normal image is trained. For example, when using uniformly distributed random numbers of V_{min} to V_{max} (theoretical minimum and maximum pixel values), random images are considered to simulate various data including anomaly images. By training to translate a

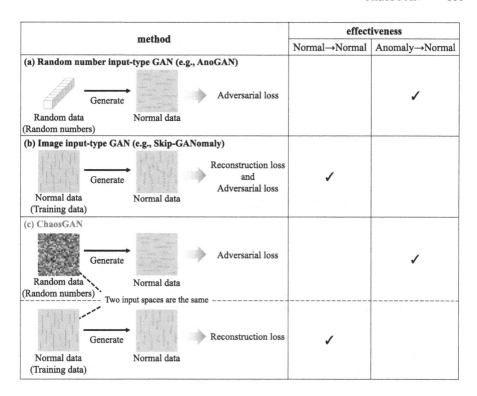

method		effectiveness	
		Normal→Normal	Anomaly→Normal
(a) Random number input-type GAN (e.g., AnoGAN)			
Random data (Random numbers) → Generate → Normal data → Adversarial loss			✓
(b) Image input-type GAN (e.g., Skip-GANomaly)			
Normal data (Training data) → Generate → Normal data → Reconstruction loss and Adversarial loss		✓	
(c) ChaosGAN			
Random data (Random numbers) → Generate → Normal data → Adversarial loss			✓
Two input spaces are the same			
Normal data (Training data) → Generate → Normal data → Reconstruction loss		✓	

Fig. 2. Combination of AnoGAN and Skip-GANomaly. Random number input-type GANs, such as AnoGAN, have strong translation from anomaly to normal. Image input-type GANs, such as Skip-GANomaly, have strong translation from normal to normal. ChaosGAN acquires both translation through combination of both methods.

random image to a normal image, epistemic uncertainty about anomaly images is reduced and (ii) will be satisfied.

This paper makes the following contributions:

- A new defect detection method is proposed that uses 2D latent space as input with a random value.
- The epistemic uncertainty (undefined behavior) on anomaly images is reduced even though there was no information on anomaly images for training.
- Requirements (i) and (ii) can be satisfied at the same time compared with other defect detection methods.

2   Fusion of Real Image Space and Latent Space

2.1   Generative Model-Based Defect Detection

In image generation-based defect detection [2, 7–10], it is necessary to construct a neural network that can generate realistic normal images no matter what type of image (normal or anomaly) is input.

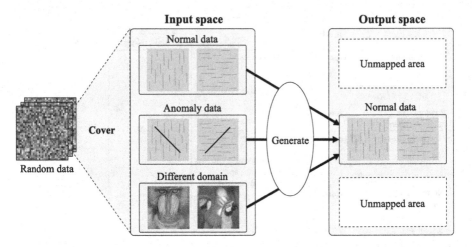

Fig. 3. Input space modeling and translation from random image to normal image. Arbitrary image in input space is formulated using random images. Translation from random image to normal image can be seen as pseudo translation from anomaly image to normal image in process of generating random numbers.

Such a method should

(i) output a normal image that is the same as the input when a normal image is input.
(ii) output a normal image with defect parts removed when an anomaly image is input.

Various GANs have been proposed as methods for generating such images.

As shown in Fig. 2(a), random number input-type GANs [2,9], such as AnoGAN, are methods for training that take random data as input in the latent space and generate an arbitrary normal image that follows the probability distribution of training data in the real image space. Since the random data as input are determined by random numbers, various values are generated to cover the latent space in each iteration of training. Therefore, all images generated from data existing in the latent space within the range where the random numbers are generated should be normal images. On the basis of this property, AnoGAN searches for a latent variable closest to the test image at testing and determines a label (normal/anomaly) so that if the difference between a generated image and test image is large, it is labeled as anomaly; otherwise, normal. This model is trained to translate from latent to real image space, but it is not trained to translate from real image space to real image space for normal images. The same is true even if it is replaced with a powerful generator [11,12]. Therefore, this method has high translation ability for satisfying (ii) but low translation ability for satisfying (i).

On the other hand, as shown in Fig. 2(b), image input-type GANs [8,10], such as Skip-GANomaly, are methods for generating a normal image that is the same as the input by using a generator (U-Net [13]) that has extremely good performance at identity mapping with the addition of spatial skip connections. It is expected to convert an anomaly image into a normal image by adding adversarial loss about the image generated from the normal image [10]. The translation from a normal image to a normal image is trained, but translation from an anomaly image to a normal image has not been explicitly trained by adversarial loss. This means that anomaly images are likely to be generated during testing. Therefore, such methods have high translation ability for satisfying (i) but low translation ability for satisfying (ii).

2.2 Basic Idea

ChaosGAN fuses two types (i.e., real image space and latent space) of input spaces by combining the real image space corresponding to the input of Skip-GANomaly's generator and the latent space corresponding to the input of AnoGAN's generator. The latent space is extended to a 2D spatial shape from a 1D dense shape with the original AnoGAN. That is, at the same time as training the translation from a normal image to a normal image, the translation from a random image generated by a random number to a normal image is also trained.

As shown in Fig. 3, the reason such a training method is effective is shown from another point of view. First, the translation for satisfying (i) can be done easily by using a generator (U-Net [13]) that is extremely good at identity mapping because normal images for training are easily available. Second, it is extremely difficult to train the translation for satisfying (ii) because it is difficult to obtain anomaly images for training. To solve this problem, we attempt to train for translating any image (including normal images, anomaly images, and images with different domains) to a normal image, instead of training for the translation from an anomaly image to a normal image. An anomaly image can be a part of any image. Therefore, if such training is possible, the translation from an anomaly image to a normal image will be in a pseudo manner. Any image can be modeled by random numbers (e.g., uniform distribution). We train the model to convert a "normal image" from a "random image" generated by random numbers. This makes it possible to generate a highly realistic normal image no matter what type of image (normal or anomaly) is input, thus satisfying (ii).

3 Proposed Method

3.1 Loss Function

Figure 4 shows the model architecture and data flow of ChaosGAN.

The model is trained to minimize the following loss function:

$$\mathcal{L} = \lambda_{rec}\mathcal{L}_{rec} + \lambda_{adv}\mathcal{L}_{adv}. \tag{1}$$

The reconstruction loss term is formulated as

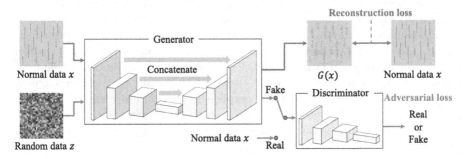

Fig. 4. Model architecture and data flow of ChaosGAN. ChaosGAN uses U-Net-based generator and DCGAN-based discriminator. Random and normal images are concatenated in mini-batch direction before being input to generator.

$$\mathcal{L}_{rec} = ||x - G(x)||_1, \tag{2}$$

and the adversarial loss term is formulated as

$$\mathcal{L}_{adv} = \begin{cases} -D(G(z)) & \text{if } G \\ -\min(D(x) - 1, 0) & \text{if } D_{real} \\ -\min(-D(G(z)) - 1, 0) & \text{if } D_{fake} \end{cases} \tag{3}$$

The total loss function $\mathcal{L}$ is expressed as the weighted sum of reconstruction loss and adversarial loss. The L_1 loss is used as reconstruction loss $\mathcal{L}_{rec}$ because sharper images can be generated in joint training with adversarial loss [14], and Hinge loss [15] is used as adversarial loss $\mathcal{L}_{adv}$ because it is stable for training a GAN. Here, x, z, G, and D indicate a normal image, random image, generator, and discriminator, respectively, and, λ_{rec} and λ_{adv} are hyper-parameters indicating the importance of each term in total loss. They were set as $\lambda_{rec} = 40$ and $\lambda_{adv} = 1$, as in previous studies [8,10].

3.2 Model Architecture

The generator of ChaosGAN requires (I) powerful identity mapping and (II) powerful translation between spaces with different expression formats. U-Net [13] has spatial skip connection to satisfy (I) and abilities of embedding and reconstruction in low-dimensional features to satisfy (II). The spatial skip connection makes it easy to reduce changes in the background texture and identify defective parts. Therefore, U-Net is used as the generator of ChaosGAN. And, a strided convolution-based model on DCGAN [16] is used as the discriminator.

Batch normalization (BN) [17] is used as the normalization of each layer since it has been reported to facilitate stable training [16]. With BN, it is assumed that mini-batch data for training are the data selected by simple random sampling from the dataset. If random and normal images are input to the generator alternately, the variance of the dataset cannot be estimated correctly, and image

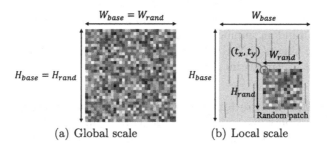

(a) Global scale   (b) Local scale

Fig. 5. Random images used for ChaosGAN. Uniformly distributed random numbers are generated on (a) global and (b) local scales. Image in (b) is generated on basis of normal image. Each random value is generated independently.

generation quality deteriorates at the time of inference. Therefore, this problem is avoided by concatenating random and normal images in the mini-batch direction and inputting them. For the activation function, a rectified linear unit (ReLU) is used in all layers of the generator, and Leaky ReLU is used in all layers of the discriminator.

3.3 Random Image Generation

As shown in Fig. 5, we evaluated two versions of ChaosGAN for generating random images. This first is ChaosGAN-G (G: global scale), which generates a random number throughout an image (Fig. 5(a)). It is suitable for detecting an anomaly at the image level. The second is ChaosGAN-L (L: local scale), which generates a random number on the local scale of an image (Fig. 5(b)). It is suitable for detecting an anomaly at the region level.

Various methods [18,19] similar to ChaosGAN have been proposed for generating artificial images in model regularization and anomaly detection. Chaos-GAN is similar to Random Erasing [18]. The main difference between these methods is the "label" given to the artificially generated image. With other methods, the generated image is defined as either always the same label as the source image (i.e., normal) or always anomaly. ChaosGAN does not define anything, i.e., it defines an arbitrary label as "normal", "anomaly" and "different domain". This is because a random image is considered to represent any arbitrary image, so the label given by force may be incorrect.

Global Scale-Based Random Numbers. Since the data format is an image, the theoretical minimum and maximum values of which are fixed, uniform distribution is used to generate random numbers. The pixel value of a random image is calculated independently for each pixel channel by

$$z(i, j, k) = U(V_{min}, V_{max}). \tag{4}$$

where $z(i, j, k)$ is the pixel value of the k-th channel in the pixel (i, j) of the random image, $U(a, b)$ is a uniformly distributed random number from a to b, and V_{min} and V_{max} are the theoretical minimum and maximum pixel values, respectively. A random number is applied as the value of all pixels; thus, this version is called ChaosGAN-G (G: global scale). ChaosGAN-G can generate any image from sets of various images in the real image space.

Local Scale-Based Random Numbers. The anomaly assumed in visual inspection occurs only in a specific part of a normal image (i.e., defect). In other words, generating random numbers in a specific part of a normal image should improve accuracy. Each random value is calculated independently for each image by using Eqs. (5)–(8) (with Eq. (4) for each pixel channel).

$$W_{rand} = U(0, W_{base}) \tag{5}$$

$$H_{rand} = U(0, H_{base}) \tag{6}$$

$$t_x = U(0, W_{base} - W_{rand}) \tag{7}$$

$$t_y = U(0, H_{base} - H_{rand}), \tag{8}$$

where W_{base}, H_{base}, W_{rand}, and H_{rand} are the width and height of the base normal image and the width and height of the random patch, respectively, and t_x and t_y are the starting point coordinates of the random patch in the x and y directions, respectively. A random number is applied to the pixel value in specific regions; thus, this version is called ChaosGAN-L (L: local scale). When W_{rand} and H_{rand} generated by the random numbers are maximum in the random patch, ChaosGAN-L provides the same result as ChaosGAN-G. Only at that time, ChaosGAN-L can generate any image from sets of various images in the real image space.

3.4 Anomaly Score

After the model is trained, the anomaly score is defined as the mean squared error between input and output by using Eq. (9) with ChaosGAN, where x_{test} is a test image and n is the number of elements (width × height × channel) of x_{test}.

$$A(x_{test}) = \frac{1}{n}||x_{test} - G(x_{test})||_2^2 \tag{9}$$

For an ideal model about image generation, (i) and (ii) are satisfied at the same time. This means that the anomaly score is small for a normal image and large for an anomaly image.

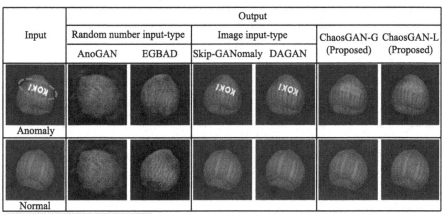

Input	Output					
	Random number input-type		Image input-type		ChaosGAN-G (Proposed)	ChaosGAN-L (Proposed)
	AnoGAN	EGBAD	Skip-GANomaly	DAGAN		
Anomaly						
Normal						

Note: ⟨= = = ⟩ = Defect region

Fig. 6. Image generation performance in MVTec AD [20]. ChaosGAN enabled high-quality translation in both cases, from anomaly to normal and from normal to normal. Other methods were only effective for one of them.

4   Experiments on Defect Detection

4.1   Settings

We used the MVTec Anomaly Detection (MVTec AD) dataset [20], which is a benchmark dataset for unsupervised defect detection, to evaluate the defect detection performance of ChaosGAN. It consists of 15 categories and contains a total of 5354 images. There are about 250 training images and about 100 test images per category. For each category, training was carried out using only normal images, and normal/anomaly classification performance was evaluated using both normal and anomaly images in the test. The area under the curve of receiver operating characteristic (AUROC) was used as a metric to evaluate classification performance at the image level (i.e., detection performance). The ROC curve was created using the threshold of anomaly score provided with each method.

To determine the effectiveness of ChaosGAN, we compared it with AnoGAN [2] and EGBAD [9] as random number input-type GANs, Skip-GANomaly [8] and DAGAN [10] as image input-type GANs. For fair comparison, all models of these methods were trained with the same input image size of 128×128 pixels, 300 epochs, batch size of 16, and using Adam optimizer [21]. If the models have the same structure (e.g., generator of Skip-GANomaly and generator of the proposed method), the number of convolution layers and kernel size are the same, and the position and type of normalization and activation functions match the specifications provided with each method.

Table 1. Detection AUROCs for various textures and objects of MVTec AD [20]. ChaosGAN had higher defect detection performance than AnoGAN and Skip-GANomaly. In particular, ChaosGAN-L performed best.

Category	AnoGAN	EGBAD	Skip-GANomaly	DAGAN	ChaosGAN-G (proposed)	ChaosGAN-L (proposed)
Carpet	0.60	0.44	0.44	0.60	**0.83**	0.56
Grid	0.30	0.71	0.16	0.61	0.08	**0.72**
Leather	0.58	0.66	0.62	0.88	0.65	**0.89**
Tile	0.48	0.63	0.91	0.90	**0.96**	0.93
Wood	0.74	0.36	0.84	0.95	**0.98**	0.95
Bottle	0.46	0.73	0.61	0.90	0.73	**0.94**
Cable	0.43	**0.65**	0.60	0.60	0.54	0.58
Capsule	0.53	0.39	0.56	0.51	0.33	**0.59**
Hazelnut	0.26	0.25	**0.89**	0.88	0.88	0.86
Metal Nut	0.56	0.44	**0.63**	0.55	0.46	0.48
Pill	0.36	0.71	0.65	0.44	0.56	**0.84**
Screw	**1.00**	**1.00**	**1.00**	0.89	**1.00**	**1.00**
Toothbrush	0.39	0.68	0.89	0.89	0.79	**0.90**
Transistor	0.24	0.19	0.49	**0.60**	0.54	0.46
Zipper	0.37	0.64	0.69	0.78	**0.83**	0.70
Average	0.49	0.57	0.67	0.73	0.68	**0.76**

4.2 Results

The normal/anomaly images used in the test and output images of each method are shown in Fig. 6. Ideally, if a normal image is input, the model should generate the same normal image as input. If an anomaly image is input, it should generate a normal image with defective parts removed. A random number input-type GAN (AnoGAN or EGBAD) is effective in generating images from anomaly to normal, but not effective from normal to the same normal. An image input-type GAN (Skip-GANomaly or DAGAN) is the opposite. In contrast, ChaosGAN is effective for both types of image generation. This shows that training using random images is effective, and it is reasonable to assume that random images represent unknown defect patterns. With ChaosGAN-L (local scale), a fairly realistic image can be generated.

Table 1 shows the AUROC for each category of MVTec AD. The AUROC of ChaosGAN was higher than that of the other methods. The algorithm of Chaos-GAN, which inputs both a random image and normal image during training, is highly versatile. The AUROC tended to be low for objects with defect similar to normal patterns such as "cable" and "transistor". The translation from an anomaly image to normal image failed. There are two main solutions to this. The first is to propose a strong model structure that can convert an anomaly image including defects similar to normal pattern into a normal image. The second is to devise a method of generating random images that are close to real anomaly images.

Table 2. Ablation study of ChaosGAN-G and -L in MVTec AD [20]. For ChaosGAN-L, defect detection performance (AUROC) was higher when two losses were combined, indicating that two types of joint translation training are important.

Method	$\mathcal{L} = \mathcal{L}_{rec}$	$\mathcal{L} = \mathcal{L}_{adv}$	$\mathcal{L} = \lambda_{rec}\mathcal{L}_{rec} + \lambda_{adv}\mathcal{L}_{adv}$
ChaosGAN-G	**0.70**	0.50	0.68
ChaosGAN-L	0.70	0.65	**0.76**

4.3 Ablation Study

We conducted an ablation study to investigate the effect of each term on the total loss function. Specifically, there are three patterns: only reconstruction loss, only adversarial loss, and both. We conducted this study using ChaosGAN-G and -L for a total of six patterns.

Table 2 shows the average AUROC in the MVTec AD dataset. The reason the result of only reconstruction loss was the same with both methods is that the training process is essentially the same. Regarding ChaosGAN-G, the pattern of with only reconstruction loss performed the best, followed by both losses. Global scale-based random number generation may not be suitable for scenes (visual inspection) in which normal and anomaly images have similar textures. Regarding ChaosGAN-L, both losses performed the best. This is thought because the random image of the local scale is more likely to occur more realistically than of the global scale, and the random patch masks the defective area. Furthermore, only reconstruction loss gave more impressive results than only adversarial loss for both ChaosGAN-G and -L. This indicates that it is better to train only the reconstruction of the normal image than to train only the translation from anomaly to normal. This can also be said from the fact that state-of-the-art methods are good at identity mapping of a normal image [8, 10].

5   Conclusion

We proposed an unsupervised defect detection method called ChaosGAN that fuses the input real image space and latent space. By training to convert a random image generated with random numbers in the real image space into an arbitrary normal image, ChaosGAN is simultaneously able to (i) convert from a normal image to the same normal image as input and (ii) convert from an anomaly image to a normal image with defective parts removed.

ChaosGAN performed better than other defect detection methods on the basis of training only normal images using the MVTec AD dataset. The average AUROC was 0.73 for the previous method and 0.76 for ChaosGAN.

For future work, we will develop a model for effectively converting a random image to a normal image and a method of generating a biased random image that is close to realistic anomaly images.

References

1. Frid-Adar, M., Diamant, I., Klang, E., Amitai, M., Goldberger, J., Greenspan, H.: GAN-based synthetic medical image augmentation for increased CNN performance in liver lesion classification. Neurocomputing **321**, 321–331 (2018)
2. Schlegl, T., Seeböck, P., Waldstein, S. M., Schmidt-Erfurth, U., Langs, G.: Unsupervised anomaly detection with generative adversarial networks to guide marker discovery. In: IPMI (2017)
3. Schölkopf, B., Platt, J.C., Shawe-Taylor, J., Smola, A.J., Williamson, R.C.: Estimating the support of a high-dimensional distribution. Neural Comput. **13**, 1443–1471 (2001)
4. Tax, D.M.J., Duin, R.P.W.: Support vector data description. Mach. Learn. **54**, 45–66 (2004)
5. Ruff, L., et al.: Deep one-class classification. In: ICML (2018)
6. Oza, P., Patel, V.M.: One-class convolutional neural network. IEEE Signal Process. Lett. **26**, 277–281 (2019)
7. Bergmann, P., Löwe, S., Fauser, M., Sattlegger, D., Steger, C.: Improving unsupervised defect segmentation by applying structural similarity to autoencoders. VISIGRAPP **5**, 372–380 (2019)
8. Akçay, S., Atapour-Abarghouei, A., Breckon, T. P.: Skip-GANomaly: skip-connected and adversarially trained encoder-decoder anomaly detection. In: IJCNN (2019)
9. Zenati, H., Foo, C. S., Lecouat, B., Manek, G., Chandrasekhar, V. R.: Efficient gan-based anomaly detection. In: ICLR Workshop (2018)
10. Tang, T.-W., Kuo, W.-H., Lan, J.-H., Ding, C.-F., Hsu, H., Young, H.-T.: Anomaly detection neural network with dual auto-encoders GAN and its industrial inspection applications. Sensors **20**(12), 3336 (2020)
11. Karras, T., Laine, S., Aila, T.: A style-based generator architecture for generative adversarial networks. In: CVPR (2019)
12. Karras, T., Laine, S., Aittala, M., Hellsten, J., Lehtinen, J., Aila, T.: Analyzing and improving the image quality of stylegan. In: CVPR (2020)
13. Ronneberger, O., Fischer, P., Brox, T.: U-Net: convolutional networks for biomedical image segmentation. In: Navab, N., Hornegger, J., Wells, W.M., Frangi, A.F. (eds.) MICCAI 2015. LNCS, vol. 9351, pp. 234–241. Springer, Cham (2015). https://doi.org/10.1007/978-3-319-24574-4_28
14. Isola, P., Zhu, J.-Y., Zhou, T., Efros, A. A.: Image-to-image translation with conditional adversarial networks. In: CVPR (2017)
15. Miyato, T., Kataoka, T., Koyama, M., Yoshida, Y.: Spectral normalization for generative adversarial networks. In: ICLR (2018)
16. Radford, A., Metz, L., Chintala, S.: Unsupervised representation learning with deep convolutional generative adversarial networks. In: ICLR (2016)
17. Ioffe, S., Szegedy, C.: Batch normalization: accelerating deep network training by reducing internal covariate shift. In: ICML (2015)
18. Zhong, Z., Zheng, L., Kang, G., Li, S., Yang, Y.: Random erasing data augmentation. In: AAAI (2020)
19. Li, C.-L., Sohn, K., Yoon, J., Pfister, T.: CutPaste: self-supervised learning for anomaly detection and localization. In: CVPR (2021)

20. Bergmann, P., Batzner, K., Fauser, M., Sattlegger, D., Steger, C.: The MVTec anomaly detection dataset: a comprehensive real-world dataset for unsupervised anomaly detection. IJCV **129**, 1038–1059 (2021)
21. Kingma, D. P., Ba, J.: Adam: a method for stochastic optimization. In: ICLR (2015)

SPNet: Multi-shell Kernel Convolution for Point Cloud Semantic Segmentation

Yuyan Li$^{(\boxtimes)}$, Chuanmao Fan, Xu Wang, and Ye Duan

University of Missouri, Columbia, USA
{yl235,cf7b6,xwf32,duanye}@umsystem.edu

Abstract. Feature encoding is essential for point cloud analysis. In this paper, we propose a novel point convolution operator named Shell Point Convolution (SPConv) for shape encoding and local context learning. Specifically, SPConv splits 3D neighborhood space into shells, aggregates local features on manually designed kernel points, and performs convolution on the shells. Moreover, SPConv incorporates a simple yet effective attention module that enhances local feature aggregation. Based upon SPConv, a deep neural network named SPNet is constructed to process large-scale point clouds. Poisson disk sampling and feature propagation are incorporated in SPNet for better efficiency and accuracy. We provided details of the shell design and conducted extensive experiments on challenging large-scale point cloud datasets. Experimental results show that SPConv is effective in local shape encoding, and our SPNet is able to achieve top-ranking performances in semantic segmentation tasks.

Keywords: Point cloud · Semantic segmentation · Attention · Deep learning

1 Introduction

Deep learning has achieved great success in image classification [9,10,12], semantic segmentation [20,35] and object detection [4,5,8]. However, deep learning based point cloud analysis is still a challenging topic. One major reason is that point clouds are non-uniformly sampled from a large, continuous 3D space, making them lack of regular grid structure. To tackle this, one straightforward approach is to voxelize point cloud into 3D regular grids and utilize standard 3D Convolutions [16,28]. But the voxelization approach has a major limitation, the discretization step inevitably loses geometric information. To address this problem, many researchers have proposed approaches to directly process point clouds. One of the seminal works is PointNet proposed by Qi et al. [23]. It uses Multi Layer Perceptron (MLP) and global pooling to preserve permutation invariance and gather a combination of local and global feature presentation. This work is further improved in their follow-up work PointNet++ [24] which adds

---

Y. Li, C. Fan and X. Wang—Equal contribution.

© Springer Nature Switzerland AG 2021
G. Bebis et al. (Eds.): ISVC 2021, LNCS 13017, pp. 366–378, 2021.
https://doi.org/10.1007/978-3-030-90439-5_29

the local geometry pooling/sampling over local neighborhood. Later works seek other ways to enhance local feature aggregation. For example, Pointweb [37] constructs a dense fully-linked web, ShellNet [36] conducts convolution based on statistics from concentric spherical shells. Besides point-based methods, several graph-based methods are proposed to capture 3D shape and structures of point clouds. Methods such as [14,15] treat point clouds as nodes in a graph whose edges carry learnable affinitiy/similarity between adjacent points.

Recently, there has been another thread of research [17,29,31,32,34] that proposes learnable kernel functions which define convolutional kernels on a continuous space. One of these approaches is KPConv [29] introduced by Thomas et al. KPConv [29] proposes kernel point operator that consists of a set of local point filters which simulate 2D image convolution processes. Features from unordered point clouds are aggregated on either rigid or deformable kernel points. Using structural kernel points makes convolution feasible on a continuous space.

Following this line of work, we propose a novel multi-shell kernel point convolution named SPConv. Our SPConv operator partitions local 3D space into shells, each shell contains a set of rigid kernel points which aggregate local supporting point features. We perform kernel point convolution on each shell individually, then integrate the output features by an additional 1D convolution operation. The last convolution learns the contributions from shells and enhances shell correlation. An illustration of our SPConv is shown in Fig. 1. Comparing to deformable KPConv [29], our method has an enhanced structure learning module, and does not require additional regularization during training. Furthermore, we find that incorporating low-level features such as color, normal, etc. in all layers for local feature re-weighting can be very effective for improving network performance. We propose two different approaches to accomplish the task, (1) Gaussian function based and (2) learning based. The first approach is hand-crafted and does not necessarily add GPU computation. The second approach has learnable weights and shows more robustness.

Using SPConv as our building block, we build a deep architecture SPNet. Similar to standard CNNs which utilize downsampling and upsampling strategy to reduce computation cost as well as to enlarge receptive field, we use Poisson disk sampling (PDS) for downsampling, and feature propagation (FP) for upsampling. In Sect. 4, we evaluate the effectiveness of our methods on the most competitive indoor segmentation datasets. Notably, experimental results show that we achieve top-ranking performances. Our main contribution is summarized as follows:

- We propose a multi-shell kernel convolution operator that shows powerful local shape encoding ability.
- We introduce a simple yet effective attention mechanism for local neighbor feature re-weighting. This attention module improves performance and speeds up convergence.
- We present a comprehensive architecture design which outperforms stage-of-the-arts on challenging large-scale indoor datasets.

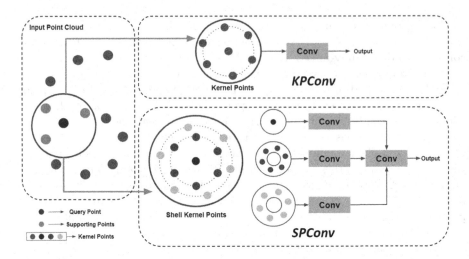

Fig. 1. Comparison between SPConv and KPConv. For a query point, a range search is performed to locate supporting points. KPConv defines a set of kernel points to aggregate local features and performs point convolution. Our SPConv has multiple shells, each shell contains one set of kernel points. Point convolutions are conducted for shells individually to encode distinctive geometric information. An additional convolution layer is used to fuse shell outputs together, as an enhancement of structure correlation.

2   Related Work

View-Based and Voxel-Based Methods. One classic category of point cloud representations is multi-view representation. MVCNN [27] renders 3D shape into images from various viewpoints and combines features from CNNs to predict point labels. However, these methods suffer from surface occlusion and density variation, which make it difficult to capture the internal structure of the shape. Another strategy is to convert point cloud into a 3D voxel structure which can be processed by standard 3D convolutions. VoxNet [21] and subsequent work [19,33] discretize point cloud into 3D volumetric grids. To improve efficiency on processing high resolution 3D voxels, recent researches [2,6] process volumetric data only on non-empty voxels.

Point-wise MLP Methods. Point-based methods receive great attention since PointNet [23] was proposed. In PointNet [23], points go through shared MLPs to obtain high dimensional features followed by a global max-pooling layer. In order to capture local neighborhood context, PointNet++ [24] is developed by hierarchically applying pointnet in local regions. There are extensive works based on PointNet++. For example, PointWeb [37] builds a dense fully connected web to explore local context, and uses an Adaptive Feature Adjustment module for feature refinement. ShellNet [36] proposes a ShellConv operator with concentric spherical shells to capture representative features.

Point Convolution Methods. Some recent works define explicit kernels for point convolution. KCNet [25] develops a kernel correlation layer to compute affinities between each point's K nearest neighbors and a predefined set of kernel points. Local features are acquired by graph pooling layers. SpiderCNN [34] designs a family of Taylor polynomial kernels to aggregate neighbor features. PointCNN [18] introduces X-transformation to exploit the canonical order of points. PCNN [31] builds a network using parametric continuous convolutional layers. SPH3D [17] uses spherical harmonic kernels during convolution on quantized space to identify distinctive geometric features. Our work is most related to KPConv [29], which defines rigid and deformable kernel points for feature aggregation. This convolution operator resolves point cloud ambiguity, alleviates varying density, and shows superior performances. Compared to KPConv [29], our SPConv enhances local structure correlation by incorporating shell-structured kernel points and learning on a larger neighborhood context.

3   Methodology

3.1   Review on Kernel Point Convolution

KPConv [29] effectively resolves the point cloud ambiguity by placing manually designed kernel points in a local neighborhood. This convolution simulates image-based convolutions. A typical image based 2D convolution with a $(2m + 1) \times (2m + 1)$ kernel at location $i, j \in \mathbb{Z}$ is defined as:

$$F * W = \sum_{x=-m}^{m} \sum_{y=-m}^{m} F(i - x, j - y)W(i, j) \tag{1}$$

where $x, y \in \{-m, ..., m\}$, W is the learnable weight, $F(i, j)$ is the feature for pixel (i, j). Image based convolution describes a one-to-one relationship between single kernel and single image pixel. Similarly, for a 3D point $p \in \mathbb{R}^3$ with a local neighborhood of radius R, point convolution can be defined as:

$$F * W = \sum_{k}^{K} F(p_k, p)W(k) \tag{2}$$

where $F(p_k, p)$ is the aggregated features on kernel point p_k. p_k carries learnable matrix $W_k \in \mathbb{R}^{C_{in} \times C_{out}}$. C_{in} and C_{out} are input and output feature channels respectively. With proper aggregation approach, the structure of supporting points can be well captured and learned by weight W. There are two key components of this convolution, placements of kernel points and aggregation function.

For a 3D point $x \in \mathbb{R}^3$ surrounded by neighboring points $x_j \in \mathbb{R}^3$ within a ball radius R, kernel points are distributed on the surface of a sphere with radius r, plus one point placed at center. Aggregated features $F(p_k, p)$ for kernel point p_k are computed as the sum of the features carried by neighboring points that fall into the influenced radius v. These neighboring features are weighted based upon the Euclidean distance between p_k and p_j. An illustration of KPConv is shown in Fig. 1.

$$F(p_k, p) = \sum_{p_j, \|p_j - p\| < R, \|p_k - p_j\| < v} F_{p_j} d(p_k, p_j) \tag{3}$$

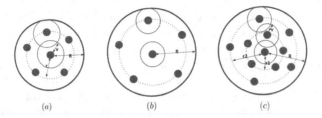

Fig. 2. A KPConv [29] operator is defined in (a) with kernel point radius r, neighborhood size R, kernel influence radius v. Kernel points have overlapping influence regions. When enlarging neighborhood size R to capture a larger context as shown in (b), kernel points become sparse and this may cause a loss of information for complex scenes with objects of different scales. Our SPConv (c) has multiple shells and keeps overlapping influence regions. r_1 and r_2 are kernel point radius for the second and third shell.

where $d(p_k, p_j)$ denotes the correlation of kernel point p_k and a neighbor point p_j. This correlation can be calculated by a linear function:

$$d(p_k, p_j) = max(0, 1 - \frac{\|p_k - p_j\|}{v})$$
(4)

3.2 SPConv

We extend the work of KPConv and propose a new point convolution operator, SPConv. SPConv divides the local 3D space into a total of N shells. Each shell has one set of kernel points. Specifically, the innermost shell contains one central kernel point p_0, for outter $n^{th}(n > 1)$ shell, a set of kernel points $p_{1,m}, m \in M_n$ scatter on the surface of a sphere with radius r_n. Central kernel point impacts on a spherical region, and the nth shell forms a ring-shaped influence area. As a result, all kernel points cover a spherical space of radius $(r_N + v)$. We perform kernel point convolution on N shells respectively, then stack shell features together along a new dimension. Finally, we use an additional convolution layer to further correlate shell structure. This convolution operator can be defined as follows:

$$(F(x) * W_1) * W_2 = \sigma(\sum_{n}^{N} \sigma(F(x) * W_1)W_{2,n})$$
(5)

where σ refers to non-linear activation function. $W_1 \in \mathbb{R}^{K \times C_{in} \times C_{out}/2}$ is the learnable weight matrix for kernel point convolution, $W_2 \in \mathbb{R}^{N \times C_{out}/2 \times C_{out}}$ is the weight matrix for shell correlation. To balance off efficiency and accuracy, we choose to use a total of 3 shells and 14 kernel points for the second and third shell respectively. An illustration of our SPConv is shown in Fig. 1.

A detailed illustration of the influence area of SPConv kernel points is shown in Fig. 2. The central kernel point encodes features from points that are spatially close to the query point. Kernel points located far from the center tend to encode more contextual information. Therefore, we learn the features by shells based on the distance from kernel point to center such that the encoded features can be representative for each shell. Furthermore, the 1D convolution layer applies weight matrix on the fused shell features, which enhances structure learning across shells. Our method aims to improve descriptive power of kernel points, so does KPConv [29] deformable version. Although deformable kernels provide more flexibility, regularization imposed on offsets is mandatory to account for mis-shifts. By contrast, our kernels are rigid and do no require regularization. In Sect. 4.4, we compare our evaluation results with deformable KPConv [29]. Our method outperforms deformable KPConv with even less parameters.

3.3   Feature Attention

To further improve local feature encoding, we propose a feature attention module using low level features such as RGB or surface normal.

We propose two approaches for local feature attention. First approach is to apply a pre-defined Gaussian function:

$$\omega_k = exp(-\frac{\|f(p) - f(s_k)\|}{2\sigma^2}) \tag{6}$$

where σ is a parameter that needs to be manually set. The second approach is to use sequential MLPs:

$$\omega_k = g(f(p) - f(s_k)), \tag{7}$$

where g is a sequence of MLPs activated by $ReLU$, except the last one which uses $sigmoid$. The final updated feature f' for point s_k can be calculated as follows with a residual connection:

$$f'(s_k) = \omega_k f(s_k) + f(s_k) \tag{8}$$

Both of the approaches improve performances and accelerate convergence speed. One issue for the first approach is that it is manually designed and not flexible. The second approach takes advantages of learnable weights and non-linear activations but adds more computation costs.

3.4   Network Architecture

We build a deep encoder-decoding network with point downsampling and upsampling to accomplish semantic segmentation task. A detailed SPNet architecture is shown in Fig. 3(a).

Downsampling Strategy. Similar to works [24,29], we adopt downsampling to reduce computation load as well as to increase receptive field. In our work, we favors Poisson disk sampling (PDS) strategy to deal with the varying density. PDS controls spatial uniformity by Poisson disk radius r_p, thus maintaining a minimal distance between points. Unlike grid sampling as used in [29] in which

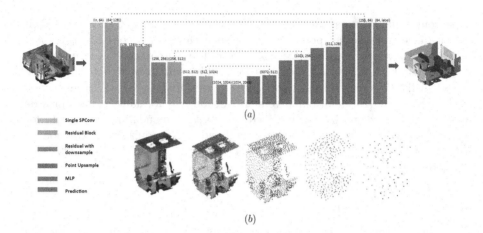

Fig. 3. (a) Illustration of the network architecture. (b) Downsampling process by PDS at each level.

downsampled location are interpolated as the barycenter of a cell, PDS keeps the original locations of sub-sets and preserves shape patterns. Comparing to farthest point sampling (FPS) [24], PDS is faster when sampling large-scale points. A downsampling process by PDS is shown in Fig. 3(b).

Upsampling Strategy. With PDS, sampled points at each level are always a sub-set from input point sets. Therefore, we can accurately recover the point sampling patterns and gradually propagate features in decoder. We adopt feature propagation module proposed in [24]. For a point p_j at level j, its propagated features f are calculated as:

$$f = \sum_k^K w_k * f_k, \; w_k = \frac{d_k^2}{\sum_k^K d_k^2} \tag{9}$$

where d_k is the inverse Euclidean Distance between p_j and its k_{th} nearest neighbor at level $j - 1$.

4   Experiments

In this section, we evaluate the performance of our network on large-scale semantic segmentation datasets. We provide extensive ablation studies to justify the effectiveness of our proposed methods. A comparison of scene segmentation results between existing methods and our is shown in Table 1.

4.1   Datasets

Stanford Large-Scale 3D Indoor Spaces (S3DIS). The S3DIS dataset [1] is a benchmark for large-scale indoor scene semantic segmentation. It consists of point clouds of six floors from three different buildings. Following the convention [18,23], We perform experiments on both 6-fold and Area 5 to evaluate our framework. For evaluation metrics, we use Overall point-wise accuracy (OA), and mean intersection over union (mIoU). The detailed results for individual class are listed in Table 2 and Table 3. We can see that our method has the highest scores for several challenging classes, such as door, wall and board.

Scannet. The Scannet [3] dataset contains more than 1500 scanned scenes annotated with 20 valid semantic classes. It provides a 1,201/312 data split for training and testing. The Scannet dataset is reconstructed from RGB-D scanner. We report the per-voxel accuracy (OA) as evaluation metrics. As shown in Table 1, our framework achieves state-of-the-art performance.

4.2 Implementation Details

Parameter Setting. SPNet uses residual block similar to [10]. Each block consists of one MLP for feature dimension reduction, one SPConv, and another MLP to increase feature dimension. SPNet consists of 5 encoding levels and 4 decoding levels, as shown in Fig. 3. The kernel influence v_0 for the first encoding level is set to $0.04m$ for both S3DIS [1] and ScanNet [3]. For subsequent level l, kernel influence is increased to $v_l = 2^l v_0$. The rest of the parameters are adjusted according to v_l. For SPConv operator, we use a total of $K = 3$ shells. Kernel points of the second and the third shell are initialized on the surfaces of spheres with radius $r_2 = 1.5v_l, r_3 = 3v_l$ respectively. Query neighborhood radius R_l is set to $4v_l$, PDS radius is set to $0.75v$. For attention module, both color and normal are used to compute the attentional scores. For the Gaussian function, we set $\sigma = v_l$ at each level.

Network Training. Our network is implemented using PyTorch [22] on a single Nvidia Titan RTX for all experiments. We use a batch size of 8, initial learning rate of 0.001. Optimization is done with Adam optimizer ($\beta_1 = 0.9, \beta_2 = 0.999$) [13]. Learning rate decays by a factor of 0.3 every 50 epoch for S3DIS [1], and every 30 epoch for ScanNet [3].

4.3 Ablation Studies

To prove the effectiveness of our proposed method, we conduct a series of experiments on S3DIS [1], evaluate on Area 5. Our baseline employs kernel point convolution with 15 kernel points. As shown in Table 4, each time we add or replace a module while keeping the rest unchanged. First, combining feature propagation (FP) with PDS produces a +2.3% boost. An explanation is that PDS preserves shape patterns in every downsampling level, FP correctly retrieves the shape patterns by interpolating features from neighborhood at upsampling level. Grid sampling loses geometric information, and this incorrectness accumulates through multiple downsampling layers. Moreover, adding local feature attention module produces +2.9% gain. Finally, SPConv improves the performance by +3.4%, showing its great capability of local feature encoding. Our full pipeline

Table 1. Comparative 3D scene segmentation scores on S3DIS [1], ScanNet [3] datasets. S3DIS [1] scores are reported in metric of mean Intersection over Union (mIoU) including Area 5 and 6-fold cross validation. ScanNet [3] scores are reported as Overall Accuracy (OA) and mIoU. The symbol '−' means the results are not available.

Methods	S3DIS (mIoU) Area 5	S3DIS (mIoU) 6-fold	ScanNet (OA)
PointNet [23]	41.1	47.6	-
PointNet++ [24]	-	54.5	84.5
DGCNN [26]	-	56.1	-
SPGraph [15]	58.0	62.1	-
ShellNet [36]	-	66.8	85.2
PointWeb [37]	60.3	66.7	85.9
GACNet [30]	62.9	-	-
RandLA-Net [11]	-	68.5	-
SPH3D-GCN [17]	59.5	68.9	-
Point2Node [7]	63.0	70.0	86.3
KPConv(R) [29]	65.4	69.6	-
KPConv(D) [29]	67.1	70.6	-
Minkowski [2]	65.4	-	-
Ours	**69.9**	**73.7**	**89.5**

Table 2. Semantic segmentation mIoU and OA scores on S3DIS [1] Area 5.

Method	mIoU	OA	ceil.	floor	wall	beam	col.	wind.	door	chair	table	book.	sofa	board	clut.
PointNet [23]	41.1	49.0	88.8	97.3	69.8	0.1	3.9	46.3	10.8	52.6	58.9	40.3	5.9	26.4	33.2
PointWeb [37]	60.3	87.0	91.9	**98.5**	79.4	0.0	21.1	59.7	34.8	76.3	88.3	46.9	69.3	64.9	52.5
Point2Node [7]	62.9	88.8	93.8	98.3	83.3	0.0	35.6	55.3	58.8	79.5	84.7	44.1	71.1	58.7	55.2
KPConv(R) [29]	65.4	-	92.6	97.3	81.4	0.0	16.5	54.5	69.5	90.1	80.2	74.6	66.4	63.7	58.1
KPConv(D) [29]	67.1	-	92.8	97.3	82.4	0.0	23.9	58.0	69.0	**91.0**	**81.5**	**75.3**	75.4	66.7	58.9
Ours	**69.9**	**90.3**	**94.5**	98.3	**84.0**	0.0	24.0	59.7	**79.8**	89.6	81.0	75.2	**82.4**	**80.4**	**60.4**

Table 3. Semantic segmentation mIoU and OA scores on S3DIS [1] 6-fold.

Method	mIoU	OA	ceil.	floor	wall	beam	col.	wind.	door	chair	table	book.	sofa	board	clut.
PointNet [23]	47.8	78.5	88.0	88.7	69.3	42.4	23.1	47.5	51.6	54.1	42.0	9.6	38.2	29.4	35.2
SPGraph [15]	62.1	85.5	89.9	95.1	76.4	62.8	47.1	55.3	68.4	69.2	73.5	45.9	63.2	8.7	52.9
PointCNN [18]	65.4	88.1	**94.8**	**97.3**	75.8	63.3	51.7	58.4	57.2	69.1	71.6	61.2	39.1	52.2	58.6
PointWeb [37]	66.7	87.3	93.5	94.2	80.8	52.4	41.3	64.9	68.1	71.4	67.1	50.3	62.7	62.2	58.5
KPConv(R) [29]	69.6	-	93.7	92.0	82.5	62.5	49.5	65.7	**77.3**	57.8	64.0	68.8	71.7	60.1	59.6
Point2Node [7]	70.0	89.0	94.1	97.3	83.4	62.7	52.3	72.3	64.3	75.8	70.8	65.7	49.8	60.3	60.9
KPConv(D) [29]	70.6	-	93.6	92.4	83.1	63.9	54.3	66.1	76.6	57.8	64.0	69.3	**74.9**	61.3	60.3
Ours	**73.7**	**90.9**	94.6	**97.3**	**85.0**	45.2	56.9	**82.1**	63.4	**73.1**	**83.4**	71.5	68.8	**68.6**	**67.8**

Table 4. Ablation studies evaluated on Area 5 of S3DIS [1].

	mIoU	GainΔ
Baseline + grid sampling	65.4	-
Baseline + grid sampling + FP	65.4	-
Baseline + PDS	66.0	+0.6
Baseline + PDS + FP	67.7	+2.3
SPConv + PDS + FP	68.8	+3.4
Baseline + Attention + PDS + FP	68.3	+2.9
SPConv + Attention + PDS + FP	69.9	+4.5

exceeds baseline with grid sample by +4.5%, which has the state-of-the-art performance on S3DIS dataset [1].

To illustrate the effectiveness of our proposed attention module, see Table 5. Learnable MLP-based method achieves better performance however it burdens the computation.

Table 5. Ablation studies with the proposed feature attention.

Approach	Input features	mIoU	Inference speed (iter/s)
Gaussian function	color	68.0	4.3
Gaussian function	normal	67.1	4.3
Gaussian function	color+normal	68.3	4.3
2layer MLP	color	68.7	4.1
2layer MLP	normal	68.2	4.1
2layer MLP	color+normal	68.7	3.0
3layer MLP	color+normal	69.9	3.0

5   Conclusions

In this work, we propose an architecture named SPNet for 3D point cloud semantic segmentation. We introduce a SPConv operator to effectively learn point cloud geometry. We demonstrate that with Poisson disk sampling as well as feature propagation, our network can go deep without losing much inherent shape patterns. Our framework outperforms many competing approaches proved by experimental results on public large-scale datasets. We will experiment our method on outdoor Lidar datasets and investigate more effective attention methods.

References

1. Armeni, I., Sax, S., Zamir, A.R., Savarese, S.: Joint 2D–3D-semantic data for indoor scene understanding. arXiv preprint arXiv:1702.01105 (2017)
2. Choy, C., Gwak, J., Savarese, S.: 4D spatio-temporal convnets: Minkowski convolutional neural networks. In: Proceedings of the IEEE Conference on Computer Vision and Pattern Recognition, pp. 3075–3084 (2019)
3. Dai, A., Chang, A.X., Savva, M., Halber, M., Funkhouser, T., Nießner, M.: ScanNet: richly-annotated 3D reconstructions of indoor scenes. In: Proceedings of the IEEE Conference on Computer Vision and Pattern Recognition, pp. 5828–5839 (2017)
4. Girshick, R.: Fast R-CNN. In: Proceedings of the IEEE International Conference on Computer Vision, pp. 1440–1448 (2015)
5. Girshick, R., Donahue, J., Darrell, T., Malik, J.: Rich feature hierarchies for accurate object detection and semantic segmentation. In: Proceedings of the IEEE Conference on Computer Vision and Pattern Recognition, pp. 580–587 (2014)
6. Graham, B., Engelcke, M., van der Maaten, L.: 3D semantic segmentation with submanifold sparse convolutional networks. In: Proceedings of the IEEE Conference on Computer Vision and Pattern Recognition, pp. 9224–9232 (2018)
7. Han, W., Wen, C., Wang, C., Li, X., Li, Q.: Point2Node: correlation learning of dynamic-node for point cloud feature modeling. arXiv preprint arXiv:1912.10775 (2019)
8. He, K., Gkioxari, G., Dollár, P., Girshick, R.: Mask R-CNN. In: Proceedings of the IEEE International Conference on Computer Vision, pp. 2961–2969 (2017)
9. He, K., Zhang, X., Ren, S., Sun, J.: Delving deep into rectifiers: surpassing human-level performance on ImageNet classification. In: Proceedings of the IEEE International Conference on Computer Vision, pp. 1026–1034 (2015)
10. He, K., Zhang, X., Ren, S., Sun, J.: Deep residual learning for image recognition. In: Proceedings of the IEEE Conference on Computer Vision and Pattern Recognition, pp. 770–778 (2016)
11. Hu, Q., et al.: RandLA-Net: efficient semantic segmentation of large-scale point clouds. arXiv preprint arXiv:1911.11236 (2019)
12. Huang, G., Liu, Z., Van Der Maaten, L., Weinberger, K.Q.: Densely connected convolutional networks. In: Proceedings of the IEEE Conference on Computer Vision and Pattern Recognition, pp. 4700–4708 (2017)
13. Kingma, D.P., Ba, J.: Adam: a method for stochastic optimization. arXiv preprint arXiv:1412.6980 (2014)
14. Landrieu, L., Boussaha, M.: Point cloud over segmentation with graph-structured deep metric learning. In: Proceedings of the IEEE Conference on Computer Vision and Pattern Recognition, pp. 7440–7449 (2019)
15. Landrieu, L., Simonovsky, M.: Large-scale point cloud semantic segmentation with superpoint graphs. In: Proceedings of the IEEE Conference on Computer Vision and Pattern Recognition, pp. 4558–4567 (2018)
16. Le, T., Duan, Y.: PointGrid: a deep network for 3D shape understanding. In: Proceedings of the IEEE Conference on Computer Vision and Pattern Recognition, pp. 9204–9214 (2018)
17. Lei, H., Akhtar, N., Mian, A.: Spherical kernel for efficient graph convolution on 3D point clouds. arXiv preprint arXiv:1909.09287 (2019)
18. Li, Y., Bu, R., Sun, M., Wu, W., Di, X., Chen, B.: PointCNN: convolution on x-transformed points. In: Advances in Neural Information Processing Systems, pp. 820–830 (2018)

19. Li, Y., Pirk, S., Su, H., Qi, C.R., Guibas, L.J.: FPNN: field probing neural networks for 3D data. In: Advances in Neural Information Processing Systems, pp. 307–315 (2016)

20. Long, J., Shelhamer, E., Darrell, T.: Fully convolutional networks for semantic segmentation. In: Proceedings of the IEEE Conference on Computer Vision and Pattern Recognition, pp. 3431–3440 (2015)

21. Maturana, D., Scherer, S.: VoxNet: a 3D convolutional neural network for real-time object recognition. In: 2015 IEEE/RSJ International Conference on Intelligent Robots and Systems (IROS), pp. 922–928. IEEE (2015)

22. Paszke, A., et al.: Automatic differentiation in pytorch (2017)

23. Qi, C.R., Su, H., Mo, K., Guibas, L.J.: PointNet: deep learning on point sets for 3D classification and segmentation. In: Proceedings of the IEEE Conference on Computer Vision and Pattern Recognition, pp. 652–660 (2017)

24. Qi, C.R., Yi, L., Su, H., Guibas, L.J.: PointNet++: deep hierarchical feature learning on point sets in a metric space. In: Advances in Neural Information Processing Systems, pp. 5099–5108 (2017)

25. Shen, Y., Feng, C., Yang, Y., Tian, D.: Mining point cloud local structures by kernel correlation and graph pooling. In: Proceedings of the IEEE Conference on Computer Vision and Pattern Recognition, pp. 4548–4557 (2018)

26. Simonovsky, M., Komodakis, N.: Dynamic edge-conditioned filters in convolutional neural networks on graphs. In: Proceedings of the IEEE Conference on Computer Vision and Pattern Recognition, pp. 3693–3702 (2017)

27. Su, H., Maji, S., Kalogerakis, E., Learned-Miller, E.: Multi-view convolutional neural networks for 3D shape recognition. In: Proceedings of the IEEE International Conference on Computer Vision, pp. 945–953 (2015)

28. Tchapmi, L., Choy, C., Armeni, I., Gwak, J., Savarese, S.: Segcloud: semantic segmentation of 3D point clouds. In: 2017 International Conference on 3D Vision (3DV), pp. 537–547. IEEE (2017)

29. Thomas, H., Qi, C.R., Deschaud, J.E., Marcotegui, B., Goulette, F., Guibas, L.J.: KPConv: flexible and deformable convolution for point clouds. In: Proceedings of the IEEE International Conference on Computer Vision, pp. 6411–6420 (2019)

30. Wang, L., Huang, Y., Hou, Y., Zhang, S., Shan, J.: Graph attention convolution for point cloud semantic segmentation. In: Proceedings of the IEEE Conference on Computer Vision and Pattern Recognition, pp. 10296–10305 (2019)

31. Wang, S., Suo, S., Ma, W.C., Pokrovsky, A., Urtasun, R.: Deep parametric continuous convolutional neural networks. In: Proceedings of the IEEE Conference on Computer Vision and Pattern Recognition, pp. 2589–2597 (2018)

32. Wu, W., Qi, Z., Fuxin, L.: PointConv: deep convolutional networks on 3D point clouds. In: Proceedings of the IEEE Conference on Computer Vision and Pattern Recognition, pp. 9621–9630 (2019)

33. Wu, Z., et al.: 3D ShapeNets: a deep representation for volumetric shapes. In: Proceedings of the IEEE Conference on Computer Vision and Pattern Recognition, pp. 1912–1920 (2015)

34. Xu, Y., Fan, T., Xu, M., Zeng, L., Qiao, Y.: SpiderCNN: deep learning on point sets with parameterized convolutional filters. In: Proceedings of the European Conference on Computer Vision (ECCV), pp. 87–102 (2018)

35. Yang, M., Yu, K., Zhang, C., Li, Z., Yang, K.: Denseaspp for semantic segmentation in street scenes. In: Proceedings of the IEEE Conference on Computer Vision and Pattern Recognition, pp. 3684–3692 (2018)

36. Zhang, Z., Hua, B.S., Yeung, S.K.: ShellNet: efficient point cloud convolutional neural networks using concentric shells statistics. In: Proceedings of the IEEE International Conference on Computer Vision, pp. 1607–1616 (2019)
37. Zhao, H., Jiang, L., Fu, C.W., Jia, J.: PointWeb: enhancing local neighborhood features for point cloud processing. In: Proceedings of the IEEE Conference on Computer Vision and Pattern Recognition, pp. 5565–5573 (2019)

Computer Graphics II

Procedural Modeling
of the Great Barrier Reef

Wanwan Li[✉]

George Mason University, Fairfax, USA
wli17@gmu.edu

Abstract. Since terrain procedural modeling is widely adopted for the virtual natural scene generations in the game design, movie industry, and digital arts, lots of advanced techniques have been explored by researchers to procedurally synthesize a large variety of different types of terrain and landscapes. In this paper, we present a novel approach to generate a special type of landscape – the Great Barrier Reef – an amazing natural landscape that is currently being ignored. We propose a hypothesis that the Great Barrier Reef is grown with the diffusion-limited aggregation (DLA) model and simulate the DLA process to generate the Great Barrier Reef procedurally. As presented in the results, the procedural Great Barrier Reef generated with our approach looks natural when compared to the photos of the real ones.

Keywords: Procedural modeling · Landscape · Terrain · Great Barrier Reef · Diffusion-limited aggregation (DLA)

1 Introduction

As one of the most popular techniques applied in terrain authoring, procedural terrain modeling has been widely studied by researchers nowadays. Understanding the natural procedure of how the landscapes are formed is the key issue for researchers to get a deeper insight into designing efficient procedural modeling algorithms. Since the early ages, different representations has been proposed for different types of terrain modelings such as the elevation models [27] (including discrete heightfields model [8] and layered mixture representations [19], etc.) and the volumetric models (including voxels representation [13] and hybrid representations [23], etc.). Given these observations, various types of procedural modeling algorithms have been applied to different types of terrain and landscapes synthesis. Fournier et al. [11] proposed a recursive midpoint displacement subdivision algorithm to add fractal details on curves which can be further modified to apply to general procedural terrains. Image filters [21] can be introduced to add fractal properties on the terrain surface such as ridge filters, multi-fractal filters, and warped filters to raise crests, ridges, and valleys, etc. [9]. De et al. [7] proposed a method for realistic procedural canyons generation. Featuring arches effect have been simulated on volumetric terrains by Becher et al. [5]. Terrains with thermal

© Springer Nature Switzerland AG 2021
G. Bebis et al. (Eds.): ISVC 2021, LNCS 13017, pp. 381–391, 2021.
https://doi.org/10.1007/978-3-030-90439-5_30

(a) Top-down view of real Great Barrier Reef.   (b) Procedural Great Barrier Reef generation.

Fig. 1. Example of procedural Great Barrier Reef generation.

erosion effects have been synthesized by Musgrave et al. [19]. Spheroidal weathering effects have been implemented by Beardall et al. [4] to synthesize realistic procedural Goblins. Recently, other types of landscapes such as riverscapes synthesized by Paris et al. [22], desertscapes synthesized by Paris et al. [20], glacierscapes synthesized by Argudo et al. [2] are well generated by the applications of existing procedural modeling techniques (Fig. 1).

However, according to the best of our knowledge, as one of the most attractive places for traveling in Australia, the Great Barrier Reef, which forms an extraordinary special landscape, has never been studied so far with respect to procedural modeling. Existing research works about the Great Barrier Reef modelings are mainly focusing on its hydrodynamic modeling [17], spectral discrimination modeling [16], water quality modeling [15], and biological population dynamics modeling [6], etc. Therefore, we open a new topic about generalizing the features observed from the Great Barrier Reef landscape and exploring an effective computer graphics algorithm to generate realistic procedural Great Barrier Reef landscapes. We conclude the contributions of our work as following:

- We initiate a discussion of an open problem about procedural Great Barrier Reef generation and propose a hypothesis that how the Great Barrier Reef is formed from a procedural modeling aspect.
- We propose a novel algorithm to procedurally synthesis the Great Barrier Reef and discuss how the parameters in our procedural model affect the landscape of the Great Barrier Reef.
- We conclude the limitations of our work and prospect the next steps to extend our work for the future study about procedural Great Barrier Reef generation and its potential applications.

2   Growth of the Great Barrier Reef: A Hypothesis

As we know, the Great Barrier Reef, as the world's largest coral reef system [18], most of its major components are individual reefs, combined with stretching islands as minor components. As coral reefs are the skeleton of coral worms, therefore, the landscape of the coral reefs' colonies looks more like living creatures rather than ordinary terrains. By assuming that coral reefs landscapes are sharing similar features with the distributions of leaving creatures that are aggregated into colonies naturally, we propose a hypothesis that the growth of the Great Barrier Reef flows the rules of diffusion-limited aggregation (DLA) process [26] which is a natural aggregation process caused by the individual particles' random walks due to their Brownian motion [25]. DLA algorithm [14] is a computational procedure that simulates the process of how random particles are aggregated into colonies within the natural environment. To describe this phenomenon, in short, DLA simulations have three main steps: (1) setup a random aggregation kernel, (2) releasing random particles with Brownian motions, and (3) aggregate those particles whenever two individual particles are neighboring to each other. When evaluating whether such a DLA process fits well our problem definition of growing the Great Barrier Reef, we need to argue that whether these three steps in DLA are able to be mapped to the growth of the Great Barrier Reef. Here is a tentative inductive reasoning proof:

Proof. Step (1) in DLA is reasonable when assuming that there is the first coral reef appearing in the Great Barrier Reef. Step (2) in the DLA can be interpreted as there is the second coral reef given birth in a random place in the Great Barrier Reef, which can be reasonable as well. Step (3) is actually the discussion that whether the second coral reef is necessarily nearby the first coral reef. Fortunately, this can be proved by the fact that the coral reef is the skeleton of the coral worms and the coral worms are actually not moving very frequently. This means coral worms tend to give birth in place and hence every two colonies will not be too far away from each other if there is an inheritance relationship between these two.

Therefore, according to this proof of concept, the DLA process is reasonable for simulating the growth of the Great Barrier Reef and this theoretically defends our hypothesis from a philosophical view. Given this theoretical hypothesis and proof, in the following sections, we will present our proposed problem formulation, discuss the experimental results, and prospect the future works.

3   Problem Formulations

3.1   Terrain Representation

In our work, we are using the discrete heightfields, also called heightmap, to represent the elevations of terrain. The heightmap is an image storing the elevation height of the terrain on arbitrary pixels. Typically, heightmap is represented as a $M \times N$ normalized scalar matrix $H_{M \times N}$ consisted with real numbers between 0 and 1. Given any 2D vector $\mathbf{p} = (u, v) \in \mathbb{R}^2$ as a location on terrain, we can calculate the elevation of terrain surface at location $\mathbf{p}$, denoted as $h(\mathbf{p})$, using interpolation methods. Assume that (u_0, v_0) and (u_1, v_1) are the two corners on the diagonals of the rectangle region of the terrain respectively, then the heightmap grids interval $(\Delta u, \Delta v) = ((u_1 - u_0)/(M - 1), (v_1 - v_0)/(N - 1)$. The terrain's corresponding location of the pixel on heightmap's i^{th} row and j^{th} column can be calculated through a mapping function $\Phi(i,j) = (u_0, v_0) + (i,j) \cdot (\Delta u, \Delta v)$ where $(i,j) \in \mathbb{I}^2$. Noted that $h(\Phi(i,j)) = h_{\max}H_{i,j}$, where $h_{\max}$ is the maximum height of the terrain. As shown in Fig. 2(a), we take a realistic terrain heightmap (gray) generated with the approach proposed by De et al. [7] with canyons effects as the base map $h_0(u,v)$ upon which our Great Barrier Reef grows.

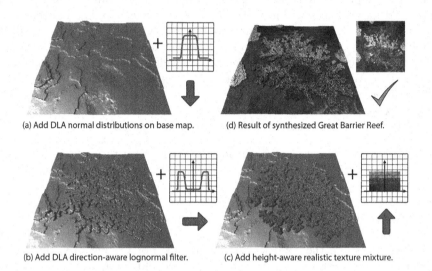

(a) Add DLA normal distributions on base map.   (d) Result of synthesized Great Barrier Reef.

(b) Add DLA direction-aware lognormal filter.   (c) Add height-aware realistic texture mixture.

Fig. 2. Overview of our technical approach.

3.2   DLA Normal Distributions

DLA normal distribution is a compound term that combines the term of DLA (short for diffusion-limited aggregation) and the term of normal distributions. As this term suggests, DLA-normal distribution is the scale mixtures of normal distributions [1] where the centers of the individual normal distributions are following a spatial distribution pattern of diffusion-limited aggregation. Mathematically, we form a DLA distribution on a 2D terrain coordinate space. First, we create a boolean matrix DLA grids mask $B_{M \times N} \in \{0,1\}_{M \times N}$. Then, we turn an arbitrary bit of the DLA grid mask on and take it as the diffusion kernel. Finally, we repeatedly sample pixel (i,j) on the terrain with random walk step $(\Delta i, \Delta j)$, turn on the pixel (i,j)'s mask $B_{i,j} = 1$ where exists any one of its eight adjacent neighbor pixels $(i', j') \in \{(i \pm k_1 \Delta i, j \pm k_2 \Delta j) | k_1, k_2 \in \{0,1\}\}$ that has mask also been turned on, namely, when $B_{i',j'} = 1$. Noted that the random walk step $(\Delta i, \Delta j)$ is also interpreted as DLA grids cell size, we will discuss more about how the grids cell size settings influence the results in the following section. After the DLA calculation step, we accumulate the convolutions between terrain's base map $h_0(\mathbf{p})$ and Gaussian function with pixel center (i, j) as a new heightmap $h_1(u,v)$ through Eq. 1:

$$h_1(\mathbf{p}) = w_0 h_0(\mathbf{p}) + w_1 \sum_{\mathbf{q} \in \{\Phi(i,j)|B_{i,j}=1\}} h_0(\mathbf{p}) \circ e^{-||\mathbf{p}-\mathbf{q}||^k} \tag{1}$$

where we empirically set $k = 10$ for a realistic result. As shown in Fig. 2(b), after this convolution process, those that belong to the DLA areas on the base map are lifted up to a certain level specified by w_1, the edges are smoothed by the Gaussian filter. This procedural is used to simulate the aggregation of the corals under the sea. As the amount of the coral reef increases, they will float above sea level and form into islands.

3.3   Directional DLA Log-Normal Filter

According to the definition of log-normal distribution in statistical science [24], it is used to describe the distributions whose logarithm is normally distributed. From the shape of the log-normal distribution function, it looks more like a biased normal distribution. As one interesting phenomenon shown in Fig. 3 which is downloaded from

Fig. 3. Edge uplift effects.

the website [3], the Great Barrier Reef is captured from a top-down view. As we can see, the edges of the coral reef are frequently uplifted due to the aggregation of corals near the seashore. Inside the edges, the corals reefs look more plat. This observation inspire us to use the log-normal distribution function as a filter to uplift the edges of the procedural landscape to generate such effect. In this scenario, we propose a directional DLA log-normal filter to convolute the edges of the DLA grids using log-normal distributions function. After adding the normal distributions in the previous step, we accumulate the convolutions between terrain's DLA normal distributions map $h_1(\mathbf{p})$ and the Log-Gaussian function with pixel centers (i, j) in the DLA grids as a final heightmap $h_2(u, v)$ through Eq. 2:

$$h_2(\mathbf{p}) = h_1(\mathbf{p}) + w_2 \sum_{\mathbf{q} \in \{\Phi(i,j)|B_{i,j}=1\}} h_0(\mathbf{p}) \circ w_d(\mathbf{p},\mathbf{q}) e^{-\ln k_1(1-||\mathbf{p}-\mathbf{q}||)^{k_2}} \tag{2}$$

where we empirically set $k_1 = 5$ and $k_2 = 10$ for a realistic rendering result. Furthermore, we add random values on k_1 to simulate the noises on the edges.

The directional weight sampler $w_d(\mathbf{p},\mathbf{q})$ returns a value between 0 and 1. $w_d(\mathbf{p},\mathbf{q})$ is calculated through the following steps: Step (1) Calculate the angle between the y-axis and $\mathbf{q} - \mathbf{p}$. The calculated angle is between 0 and 360°. Step (2) we divide the 360-degree angles into eight directions and check out the calculated angle belongs to which direction. Step (3), we search the current pixel index (i, j) of the location $\mathbf{q}$ and its adjacent neighbor pixels at that calculated direction, if that neighbor belongs to the DLA grids, then we set the weight of that direction into 0, otherwise, we set $w_d(\mathbf{p},\mathbf{q}) = 1$. As shown in Fig. 2(c), after applying the directional DLA log-normal filter, those lifted regions' edges are furtherly lift up to a certain level specified by w_2. The edges are noised. The inner area is not lifted as much as the edges due to the directional weight multiplier. This procedural is used to realistically simulate the effects shown in Fig. 3. After applying these two major steps of the convolutions on the terrain map, another two optional minor steps are applied on the terrain heightmap including a blurring step to remove high-frequency artefacts and a normalization step to refine the heightmap values ranging between 0 and 1.

3.4   Height-Aware Terrain Texture Synthesis

Texture synthesis is an important step to generate a realistic terrain appearance. There are lots of different types of texture synthesis methods such as pixel-based non-parametric sampling methods proposed by Efros et al. [10] and its applications on terrain texture [12]. In our work, we consider the terrain characteristics such as the absolute elevation function $h_2(\mathbf{p})$ calculated from the above steps. According to the observation, the deep sea areas has texture with dark blues, shallow sea ares are colored with light blues, and the coral reef island has a green blue texture. Therefore, in order to blend the textures smoothly, we propose two functions as the alphamap values for texture mixture: Lowpass Function P_{low} and Highpass Function P_{high} which are defined in Eq. 3 and Eq. 4 respectively:

$$P_{\text{low}}(h(\mathbf{p}), h_{\text{low}}) = \begin{cases} 1 & h(\mathbf{p}) \leq h_{\text{low}} \\ P_{\text{error}}(|h(\mathbf{p}) - h_{\text{low}}|, \epsilon_{\text{low}}) & h(\mathbf{p}) > h_{\text{low}} \end{cases} \tag{3}$$

$$P_{\text{high}}(h(\mathbf{p}), h_{\text{high}}) = \begin{cases} 1 & h(\mathbf{p}) \geq h_{\text{high}} \\ P_{\text{error}}(|h(\mathbf{p}) - h_{\text{high}}|, \epsilon_{\text{high}}) & h(\mathbf{p}) < h_{\text{high}} \end{cases} \tag{4}$$

where Errorpass Function $P_{\text{error}}(d, \epsilon)$ compare the distance d and the error ϵ as shown in Eq. 5:

$$P_{\text{error}}(d, \epsilon) = \begin{cases} 0 & d \geq \epsilon \\ 1 - d/\epsilon & d < \epsilon \end{cases} \tag{5}$$

Then, we have the final alphamap values for deep sea texture α_{d}, shallow sea texture α_{s}, and coral reef island texture α_{c} are calculated through Eq. 6:

$$\begin{bmatrix} \alpha_{\text{d}}(\mathbf{p}) \\ \alpha_{\text{s}}(\mathbf{p}) \\ \alpha_{\text{c}}(\mathbf{p}) \end{bmatrix} = \begin{bmatrix} P_{\text{low}}(h(\mathbf{p}), h_{\text{low}}) \\ (1 - P_{\text{low}}(h(\mathbf{p})))(1 - P_{\text{high}}(h(\mathbf{p}))) \\ (1 - P_{\text{low}}(h(\mathbf{p}))P_{\text{high}}(h(\mathbf{p})) \end{bmatrix} \tag{6}$$

Empirically, we have set height texture borderlines $h_{\text{low}} = 0.3$ and $h_{\text{high}} = 0.5$ Borderlines errors are set as $\epsilon_{\text{low}} = 0.1$ and $\epsilon_{\text{high}} = 0.05$ respectively. As shown in Fig. 2(d), the final terrain mesh generated with our approach has been colored with this proposed height-aware texture synthesis method mentioned above. As we can see, those areas that belong to the DLA areas on the heightmap are colored as dark green-blue texture. This mimics the green island floating above the sea. In the middle area, they are shallow water with light bright blue. As the deeper blue highlight the areas where belong to the deep sea. This rendering's visual effects look realistic as the texture synthesis methods obey the natural rules observed from real photography as we explained above.

4   Experimental Results

We have implemented the proposed approach to synthesize the Great Barrier Reef using Unity 3D with the 2019 version. The hardware configurations contain Intel Core i5 CPU, 32 GB DDR4 RAM, and NVIDIA GeForce GTX 1650 4 GB GDDR6 Graphics Card. Our proposed algorithm is implemented on the CPU. We have tested our synthesized Great Barrier Reef landscapes with different settings. In this section, we will demonstrate the robustness of our proposed approach by changing the input terrains, changing the DLA aggregation centers, changing the DLA grids sizes, and changing the textures.

4.1   Changing Input Terrains

As shown in Fig. 4, we have synthesized Great Barrier Reef landscapes with three different terrain inputs. All of the terrains are randomly generated with the same parameter settings but with different random numbers generator seeds inputs. All terrains are generated with a heightmap of 4096×4096 pixels. The terrain's real width is 10 km and its real height is 500 m. Among these three results, the DLA grid size is set to 150 (dimension of the DLA grids), the grids radius is 40 (convolution kernel size) and the aggregation center is (120, 120). The DLA particle shooting number is 3000. The maximum Brown motion random walk steps are 30000. The heightmap blending weights for base map h_0, DLA normal distribution map h_1 and the DLA log-normal filter map h_2 are $w_0 = 0.5$,

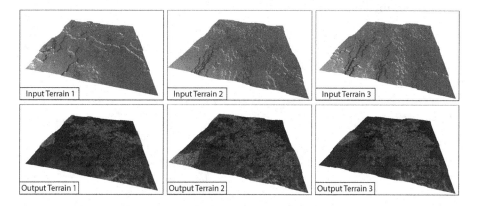

Fig. 4. Experiments results of changing input terrains.

$w_1 = 0.2$, and $w_2 = 0.1$ respectively. The execution times for these three terrain synthesis results are 21 s, 26 s, and 24 s respectively. As we can see, our approach is robust to different kinds of terrain inputs.

4.2   Changing Aggregation Centers

Another interesting phenomenon to show is that our approach is robust to aggregation centers settings as well. As shown in Fig. 5, we have three different aggregation center settings respectively. The three centers are labeled through three red pins. In this test, we have the DLA grids settings as same as above where the DLA grid size is set to 150 and the grids radius is 40. However, we have three different aggregation centers settings are left bottom (20, 130), middle center (80, 80), and right top (130, 20) respectively. The aggregation center is the DLA kernel where the first particle is put in DAL girds. Then other particles will be aggregated around this kernel. As we can see, different DLA kernels will affect the overall distributions of the coral reefs in our synthesized Great Barrier Reef. The shape of the landscape is smoothly moving from the left bottom (left subfigure) towards the middle center (middle subfigure) and finally move to the right top (right subfigure).

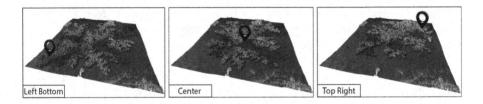

Fig. 5. Experiments results of changing aggregation centers.

4.3   Changing DLA Grid Sizes

The DLA grid size settings are essential for our algorithm as it adjusts the resolution of our synthesized Great Barrier Reef. As shown in Fig. 6, we have three different grid Sizes settings respectively.

Fig. 6. Experiments results of changing DLA grid sizes.

The left subfigure shows the result synthesized with the grid size of 50, grids radius of 120, and the aggregation center is (40, 40), the particle shooting number is 500, and its running time is 19 s. The middle subfigure shows the result synthesized with the grid size of 100, grids radius of 60, and the aggregation center is (80, 80), the particle shooting number is 2000, and its running time is 22 s. The right subfigure shows the result synthesized with the grid size of 200, grids radius of 30, the aggregation center is (180, 180), the particle shooting number is 8000, and its running time is 28 s. As we can see, as the grid size decreases, more particles are needed to aggregate into the same large-scale terrain and in turn, it takes more time for running, and it results in more details of the synthesized terrain.

4.4 Changing Textures

For showing some special visual effects, we have generalized the idea of "Great Barrier Reefs". Hereby, we have used three different texture styles to synthesize the Great Barrier Reefs. As shown in Fig. 7, the left subfigure shows the Great Barrier Reefs rendered with a stony mountain style. In this case, the lower part is filled with stones and grass, the middle part is the stony hills, and the upper parts are filled with green vegetation. The middle subfigure shows the Great Barrier Reefs rendered with a desert hill style. In this case, the lower part is filled with yellow sands, the middle part is filled with some sparse vegetation, while the upper parts are filled with sandy hills. The subfigure on the right shows the Great Barrier Reefs rendered with a volcano style. In this case, the lower part is filled with burned stones, the middle part is filled with red lava, while the upper parts are filled with volcano outbreaks. As we can see, the results shown here look realistic and is ready to be considered to be used in the movie for rendering some special visual effects.

Fig. 7. Experiments results of changing textures.

5 Conclusion

In this paper, we have proposed an interesting question about how to generate the Great Barrier Reef using procedural modeling techniques. By proposing a hypothesis that the Great Barrier Reef is formed through the diffusion-limited aggregation (DLA) process, we have simulated the DLA process and combining it onto a realistic terrain through two types of convolutional kernels: DLA normal distribution kernel and the DLA log-normal edge enhancement kernel. After applying directionally weighted randomized DLA log-normal filters, we can synthesize the terrains with realistic visual effects. As shown in the experimental results, We have visually proved the robustness of our proposed approach by changing the parameters such as changing the input terrains, changing the DLA aggregation centers, changing the DLA grids sizes, and changing the textures.

In the future work, we will further explore our approach by adding more details such as including the corals and marine environment on the generated Great Barrier Reef. This will prepare our work ready to be used in the movie industry and game industry for the scenarios that are near the seashore with a special landscape that looks like the Great Barrier Reef. We believe our work will inspire more researchers to follow up and generate more eye-catching results about realistic procedural modelings of the Great Barrier Reef.

References

1. Andrews, D.F., Mallows, C.L.: Scale mixtures of normal distributions. J. Roy. Stat. Soc.: Ser. B (Methodol.) **36**(1), 99–102 (1974)
2. Argudo, O., Galin, E., Peytavie, A., Paris, A., Guérin, E.: Simulation, modeling and authoring of glaciers. ACM Trans. Graph. (TOG) **39**(6), 1–14 (2020)
3. Arikoglu, L.: Scientists discover secret reef...behind the Great Barrier Reef (2016). https://www.cntraveler.com/story/scientists-discover-secret-reef-below-the-great-barrier-reef
4. Beardall, M., Farley, M., Ouderkirk, D., Smith, J., Jones, M., Egbert, P.K.: Goblins by spheroidal weathering. In: NPH, pp. 7–14 (2007)
5. Becher, M., Krone, M., Reina, G., Ertl, T.: Feature-based volumetric terrain generation. In: Proceedings of the 21st ACM SIGGRAPH Symposium on Interactive 3D Graphics and Games, pp. 1–9 (2017)
6. Chaloupka, M.: Stochastic simulation modelling of southern Great Barrier Reef green turtle population dynamics. Ecol. Model. **148**(1), 79–109 (2002)
7. De Carli, D.M., Pozzer, C.T., Bevilacqua, F., Schetinger, V.: Procedural generation of 3D canyons. In: 2014 27th SIBGRAPI Conference on Graphics, Patterns and Images, pp. 103–110. IEEE (2014)
8. De Carpentier, G.J., Bidarra, R.: Interactive GPU-based procedural heightfield brushes. In: Proceedings of the 4th International Conference on Foundations of Digital Games, pp. 55–62 (2009)
9. Ebert, D.S., Musgrave, F.K., Peachey, D., Perlin, K., Worley, S.: Texturing & Modeling: A Procedural Approach. Morgan Kaufmann, San Francisco (2003)
10. Efros, A.A., Leung, T.K.: Texture synthesis by non-parametric sampling. In: Proceedings of the Seventh IEEE International Conference on Computer Vision, vol. 2, pp. 1033–1038. IEEE (1999)
11. Fournier, A., Fussell, D., Carpenter, L.: Computer rendering of stochastic models. Commun. ACM **25**(6), 371–384 (1982)
12. Gain, J., Merry, B., Marais, P.: Parallel, realistic and controllable terrain synthesis. In: Computer Graphics Forum, vol. 34, pp. 105–116. Wiley Online Library (2015)
13. Geiss, R.: Generating complex procedural terrains using the GPU. GPU Gems **3**, 7–37 (2007)

14. Hurd, A.J., Schaefer, D.W.: Diffusion-limited aggregation in two dimensions. Phys. Rev. Lett. **54**(10), 1043 (1985)
15. Khan, U., et al.: Development of catchment water quality models within a realtime status and forecast system for the Great Barrier Reef. Environ. Model. Softw. **132**, 104790 (2020)
16. Kutser, T., Dekker, A.G., Skirving, W.: Modeling spectral discrimination of Great Barrier Reef benthic communities by remote sensing instruments. Limnol. Oceanogr. **48**(1part2), 497–510 (2003)
17. Legrand, S., Deleersnijder, E., Hanert, E., Legat, V., Wolanski, E.: High-resolution, unstructured meshes for hydrodynamic models of the Great Barrier Reef, Australia. Estuar. Coast. Shelf Sci. **68**(1–2), 36–46 (2006)
18. Lucas, P., Webb, T., Valentine, P., Marsh, H.: The outstanding universal value of the Great Barrier Reef world heritage area (1997)
19. Musgrave, F.K., Kolb, C.E., Mace, R.S.: The synthesis and rendering of eroded fractal terrains. ACM SIGGRAPH Comput. Graph. **23**(3), 41–50 (1989)
20. Paris, A., Peytavie, A., Guérin, E., Argudo, O., Galin, E.: Desertscape simulation. In: Computer Graphics Forum, vol. 38, pp. 47–55. Wiley Online Library (2019)
21. Perlin, K.: An image synthesizer. ACM SIGGRAPH Comput. Graph. **19**(3), 287–296 (1985)
22. Peytavie, A., et al.: Procedural riverscapes. In: Computer Graphics Forum, vol. 38, pp. 35–46. Wiley Online Library (2019)
23. Peytavie, A., Galin, E., Grosjean, J., Mérillou, S.: Arches: a framework for modeling complex terrains. In: Computer Graphics Forum, vol. 28, pp. 457–467. Wiley Online Library (2009)
24. Siano, D.B.: The log-normal distribution function. J. Chem. Educ. **49**(11), 755 (1972)
25. Uhlenbeck, G.E., Ornstein, L.S.: On the theory of the Brownian motion. Phys. Rev. **36**(5), 823 (1930)
26. Witten, T.A., Jr., Sander, L.M.: Diffusion-limited aggregation, a kinetic critical phenomenon. Phys. Rev. Lett. **47**(19), 1400 (1981)
27. Zhou, H., Sun, J., Turk, G., Rehg, J.M.: Terrain synthesis from digital elevation models. IEEE Trans. Visual Comput. Graphics **13**(4), 834–848 (2007)

Art-Directable Cloud Animation

Yiyun Wang and Tim McGraw[✉]

Purdue University, West Lafayette, IN 47907, USA
tmcgraw@purdue.edu

Abstract. Volumetric cloud generation and rendering algorithms are well-developed to meet the need for a realistic sky appearance in animation or games. However, it is challenging to create a stylized or designed animation for volumetric clouds using physics-based simulation methods in real-time. The purpose of this project is to implement an animation technique for volumetric clouds with art-directable controllers. Using this method, a designer can easily control the cloud's motion in a reliable way. Users can animate the cloud with a sparse set of control vectors which are interpolated to create a physically plausible velocity field.

Keywords: Animation · Clouds · Smoke

1 Introduction

Many interactive applications, like video games, simulate natural phenomena to provide users a more realistic scene and a better immersive experience. Cloud simulation can be used in video games to improve sky scenes or weather systems. A common way to display the cloud is to treat it as volume and perform volume rendering. Most volumetric cloud generation processes will use noise textures to imitate the shape and texture of clouds (see Fig. 1). Many volumetric cloud rendering systems can be calculated fast enough on modern computers to be feasible in real-time rendering applications.

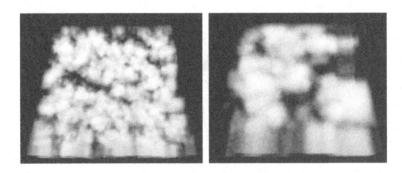

Fig. 1. Volume rendered clouds.

© Springer Nature Switzerland AG 2021
G. Bebis et al. (Eds.): ISVC 2021, LNCS 13017, pp. 392–399, 2021.
https://doi.org/10.1007/978-3-030-90439-5_31

Video game developers have made many improvements in cloud generation and rendering processes in recent years, such as the dynamic atmosphere system in Red Dead Redemption 2 [1] and the real-time cloudscapes in Horizon: Zero Dawn [2]. These generation and rendering processes are well developed, and the cloud rendering results are realistic. However, those methods can only work for natural weather systems or skyboxes, which means they can not generate clouds in a given shape or animate the cloud in a specific way desired by a designer or director.

Although physics-based simulation of clouds can provide realistic results, achieving a specific cloud shape or motion is not easy using simulation. Animators would need to adjust many physical parameters by trial-and-error to reach a desired result [3]. Stam [4] implemented methods to solve Navier-Stokes equations using both Lagrangian and implicit methods, which provide a stable algorithm to solve the full Navier-Stokes equation. Stam used his method to display volumetric clouds as well, but his method can not shape or animate the cloud in an art-directable way. The parameters of Stam's method and other physics-based methods include variables like viscosity, diffusion rate, and dissipation rate, which are not intuitive to many artists.

We propose a more direct solution of constrained cloud animation which does not rely on fluid simulation and can be performed interactively. By advecting a cloud volume with a divergence-free vector field we can achieve a physically-plausible fluid motion. The vector-field is determined by a sparse set of scattered control vectors which can easily and intuitively be manipulated by the user. The dense field can be generated at interactive framerates.

2   Related Work

Many approaches to controlled animation of fluids have been proposed in the literature. However, many are based on unintuitive physical parameters, and most do not work at interactive rates which would allow a designer to efficiently iterate on the animation.

Hong and Kim [5] developed a shape control method that can fill the volume clouds into a certain shape. The filling process is still physics-based, which means solving the Navier-Stokes equations. The results are high-quality, but the method is not interactive. Hong et al.'s method aims to set the start and end shape of the cloud and let fluid simulation interpolate in between. An interactive cloud generation method has been proposed by Dobashi, Kusumoto, Nishita, et al. [6]. By setting new edges of the volume cloud, the cloud will be generated and grow to meet the edges. By setting a target contour line, they generate a 3D target shape. Their simulation is constrained to minimize the difference between the current cloud shape and the target shape. Dobashi, Iwasaki, Yue, et al. [3] improved upon this algorithm and compared the rendering result with real photos. The improved method can generate inorganic shapes of clouds, such as a cloud shaped like a human skull. Dobashi et al.'s method has a similar idea as Hong et al., setting the cloud's target shape and letting the fluid simulation perform interpolation between the target shapes. However, interaction requires modification of physical parameters. For example, they set a higher temperature at the bottom of the scene to force the cloud to rise. Treuille, McNamara, Popović, et al. [7] implemented a key frame control for smoke simulation. They let the user set keyframes for the smoke and formulate an objective function quantifying the difference between the simulation and the keyframe. They then solve for the force parameters which minimize that function. Their solution is time-consuming and not interactive. Treuille et al. used a velocity vector field as control parameters. McNamara, Treuille, Popović, et al. [8] use the adjoint method to control a large 3D physics-based simulation of fluid. They use Gaussian wind forces presented by Treuille et al. and add sources to their control parameters. McNamara et al.'s method produces very close matches to the keyframes and works both for water and smoke. However, their method takes hours, sometimes even days, to calculate.

Fattal and Lischinski [9] implemented a target-driven method for smoke simulation. Their method uses two terms, a driving force term to carry the smoke towards the target state and a gathering term to prevent over-diffusion. Their method is much faster than the methods previously discussed, but still can not provide a real-time performance in 3D.

Stam [4] implemented methods to solve the Navier-Stokes equations using both Lagrangian and implicit methods, which provides a stable algorithm to solve the full Navier-Stokes equation. Harris, Baxter, Scheuermann, et al. [10] also implement a physics-based animation process for 3D clouds. However, their algorithm does not support interaction between the users and the clouds. The simulation is based on the Navier-Stokes equation, but they only show 2D results of clouds affected by the fluid.

Alex [11] introduced the idea of flow maps in games. They precompute a 2D flow map based on their level geometry in Houdini using fluid simulation. The flow map provides unique 2D vectors for each point on the water surface. They then use the flow map to distort the water surface's normal map, which provides a real-time water flowing animation. Simon [12] implemented software to generate flow maps. However, these flow map generators can not operate interactively, and the results are only 2-dimensional since they are intended to represent the surface of a body of water.

An alternative method to simulation for generating user-controllable vector fields that represent plausible wind velocity fields is to impose mathematical constraints on the vector field. Arbitrary vector fields are not plausible for cloud deformation if they do not represent incompressible flow. One way of imposing this constraint is to generate vector fields which are divergence-free. Yassine and McGraw [13,14] developed methods for interpolating tensor fields of arbitrary order (including vector fields) while imposing constraints on the divergence and curl of the resulting field. However, these methods require that the interpolated data lie on a regular grid. To provide more general artistic freedom to specify vectors at any location, a scattered-data interpolation technique is more practical. McNally [15] and Mitrano and Platte [16] developed scattered-data interpolation methods for divergence-free vector fields in 2D and 3D. The technique we developed makes use of their techniques to create vectors fields to control cloud animation. Artists can control a few scattered vectors, and a dense field can be automatically generated interactively. Since the dense field has a divergence minimizing property it has a physically-plausible appearance, even though no simulation is performed.

3 Methods

Our system allows the user to generate the initial volumetric cloud and create a time-varying vector field before animating the cloud by texture advection. Users can add control vectors into the vector field and change their orientation and magnitude on an animation timeline. The program will calculate a divergence-free interpolation vector field for each frame of animation. The vector field and clouds are stored in a 3D buffers. After the user starts the advection calculation, the system will update the cloud buffer based on the current vector field.

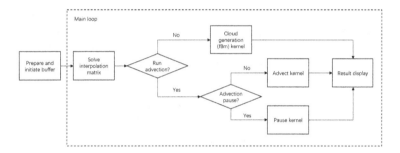

Fig. 2. Flowchart of the cloud animation system.

Our system was implemented in OpenGL 4.6 and CUDA 11.1. Figure 2 gives a flowchart of the primary process of the program. The program starts with the creation and initialization of multiple buffers, including those for the vector field, cloud density, 3D noise textures, input control vectors, and the basis matrices used during interpolation. While shaping the volumetric clouds, the program will run the cloud generation kernel. The user can modify the vector field by adding or adjusting the input control vectors. The program will solve for the coefficients of the divergence-free vector field and update the buffer on the device. The user can change the cloud appearance in this kernel by modifying the noise parameters. The cloud's shape will be stored as a 3D density buffer on the device. The cloud density is advected based on the velocity values from the current vector field. The user can pause the advection calculation and rotate or scale the volume to observe it under different views.

The program generates two types of 3D textures to represent the cloud: a shape texture and a detail texture. The shape texture uses RGBA color channels, and its resolution is $128 \times 128 \times 128$. The basic shape of the clouds is sampled from the shape texture. The detail texture is a $32 \times 32 \times 32$ volume which includes Perlin noise and Worley noise in the color channels and is seamlessly repeatable, so that the user can scale it without limit. Both noise textures are copied to the device as CUDA textures.

Clouds are displayed by raycasting using a box as proxy geometry. If view ray intersects the box containing the volumetric clouds, the marching will proceed between the entry and exit points. For each step of the marching, the program will sample the shape and detail textures, and combine those values to obtain the density at the current point. The program will then cast a ray from the current point to the light source and to calculate the lighting. After lighting calculation, we check to see if the position has reached the exit point or the density is already opaque. If not, raymarching proceeds and density and lighting results are accumulated. If so, the marching is stopped, and the output color is written to the framebuffer.

Advection of the cloud texture, d, is performed as

$$d_{t+1}(\mathbf{p}) = d_t(\mathbf{p} - v_t(\mathbf{p})\Delta t) \tag{1}$$

at each point, $\mathbf{p}$, in the domain of d where v_t is the divergence-free dense texture field and Δt is the time step.

The interpolated vector field v is represented as a combination of divergence-free basis functions, $\Phi()$, each centered at the N scattered input vector locations,

$$v(\mathbf{p}) = \sum_{k=1}^{N} c_k \Phi(\epsilon||\mathbf{p} - \mathbf{p_k}||). \tag{2}$$

The coefficients, c_k, can be found by solving the linear system

$$\begin{bmatrix} \Phi(\epsilon||\mathbf{p_1} - \mathbf{p_1}||) & \Phi(\epsilon||\mathbf{p_1} - \mathbf{p_2}||) & \cdots & \Phi(\epsilon||\mathbf{p_1} - \mathbf{p_N}||) \\ \Phi(\epsilon||\mathbf{p_2} - \mathbf{p_1}||) & \Phi(\epsilon||\mathbf{p_2} - \mathbf{p_2}||) & \cdots & \Phi(\epsilon||\mathbf{p_2} - \mathbf{p_N}||) \\ \vdots & \vdots & \ddots & \vdots \\ \Phi(\epsilon||\mathbf{p_N} - \mathbf{p_1}||) & \Phi(\epsilon||\mathbf{p_N} - \mathbf{p_2}||) & \cdots & \Phi(\epsilon||\mathbf{p_N} - \mathbf{p_N}||) \end{bmatrix} \begin{bmatrix} c_1 \\ c_2 \\ \vdots \\ c_N \end{bmatrix} = \begin{bmatrix} \mathbf{V_1} \\ \mathbf{V_2} \\ \vdots \\ \mathbf{V_N} \end{bmatrix} \tag{3}$$

where $\mathbf{V_k}$ are the input vectors located at points $\mathbf{p_k}$. The equation for basis function, Φ can be found in [16], and the shape parameter ϵ can be chosen by the user. It represents the support of the basis functions, and should be smaller when input vectors are close together and larger when the inputs are more dispersed. It can be chosen interactively during design of the vector field. A visual indicator that ϵ should be larger is when the field decays to zero magnitude away from the inputs. The dense $3N \times 3N$ positive-definite linear system is solved using Cholesky decomposition each time the user interacts with the input vectors.

An issue we encountered during testing is that when two input vectors are near to each other, the interpolation result can blow up. The vector field's divergence is still minimized, but the vector magnitude may become very large, leading to extreme deformations of the cloud during advection. We clamp the maximum length of each vector to 2 voxels. We have also observed that the interpolated vector field may have some small nonzero divergence values at some locations with some specific inputs, so the resulting animation may not represent a perfectly incompressible flow. However, even when this occurs the result is still visually plausible.

4   Results

We performed preliminary tests on the vector field interpolation technique to assess the quality of the vector fields. Figure 3 shows an interpolation result in 2D. The input control vectors are shown in red and the dense divergence-free interpolated result is shown in blue. The dense vector field has the rotational flow characteristic of incompressible fluids, even though no simulation is performed. The effect of the shape parameter, ϵ, can be seen where the field magnitude becomes small far from the input vectors. While interacting with this 2D sample we found that since the field exactly interpolates the inputs we were able to direct flow at given locations exactly how we wanted. Away from the inputs the field may behave in unexpected ways, due to the creation of swirls and vortices in the flow. But this could be counteracted by adding additional control vectors in locations where a specific flow direction was desired.

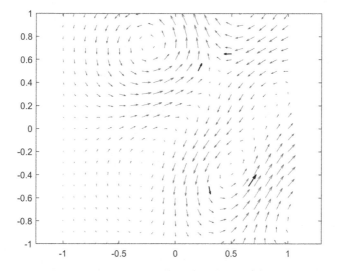

Fig. 3. Red vectors are the input vectors $\mathbf{V_k}$ at points $\mathbf{p_k}$, and blue vectors are the divergence-free interpolated result $v(\mathbf{p})$. (Color figure online)

Figure 4 shows the vector fields and cloud renderings during animation from two different interactive sessions. Our user interface allows the user to click and drag to place vectors on plane that may be positioned in the domain of the cloud texture. Existing vectors may be selected with the mouse to be deleted or dragged to change magnitude and direction.

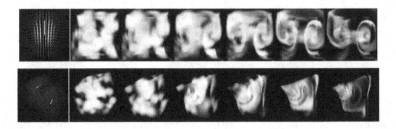

Fig. 4. Captures from two interactive sessions of cloud animation. The leftmost image shows the vector field and the remain images were captured during animation of the cloud.

Table 1 shows our system's performance with different buffer sizes on a PC with Intel Core i7-9700K 3.60 GHz CPU, 32 GB RAM and NVIDIA GeForce RTX 2080 SUPER. Increasing the vector field buffer size increases GPU memory usage, but at the largest size is well within the limits of modern videocards (10 to 12 GB). Larger buffer sizes decrease the framerate, mostly due to the increased number of calculations when advecting the cloud textures. At the highest resolution we do not achieve realtime performance, but user interaction is still possible at this framerate.

Table 1. Memory usage and framerate for several vector field buffer sizes.

VF buffer scale	FPS	GPU memory usage
$512 \times 512 \times 512$	11	4.2 GB
$256 \times 256 \times 256$	33	0.8 GB
$128 \times 128 \times 128$	>120	0.3 GB

5   Conclusion

In this work we have described our system for art-directable cloud animation. The problem addressed by this project is that a pure physics-based simulation of volumetric clouds can not provide a flexible controller to designers and animators in real-time. We used vector field interpolation with divergence minimization which we used to advect a cloud volume to produce a plausible cloud animation while giving artists control over the final result. In this research, the user can animate the shape of volumetric clouds using a few inputs. By adding and modifying input vectors, the user can interactively animate the clouds as they wish.

Our approach to uses a 3D interpolation vector field which is similar, in some respects, to the flow map approach previously used in 2D applications. The flow map uses physics-based algorithms and takes a much longer time to calculate, while the divergence-free interpolation we use is much faster. The output of these two processes are both textures storing vectors at each point and used to advect another texture to give the appearance of fluid. Though the animations produced by our system look plausible, the volumetric clouds are not conservative under the advection process. That means, for most interpolation vector fields, the total density of clouds inside the vector field will gradually decrease over time. In future work we will address these issues and explore other approaches to animating clouds and smoke using constraints to achieve physically-plausible motion.

References

1. Bauer, F.: Creating the atmospheric world of red dead redemption 2: a complete and integrated solution. In: SIGGRAPH 2019, SIGGRAPH Courses, June 2019
2. Schneider, A.: The real-time volumetric cloudscapes of horizon: zero dawn. In: SIGGRAPH 2015, SIGGRAPH Courses, August 2015
3. Dobashi, Y., Iwasaki, K., Yue, Y., Nishita, T.: Visual simulation of clouds. Vis. Inf. **1**(1), 1–8 (2017)
4. Stam, J.: Stable fluids. In: Proceedings of the 26th Annual Conference on Computer Graphics and Interactive Techniques, SIGGRAPH 1999, pp. 121–128 (1999)
5. Hong, J.-M., Kim, C.-H.: Controlling fluid animation with geometric potential. Comput. Anim. Virtual Worlds **15**(34), 147–157 (2004)
6. Dobashi, Y., Kusumoto, K., Nishita, T., Yamamoto, T.: Feedback control of cumuliform cloud formation based on computational fluid dynamics. ACM Trans. Graph. **27**(3), 1–8 (2008)
7. Treuille, A., McNamara, A., Popović, Z., Stam, J.: Keyframe control of smoke simulations. ACM Trans. Graph. **22**(3), 716–723 (2003)
8. McNamara, A., Treuille, A., Popović, Z., Stam, J.: Fluid control using the adjoint method. ACM Trans. Graph. **23**(3), 449–456 (2004)
9. Fattal, R., Lischinski, D.: Target-driven smoke animation. ACM Trans. Graph. **23**(3), 441–448 (2004)
10. Harris, M.J., Baxter, W.V., Scheuermann, T., Lastra, A.: Simulation of cloud dynamics on graphics hardware. In: Proceedings of the ACM SIG-GRAPH/EUROGRAPHICS Conference on Graphics Hardware, ser. HWWS 2003. Eurographics Association, San Diego (2003)
11. Alex, V.: Water flow in portal 2. In: SIGGRAPH 2019, SIGGRAPH Courses, July 2010
12. Simon, B.: Flowmap generator (2021). http://www.superpositiongames.com/products/flowmap-generator
13. Yassine, I., McGraw, T.: 4th order diffusion tensor interpolation with divergence and curl constrained Bézier patches. In: 2009 IEEE International Symposium on Biomedical Imaging: From Nano to Macro, pp. 634–637. IEEE (2009)
14. Yassine, I., McGraw, T.: A subdivision approach to tensor field interpolation. In: Workshop on Computational Diffusion MRI, pp. 117–124 (2008)
15. McNally, C.P.: Divergence-free interpolation of vector fields from point values— exact $\nabla \cdot B = 0$ in numerical simulations. Monthly Not. R. Astron. Soc.: Lett. **413**(1), L76–L80 (2011)
16. Mitrano, A.A., Platte, R.B.: A numerical study of divergence-free kernel approximations. Appl. Numer. Math. **96**, 94–107 (2015)

Physically Based Rendering of Simple Thin Volume Natural Nanostructures

Daljit Singh J. Dhillon[(⊠)]

School of Computing, Clemson University, Clemson, SC 29634, USA
djsingh@clemson.edu

Abstract. Thin volumes of semi-transparent nanostructures present on outer layers of organic embodiments often interact coherently with incident light waves to produce nuanced structural coloration. Such mechanisms are further complicated through incoherent scattering by accompanying micro-geometries. We present a simple physically based approach to directly use the sub-microscopic scans of quasi-periodic, one-dimensional modulations in such volumes to render them realistically. Our method relies on prior knowledge of quasi-periodicity to process the scan data in the Fourier space for recreating nuanced coloration effects. We demonstrate the working of our method with the actual scanned data of an egg-sac that shows coloration only when immersed in water. Proposed method can be used by bio-physicists for visual conformity of such mechanisms at a macro-scale as well as graphical rendering pipelines can employ it for scientific recreations or artistic renditions.

Keywords: Structural colors · Physically based rendering · Wave optics · Wave interference · Diffraction · Photonics · Natural phenomena · Sub surface scattering · Volumetric rendering

1 Introduction

Several natural surfaces are made up of organic matter consisting of thin, composite layers of translucent nanostructures (see Fig. 1). These thin-volumes exhibit a mix of coherent and incoherent interactions with the incident light waves. Many of these nanostructural compositions have geometric or statistical regularities to bring about stationary interference that result in magnificent, iridescent structural colors. Common examples include insect wings, bird feathers, animal or fruit skins and pearls. Devising photo-realistic models for reproducing their appearance characteristics is still largely an open research problem. Efficient computational methods find applications in domains ranging from computer graphics (VFX effects, animations, gaming) to scientific studies by bio-physicists and even in medicine.

In general, we need to solve Maxwell's equations to model the wave interactions under discussion for reproducing stationary interference patterns. More importantly, we need to represent and appropriately apply coherence spans (spatial as well as temporal) for the incident light over the nanostructural volumes

© Springer Nature Switzerland AG 2021
G. Bebis et al. (Eds.): ISVC 2021, LNCS 13017, pp. 400–413, 2021.
https://doi.org/10.1007/978-3-030-90439-5_32

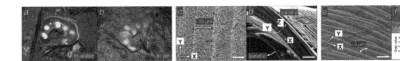

Fig. 1. Images showing structural coloration and microscopic scans for an egg-sac. Reproduced from [16] with permission from the Royal Society of Chemistry. (Color figure online)

to separate out the coherent and incoherent interactions for accurate modeling. Several methods such as those based on Kirchhoff integral theorem [4,5,7,12] and Harvey-Shack model for diffraction [3,6,8,15] have been proposed in existing literature to model simple diffraction mechanisms. Some even make good use of the spatial coherence properties of sunlight for photo-realistic reconstruction [4,15]. However, for complex volumes of nanostructures with varying optical properties, existing methods mainly rely on computationally expensive *finite difference time domain* (FDTD) based formulations [10] or full-blown light transport frameworks with coherence/phase propagation mechanism [11,13] for accurate reconstructions. Furthermore, evaluating such volumetric formulations involve an added challenge in generating or acquiring the volumetric data for natural compositions in order to model their nuanced light interactions accurately.

In this paper, we propose a physically based method to deal with a class of thin volume nanostructures that exhibit quasi-periodic modulations along a single dimension. Furthermore, these structures have a layered composition of similar modulations in each layer. The layering process may lend micro-geometric variations that cause incoherent light-scattering within the thin volume. This results in glossy specular highlights and blurring of the structural coloration patterns that emerge from coherent interference due to the nanostructural modulations. Our method uses prior information of the mean periodicity for the modulations to perform Fourier domain filtering of the structural information as explained later, in detail. It further accommodates multi-layer effects using simple image processing techniques. In summary, our main contribution in this paper is a novel physically based rendering method that: (a) adapts actual sub-microscopic scan data of a single representative layer, (b) for thin volumes with nanostructural layered modulations, (c) and simplifies application of Fourier optics to accurately reproduce their nuanced structural coloration, (d) at interactive speeds.

2   Thin Volume Nanostructures and Layer Surface Modulations

Thin volumetric nanostructural compositions may occur in several configurations. At a broader level, those are classified as 1D-, 2D- or 3D- photonic structures depending on the number of dimensions over which they exhibit observable modulations. In lack of any semblance of periodic modulations, they are generally referred to being stochastic. The most basic nanostructural compositions

402   D. S. J. Dhillon

are made up of a single layer that causes off-surface wave diffraction to produce structural colors. Such surfaces are easy to model. Unlike diffractive surfaces, thin volumes may be organized into multilayers of same or near similar structures. Furthermore, they may exhibit shape modulations with quasi periodicity along multiple dimensions to cause volumetric wave interactions and complex interference patterns. Apart from structural complexities, the material (optical) properties of the basic components in the composition may as well vary spatially. While one needs a generic implementation like an FDTD solver for an arbitrary composition, we can always exploit some prior knowledge about the overall structural layout to develop an efficient rendering model. With this generic strategy we devise a physically based model that can be used to render structural colors at interactive rates for thin volume nanostructures that satisfy the following criteria for its layout: (a) the whole thin volume is composed of basically the same material, (b) the volume is essentially laid out in multiple layers that are structurally similar to each other, (c) each layer exhibits quasi-periodic modulations at nanoscale, (d) the structure of an individual layer is available through scanning or construction, and (e) the range for quasi periodicities is known.

As a concrete example, we work with the data for an egg-sac (Hynobius Kimurae) provided by Zabuga et al. [16]. This egg-sac does not exhibit any structural coloration when placed in open air (see Fig. 1b). However, it shows nuanced blueish-green and greenish-yellow colors in peripheral regions when placed in water as shown in Fig. 1a. The egg-sac has a tubular structure and it is made up of translucent fibrous elements that are individually 2–5 μm thick and tightly packed into layers ranging in their depth from 350–1000 nm. The total thickness of the egg-sac is about 100 μm. We assign a local frame of reference to each surface point on the sac where the X-axis is tangential to the circular cross-section, the Y-axis runs along the sac length (top to bottom) and the Z-axis traverses the sac depth. A closer, microscopic examination performed by Zabuga et al. [16] using a *focused ion beam-scanning electron microscope* (FIB-SEM) scanner reveals the volumetric structure as shown in Fig. 2. They discuss the nano-structure with painstaking details. Importantly, each layer of fibrous composition exhibits fine, quasi-periodic folds. These folds vary spatially in their

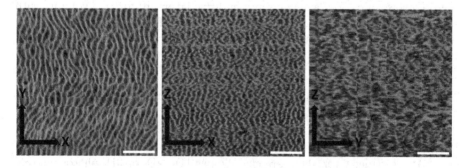

Fig. 2. Volumetric FIB-SEM scan slices for the egg-sac. White bar → 1 μm.

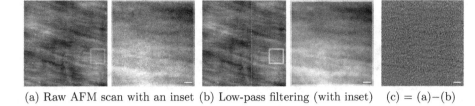

(a) Raw AFM scan with an inset (b) Low-pass filtering (with inset)   (c) = (a)−(b)

Fig. 3. An AFM scan of the inner surface of the egg-sac shown as a height-field. The grayscale for the inset images spans the height-range from 0–502 nm. (a) is the raw scan image. (b) Spatial low-pass filtering removes frequencies causing diffraction in the visible spectrum. (c) Spatially filtered nano-gratings.

mean periodicity from 170–230 nm. In this local frame of reference, the quasi-periodic 1D modulations are primarily oriented along the X-axis. An *atomic force microscope* (AFM) scan for the inner surface reveals these modulations as shown in Fig. 3.

3 Fourier Optics and Physically Based Rendering

For the type of quasi-periodic, multi-layer structures under discussion, we begin with the clarity that all layers are similar if not the same. We may thus think in terms of wave interference caused by these layers individually and the combined effect across them all. For natural compositions, the layers that lie close enough to cause coherent interactions, we found that such layers don't vary much structurally. We thus take an individual layer and consider it as the representative of local coherent wave interactions. This simplifies wave interference effects to be represented through a simple diffraction mechanism. This indeed is one of the main conclusions made by Zabuga et al. [16] in their detailed physical studies of such coloration effects in the case of egg-sacs. For diffraction caused by the roughness around a surface point, we can first measure and express surface bumps as a discretized height-field $h(x, y)$ in the local tangent plane at that point. We can then model the spectral *bidirectional reflectance distribution function* (BRDF) due to $h(x, y)$ with an application of Kirchhoff integral theorem [4,12].

For layers that are mutually incoherent, their local coherent interference patterns add up in the Fourier power space [16]. We study the net impact of this Fourier power accumulation on the distribution profile for the Fourier power of the phasor function for Kirchhoff integral. We do these studies using the actual FIB-SEM data for the egg-sac case. Next, we define an image processing technique to emulate those effects over the Fourier power distribution computed from the height-field data for an individual layer. This physically based approach for incoherent mixing of coherent interference effects across crudely separated layer-sets that is both a computational simplification as well a data-reduction step. We thus can use a single 2D AFM scan for acquiring nanostructural details instead of requiring a full-blown 3D volumetric scan.

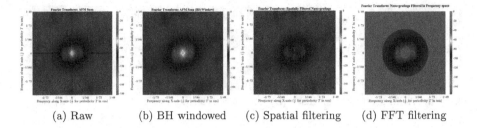

(a) Raw   (b) BH windowed   (c) Spatial filtering   (d) FFT filtering

Fig. 4. Extracting nanostructural gratings through frequency-domain filtering.

Next, we consider the incoherent scattering due to micro-geometric variations in the layer's height-field. They cause glossy specular highlights instead
of sharp mirror like reflections. Figure 1(a) shows few such glossy highlights, for
example. To this end, we propose to separate nano-structural variations from
the micro-structural variations in a layer and use an approach similar to [6].
Next, we empirically approximate an isotropic Beckmann distribution through
Blinn-Phong modeling of glossy reflectances due to micro-facets.

Finally, we model the incoherent scattering of the coherent diffractive coloration effects from lower layers as those reflections permeate through the micro-
faceted structuring of higher-up layers. Thinking in terms of layered interactions,
one may be motivated to accurately model these scatterings into a *bidirectional scattering distribution function* (BSDF). This would involve a convolution
between the specular *bidirectional transmittance distribution function* (BTDF)
and the diffractive BRDF forms [6]. In our method we propose using a simple
light cone to emulate this convolution for mixing the back-scattered diffraction
colors.

3.1   Proposed Method

We now present our proposed method in detail. Pseudo-code [1] gives the computational steps that a pixel shader needs to execute to render natural photonic
structures under discussion. While this code-block is sequential, initial three
steps and parameter estimation is performed in an offline manner to produce a
lookup texture that can be used as at runtime. This allows us to achieve interactive performance for our method. Next, we explain the key steps in our proposed
algorithm along with their application to the egg-sac case, in detail.

[STEP 1] Extracting Grating Structure. For the nanostructures under discussion, the key feature that result in nuanced appearances include natural mean-
derings of biologically laid out gratings that are quasi-periodic at large. Thus
the variations in the periodicity and local orientations lend a richer, natural
appearance to such compositions. To extract these features, we rely on prior
knowledge of the mean periodicity of the key grating structures and variance
in this periodicity measure. Using these two statistics, we devise a bandpass
filter in the frequency space. While spatial domain filtering may produce a visually convincing representation of the key grating structures, operating in the

---

Pseudo-Code 1. Pixel Shader for Natural Layered Photonics

Input:

(a) Measured discrete height-field $h(x, y)$, (b) Light and view directions ω_i and ω_o, respectively, (c) Mean and variance in 1D/2D quasi-periodicities T_{mean} and T_{var}, (d) Surface normal ω_N, (e) Half-vector ω_H, (f) Medium and material refractive indices $n1, n2$, respectively, and (g) Incident radiance $\mathbf{L}_R$ in RU units.

Initialize: $(u, v, w) = -(\omega_i + \omega_o)$.

Begin{Main}

—— {*Offline Processing*} ————————————————————————

   Begin{Extract grating structure }   ▷ See Section 3.1 Step(1) for details

  1. Compute bandpass filter $\mathcal{B}(\omega_u, \omega_v)$ in *Frequency Space* using T_{mean} and T_{var}.

  2. Filter height-field data in Frequency Space as: $\mathcal{H}_f(\omega_u, \omega_v) = \mathcal{B}(\omega_u, \omega_v) \cdot \mathfrak{F}\{h(x, y)\}(\omega_u, \omega_v)$

   End

   Begin{Model surface diffractions with first-order approximations and a coherence window $\mathcal{W}$, See [4]}

     $\mathbf{D}^\lambda(\omega_i, \omega_o) = |(\mathcal{W} * \mathcal{H}_f)(u/\lambda, v/\lambda)|^2$ ▷ ω_i:light direction,ω_o:view direction, λ: light wavelength

   End

   Begin{Consolidate multi-layer interference effects}   ▷ See Section 3.1 Step(2) for details

  1. Set blurr filter $\mathcal{M}(\omega_u, \omega_v)$

  2. Compute $\mathbf{D}_m^\lambda(\omega_i, \omega_o) = (\mathcal{M} * \mathbf{D}^\lambda)(u/\lambda, v/\lambda)$

   End—— {*Of Offline Processing*} ————————————————————

   Begin{Model specular highlight}   ▷ See Section 3.1 Step(3) for details

  1. Use (a) Blinn-Phong model or (b) Fit an isotropic Beckmann distribution for a micro-faceted

    specular BRDF: $\mathbf{S}(\omega_i, \omega_o) = (\omega_N \cdot \omega_H)^n$ or $\mathbf{S}(\omega_i, \omega_o) = \frac{\exp(-\tan^2\alpha/\tan^2\theta)}{\pi\tan^2\theta\cos^4\alpha}$, where $\alpha = \arccos(\omega_N \cdot \omega_H)$

   End

   Begin{Incorporate incoherent scattering of diffraction colors due to microfacet geometry} ▷ Sec.3.1 Step(4)

  1. Estimate a Box blurr filter for light directions $\mathcal{G}(\omega_u, \omega_v)$ corresponding to $\mathbf{S}(\omega_i, \omega_o)$

  2. Compute $\mathbf{D}_g^\lambda(\omega_i, \omega_o) = (w/\lambda)^2(\mathcal{G} * \mathbf{D}_m^\lambda)(u/\lambda, v/\lambda)$ by sampling the light cone

   End

   Begin{Perform spectral rendering to compute pixel intensities}

  1. Perform Fresnel factor using Schlick's approximation $\mathbf{F}_{\text{raw}} = R_0 + (1 - R_0)(1 - \cos\theta_i)^5$, where $R_0 = (n_2 - n_1)^2/(n_2 + n_1)^2$, θ_i is the incident angle.

  2. Normalize $F = F_{\text{raw}}/(R_0 \cdot w \cdot w)$ to work with relative units (RU) for radiance. ▷ See [4] for details.

  3. Estimate geometric attenuation $\mathbf{G}(\omega_i, \omega_o)$ including a Cook-Torrance shadowing function

  4. Set CIE-X,-Y,-Z color matching functions $C_i(\lambda)$, where $i \in \{X, Y, Z\}$

  5. Set $D65$ spectral power distribution as $\mathbf{I}(\lambda)$

  6. Compute pixel color in CIE-X,Y,Z color space as: $\mathbf{P}_i(\omega_i, \omega_o) = \int_\Omega \mathbf{L}_R(\omega_i) \cos\theta_i d\omega_i \int_\lambda \mathbf{I}(\lambda)\mathbf{C}_i(\lambda)(\mathbf{F} \cdot \mathbf{G} \cdot (\mathbf{S} + \mathbf{D}_g^\lambda))(\omega_i, \omega_o)d\lambda$

  7. Tone-map and gamma-correct pixel colors

   End

End

---

frequency space is critical. For example, the FFT for spatially filtered grating structures shown in Fig. 3c still contains low frequency components as shown in Fig. 4c. Clearly, applying first-order approximations as used by [14] will result in systematic errors. We hypothesize that for the photonic thin-volumes of natural origin such lower frequency components that are far removed from the quasi-periodic frequency bands could in general be ineffective in producing stationary interference and need discounting. This hypothesis holds true for cases like the egg-sac. It is confirmed visually with the lack of any coloration while the sac is in air and through detailed physical experiments on it by Zabuga et al. [16]. For the representative case-study of the egg-sac, using mean periodicity $\mu = 230$ nm and standard deviation $\sigma = +/- 72$ nm, we devise a frequency-domain, bandpass filter $\mathcal{B}$ with the pass-band $[\mu - \sigma, \mu + \sigma]$ radially. Figure 4d shows the filtered frequency response $\mathcal{H}_f$ for the egg-sac case. Using $\mathcal{H}_f$ as the first and only Fourier term in Equations (6) and (8) from [4] results in first-order approximation for diffraction effects from an individual layer as shown in Fig. 5b for the egg-sac data. Next,we look at consolidating these coloration effects across multiple layers.

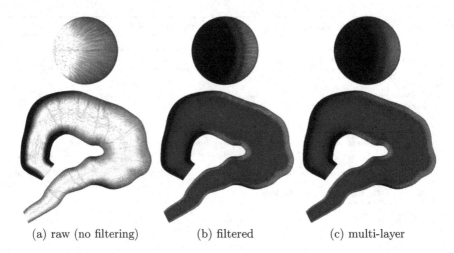

| (a) raw (no filtering) | (b) filtered | (c) multi-layer |

Fig. 5. Rendering structural colors for the egg-sac with differently filtered height-fields. Filtered FFT is used in a spectral BRDF formulation [4]. Top row shows example BRDF slices for the light source at a grazing angle along X-axis. Refer to Sect. 4 (*Setup*) for more information on BRDF slices.

[STEP 2] Consolidate Coherent Interference from Multiple Layers.
For accumulating interference effects across multiple layers, we make note of two practical considerations: (a) for two layers close enough to cause coherent light wave interactions, their height-field profiles are very similar, and (b) for two layers that are far removed to cause coherent inter-layer light interactions, the spectral power distributions from their individual interference patterns add up to produce net effects like any two co-located, non-coherent light interaction events. For the class of photonic structures that have slow varying, 1D/2D quasi periodic layer surface modulations, both of the above assumptions hold true. These two assumptions also form the basis for the statistical analysis put to use in the actual physical experiments by [16]. With these two assumptions we are able to formulate a strategy for modeling multi-layer coherent interactions effectively. We assume that the whole volumetric mass can be approximated by non-overlapping slabs where the adjacent slabs only cause incoherent wave-interactions. Secondly, for each slab we assume that a single representative layer can be used to estimate the diffraction effects caused by the entire slab. These assumptions do not hold true in general. However, for the modulations that vary very slowly across the depth dimension, [16] empirically found these assumptions to be consistent with their physical experiments. In our method, we make use of the fact that the adjacent slabs are progressively but only slightly differing in their structural composition while remaining within the same range of quasi-periodic bandwidth. It implies that the Fourier transforms of the representative layers for individual slabs do not change much in the critical frequency band and adding up the resulting power spectrums is akin to low-pass filtering of the Fourier transform of an individual representative layer. We thus consolidate the

net effect of multiple layers by simply filtering the power distribution in the frequency space. See Pseudo-Code [1] and Sect. 4 for further details.

[**STEP 3**] **Model Microfacet-Based Glossy Specular Highlight: S.** With the filtering process used in STEP_1 all micro-scale variations are removed from the height-field. [6] suggest that the micro-geometric and nano-geometric effects can be modeled separately and then superimposed in a BRDF. We note that for the achromatic, incoherent scattering behavior of our class of photonic structures, each individual layer is statistically similar and thus either of them is a good enough representative for the entire volume. We empirically fit a Blinn-Phong model to model the specular highlights.

[**STEP 4**] **Accommodate Incoherent Scattering of Structural Colors.** In one last final step, we take care of the nanostructural coloration effects getting modulated by the micro-structures. Since the extracted nano-structures are maneuvered by the underlying micro-structures, the diffraction colors arising from coherent scattering in the underlying layers are expected to undergo incoherent scattering as the diffracted light waves pass through the upper layers. As a simple method to accommodate these cascaded, mixed scattering events, we can expect the convolution of the achromatic, specular BRDF model $\mathbf{S}$ with the spectral diffractive coloration BRDF $\mathbf{D}_m^\lambda$ to suffice. To keep things even simpler, we instead emulate a low-pass filter kernel $\mathcal{G}$ that approximates $\mathbf{S}$ and convolve $\mathcal{G}$ with $\mathbf{D}_m^\lambda$.

4   Experiments and Results

In this section we present our various experiments for the filtering steps discussed in the previous section. We share the final implementation details that work the best and demonstrate the working of our method with the rendering results.

Implementation Details. Most of the implementation details are presented in the Pseudo-Code 1 for the pixel shader. Here we note that the diffraction BRDF is normalized to just saturate the reflectance from the perfectly planar surface of the same base material when viewed opposite to the surface normal with the light placed at the camera origin. This requires the incident light radiance to be expressed on a scale relative to this normalization step. We adopt the same nomenclature of expressing light intensity in RU or relative units as done by Dhillon et al. [4]. Likewise, for subjective comparability, we scale all final filtered FFT forms to have equal average power in the frequency band $\mu \pm \sigma$ for the mean periodicity μ and periodicity standard deviation σ. We use the total Fourier spectral power in the same band for a perfectly circular grating with periodicity same as given μ as the reference for scaling. We prefilter all height-fields with a Blackman-Harris window to avoid windowing artifacts in the renderings. The height-field patch for the egg-sac is about 72×72 microns at a resolution of 3000×3000 pixels. We use the spatial coherence length with its *full width at half maximum* (FWHM) set at $65\,\mu m$ for the sunlight [9].

We perform spectral integration at runtime with a sampling of 3–10 nm for most results.

Setup. Unless specified otherwise, we place a point light at the camera center itself for rendering surfaces. The tubular egg-sac is about 2 cm thick and 12.5 cm long. Its medial axis was traced in the reference image to reconstruct the surface mesh by hand. It is viewed from a close shot with the field of view of about 2°. The actual egg-sac is translucent. However, since our main focus in on iridescent back-scattering, we simply the setup by assuming that it has an opaque base. Unless specified otherwise, we assume that the surface is submerged in water and use its refractive index $n = 1.33$ to shift the visible spectrum for computing correct diffraction effects. We show BRDF slices with fixed incident light directions ω_i as circular maps. The disk center corresponds to the view direction being fronto-parallel to the surface $\theta_o = 0$ for ω_0. Each point on the map represents a view direction. The radial distance from this disk center to any point the map equals the sine of the angle for the view direction ($\sin \theta_0$) for that point. Also, the angle between the radial vector for that point and the X-axis equals the azimuth angle ϕ_o for the view direction represented at that point.

Experiments with Grating Approximations. We tried few simple experiments to study if the natural gratings can be reduced to some standard form. Using the known mean periodicity of $\mu = 190$ nm, we devised two regular gratings: (a) a 1D horizontal grating, and (b) a radial grading. We constructed their corresponding diffraction BRDFs and rendered the egg-sac geometry with it. Resulting BRDF maps are empty except for the specular highlight when the surrounding medium is air. Changing the medium to water only shows coloration in backscattering when the incident light is closer to the grazing angles. The light source for the BRDF slices shown in Fig. 6 is set horizontally at a grazing angle along the X-axis. For 1D grating, the scattered coloration is limited to only few view directions. As seen in Fig. 6a, it fails to produce any remarkable pattern over the egg-sac surface. A circular 2D grating produces back-scattered colors in a much larger range of view directions. It produces coloration in the peripheral regions for the egg-sac that are consistent with the photograph in Fig. 1a. However, the colors in Fig. 6b are too well-resolved and lack any nuances. Actual image shows meandered mixing of multiple wavelengths. We also changed the grating periodicity to 225 nm to match the variations in the inner curvature for the egg-sac. Figure 6c shows that doing so produces a greater range of visible colors when the specimen is in water. However, it lacks in wavelength mixing as well. We thus conclude that such simple structures cannot produce visually convincing renderings. The model needs to represent and use the large variations in natural gratings to produce realistic appearances. In our method, we are able to directly process the AFM height-fields for computing the diffraction part of the BRDF response as shown in Fig. 5c.

Experiments with the Bandpass Filtering Kernel $\mathcal{B}$. As discussed in Sect. 3.1 we need to filter the height-field $h(x, y)$ to extract the gratings. The importance of this step is discussed here along with several different kernels for

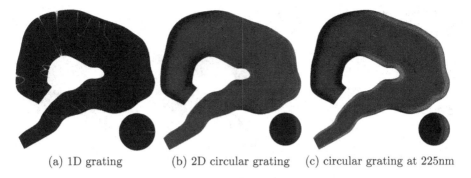

(a) 1D grating   (b) 2D circular grating   (c) circular grating at 225nm

Fig. 6. Experiments with regular gratings as height-fields (Insets: BRDF slices).

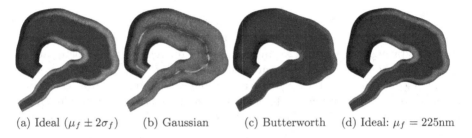

(a) Ideal ($\mu_f \pm 2\sigma_f$)   (b) Gaussian   (c) Butterworth   (d) Ideal: $\mu_f = 225$nm

Fig. 7. Experiments with the frequency domain filtering $\mathcal{B}$. Radial forms of ideal, Gaussian and Butter-worth bandpass filters were devised with lower and upper cut-off frequencies derived from the mean periodicity μ and its variance σ^2. (Color figure online)

the filter $\mathcal{B}$. Figure 5a shows that the raw data does not produce any similarity to the observed coloration effects when used directly in our method. Removing lower frequencies is impervious to coloration from the gratings. Also, not removing frequencies higher than those in the bandwidth defined by the mean periodicity μ and its standard deviation σ can produce unwanted visual artifacts. We thus device bandpass filters using known μ and σ statistics for the given height-field and apply them in Fourier space. We experimented with three different types of bandpass filters, namely: Ideal, Gaussian and Butterworth filters and our results are illustrated in Figs. 5 and 7. Figure 5b shows that an ideal filter with the bandwidth $\mu \pm \sigma$ provides good separation and coloration starts to resemble with observations. Although, the renderings are not soft enough and significant amount of streaking is produced. We increased the bandwidth to $\mu \pm 2\sigma$ but this causes the streaks to spread out unwantedly to adjacent regions (see Fig. 7a). Using a Gaussian filter with the lower cut-off corresponding to time-period $T = \mu + \sigma$ and the higher cut-off set at $T = \mu - \sigma$ fails completely. A Butterworth filter with the same stop-band works far better (Fig. 7c). However, its results are visually similar to those for the ideal filter as it does not extract any more useful information from the natural gratings that we work with.

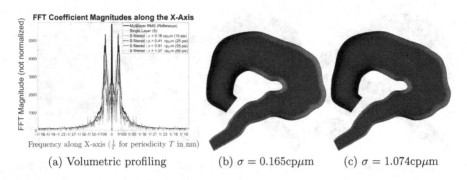

(a) Volumetric profiling   (b) $\sigma = 0.165\text{cp}\mu\text{m}$ (c) $\sigma = 1.074\text{cp}\mu\text{m}$

Fig. 8. Experiments with the Gaussian kernel ($\mathcal{M}$) used in blurring of the frequency spectrum for consolidating multi-layer coherent scattering.

We thus resolve to use the simpler ideal filter in our pipeline. Figure 7d shows that for gratings with $\mu = 225$ nm we notice stronger yellowish colors at the egg-sac peripheries. This is the desired coloration for the inner curvature of the actual egg-sac which had a larger μ [16]. While extracting the gratings from a single layer works in principle, it shows a lot of color streaking. This is understandable as we know that the combined effect of multiple layers produces softer color mixes over the egg-sac surface.

Experiments with the Frequency-Space Blurring Kernel $\mathcal{M}$. As discussed in Sect. 3.1, we convolve the frequency spectrum magnitudes with a blurring kernel to consolidate for the variations and mixing in coherent interference coloration effects arising from different layers. To study these effects, we first used the volumetric data for the egg-sac. Slices of this data set are depicted in Fig. 2. We first compute the root-mean-squared (RMS) Fourier term magnitudes across all the $X - Y$ slices. The black solid curve in Fig. 8a shows this RMS Fourier spectral magnitude for the frequencies along the reference X-axis. The smoothness of this curve confirms structural similarity across the layers. Also, the peak seen at $f_s = \frac{1}{172}$ nm^{-1} for the FIB-SEM sample, which shrinked due to scanning preparation processes, is equivalent to $\frac{1}{210}$ nm^{-1} for the living specimen. This peak is consistent and close enough to the mean grating period $T = 230$ nm for the outer curvature of the egg-sac (see [16] for details). Also, we use the volumetric data only to guide our multilayer related filtering process and not in the actual renderings. Next, we compute and show a similar curve for an individual layer in red color, in the same plot. Both the curves have similar profiles overall. The red curve has many exaggerated fluctuations that result in color streaking as seen in Fig. 7. We perform low-pass Gaussian filtering of the red curve with different σ_m values and smoother curves are shown in green, blue, magenta and orange colors. For $\sigma_m = 0.91$cpμm, the (magenta) curve profile better matches with the reference (black). However, it is significantly lower in its peak and lack consolidated local fluctuations seen in the reference (black) curve. For, $\sigma_m = 0.41$cpμm, the filtered (blue) profile tames and retains these local fluctuations while maintaining the peak at a reasonable high. Deriving similar Gaussian filtering parameters from this study, we filtered the Fourier spectral magnitudes for the AFM height-field data and used resulting filtered FFTs $\mathcal{M} * \mathbf{D}^\lambda$ in rendering experiments. Figures 8b,c show softer color mixing due to such filtering. These renderings are photo-realistically much closer to observations. We found no significant advantage in using a Gaussian kernel $\mathcal{M}$ with $\sigma_m > 0.41 \text{cp}\mu\text{m}$ and thus resolved to use this empirical value in our method. Finally, we note that filtering with $\mathcal{M}$ leaks some energy outside the stop-band for the filter $\mathcal{B}$. So we repeat bandpass filtering with $\mathcal{B}$ after this step.

Experiments with the Incoherent Scattering Model. For the specular highlight due to incoherent scattering, we fall-back to the empirical equivalence established between the Blinn-Phong NDFs and the Beckmann distribution to be used in a standard Cook-Torrance formulation for $\mathbf{S}$ (refer to Fig. 9.36 in the book Real-Time Rendering by Akenine-Möller et al. [2]). For the Blinn-Phong kernel, an exponent n between 250–2000 works well for the structures under consideration. We empirically set it to 500 for the egg-sac.

Also, to model the convolution between $\mathbf{S}$ and $\mathbf{D}_g^\lambda$ we use a screen-space approach by modeling the incident light with an elliptic cone. The span for the light cone along the incident plane is scaled to vary the projection of the light direction along the surface normal by a fixed proportion $p\%$. Similarly, the cone spans the off-plane perpendicular to the incident plane (while containing the light direction vector) to vary the projection of the light direction along the surface tangent-plane by a fixed proportion $p\%$. Apart from the original light direction, we draw 6 samples along the incident plane and 6 samples along the off-plane within the light cone. Setting p at 30% gave us the best smoothing of the remnant color streaks from the previous steps. Figure 9 shows the output of our incoherent scattering model for the egg-sac along side the actual photo. We positioned the specimen and the point light in the renderings as best to match the impressions from the photo. The photo has multiple light source while we use a single light source. Yet, the level of softness and color gamut for the back-scattered diffractions are subjectively similar between the rendering and the image. The specular highlights and the peripheral color bands occur in similar regions over the surface. We rendered the same specimen with several other positions, orientations, with alpha blending for a diffuse component and also with a different mean periodicity $T = 230 \, \text{nm}$. The renderings are shown in Fig. 9c.

Performance. We performed several runtime performance tests for our method on a Windows Surface Note Book 2 with an NVIDIA GPU GeForce GTX1050. It has a display memory (VRAM) of 1979MB and shared memory of 8150MB. We animated images similar to those in Fig. 9(c) including diffuse color blending and all the filtering steps discussed above and bench-marked performances using FRAPS [1]. Except for: (a) the spectral computations at a resolution of 10–50 nm, and (b) the screen-space light cone sampling with 13 samples, rest of the filtering operations are done offline for this exercise. Our display screen spanned a resolution of 2000×3000 pixels. With a simple rectangular animated object

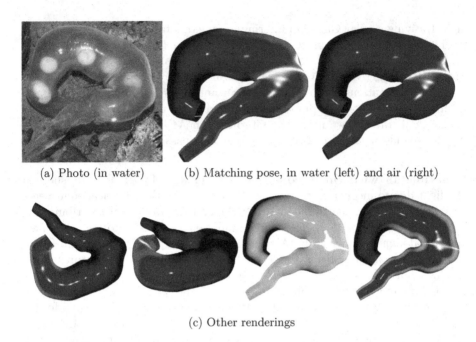

(a) Photo (in water)   (b) Matching pose, in water (left) and air (right)

(c) Other renderings

Fig. 9. Final rendering results with all filtering steps incorporated in the method.

spanning between 800 × 600 sub-window, at spectral sampling of 50 nm, we achieved an average performance of 10.12 fps. With a resolution of 1300 × 900 pixels it dropped to 5.44 fps. With the spectral sampling rate of 10 nm it further dropped to 3.88 fps. For the egg-sac surface at the resolution of 1800 × 1600 it performed at about 2 fps. Here we note Dhillon et al. [4] use pre-computed lookup tables to collapse the spectral rendering integral. We claim that with their proposed pre-computations for our data, our method can perform in realtime.

5   Conclusion

In this paper, we have presented a physically based method for rendering simple thin-volume photonic structures on natural surfaces. Our method, employs separation of nano-gratings from the micro-geometries through frequency domain filtering of the nanostructures represented as height-fields. Our method consolidates the incoherent mixing of coherently scattered coloration effects from multiple layers with a simple low-pass filtering of Fourier domain magnitudes. We further model incoherent scattering of diffracted colors by the micro-geometries using simple light cones. We demonstrated the working of our method with an actual AFM scan of an example data set. Our method produces photo-realistic softness and gamut for the reference nanostructures. We also show that our method works interactively and can be further optimized for performance. Also, adapting our method for importance sampling will be an interesting challenge for future. More importantly, we would like to adapt our proposed method to work with far more complex thin-volume surfaces or tubular compositions through efficient application of spatio-temporal light coherence properties and volumetric processing of microscopically acquired data for them.

Acknowledgments. I thank Prof. Milinkovitch, Ms. Arrigo and Dr. Zabuga from Univ. of Geneva (https://www.lanevol.org) for providing microscopic scans. I thank them along with Prof. M. Zwicker (UMD) and Dr. A. Ghosh (ICL) for having valuable discussions relating to this work. This work was partly supported by SNSF Early Postdoc. Mobility Fellowship P2BEP2 165343 and partly by NSF Grant No. 2007974.

References

1. Frames-per-second benchmarking tool (FRAPS) v3.5.99 (2021). http://www.fraps.com/. Accessed 14 Aug 2021
2. Akenine-Möller, T., Haines, E., Hoffman, N., Pesce, A., Iwanicki, M., Hillaire, S.: Real-Time Rendering, 4th edn. A.K. Peters Ltd, USA (2018)
3. Belcour, L., Barla, P.: A practical extension to microfacet theory for the modeling of varying iridescence. ACM Trans. Graph. (TOG) **36**(4), 1–14 (2017)
4. Dhillon, D.S., Teyssier, J., Single, M., Gaponenko, I., Milinkovitch, M.C., Zwicker, M.: Interactive diffraction from biological nanostructures. Comput. Graph. Forum **33**(8), 177–188 (2014)
5. He, X.D., Torrance, K.E., Sillion, F.X., Greenberg, D.P.: A comprehensive physical model for light reflection. ACM, New York (1991)
6. Holzschuch, N., Pacanowski, R.: A two-scale microfacet reflectance model combining reflection and diffraction. ACM Trans. Graph. (TOG) **36**(4), 1–12 (2017)
7. Levin, A., et al.: Fabricating BRDFS at high spatial resolution using wave optics. ACM Trans. Graph. (TOG) **32**(4), 1–14 (2013)
8. Löw, J., Kronander, J., Ynnerman, A., Unger, J.: BRDF models for accurate and efficient rendering of glossy surfaces. ACM Trans. Graph. **31**(1), 1–14 (2012)
9. Mashaal, H., Goldstein, A., Feuermann, D., Gordon, J.M.: First direct measurement of the spatial coherence of sunlight. Opt. Lett. **37**(17), 3516–3518 (2012)
10. Musbach, A., Meyer, G., Reitich, F., Oh, S.H.: Full wave modelling of light propagation and reflection. In: CGF, vol. 32, pp. 24–37 (2013)
11. Oh, S.B., Kashyap, S., Garg, R., Chandran, S., Raskar, R.: Rendering wave effects with augmented light field. In: CGF, vol. 29, pp. 507–516 (2010)
12. Stam, J.: Diffraction shaders. In: Proceedings of the 26th Annual Conference on Computer Graphics and Interactive Techniques, SIGGRAPH 1999, pp. 101–110. ACM Press/Addison-Wesley Publishing Co., USA (1999)
13. Steinberg, S., Yan, L.Q.: A generic framework for physical light transport. ACM Trans. Graph. (TOG) **40**(4), 1–20 (2021)
14. Toisoul, A., Ghosh, A.: Practical acquisition and rendering of diffraction effects in surface reflectance. ACM Trans. Graph. **36**(5), 1–16 (2017)
15. Werner, S., Velinov, Z., Jakob, W., Hullin, M.B.: Scratch iridescence: wave-optical rendering of diffractive surface structure. ACM Trans. Graph. (TOG) **36**(6), 1–14 (2017)
16. Zabuga, A.V., et al.: Translucent in air and iridescent in water: structural analysis of a salamander egg sac. Soft Matter **16**(7), 1714–1721 (2020)

Deep Tiling: Texture Tile Synthesis Using a Constant Space Deep Learning Approach

Vasilis Toulatzis and Ioannis Fudos[(⊠)]

University of Ioannina, Ioannina, Greece
{vtoulatz,fudos}@cse.uoi.gr

Abstract. Texturing is a fundamental process in computer graphics. Texture is leveraged to enhance the visualization outcome for a 3D scene. In many cases a texture image cannot cover a large 3D model surface because of its small resolution. Conventional techniques like repeating, mirroring or clamping to edge do not yield visually acceptable results. Deep learning based texture synthesis has proven to be very effective in such cases. All deep texture synthesis methods that attempt to create larger resolution textures are limited in terms of GPU memory resources. In this paper, we propose a novel approach to example-based texture synthesis by using a robust deep learning process for creating tiles of arbitrary resolutions that resemble the structural components of an input texture. In this manner, our method is firstly much less memory limited owing to the fact that a new texture tile of small size is synthesized and merged with the existing texture and secondly can easily produce missing parts of a large texture.

Keywords: Texture synthesis · Deep learning

1 Introduction

Texture synthesis aims at generating a new texture such that its resolution and structure are appropriate for using it on wrapping a 3D model. Texture expansion plays a cardinal role in many applications where a large texture is required. Games along side with Geographic Information System (GIS) apps are such cases in which large unbounded resolution textures are needed. In addition, the same applies not only for diffuse textures but also for specular, normal, bump and height maps.

Structure similarity with the original input texture is one of the most investigated topics on texturing. Many texture synthesis methods aim at expanding a

---

This work has been co-financed by the European Union (European Regional Development Fund-ERDF) and Greek national funds through the Interreg Greece Albania 2014–2020 Program (project VirtuaLand).

G. Bebis et al. (Eds.): ISVC 2021, LNCS 13017, pp. 414–426, 2021.
https://doi.org/10.1007/978-3-030-90439-5_33

texture and usually on doubling its width and height. However, they simultaneously introduce an increased consumption of memory resources which severely restricts its scalability. To this end, many such methods end up on running on CPU without leveraging the power and speed of GPU. Consequently, memory efficiency is a key factor for texture synthesis and expansion.

Example-based texture synthesis techniques employ deep learning based optimization processes that seek larger resolution textures that resemble an input texture. Such methods by targeting on producing synthesized images of larger resolution textures [17,19] do not have the capacity to create smaller or arbitrary resolution textures. Tiling is the only alternative for building arbitrary texture images. Therefore, tiling texture synthesis [2,6,7], is not only capable of synthesizing larger textures but also a novel way of constructing step by step a brand-new texture or for completing missing parts of a larger texture.

In this work, we propose a new texture synthesis approach that follows the aforementioned procedure. Thus, our method is capable of generating new tiles that match structurally and have the same morphology with the original input texture. We utilize a space invariant deep neural network to produce a new tile that can be used to expand the original texture. Subsequently our system builds a new texture of arbitrary shape and size by artificially synthesizing tiles in any direction by using constant memory.

2   Related Work

2.1   Texture Synthesis

Texture synthesis is a field of research that has drawn the attention of researchers for many years. Starting from simple ideas of tiling patterns and stochastic models to state of the art techniques based on exemplars all of them aim to produce new synthetic visually acceptable textures.

The most effective approaches have proven to be example-based methods that employ deep learning approaches [8], optimization-based techniques [12], pixel-based [5,18] and patch-based methods [4,13].

Expanding texture synthesis is the most challenging among the texture synthesis goals. Therefore, several techniques that aim at expanding texture synthesis have been developed [10,19]. The most recent ones rely on deep learning by producing remarkable results on expanding and even for super-resolution texture synthesis [14]. By using Convolutional Neural Networks (CNNs) of many layers [17] or Generative Adversarial Networks (GANs) [6,19] these methods correlate image features to produce a new synthesized high resolution texture map and constitute the state-of-the-art methods on texture expansion. Nevertheless, except for their efficacy on visually acceptable results they do have some limitations like memory consumption and a very restricted either on the way of new texture shapes are generated [19] (fixed new texture dimensions) or on adding new patterns not included in the input image [6] (huge data-set of images that contain different patterns) which in some cases is not the intention on texture expansion.

Another work utilizing a Generative Adversarial Network (GAN) trained to expand a texture in a uniform manner is [9]. On the other hand, there are optimization techniques like Self Tuning [3,13], which is a method that extends texture optimization, that accomplish visually acceptable results.

2.2 Texture Tiling

The drawback of the aforementioned approaches is the large requirement of memory resources that makes them unsuitable for GPUs. To this end, tiling seems to be the only viable approach for synthesizing large textures.

One of the simplest texture design techniques is repeating tile patterns such that the produced texture does not include seams. Moreover, methods generating stochastic tiles have been developed [2,7] for the same purpose. However, texture tiling is still an open field of research in terms of increasing texture resolution without considerable performance downgrade.

Thus, tiling forms a new challenge for texture synthesis and deep learning methods have already started being used to this end. Their main advantage is the capability of synthesizing new textures that are not repeated. Instead, they use one or more original input textures and produce random texture tiles in any direction matching the original structure. One recent work that focuses on creating high resolution texture tiles is [6]. This work introduces an approach to homogenizing texture tiles outputs of GANs trained on lower resolution textures to produce a high resolution texture with no seam artifacts by using Markov Random Fields (MRF). However, this method has very high GPU memory space requirements making it inappropriate for medium GPU configurations.

3 Deep Texture Tiling

The main issue of most of state-of-the-art methods is memory consumption that is a key factor both on computation but also hardware cost which is more obvious on using GPU for texture synthesis. To this end, we are focusing on creating smaller textures that are merged together to form a new synthesized texture of greater size but with respect on keeping the seamless manner of expanding in every direction with new tiles.

We propose a novel algorithm for synthesizing tiles by extending the fundamental work by [8] on neural texture synthesis. In general, by leveraging the power of a CNN of multiple layers we extract and correlate feature maps across layers of two instances of a VGG19 [15] network given two different resolution textures in each network. Our algorithm has the ability to synthesize texture tiles in a seamless manner by optimizing the distance of feature maps across the layers of our model by using as input textures the original and a new white noise tile merged with the original texture towards a specific orientation (up, down, right, left tiling).

Consequently, we embrace the main idea of deep texture synthesis but we abandon the specific size expansion and replace it with tiling. More specifically,

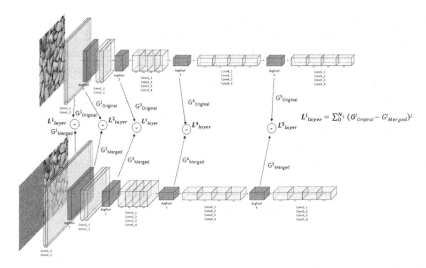

Fig. 1. Deep texture tiling: G^l_{layer} is the Gram Matrice of feature maps in layer l which depends on the number of filters N_l. The network structure adopted is VGG19 [15] by changing $MaxPooling$ layers to $AvgPooling$ layers. This figure is generated by PlotNeuralNet (https://github.com/HarisIqbal88/PlotNeuralNet) and then modified.

we correlate feature spaces targeting to produce similar representations across network layers. On the first network we forward the original image while on the second network we utilize two user input tiling factors for width and height for a new white noise tile creation that is forwarded along with the original as a merged input texture.

To capture correlations among network layers we extract their feature space representation F^l_{li} of a general feature map $F^l \in R^{n_f \times vs_f}$, where l is a layer having n_f filters of size vs_f reshaped into one dimensional vectors. This is achieved by the use of Gram Matrices:

$$G^l_{rc} = \sum_i F^l_{ki} F^l_{li} \tag{1}$$

The total layer loss is the sum of all layer losses that are computed as the mean squared displacement of the Gram Matrices of the two VGG19 instances. As a consequence, the total loss function is defined as follows:

$$L_{total}(I_{original}, I_{merged}) = \sum_{l=1}^{N^L} \frac{w^l}{4n_f^{l\,2} vs_f^{l\,2}} \sum (G^l_{original} - G^l_{merged})^2 \tag{2}$$

where $I_{original}$ is the original texture and I_{merged} is a white noise texture merged with the original one having been forwarded to our system as described above and N^L is the number of contributory layers. The whole process and the layers contributing to the total loss function are shown in Fig. 1. We correlate feature representations along *layer*1, *pool*1, *pool*2, *pool*3, *pool*4 and the corresponding weight setting for every layer contributory factor is $\frac{1}{5}$.

In some texture input cases the output of our method produces some noise in the boundaries of the original and deep generated tile. Therefore, we have developed an additional preprocessing phase we call Seam Removal in which we attempt to vanish the seam effect of deep texture tiling method. In the noise part of the second network instance (*Merged* in Fig. 1) instead of using a simple noise we utilize a mirrored version of the input original texture and then we apply noise that increases exponentially based on the distance of each column from the seam. Specifically, every pixel for the *Merged* part of our model is computed as:

$$Noise(i,j) = w_1 Original(i, width - j - i) + w_2 RandomColor \qquad (3)$$

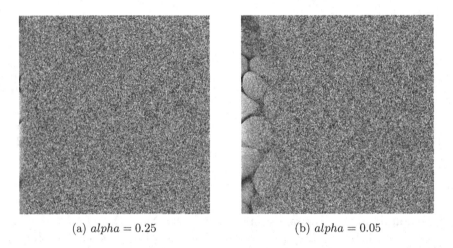

(a) *alpha* = 0.25   (b) *alpha* = 0.05

Fig. 2. Seam removal: exponentially fading column mirroring

where $w_1 = e^{-\alpha j}$ with $\alpha \in (0,1)$, $w_2 = 1 - w_1$, i and j rows and columns accordingly. The produced noise outcome with $\alpha = 0.25$ and 0.05 is illustrated in Figs. 2a and 2b respectively. An optimal α can been determined by

$$\alpha = -\frac{50\ ln(0.5)}{c}$$

where $c \times r$ is the resolution of the input texture. To obtain this we have determined experimentally running our whole methodology in the same input texture that the optimal visual result is derived by setting as target an attenuation of 50% (i.e. $w_1 = 0.5$) of the original mirrored image when we reach the 2% of the total number of columns (i.e. $j = c/50$). By doing so we achieve a seamless join of the two images without the mirroring effect being noticeable.

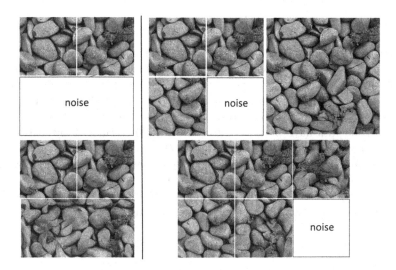

Fig. 3. The two Deep Texture Tiling Expansion methods. (left) Simple Right & then Down Tiling, (right) Create tiles of equal size - Right & Down Tiling are performed and then the Bottom Right Tile is produced by training our model lowering the mean square displacement of all 4 merged tiles to an original texture of double size. The second method is capable of keeping constant the amount of memory needed to expand a texture on any direction by following the exact same steps. Both methods are able to generate tiled textures of arbitrary size.

Texture expansion can be accomplished utilizing the aforementioned method in all directions by comparing input image with noise that is merged with a non noise part, using Gram matrices of arbitrary size. We have developed two different ways of creating large non-homogeneous textures.

The first one is a two step method. Firstly, a tile expansion to one of the four directions is performed with scaling factor that makes height or width of the starting image being doubled. For example, by doing a right tiling the original texture is doubled in width. Secondly, a tiling step is conducted, so that the other dimension is doubled. In the aforementioned case a down tiling follows to double the height, as well.

For limiting GPU memory requirements, we have developed an additional tiling method that it is slower but needs constant memory on the GPU. The method comprises three tiling steps. First we perform a side tiling, then a down tiling and eventually we end up merging the three tiles with a noise and our method goal is to converge on resembling to a fixed size original texture that we additionally provide as input. This approach is capable of serving as a missing tile filling method and it is presented along with the aforementioned Simple Tiling method in Fig. 3. The drawback of this method that needs to be improved in the future is the forwarding of noise that is incrementally passed on to the new synthesized tiles.

4   Results and Evaluation

Our method has been developed on Python, using Tensorflow [1] and it has been tested on an NVIDIA GeForce RTX 2080 Ti with 11 GB GDDR6 RAM and 1350 MHz base clock. Input texture resolution was 256×256 and we used a tiling factor of 1 for both width and height of the generated input noise in both right and up tiling with which the original textures were merged (second VGG19 input). All outputs have been produced by 100000 *iterations* by utilizing the Adam optimizer [11] with *learning rate* = 0.0005 on our system learning process and the running average time was $\approx$2400 secs. However, using this learning rate to which we concluded experimentally we observe after 50000 epochs our method has already converged (Fig. 4) in all input cases and it is just searching for a better minima and visual outcome with minor changes on loss value.

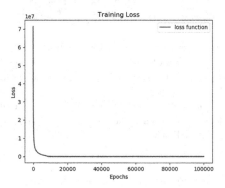

Fig. 4. Loss function per epoch during training for producing a new right tile with Adam optimizer [11] and *learning rate* = 0.0005 on a range of 100000 *iterations*.

In Figs. 5 and 6 results of our algorithm are presented showing that synthesis of texture tiles which highly match an original texture is plausible by using our deep learning system with acceptable visual quality. In addition, Fig. 7 depicts how effective is our method producing synthesized textures (consisted of new synthetic tiles) of larger size comparing to the original input tile. In this specific case, our method produces textures of double size (256×256 to 512×512) and in all cases Seam Removal with $a = 0.15$ is used. Our method is able to be used in left and down tiling and in cases in which a part of texture is missing, as well. In the latter case, the merged texture is the union of all other tiles surrounding the missing part (noise) which should resemble to a fixed size image, as presented in Sect. 3.

Finally, we compare our method with state-of-the-art methods as shown in Figs. 8a and 8b with [19] and [6] being the corresponding methods accordingly. Both methods are designed for different applications. However, this is a valid informal comparison of our method with two of the most competent methods in texture synthesis.

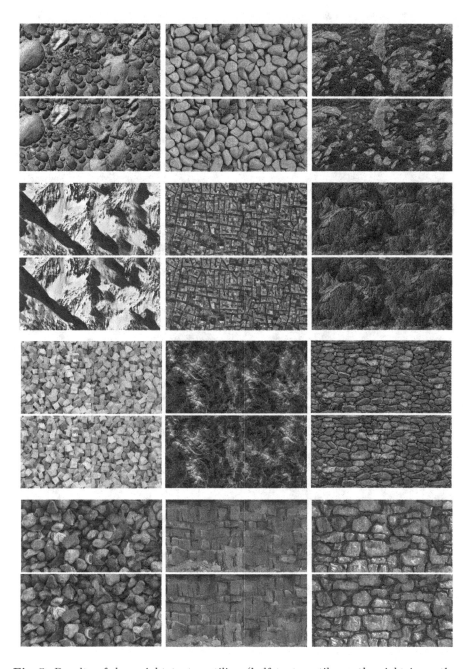

Fig. 5. Results of deep right texture tiling (half texture tile on the right is synthesized): odd rows have been generated by deep texture tiling for right tile construction without seam removal applied, even rows illustrate the same but with seam removal by exponential column mirroring with $\alpha = 0.15$.

Fig. 6. Results of deep up texture tiling (upper half texture tile is synthesized): tiles synthesized on up direction with no seam removal.

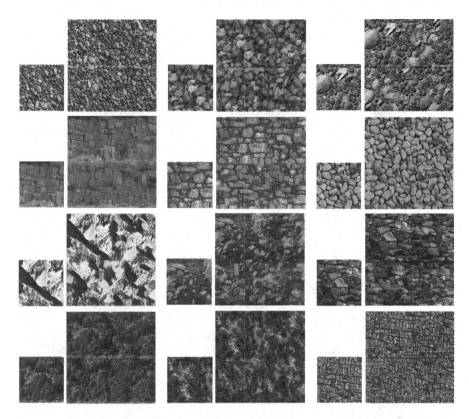

Fig. 7. Results for doubling the texture size with deep tiling: first, a right tiling is performed to produce a 512×256 tile and then a down tiling to produce the final 512×512 outcome. Seam removal by exponential column mirroring with $\alpha = 0.15$ is used. The last two input images are part of Pindos mountains and Athens city respectively and they have been extracted from Google Maps.

Our method based on the outcome of running it in non-stationary textures is not capable of synthesizing new seamless tiles. Thus, this constitutes one of the limitations of our method. This is mainly because our method is not designed to capture such patterns as [19] does and due to the tiling nature. Therefore, we see our method failing and not capturing well such type of textures on a seamless manner. However, [19]'s goal is generating such textures mainly. As a consequence, it makes it not compatible for comparing our method with, in a formal way.

On the other hand, although TileGAN [6] is closer to our rational and way of producing new textures, it is not targeting to expand a texture towards a direction as we do, but their outcome is a synthesized texture of greater size trying to keep the structure as it is shown in sub-Fig. 8b. To this end, this method cannot be formally compared with ours owing to the fact that the two approaches

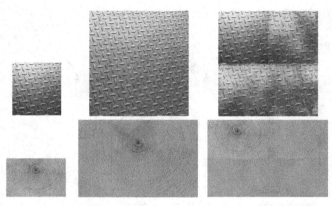

(a) Visual comparison with [19]. Generating from 256×256 texture a synthesized of 512×512 size.

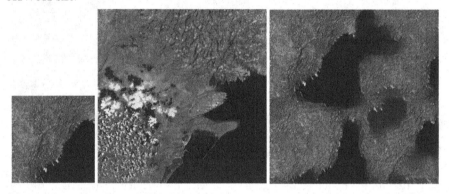

(b) Visual comparison with TileGAN [6]. Guidance images resolutions for TileGAN used on this experiment is 32×32 so that the output of this method being a 512×512 image. In this manner, we are able to make our method comparable to the aforementioned work.

Fig. 8. Non-stationary expansion sub-figure (a) and TileGAN sub-figure (b) outputs are presented in second column and ours in last column.

are targeting into tackle different problems. Nevertheless, the results of both techniques are visually and perceptually acceptable as synthesized textures.

5   Conclusions and Future Work

We presented an innovative tiling synthesis method that is capable of producing new texture tiles in any direction. Moreover, we have introduced a new method for reducing the seam effect in texture synthesis. Based on the results, our method has proven to be very effective on tile texture synthesis bearing an essential advantage due to the fact that tiles can be generated in small resolutions step by step, making even low memory GPUs capable of synthesizing high resolution textures. A limitation of our approach is that noise is passed on from one tile to another and this is an issue that could be reduced using Gaussian pyramid as in [16]. As future work, we are also targeting at expanding our method with style transfer by creating new tiles of mixed styles. This is required for generating high resolutions textures or terrains that differ from area to area.

References

1. Abadi, M., et al.: TensorFlow: a system for large-scale machine learning. In: Proceedings of the 12th USENIX Conference on Operating Systems Design and Implementation, OSDI 2016, pp. 265–283. USENIX Association, USA (2016)
2. Cohen, M., Shade, J., Hiller, S., Deussen, O.: Wang tiles for image and texture generation. ACM Trans. Graph. **22**, 287–294 (2003). https://doi.org/10.1145/1201775.882265
3. Darabi, S., Shechtman, E., Barnes, C., Goldman, D.B., Sen, P.: Image melding: combining inconsistent images using patch-based synthesis. ACM Trans. Graph. **31**(4), 82:1–82:10 (2012). https://doi.org/10.1145/2185520.2185578
4. Efros, A.A., Freeman, W.T.: Image quilting for texture synthesis and transfer. In: Proceedings of the 28th Annual Conference on Computer Graphics and Interactive Techniques, SIGGRAPH 2001, pp. 341–346. ACM, New York (2001). https://doi.org/10.1145/383259.383296
5. Efros, A.A., Leung, T.K.: Texture synthesis by non-parametric sampling. In: Proceedings of the International Conference on Computer Vision, ICCV 1999, vol. 2. p. 1033. IEEE Computer Society, Washington (1999). http://dl.acm.org/citation.cfm?id=850924.851569
6. Frühstück, A., Alhashim, I., Wonka, P.: TileGAN: synthesis of large-scale non-homogeneous textures. ACM Trans. Graph. **38**(4), 1–11 (2019). https://doi.org/10.1145/3306346.3322993
7. Fu, C.W., Leung, M.K.: Texture tiling on arbitrary topological surfaces using wang tiles, pp. 99–104 (2005). https://doi.org/10.2312/EGWR/EGSR05/099-104
8. Gatys, L.A., Ecker, A.S., Bethge, M.: Texture synthesis using convolutional neural networks. In: Proceedings of the 28th International Conference on Neural Information Processing Systems, NIPS 2015, vol. 1, pp. 262–270. MIT Press, Cambridge (2015). http://dl.acm.org/citation.cfm?id=2969239.2969269
9. Goodfellow, I.J., et al.: Generative adversarial nets. In: Proceedings of the 27th International Conference on Neural Information Processing Systems, NIPS 2014, vol. 2, pp. 2672–2680. MIT Press, Cambridge (2014). http://dl.acm.org/citation.cfm?id=2969033.2969125
10. Kaspar, A., Neubert, B., Lischinski, D., Pauly, M., Kopf, J.: Self tuning texture optimization. Comput. Graph. Forum **34**(2), 349–359 (2015). https://doi.org/10.1111/cgf.12565
11. Kingma, D., Ba, J.: Adam: a method for stochastic optimization. International Conference on Learning Representations, December 2014
12. Kwatra, V., Essa, I., Bobick, A., Kwatra, N.: Texture optimization for example-based synthesis. ACM Trans. Graph. **24**(3), 795–802 (2005). https://doi.org/10.1145/1073204.1073263
13. Kwatra, V., Schödl, A., Essa, I., Turk, G., Bobick, A.: Graphcut textures: image and video synthesis using graph cuts. In: ACM SIGGRAPH 2003 Papers, SIGGRAPH 2003, pp. 277–286. ACM, New York (2003). https://doi.org/10.1145/1201775.882264

14. Sajjadi, M.S.M., Schölkopf, B., Hirsch, M.: EnhanceNet: single image super-resolution through automated texture synthesis (2017)
15. Simonyan, K., Zisserman, A.: Very deep convolutional networks for large-scale image recognition. arXiv:1409.1556 (2014)
16. Snelgrove, X.: High-resolution multi-scale neural texture synthesis, pp. 1–4, November 2017. https://doi.org/10.1145/3145749.3149449
17. Toulatzis, V., Fudos, I.: Deep terrain expansion: terrain texture synthesis with deep learning. In: Vidal, F.P., Tam, G.K.L., Roberts, J.C. (eds.) Computer Graphics and Visual Computing (CGVC). The Eurographics Association (2019). https://doi.org/10.2312/cgvc.20191262
18. Wei, L.Y., Levoy, M.: Fast texture synthesis using tree-structured vector quantization. In: Proceedings of the 27th Annual Conference on Computer Graphics and Interactive Techniques, SIGGRAPH 2000, pp. 479–488. ACM Press/Addison-Wesley Publishing Co., New York (2000). https://doi.org/10.1145/344779.345009
19. Zhou, Y., Zhu, Z., Bai, X., Lischinski, D., Cohen-Or, D., Huang, H.: Non-stationary texture synthesis by adversarial expansion. ACM Trans. Graph. **37**(4), 49:1–49:13 (2018). https://doi.org/10.1145/3197517.3201285

BEAPS: Integrating Volumetric Dynamics in Virtual Agent Prototyping

Abishek S. Kumar and Stefan Rank$^{(\boxtimes)}$

PerCubed Lab, Drexel University, Philadelphia, PA, USA
stefan.rank@drexel.edu

Abstract. Interactive real-time virtual worlds benefit from agents with complex shapes and geometry, imbued with a repertoire of expressive actions suitable for engaging narrative settings. Volumetric simulations like position-based dynamics, often used for motion picture graphics or interactive material simulations, offer a way towards increased expressivity. We describe a proof-of-concept real-time simulation testbed that integrates animated agent behaviors with deformable geometries, specifically GPU-accelerated volumetric soft body dynamics, and custom planners that expand the agents' behavioral action space. We introduce these simulations in a modular hierarchical event-driven agent prototyping framework aiming for minimal message passing between the CPU and GPU. As a result, more diverse animations, beyond skeletal animation and Inverse Kinematics, are afforded to virtual agents that can be incorporated directly in a narrative setting.

Keywords: Virtual agents · Volumetric simulations · Expressive actions

1 Introduction

A virtual agent prototyping test-bed is a flexible platform for designing and authoring functional, purposeful behavioral animation [14], affording animated agents high-level actions such as locomotion, navigation, reaching, gesturing, or collision detection, most commonly in narrative settings [10]. Agents portray an understanding about their surroundings and can have unconventional action states [16], not limited to inverse kinematics, but potentially real time physics systems as well that can produce varied articulated geometry, material properties or dynamic constraints [17]. Real-time graphics research has allowed for simulating various dynamic effects on the GPU such as soft body/rigid body dynamics, destructible physics and smooth particle hydrodynamics. An ideal modular IVA (Intelligent virtual agent) control architecture should be able to integrate these simulations to expand the agents' action space and provide the user with a greater variety in behaviors to author while not interrupting other

We would like to thank Dr. Mubbasir Kapadia and his team at Rutgers' Intelligent Visual Interfaces lab for their support.

G. Bebis et al. (Eds.): ISVC 2021, LNCS 13017, pp. 427–438, 2021.
https://doi.org/10.1007/978-3-030-90439-5_34

controllers in the test-bed [9]. Integrating multiple character control architectures for these behaviors requires a deep understanding of each controller's design and their interaction with the virtual world so that they may communicate with one another seamlessly [10].

In this regard, an agent control system is a modular event-driven framework that allows for various controllers to coordinate with one another while not overriding one another. This complexity of coordination is amplified if we increase the degree of sophistication of representing characters by including controllers for dynamic simulations. Furthermore, in terms of behavior authoring, a virtual agent's actions are usually limited to the actions the performance capture allows for [7]. In order to make virtual agents more versatile, by including sophisticated simulations in their actions, a character animation system should allow a designer to integrate multiple different techniques/simulations for authoring a particular behavior and not be limited to the behaviors provided by the system's performance capture database [10].

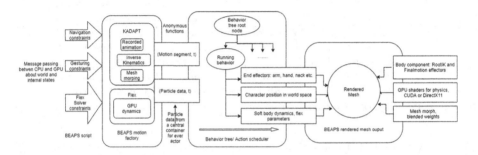

Fig. 1. High-level data flow in the BEAPS system.

We present BEAPS (Behaviors for Expressive and Adaptive Particle Simulations), an agent control system that allows for CPU-GPU communication to incorporate volumetric dynamics to expand the high-level authored behaviors of animated virtual agents. See Fig. 1 for an overview of the data flow between volumetric simulations, motion segmentation and planning via a behaviour tree in the BEAPS system. Simulations, taking advantage of the GPU, allow for creating immersive visual effects like real-time interactive physically based animations [2]. Our contribution extends a modular agent authoring system with a set of methods that allow controlling embedded interactive volume lattices in agents [1] whose physical constituents can be made to communicate with the other controllers in the system. All modules are managed by a behavior coordinator, which acts as a central point of contact for manipulating the virtual character's pose, internal material structures and rendered mesh in real-time. We primarily experiment with volume preserving GPU-accelerated soft body dynamics (specifically position-based dynamics), in order to determine the feasibility and performance of integrating this volumetric simulation with agent prototyping; in particular, a soft body skeletal animation directed by user defined free deformations parsed by an agent control system, expressive gesturing by blending soft body with reference animations, and volumetric shock propagation.

2   Related Work

There are many methods of creating volumetric deformable soft bodies like position-based dynamics on the GPU [1], or lattice shape matching [2]. Using soft body volumes can enhance the physicality of motion and interaction with objects in the form of collisions or secondary physical motion of simulated materials [3,4]. Chuah et al. [5] defined an IVA's physicality to include the physical size, volume, and position it occupies and its ability to interact with its surrounding environment, albeit this inference was made in a medical simulation setting. From an animated intelligent agent standpoint, this physicality may prove useful in modifying motion for expressiveness [7] or naturalness of motion [6].

From the perspective of expanding and parameterizing an animated humanoid virtual agent's action space [15], involving volumetric simulations and the actions it provides, requires a few additions to agent control architectures. Gaisbauer et al. [9] profess the need for additive motion model units to be interfaced with a central event driven prototyping testbed for expanding the actions of embodied expressive agents. Common formats for exchanging motion information, such as Biovision Hierarchy (bvh) and Filmbox (fbx) are static [9], so they use motion model units, an interface (similar to FMI - functional mockup interface) to run data-driven (mocap-based) and model-based (physics-based) heterogeneous simulations concurrently. Shoulson et al. [10] created a modular event-driven agent framework named ADAPT aimed at combining heterogeneous simulation models in a single agent testbed, allowing GPU-based simulations as an extension to procedural behavioral animation. They implement a functional programming interface which affords agent behaviors to be passed as code parameters to high-level agent narrative controls/sequences without interrupting or explicitly communicating with other controllers. This allows programs to be written in a declarative and composable style, as seen in [10] for narrative sequences, for smooth transitions in animation as shown by Reach et al. [18], and very early on game for AI behavior signaling by Khoo et al. [19].

Reviewing related work has shown that creating and controlling deformable, volumetric characters is an active area of research in computer graphics, specifically GPU-accelerated physics simulation environments [17], but has also shown there is a lack of research on the design and implementation of GPU-based volumetric virtual agent control modalities or even game mechanics [11]. Previous flagship agent testbeds such as virtual human toolkit [14] do not easily allow for designers or programmers to interface additional layers of simulation as controllers using the central event-driven model [9]. We aim to pass GPU-data to high-level behaviors that parameterize agents' action representations [10], beyond the usage of IK (Inverse Kinematic) end effectors to create empathic bodily animations [12].

3   Methodology

BEAPS provides a hierarchical behavior authoring system empowering agent designers to orchestrate fine-grained character movements beyond skeletal animation using embedded volumetric GPU-accelerated dynamics. In our system, interactions with the particle level data layer provide information about the world that can be passed as parameters to controllers that make decisions based on it and subsequently react by running sub-trees that affect particle data, refer to the data flow graph in Fig. 1. We integrate Nvidia FleX (a GPU-accelerated particle-oriented physics simulation system, used via the Unity plug-in) with the skeletal agent animation system KADAPT (an extension of ADAPT [10]), in a robust behavior tree framework working with existing animation controllers. The term controller is used to denote behavior choreographers (node classes in the terminology of behavior trees) that manipulate some kind of data as low-level actions for high-level narrative behaviors. Within our system, there are controllers that handle narrative-directed agent interactions with the virtual world, and controllers that interface with the GPU that handle vector data for particles if required during said interactions. The communication between both sets of controllers is used to create a few novel and interesting behaviors.

The system was developed in the Unity engine combining the KADAPT (which uses RootMotion's FinalIK) and Nvidia FleX libraries. In the next sections, we present the control architecture used and subsequently the methods that allow aforementioned behaviors.

3.1   Nvidia FleX

FleX is meant to bring the capabilities of offline volumetric material simulations to real-time computer graphics [13]. The FleX API allows to create deformable meshes that are then subject to a constraint-based solver while still providing methods for accessing and manipulating particle data residing in GPU memory in a simple format, see Listing 1.1.

Listing 1.1. Structure of a particle in FleX

```
struct Particle
{
    float x [3];
    float v [3];
    float invmass;
    int phase;
}
```

Primarily designed for visual effects, there is limited support for animations requiring real-time adaptive manipulation of GPU data, or function primitives for handling particle data in real time like moving assets in world space, integrating skeletal animation or user-defined free form deformations. Soft assets and their constituent lattice particles are stored in a container as an array of vectors. Using the FleX API, we can access and modify these particles, see pseudo-code Listing 1.2.

Listing 1.2. Structure of FleX particle data in GPU accessed through a container structure

```
struct ParticleData
{
    Int Pointer to the particle position and mass data
    Int Pointer to the particle's rest position
    Int Pointer to the particle velocity data
    Int Pointer to the particle phase data
    Int Pointer to the particle normal data with 16 byte stride in
        format [nx, ny, nz, nw]
    Int Pointer to the particle lower bounds [x, y, z]
    Int Pointer to the particle upper bounds [x, y, z]
}
```

In FleX's Unity plug-in, a central update function, OnFlexUpdate(), coordinates particle interactions with the GPU solver through the FleX API (see Table 1), both for acquiring data and modifying it. BEAPS' design aims to minimize the need to copy data to and from GPU memory.

Table 1. Helper functions in the Flex API for accessing particle data

Commands	Description
NvFlexContainer()	For high performance NvFlexContainer() creates a wrapper object around a Flex solver that can hold assets/instances, the container manages sending and retrieving particle data to/from the solver
NvFlexExtMapParticleData()	Returns pointers to the internal data stored by the container. These are host-memory pointers, and will remain valid until NvFlexExtUnmapParticleData() is called
NvFlexExtTickContainer()	Updates the container, applies force fields, steps the solver forward in time, updates the host with the results synchronously
NvFlexExtPushToDevice()	Updates the device asynchronously, transfers any particle and constraint changes to the flex solver, expected to be called in the following sequence: NvFlexExtPushToDevice, NvFlexUpdateSolver, NvFlexExtPullFromDevice, flexSynchronize
NvFlexExtPullFromDevice()	Updates the host asynchronously, transfers particle and constraint data back to he host, expected to be called in the following sequence: NvFlexExtPushToDevice, NvFlexUpdateSolver, NvFlexExtPullFromDevice

3.2   KADAPT - A Virtual Agent Prototyping Test-Bed

KADAPT is a lightweight library for authoring both high level decision-making and complex interactions between actors using a centralized behavior tree model. It originated as an extension of ADAPT [10]. It provides an array of character choreographers, also known as shadow coordinators, for animating fully articulated, expressive humanoid characters. Shadows replicate the skeletal structure and functionality of a regular character model to each influence the skeleton without interrupting other choreographers. Base functionality is provided by RootMotion's FinalIK and a behavior tree implementation called TreeSharp-Plus. The latter takes advantage of more recent additions to the C# language, such as closures and anonymous functions, to provide an intuitive interface for authoring agent behavior while avoiding code duplication. This flexible behavior tree setup allows BEAPS to seamlessly integrate the manipulation of particle data that is fetched from and pushed to the GPU in a similar manner as the shadows used for skeletal coordinators.

This setup allows a designer to add additional choreographers that can extend high-level narrative control, with new techniques affecting not only the skeleton but the agent's rendered mesh or internal volumes via GPU data access, and easily exchange generic choreographers with more specialized alternatives.

KADAPT and Flex: BEAPS directly incorporates properties and parameters of FleX's volumetric simulation in controllers that are coordinated with KADAPT's action choreographers. The effects denoted in this section manipulate particle data on the fly by communicating with the GPU. Furthermore, the high level controllers for these effects can be passed as parameters to choreographers in KADAPT.

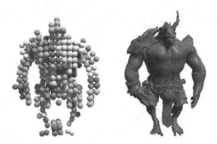

Fig. 2. Soft body particle simulation influenced by skeletal reference animation: left is the FleX soft asset with shapes (denoted by clusters of differently colored particles), right is the resulting skinned mesh

Soft Body Procedural Animation - Volumetric Soft Skinning: Soft skinning to form a deformable skeletal animation can be used to provide a naturalness to motion when blended with a running animation from KADAPT and a physicality when interacting with objects in a virtual space [4]. Soft body assets created by the Nvidia Flex API cannot be animated straightforwardly by a skeletal rig as they do not possess a hierarchical rig system, but rather a collection of shapes derived from the set of particles initially created for the asset. Shape animation for soft body dynamics and interfacing a particle/voxel lattice with skeletal animation [2] is not possible without first allowing for the soft body mesh's skinning weights to be driven by traditional bones. To enable the coordination of particle simulation and skeletal animation, we first dynamically manipulate the underlying particle data for agents with a skeletal rig corresponding to the soft body, by applying appropriate forces to every particle in the agent every frame to follow the current vertex positioning of the particle's reference mesh vertex, i.e. the nearest (shortest euclidean distance in local space) vertex. The method mentioned here is purely for procedural animation of a soft asset, no performance metrics are provided, however it works at interactive frame rates even for assets containing many thousands of particles.

We transfer the bone weights of the reference animation's bones and apply them as transformation matrices for the particles in world space, then apply a resultant force to each particle based off of the displacement of the particle relative to the intended positions in the reference animation, refer to Algorithm 1 and Fig. 2.

Result: Updating particle positions via forces based on skinning weights from a reference rig
```
// Initialize local arrays for copying data from container and
   calculate particle displacements
```
particles = Vector4[actor.indexCount];
velocities = Vector3[particles.length];
displacementVector = Vector3[particles.length];
```
// Initialize a mapping from bone to vertex to particle
```
Pull particle data for actor from container;
Cache mesh vertices from rest pose of reference animation's skinned mesh;
Calculate nearest particle position to cached vertices;
Record bone weights for corresponding particle;
while *waiting for frame update* **do**
    Pull particle data for actor from container;
    ```
// Update particle positions
```
    for *all-particle-bone-weights* **do**
        calculate local space transforms for every particle position;
    end
    for *all-local-space-particle-positions* **do**
        calculate world space transforms, update displacement vector for each particle based on world space transform matrix;
        update particle velocities by multiplying displacement vector with each particles mass;
    end
    Push particle velocities for actor to container and then GPU solver;
end

Algorithm 1: Soft body skeletal animation: transferring skinning weights to particles and applying relevant forces

---

The soft body animation mimics the reference animation, e.g. the ones that are created by choreographers in KADAPT to provide good visual fidelity to the original animated agent's movement. The more shapes the more degrees of freedom the soft body object has, allowing it to track the reference animation with greater exaggerated motion akin to cartoonish motion. The soft body provides physicality to the agent and below we provide details on how to use KADAPT to leverage said physicality via custom controllers to create expressive and stylized motion.

Table 2. Composite behaviour tree node types in KADAPT

Commands	Description
Selector()	This node will attempt to execute all branches, until one succeeds. This composite will fail only if all branches fail as well
Sequence()	This node will execute each branch, in order. If all branches succeed, this composite will return a successful run status. If any branch fails, this composite will return a failed run status
Parallel()	Parallel nodes execute all of their children simultaneously, with varying termination conditions

Coordinating KADAPT's Behavior Tree with Flex Dynamics: BEAPS allows for post-processing of skeletal reference animations via the soft body physics animation that tracks the same. A few coordinated actions combining KADAPT and Flex are shown as pseudo-code below with an example root node that integrates said choreographers in a behavior tree model. KADAPT's behavior tree has various composite node types for sequencing or running behaviors in parallel (see Table 2). This allows for complex narrative actions by combining said nodes with those that require the dynamics of Flex as low level actions.

Below, we describe example controllers such as: user defined free form deformation states that can be serialized and used in future prototypes, a blend function between the reference animation and the physic-based animation to showcase some realism by secondary motion (the behavior tree can alter the blend weights as well) and a volumetric shiver/shock controller to showcase a simulation that can parameterize low-level behaviors by the behavior tree.

- User defined free-form deformation: An example of fine grained control over lattice particles of the soft body. The lattice and bones of the soft body allow for multiple configurations to take place while also providing creative control. Deformed physically exaggerated states (Fig. 3) are serialized dictionaries containing particle index and vector data which can be applied to any other behavior in the behavior tree.
- Secondary motion via soft body animation in agents: Blending between FleX objects and a reference animation (Fig. 4). The blending is used to add a naturalness to motion. For example the designer may want the original animation as is and only use the physics of the soft body for expressive exaggeration of certain motions like gesturing. Blending uses a naive interpolation of mesh vertices and the resulting effects are not always obvious.

Fig. 3. Idle animation mimicked by soft body enhanced with user-defined deformations, akin to stop motion or claymation. Deformed states are serialized and accessible from high-level behavior nodes.

Fig. 4. The blended mesh (right) interpolated between the original animation (left) and physics animation (center) for creating a natural motion parameterized by the physics object. The current blending method allows for limiting deformations to certain parts of characters, in this case even though the arms are deformed the motion is blended only in the head and shoulders. The blend function can be called as needed when expressive motion is required in nodes of the behavior tree root (refer to Listing 1.3).

Fig. 5. Illustration of the behavior tree sequence (refer to Listing 1.4) implementing the Shock propagation processor. The soft body physics is blended as necessary in the logic of the root node

– Shiver/Shock propagation processor: The root node in the example behavior tree (see Listing 1.4) will traverse its children and complete tasks while communicating with the flex choreographers as well. The struct ParticleData 1.2 is used to pull velocity data from the GPU on a frame's OnFlexUpdate() and a method is passed to a behavior tree node which applies randomized velocities as necessary once pushed back to the GPU; this produces a shock effect or shivering effect during interaction with the environment (Fig. 5). Choreographers are supplied as parameters for nodes in the behavior tree.

Listing 1.3. Behavior Node for blending between meshes at runtime. Anonymous functions are used to pass soft body animation class and associated particle data as parameters to blending function

```
BEAPS_Node_blend(Mesh reference_anim, Mesh soft_body_anim,
      Runtime_blended_mesh morph_target, float blend_weight)
{
    // Create a runtime mesh that linearly interpolates between
        reference and soft body animation using a weight
    // Return local copy of blended mesh
    return Selector (blend_mesh(() => reference_anim, soft_body_anim,
        blend_weight))

}
```

Listing 1.4. High-level representation of behaviors in the root node which is a loop of action nodes. Tasks that require the use of GPU dynamics are embedded in the script of the narrative scene and not just a stand alone simulation. Functions defined for blending or naturalness of motion are passed to children in the root node. The effects from flex are blended with the running behaviors and can be run in parallel with other nodes using the Parallel() node

```
BEAPS_Node BuildTreeRoot() // A root node example
{
    // loop_indefinitely while character is in locomotion
    return (new Sequence(
      Sequence (Approach a target,
        Selector(BEAPS_Node_Blend(KADAPT mesh, physics animation mesh)),
        Orient towards target),
      new Parallel(
        Selector(Wait at the location for 1000s),
        Selector(Node_Shock(
        trigger shock (
        OnFlexUpdate( for all particles (scale velocity by a factor)))))
        ),
      Selector(Go to new location)));
}
```

4   Conclusion

In this paper, we presented BEAPS which embeds simulations of dynamic material physics on the GPU within an agent control architecture in order to expand the agent's action portfolio, specifically with a physics-based element to its animations involving position-based dynamics. A behavior tree model was used to coordinate actions involving said materials and higher level behaviors. Using BEAPS, we can integrate a volumetric dynamics layer based on Nvidia Flex for creating expressive virtual agents. Using a behavior tree as a scheduler proves to be suitable for extensibility and could lead to more versatile use of GPU-based simulations.

Informal testing of performance shows that the current setup allows for sufficient temporal resolution for five characters, using a single container in the scene. Regarding future work, one point of possible investigation is based on the fact that FleX is not designed to build gameplay-affecting physics interactions, as it lacks functionality such as trigger events, contact callbacks, ray-casting or serialization. For this reason, we built extensions for animation, movement control, and trigger events that integrate with the rest of Unity's framework.

In the future, we will extend our prototypes to allow for novel gameplay mechanics using multiple parallel nodes accessing the features and facets of soft bodies such as individual or chunks of particles in authoring agent control [11], for example to control effects like adhesion or melting. This requires registering collisions involving individual particles. This computationally expensive requirement can potentially be met with accelerated data structures for particle access such as VDB or its GPU-accelerated implementations GVDB or nanoVDB. We will also look into integrating high resolution methods like smoothed-particle hydrodynamics (SPH), as well as into improving the visual appeal of blending between different animation choreographers, such as replacing linear interpolation with rig-space blending.

References

1. Bender, J., Müller, M., Macklin, M.: A survey on position based dynamics. In: 2017 Proceedings of the European Association for Computer Graphics: Tutorials, pp. 1–31 (2017)
2. Rivers, A.R., James, D.L.: FastLSM: fast lattice shape matching for robust real-time deformation. ACM Trans. Graph. (TOG) **26**(3), 82-es (2007)
3. Rohmer, D., et al.: Velocity skinning for real-time stylized skeletal animation. In: Computer Graphics Forum, vol. 40, no. 2 (2021)
4. Iwamoto, N., et al.: Multi-layer lattice model for real-time dynamic character deformation. In: Computer Graphics Forum, vol. 34, no. 7 (2015)
5. Chuah, J.H., et al.: Exploring agent physicality and social presence for medical team training. Presence: Teleoper. Virtual Environ. **22**(2), 141–170 (2013)
6. Van Welbergen, H., et al.: Real time animation of virtual humans: a trade-off between naturalness and control. In: Computer Graphics Forum, vol. 29, no. 8. Blackwell Publishing Ltd., Oxford (2010)
7. Badler, N.I., Reich, B.D., Webber, B.L.: Towards personalities for animated agents with reactive and planning behaviors. In: Trappl, R., Petta, P. (eds.) Creating Personalities for Synthetic Actors. LNCS, vol. 1195, pp. 43–57. Springer, Heidelberg (1997). https://doi.org/10.1007/BFb0030569
8. Badler, N.I., et al.: A parameterized action representation for virtual human agents, p. 256 (2000)

9. Gaisbauer, F., Lampen, E., Agethen, P., Rukzio, E.: Combining heterogeneous digital human simulations: presenting a novel co-simulation approach for incorporating different character animation technologies. Vis. Comput. **37**(4), 717–734 (2020). https://doi.org/10.1007/s00371-020-01792-x

10. Shoulson, A., et al.: ADAPT: the agent development and prototyping testbed. IEEE Trans. Vis. Comput. Graph. **20**(7), 1035–1047 (2013)

11. Clarke, G.: Creating gameplay mechanics with deformable characters. In: 19th annual European GAME-ON Conference (GAME-ON 2018) on Simulation and AI in Computer Games. EUROSIS (2018)

12. Bishko, L.: Animation principles and Laban movement analysis: movement frameworks for creating empathic character performances. Nonverbal Commun. Virtual Worlds 177–203 (2014)

13. Macklin, M., et al.: Unified particle physics for real-time applications. ACM Trans. Graph. (TOG) **33**(4), 1–12 (2014)

14. Hartholt, A., et al.: All together now. In: Aylett, R., Krenn, B., Pelachaud, C., Shimodaira, H. (eds.) IVA 2013. LNCS (LNAI), vol. 8108, pp. 368–381. Springer, Heidelberg (2013). https://doi.org/10.1007/978-3-642-40415-3_33

15. Rodriguez, A.M.R., et al.: Parameterized animated activities. In: Motion, Interaction and Games, pp. 1–9 (2019)

16. Pitiot, T., et al.: Deformable polygonal agents in crowd simulation. Comput. Anim. Virtual Worlds **25**(3–4), 341–350 (2014)

17. Austin, J., et al.: Titan: a parallel asynchronous library for multi-agent and soft-body robotics using NVIDIA CUDA. In: 2020 IEEE International Conference on Robotics and Automation (ICRA). IEEE (2020)

18. Reach, A.M., North, C.: The signals and systems approach to animation. arXiv preprint arXiv:1703.00521 (2017)

19. Khoo, A., et al.: Efficient, realistic NPC control systems using behavior-based techniques. In: Proceedings of the AAAI 2002 Spring Symposium Series: Artificial Intelligence and Interactive Entertainment (2002)

3D Vision

IVS3D: An Open Source Framework for Intelligent Video Sampling and Preprocessing to Facilitate 3D Reconstruction

Max Hermann[1,2]([✉]), Thomas Pollok[1], Daniel Brommer[1], and Dominic Zahn[1]

[1] Video Exploitation Systems, Fraunhofer Institute of Optronics, System Technologies and Image Exploitation IOSB, Karlsruhe, Germany
{max.hermann,thomas.pollok,daniel.brommer,
dominic.zahn}@iosb.fraunhofer.de
[2] Institute of Photogrammetry and Remote Sensing,
Karlsruhe Institute of Technology, Karlsruhe, Germany
max.hermann@kit.edu

Abstract. The creation of detailed 3D models is relevant for a wide range of applications such as navigation in three-dimensional space, construction planning or disaster assessment. However, the complex processing and long execution time for detailed 3D reconstructions require the original database to be reduced in order to obtain a result in reasonable time. In this paper we therefore present our framework iVS3D for intelligent pre-processing of image sequences. Our software is able to down sample entire videos to a specific frame rate, as well as to resize and crop the individual images. Furthermore, thanks to our modular architecture, it is easy to develop and integrate plugins with additional algorithms. We provide three plugins as baseline methods that enable an intelligent selection of suitable images and can enrich them with additional information. To filter out images affected by motion blur, we developed a plugin that detects these frames and also searches the spatial neighbourhood for suitable images as replacements. The second plugin uses optical flow to detect redundant images caused by a temporarily stationary camera. In our experiments, we show how this approach leads to a more balanced image sampling if the camera speed varies, and that excluding such redundant images leads to a time saving of 8.1 % for our sequences. A third plugin makes it possible to exclude challenging image regions from the 3D reconstruction by performing semantic segmentation. As we think that the community can greatly benefit from such an approach, we will publish our framework and the developed plugins open source using the MIT licence to allow co-development and easy extension.

Keywords: 3D reconstruction · Preprocessing · Video sampling · Open source framework

---

D. Brommer and D. Zahn—Contributed equally to this work.

© Springer Nature Switzerland AG 2021
G. Bebis et al. (Eds.): ISVC 2021, LNCS 13017, pp. 441–454, 2021.
https://doi.org/10.1007/978-3-030-90439-5_35

1   Introduction

Photogrammetric approaches like Structure-from-Motion require a set of images in order to reconstruct a 3D scene. In the case of video sequences, not every frame provides additional information that has not been already been available through a previous frame. The manual preprocessing of image or video sequences can require intensive manual labour, that can be easily automated. In the case of recorded videos using an drone, there could be situations, where an operator keeps the drone still at a location, before flying to the next location. This means that the input video would contain a large set of redundant frames with very similar image content, while the use of more frames slows down the reconstruction process drastically. Naive approaches, where the original frame rate is down sampled to a lower frame rate, reduce the number of images in the data set drastically, which in turn will have impact on the reconstruction speed as only a subset of images has to be processed in the reconstruction pipeline. However, the naive approach will not always result in a good selection of keyframes. Blurry images impact the image matching and texturing process, where neighbouring frames in the local neighbourhood of the sequence would provide a higher image quality. Also images with a lot of dynamic objects like moving persons can impact the reconstruction quality. Also situations in which the camera is not moving, a selection of a frame with lower individually moving objects or low dynamic static pixel ratio could also contribute to a higher quality. Popular reconstruction approaches like COLMAP [15] allow to provide an additional binary mask per frame in order to prevent mismatches from regions with dynamic objects. Our framework allows to create such masks automatically using a Mask R-CNN [10] plugin. In this paper we present our framework iVS3D to tackle the task of intelligent image preprocessing of videos or continuous image sequences for high quality 3D reconstruction purpose. Our framework consists of a plugin based architecture for extensibility. Our framework provides a COLMAP integration and can be extended with further reconstruction tools. The code[1] is released using the MIT open source license. We hope that we can facilitate the task of 3D reconstruction from 2D images with this contribution and invite the community for further contributions and improvements.

The paper is structured as follows: first related work is presented. Afterwards, our approach and architecture is presented in Sect. 3. Experiments using our framework are discussed in Sect. 4 and finally a conclusion is presented.

2   Related Work

Pre-processing strategies of video and image sequences for the photogrammetric application of 3D reconstruction can be mainly divided into two categories. The first category tries to reduce the number of frames in favour of a lower computational run-time cost and the second category tries to improve the quality in terms of total 3D point reprojection error and visual quality after texture mapping. The

---

[1] https://github.com/iVS3D/iVS3D.

first category is extensively used by and integrated in visual SLAM techniques [4,7], in order to reduce the memory footprint and optimization cost of Bundle Adjustment. New keyframes are sampled from the input sequence only if the relative translation and rotation to the previous keyframe exceeds a manually specified threshold. Additionally, keyframes are removed by these methods during run-time, in case a loop has been detected and the occurrence of redundant keyframes from very similar views. This can result in a better set of keyframes compared to the naive approach, where the complete sequence is simply sampled to a lower frame rate. Bellavia et al. [2] proposed an online method to detect and discard bad frames, i.e. blurry frames, resulting in a better reconstruction quality. Ballabeni et al. [1] propose an image enhancement preprocessing strategy to improve the reconstruction quality. It consists of multiple stages like color balancing, exposure equalization, image denoising, rgb to grayscale conversion and finally an adaptive median filtering. In this paper we do not propose a new preprocessing strategy. The main contribution of our paper is the contribution of an extensible open source framework with a number of baseline plugins to the community, for preprocessing of image and video sequences in the context of photogrammetric applications.

3   Approach

Our framework has two main goals: One is to speed up the downstream 3D reconstruction by filtering images without enough novel image content while maintaining the reconstruction quality. Secondly, the enhancement of the source material by removing challenging areas. In this context, we mainly focus on masking regions with a high degree of movement, such as pedestrians, cars or vegetation. For easy extensibility and quick addition of new algorithms, we have decided to use a plugin-based architecture. All of our baseline methods presented below are encapsulated as plugins and can thus be individually added to the processing chain. In the following, we will first discuss the basic architecture of our framework and then describe the individual plugins with regard to frame filtering and image region masking. Finally, we outline our ability to define, save and execute specific workflows for batch processing.

3.1   Architecture Overview

We have designed the application as a model-view-controller architecture that can integrate algorithms via two distinct interfaces. iVS3D is implemented with the Qt framework using the programming language C++ and is therefore cross platform capable. To allow everyone to add algorithms to iVS3D and to easily share them we are using a plugin-based approach for all the algorithms. Plugins can either extract specific images from the provided image sequences or generate additional image information. These explicitly selected images are called keyframes in the following. For this architecture we rely on the plug-in functionality in Qt. As baseline methods we implemented four plugins, which are the

Nth frame plugin for fixed frame subsampling, the camera movement detection plugin, the blur detection plugin and the plugin for semantic segmentation.

The graphical user interface shown in Fig. 1 gives an impression of the individual components of our framework, which we will discuss in more detail in the following. Our processing pipeline consists of a defined input that receives either a video or a collection of individual images. These are transformed by one or more plugins and then exported to a new location. In addition, the software COLMAP can be started directly from our application with automatically generated project files. In the following, the individual steps of the pipeline are explained in more detail, whereby the sections are structured according to the components marked in Fig. 1.

1 Input. To start the process, you can either open a project that is already in progress or begin importing new data. For this we accept a folder with single images as well as videos in the common formats. The project file contains the source of the imported data as well as the settings and sampled key frames. If a video file was imported the graphical user interface will display additional information in the input section like the frames per second, resolution and duration.

2 Plugins. To process the input data we offer two types of plugins. The first one represents the possibility to select keyframes from the currently loaded image sequence, while the second one generates additional information for each image. In order to enable the user to set parameters for the plugin, every plugin has its own user interface where all necessary settings can be applied, which gets embedded in the main application. For more complex plugins with several parameters, we offer an optional interface that allows the plugin to use heuristics to determine suitable settings in advance based on a subset of the input data. This allows, for example, algorithms whose parameters depend indirectly on the image resolution to set more suitable default parameters. In contrast to this there are some functions that need to be implemented to ensure that the plugin will work correctly. The *sampleImages* function is the core of each plugin. It receives access to the input data and returns a vector of indices of keyframes based on the given image sequence. To start the sampling process a plugin has to be selected and configured by the user. With the brackets in the timeline **5** the amount of images which are sampled can be reduced by excluding images on the respective left or right side. In this way, parts of videos can be removed that show, for example, a starting or landing unmanned aerial vehicle (UAV). After the sampling is done the timeline will show the sampled key frames as red bars. Using multiple sampling processes in sequence is supported as well as manual selecting and removing keyframes. The second type of plugin focuses on creating additional information that belong to a specific input image. Like the plugins of the first type, these plugins have their own user interface, which is embedded in the main window when the plugin is selected. The core of these plugins is the *transform* function where they are given a image and return a vector of images. It has the ability to show the newly generated images on the graphical user interface and to export the newly generated images among the sampled images. A deeper explanation of the already implemented plugins is given in Sect. 3.2.

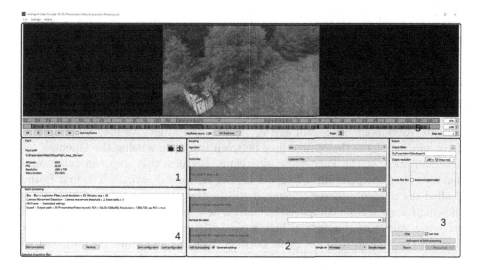

Fig. 1. Graphical user interface which is split in five different sections. 1. Input, 2. Plugins, 3. Export, 4. Batch processing and 5. Video player with the timeline for keyframes

3 Export. The last step of the processing pipeline is to export the sampled images to the desired location. In addition to the export of the sampled images, the export step offers additional functionality. Images can be cropped to e.g. remove unwanted timestamps visible in the images and the resolution can be changed. Every export creates a project file containing the import source, the indexes of the sampled keyframes. After an export is finished a 3D reconstruction tool can be started from iVS3D. So far, we have integrated the software COLMAP and generate project file and database. If binary masks for the images were created these will be included to the project file as well. COLMAP then starts with these files already imported which allows the user to start the reconstruction process without having to manually set the input data again. Furthermore, the direct start of a headless reconstruction with COLMAP is possible with our application.

3.2 Baseline Plugins Already Developed

The time complexity of methods such as feature matching or structure from motion often scale quadratic, which makes processing large image data sets very difficult. Choosing the right images is therefore crucial to avoid unnecessary processing time. We have implemented three filtering plugins as baseline methods. Firstly, a simple down-sampling to a fixed fps value, then the detection of redundant frames by determining the optical flow and thirdly the filtering of blurred images. We have also developed a plugin that uses semantic segmentation to exclude regions from the image that are unusable for 3D reconstruction.

Plugin to Exclude Redundant Images. If the images for the 3D reconstruction are extracted from a video, it can happen that the camera is stationary for some time and therefore the following images are nearly identical. To detect and filter these redundant images, we identify missing camera movement by calculating the optical flow following the method of Farnebäck [8] and specify a threshold for minimum camera movement. The total algorithm can be split in three major steps: 1.) Calculate optical flow with the method of Farnebäck 2.) Estimate movement of the camera 3.) Select keyframes. As mentioned before the plugin calculates the optical flow between two frames using the OpenCV [3] implementation of the Farnebäck algorithm. Because this step can take some time we added the possibility to use a CUDA optimised variant. The first frame is called the reference image because it will be the starting point to which every following image will be compared to until a new keyframe is selected. From the estimated values of the optical flow we calculate the trimmed mean to get a score for the amount of movement between two images, which is compared to the parameter *movement threshold*. This approach is methodologically difficult if two images are compared that do not show sufficient similarity. To prevent this from happening the plugin uses a second parameter named *reset delta*. It determines how many frames are allowed to be between two compared images until in each case a new reference frame is set and the process starts again from the beginning. In contrast to approaches such as simultaneous localization and mapping (SLAM), we do not need any further information in addition to the images. This includes the fact that a calibrated camera is not required to use this plugin.

Plugin to Exclude Images Affected by Motion Blur. Sudden movements can lead to motion blur, which significantly reduces the quality of such images. Using a sliding window approach, we search for images without motion blur and, if motion blur is detected, for spatially close replacement images. We calculate a sharpness score for each image and compare it with the values of surrounding images to get a relative score for the sharpness of the image. To calculate this score, we rely on established methods. Pertuz et al. state in their work that depending on the image content, type of camera and level of noise, different algorithms produce competitive results [14]. We therefore offer two options as baseline methods. First, the Tenegrad algorithm using Sobel operators according to the implementation described in [14] and second a technique utilising the variance of the image Laplacian [13]. If the sharpness score of an image divided by the average value of its window is bigger than a defined threshold, this image is considered sharp and will be selected as keyframe. In case keyframes are already sampled, we can try to obtain keyframes with a lower motion blur by taking the neighbouring images into account. A window of a certain size is created around each keyframe, in which the image with the highest sharpness value is selected as the substitute keyframe.

Enrichment with Additional Information by Semantic Segmentation. Objects such as pedestrians or cars that move dynamically in the scene hinder 3D reconstruction because it is more difficult to find correspondences between images. Instead of selecting keyframes as previously explained, this plugin generates additional information by masking the challenging areas in the input images by incorporating semantic information. In this way we prevent not only unstable matches of feature points between images but also that these regions have to be processed at all. For this we use the ability of COLMAP to use binary masks as input in addition to the images. We generate these masks through semantic segmentation by transferring the included classes into the binary mask. For our baseline plugin we use neural networks consisting of a DeepLabv3+ [5] model with a ResNet101 [11] backbone. For a faster execution speed on weaker hardware, we provide networks trained on different resolutions. All networks are trained on the Cityscapes data set [6] and provide segmentations for 19 classes. However, it is very easy to add additional neural networks with different architectures or which have been trained on other data sets. Our developed plugin is able to display a live preview of the segmentations as well as the binary mask. In this way, combinations of classes or different deep learning models can be tested quickly. For broad compatibility we use OpenCV as inference framework which allows a fallback to the CPU if no CUDA compatible graphics card is available.

3.3   Batch Processing

To prevent the user from having to perform all the steps described above for every image sequence batch processing can be used. Every sampling plugin can be added multiples times with any configuration wanted. Likewise, multiple export steps with different settings can be added to the workflow. Multiple exports can be useful to e.g. export images with different resolutions or with varying frame rate to different locations. The currently selected workflow can be seen and edited in 4 on the graphical user interface shown in Fig. 1. Starting the batch processing will run every step in the workflow in the defined order. The specified workflow can be saved and loaded into other projects, and also used to start our software in headless mode. In this case, an input sequence must be specified for which batch processing is then performed.

4   Experiments

To evaluate the advantage of our framework, we compare the output with the widely used approach of sub-sampling the input image sequences to a fixed fps rate. We will first focus on the evaluation of our plugins for frame selection and to what extent they have an influence on the quality and duration of the 3D reconstruction. In addition, the following section examines if the quality of the reconstructions can be further improved by removing challenging image regions. For this, complete 3D reconstructions are created with COLMAP for the sequences preprocessed by our framework and a corresponding 1 fps baseline. Our video data sets for this come from two different sources. The first consists of aerial imagery taken from oblique view by an UAV flying around a point of interest. This scenario features a rural setting where buildings and objects were captured at different altitudes and camera angles by a DJI Phantom 3 Pro. The flight altitude varies across the sequences from 2 m to 18 m and cars as well as moving people are visible in some scenes. They also include motion blur and scenes where the UAV is stationary. Due to the lack of ground truth data, we can evaluate the achieved results here mainly qualitatively and measure the speed increase of the reconstruction by excluding redundant images. In order to quantitatively evaluate the quality of the estimated camera trajectories and depth maps from COLMAP, we therefore additionally recorded synthetic sequences. We use a modification of the code from Johnson-Roberson et al. [12] to gather data from the video game GTAV. This allows us to extract ground truth depth maps and camera trajectories from the GPU. Unfortunately, there is no way to access the underlying 3D models and simple back projection of the depth maps only works if the scene does not contain moving objects, otherwise artefacts will occur. For the evaluation, we recorded eight synthetic video sequences and their ground truth, which contain areas with a lot of movement and sections where the flight speed of the UAV varies. The synthetic sequences differ from the real-world data set mainly by the urban setting and a partly higher flight altitude. Examples of the two data sets are visible in Fig. 2.

Fig. 2. The first row shows examples of the rural real-world data set and the second row from the urban synthetic data set. The sequences containing the last three images of the second row are referred to as A, B and C in the following evaluation.

4.1   Experimental Setup for the Frame Selection

For our frame selection we rely on the following three plugins: 1) First we filter out redundant frames 2) Then we down sample the video to 1 fps 3) In the last step we look for blurred images and try to replace them with better neighbouring frames. To evaluate this, we perform dense COLMAP reconstructions at both full frame rate as well as at 1 fps and using our approach described above. All reconstructions were carried out on a Nvidia Tesla P40 with a Xeon E5-2650 CPU. To assess the performance of our framework, we compare the results achieved with COLMAP to the ground truth of our synthetic data set. As a metric for evaluating the quality of our depth maps in this context, we use the accuracy δ_θ, which is defined as follows:

$$\delta_\theta \left(d, \hat{d} \right) = \frac{1}{m} \sum_{i=1}^{m} \max \left(\frac{d_i}{\hat{d}_i}, \frac{\hat{d}_i}{d_i} \right) < \theta. \tag{1}$$

It classifies a pixel in the estimated depth map as correct if the estimate is within a certain threshold θ to the corresponding measurement. $\delta_{1.25}$ for example describes the proportion of pixels, relative to the number of pixels m, for which an estimate exists and for which the difference between the estimate d and the ground truth $\hat{d}$ is not greater than 25 of $\hat{d}$. For the evaluation of the camera trajectory, we use the Root Mean Square Error (RMSE) to measure the deviation of the estimated camera position from the ground truth pose. We use the library evo [9] for the quantitative evaluation and visualisation of the camera trajectories.

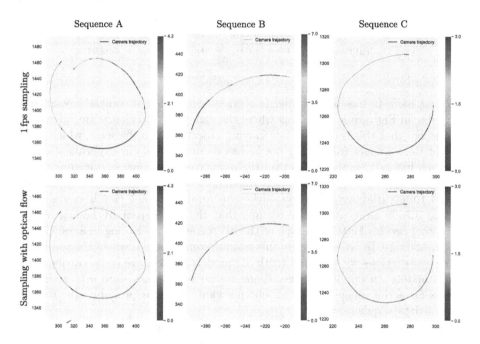

Fig. 3. Exemplary comparison of the three trajectories sampled in the first row using 1 fps and in the second row using optical flow. The trajectories show the flight path of a UAV in metres, projected onto the XY-plane, with the distance to the previous image position colour-coded. Especially in regions with high flight speed it is visible that our sampling using the optical flow is more balanced.

Both quantitatively and qualitatively from the colouring of the trajectories in Fig. 3, it can be seen that for most cases the sampling through our framework leads to a more balanced camera trajectory than sampling based on frame rate alone. As shown in Table 1, the 10 % percentile of the distance to the previous camera position is almost everywhere above and the 90 % percentile below the baseline method of 1 fps sampling. In addition, the standard deviation of our sampling approach through the optical flow is noticeably lower. This shows that not only are fewer images sampled in regions with little camera movement, but

Table 1. Quantitative results for three sequences reconstructed with COLMAP, once using 1 fps as well as using optical flow based sampling. In almost all cases, the 10% percentile is higher and the 90% percentile is lower than the baseline of the 1 fps sampling. Furthermore, all three sequences have a lower standard deviation with our approach. The two columns on the right show that our approach does not lead to inferior quality, as the errors for pose and depth estimation indicate.

Sequence	Sampling method	σ	$Q_{0.1}$	$Q_{0.9}$	RMSE pose	$\delta_{0.05}$ accuracy
A	1 fps	1.26 m	0.70 m	4.20 m	0.0329 m	0.9417 %
	Optical flow	0.95 m	0.65 m	3.60 m	0.0296 m	0.9420 %
B	1 fps	0.90 m	0.70 m	2.80 m	0.0066 m	0.9596 %
	Optical flow	0.64 m	0.90 m	2.40 m	0.0052 m	0.9594 %
C	1 fps	1.95 m	0.80 m	6.68 m	0.0245 m	0.8886 %
	Optical flow	1.62 m	1.03 m	6.00 m	0.0311 m	0.8894 %

also that more frames are selected in sections with a lot of camera movement. As visible in Fig. 3, not all images where the camera is stationary are excluded. We suspect that this is due to some moving objects within the scene which may prevent these images from being marked as redundant. In our experiments, our approach has no negative impact on the quality of the camera trajectories and depth maps. As shown in Table 1, the differences are small and can be explained by run time variability. However, since the resulting point clouds contain on average 5.76 % more points, we assume that the more spatially homogeneous sampling provides better coverage of the 3D scene than selecting images with a fixed frame rate. In order to verify this assumption, a comparison of the resulting 3D reconstructions with ground truth 3D models would have to be carried out. Unfortunately, to our knowledge, there are no benchmark data sets with 3D models for aerial imagery from an oblique view, which is probably due to the difficult data acquisition.

In contrast to this approach, however, sampling through optical flow can also be used to reduce the amount of data to be processed by excluding redundant images. As before, sections in which the UAV is stationary are filtered out, but in contrast, no more additional frames are placed elsewhere. Especially due to the often quadratic run time complexity of global methods such as COLMAP, the reduction of a few redundant images can make a significant difference with large data sets. For a sequence with initially 1,056 images, our approach leads to a reduction in images of approx. 5 % especially in regions with little camera movement. This reduces the processing time from 1,510.24 min to 1,388.25 min which corresponds to a decrease of 8.1 %. For this, we measured the individual duration of all steps in COLMAP's 3D reconstruction pipeline. Since the speedup is divided into 10.52% for the sparse reconstruction and 4.95% for the dense reconstruction, especially feature matching and sparse mapping seem to benefit from our filtering in advance, as the savings are disproportionately high.

To further avoid processing images that do not provide novel content, we have developed a plugin that can detect and replace images affected by motion

Fig. 4. As can be seen in the images I_1 to I_5, the camera rotates quickly within approx. 2 s by 180° and therefore causes significant motion blur. The timeline below shows the entire sequence, with each red bar corresponding to an image that is considered sharp. The blurred images shown above are located in the middle of the highlighted area and are successfully detected and excluded. (Color figure online)

blur. The sequence we use for this shows usable images for most of the flight, but it includes a section where the camera rotates 180° in about 2 s and the corresponding images become unusable due high degrees of motion blur. In Fig. 4 the corresponding section is shown, once by exemplary images and on the timeline below as an area marked in blue. Each red bar corresponds to an image that is considered sharp enough. As can be seen here, the area with motion blur is reliably detected and no images are selected here. However, it is also visible that key frames accumulate around this point. This occurs because although our plugin searches for a spatially close replacements, the search for better neighbouring images on this explicit sequence does not work optimally due to the fact that the blurred section is too long and therefore no better images exist. When selecting replacement images, the current image density should be taken into account in the future or the replacement should be made optional.

4.2 Semantic Segmentation for Masking Potentially Moving Objects

In addition to the reduction to the most significant images, our framework has as a second type of plugins for the enrichment with additional information. Currently, we focus on masking challenging image areas through semantic segmentation. For this purpose, we provide a plugin that allows deep learning models with different depths and architectures to be imported and applied to the images. Since there are currently hardly any data sets for semantic segmentation of aerial images from oblique view, all neural networks for this purpose were trained on the Cityscapes data set. Being an autonomous driving data set, the domain gap with regard to the camera angle is in some cases large, which can also be seen in the results. However, as visible in Fig. 5, reasonable results are achieved for relatively flat camera angles. Vegetation is reliably detected from all camera angles, but due to only one class available, a distinction between not problematic vegetation and trees moving in the wind is not possible. Since we filter out all objects that could be moving, objects such as parked cars are also excluded, which may be undesirable depending on the type of application.

In our experiments with aerial images, masking people and vehicles did not lead to a quantitatively better quality of the 3D models. We attribute this to

| Input image | Semantic segmentation | Binary mask |

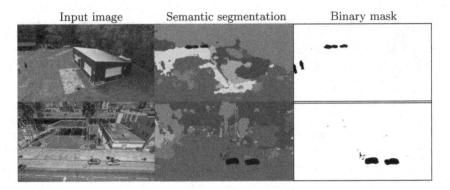

Fig. 5. Examples of our semantic segmentation plugin. From left to right: input image, semantic segmentation and binary mask excluding the classes car and person.

sub-optimal segmentations, as the neural networks we use were not trained for oblique-view aerial imagery and thus contain a high rate of errors when the camera angle is very different from that of the training data. In addition, COLMAP already has photometric and geometric consistency verification techniques that can compensate for some artefacts induced by movement [16]. During our tests, however, we noticed that especially scenarios with a large amount of movement, e.g. next to a motorway, often did not yield a useful sparse reconstruction. Although in some cases a useful sparse reconstruction can be obtained by starting the reconstruction several times, it is here in particular that we see potential for semantic segmentation to ease 3D reconstruction. Once the sparse reconstruction succeeds, the results for the dense reconstruction are quite good, as can be seen from sequence C in Table 1. However, the drop in $\delta_{0.05}$ accuracy of the depth maps compared to both sequences A and B with less movement within the scene is worth noting. This is probably because moving objects are filtered out in the reconstruction but are present in the ground truth depth maps.

5   Conclusion and Future Work

In this paper, we presented a new framework for pre-processing image sequences to facilitate 3D reconstruction, which we publish open source using the MIT licence. The modular architecture allows for easy customisation and integration of already existing algorithms by encapsulating them in plugins using our simple interfaces. This provides the opportunity to participate in the development of the core application or individual plugins. So far, we have developed plugins that can detect redundant frames, replace blurred images and also mask potentially moving objects. As shown in the previous section, these baseline methods are already capable of accelerating a downstream 3D reconstruction by 8.1 % through reducing redundant images. By creating a dedicated workflow for batch processing, large quantities of images can be edited with little effort, e.g. by specifying frame rate, resolution, cropping and the utilised plugins only once and then processing multiple videos with them. In the future, we focus on extending our current plugins and the development of further ones. One possibility here would be to perform a real-time SLAM algorithm such as ORB-SLAM3 [4] and extract the key frames or incorporate metadata present in the input videos. Similarly, we plan to further enhance the semantic segmentation plugin by incorporating additional models trained on other data sets, as it has been shown that the domain gap can be very high for aerial imagery depending on the camera angle. We are convinced that the framework we provide offers great added value, especially when more plugins become available in the future.

References

1. Ballabeni, A., Apollonio, F., Gaiani, M., Remondino, F.: Advances in image preprocessing to improve automated 3D reconstruction. In: ISPRS - International Archives of the Photogrammetry, Remote Sensing and Spatial Information Sciences XL-5/W4, pp. 315–323, February 2015. https://doi.org/10.5194/isprsarchives-XL-5-W4-315-2015
2. Bellavia, F., Fanfani, M., Colombo, C.: Fast adaptive frame preprocessing for 3D reconstruction, vol. 3, March 2015. https://doi.org/10.5220/0005272702600267
3. Bradski, G.: The OpenCV library. Dr. Dobb's J. Softw. Tools **120**, 122–125 (2000)
4. Campos, C., Elvira, R., Rodríguez, J.J.G., M. Montiel, J.M., D. Tardós, J.: ORB-SLAM3: an accurate open-source library for visual, visual-inertial, and multimap slam. IEEE Trans. Robot. 1–17 (2021). https://doi.org/10.1109/TRO.2021.3075644
5. Chen, L., Papandreou, G., Schroff, F., Adam, H.: Rethinking atrous convolution for semantic image segmentation. CoRR abs/1706.05587 (2017). http://arxiv.org/abs/1706.05587
6. Cordts, M., et al.: The cityscapes dataset for semantic urban scene understanding. In: Proceedings of the IEEE Conference on Computer Vision and Pattern Recognition, pp. 3213–3223 (2016)
7. Engel, J., Schöps, T., Cremers, D.: LSD-SLAM: large-scale direct monocular SLAM. In: European Conference on Computer Vision (ECCV), September 2014
8. Farnebäck, G.: Two-frame motion estimation based on polynomial expansion. In: Bigun, J., Gustavsson, T. (eds.) SCIA 2003. LNCS, vol. 2749, pp. 363–370. Springer, Heidelberg (2003). https://doi.org/10.1007/3-540-45103-X_50
9. Grupp, M.: EVO: Python package for the evaluation of odometry and SLAM (2017). https://github.com/MichaelGrupp/evo
10. He, K., Gkioxari, G., Dollár, P., Girshick, R.: Mask R-CNN. In: 2017 IEEE International Conference on Computer Vision (ICCV), pp. 2980–2988 (2017). https://doi.org/10.1109/ICCV.2017.322
11. He, K., Zhang, X., Ren, S., Sun, J.: Deep residual learning for image recognition. In: Proceedings of the IEEE Conference on Computer Vision and Pattern Recognition, pp. 770–778 (2016)
12. Johnson-Roberson, M., Barto, C., Mehta, R., Sridhar, S.N., Rosaen, K., Vasudevan, R.: Driving in the matrix: can virtual worlds replace human-generated annotations for real world tasks? In: IEEE International Conference on Robotics and Automation, pp. 1–8 (2017)

13. Pech-Pacheco, J.L., Cristóbal, G., Chamorro-Martinez, J., Fernández-Valdivia, J.: Diatom autofocusing in brightfield microscopy: a comparative study. In: Proceedings 15th International Conference on Pattern Recognition. ICPR-2000, vol. 3, pp. 314–317. IEEE (2000)
14. Pertuz, S., Puig, D., García, M.: Analysis of focus measure operators in shape-from-focus. Pattern Recogn. **46**(5), 1415–1432 (11 2012). https://doi.org/10.1016/j.patcog.2012.11.011
15. Schönberger, J.L., Frahm, J.M.: Structure-from-motion revisited. In: Proceedings of IEEE Conference on Computer Vision and Pattern Recognition, pp. 4104–4113 (2016)
16. Schönberger, J.L., Zheng, E., Frahm, J.M., Pollefeys, M.: Pixelwise view selection for unstructured multi-view stereo. In: Proceedings of European Conference on Computer Vision, pp. 501–518 (2016)

3D Registration of Deformable Objects Using a Time-of-Flight Camera

Su Wai Tun[1], Takashi Komuro[1(✉)], and Hajime Nagahara[2]

[1] Saitama University, Saitama 338-8570, Japan
tun.s.w.748@ms.saitama-u.ac.jp, komuro@mail.saitama-u.ac.jp
[2] Osaka University, Suita 565-0871, Japan

Abstract. We propose a framework for 3D deformable object registration using both texture and shape information. Registration is performed using depth and infrared (IR) images captured with a Time-of-Flight (ToF) camera. Our method can register objects that have sparse texture and little concavity/convexity, and can be applied to human organs for surgery assistance. We demonstrate the effectiveness of our approach using videos of densely and sparsely textured paper sheets and an endoscopic stereo video by comparing the performance of our method with the methods using only shape or texture information. The experimental results showed that our method has good registration capability in terms of both texture and shape.

Keywords: Non-rigid registration · RGB-D camera · Surgery assistance

1 Introduction

3D deformable object registration is an active research topic in computer vision and its application fields. The deformable registration is to find the geometrical transformation to align an image with a reference image. If this technology could be applied to living human organs, it would be possible to assist the surgery by overlaying the vessels and tumors, which were measured in advance, onto the organs in real time.

In the medical field, non-rigid registration is mostly applied on CT or MRI images [8,14] and it can be used for the preoperative treatment planning. On the other hand, in the robotic research field, deformable registration is often performed on 3D point clouds for complex-shaped objects [4].

There are some studies to recover the 3D shape of the deformable objects from monocular images using deformable registration. Some of them use prior deformation model to recover the shape of deformable surfaces [3,10]. In [10], they constructed the textured 3D model of the object to compute correspondences between 3D surface locations and 2D image features. Salzmann et al. [11] presented the closed-form solution to recover the shape of non-rigid inelastic surface without any initial shape estimation. In this work, they generated

ⓒ Springer Nature Switzerland AG 2021
G. Bebis et al. (Eds.): ISVC 2021, LNCS 13017, pp. 455–465, 2021.
https://doi.org/10.1007/978-3-030-90439-5_36

the synthetic textured image correspond to the reference image by using the recovered shape.

It becomes difficult to perform registration when the deformable surface has sparse texture since sparse texture on the surface does not provide useful information for registration. Ngo et al. proposed a method for monocular 3D reconstruction of sparsely textured and occluded surfaces [9]. They introduced gradient-based pixel descriptors for robust template matching and the isometric deformation constraints enforcing that the surface should not stretch or shrink. Although they used a Kinect camera for creating the dataset, the depth information was used only for generating the ground truth surfaces and used only image information for 3D reconstruction. Therefore, their method has a limitation that template images need to be obtained from a flat surface.

Our approach is based on [9] but we use depth and IR images captured with a ToF camera to obtain shape and texture information. The main difference is that our method can use a non-flat surface as the reference surface, which allows our method to be applied to human organs for surgery assistance. Our method can register objects with sparse texture and with little concavity or convexity. We demonstrate the effectiveness of our approach using videos of textured paper and an endoscopic stereo video by comparing with the methods using only texture or shape information.

2   Related Work

3D deformable object registration is a challenging task in computer vision. Many approaches have been proposed for deformable registration. Existing approaches can be roughly categorized into shape-based registration and texture-based registration.

Shape-Based Registration. Many studies have been conducted on registration of deformable objects using shape information. Salzmann et al. [10] introduced a deformation model for deformable 3D surfaces. They used a small subset of the angles between facets to parameterize the shape of triangulated mesh and created a representative sample of possible shapes. To produce the low-dimensional models, they performed dimension reduction by using principal component analysis (PCA). To recover the shape of deformable surfaces, their approach needs to create the samples. They assume all shapes are equally probable and so similarly influence the model deriving from these samples.

Dyke et al. [2] proposes two distinct changes to a typical non-rigid Iterative Closet Point (N-ICP) registration pipeline for large-scale and non-isometric deformations. Firstly, they describe a method using the principal scaling factor to estimate anisotropic deformations on a discrete mesh and incorporate it into N-ICP pipeline. Secondly, they introduce correspondence generation in non-isometrically deformation regions and inconsistent correspondence pruning method based on local geodesics. To effectively handle large deformations, they incorporate r-ring as-rigid-as-possible (ARAP) formulation into their N-ICP registration pipeline. However, if the initial correspondences are largely wrong, the performance of their method is poor. Therefore, their method relies on the initial correspondences.

To track deformation from image to image, some existing approaches need to estimate the initial shape. Salzmann et al. [11] proposed a close-form solution to detect and reconstruct the 3D shape for a non-rigid inelastic surface from 3D to 2D correspondences. Their approach does not need the initial shape estimation. Haung et al. [4] presents pairwise non-rigid registration algorithm for partially overlapped point cloud surface. They define non-rigid registration as an optimization problem. Therefore, deformation optimization is solved by alternating correspondences computation. In their approach, geodesic distance between a set of correspondences is preserved to be stable correspondences. Due to the topology changing, geodesic consistency preservation is invalid. Therefore, their method will fail in this condition.

In medical field, tracking organs deformation due to our respiration system is a challenging task. Lu et al. [7] proposed a non-rigid registration method based on linear elastic model. In their approach, the image region of interest was divided in triangular grid. Extracted image feature point are used to form the irregular triangular grid. For similarity measure, the minimum potential energy was used to achieve their registration. They validated the robustness of their method on 2D CT heart image time series dataset. Due to the large number of triangular and small shape of the triangular, their method still needs many iterations to converge. Kajihara et al. [5] proposed a feature-based non-rigid registration method that establishes the transformation field and estimates the rigid transform in local region and then blends them to interpolate the transform at every pixel. Since their approach is feature-based, their method may not work well if sufficient number of feature points are not extracted.

Texture-Based Registration. Some studies uses texture information for registration of deformable objects. Sidorov et al. [13] proposed groupwise non-rigid registration for textured surfaces such as human faces that were obtained using a 3D scanner. Their method finds correspondences between meshes and build high quality 3D appearance models.

Savran et al. [12] presented an automated non-linear elasticity surface registration method by using both attraction forces originating from geometrical and textural similarities. To avoid the loss of information during mapping between 2D and 3D, they use mesh parameterization approach instead of using projection. Although their approach handles the large deformation, if human surface topology changes such as open mouth expression, their approach cannot solve such kind of changes.

In texture-based registration, less texture and occlusions on surface are more challenging problems. Ngo et al. [9] addressed these problems by proposing a template-matching approach. Moreover, they added the additional constraint for 3D shape of the surface that do not stretch or shrink. In their work, they used gradient-based pixel descriptors for robust template matching and compute the relevancy score for each pixel to handle surface occlusions. Their approach can track well-textured and sparsely textured deforming surfaces in monocular video dataset with presence of occlusion or without occlusion. However, their method has a limitation that template images need to be obtained from a flat surface.

3   Proposed Framework

We propose a framework that uses a ToF camera for 3D registration of deformable objects. We use IR images for texture registration and depth images for shape registration.

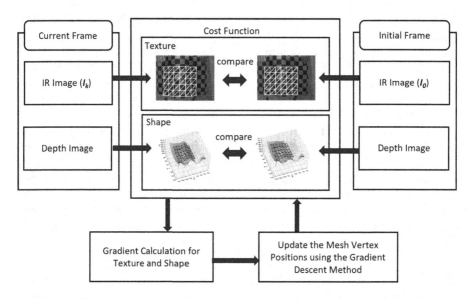

Fig. 1. Overview of our method. The cost function is defined using texture and shape differences between the initial frame and the input frame. The gradient of the cost function is calculated to minimize the function with respect to the 2D positions of the mesh vertices.

3.1   Methodology

Assume that the IR image in the initial frame $I_0(\mathbf{x})$ and the IR image of the current frame $I_k(\mathbf{x})$ are given, where $\mathbf{x} = (x, y)$ is the pixel coordinates. We set the 2D vertex positions of the triangular meshes for the initial frame, $\mathbf{v}_{i,j}^0$, on a regular grid. We perform registration by finding the corresponding 2D vertex positions, $\mathbf{v}_{i,j}$.

For texture registration, the texture patterns in each mesh between the initial IR image and the current IR image are compared. The warping function $\mathbf{W}(\mathbf{x}; V)$ is determined from the 2D positions of the mesh vertices $\mathbf{V} = \{\mathbf{v}_{0,0}, \mathbf{v}_{1,0}, \ldots\}$. Using the warping function, a pixel in the initial frame image is mapped to a

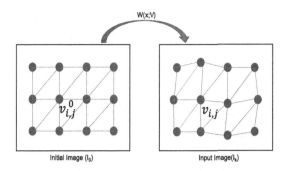

Fig. 2. The warping function $\mathbf{W}(\mathbf{x}; V)$ is determined from the 2D positions of the mesh vertices $\mathbf{v}_{i,j}$. Using this function, a pixel in the initial frame image is mapped to a pixel in the current frame image.

pixel in the current frame image as illustrated in Fig. 2. We define the cost for texture registration:

$$E_{img} = \sum_x \{I(\mathbf{W}(\mathbf{x}; V)) - I_0(\mathbf{x})\}^2 \tag{1}$$

For shape registration, we assume that the deformed surface should not stretch or shrink as in [9]. Therefore, the lengths in 3D space between two adjacent vertices before and after deformation are compared. The 3D positions of the vertices are obtained using the depth images. We define the cost for shape registration:

$$E_{len} = \sum_{i,j} \{(||\mathbf{X}_{i,j} - \mathbf{X}_{i+1,j}|| - ||\mathbf{X}^0_{i,j} - \mathbf{X}^0_{i+1,j}||)^2 \\ + (||\mathbf{X}_{i,j} - \mathbf{X}_{i,j+1}|| - ||\mathbf{X}^0_{i,j} - \mathbf{X}^0_{i,j+1}||)^2\} \tag{2}$$

where $\mathbf{X}^0_{i,j}$ are the 3D positions of the vertices in the initial frame, $\mathbf{v}^0_{i,j}$, and $\mathbf{X}_{i,j}$ are the 3D positions of the vertices in the current frame, $\mathbf{v}_{i,j}$. By combining these costs, we obtain the total cost function considering both texture and shape:

$$E = \lambda_1 E_{img} + \lambda_2 E_{len} \tag{3}$$

where, λ_1 and λ_2 are the weights for texture and shape costs, respectively. To minimize the cost function for texture and shape, we use the gradient descent method with respect to $\mathbf{V}$ [1]. The gradient of the texture cost is calculated as

$$\frac{\partial E_{img}}{\partial v_{i,j}} = 2\sum_x \{\nabla I \frac{\partial W}{\partial p}\}^T \{I(\mathbf{W}(\mathbf{x}; V)) - I_0(\mathbf{x})\} \tag{4}$$

The gradient of the shape cost is calculated as

$$\frac{\partial E_{len}}{\partial v_{i,j}} = 2\sum_{i,j} \{(||\mathbf{X}_{i,j} - X_{i+1,j}|| - ||\mathbf{X}^0_{i,j} - \mathbf{X}^0_{i+1,j}||)\frac{\partial}{\partial p}||\mathbf{X}_{i,j} - \mathbf{X}_{i+1,j}|| \\ + (||\mathbf{X}_{i,j} - \mathbf{X}_{i,j+1}|| - ||\mathbf{X}^0_{i,j} - \mathbf{X}^0_{i,j+1}||)\frac{\partial}{\partial p}||\mathbf{X}_{i,j} - \mathbf{X}_{i,j+1}||\} \tag{5}$$

The 2D vertex positions of the meshes are updated according to the gradient calculation as below:

$$\mathbf{v}_{i,j} = \mathbf{v}_{i,j} - w\left(\lambda_1\frac{\partial E_{img}}{\partial v_{i,j}} + \lambda_2\frac{\partial E_{len}}{\partial v_{i,j}}\right) \qquad (6)$$

where, w is a weight for the gradient descent method.

This is iteratively performed until the cost function is approximately converged. The overview of our method is shown in Fig. 1.

4   Experimental Results

We implemented our method and conducted experiments using two types of datasets. Our method was compared with the methods using only texture and only shape information.

4.1   Densely and Sparsely Textured Paper Sheets

The videos of densely and sparsely textured paper sheets were used in the experiment. These videos were captured by DepthSense 325 ToF camera. These paper sheets were pushed and pulled from both sides by hand to be deformed. The camera was about 0.3 m away from the sheets. The number of frames were 32 for each video. We made shading correction to compensate unequal lighting on the sheets. The resolution of both IR images and depth images was 320×240 pixels.

We set the number of mesh vertices to 7×6. We used the following parameter values: $\lambda_1 = 1$, $\lambda_2 = 10^5$ and $w = 10^{-7}$. We set λ_1 or λ_2 to be zero for the methods using only shape or texture information.

To evaluate the quality of registration, the input images were warped back into those in the coordinate system of the initial frame image, which we call restored images. The registration and restoration results for densely and sparsely textured paper sheets are shown in Figs. 3 and 4, respectively. For both densely and sparsely textured paper sheets, we can see the texture in the restored images is similar to that of the initial frame image. Although the registration using texture only was able to register the texture well, the meshes were distorted a little because the shape of the meshes is not considered in the texture-based registration. The 3D shapes of the sheet and meshes are shown in Fig. 5. In the registration using shape, we can see that the shape of the meshes was more stationary than registration using texture only.

To evaluate the registration performance in terms of texture, we calculated peak signal to noise ratio (PSNR) between the restored images and the initial frame image. To evaluate the registration performance in terms of shape, we calculated Mean Square Error (MSE) between the inter-vertex lengths of the initial mesh and those of the registered mesh. The PSNR and MSE results for densely and sparsely textured paper sheets are shown in Figs. 6 and 7, respectively. The results showed that the proposed method was as good as the texture-only method and was better than the shape-only method. MSE results showed that the proposed method was better than the texture-only method but was worse than the shape-only method. These results showed that our proposed method has good registration capability in terms of both texture and shape.

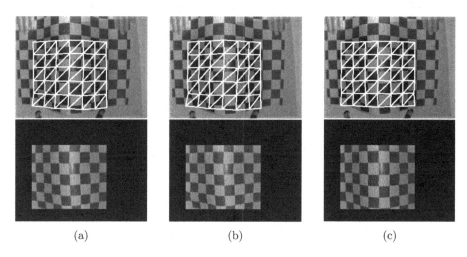

(a)   (b)   (c)

Fig. 3. The registration and restoration results for densely textured paper sheet: (a) Registration using both texture and shape (b) Registration using texture only, and (c) Registration using shape only.

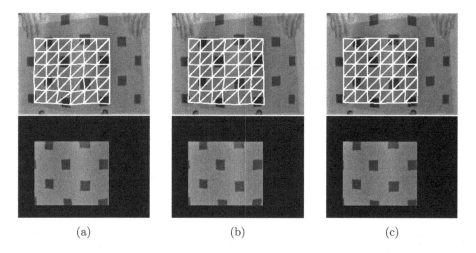

(a)   (b)   (c)

Fig. 4. The registration and restoration results for sparsely textured paper sheet: (a) Registration using both texture and shape (b) Registration using texture only, and (c) Registration using shape only.

4.2   Endoscopic Stereo Video

We also applied our method to a publicly available endoscopic stereo video that contained a deforming heart from the Hamlyn Center Laparoscopic/Endoscopic Dataset [6]. To reconstruct the 3D shapes from the stereo video, we estimated the disparity maps by using the semi-global block matching (SGBM) algorithm.

(a)   (b)

Fig. 5. The registration of the deformed surface of the both densely and sparsely textured paper sheets: (a) Registration using texture only, registration using shape only and registration using both texture and shape of densely textured paper respectively, (b) Registration using texture only, registration using shape only and registration using both texture and shape of sparsely textured paper respectively.

The estimated disparity maps are converted into depth images by using the following equations:

$$z = f\frac{b}{d} \tag{7}$$

where, z is the depth, f is the focal length, b is the baseline, d is the disparity.

We used 194 frame images in the video. The number of mesh vertices was 5×4. For this dataset, we used the parameters $\lambda_1 = 4$ and $\lambda_2 = 10^3$ for both texture and shape information, $\lambda_1 = 1$, $\lambda_2 = 0$ for texture only information, and $\lambda_1 = 0$, $\lambda_2 = 10^5$ for shape only information. The qualitative results for stereo video dataset are shown in Fig. 8. We can see the texture in the restored image was similar to that in the initial image. The heart in the video has sparse texture, so it was more challenging to register.

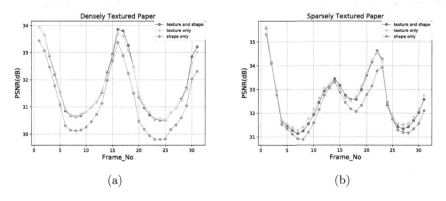

Fig. 6. PSNR results for densely and sparsely textured papers in each frame: (a) PSNR results for densely texture paper, (b) PSNR results for sparsely textured paper.

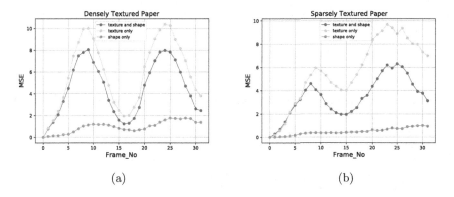

Fig. 7. MSE results for densely and sparsely textured papers per frame number: (a) MSE results for densely textured paper, (b) MSE results for sparsely textured paper.

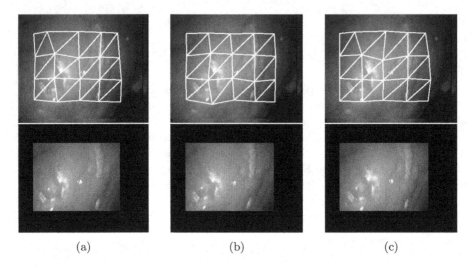

(a)   (b)   (c)

Fig. 8. The registration and restoration results for the endoscopic stereo video: (a) Registration using both texture and shape, (b) Registration using texture only, and (c) Registration using shape only.

5   Conclusion and Future Work

We proposed a framework for 3D deformable objects registration using both texture and shape information obtained using a ToF camera. We demonstrated the effectiveness of our proposed method by using videos of textured paper sheets captured with a ToF camera and an endoscopic stereo video. The experimental results showed that our method has good registration capability in terms of both texture and shape. Future work includes conducting experiments using real organ images captured with a ToF camera and extending our framework for real time registration.

References

1. Baker, S., Matthews, I.: Lucas-Kanade 20 years on: a unifying framework. Int. J. Comput. Vis. **56**, 221–255 (2004)
2. Dyke, R.M., Lai, Y.K., Rosin, P.L., Tam, G.K.: Non-rigid registration under anisotropic deformations. Comput. Aided Geom. Des. **71**, 142–156 (2019)
3. Ellingsen, L.M., Chintalapani, G., Taylor, R.H., Prince, J.L.: Robust deformable image registration using prior shape information for atlas to patient registration. Comput. Med. Imaging Graph. **34**(1), 79–90 (2010)
4. Huang, Q.X., Adams, B., Wicke, M., Guibas, L.J.: Non-rigid registration under isometric deformations. Comput. Graph. Forum. **27**(5), 1449–1457 (2008)
5. Kajihara, T., et al.: Non-rigid registration of serial section images by blending transforms for 3D reconstruction. Pattern Recogn. **96**, 106956 (2019)
6. London, I.: Hamlyn Centre laparoscopic/endoscopic video datasets (2019). http:// hamlyn.doc.ic.ac.uk/vision/. Accessed 15 Jan 2019

7. Lu, X., Ma, H., Zhang, B.: A non-rigid medical image registration method based on improved linear elastic model. Optik **123**(20), 1867–1873 (2012)
8. Lu, X., Zhao, Y., Zhang, B., Wu, J., Li, N., Jia, W.: A non-rigid cardiac image registration method based on an optical flow model. Optik **124**(20), 4266–4273 (2013)
9. Ngo, D. T., Park, S., Jorstad, A., Crivellaro, A., Yoo, C., Fua, P.: Dense image registration and deformable surface reconstruction in presence of occlusions and minimal texture. In: Proceedings of the IEEE International Conference on Computer Vision, pp. 2273–2281 (2015)
10. Salzmann, M., Pilet, J., Ilic, S., Fua, P.: Surface deformation models for nonrigid 3D shape recovery. IEEE Trans. Pattern Anal. Mach. Intell. **29**(8), 1481–1487 (2007)
11. Salzmann, M., Moreno-Noguer, F., Lepetit, V., Fua, P.: Closed-form solution to non-rigid 3D surface registration. In: Proceedings of European Conference on Computer Vision, pp. 581–594 (2008)
12. Savran, A., Sankur, B.: Non-rigid registration of 3D surfaces by deformable 2D triangular meshes. In: Proceedings of IEEE Computer Society Conference on Computer Vision and Pattern Recognition Workshops, pp. 1–6 (2008)
13. Sidorov, K. A., Richmond, S., Marshall, D.: Efficient groupwise non-rigid registration of textured surfaces. In: Proceedings of the IEEE Conference on Computer Vision and Pattern Recognition (2011)
14. Wang, J., Jiang, T.: Nonrigid registration of brain MRI using NURBS. Pattern Recogn. Lett. **28**(2), 214–223 (2007)

Pose Estimation of Texture-Less Targets for Unconstrained Grasping

Sixiong Xu[1], Pei Gong[1], Yanchao Dong[1(✉)], Lingling Gi[1], Cheng Huang[2], and Sibiao Wang[2]

[1] College of Electronic and Information Engineering, Tongji University, Shanghai 201804, People's Republic of China
dongyanchao@tongji.edu.cn
[2] Shanghai Waigaoqiao Power Generation CO., LTD., Shanghai 200137, People's Republic of China

Abstract. With the advent of Industry 4.0, the demand for estimating target pose keeps increasing. However, the accuracy of the existing pose estimation algorithms for texture-less targets is still poor. Traditional methods require approximately accurate initial pose or else they are easy to fall into a local optimum while the deep learning methods are limited in unconstrained environments where the unpredictable data can not be captured ahead for model training. Therefore, the paper proposes an innovative method which can cover the shortage of these two classes of methods. In our method, a multi-task model which can predict the pose of target and simultaneously obtain the edge map is designed. Then, the predicted pose and edge map are transferred to pose optimization module which is implemented based on edge matching. In addition, considering the lack of the pose datasets for texture-less objects, we design an effective pose dataset generation method based on 3D reconstruction. At last, the proposed system is tested on the public dataset and the rendered dataset. Experimental results demonstrate that the proposed algorithm is more accurate compared with the state-of-the-art methods.

Keywords: Pose estimation · Texture-less targets · Multi-task learning

1 Introduction

Vision-based pose estimation of target objects plays an important role in the fields of manufacturing and modern logostics as it can be used for robotic grasping. It is a challenging task and arouses the interest of some companies. For

Supported by the National Key R&D Program of China under Grant No. 2018YFB1 305300, the National Natural Science Foundation of China under Grant No. 61873189, the Natural Science Foundation of Shanghai under Grant No. 18ZR1442500, Shanghai Municipal Science and Technology Major Project under Grant No. 2021SHZDZX0100 and Shanghai Municipal Commission of Science and Technology Project under Grant No. 19511132101.

© Springer Nature Switzerland AG 2021
G. Bebis et al. (Eds.): ISVC 2021, LNCS 13017, pp. 466–477, 2021.
https://doi.org/10.1007/978-3-030-90439-5_37

example, the Amazon Picking Challenge whose task is to identify the objects on shelves, and to complete the target items transition through robotic grasping. To realize this goal, it requires accurate and fast pose estimation for target objects. Currently, the poses of industrial parts on assembly line are determined by fixtures or localization methods based on feature points. The detection and positioning performance will be significantly reduced, if working conditions are away from the structured assembly line. In addition, methods based on feature points are not suitable as the surfaces of industrial parts usually are texture-less. Therefore, research on pose estimation of texture-less targets for unconstrained grasping is still needed both for academic community and modern industry.

Traditional methods estimate optimal object pose based on image appearance and prior 3D model. Prisacariu et al. proposed a method [11] that can track and reconstruct objects in real time on mobile phone. The method uses an approximation of the standard distance field in the pose optimization process but needs IMU on mobile phone to operate. Works like D2CO [2,5] use global optimization methods for edge matching, which guarantee the accuracy and robustness of the pose tracking method. However, when the target objects are in the complex backgrounds, the accuracy and robustness will decrease due to the bad performance on edge detection by LSD and Canny detectors.

In recent years, deep learning methods have achieved excellent performance in many computer vision applications, such as object detection, classification and segmentation. Pose estimation algorithms based on deep learning are also increasingly emerging. Techniques such as viewpoints and keypoints in [17] and rendering [14] turn 3D pose estimation into a classification task through discretizing the pose space of an object. The method proposed by Tekin [15] follows the idea of the YOLO [12] algorithm, which is an end-to-end network that directly classifies the object and predicts the nine 2D projection points corresponding to the 3D bounding box of the target object, including the 8 vertices and center points of the 3D bounding box. Then the PnP algorithm is used to obtain the pose of the object. However, this method is not effective in estimating the poses of axisymmetric objects. Although many pose estimation methods have been demonstrated with satisfactory results, the accuracy decreases when the target object appears more refined. To reduce the error of pose estimation, further optimization algorithm is needed to be developed. Inspired by the edge tracking algorithm, Manhardt [8] et al. proposed an edge alignment method to optimize the pose without segmenting the scene. DeepIM [6] optimizes the pose of the object based on the iterative method. Given an initial pose, it iteratively refine the pose by matching the rendered image against the observed image. The HybridPose [13] method combines pose initialization and pose refinement to maximize the quality of the resulting object pose, and optimizes the pose by solving unconstrained nonlinear problems. These methods are effective when the initial pose is accurate. Hence, high precision initial pose is critical in the process of pose optimization.

In this paper, we combine traditional method with deep learning in our proposed algorithm considering the importance of edge map and initial pose in pose estimation for industrial parts. Firstly, the multi-task learning algorithm is used to estimate the initial pose of the object and extract the edge map of the scene. The initial pose is subsequently optimized based on edge matching for more precise grasping task. In view of the lack of pose datasets for texture-less objects, we build the industrial parts dataset based on 3D reconstruction. The main framework of our proposed algorithm is shown in Fig. 1. The main contributions in this paper are as follows:

1) Since the quality of the edge map and the initial pose will directly affect the speed and accuracy of latter pose optimization, a multi-task learning for 3D bounding box and edge map of target object is proposed.
2) There are few datasets for texture-less target objects, especially for industrial parts, and the production of these datasets is complicated. Hence, we propose an efficient method for generating pose dataset based on 3D reconstruction.

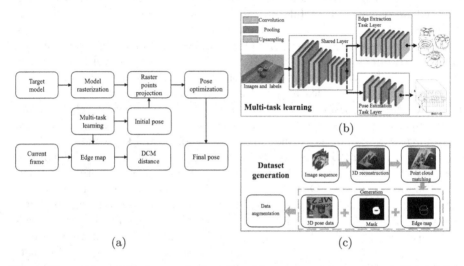

Fig. 1. Illustration of our proposed algorithm. (a) represents the overall pipeline of the recognition process from input data to final pose result. Details of multi-task learning included in (a) are shown in (b). The dataset generation method for the network is shown in (c).

2   Multi-task Learning for Initial Pose Estimation

We propose a pose estimation oriented multi-task learning method where the 3D bounding box coordinates, object class and edges of the current scene graph can be simultaneously detected through a single model. In this paper, we use hard parameter sharing mechanism to design multi-task network. Several convolutional layers are shared among multiple tasks. The structure of network is shown in Fig. 1(b). The multi-task learning network is based on the Dense Extreme Inception Network [10], which is a single task network and borrows the idea from Xception [3]. The network takes the input of the images and ground truth into the model, followed by extracting low-level features through the shared layer which contains a total of 18 convolutional layers and 3 maximum pooling layers. These features are then fed into the special layers of the two tasks respectively. The edge extraction network uses the DexiNet network proposed by Soria et al. [10]. The method of pose estimation is inspired by Tekin et al. [15], which predicts the image pixels of 3D bounding boxes instead of immediate 6D pose.

Pose estimation task and edge extraction task are the two tasks in the model. To make the network learn features effectively, we design two loss functions for these two tasks. In the pose estimation network, the network firstly detects the 3D bounding box of the object, and then uses the PnP algorithm to solve the pose of the object according to the 2D-3D correspondences. The algorithm based on YOLO treats the detection problem as a regression problem and predict the offset between the center point of the bounding box and the upper left corner of the corresponding grid. To constrain the center point of the bounding box in the current grid, we use a sigmoid function so that the predicted offset value is in the range of (0,1) (the scale of each cell is 1), then the network is trained by minimizing the Eq. (1):

$$\mathcal{L}_1 = \lambda_{pt}\mathcal{L}_{pt} + \lambda_{conf}\mathcal{L}_{conf} + \lambda_{id}\mathcal{L}_{id} \tag{1}$$

Where $\mathcal{L}_{pt}$, $\mathcal{L}_{conf}$ and $\mathcal{L}_{id}$ are the loss functions of point coordinate, confidence and category, respectively. The mean square error is used to calculate the loss values of the point coordinate and the confidence. The cross entropy is used to calculate the classification loss. If there is no target object in a grid, the coefficient of the confidence loss is reduced to 0.1.

The edge extraction task can be regarded as a regression problem. Here we use a weighted cross-entropy loss function [10], as shown in Eq. (2):

$$\begin{aligned} \imath^n\left(W, w^n\right) \\ = -\beta \sum_{j \in Y^+} \log\sigma\left(y_j = 1 \mid X; W, w^n\right) - (1 - \beta) \sum_{i \in Y^-} \log\sigma\left(y_i = 0 \mid X; W, w^n\right) \end{aligned} \tag{2}$$

Where X is the input image, and Y represents the ground truth of the corresponding edge image. Then, the loss function can be defined as:

$$\mathcal{L}_2(W, w) = \sum_{n=1}^{N} \delta^n \times \imath^n\left(W, w^n\right) \tag{3}$$

Whre W represents the parameters of the network, ω represents the n corresponding parameters, δ represents the weight for every scale. $\beta = |Y^-|/|Y^+ + Y^-|$, $1 - \beta = |Y^+|/|Y^+ + Y^-|$. $|Y^-|$ and $|Y^+|$ are respectively represent the edge and non-edge in truth. Therefore, the loss function of network training is shown in Eq. (4):

$$\text{Loss} = \lambda\mathcal{L}_1 + (1 - \lambda)\mathcal{L}_2 \tag{4}$$

Where λ is the reconciliation parameter, it is used to adjust the contribution of the loss function of the two tasks to the total loss function.

3   Generation of Pose Dataset Based on 3D Reconstruction

As the proposed pose estimation method is based on deep learning, the authenticity and accuracy of the dataset will directly affect the pose precision. Meanwhile, the existing public datasets such as Rigid Pose dataset [9] are not suitable for texture-less objects, especially for industrial parts. We propose a method for generating pose dataset based on 3D reconstruction. The flowchart of the dataset creation method is shown in Fig. 1(c). When the scene contains 8 objects, we capture 70 image sequences and use 3D reconstruction technique to obtain the point cloud data. Then we match the known 3D model of the target object with the point cloud data to retrieve the target object's pose and generate the mask and edge map of the object through projection. Finally, the data is expanded and augmented to achieve 1000 data sets.

In the period of image capturing, we need cover all the angles of the scene as much as possible. We screen out the image sequences where there should be a certain overlapped area between each two sequential frames for 3D reconstruction. 3D reconstruction is a general-purpose Structure-from-Motion (SfM) and Multi-View Stereo (MVS) pipeline with a graphical and command-line interface. Through the 3D reconstruction, the camera internal parameters, external parameters corresponding to each image and dense 3D point clouds can be obtained. Among them, the camera external parameters represent the pose transformation between the camera coordinate system and the world coordinate system.

Since the real 3D coordinates of the target point cloud cannot be directly obtained. We use the method of point cloud registration to retrieve the world coordinates of the 3D bounding box for each target object. To ensure the 3D model of the industrial part and the point cloud are consistent in the same scale, it is necessary to select special points for size measurement, and to adjust the size of the 3D model according to the scale. After the size is adjusted, the coordinates of the vertices and center points for 3D model's bounding box are found. Next, we split the point cloud of the industrial part from the whole model, eliminating the effects of irrelevant point clouds for model matching. The adjusted 3D model and the segmented dense point cloud are shown in Fig. 2. The left is the imported accurate 3D model, and the right is the segmented target point cloud. In order to improve the performance of matching, the model is manually aligned with the reconstructed point cloud. After the rough matching, we use the interactive closet point (ICP) algorithm to automatically register the reconstructed point cloud with the model. The purpose of the ICP algorithm is to find the pose transformation between the pending point cloud and the reference model, so that the two entities are optimally matched under the given measurement criteria. The registration result is shown in Fig. 3. The green part in the figure is the 3D model of the target part.

Suppose the coordinate of the bounding box after the scale adjustment is p_i and the coordinate after two transformations is p_j. In addition, the two transformation matrices are respectively described as $T_1 = \begin{bmatrix} R_1 & t_1 \\ 0 & 1 \end{bmatrix}$ and $T_2 = \begin{bmatrix} R_2 & t_2 \\ 0 & 1 \end{bmatrix}$,

Fig. 2. Before registration.   **Fig. 3.** After Registration.   **Fig. 4.** Demonstration of pose data. (Color figure online)

where R_i represents 3×3 rotation matrix, t_i represent 3×1 translation vector and i belongs to the set $\{1, 2\}$. Then the 3D coordinates of the bounding box for the target part in the world coordinate system can be calculated by $p_j = R_2 (R_1 p_i + t_1) + t_2$, and the corresponding pixel coordinates can be calculated through perspective projection model. The demonstration of final result is shown in Fig. 4.

The mask and edge map are both generated by means of the known 3D model and camera parameters. Take the mask image for example. We extract the coordinates of mesh vertices from model and project them onto the image plane through perspective projection model. At last, the triangle areas are filled with the target color and the mask image is completed.

Data augmentation is the last step in dataset generation. The dataset is created to cover as many scenes as possible in different situations by geometric transformations, such as cropping, scaling, perspective transformation, or randomly adjusting the brightness and saturation of the images, as well as adding noise and blurring components. Furthermore, we also arbitrarily replace image backgrounds to improve the generalization ability and robustness of multi-task learning models.

4   Pose Optimization of Texture-Less Targets

Generally, it is difficult to extract rich features from smooth and texture-less objects. In industrial applications, as most objects are produced on fixed precise CAD model. A more reliable method is to extract the edges of the target object and optimise the pose based on edge matching.

We use OpenGL's Z-Buffer to extract the edges of the target object model. These edges are then rasterized into a set of raster points, which is denoted as $P = \{o_1, o_2, o_3 \dots, o_m\} \in R^3$. Beyond that , the set of raster point $\bar{P} = \{\bar{o}_1, \bar{o}_2, \bar{o}_3, ..., \bar{o}_m\} \in \mathbb{R}^3$ is also sampled, and satisfies the Eq. (5).

$$\bar{o}_i = o_i + \hat{\tau}(o_i) \cdot dr \tag{5}$$

Where $\hat{\tau}(o_i)$ represents the unit tangent vector of the edge, dr represents a small increment of the image distance. The raster points are then projected onto the image through perspective camera model. Assuming that the pose $g \in SE(3)$ to be optimized represents the object pose with respect to the camera coordinate system. The 3D point set P and $\bar{P}$ are mapped into the image using Eq. (6).

$$\begin{cases} x_i = \pi(o_i, g) \in \mathbb{R}^2, i = \{1, 2, 3, ..., m\} \\ \bar{x}_i = \pi(\bar{o}_i, g) \in \mathbb{R}^2, i = \{1, 2, 3, ..., m\} \end{cases} \tag{6}$$

Where x_i and $\bar{x}_i$ represent the projection points in image corresponding to o_i and $\bar{o}_i$. $\pi(\cdot) : \mathbb{R}^3 \rightarrow \mathbb{R}^2$ represents the camera projection model. Then the edge direction of the projected model can be calculated by x_i and $\bar{x}_i$. Subsequently, we use the Directional Chamfer Matching (DCM) [7] to describe error considering the DCM-based matching method can effectively reduce the matching error and is more robust to occlusion and complex background. As the initial pose of the target object and the scene edge map could be obtained from multi-task model, the DCM distance calculation based on the scene edge map could be calculated with reference to [7]. DCM distance transformation represents an image using minimal pixel distance to the pixel's nearest image edge point, simultaneously considering the pixel's directional factor. In this paper, we represent the DCM distance of an image using $DT3_V$. At last, we use the DCM distance and model raster points to construct the objective function. For each pixel on the edge of the image, a residual function is constructed, as shown in Eq. (7), where n represents the number of edge points on the model, and $\hat{\phi}(x_i)$ represents the direction of the edge point.

$$E_{DCM} = \frac{1}{n} \sum_{i=1}^{n} DT3_V(x_i, \hat{\phi}(x_i)) \tag{7}$$

The matching problem is transformed into an optimization problem through constructing a residual function, and the pose can be solved by minimizing the residual between the projection points of raster points and the edge points from edge map. Assuming that the pose of the object relative to the camera is represented by a rotation vector R and a translation vector T, then the objective function to be optimized can be expressed as:

$$E(T, R) = \frac{1}{2} \sum_{i=1}^{n} DT3_V[\pi(o_i, g(T, R)), \hat{\phi}(\pi(o_i, g(T, R)))]^2 \tag{8}$$

Where o_i is the raster point of the object model, and $g \in \mathbb{R}^6$ represents the object pose with respect to the camera coordinate system. The accurate object pose can be retrieved by optimizing the objective function.

5 Experiments

In the experiments, we use Balser camera as vision sensor. The platform to implement and test is a workstation with AMD Ryzen 1950x CPU with 32G RAM and NVIDIA GeForce Titan x GPU. Multi-task learning model is implemented based on deep learning framework Pytorch 1.0.1, which is an open-source machine learning framework developed by Facebook's AI research team. The algorithm of pose optimization is implemented using C++ and CUDA. The initial pose estimation module in multi-task learning and pose optimization module are connected after completing the model analysis by Libtorch API.

The datasets used to do quantitative experimental analysis include the publicly available RBOT dataset [16] and CG-rendered dataset which is generated using similar method from [18]. The state-of-the-art methods used in this section to compare with the proposed method are listed as follows:
1) Single-Shot [15], which uses CNN to detect and predict object poses;
2) D2CO [5] and our previously proposed algorithm [4], which use similar technique comparing with the proposed system.

5.1   Object Detection and Edge Extraction Tests

First of all, we test our proposed multi-task model on the rendered dataset. The same dataset and training parameters are used in the test of Single-shot based on single task model in order to compare the accuracy of object detection. The model learning is carried out by joint training as the multi-task network learning in this paper only involves a single dataset. The input of the network are the scene image sequence and a serious of data labels including the edge images and the mask images corresponding to scene image sequence, the positions of the 3D bounding boxes and the classes of objects. The output of the network are the edge images, the positions of the 3D bounding boxes and the classes of objects. Since the pose estimation network predicts the pixel coordinates of the 3D bounding box for target object, it can be directly evaluated by a total of 9 coordinates of points which includes 1 center point and 8 vertices of the bounding box. Suppose that there are n sequences, the accuracy of detection can be defined as:

$$Error_{pixel} = \frac{1}{n} \sum_{i=1}^{n} \sum_{j=1}^{9} \sqrt{(pr[i][j] - gt[i][j])^2} \tag{9}$$

Where the $pr[i][j]$ and $gt[i][j]$ are separately represent the predicted and true values of the j-th point coordinate of the i-th image. The accuracy of object recognition will be evaluated by the precision of network.

Table 1. Accuracy comparison of single task model and multi-task model.

	Single task model [15]		Multi-task model(Proposed)	
	Recognition accuracy (%)	Detection accuracy (pixel)	Recognition accuracy (%)	Detection accuracy (pixel)
Gear	98	1.94	**98.6**	**1.61**
Nut	96.5	5.49	**99.3**	**1.32**
Bearing	96.9	7.68	**98.9**	**1.61**
Flange	97.2	6.17	**99.1**	**1.35**

S. Xu et al.

Fig. 5. Results of multi-task model test on rendered dataset and comparision on different algorithms of edge detection.

We test the 4 different targets in the same image sequences, and the results are shown in Table 1. It can be seen that the effect of multi-task learning on 3D detection and recognition is significantly improved as the associated tasks complement each other by sharing information. The test results of the multi-task model on the rendered dataset are shown in first three columns of Fig. 5. The first column of images are the original images. The second column of images are the edge images. The third column of images are the pose results including the true value denoted by the green box and the predicted value denoted by the blue box. For the test of the edge detection algorithm, F-Measure is selected to measure the effect of the edge map of the scene [1], and the definition of F-Measure is shown in Eq. (10).

$$F-measure = \frac{(1+\beta^2) \times precision \times Recall}{(\beta^2 \times precision) + Recall} \tag{10}$$

Where Recall represents the recall rate, described as $\frac{TP}{TP+FN}$, TP represents the number of overlapped edge pixels from true value and model, FN represents the number of non-overlapped non-edge pixels from true value and model. Precision represents the accuracy rate, described as $\frac{TP}{TP+FP}$, FP represents the number of non-overlapped edge pixels from true value and model. The weight of the precision rate and recall rate are the same. We set β to 1 and choose 100 edge images for test. The result of average precision (AP) is 0.84. This demonstrates that the edge detection based on multi-task learning has better performance compared with the traditional edge detection algorithms where the noise inevitably appears although with image preprocessing, which can be seen in the rightmost column of Fig. 5.

5.2   Pose Accuracy Test

Next, the accuracy of the pose optimization on texture-less targets for unconstrained grasping is tested. Objects from different perspectives are tested on the public dataset RBOT and the rendered dataset. To evaluate the performance of the proposed method, we compare it with D2CO and our previous algorithm using following criteria:

1) Average absolute error (AAE). AAE is the average of the absolute error between the measured position t_{obj} and the ground truth position t_{gt} accross a group of N tracked objects. As is shown in Eq. (11):

$$AAE = \frac{1}{N} \sum_{i=0}^{N} \|t_{obj} - t_{gt}\| \tag{11}$$

2) Average relative error (ARE). ARE is the average of the percentage comparing absolute error with the objects' distance to the camera accross a group of N tracked objects. As is shown in Eq. (12):

$$ARE = \frac{1}{N} \sum_{i=0}^{N} \frac{\|t_{obj} - t_{gt}\|}{\|t_{gt}\|} \tag{12}$$

3) Average rotational error (AQE). AQE is the average of the distance between the measured rotation vector r_{obj} and the true value r_{gt} accross a group of N tracked objects. As is shown in Eq. (13):

$$AQE = \frac{1}{N} \sum_{i=0}^{N} \|r_{obj} - r_{gt}\| \tag{13}$$

The results of pose error for the target object on RBOT dataset and rendered dataset are shown in Table 2. We selected four different texture-less objects as test objects in the RBOT dataset. It can be seen that our previous method and the method proposed in this paper have better accuracy than the D2CO method in translation error and rotation error. The reason is that the resolution of image in RBOT data is a bit lower at 640 * 480, and the objects in the image have a certain amount of motion blur, leading to the large noise on edge detection in the D2CO method. It shows that the method proposed in this paper has a certain anti-interference ability against blurry images. Meanwhile, we can see that the accuracy of the three methods has been greatly improved relative to the RBOT dataset. This is due to the fact that the image quality of the rendered dataset is high, and the effect of edge detection is better. Our previous method adds an analytical Jacobian matrix and an adaptive weight optimization method on the basis of the D2CO method. Therefore, the accuracy of the pose estimation is significantly improved. The proposed method in this paper has more advantages in accurate edge and initial pose than our previous method, so the highest precision can be retrieved from optimization compared with other methods.

Table 2. Object pose error on RBOT dataset and rendered dataset.

		RBOT dataset				Rendered dataset			
		Cat	Ape	Can	Clown	Gear	Nut	Bearing	Flange
D2CO [5]	AAE (mm)	26.42	93.48	168.05	95.42	8.29	8.85	7.63	11.44
	ARE (%)	3.13	10.3	18.95	10.46	0.69	0.69	0.57	0.86
	AQE (rad)	0.130	0.82	1.068	0.123	0.0120	0.3468	0.0761	0.0144
Previous method [4]	AAE (mm)	22.96	50.57	8.78	88.39	2.48	8.28	7.60	4.28
	ARE (%)	2.67	5.91	0.99	8.69	0.21	0.69	0.57	0.30
	AQE (rad)	0.125	0.557	0.049	0.344	0.0055	0.1976	0.0731	0.0039
Proposed method	AAE (mm)	**19.08**	**41.56**	**7.19**	**67.39**	**2.16**	**7.42**	**5.58**	**2.67**
	ARE (%)	**2.54**	**4.01**	**0.92**	**7.91**	**0.19**	**0.59**	**0.49**	**0.17**
	AQE (rad)	**0.119**	**0.428**	**0.037**	**0.205**	**0.0046**	**0.0512**	**0.064**	**0.0032**

6   Conclusion

This paper proposes a pose estimation and optimization method combined traditional method and deep learning for more precise unconstrained grasping. Our method is mainly consisted by two parts: initial pose estimation and pose optimization. The pose estimation is implemented by multi-task learning which can also generate the edge map for the latter optimization. The pose optimization is implemented by DCM based edge matching. The pose estimation method based on deep learning requires a large amount of data for training and testing, and the quality of the training data directly affects the result of pose estimation. Accordingly, this paper proposes a flexible and fast pose dataset generation method. At last, the proposed algorithm is tested on the public dataset RBOT and the rendered dataset, and the improvment on accuracy is validated.

References

1. Arbeláez, P., Maire, M., Fowlkes, C., Malik, J.: Contour detection and hierarchical image segmentation. IEEE Trans. Pattern Anal. Mach. Intell. **33**(5), 898–916 (2011). https://doi.org/10.1109/TPAMI.2010.161
2. Choi, C., Christensen, H.I.: Real-time 3D model-based tracking using edge and keypoint features for robotic manipulation. In: 2010 IEEE International Conference on Robotics and Automation, pp. 4048–4055 (2010). https://doi.org/10.1109/ROBOT.2010.5509171
3. Chollet, F.: Xception: Deep learning with depthwise separable convolutions. In: Proceedings of the IEEE Conference on Computer Vision and Pattern Recognition, pp. 1251–1258 (2017)
4. Dong, Y., et al.: Accurate 6dof pose tracking for texture-less objects. IEEE Trans. Circuits Syst. Video Technol. **31**(5), 1834–1848 (2021). https://doi.org/10.1109/TCSVT.2020.3011737

5. Imperoli, M., Pretto, A.: D^2CO: fast and robust registration of 3D textureless objects using the directional chamfer distance. In: Nalpantidis, L., Krüger, V., Eklundh, J.-O., Gasteratos, A. (eds.) ICVS 2015. LNCS, vol. 9163, pp. 316–328. Springer, Cham (2015). https://doi.org/10.1007/978-3-319-20904-3_29

6. Li, Y., Wang, G., Ji, X., Xiang, Yu., Fox, D.: DeepIM: deep iterative matching for 6D pose estimation. In: Ferrari, V., Hebert, M., Sminchisescu, C., Weiss, Y. (eds.) ECCV 2018. LNCS, vol. 11210, pp. 695–711. Springer, Cham (2018). https://doi.org/10.1007/978-3-030-01231-1_42

7. Liu, M.Y., Tuzel, O., Veeraraghavan, A., Chellappa, R.: Fast directional chamfer matching. In: 2010 IEEE Computer Society Conference on Computer Vision and Pattern Recognition, pp. 1696–1703 (2010). https://doi.org/10.1109/CVPR.2010.5539837

8. Manhardt, F., Kehl, W., Navab, N., Tombari, F.: Deep model-based 6D pose refinement in RGB. In: Ferrari, V., Hebert, M., Sminchisescu, C., Weiss, Y. (eds.) Computer Vision – ECCV 2018. LNCS, vol. 11218, pp. 833–849. Springer, Cham (2018). https://doi.org/10.1007/978-3-030-01264-9_49

9. Pauwels, K., Rubio, L., Díaz, J., Ros, E.: Real-time model-based rigid object pose estimation and tracking combining dense and sparse visual cues. In: 2013 IEEE Conference on Computer Vision and Pattern Recognition, pp. 2347–2354 (2013). https://doi.org/10.1109/CVPR.2013.304

10. Poma, X.S., Riba, E., Sappa, A.: Dense extreme inception network: towards a robust CNN model for edge detection. In: Proceedings of the IEEE/CVF Winter Conference on Applications of Computer Vision, pp. 1923–1932 (2020)

11. Prisacariu, V.A., Kähler, O., Murray, D.W., Reid, I.D.: Real-time 3D tracking and reconstruction on mobile phones. IEEE Trans. Visual Comput. Graphics **21**(5), 557–570 (2015). https://doi.org/10.1109/TVCG.2014.2355207

12. Redmon, J., Farhadi, A.: Yolo9000: better, faster, stronger. In: Proceedings of the IEEE Conference on Computer Vision and Pattern Recognition, pp. 7263–7271 (2017)

13. Song, C., Song, J., Huang, Q.: HybridPose: 6D object pose estimation under hybrid representations. In: Proceedings of the IEEE/CVF Conference on Computer Vision and Pattern Recognition, pp. 431–440 (2020)

14. Su, H., Qi, C.R., Li, Y., Guibas, L.J.: Render for CNN: viewpoint estimation in images using CNNs trained with rendered 3D model views. In: Proceedings of the IEEE International Conference on Computer Vision, pp. 2686–2694 (2015)

15. Tekin, B., Sinha, S.N., Fua, P.: Real-time seamless single shot 6D object pose prediction. In: Proceedings of the IEEE Conference on Computer Vision and Pattern Recognition, pp. 292–301 (2018)

16. Tjaden, H., Schwanecke, U., Schomer, E., Cremers, D.: A region-based gauss-newton approach to real-time monocular multiple object tracking. IEEE Trans. Pattern Anal. Mach. Intell., 1 (2018). https://doi.org/10.1109/TPAMI.2018.2884990

17. Tulsiani, S., Malik, J.: Viewpoints and keypoints. In: Proceedings of the IEEE Conference on Computer Vision and Pattern Recognition, pp. 1510–1519 (2015)

18. Wang, S., Yue, J., Dong, Y., He, S., Wang, H., Ning, S.: A synthetic dataset for visual slam evaluation. Robot. Auton. Syst. **124**, 103336 (2020). https://doi.org/10.1016/j.robot.2019.103336

Virtual Reality

Wearable Augmented Reality System Using Head-Mounted Projector

Masamichi Iimori and Takashi Komuro$^{(\boxtimes)}$

Saitama University, 255 Shimookubo, Sakura-ku, Saitama-city, Saitama, Japan
iimori@is.ics.saitama-u.ac.jp, komuro@mail.saitama-u.ac.jp

Abstract. In this paper, we propose a wearable augmented reality system that can be used without restrictions on location and can present images that are fixed in the real environment. In the proposed system, a projector is mounted on the head so that an image is always projected in the user's line of sight. By estimating the position and orientation of the head in real time, the system presents images of objects in the virtual space as if the objects were fixed in the real space. In addition, by placing the projector close to the viewpoint, the user can see an image without distortion regardless of the shape of the projection surface. Using this system, a pseudo-large screen is realized by fixing a virtual object on the projected surface, which realizes the expansion of work space. The prototype system was developed using a small, lightweight projector and a tracking camera. We confirmed that the virtual object were fixed in the real space even if the user is moving the head. We also confirmed that the user was able to see an undistorted image regardless of the shape of the projection surface.

Keywords: Augmented reality · Projector camera system · Tracking camera

1 Introduction

In recent years, systems using smart glasses, which are eyeglass-type wearable devices, have begun to be introduced in the fields of work support. Since such wearable devices can be used without restrictions on location, making user's both hands free, they can replace conventional systems such as tablet devices in manufacturing and distribution sites. However, while smart glasses can always present an image to the user's field of view, there is a problem that the display area is narrow and much information cannot be displayed.

There is a technology of augmented reality (AR), which superimposes images such as annotation and navigation information in the real world, using a see-through head mounted display (HMD) [4,12]. To fix virtual objects in the real space, the displayed image is changed depending on the place to be viewed, which enables to display the image on a wide area. However, there are problems that the device tends to be large and heavy and that the real scene seen through

© Springer Nature Switzerland AG 2021
G. Bebis et al. (Eds.): ISVC 2021, LNCS 13017, pp. 481–491, 2021.
https://doi.org/10.1007/978-3-030-90439-5_38

the half mirror becomes dark. Also, eye strain sometimes occurs due to the discrepancy between the convergence distance and the focal length.

On the other hand, there are systems that present information on a surface in the real space using a projector [1,7,17]. An image is projected on a flat surface by the projector, and the user can receive information interactively by touch operations. Compared to HMDs, it is possible for the user to view images with the naked eyes without any obstruction. However, in order to widen the projection area to display a lot of information, it is necessary to increase the distance between the projector and the projection surface or install multiple projectors, which restricts the installation locations.

To solve this problem, there are studies using a handheld projector [9,16]. By changing the image according to the direction and position of the projector, which is holded by the user, it is possible to virtually enlarge the display area. However, in these studies, the user needs to point the projector to the place where the user wants to project the image, which takes effort to move the projector. In addition, there is a problem that a wide flat surface is required to realize a large effective screen, and also the projected image becomes distorted if the projection surface is not flat.

Kemmoku et al. [10], have developed a tabletop interface using a projector and a camera mounted on the user's head, and that realizes a large effective display without restrictions on the installation location. This system estimates the position and orientation of the head using the plane detected from the image taken by the depth camera. However, this approach is also limited to use on flat surface.

To eliminate this limitation, we introduce a tracking camera, which can estimate the self position of the camera, so that the system can estimate the position and orientation of the user's head without a flat surface. By doing so, it is possible to present an image according to the orientation and position of the head, and thus to fix a virtual object in the real environment. As a result, the work space can be expanded, and it is possible to display an image that is not restricted by the limitation of the display range of the projector. In addition, since the positions of the projector and the user's viewpoint are close to each other, there is also an advantage that the image looks undistorted even when projected on an uneven surface. Therefore, the system can be used even in an environment where there is no flat surface large enough to project the image.

2   Related Work

2.1   AR Systems Using a Head-Mounted Display

There have been studies on UIs in which the user wears a head-mounted display (HMD) and virtual information is superimposed on the real space [4,12]. An HMD is a display worn on the head, which can always displays images in the wearer's field of view.

Grubert et al. have developed MultiFi, a system that combines a smartphone display and an HMD [4]. The system realizes a larger display area by presenting images in the area around the smartphone display using an HMD. This allows for the presentation of additional information to the user. However, such HMD-type devices tend to be heavy, and also can greatly block the user's view.

2.2   AR Systems Using a Projector

There is research on AR systems using projectors that allow interaction by touching the projected image on a plane [1,7,17]. Jones et al. developed RoomAlive, a system consisting of multiple units in a room with a projector and a depth camera, which enables users to interact with virtual objects such as enemy characters by touching or shooting them [7]. This system can project virtual objects over the whole room, so the user can have an immersive experience of AR. However, it is necessary to arrange multiple projectors so that they can project images on the entire room, and the number of projectors must be increased if the room is large.

In addition, Benko et al. have developed MirageTable, a system that allows bare hand interaction with a virtual object by combining a depth camera and a projector with a curved screen [1]. By tracking the user's eye position and changing the appearance of the displayed image according to the eye position, a stereoscopic view of a virtual object is possible. Also, by acquiring the shape of a real object in front of the camera and detecting its contact with a virtual object, the user can interact with the object, such as, lifting the object by hand.

2.3   Wearable AR Systems Using a Portable Projector

There is research on systems that allow users who wear a projector and a camera on their body to operate on the projected image performing gestures and touches [5,13]. By recognizing a marker attached to the fingertip of a user or recognizing a touch operation from images captured by a depth camera, they have realized an AR system that can be used without restrictions on the location.

There is research on projecting images using a projector and a half mirror worn on the user's hand [3,6,11]. An image is projected at a position optically conjugate with the observer's eye, and is reflected by an object coated with a retroreflective material to show the image on the eye through a half mirror. Also, there are systems in which images from a projector are directly projected on a flat surface on which a retroreflective material is applied, without using a half mirror [2,8,18].

Yoshida et al. have developed ARScope [18]. In this system, the device looks transparent when a user who wears a projector on his or her head looks into the device. Also, even if the user's viewpoint position changes, the projected images seem to be consistent with the real world.

There is also research that allows users to manipulate the projected object by wearing a camera and a projector on their ears or head and making gestures on the image [14,15].

In these studies, the user mounts a projector on the head, and the place to project changes depending on the direction of the head, so it is possible to always project the image ahead of the line of sight. However, their systems were not designed to expand the user's work space.

3   System Design

This section describes the design of our proposed wearable AR system. We aim at a compact and lightweight system in order to reduce the physical burden of the device, which was a problem of AR systems using an HMD. In addition, we propose a system that can expand the virtual work space and present images without depending on the shape of the projection surface.

3.1   Wearable AR System Using Head-Mounted Projector

In the proposed system, the user wears a small projector and a tracking camera on his or her head. The position and orientation of the head estimated by the tracking camera can be reflected in the projection image in real time. By changing the position and orientation of the viewpoint in the virtual space according to those of the user's head, the object placed in the virtual space appears to be fixed in the real space as shown in the Fig. 1. This enables the field of view to be expanded.

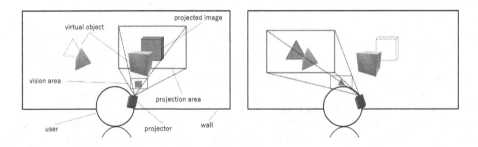

Fig. 1. Overview of the proposed system

3.2   Image Projection Independent of the Shape of the Projection Surface

In order to present an image with a projector, a flat surface for projection is generally required. However, since a flat surface is not always around the user, the environment that can be used by conventional projectors is limited. In the proposed system, by mounting a small projector near the wearer's viewpoint, even if the image is projected on a flat surface that is not flat, the image can be presented without distortion when viewed from the wearer.

For example, consider the case where an image is projected on a curved surface as shown in the Fig. 2(a). The projected image is distorted on the surface as shown in Fig. 2(a). However, by mounting the projector on the head, the position of the viewpoint and the position of the projector are close, so the projected image (2D image in Fig. 2(a)) and the image seen by the user (2D image in Fig. 2(b)) are almost the same. This allows the user to observe a virtual object with the same appearance as when projected onto a flat surface even when projected onto a curved surface.

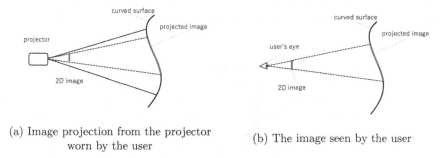

(a) Image projection from the projector worn by the user

(b) The image seen by the user

Fig. 2. Image projection on a curved surface

3.3 Work Space Expansion

Conventional projectors have a limitation in the displayable area, and there is a constraint that the distance between the projection surface and the projector has to be increased in order to expand the area. In the proposed system, the position and orientation of the head are estimated in real time and are reflected to the position in the virtual space displayed by the projector. By moving the position of the camera in the virtual space according to the movement of the head, it is possible to present an image in which the virtual object is fixed in the real space. By changing the image to be displayed depending on the viewing location and the image can be projected on any area of the surface, a large effective screen can be realized.

4   Implementation and Evaluation

In order to confirm the effectiveness of the proposed system, we have developed a system that implements the design described in Sect. 3. Furthermore, we comfirmed the basic functions of the prototype system.

4.1 System Overview

Using a mobile projector and a tracking camera, we have created a prototype system as shown in Fig. 3. We used SEKONIX's MiNi-Ray mobile projector, and Intel's RealSense T265 tracking camera. This tracking camera is
equipped with two fisheye cameras and an inertial measurement unit, and can
execute a high-speed self-position estimation. It offers sub 6 ms latency between
movement and reflection of movement in the pose. The size of the projector
is $44 \times 44 \times 14$ mm/27 g, and the size of the camera is $108 \times 25 \times 13$ mm/55 g,
which are light enough not to be a burden on the user when worn on the head.
The projector and tracking camera are connected to a desktop PC (CPU: Intel
Core i7-6700 3.4 GHz RAM: 8 GB), which was used for calculations.

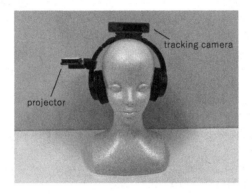

Fig. 3. Appearance of prototype system

We used the RealSense SDK, which can estimate the position and orientation
of the head with a tracking camera, and used the estimated position to reflect
the acquired position in the virtual space. The virtual scene is rendered in the
virtual camera and the projector projects the rendered image over the real scene.
We used Unity for rendering the virtual scene.

4.2 Image Projection Independent of the Shape of the Projection
Surface

By arranging the projector near the position of the user's viewpoint, the image
seen by the user and the original image projected by the projector are almost the
same, so it is possible to present an image that does not depend on the shape of
the projection surface. In order to evaluate the effectiveness of the method, the
appearance of the image viewed from the user is compared with the appearance
of the image viewed from a different position from the wearer. The user sat
at a position 125.5 cm from the wall and projects an image on the boundary
between the wall and the ceiling. The height from the floor to the projector of

the device was 112 cm, and the height from the floor to the ceiling was 258 cm. Figure 4 (a) shows the view from the user, and Fig. 4 (b) shows the view from the position moved to the right 82 cm from the user. We can confirm that even if the projection surface is not flat, the appearance of the image is not much distorted compared to when projected on a flat surface, and that the image can be presented regardless of the shape of the projection surface.

(a) The view from the user

(b) The view from the position moved to the right 82 cm from the user

Fig. 4. The appearance of the image when projected on a curved surface

4.3   Work Space Expansion

Since the prototype system can present an image that is fixed in the real space, it is possible to present the image over a large screen and expand the work space.

Consider the case where a virtual object is fixed on a plane in the real space. By drawing an object inthe virtual space at a position that is equidistant from the user to the projection plane, it is possible to present the image that the virtual object is fixed on the projection plane. In this evaluation, the user sat at a position 125.5 cm away from the wall, and at a position 125.5 cm from the camera in the virtual space, square images with 25 cm on each side were placed at three locations. At this time, the height from the floor to the projector of the device were 130 cm. Figure 5(a) to (d) show the user moving his head and projecting an image on the wall.

In order to show that the images were fixed on the plane, the composite image of Fig. 5(a) to (d) is shown in the Fig. 5(e). It can be confirmed that even if the head is moved, the image looks fixed on the wall on the projection surface.

5   Applications

We implemented some application examples into the system to demonstrate the use cases of the proposed system.

Figure 6(a) shows a world map application. The user can project a part of the world map on the wall and use the entire wall as a large screen. Figure 6(b) shows

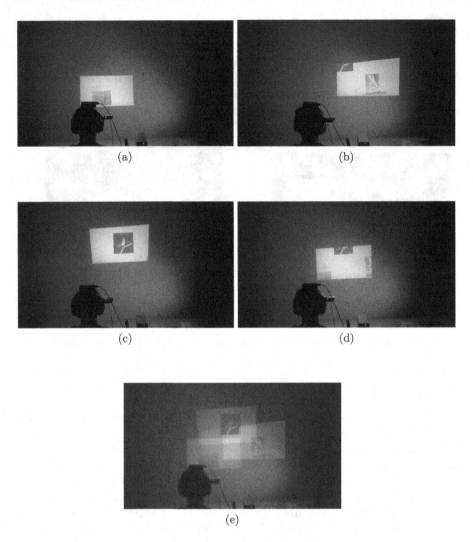

Fig. 5. Projecting an images with the user moving his head

an aquarium application. The user can see various fishes swimming in the virtual aquarium by looking around. Figure 6(c) shows a planetarium application. The user can look around the stars and constellations projected on the walls and ceiling. Figure 6(d) shows a bird watching application. The user can see birds flying from tree to tree.

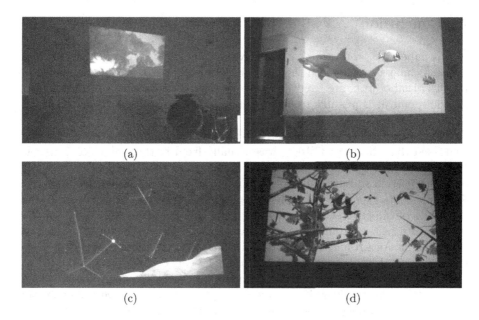

Fig. 6. Application examples. (a) The view from behind the user, (b) (c) (d) The view from the user.

6 Limitataions

In the proposed system, the virtual object is placed regardless of the shape of the real environment, so the virtual object may move to a space that is hidden by or inside other objects the real space. Therefore, it may not be possible to present the correct appearance of the object.

The projector used in our prototype system is small and lightweight enough to be worn on the head, but has a brightness of only 30 lm, which is darker than that of a general projector, so it is difficult to use the prototype system in a bright room or outdoors. In addition, there is a slight delay in reflecting the position acquired by the tracking camera to the projected image, so it is necessary to use it with the constraint that the head should not move quickly. Also, this system is currently connected to a PC with a camera and projector, so it is difficult to use while moving around, but this problem can be solved by using a portable computer such as a stick PC.

The focus of the projector can be an issue with our current prototype of proposed system. Since the user can move around, the projection may be done at closer or further distances than the one on focus. This issue can be solved by using either a laser projector or autofocus algorithms.

7   Conclusion

In this paper, we proposed a wearable AR system with a small projector and a tracking camera mounted on the user's head and that can present the image in which virtual objects are fixed in the real space. By installing a projector near the viewpoint, it is possible to present images that do not depend on the shape of the projection surface.

We also created a prototype system based on the proposed system design and confirmed that the virtual object was actually fixed in the real space. Furthermore, we confirmed that the workspace can be expanded by fixing a virtual object on the projection surface and projecting a part of a wide image with a projector. We implemented some application examples into the system to demonstrate the usefulness of the proposed system.

A future task is to arrange virtual objects based on the shape of the real environment. As a result, virtual objects can be placed so that they do not overlap with real objects, and more realistic image can be presented. In addition, practical applications such as work support and navigation using the proposed system should be considered. As an example of work support, we will create an environment assuming the site of equipment maintenance and inspection, and implement an application that presents work procedures and locations to workers. Then, we plan to collect participants and perform experiments to evaluate the effectiveness of the system.

References

1. Benko, H., Jota, R., Wilson, A.: MirageTable: freehand interaction on a projected augmented reality tabletop. In: Proceedings of the SIGCHI Conference on Human Factors in Computing Systems, pp. 199–208 (2012)
2. Bolas, M., Krum, D.M.: Augmented reality applications and user interfaces using head-coupled near-axis personal projectors with novel retroreflective props and surfaces. In: Proceedings of Pervasive 2010 Ubiprojection Workshop. vol. 22, p. 23 (2010)
3. Fergason, J.L.: Optical system for a head mounted display using a retro-reflector and method of displaying an image, 15 April 1997. uS Patent 5,621,572
4. Grubert, J., Heinisch, M., Quigley, A., Schmalstieg, D.: MultiFi: multi fidelity interaction with displays on and around the body. In: Proceedings of the 33rd Annual ACM Conference on Human Factors in Computing Systems, pp. 3933–3942 (2015)
5. Harrison, C., Benko, H., Wilson, A.D.: OmniTouch: wearable multitouch interaction everywhere. In: Proceedings of the 24th Annual ACM Symposium on User Interface Software and Technology, pp. 441–450 (2011)
6. Inami, M., Kawakami, N., Sekiguchi, D., Yanagida, Y., Maeda, T., Tachi, S.: Visuo-haptic display using head-mounted projector. In: Proceedings of IEEE Virtual Reality 2000, pp. 233–240. IEEE (2000)
7. Jones, B., et al.: RoomAlive: magical experiences enabled by scalable, adaptive projector-camera units. In: Proceedings of the 27th Annual ACM Symposium on User Interface Software and Technology, pp. 637–644 (2014)

8. Kade, D., Akşit, K., Ürey, H., Özcan, O.: Head-mounted mixed reality projection display for games production and entertainment. Pers. Ubiquit. Comput. **19**(3–4), 509–521 (2015)
9. Kaufmann, B., Hitz, M.: X-large virtual workspaces for projector phones through peephole interaction. In: Proceedings of the 20th ACM International Conference on Multimedia, pp. 1279–1280 (2012)
10. Kemmoku, Y., Komuro, T.: AR tabletop interface using a head-mounted projector. In: Adjunct Proceedings of 2016 IEEE International Symposium on Mixed and Augmented Reality (ISMAR-Adjunct), pp. 288–291. IEEE (2016)
11. Kijima, R., Hirose, M.: A compound virtual environment using the projective head mounted display. In: Proceedings of International Conference on Virtual Reality Software and Technology, vol. 95, pp. 111–121 (1995)
12. Lee, G.A., Billinghurst, M., Kim, G.J.: Occlusion based interaction methods for tangible augmented reality environments. In: Proceedings of the 2004 ACM SIG-GRAPH International Conference on Virtual Reality Continuum and Its Applications in Industry, pp. 419–426 (2004)
13. Mistry, P., Maes, P.: SixthSense: a wearable gestural interface. In: Proceedings of ACM SIGGRAPH ASIA 2009 Art Gallery & Emerging Technologies: Adaptation, pp. 85–85 (2009)
14. Mistry, P., Maes, P., Chang, L.: WUW-wear Ur world: a wearable gestural interface. In: CHI 2009 Extended Abstracts on Human Factors in Computing Systems, pp. 4111–4116 (2009)
15. Tamaki, E., Miyaki, T., Rekimoto, J.: Brainy hand: an ear-worn hand gesture interaction device. In: CHI 2009 Extended Abstracts on Human Factors in Computing Systems, pp. 4255–4260 (2009)
16. Willis, K.D., Shiratori, T., Mahler, M.: HideOut: mobile projector interaction with tangible objects and surfaces. In: Proceedings of the 7th International Conference on Tangible, Embedded and Embodied Interaction, pp. 331–338 (2013)
17. Wilson, A.D., Benko, H.: Combining multiple depth cameras and projectors for interactions on, above and between surfaces. In: Proceedings of the 23nd Annual ACM Symposium on User Interface Software and Technology, pp. 273–282 (2010)
18. Yoshida, T., Kuroki, S., Nii, H., Kawakami, N., Tachi, S.: Arscope. In: Proceedings of the 35th International Conference on Computer Graphics and Interactive Techniques, p. 4 (2008)

Generation of Virtual Reality Environment Based on 3D Scanned Indoor Physical Space

Satoshi Moro and Takashi Komuro[✉]

Saitama University, 255 Shimo-Okubo, Sakura-ku, Saitama 338-8570, Japan
moro@is.ics.saitama-u.ac.jp, komuro@mail.saitama-u.ac.jp

Abstract. In this paper, we propose a method for generating a virtual environment in which users can avoid surrounding obstacles and also get haptic feedback from physical objects. By performing plane detection and clustering on the 3D point cloud acquired using a mobile device, and optimizing the layout of virtual objects using a cost function, a virtual environment based on the structure of the physical space is generated. In addition, by performing plane detection with normal constraints, surfaces that the user can touch are presented, and the user can touch objects in the physical space through the virtual environment with haptic feedback. We implemented the proposed method and conducted an experiment in an actual indoor physical space. As the result, we confirmed that a virtual environment was properly generated with many touchable surfaces based on the physical space, and that a user can touch a surface in the physical space.

Keywords: VR environment generation · Layout optimization · Obstacle avoidance · Passive haptics

1 Introduction

In recent years, VR devices that can be used at home, such as PlayStation VR and Oculus Quest, have been increasing. Such devices provide users with an immersive experience, but users wear a head-mounted display (HMD) during the VR experience and cannot see the surrounding physical space, which may compromise their safety. In addition, some VR devices allow users to use their own hands as a VR controller. However, unlike the case of using physical controllers, users cannot get haptic feedback.

In order to realize obstacle avoidance, methods of incorporating information about the physical space into the virtual environment in the form of images, point clouds, and wireframes have been proposed [1,5–10,16]. These methods make it easier for users to recognize the surrounding environment, but they embed information that is out of the context of the VR environment, which could negatively affect the sense of presence.

© Springer Nature Switzerland AG 2021
G. Bebis et al. (Eds.): ISVC 2021, LNCS 13017, pp. 492–503, 2021.
https://doi.org/10.1007/978-3-030-90439-5_39

On the other hand, there have been methods of placing virtual objects in the virtual environment that reflect the positions of obstacles in the physical space [3,12–15,17]. These methods allow users to have a VR experience that corresponds to physical objects without destroying the atmosphere of the VR environment, but when a user tries to touch a virtual object, the physical object that corresponds to it may not exist and the user cannot touch it.

There have also been methods of generating a virtual environment in which users can avoid obstacles in real-time using multiple sensors such as a depth camera and GPS [2,18]. While these methods provide a safe VR experience without prior preparation such as 3D scanning but focus on allowing users to avoid obstacles and are not intended to use physical objects for providing haptic feedback.

In this paper, we propose a method for generating a virtual environment in which users can avoid surrounding obstacles and also get haptic feedback from the environment.

In the proposed method, we first obtain a 3D point cloud by scanning the indoor space using a mobile device equipped with a depth camera and an inertial measurement unit (IMU) for self-position estimation. By performing plane detection and clustering on the acquired point cloud, and optimizing the layout of the virtual objects using a cost function, and a virtual environment based on the structure of the physical space is generated. In addition, by performing plane detection with normal constraints, the surfaces that the user can touch are presented, and the user can touch objects in the physical space through the virtual environment with haptic feedback.

The contributions of this paper are as follows.

1. A new pipeline for semi-automatically generating a virtual environment based on the indoor physical space.
2. Layout optimization of virtual objects using a cost function to cover obstacles and increase the user's walkable area.
3. Presentation of the surfaces that the user can touch and get passive haptic feedback.

2   Generation of Virtual Reality Environment Based on 3D Scanned Indoor Physical Space

The proposed method consists of five steps: indoor 3D scanning, ceiling and floor removal, clustering of obstacle points, layout optimization of virtual objects by using a cost function, and detection of touchable surfaces. An overview of the method is shown in Fig. 1.

2.1   Ceiling and Floor Removal

All points in the point cloud acquired by 3D scanning except for the ceiling and floor are considered as obstacles and are replaced by virtual objects. Therefore, the ceiling and floor are removed by plane detection.

We use RANSAC [4] for plane detection. RANSAC is a model fitting algorithm that is robust to outliers and is often used for plane detection.

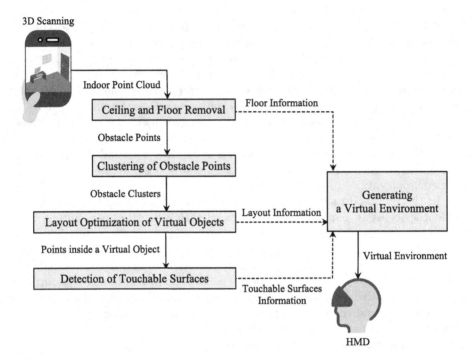

Fig. 1. Overview of generating the virtual environment

The number of random samples is set to 10^4, and the tolerance is set to 0.05 m. By removing the points of the detected plane from the point cloud and applying RANSAC repeatedly, multiple planes are detected. This process is terminated when the number of points in the point cloud becomes less than 30%. The ceiling is the plane with the largest minimum z-coordinate value among the planes, and the floor is the plane with the smallest maximum z-coordinate value. The ceiling and floor planes are removed from the point cloud.

The points that are not properly detected as a part of the ceiling or floor become noise in the subsequent processing, which may negatively affect the result. Therefore, the points that are higher than the ceiling or lower than the floor are removed as noise.

2.2   Clustering of Obstacle Points

Clustering is applied to all the remaining points in the point cloud to roughly group the points into obstacles. We use the Euclidean Cluster Extraction method [11], which is the clustering method based on the Euclidean distance between points. The maximum distance to be integrated as a cluster is set to 0.2 m, and the minimum number of points to be included in a cluster is set to 500.

2.3   Layout Optimization of Virtual Objects

Optimization using a cost function is applied to determine the size and position of a single virtual object. This optimization is repeated to determine the sizes and positions of multiple virtual objects and to obtain an entire layout.

By projecting the points of each clustered obstacle onto the $x - y$ plane, the 3D point cloud is transformed into a 2D image. After that, closing is applied to the cluster image to fill the holes. Examples of a cluster image and its closing result are shown in Fig. 2. Then, we consider a bounding box that surrounds the entire obstacle region. If the size of the bounding box is larger than a threshold, the bounding box is divided into parts of equal width and height. We set the threshold size to $(w_{\max}, h_{\max}) = (0.5\,\mathrm{m}, 0.5\,\mathrm{m})$. Figure 3 shows examples of a bounding box and divided rectangles. The filled cluster image is cropped by divided rectangles. We use each divided rectangle as the initial rectangle for optimization. The results of determining the initial rectangle and layout optimization are shown in Fig. 4.

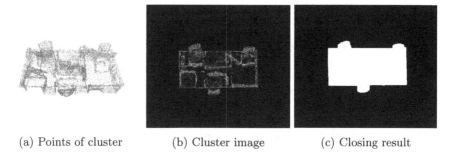

(a) Points of cluster   (b) Cluster image   (c) Closing result

Fig. 2. Examples of transformation to cluster image and closing result

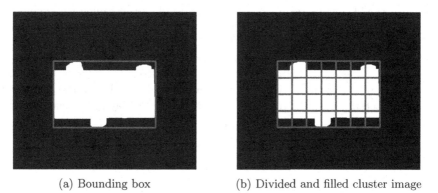

(a) Bounding box   (b) Divided and filled cluster image

Fig. 3. Examples of a bounding box and divided rectangles

(a) Initial rectangle for optimization   (b) Results of optimization in Fig 4a

(c) Results of layout optimization

Fig. 4. Examples of cluster layout optimization

To optimize the size and the position of a single rectangle, we define a cost function as Eq. 1.

$$C(\rho) = \beta S_{\text{intersection}} - \gamma S_{\text{rect}}$$
$$\rho = (x, y, w, h, \theta)$$
$$(1)$$

$S_{\text{intersection}}$ is the area of the intersection between the filled rectangle image and the filled cluster image, S_{rect} is the area of the filled rectangle image, and β and γ are the weights of the terms. ρ is a parameter of the rectangle to be changed by optimization, w is width, h is height, and θ is a rotation angle around the center of the rectangle. (β, γ) are set to $= (1, 0.5)$.

A gradient descent method is used for optimization, and learning rates of the parameters x, y, w, h, and θ are $\alpha_x, \alpha_y, \alpha_w, \alpha_h$, and α_θ. In order to ensure the convergence of the optimization, learning rates are decayed with the number of iterations. Letting n be the number of iterations, the decay of the learning rate is written as Eq. 2.

$$(\alpha_x, \alpha_y, \alpha_w, \alpha_h, \alpha_\theta) = (0.05, 0.05, 0.005, 0.005, 0.01)$$
$$\boldsymbol{\alpha}(0) = (\alpha_x, \alpha_y, \alpha_w, \alpha_h, \alpha_\theta) \qquad (2)$$
$$\boldsymbol{\alpha}(n) = \frac{1}{1 + kn}\, \boldsymbol{\alpha}(n - 1) \quad (n \geq 1)$$

$k = 5 \times 10^{-6}$ is a parameter that controls the decay of the learning rate. This optimization is terminated when the difference of the cost function becomes zero or the number of iterations n becomes greater than a threshold $N = 10^2$.

Once the optimization is completed, the size and position of a single rectangle in the x-y plane are determined. This 2D rectangle is transformed into a 3D virtual object. The size of the virtual object in the z-axis is determined from the maximum and minimum z-coordinates of the obstacle points inside the rectangle.

2.4 Detection of Touchable Surfaces

In order to show touchable surfaces to users, plane detection with normal constraints on the points inside each virtual object is performed. Figure 5 shows the overview of touchable surface detection. The plane that is parallel to any of the five faces except for the bottom of the virtual object, with a distance x'_d to any of the five faces below a threshold is detected as a touchable surface. This plane detection is performed by adding normal constraints in the x'-axis direction, which passes through the center of the virtual object and is perpendicular to two planes. Letting $\boldsymbol{n}$ be the normal vector of the plane detected by RANSAC, normal constraints can be expressed by Eq. 3.

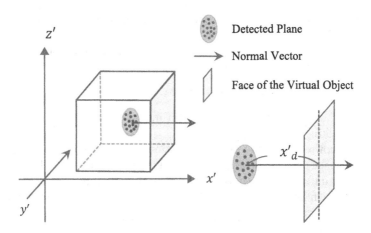

Fig. 5. Touchable surface detection

$$n = tx' \quad (t \neq 0) \tag{3}$$

To increase the number of detected planes, we relax the constraint by setting an error of $\pm 10°$ in the angle between n and x'. This relaxation allows detecting a plane that is approximately parallel to any of the five faces of the virtual object. In addition, letting $\varepsilon_d = 0.05$ m be the allowable distance between the detected plane and any of the five faces, x'_p be the coordinates of the detected plane in the x'-axis, and x''_{max} and x''_{min} be the maximum and minimum coordinates of the virtual object in the x'-axis, touchable surfaces are the planes that satisfy Eq. 4.

$$x'_d = x''_{max} - x'_p, \; x'_p - x''_{min}$$
$$0 \leq x'_d \leq \varepsilon_d \tag{4}$$

The constraints of Eq. 4 are applied in the direction of three axes x', y', and z', and detected planes are presented as touchable surfaces to the user.

3 Experiment

3.1 System

We implemented the proposed method into the system consisting of three devices: a mobile device with 3D scanning capability (Lenovo Phab2 Pro with Google Tango), an HMD (Oculus Quest), and a PC (Dell Precision T3420).

We used Constructor Developer Tool for 3D scanning of indoor environments, Point Cloud Library for point cloud processing, OpenCV for image processing, and Unity for constructing virtual environments.

We prepared three types of virtual objects: obstacles, floors, and touchable surfaces. In addition, to allow the user to touch presented touchable surfaces, the user's hand was displayed as an avatar in the virtual environment.

3.2 Generated Virtual Environment

We performed 3D scanning of a 7 m × 8 m indoor room by holding the mobile device and walking around.

Figure 6 shows the results of layout optimization. In addition, Fig. 7 shows the physical space used in the experiment and the generated virtual environment. Bricks are virtual objects that correspond to obstacles and touchable surfaces are indicated with light blue ellipses. We confirmed that the virtual environment was properly generated based on the physical space. In addition, many touchable surfaces were presented on planar areas, such as the top of tables. Figure 8 shows the user touching a virtual object in the virtual environment and a corresponding table in the physical space. The user was able to touch the table in the physical space through the virtual environment. The time required for each process in generating the virtual environment was 26 s for removing the ceiling and floor, 4 s for clustering of obstacle points, 863 s for optimizing the layout of virtual objects, and 31 s for detecting touchable surfaces.

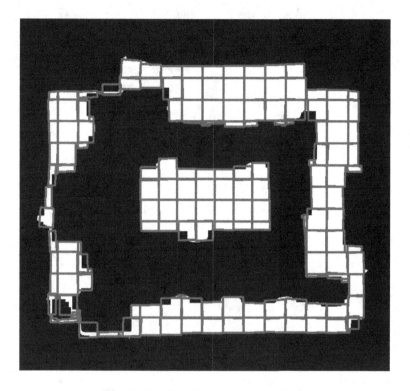

Fig. 6. Results of layout optimization.

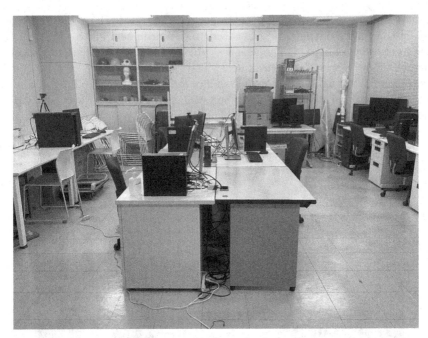

(a) 3D scanned indoor physical space

(b) Generated virtual environment

Fig. 7. Results of generation

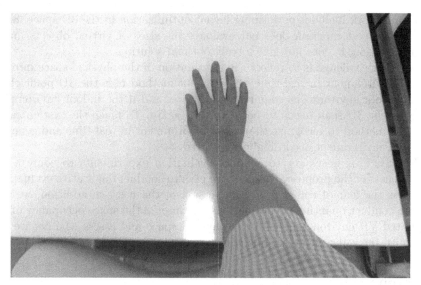

(a) The user touching a physical surface

(b) Virtual object corresponding to Fig. 8a

Fig. 8. Results of haptic experiences

4   Conclusion and Future Work

In this paper, we proposed a method for generating a virtual environment in which users can avoid surrounding obstacles and that allows the user to touch objects in the physical space.

Future work includes performing layout optimization in the 3D space. Since the current cost function does not evaluate the sizes of virtual objects in the z-axis direction, it does not give a truly optimal solution.

Another challenge is to reflect the information of the physical space into the virtual environment in real-time. The current method uses the 3D point cloud of the indoor environment acquired in advance, and if the indoor environment changes, the 3D scan needs to be performed again. To make the system easier to use, a method to recognize the indoor environment in real-time and generate a virtual environment accordingly is required.

Finally, it is necessary to conduct evaluation experiments to confirm the effectiveness of the proposed method. We plan to conduct qualitative evaluations to assess the fear of collision and immersion of the user. In addition, we also plan to conduct quantitative evaluations to compare the space occupancy of the generated VR environment with the physical space and assess whether we can maximize the walkable area while covering obstacles.

References

1. Budhiraja, P., Sodhi, R., Jones, B., Karsch, K., Bailey, B., Forsyth, D.: Where's my drink? Enabling peripheral real world interactions while using HMDs. arXiv preprint arXiv:1502.04744 (2015)
2. Cheng, L.P., Ofek, E., Holz, C., Wilson, A.D.: Vroamer: generating on-the-fly VR experiences while walking inside large, unknown real-world building environments. In: Proceedings of the 2019 IEEE Conference on Virtual Reality and 3D User Interfaces (VR), pp. 359–366 (2019). https://doi.org/10.1109/VR.2019.8798074
3. Eckstein, B., Krapp, E., Lugrin, B.: Towards serious games and applications in smart substitutional reality. In: Proceedings of the 2018 10th International Conference on Virtual Worlds and Games for Serious Applications (VS-Games), pp. 1–8 (2018). https://doi.org/10.1109/VS-Games.2018.8493444
4. Fischler, M., et al.: Random sample consensus: a paradigm for model fitting with applications to image analysis and automated cartography. Commun. ACM **24**(6), 381–395 (1981). https://doi.org/10.1145/358669.358692
5. Hartmann, J., Holz, C., Ofek, E., Wilson, A.D.: Realitycheck: blending virtual environments with situated physical reality. In: Proceedings of the 2019 CHI Conference on Human Factors in Computing Systems, pp. 1–12 (2019). https://doi.org/10.1145/3290605.3300577
6. Hettiarachchi, A., Wigdor, D.: Annexing reality: enabling opportunistic use of everyday objects as tangible proxies in augmented reality. In: Proceedings of the 2016 CHI Conference on Human Factors in Computing Systems, pp. 1957–1967 (2016). https://doi.org/10.1145/2858036.2858134
7. Kanamori, K., Sakata, N., Tominaga, T., Hijikata, Y., Harada, K., Kiyokawa, K.: Obstacle avoidance method in real space for virtual reality immersion. In: Proceedings of the 2018 IEEE International Symposium on Mixed and Augmented Reality (ISMAR), pp. 80–89 (2018). https://doi.org/10.1109/ISMAR.2018.00033
8. Keller, M., Tchilinguirian, T.: Obstacles awareness methods from occupancy map for free walking in VR. In: Proceedings of the 2019 IEEE Conference on Virtual Reality and 3D User Interfaces (VR), pp. 1012–1013 (2019). https://doi.org/10.1109/VR.2019.8798260

9. McGill, M., Boland, D., Murray-Smith, R., Brewster, S.: A dose of reality: overcoming usability challenges in VR head-mounted displays. In: Proceedings of the 33rd Annual ACM Conference on Human Factors in Computing Systems, pp. 2143–2152 (2015). https://doi.org/10.1145/2702123.2702382
10. Rauter, M., Abseher, C., Safar, M.: Augmenting virtual reality with near real world objects. In: Proceedings of the 2019 IEEE Conference on Virtual Reality and 3D User Interfaces (VR), pp. 1134–1135 (2019). https://doi.org/10.1109/VR.2019.8797873
11. Rusu, R.: Semantic 3D object maps for everyday manipulation in human living environments. KI-Künstliche Intelligenz **24**(4), 345–348 (2010). https://doi.org/10.1007/s13218-010-0059-6
12. Shapira, L., Freedman, D.: Reality skins: creating immersive and tactile virtual environments. In: Proceedings of the 2016 IEEE International Symposium on Mixed and Augmented Reality (ISMAR), pp. 115–124 (2016). https://doi.org/10.1109/ISMAR.2016.23
13. Simeone, A.L., Velloso, E., Gellersen, H.: Substitutional reality: using the physical environment to design virtual reality experiences. In: Proceedings of the 33rd Annual ACM Conference on Human Factors in Computing Systems, pp. 3307–3316 (2015). https://doi.org/10.1145/2702123.2702389
14. Sra, M., et al.: Oasis: procedurally generated social virtual spaces from 3D scanned real spaces. IEEE TVCG **24**(12), 3174–3187 (2017). https://doi.org/10.1109/TVCG.2017.2762691
15. Valentini, I., Ballestin, G., Bassano, C., Solari, F., Chessa, M.: Improving obstacle awareness to enhance interaction in virtual reality. In: Proceedings of the 2020 IEEE Conference on Virtual Reality and 3D User Interfaces (VR), pp. 44–52 (2020). https://doi.org/10.1109/VR46266.2020.00022
16. Wu, F., Rosenberg, E.S.: Combining dynamic field of view modification with physical obstacle avoidance. In: Proceedings of the 2019 IEEE Conference on Virtual Reality and 3D User Interfaces (VR), pp. 1882–1883 (2019). https://doi.org/10.1109/VR.2019.8798015
17. Yabe, H., Ono, D., Horikawa, T.: Space fusion: context-aware interaction using 3D scene parsing. In: Proceedings of the SIGGRAPH Asia 2018 Virtual & Augmented Reality, pp. 1–2 (2018). https://doi.org/10.1145/3275495.3275498
18. Yang, J., Holz, C., Ofek, E., Wilson, A.D.: Dreamwalker: substituting real-world walking experiences with a virtual reality. In: Proceedings of the 32nd Annual ACM Symposium on User Interface Software and Technology, pp. 1093–1107 (2019). https://doi.org/10.1145/3332165.3347875

Omnichannel Retail Customer Experience with Mixed-Reality Shopping Assistant Systems

Shubham Jain[✉], Thomas Schweiss, Simon Bender, and Dirk Werth

August-Wilhelm Scheer Institute, Saarbrücken, Germany
{thomas.schweiss,simon.bender,dirk.werth}@aws-institut.de

Abstract. Mixed reality has been identified as one of the technologies that can be deployed in omnichannel retail to improve the customer shopping experience. The article presents a mixed reality based digital shopping assistant which aims to provide retail customers with a holistic shopping experience. Design science research methodology is used to develop this physical artifact that comprises of assisting elements: product information, reviews, recommendations and a buy button. A study was conducted with two different head-mounted displays (Microsoft HoloLens and HoloLens 2) where 29 participants evaluated the proposed physical artifact and brings out the relationship between shopping experience constructs that constitutes a modern omnichannel retail customer experience. Results show a positive attitude of customers towards the technology. Differences between the two-head mounted displays were observed in terms of perceived privacy issues. Technology adoption, enjoyment and security beliefs of the customers are observed to have a significant effect on the user's intention to use the technology. The results also reveal that a customer's perceived convenience, perceived service quality, attitude towards the retailer and the word of mouth are affected significantly by their intention to use the technology. These results, along with qualitative comments from the participants are used to extract research, development and deployment implications for future iterations of shopping assistant systems based on mixed reality.

Keywords: Mixed reality · Omnichannel retail · Digital retail · Customer experience

1 Introduction

The concept of 'omnichannel retail' is centered around providing customers with a holistic shopping experience [1]. It has been established as the next step to digital retail [2] that makes it important for the retailers to stay relevant in the business. Several retailers have already started with this transition to omnichannel and have benefited from it [3]. Omnichannel retail has also been suggested as one of the tools to battle the 'retail apocalypse' [4], and consequently meet the expectations of a progressive retail customer. Along with this, research around digital and omnichannel retail has become more important as a consequence of COVID-19 where traditional retail environments are forced to adopt newer models and technologies [5].

© The Author(s) 2021
G. Bebis et al. (Eds.): ISVC 2021, LNCS 13017, pp. 504–517, 2021.
https://doi.org/10.1007/978-3-030-90439-5_40

An omnichannel customer expects their shopping journey to be seamless and attributed with utilitarian and hedonic values, while they evaluate their shopping experience by interacting with the shopping environment [1]. One of the key attributes of an omnichannel retail environment is the optimal deployment of novel digital technologies like digital realities, smartphones and recommender systems to enhance the customer's shopping journey [6]. Among these technologies, Mixed Reality (MR) has emerged as one of the key technology megatrends that has the potential to revolutionize the retail sector in the next decade [7]. MR has a unique capability to bridge the gap between online and offline environments which fits right into the concept of omnichannel retail where multiple channels are integrated into a single seamless customer journey. Furthermore, a shopping assistant system that leverages the qualities of MR technology to tackle customers' needs and improve their experience is one of the preeminent ways to row through the transition to omnichannel retail [8].

Design Science Research (DSR) methodology can be used to develop such systems, as it provides a rigid framework to produce physical artifacts that can solve real-world organizational problems [9–11]. This is an iterative approach where the evaluation of the physical artifact is an important step to optimize the next iteration. Traditionally, Technology Acceptance Model (TAM) [12] has been used in this regard to capturing user perception over innovative technologies. While the literature advances, a number of authors have manifested TAM to fit better into their particular context, for e.g., the authors in [13] added the hedonic element 'enjoyment' to their studies. Other constructs like user's privacy and trust have also been studied to influence the perception of retail customers as they emerge as a topic of concern in the current literature [14]. These factors can influence the customer's overall perception of retail technologies which can affect different shopping outcomes for retailers and their businesses.

Although the present literature brings out a lot of different advantages of MR, and several application designs towards retail [15], more research is required towards the understanding of user's perception towards the technology. This is the targeted research gap, which also builds upon the research framework mentioned in [16]. Towards this, we firstly use DSR to design an omnichannel retail shopping assistant system using 'optical see-through mixed reality' and Microsoft (MS) HoloLens and Microsoft HoloLens 2 as two different hardware archetypes. We use the present industry and academic standards to develop a pseudo-optimal system, hence contributing a physical instantiation as the research outcome.

Furthermore, we captured user perception towards the designed artifact in a laboratory study with 29 participants. An extended TAM was used to study users' behavioral intentions. The results reveal the relationship between the different shopping constructs. These results along with the qualitative comments from the participants during the study are used to extract research, development and deployment implications. These implications aim to contribute towards a better understanding of the general user perception towards MR-based retail systems and suggest improvements over the next iteration of the prototype. Hence, we add to the current literature of MR systems in retail environments.

2 Background and Previous Work

2.1 Optical-See Through Mixed Reality

The 'Virtuality continuum' defined by Paul Milgram [17] categorizes optical see-through mixed reality (OSTMR) as class 3 displays. These devices are "head-mounted displays equipped with a see-through capability, with which computer-generated graphics can be optically superimposed" [17, p. 3]. As there is limited literature on the deployment of OSTMR in retail, we first reviewed some literature from similar technologies. For example, Authors in [18] and [15] deployed smartphone-based MR applications that aim to enhance the in-store shopping experience. However, smartphones are limited in terms of providing a natural posture for interaction and communicating tangible characteristics of a product to the customer. Other devices like Oculus [19], which uses the concept of fully immersive virtual reality (VR) also has been studied in this regard. Fully immersive VR poses a challenge for customers as it occludes the vision of a user and hence, obstructs their primary tasks in a natural environment. Also, non-immersive technologies like display screen monitors have been used in this regard to develop physical artifacts for an enhanced customer journey. A 2D display like a monitor screen or a smartphone is unable to project an organic environment even with touch and sensor-based input methods. These technologies have proven their significance for a long time but still is abstain from providing hedonism and natural interactions [20]. OSTMR complements these technologies by having the capability of not completely occluding the vision of a user during the use, and creating a pseudo immersive environment where digital and physical objects co-exist and interact with each other. This makes the experience more tangible, interactive, and exciting for customers as compared to other display and interaction technologies. MS HoloLens executes this task using a holographic display that projects 'holograms', which are digital objects rendered into the real world. These holograms are enhanced by sound and light and can be interacted with, using interaction techniques provided by the device [21].

2.2 MR Shopping Assistant System

A contemporary customer has high expectations in terms of their shopping experience due to the development of technologies. Retailers need to address these needs and expectations to stay relevant in the business [22]. This can be done by providing personalized and tailored assistance with digital shopping assistants [7]. Personal MR devices can provide this assistance putting the customers in control of their shopping journey and helping them towards comparing products, finding alternatives, and feeling more confident in their decision-making at the purchase. Previous authors have used OSTMR to develop such systems in different settings. Recent literature shows examples such as [23] where the authors used this technology to develop an in-store recommender system that can provide tailored recommendations to customers. Other examples brought out features like product detection [24] and Natural User Interaction (NUI) [25] that can be used in an optimal MR shopping assistant design. Authors in [26] suggest the use of product information and reviews in a shopping assistant system while mentioning the importance of hardware design. Authors in [27] point out the significance of the 'buy' button in a shopping interface. Collectively, these shopping elements and MR features can help design a pseudo-optimal MR shopping assistant system.

2.3 Customer Experience and Hypotheses Development

Customer experience is considered to be the center of omnichannel retail business models [2]. It has been defined to be "holistic in nature and involves the customer's cognitive, affective, emotional, social and physical responses to the retailer" [28, p. 70]. Thus, it is absolutely important to understand customers' perceptions and responses in order to create digital solutions towards enhancing their shopping journey [1]. The customer experience can consist of a plethora of constructs that can be based on subjective and objective attributes. The current work does not aim to report an exhaustive account of all the customer experience constructs but works on a set of constructs that have been either studied extensively in academic literature or are relevant in the current age. One of the most used models to test the usability, and capture the user perception towards a new technology-based system is TAM (Davis 1985), which predicts the user's Intention to use (ITU) a system using 'Perceived usability' (PU), and 'Perceived ease of use' (PEOU). PU and PEOU are collectively used to define 'technology adoption' in the current work. Along with the utilitarian assistance provided by the desired solution, hedonic motivations such as fun, pleasure, and enjoyability [29] are crucial factors influencing customers' shopping experience. 'Enjoyability' has been used as an added parameter of technology adoption [30, 31], even especially for MR [32], where the authors bring out the importance of the construct and its positive effect on factors like purchase intention and the attitude of the customers in a shopping journey. Developing on these findings, we propose the first hypothesis:

H1: Perceived usefulness (H1a), perceived ease of use (H1b), and perceived enjoyment (H1c) have a significant effect on the intention to use the MR shopping assistant in omnichannel retail.

'Security beliefs' consisting of 'Privacy concerns' and 'Trust' are adapted from [26]. The authors argued that trust and privacy concerns play an important role in the general perception of the shopping environment and whether customers will use the technologies or not. The authors used two shopping assistance systems that leverage either bar-code scanner or radio frequency identification (RFID) reader as the hardware design, while we want to study the effects in MR technology. The authors in [14] state that security concerns have risen with technologies like MR, which can affect the customer perception in a retail environment. Hence, we propose the second hypothesis as:

H2: Privacy concerns (H2a) and trust (H2b) have a significant effect on the intention to use the MR shopping assistant in omnichannel retail.

Shopping outcomes comprise of 'Convenience', 'Word-of-mouth', 'Attitude towards a retailer', and 'Customer service quality' [26]. These outcomes are some of the widely studied constructs in context to customer experience and perception [33–35]. These constructs have been mentioned in the literature to have a great impact on the retailer's businesses, and hence are important to be researched. As digital technology is an important part of an omnichannel retail environment, we believe that the intention to use the system can shape these outcomes. Hence, we propose the following hypothesis.

H3: The intention to use the MR shopping assistant in omnichannel retail has a significant effect on the shopping outcomes: Convenience (H3a), Word-of-mouth (H3b), Customer service quality (H3c) and Attitude towards a retailer (H3d).

3 MR Shopping Assistant System

The designed system is summarized below using the eight components of the information systems design science principles mentioned in [9].

Purpose and Scope: The mixed-reality digital shopping assistant application was designed to provide customers with an exciting and helpful shopping journey.

Constructs: Technology adoption (perceived usefulness, perceived ease-of-use), intention to use, enjoyment, security beliefs (privacy concerns, trust), shopping outcomes (convenience, word-of-mouth, customer service quality, attitude towards a retailer).

Principle of Form and Function: The blueprint of the IT artifact involved hardware and software design:

Hardware Design (MS HoloLens and MS HoloLens 2): The produced artifact in the form of a digital shopping assistant is deployed over two different OSTMR devices of the same family: MS HoloLens and HoloLens 2. The first generation of MS HoloLens introduced a whole new ecosystem of immersive technology devices and was projected as the 'The future of augmented reality' [21]. Despite its success as a developer prototype, certain limitations of the hardware were reported like the narrow field of view, the complexity of interaction methods, ergonomics, etc. The second generation, HoloLens 2 brings several improvements for the first-generation device such as a dedicated DNN core, wider field of view, improved ergonomics, articulated hand tracking, and eye gaze tracking [36]. Both devices aim to deploy a multimodal NUI based on hand gestures and voice interaction, but HoloLens 2 claims to have a more natural interaction as the digital holograms can be 'touched' like physical objects as compared to the 'gaze and commit' scheme of HoloLens. However, the shortcomings of the earlier device can be compensated by using the HoloLens Clicker, which is a handheld click-based interaction device, which reduces the physical complexity of the HoloLens interaction schema. Arguably, this reduction in the physical complexity of interaction can take over the reward of naturalness in HoloLens 2. This will lead to a similar perception for both of the devices which also implies higher scalability of the designed interface.

Software Design (Information, Recommendation, Reviews, and a Buy Button). The system largely builds over the requirements developed by the authors in [23]. We deployed image recognition using Vuforia Engine [37] that enables the system to detect the product of interest that is brought on to its field of view (FOV). Once the device recognizes

Fig. 1. Application design: HoloLens 2 (left), HoloLens (right); Participant interacting with the application (center)

the product, a 3D digital interface is placed around the object as shown in Fig. 1 (left and right).

The interactive user interface is designed with the help of standardized tools: Mixed Reality Toolkit (MRTK and MRTK2) for HoloLens1 and HoloLens 2 [38]. The UI contains four major elements: 'Information,' 'Recommendations,' 'Reviews,' and 'Buy' as shown in Fig. 1. These elements are represented as 3D buttons that are anchored on to the product. Information and reviews, as a shopping assistant element has been adapted from [26, 39] where the combination of these two elements in the artifact was preferred by the customers in comparison to the absence of them or presence of only one of the elements. Mining data from different channels to provide a customized service such as product recommendations on ubiquitous devices, such as the HoloLens could create multiple benefits in the retail ecosystem [40]. For retail customers, the product recommendations boost the efficiency in finding preferential products, provide more confidence in making a purchase decision, and give a potential chance to discover something new. These assistance items aim to reduce information overload and enhance decision-making [41] as the customer is more confident in the buying process. Furthermore, it was necessary to introduce a one-click checkout UI item [42], following web-based shopping interfaces. This is addressed with the 'Buy' button in the UI, which eases the customer's path-to-purchase and target the customer's need to buy the product immediately, raising customer satisfaction, solving the 'crisis of immediacy' [22], and integrating the customer journey into one channel/touchpoint. Both devices are rigged with a voice recognition system which can be used by the user to disable or enable the holograms attached to the product by saying 'start' and 'stop' respectively.

Artifact Mutability: The artifact designs were developed toward scalability. Although during the tests, the application content was static, a retailer's databases could be linked to the artifacts. By having access to real-time data, the artifacts could adjust to the dynamic retail environment.

Testable Propositions: Nine prepositions were constructed based on the present literature (see Sect. 2).

Justificatory Knowledge: Drawing on existing literature, generalizations were constructed from patterns observed in academic literature and industry trends.

Principles of Implementation: Several recommendations for implementing the learnings in future research and iterations are provided in the form of implications.

Expository Instantiation: The MR shopping artifacts were implemented in a simulated omnichannel retail environment.

4 Experiment Setup

The study was conducted with 29 participants who tried the MR application on both devices (HoloLens, HoloLens 2). The participants were recruited using e-mail and instant message-based invitations. The order of the devices was randomized and distributed evenly among the population. Sixteen (55%) of the participants were male while the other 45% were female. The participants were from ten different nationalities, however, 17 (59%) were German. The mean age of the participants was 28 years with a standard deviation of 4.8. Eighteen (62%) of the participants answered "yes" to the question "Have you had any experience with Mixed-Reality before this study?", and hence had prior experience with MS HoloLens or similar immersive environments. The participation was voluntary, and no financial compensation was provided.

An omnichannel retail environment was simulated in a laboratory with a hypothetical retailer 'AWS'. The setting consisted of two different categories of products that are considered to diversify the product assortment in the setting: Search products (a pack of milk, a computer monitor, a pair of sneakers, a package of soft-drinks, a pack of coffee beans) and experience products (i.e., a box of chocolate, a tech magazine, a bottle of rum, a video game disc, a 6-pack of beer).

The setup was made to look casual, and less like a traditional brick-and-mortar store. Written consent was obtained from the participants which was followed by a short introduction to the application and the environment. Then, the participants were assigned the task of 'general browsing' where they were asked to browse and buy the available products as they want. This was done using verbal and written instructions. No real money was involved in the buying process and the task was more oriented towards testing the functionalities of the application and experiencing the shopping environment. General browsing was chosen over goal-oriented because the goal of the study focused more on a participant's perception and opinion about technology and less on the efficiency of the application during the shopping journey. The participants were then asked to complete a questionnaire that consisted of 34 items. They rated their responses on a 7-point Likert Scale. Scales were adopted from [26] for technology adoption, intention to use, security beliefs, and customer shopping outcomes. Items in the scale for enjoyability were adopted from [13, 32]. The complete questionnaire is attached in the appendix Table A1. The study took less than 60 min per participant with an exposure of approximately 30 min to the MR devices ensuring that there is no simulation sickness to deviate the user's opinion towards the technology.

5 Results

The scales' reliability was tested, and the cronbach's alpha was greater than 0.90 with both the devices, hence making the scale reliable. Table 1 summarizes the participants' response towards the technology, with both the hardware devices. Paired t-test was used to compare the two hardware and the results show a significant difference between the perceived privacy concerns in HoloLens (HL1) and HoloLens 2 (HL2). As a higher value with privacy concerns means fewer privacy concerns (see Table A1), it can be interpreted that the participants felt more comfortable with HoloLens 2 towards their privacy.

Table 1. Mean and Standard deviation (SD) for HoloLens1 and HoloLens 2

Construct	Mean (HL1)	SD	Mean (HL2)	SD	P-value with paired t-test
Intention to use	5.21	1.59	5.44	1.11	0.17
Perceived usefulness	5.23	1.23	5.31	1.15	0.35
Perceived ease of use	5.56	1.36	5.35	1.01	0.25
Enjoyability	5.68	1.31	5.98	0.93	0.16
Privacy concerns	**4.42**	**1.22**	**4.70**	**1.20**	**0.04**
Trust	4.61	0.71	4.65	0.67	0.39
Convenience	5.05	0.99	5.21	0.94	0.23
Word-of-mouth	5.53	1.14	5.52	1.08	0.48
Customer service quality	5.15	1.22	5.14	1.28	0.48
Attitude toward the retailer	5.56	1.25	5.76	1.04	0.21

5.1 Regression Analysis

The Hypotheses proposed in Sect. 2 were tested using linear regression analysis. The regression coefficient was calculated along with the significance (p-values) of the relationships. Figure 2 presents the results from the analysis. The hypotheses are tested with the criteria that if $p < 0.05$, the null hypothesis can be rejected and the proposed hypothesis is supported. The results show that perceived usefulness, perceived ease of use and enjoyment has a significant effect on the intention to use, thus supporting H1a-c. The results also show a significant effect of privacy concerns and trust on intention to use with both hardware even though privacy concerns have a higher effect in the case of HoloLens 2. Also, intention to use is seen to have a significant effect on all the shopping outcomes (convenience, word-of-mouth, customer service quality and attitude towards a retailer). Hence, H2a-b and H3a-d are fully supported.

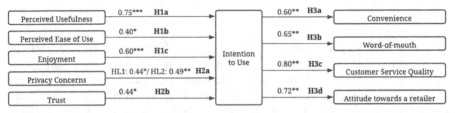

Fig. 2. Hypotheses testing using simple linear regression, Note: * p < .05, ** p < .01, *** p < .001

5.2   Qualitative Comments from the Participants

During the study, the participants were allowed to make comments and ask questions about the use of the prototype. As HoloLens and HoloLens 2 are not designed in the current age to be used by naïve customers, participants mentioned a number of ergonomic issues with the hardware. This was observed with both devices in terms of heaviness and general comfort. The participants also mentioned interaction and visualization problems, for e.g., the clipping of 3D objects in the case of HoloLens. The users responded positively towards the overall usability of the interface and made some suggestions for the next iteration. This includes changing the 'one-touch' buying mechanism to a more secure virtual cart-based process that gives them a chance to review the products before the payment. Another suggestion was made to add meta-information elements that are either unique to an MR experience, or that combine online e-commerce and the traditional brick and mortar retail environment.

6   Discussion and Implications

The quantitative results along with the qualitative comments from the participants can have several implications for future research and development. The quantitative results in Table 1 show a positive reaction towards the MR shopping assistant system, while the quantitative comments suggest improvement over the next iteration of the prototype. The implications from these results are as follows:

Research Implications

- As participants made valuable suggestions and comments during the quantitative study, we motivate researchers to follow a mixed-method research method that aims to qualitatively triangulate the quantitative findings to confirm and expand the knowledge and causes of the proposed hypothesis [43].
- Following simple linear regression, multiple linear regression and mediation analysis should be used to better model the omnichannel retail customer experience in MR environments.
- With HoloLens 2, participants showed fewer concerns towards privacy issues which calls for further privacy research with mixed reality environments.

Development Implications

- Virtual shopping carts should be used in an MR shopping assistance system to facilitate shopping for customers.
- Developers should highlight the novelty of MR environments by integrating shopping assistant elements that provide unique value to the customers. This can be done by integrating online and offline elements into a single application.
- An MR shopping assistant application should focus on the efficiency of interactions and the effects of visualization. This can be done by either iterating the prototypes repeatedly using subjective evaluations or providing an option to tailor the user interface according to the customer's needs.

Deployment Implications

- MR shopping assistant systems are constrained by a number of constructs. These include technology adoption constructs (PU, PEOU), enjoyability privacy concerns and trust among others that can influence the intention to use the technology, which further affects a customer's perceived convenience, word-of-mouth towards the retailers, perceived service quality and attitude towards the retailer.
- Even though the results suggest a positive perception of MR technology in retail, as in Table 1, the retailers should be mindful of the deployment constraints and customize their omnichannel solutions according to their business needs and customer perception.

7 Conclusion

In the current age where the retail sector is forced to transition into an omnichannel paradigm due to industry trends and environmental factors like COVID-19, it is important for retailers to deploy innovative retail solutions in their businesses to enhance their customer's shopping experience. In the current research, we first designed an OSTMR shopping assistant system using MS HoloLens and HoloLens 2 as the hardware archetypes. We integrated product information, reviews, recommendations, and a buy button into a 3D interface using the DSR approach. The evaluation of the system in a laboratory study suggests a positive perception of a user towards the technology, while several research, development and deployment implications are extracted from the quantitative results and the qualitative comments.

Acknowledgement. This research is a part of the European Training Network project PERFORM that has received funding from the European Union's Horizon 2020 research and innovation programme under the Marie Skłodowska- Curie grant agreement No. 765395. This research reflects only the authors' view, the European Commission is not responsible for any use that may be made of the information it contains.

Appendix

Table A1. Scales Used, Note: *This item was reverse coded

Item no.	Items
Intention to use	
1.	I would use Mixed Reality shopping to shop in the store
2.	I intend to use Mixed Reality shopping the next time I see it in the store
3.	I will not use Mixed Reality shopping the next time I see the system in the store*
Technology adoption	
	Perceived usefulness
4.	Using Mixed Reality shopping in the store added value to my shopping experience
5.	The experience of using Mixed Reality shopping in the store was useful to me
6.	I believe that the experience of using Mixed Reality shopping in the store added value to the overall service
	Perceived ease of use
7.	My interaction with Mixed Reality shopping in the store was clear and understandable
8.	It was easy for me to become skilful at using Mixed Reality shopping in the store
9.	I found Mixed Reality shopping easy to use in the store
10.	Learning to operate Mixed Reality shopping in the store was easy for me
Enjoyability	
11.	Using Mixed Reality for shopping was fun
12.	Using Mixed Reality shopping was enjoyable
13.	Using Mixed Reality shopping was exciting
Security beliefs	
	Privacy concerns
14.	I feel comfortable giving personal information on this retailer
15.	I feel comfortable shopping at this retailer
16.	The retailer clearly explained how user information will be used
17.	Information regarding security of payments is clearly presented
	Trust
18.	This store is trustworthy
19.	I trust this store keeps my best interests in mind
20.	I think it makes sense to be cautious with this store
21.	This retailer has more to lose than to gain by not delivering on their promises
22.	This store's behavior meets my expectations
Shopping outcomes	
	Convenience
23.	It was convenient to find information on products
24.	I found it complicated to find products at this store*

(continued)

Table A1. (*continued*)

Item no.	Items
25.	It is convenient to shop from this retailer
	Word-of-mouth
26.	I would recommend visiting this retailer to friends
27.	I would say good things about this retailer to others
28.	I would encourage friends and relatives to visit this retailer
	Customer service quality
29.	The retailer's customer service was of high quality
30.	The retailer's customer service was always functional
31.	The retailer's customer service was very reliable
	Attitude towards a retailer
32.	My overall attitude toward the retailer is favorable
33.	My overall attitude toward the retailer is good
34.	My overall attitude toward the retailer is positive

References

1. Lemon, K.N., Verhoef, P.C.: Understanding customer experience throughout the customer journey. J. Mark. **80**, 69–96 (2016). https://doi.org/10.1509/jm.15.0420
2. Rigby, D.K.: The future of shopping. Harv. Bus. Rev. **89**, 65–76 (2011)
3. Zhang, M., Ren, C., Wang, G.A., He, Z.: The impact of channel integration on consumer responses in omni-channel retailing: the mediating effect of consumer empowerment. Electron. Commer. Res. Appl. **28**, 181–193 (2018). https://doi.org/10.1016/j.elerap.2018.02.002
4. Berman, B.: Flatlined: combatting the death of retail stores. Bus. Horiz. **62**, 75–82 (2019). https://doi.org/10.1016/j.bushor.2018.08.006
5. Shankar, V., et al.: How technology is changing retail. J. Retail. **97**, 13–27 (2021). https://doi.org/10.1016/j.jretai.2020.10.006
6. Burke, R.R.: Technology and the customer interface: what consumers want in the physical and virtual store. J. Acad. Mark. Sci. **30**, 411–432 (2002). https://doi.org/10.1177/009207002236914
7. von Briel, F.: The future of omnichannel retail: a four-stage Delphi study. Technol. Forecast. Soc. Chang. **132**, 217–229 (2018). https://doi.org/10.1016/j.techfore.2018.02.004
8. Competing in the age of omnichannel retailing (2013)
9. Gregor, S., Jones, D.: The Anatomy of a Design Theory, pp. 1536–9323 (2007)
10. Hevner, A.R., Chatterjee, S.: Design research in information systems. Theory and practice. In: Hevner, A., Chatterjee, S. (eds.). Forewords by Paul Gray and Carliss Y. Baldwin. Springer, New York, London (2010)
11. Peffers, K., Tuunanen, T., Rothenberger, M.A., Chatterjee, S.: A design science research methodology for information systems research. J. Manag. Inf. Syst. **24**, 45–77 (2007). https://doi.org/10.2753/MIS0742-1222240302
12. Davis, F.: A technology acceptance model for empirically testing new end-user information systems, theory and results. Doctoral dissertation, Massachusetts Institute of Technology (1985)

516   S. Jain et al.

13. Rasimah, C.M.Y., Ahmad, A., Zaman, H.B.: Evaluation of user acceptance of mixed reality technology. AJET **27** (2011). https://doi.org/10.14742/ajet.899
14. Pizzi, G., Scarpi, D.: Privacy threats with retail technologies: a consumer perspective. J. Retail. Consum. Serv. **56**, 102160 (2020). https://doi.org/10.1016/j.jretconser.2020.102160
15. Spreer, P., Kallweit, K.: Augmented reality in retail: assessing the acceptance and potential for multimedia product presentation at the PoS. SOP Trans. Market. Res. **1**(1), 23–31 (2014). https://doi.org/10.15764/MR.2014.01002
16. Jain, S., Werth, D.: Current state of mixed reality technology for digital retail: a literature review. In: Nah, F.-H., Siau, K. (eds.) HCII 2019. LNCS, vol. 11588, pp. 22–37. Springer, Cham (2019). https://doi.org/10.1007/978-3-030-22335-9_2
17. Milgram, P., Kishino, F.: A Taxonomy of Mixed Reality Visual Displays (1994)
18. Meegahapola, L., Perera, I.: Enhanced in-store shopping experience through smart phone based mixed reality application. In: Regions, I.C.o.A.i.I.f.E. (ed.) 17th International Conference on Advances in ICT for Emerging Regions (ICTer) - 2017. Conference Proceedings: 07th & 08th of September 2017, Vidya Jyothi Prof. V. Samaranayaka Auditorium, University of Colombo School of Computing, Colombo, Sri Lanka, pp. 1–8. IEEE, Piscataway (2017). https://doi.org/10.1109/ICTER.2017.8257810
19. Márquez, J.O.Á., Ziegler, J.: Augmented-reality-enhanced product comparison in physical retailing. In: Alt, F., Bulling, A., Döring, T. (eds.) Mensch und Computer 2019 - Tagungsband, pp. 55–65. The Association for Computing Machinery, Inc., New York (2019). https://doi.org/10.1145/3340764.3340800
20. Flavián, C., Ibáñez-Sánchez, S., Orús, C.: The impact of virtual, augmented and mixed reality technologies on the customer experience. J. Bus. Res. **100**, 547–560 (2019). https://doi.org/10.1016/j.jbusres.2018.10.050
21. Furlan, R.: The future of augmented reality: Hololens – Microsoft's AR headset shines despite rough edges [Resources_Tools and Toys]. IEEE Spectr. **53**, 21 (2016). https://doi.org/10.1109/MSPEC.2016.7473143
22. Parise, S., Guinan, P.J., Kafka, R.: Solving the crisis of immediacy: how digital technology can transform the customer experience. Bus. Horiz. **59**, 411–420 (2016). https://doi.org/10.1016/j.bushor.2016.03.004
23. Mora, D., Jain, S., Nalbach, O., Werth, D.: Holographic recommendations in brick-and-mortar stores. In: AMCIS 2020 Proceedings (2020)
24. Fuchs, K., Grundmann, T., Fleisch, E.: Towards identification of packaged products via computer vision. In: Proceedings of the 9th International Conference on the Internet of Things, pp. 1–8. ACM, New York (10222019). https://doi.org/10.1145/3365871.3365899
25. Cheng, K., Nakazawa, M., Masuko, S.: MR-Shoppingu: physical interaction with augmented retail products using continuous context awareness. In: Munekata, N., Kunita, I., Hoshino, J. (eds.) ICEC 2017. LNCS, vol. 10507, pp. 452–455. Springer, Cham (2017). https://doi.org/10.1007/978-3-319-66715-7_61
26. Venkatesh, V., Aloysius, J.A., Burton, S.: Design and evaluation of auto-ID enabled shopping assistance artifacts in customers' mobile phones: two retail store laboratory experiments. MISQ **41**, 83–113 (2017). https://doi.org/10.25300/MISQ/2017/41.1.05
27. Loureiro, S.M.C., Breazeale, M.: Pressing the buy button. Cloth. Text. Res. J. **34**, 163–178 (2016). https://doi.org/10.1177/0887302X16633530
28. Verhoef, P.C., Lemon, K.N., Parasuraman, A., Roggeveen, A., Tsiros, M., Schlesinger, L.A.: Customer experience creation: determinants, dynamics and management strategies. J. Retail. **85**, 31–41 (2009). https://doi.org/10.1016/j.jretai.2008.11.001
29. Juaneda-Ayensa, E., Mosquera, A., Sierra Murillo, Y.: Omnichannel customer behavior: key drivers of technology acceptance and use and their effects on purchase intention. Front. Psychol. **7**, 1117 (2016). https://doi.org/10.3389/fpsyg.2016.01117

30. Peukert, C., Pfeiffer, J., Meissner, M., Pfeiffer, T., Weinhardt, C.: Acceptance of imagined versus experienced virtual reality shopping environments: insights from two experiments. Research Papers (2019)
31. Roy, S.K., Balaji, M.S., Sadeque, S., Nguyen, B., Melewar, T.C.: Constituents and consequences of smart customer experience in retailing. Technol. Forecast. Soc. Chang. **124**, 257–270 (2017). https://doi.org/10.1016/j.techfore.2016.09.022
32. Poushneh, A., Vasquez-Parraga, A.Z.: Discernible impact of augmented reality on retail customer's experience, satisfaction and willingness to buy. J. Retail. Consum. Serv. **34**, 229–234 (2017). https://doi.org/10.1016/j.jretconser.2016.10.005
33. Intention to Use Digital Banking Services of Young Retail Customers in Vietnam (2021)
34. Deepthi, P.M., Purna, G.V.: Evolution of E-commerce in indian retail market and its future trends. In: Dynamic Business Trends and Innovations in Contemporary Times. Para-manount Publishing, pp. 162–168 (2021)
35. Reimann, O., Thomas, O., Kucza, G., Schuppisser, S.: First insights on brand attitude towards a retailer's individual private labels. In: Martínez-López, F.J., Gázquez-Abad, J.C. (eds.) NB-PL 2021. SPBE, pp. 20–23. Springer, Cham (2021). https://doi.org/10.1007/978-3-030-769 35-2_3
36. Ungureanu, D., et al.: HoloLens 2 Research Mode as a Tool for Computer Vision Research (2020)
37. PTC, Inc.: Vuforia - Engine (2020). https://engine.vuforia.com/engine
38. Microsoft: Mixed Reality Toolkit (2020). https://microsoft.github.io/MixedRealityToolkit-Unity/README.html
39. Forman, C., Ghose, A., Wiesenfeld, B.: Examining the relationship between reviews and sales: the role of reviewer identity disclosure in electronic markets. Inf. Syst. Res. **19**(3), 291–313 (2008). https://doi.org/10.1287/ISRE.1080.0193
40. Pu, P., Chen, L., Hu, R.: A user-centric evaluation framework for recommender systems. In: Mobasher, B. (ed.) Proceedings of the Fifth ACM Conference on Recommender Systems. ACM Digital Library, p. 157. ACM, New York (2011). https://doi.org/10.1145/2043932.204 3962
41. Huddleston, P.T., Behe, B.K., Driesener, C., Minahan, S.: Inside-outside: using eye-tracking to investigate search-choice processes in the retail environment. J. Retail. Consum. Serv. **43**, 85–93 (2018). https://doi.org/10.1016/j.jretconser.2018.03.006
42. Shankar, V., Inman, J.J., Mantrala, M., Kelley, E., Rizley, R.: Innovations in shopper marketing: current insights and future research issues. J. Retail. **87**, S29–S42 (2011). https://doi.org/10.1016/j.jretai.2011.04.007

Motion and Tracking

MissFormer: (In-)Attention-Based Handling of Missing Observations for Trajectory Filtering and Prediction

Stefan Becker[1]($\boxtimes$) (ID), Ronny Hug[1] (ID), Wolfgang Huebner[1] (ID), Michael Arens[1] (ID), and Brendan Tran Morris[2] (ID)

[1] Fraunhofer IOSB, Ettlingen, Germany
{stefan.becker,ronny.hug,wolfgang.huebner,
michael.arens}@iosb.fraunhofer.de
[2] University of Nevada, Las Vegas, USA
brendan.morris@unlv.edu
https://www.iosb.fraunhofer.de/

Abstract. In applications such as object tracking, time-series data inevitably carry missing observations. Following the success of deep learning-based models for various sequence learning tasks, these models increasingly replace classic approaches in object tracking applications for inferring the objects' motion states. While traditional tracking approaches can deal with missing observations, most of their deep counterparts are, by default, not suited for this.

Towards this end, this paper introduces a *transformer*-based approach for handling missing observations in variable input length trajectory data. The model is formed indirectly by successively increasing the complexity of the demanded inference tasks. Starting from reproducing noise-free trajectories, the model then learns to infer trajectories from noisy inputs. By providing missing tokens, binary-encoded missing events, the model learns to in-attend to missing data and infers a complete trajectory conditioned on the remaining inputs. In the case of a sequence of successive missing events, the model then acts as a pure prediction model. The abilities of the approach are demonstrated on synthetic data and real-world data reflecting prototypical object tracking scenarios.

Keywords: Transformer · Trajectory data · Missing Input Data · Filtering · Trajectory prediction · Missing observations

1 Introduction and Related Work

One crucial task for autonomous systems is estimating the agents' motion states based on observations. Following the success of deep learning-based models in various sequence processing tasks, like speech recognition [7,12] and caption generation [10,37], these models are successfully utilized for trajectory prediction.

Fraunhofer IOSB is a member of the Fraunhofer Center for Machine Learning.

© Springer Nature Switzerland AG 2021
G. Bebis et al. (Eds.): ISVC 2021, LNCS 13017, pp. 521–533, 2021.
https://doi.org/10.1007/978-3-030-90439-5_41

In trajectory prediction applications, deep learning-based approaches are increasingly replacing classic approaches due to their ability to capture better contextual cues from the static (e.g., obstacles; *scene cues*) or dynamic environment (e.g., other objects in the scene; *social cues*)[29]. Commonly used approaches for encoding object motions rely on *recurrent neural networks* (RNNs) [1,14], *temporal convolution networks* (TCNs) [2,24], or *transformers* [11,30]. The reader is referred to these surveys [20,28,29] for a comprehensive overview of current deep learning-based approaches for trajectory prediction. Since these models have the ability to consider *social cues* and *scene cues*, the focus of most research is how to incorporate these cues better. Although this research direction offers the strongest performance boost, problems such as missing observations are partly ignored or mainly addressed with data imputation and omitting the missing data [32]. To be more specific, this applies to trajectory prediction relying on observation extracted from an agent's trajectory as basic input (e.g., positions). Only this type of prediction problem is considered here and is referred to as *trajectory cues*-based prediction in the remainder. For example, RNNs are designed to receive input data in every step and therefore are by default not suited to deal with missing inputs. In contrast, *transformers* offer an alternative to the step-by-step processing in the form of the underlying attention mechanisms in combination with positional encoding. In general, data imputation means to substitute the missing values with methods like interpolation [21] or spline fitting [8] which results in a process where imputation and prediction models are separated [6]. Thus, only suboptimal results are achieved since the model does not effectively explore the missing pattern. The simplest strategy for omitting is to remove samples in which a value is missing. While for RNNs this may work for training but cannot be applied during inference, omitting the missing value can be applied with *transformers*. Giuliari et al. [11] suggested omitting data with a *transformer* model for trajectory prediction as an advantage compared to RNN-based models. They analyzed the effect of omitting the last observations of a fixed-length input sequence. Alternatively, and in particular for RNNs, the problem can be modeled with marked missing values. A missing value can be masked and explicitly excluded, or the model can be encouraged to learn that a specific value represents the missing observation (*missing tokens*) [5]. Most approaches are for healthcare applications [34] or in the field of speech recognition [25]. In the field of trajectory prediction, Becker et al. [3] introduced an RNN-based full temporal filtering cycle for motion state estimation to better deal with missing observations. The Kalman filter-inspired model learns to weigh between its short-term predictions and observations enriched with missing tokens. In cases of missing inputs, the model entirely relies on predictions. Due to the recursive incorporation of new observations, deep Kalman models can be adapted similarly.

In this paper, we further explore the ability of *transformer* networks to handle missing observations. Compared to the work of Giuliari et al. [11], we utilize a modified encoder-only *transformer* model and provide missing tokens. Thus, the model is encouraged to learn specific placeholder values representing the missing observations. We analyze to what extent the combination of the underlying attention mechanisms with the positional encoding is able to then handle missing inputs along a variable length trajectory. Further, our model is not primarily designed as a prediction model, but in contrast, the model is formed indirectly by successively increasing the complexity of the demanded inference tasks. Starting from reproducing noise-free trajectories, the model then learns to infer trajectories from noisy inputs. The model outputs a full trajectory despite only being given partly observed trajectory data. Thus, for a sequence of successive missing events, the model then acts as a mere prediction model. The analysis of the model ability is performed under controlled conditions using synthetic data. For a comparison to other prediction models, the commonly used, publicly available *BIWI* [27] and *UCY* [22] datasets are used.

In the following, a brief formalization of the problem and a description of the proposed *transformer* model are provided in Sect. 2. The achieved results are presented in Sect. 3. Finally, a conclusion is given in Sect. 4.

2   MissFormer

The goal is to devise a model that can successfully infer the trajectory of a tracked agent conditioned on *trajectory cues* (e.g., positions, headings, velocities) with missing observations. Trajectory prediction is formally stated as follows. Given an input sequence $\mathcal{X}$ of consecutively observed positions $\vec{x}^k = (p_x^k, p_y^k)$ (or other *trajectory cues*) at time step k along a trajectory, the task is to generate predictions for future positions $\{\vec{x}^{k+1}, \vec{x}^{k+2}, \ldots\}$ Here, we adapt the formal description as follows. Given a sequence of noisy, potentially missing observations $\tilde{\vec{x}}^k$, the task is to estimate the noise-free positions of the trajectory $\vec{x}^k$. So, $\tilde{\vec{x}}^k$ is a realization of $\vec{x}^k$ despite the fact the inputs of a *transformer* are deterministic. In case the observations are noise-free, the task is to reproduce the trajectories. Although this might sound trivial, there exists no commonly accepted standards on encoding trajectory data in a deep learning model [15]. When noise is present, the task is filtering. In addition to learning an adequate representation, the model needs to compensate input noise. If observations are missing at the end of the input sequence, the model acts as a prediction model and still infers the complete trajectory. Disregarding *scene* and *social cues*, trajectory prediction is here divided into different inference tasks with increasing complexity which the model can learn successively.

Input/Output: For an agent, the *transformer* network outputs the complete trajectory $\{\vec{x}^1, \ldots \vec{x}^k\}$ up to time step k conditioned on $\{\tilde{\vec{x}}^1, \ldots \tilde{\vec{x}}^k\}$. To encourage the model to learn that a specific value represents missing, a binary-coded missing pattern is provided. The missing token is chosen as $(\vec{0}^k, 1^k)$ for a missing observation and, respectively, $(\tilde{\vec{x}}^k, 0^k)$ for a default input, where $k \in \{1, k_{max}\}$. The adapted input is embedded onto a higher d_{model}-dimensional space by means of a linear mapping $\vec{e}^k = \text{EMB}(\tilde{\vec{x}}^k; \vec{\Theta}_e)$. Accordingly, the output of the *transformer* model is re-mapped to the 2-dimensional coordinate system. Since *transformers* contain no recurrence and no convolution, information about the position in the sequence must be injected. *Positional encodings* are added to the input embeddings in accordance to the original *transformer* [35]. The *positional encodings* have the same dimension d_{model} as the embeddings, so that both can be summed up. Hence, the embedded input is time-stamped at time step k by adding a *positional encoding* vector PE^k. Following [35], sine and cosine functions of different frequencies are used to define $PE^k = \{PE_{k,d}\}_{d=1}^{d_{\text{model}}}$ with

$$
PE_{k,d} = \begin{cases} \sin\left(\frac{k}{10000^{d/d_{\text{model}}}}\right) & \text{for } d \text{ even} \\ \cos\left(\frac{k}{10000^{d/d_{\text{model}}}}\right) & \text{for } d \text{ odd} \end{cases}. \tag{1}
$$

The time step k corresponds to the position in the sequence and d is the dimension. Each dimension of the positional encoding varies in time according to a sinusoid of different frequencies, from 2π to $10000 \cdot 2\pi$. That way, unique timestamps for sequences of up to 10000 elements are ensured.

MissFormer: Both the encoder and the decoder of a *transformer* are composed of a stack of identical layers consisting of two sub-layers. Firstly, an attention module, and secondly, a feed-forward fully-connected module. Around each sublayer, a residual connection followed by layer normalization is employed. Here, we only use the encoder and directly map the encoded state to an entire estimated trajectory instead of an auto-regressive generation with a decoder. Contrary to using a step-by-step processing of RNNs or convolution, *transformers* rely entirely on self-attention to compute representations of its input and output. The attention function used by *transformers* is the so-called scaled dot-product attention. The inputs consists of *queries* and *keys* of dimension d_k, and *values* of dimension d_v packed into matrices Q, K and V. The attention layer is given by:

$$
\text{Attention}(Q, K, V) = \text{softmax}\left(\frac{QK^\intercal}{\sqrt{d_k}}\right)V \tag{2}
$$

So, the attention layer computes a dot product of the *query* with all *keys*, divided by d_k, and followed by a softmax function to obtain the weights on the values. Multi-head attention performs several attention functions in parallel, yielding to d_v-dimensional outputs. These values are concatenated before projected to the final value. The *transformer* uses multi-head attention in different ways, whereas for an encoder-only architecture, solely the self-attention layer in the encoder is important. For more details, we refer to [35]. In a self-attention layer of the encoder, all of the *keys*, *values* and *queries* come from the same place, in this case the output of the previous layer in the encoder. On a high level, attention can be seen as routing of information. Thus, each position in the encoder can attend to all positions of the previous encoder layer or rather over all positions in the input sequence. The encoder creates a representation given the observation sequence resulting in the memory - the encoder state. In

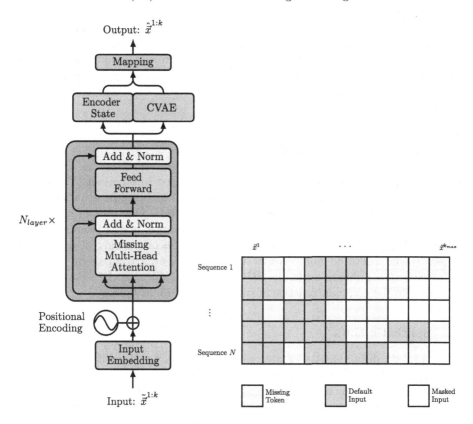

Fig. 1. (Left) Visualization of the adapted *transformer* network - MissFormer. (Right) Visualization of the adapted input data for the missing multi-head attention.

an encoder-decoder set-up, the encoder state is used to generate a *key* and *value* passed to the decoder. Since no new observations are provided to the decoder, we only used the encoder part. For every new observation, the extended input sequence is given to the model. As described, the model infers a sequence with a similar length to the input sequence. Our focus is on how well the described attention mechanism can route information to deal with missing observations and reconstruct complete, noise-free trajectories from the data. Further, the model is encouraged to still produce a meaningful representation and in-attend to useless placeholder values in the input sequence. The adapted *transformer* model, referred to as MissFormer, together with modified input data with missing tokens, is visualized in Fig. 1.

On the left, the MissFormer with the missing self-attention sub-layer is shown. On the right, the *missing tokens* are highlighted in yellow and default inputs are highlighted in blue. The Missformer is trained by minimizing the L2-loss in the form of the mean squared error between the ground truth trajectories and the estimated trajectories. Exemplary, the encoded state is combined with

a conditional *variational auto encoder*(VAE) [18] for producing multiple outputs and capturing the uncertainty of the estimation. Thus, the *evidence-based
lower bound* ELBO term is added as a second factor to the loss function (see for
example [4]). However, capturing the multi-modality of trajectory prediction is
out of the scope of this paper. For example, this component can be replaced by
flow-based models [9] or $\mathcal{N}$-*curve* models [17].

3   Evaluation and Analysis

This section consists of an evaluation of the proposed MissFormer. The evaluation concerns with verifying the approach's overall viability in situations with
missing observations in variable-length trajectory data. One part of the evaluation is done with synthetically generated data because, firstly, reference models can not handle mission observation by default. Secondly, current pedestrian
trajectory data sets do not consider this aspect. For a comparison to other
approaches, the publicly available *BIWI* [27] and *UCY* [22] datasets are used
according to the common practice of fully observed input data.

3.1   Synthetic Data

The synthetic data consists of diverse trajectories covering different types of
prototypical object motion present in trajectory datasets [16]. The generated
trajectories include the motion patterns of constant velocity, curvilinear motion,
acceleration and deceleration motion. For generating synthetic trajectories of
a basic object motion on a ground plane, random agents are sampled from
a uniform distribution of speeds $(\mathcal{U}(5.0\,\mathrm{m/s}, 10.0\,\mathrm{m/s}))$. The frame rate is set
to 1 fps. The heading direction is sampled from $\mathcal{U}(0°, 360°)$ with a change of
heading during a sampling period also sampled from uniform distribution of
$\mathcal{U}(-20°, 20°)$. The de- and acceleration during a sampling period is sampled
from $\mathcal{U}(-0.8\,\mathrm{m/s^2}, 1.5\,\mathrm{m/s^2})$. Missing events are drawn from a Bernoulli distribution $\mathcal{B}(\cdot, \cdot)$. The positional observation noise is assumed to follow a zero-mean
Gaussian distribution $\mathcal{N}(0\,\mathrm{m/s}, (\cdot\,\mathrm{m/s})^2)$. The evaluation set includes always 5000
samples. The number of training samples is varied thought-out the experiments.
The models have been implemented using *Pytorch* [26]. For training, an ADAM
optimizer variant [19,23] with a learning rate of 0.001 is used.

   In order to emphasize some statements, parts from the first experiments
are summarized in Table 1. For comparison of the different trained MissFormer
models, the average displacement error (ADE) is calculated as the average L2
distance between the estimated positions and the ground truth positions. It
should be noted that the model directly infers positions. Typically, only velocities
or rather offsets are predicted and the last observation is used as a reference
point. Since the amount of variation for offsets is lower compared to positions
and the range in the data is more limited, less modeling effort and less data is
required for model training (see from example [2]). Because the last observation
is affected by noise or even missing, this practice is not applicable. Thus, here

Table 1. Results for a comparison between several trained MissFormer models for different inference tasks. The inference tasks are reconstruction, filtering and prediction. Reconstruction: In case the observations is noise-free, the task is to reproduce the trajectories. Filtering: Here positional observation noise is added and the model has to filter out this noise to generate noise-free trajectories. Prediction: Future object locations are inferred from noisy, observed trajectories.

Task: Encoding / Reconstruction

Input	Output	obs.	pred.	#samples	#epochs	Noise	Missing	ADE	σ_{ADE}
pos.	pos.	8-20	✗	1000	1000	✗	✗	0.067	0.013
off.	pos.	8-20	✗	1000	1000	✗	✗	0.061	0.012
pos.	pos.	8-20	✗	1000	1000	✗	$\mathcal{B}(0.1,0.9)$	0.377	0.403
off.	pos.	8-20	✗	1000	1000	✗	$\mathcal{B}(0.1,0.9)$	0.175	0.154
pos.	pos.	8-20	✗	3000	1000	✗	$\mathcal{B}(0.1,0.9)$	0.138	0.074
off.	pos.	8-20	✗	3000	1000	✗	$\mathcal{B}(0.1,0.9)$	0.155	0.079
pos.	pos.	8-20	✗	3000	3000	✗	✗	0.030	0.020
off.	pos.	8-20	✗	3000	3000	✗	✗	0.039	0.013
pos.	pos.	8-20	✗	3000	3000	✗	$\mathcal{B}(0.1,0.9)$	0.087	0.060
off.	pos.	8-20	✗	3000	3000	✗	$\mathcal{B}(0.1,0.9)$	0.095	0.065
pos.	pos.	8-20	✗	4000	4000	✗	✗	0.028	0.015
pos.	pos.	8-20	✗	4000	4000	✗	$\mathcal{B}(0.1,0.9)$	0.081	0.015
off.	pos.	8-20	✗	4000	4000	✗	✗	0.031	0.014
off.	pos.	8-20	✗	4000	4000	✗	$\mathcal{B}(0.1,0.9)$	0.084	0.014

Task: De-Noising / Filtering

Input	Output	obs.	pred.	#samples	#epochs	Noise	Missing	ADE	σ_{ADE}
pos.	pos.	8-20	✗	4000	4000	$\mathcal{N}(0,1^2)$	✗	0.126	0.049
pos.	pos.	8-20	✗	4000	4000	$\mathcal{N}(0,1^2)$	$\mathcal{B}(0.1,0.9)$	0.165	0.071
offs.	pos.	8-20	✗	4000	4000	$\mathcal{N}(0,1^2)$	✗	0.148	0.055
offs.	pos.	8-20	✗	4000	4000	$\mathcal{N}(0,1^2)$	$\mathcal{B}(0.1,0.9)$	0.222	0.137

Task: Prediction

Input	Output	obs.	pred.	#samples	#epochs	Noise	Missing	ADE	σ_{ADE}
pos.	pos.	8-14	6-12	4000	4000	$\mathcal{N}(0,1^2)$	✗	0.809	0.514
pos.	pos.	8-14	6-12	4000	4000	$\mathcal{N}(0,1^2)$	$\mathcal{B}(0.1,0.9)$	0.920	0.422
offs.	pos.	8-14	6-12	4000	4000	$\mathcal{N}(0,1^2)$	✗	1.186	0.583
offs.	pos.	8-14	6-12	4000	4000	$\mathcal{N}(0,1^2)$	$\mathcal{B}(0.1,0.9)$	1.221	0.734

the outputs of the model are positions, and the inputs are varied between using positions or using offsets to infer positions by path integration.

The results show that the MissFormer is able to successfully in-attend to the missing tokens and successfully only uses the remaining inputs for conditioning. The difference between the model's estimate without missing observation and a missing probability $\mathcal{B}(0.1,0.9)$ is very low. Of course, there is a drop in performance which can best be seen when looking at the reconstruction task. But the model can there basically learn a trivial solution of the identity of the input. Even when a trivial solution exists for using positions as inputs, the error does not drop to zero. Positional trajectory data can be seen as some sort of an increasing trend that cannot be fully captured by using non-linear activation functions. However, deep networks can achieve outputs greater than the bound of single activation functions, but they can saturate at minimum or maximum values, particularly for trending input data. For all inference tasks, but in particular for reconstruction, the model requires enough variation and training time to handle missing data. At first, the model simply reproduces placeholder values as outputs. By increasing the number of provided samples, the MissFormer starts to better route the information to compensate for outages. When the model has to additionally compensate for noise, the difference between missing and no-missing decreases. Here, the MissFormer has to generalize and filter out the noise. Thus, input identity mapping cannot be applied. When switching to a prediction task by replacing the last inputs with missing tokens, the difference between the models' estimates of fully observed and missing data decreases further.

In the experiments for all tasks, using positions as inputs works slightly better. The increased modeling effort is compensated by providing more variation during training. Since the error by using path integration for estimating the true position is propagated, the result is comprehensible. Further, in the context of a *dynamical* system, only observing offsets is an unobservable system where it is impossible to identify the initial condition uniquely. Thus, the error in the first positional estimate cannot be compensated. However, without missing observations and low positional observation noise, choosing offsets over positions has shown superior results on public trajectory prediction benchmarks ([2]).

For these experiments only one attention head ($N_{\text{head}} = 1$) and one attention layer ($N_{\text{layer}} = 1$) is used. Firstly, this allows a better understanding of the resulting attention because the attention filter directly shows what input information is used to encode a current trajectory. Secondly, compared to a *nature language processing* (NLP) or a vision task, single trajectory processing requires no attention to several aspects of the input data (e.g., a second attention filter on context information in the background). Some exemplary estimates from the MissFormer with corresponding attention filters are depicted in Fig. 2. The values of the attention filter are color-coded ($0 \blacksquare\!\!\longrightarrow \blacksquare$ max.). Here, results for the prediction tasks are shown where the last inputs are purposely missing tokens. The time steps where the input data is missing are marked with a cross and missing input indexes are shown above the attention filters. The input length k varies between 8 and 14 for a maximum length of $k_{max} = 20$ with a missing probability of $\mathcal{B}(0.1, 0.9)$.

The shown examples highlight several things. Firstly and most importantly, it can be seen that the models learned to in-attend to missing observation and to encode the trajectories based on the other inputs. Secondly, that the attention filters do not necessarily follow the typical look of high values along the diagonal

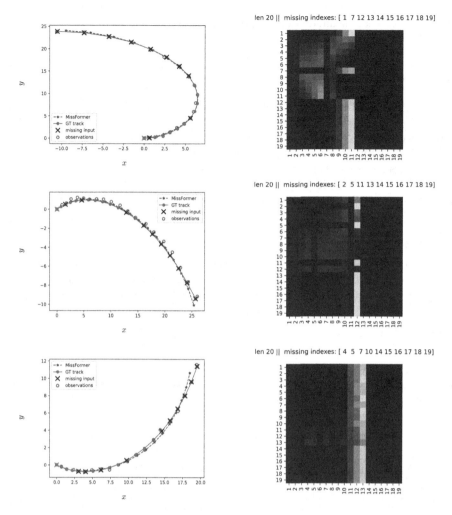

Fig. 2. (Left) Some exemplary estimates from the MissFormer with missing observations. The time steps where the input data is missing are marked with an cross. (Right) Corresponding attention filters. The attention filter values are color-coded (0 ■ → ▨ max.). (Color figure online)

as in an *NLP* task. This can be explained by the fact that there are many possibilities for trajectory generation from the given inputs although solutions with predominantly high values along the diagonal can also result. Further, the examples show how the MissFormer filters out the noise and estimates relatively smooth outputs. And lastly they demonstrate, how prediction is done mainly relying on the last inputs, which corresponds to the common assumption that the last observations mainly influence motion. In summary, when providing the MissFormer with enough variation in terms of diversity and amount of training data, the model can handle missing observations and ignore placeholder values provided as missing tokens.

3.2 Real-World Data

For real-world data and comparing the model to recent reference models, the publicly available *BIWI* [27] and *UCY* [22] datasets are used. Combined, these datasets contain five sequences from an oblique view capturing scenes with pedestrians in a shopping street and on a university campus. As mentioned before, most reference models cannot handle mission observation and this problem is not considered in their corresponding evaluation. For the sake of completeness and in order to compare the approach to others, we follow the common trajectory prediction protocol. So, evaluation is done by leaving one-out cross-validation for the 5 sequences. For conditioning, a fixed-length, fully observed trajectory of 8 points (3.2 s) is provided before predicting 12 points (4.8 s) into the future. The average displacement error (ADE) and the final displacement error (FDE) are used as error metrics. The ADE is defined as the average L2 distance between ground truth and the prediction over all predicted time steps and the FDE is defined as the L2 distance between the predicted final position and the actual final position.

Table 2. Results for a comparison between the Missformer and a selection of recent prediction models following the single trajectory deterministic protocol. The prediction is done for 12 time steps into the future conditioned on 8 observations. Results are partly taken from [11, 24, 31]

Approach	cues traj.	social	scene	model type	ADE/FDE in meters					
					dataset					average
					BIWI:ETH	BIWI:Hotel	UCY:Univ	UCY:Zara1	UCY:Zara2	
Linear interpolation	✓	✗	✗	classic	1.33/2.94	0.39/0.72	0.82/1.59	0.62/1.21	0.77/1.48	0.79/1.59
LSTM	✓	✗	✗	RNN	1.09/2.94	0.86/1.91	0.61/1.31	0.41/0.88	0.52/1.11	0.70/1.52
GAN (Ind.)[13]	✓	✗	✗	RNN	1.13/2.21	1.01/2.18	0.60/1.28	0.42/0.91	0.52/1.11	0.74/1.54
Social-LSTM [1]	✓	✓	✗	RNN	1.09/2.35	0.79/1.76	0.67/1.40	0.47/1.00	0.56/1.17	0.72/1.54
Social-Att. [36]	✓	✓	✗	RNN	0.39/3.74	0.29/2.64	0.33/3.92	0.20/0.52	0.30/2.13	0.30/2.59
Trajectron++[31]	✓	✓	✓	RNN	0.50/1.19	0.24/0.59	0.36/0.89	0.29/0.72	0.27/0.67	0.34/0.84
TCN [24]	✓	✗	✗	TCN	1.04/2.07	0.59/1.17	0.57/1.21	0.43/0.90	0.34/0.75	0.59/1.22
TF [11]	✓	✗	✗	*transformer*	1.03/2.10	0.36/0.71	0.53/1.32	0.44/1.00	0.34/0.76	0.54/1.17
MissFormer (ours)	✓	✗	✗	*transformer*	0.99/1.94	0.36/0.89	0.51/1.29	0.43/0.89	0.34/0.74	0.53/1.15

The results are summarized in Table 2. In the comparison, a collection of recent approaches is considered where in terms of models relying solely on *trajectory cues* at least one reference approach from the basic concepts of deep sequential trajectory processing and one classic approach is included (see column model type). The best performing models incorporate additional *scene cues* (e.g., semantic segmentation), *social cues* (e.g., interactions with other pedestrians) or both. When considering only *trajectory cues*, the MissFormer achieves a better or similar performance. Without any outage in conditioning trajectory, the *transformer* model of [11] and our MissFormer model are very similar.

Whereas Giuliari et al. utilize an encoder-decoder network with offsets as inputs and outputs, we use an encoder-only model with positional in- and outputs. To counter the lesser modeling effort of offset data, we pre-train the model on a diverse set of synthetically generated trajectories covering all types of prototypical pedestrian motion patterns. Therefore, the distribution and settings from Sect. 3.1 for synthetic trajectory generation are adapted to match the underlying data better. For example, the frame rate is set to 2.5 fps and random agents are sampled from a Gaussian distribution according to a preferred pedestrian walking speed [33] ($\mathcal{N}(1, 38\,\mathrm{m/s}, (0.37\,\mathrm{m/s})^2)$). The model is pre-trained on a diverse set of 4000 synthetic trajectories for 4000 epochs. For the first half of training, the full trajectories are provided. Then, corresponding to the prediction length, the last inputs are replaced with missing tokens. Here, the number of heads and attention layer is set to 2 ($N_{\mathrm{head}} = 2$, $N_{\mathrm{layer}} = 2$) and the model dimension is set to $d_{\mathrm{model}} = 256$. However, the achieved results for these datasets are very similar and the scope of this paper aims at further exploring the *transformers'* ability to deal with missing observations. On the *BIWI* [27] and *UCY* [22] datasets, there is no clearly best-performing individual *trajectory cues*-based model. Overall, different models partly require different concepts for improving their performance or overcoming shortcomings. The presented results show that *transformers* are a good choice for estimating trajectories and offer an built-in concept of dealing with missing inputs.

4   Conclusion

In this paper, a *transformer*-based approach for handling missing observations has been presented. The *transformers'* built-in attention mechanisms in combination with positional encoding is analyzed in terms of exploring the remaining inputs for inference with outages. By providing encoded missing information (*missing tokens*), the model is encouraged to learn that specific values represent missing. The presented results show that the model can in-attend to the placeholder values and successfully route the information from the remaining inputs to infer a full trajectory. The abilities of the approach are demonstrated on synthetic data and real-world data reflecting prototypical object tracking scenarios.

References

1. Alahi, A., Goel, K., Ramanathan, V., Robicquet, A., Fei-Fei, L., Savarese, S.: Social LSTM: human trajectory prediction in crowded spaces. In: Conference on Computer Vision and Pattern Recognition (CVPR), pp. 961–971 (2016)
2. Becker, S., Hug, R., Hübner, W., Arens, M.: RED: a simple but effective baseline predictor for the *TrajNet* benchmark. In: Leal-Taixé, L., Roth, S. (eds.) ECCV 2018. LNCS, vol. 11131, pp. 138–153. Springer, Cham (2019). https://doi.org/10.1007/978-3-030-11015-4_13
3. Becker, S., Hug, R., Hübner, W., Arens, M., Morris, B.T.: Handling missing observations with an RNN-based prediction-update cycle (2021)

4. Bishop, C.M.: Pattern Recognition and Machine Learning (Information Science and Statistics). Springer, Heidelberg (2006)
5. Brownlee, J.: Introduction to Time Series Forecasting with Python: How to Prepare Data and Develop Models to Predict the Future (2017)
6. Che, Z., Purushotham, S., Cho, K., Sontag, D., Liu, Y.: Recurrent neural networks for multivariate time series with missing values. Sci. Rep. (SREP) **8**(6085), 1–12 (2018)
7. Chung, J., Kastner, K., Dinh, L., Goel, K., Courville, A., Bengio, Y.: A recurrent latent variable model for sequential data. In: Advances in Neural Information Processing Systems (NeurIPS) (2015)
8. De Boor, C.: A Practical Guide to Splines, rev Applied mathematical sciences. Springer, Heidelberg (2001)
9. Dinh, L., Krueger, D., Bengio, Y.: NICE: non-linear independent components estimation. In: Bengio, Y., LeCun, Y. (eds.) 3rd International Conference on Learning Representations, ICLR 2015, Workshop Track Proceedings, San Diego, CA, USA, 7–9 May 2015 (2015)
10. Donahue, J., et al.: Long-term recurrent convolutional networks for visual recognition and description. In: Conference on Computer Vision and Pattern Recognition (CVPR). IEEE (2015)
11. Giuliari, F., Hasan, I., Cristani, M., Galasso, F.: Transformer networks for trajectory forecasting. In: International Conference on Pattern Recognition (ICPR) (2020)
12. Graves, A., Mohamed, A., Hinton, G.: Speech recognition with deep recurrent neural networks. In: International Conference on Acoustics, Speech and Signal Processing, pp. 6645–6649 (2013)
13. Gupta, A., Johnson, J., Fei-Fei, L., Savarese, S., Alahi, A.: Social GAN: socially acceptable trajectories with generative adversarial networks. In: Conference on Computer Vision and Pattern Recognition (CVPR). IEEE (2018)
14. Hug, R., Becker, S., Hübner, W., Arens, M.: On the reliability of LSTM-MDL models for pedestrian trajectory prediction. In: Chen, L., Ben Amor, B., Ghorbel, F. (eds.) RFMI 2017. CCIS, vol. 842, pp. 20–34. Springer, Cham (2019). https://doi.org/10.1007/978-3-030-19816-9_2
15. Hug, R., Becker, S., Hübner, W., Arens, M.: A complementary trajectory prediction benchmark. In: ECCV Workshop on Benchmarking Trajectory Forecasting Models (BTFM) (2020)
16. Hug, R., Becker, S., Hübner, W., Arens, M.: Quantifying the complexity of standard benchmarking datasets for long-term human trajectory prediction. IEEE Access **9**, 77693–77704 (2021)
17. Hug, R., Hübner, W., Arens, M.: Introducing probabilistic bézier curves for n-step sequence prediction. Proceedings of the AAAI Conference on Artificial Intelligence, vol. 34, no. 06, pp. 10162–10169, April 2020
18. Kingma, D.P., Welling, M.: Auto-encoding variational Bayes. In: 2nd International Conference on Learning Representations, ICLR 2014, Conference Track Proceedings, Banff, AB, Canada, 14–16 April 2014 (2014)
19. Kingma, D., Ba, J.: Adam: a method for stochastic optimization. In: International Conference on Learning Representations (ICLR) (2015)
20. Kothari, P., Kreiss, S., Alahi, A.: Human trajectory forecasting in crowds: a deep learning perspective. arXiv preprint arXiv:2007.03639 (2020)
21. Kreindler, D., Lumsden, C.J.: The effects of the irregular sample and missing data in time series analysis. Nonlinear Dyn. Psychol. Life Sci. **10**(2), 187–214 (2006)

22. Lerner, A., Chrysanthou, Y., Lischinski, D.: Crowds by example. In: Computer Graphic Forum, vol. 26, no. 3, pp. 655–664 (2007)
23. Loshchilov, I., Hutter, F.: Decoupled weight decay regularization. In: International Conference on Learning Representations (ICLR) (2019)
24. Nikhil, N., Morris, B.: Convolutional neural network for trajectory prediction. In: The European Conference on Computer Vision (ECCV) Workshops (2018)
25. Parveen, S., Green, P.: Speech recognition with missing data using recurrent neural nets. In: Advances in Neural Information Processing Systems (NeurIPS), pp. 1189–1195. MIT Press (2002)
26. Paszke, A., et al.: PyTorch: an imperative style, high-performance deep learning library. In: Advances in Neural Information Processing Systems (NeurIPS), pp. 8024–8035. Curran Associates, Inc. (2019)
27. Pellegrini, S., Ess, A., Schindler, K., van Gool, L.: You'll never walk alone: modeling social behavior for multi-target tracking. In: International Conference on Computer Vision (ICCV), pp. 261–268. IEEE (2009)
28. Rasouli, A.: Deep learning for vision-based prediction: a survey. arXiv preprint arXiv:2007.00095 (2020)
29. Rudenko, A., Palmieri, L., Herman, M., Kitani, K.M., Gavrila, D.M., Arras, K.O.: Human motion trajectory prediction: a survey. Int. J. Robot. Res. **39**, 895–935 (2020)
30. Saleh, K.: Pedestrian trajectory prediction using context-augmented transformer networks. arXiv preprint arXiv:2012.01757 (2020)
31. Salzmann, T., Ivanovic, B., Chakravarty, P., Pavone, M.: Trajectron++: dynamically-feasible trajectory forecasting with heterogeneous data. In: Vedaldi, A., Bischof, H., Brox, T., Frahm, J.-M. (eds.) ECCV 2020. LNCS, vol. 12363, pp. 683–700. Springer, Cham (2020). https://doi.org/10.1007/978-3-030-58523-5_40
32. Schafer, J.L., Graham, J.W.: Missing data: our view of the state of the art. Psychol. Meth. **7**(2), 147–177 (2002)
33. Teknom, K.: Microscopic pedestrian flow characteristics: development of an image processing data collection and simulation model. Ph.D. thesis, Tohoku University (2002)
34. Tresp, V., Briegel, T.: A solution for missing data in recurrent neural networks with an application to blood glucose prediction. In: International Conference on Neural Information Processing Systems (NeurIPS). pp. 971–977. MIT Press, Cambridge (1997)
35. Vaswani, A., et al.: Attention is all you need. In: Guyon, I., et al. (eds.) Advances in Neural Information Processing Systems 30: Annual Conference on Neural Information Processing Systems 2017, Long Beach, CA, USA, 4–9 December 2017, pp. 5998–6008 (2017)
36. Vemula, A., Muelling, K., Oh, J.: Social attention: modeling attention in human crowds. In: International Conference on Robotics and Automation (ICRA), pp. 1–7 (2018)
37. Xu, K., et al.: Show, attend and tell: neural image caption generation with visual attention. In: International Conference on Machine Learning (ICML). Proceedings of Machine Learning Research, Lille, France, vol. 37, pp. 2048–2057. PMLR (2015)

Compressed Domain Consistent Motion Based Frame Scoring for IoT Edge Surveillance Videos

Lakshya Lakshya[1]([✉]), Venkata Suneel Kota[1], Mallikarjuna Rao Voleti[1], and Shivraj Singh[2]

[1] Samsung R&D Institute India - Bangalore, Bangalore, India
{lakshya.01,suneel.kota,vm.arjun}@samsung.com
[2] CCS University, Meerut, India

Abstract. IoT Edge is a major active technical front. Among others, video surveillance is one of the most common use cases for IoT Edge. However, there is a need to analyze the surveillance stream, due to the sheer size of the generated data. The stream can be analyzed in either the Edge environment itself or send to a cloud for analysis. There are two main constraints to be considered. First is the associated bandwidth cost to send the data to a cloud server for processing. It underlines the need to reduce the data sent to a cloud. Second is the computational and memory constraints of the devices in the IoT Edge Environment. It implies that only computationally cheap and fast algorithms can be allowed to run in the Edge Environment. However, generally highly effective algorithms require more computational resources and memory. Pruning of uninterested frames is a viable methodology that can potentially reduce the bandwidth cost and the resources utilized. We have developed a fast, computationally cheap, and effective frame scoring algorithm that scores frames based on the consistent motion. The algorithm works in the compressed domain using H.264 encoded motion vectors, by which it saves on the resources spent to decode the video stream. The algorithm can be used to prune uninteresting frames, while the interesting frames can be send either to the cloud or processed further in the edge itself.

1 Introduction

Video surveillance is one of the most frequent use cases for home monitoring services. Naturally, due to the sheer size of data being generated as a video feed, there is a need to analyze the data and extract useful information. It is preferable that the generated data be processed inside the Edge environment only. However, there is generally a lack of resources available to run such services. Not only are the devices available in Edge already resource-constrained, but there is a multitude of other essential services like WebRTC running on them.

It is also generally true that there is a correlation between the effectiveness of an analyzing service and the resources utilized. Consequently, either the algorithm needs to be run on the cloud or compromise has to be made on the effectiveness of the results. However, there is a middle ground available through pruning. In a typical video surveillance situation, most of the frames that do not contain consistent motion are "uninteresting" and need not be considered. Hence, a fast, computationally cheap, and effective frame scoring algorithm can be utilized to weed out "uninteresting" frames.

© Springer Nature Switzerland AG 2021
G. Bebis et al. (Eds.): ISVC 2021, LNCS 13017, pp. 534–545, 2021.
https://doi.org/10.1007/978-3-030-90439-5_42

We focus our attention on the compressed-domain to realize the frame scoring algorithm, the reason being the processing and storage cost incurred to decode and store the stream in the pixel domain. We only analyze motion vector (MV) information available in the compressed stream to generate frame scoring. There is extra information [17] that can be further utilized to refine the results, such as DCT (Discrete Cosine Transform) coefficients and the Macroblock (MB) type. However, they would incur additional processing and memory costs.

Although, since single MV is assigned to entire MB whose minimum size is 4×4, we work at the level of 4×4 MBs. It implies, we use a MV field size is 4×4 times less than the size of original frame, which also helps in reducing execution time.

We provide the following contributions through this paper.

- We make novel observations regarding the limitations of existing approaches to capture orientation consistency information in videos.
- Based on these observations, we propose our RLV function.
- We use this function to develop a fast, computationally cheap and efficient frame scoring algorithm that can be used to prune uninteresting frames.

2 Related Works

There are several tasks for which compressed domain techniques have been proposed. [3] used mean, standard deviation and saliency percentage values of x and y components of motion vectors and DCT coefficients to define frame feature vector. The task of high-speed action recognition is undertaken by [18]. They used motion vector approximated optical flow based similarity between query video and input video. The authors of [6,7] propose to consider Group of Pictures (GoP - P and B frames between two I frames) as a single unit and analyze DCT image of I-Frames to provide GoP scoring. [4,13] provide task specific video summarization techniques.

With respect to motion vector analysis following motion detection and video summarization tasks have interesting techniques. In [9,19] intensity, spatial orientation and temporal orientation maps are extracted from MVs. The spatial and temporal orientation maps are created by applying entropy functions to the values in a fixed spatial and temporal neighborhood of the point, respectively. [16] builds on the pixel domain video synopsis technique of [12]. They first apply median filter to the motion vector field and then extract LBP (Local Binary Pattern) features for each sub-macroblock They then use kernel density estimation on extracted LBP features to extract objects in the frame. While performing the task of moving object extraction in [2], the authors first perform global motion estimation, followed by a median filter. Then, weights are assigned to each MB based on the maximum difference with the 8 spatial neighbors. They go on to apply clustering and MRF to perform segmentation. In [20] first motion vector clipping is done. Then, the absolute difference of angle of a given point is calculated with the angle of spatial neighbors to gain confidence for the point. The authors of [1] present an interesting bi-directional motion vector accumulation technique. In which motion vectors of previous and forward frames are projected back to the current frame based on their motion vectors. Authors of [14] threshold the difference between intensity and angle of the MVs of a macroblock and its reference MB. Although authors of [10]

instead of using MV, use information like the type of sub-macroblocks and quantization parameter information in their work, they present the interesting idea of either one-
step spatiotemporal processing or two-step spatial and temporal processing. In [8, 15]
permutation and combination of techniques mentioned above is used.

3 Background

It can be seem from the previous Sect. (2), that for us baseline contains not only the
group of approaches for motion detection, but, also the pre-processing steps involved
in video summarization activities, which also try to capture the consistent motion information for the frame. For example, In [19], intensity, spatial orientation, and temporal
orientation maps are extracted from MVs, before combining them with visual maps
extracted from RGB image pixels. However, there is no unique identifier for these pre-
processing techniques, due to which in this section we give a brief description for the
components used in this technique.

But before that, we describe a general template that we have observed in prior-arts
to perform MV Analysis. We have observed that related works have closely followed
this template to perform MV analysis.

3.1 MV Analysis General Template

- Calculate multiple maps using the MVs. A map can be created by defining a neighborhood set around a point, for each point in the MV field and a function to operate
on the neighborhood set. A special Intensity Map - (shows intensity of MV at each
pixel) is also generally used.
- Transform all maps, except Intensity map, using the following function.

$$f(a) = \begin{cases} 0, & a > NBH_{th} \\ NBH_{th} - a & a \leq NBH_{th} \end{cases},$$

where NBH_{th} is a threshold whose value is set based on desired expected upper
bound of function operating on the neighborhood.
- Multiply the maps together to get a Final Map.
- Score of a frame is simply the mean of all the values in the Final map.
- If the score is below defined threshold ($frame_{th}$) the frame can be pruned.

Figure 1, shows an example of MV analysis algorithm with this template. Map-1
uses Neighborhood Set-1 and f_1. Similarly Map-2 uses Neighborhood Set-2 and f_2.
Map-3 corresponds to special Intensity Map.

3.2 Prior-Arts

We have observed following definitions of neighborhood set around a point and functions operating on them.

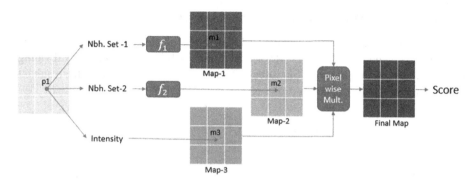

Fig. 1. Template example with two custom Maps (Map-1, Map-2) and one Intensity Map (Map-3).

Neighborhood Set Definitions for a Point

First, let

$$H(x) = \frac{x-1}{2} \tag{1}$$

Spatial Neighborhood. The spatial neighborhood(NBH) of a point/pixel p_{i_0,j_0,t_0} (i_0^{th} row and j_0^{th} column on the t_0^{th} frame in a video) with respect to a size NxN spatial window is defined as following set

$$NBH_{i_0,j_0,t_0} = \{p_{i,j,t} : i_0 - H(N) \le i \le i_0 + H(N), j_0 - H(N) \le j \le j_0 + H(N), t = t_0\} \tag{2}$$

In above equation, we assumed that N is an odd integer, as usually is the case, but similar equation can be written for even case. Also, note that current pixel is also considered as part of the Spatial Neighborhood.

Temporal Neighborhood. The temporal neighborhood of a point p_{i_0,j_0,t_0} with respect to a size N temporal window is defined as following set

$$NBH_{i_0,j_0,t_0} = \{p_{i,j,t} : i = i_0, j = j_0, t_0 - H(N) \le t \le t_0 + H(N)\} \tag{3}$$

SpatioTemporal Neighborhood. The spatiotemporal neighborhood of a point p_{i_0,j_0,t_0} with respect to a size $N \times N \times M$ temporal window is defined as following set

$$NBH_{i_0,j_0,t_0} = \{p_{i,j,t} : i_0 - H(N) \le i \le i_0 + H(N), j_0 - H(N) \le j \le j_0 + H(N),$$
$$t_0 - H(M) \le t \le t_0 + H(M)\} \tag{4}$$

Forward and Backward Accumulated Temporal Neighborhood. We refer the readers to [1] for the explanation of this neighborhood set.

Functions Used to Operate on the Neighborhood Set

Entropy Over Angle Values - Entropy. A histogram is created using the angles of the MVs in the neighborhood of $p_{i,j,t}$. Respective bin probability is calculated by dividing the bin value with summation of bin values. Then entropy is calculated over the resultant probabilities of the histogram as

$$Entropy_{i,j,t} = -\sum_{b=1}^{b=N} P(b)log(P(b)), \tag{5}$$

where N is the number of bins and $P(b)$ represents the probability of bth bin.

Average of Absolute Difference. Absolute difference between the certain aspect of the pixel and its neighborhood is used. For a point $p_{i,j,t}$,

$$ABSD_{i,j,t} = \frac{1}{N}\sum_{k=1}^{k=N} |f(MV_{i,j,t}) - f(MV_{NBH_{i,j,t}(k)})|, \tag{6}$$

where N is the number of points in the neighborhood, $NBH_{i,j,t}(k)$ represents the kth point in set NBH and $|.|$ represents the absolute function. f is a function that can be intensity of the vector or angle of the input vector. We refer to former as $ABSDoI$ and later as $ABSDoA$. The angle in $ABSDoA$ for a vector V is calculated as $A(V) = arctan(\frac{Vy}{Vx})$

4   Observations

After checking multiple maps generated from prior art methods, we have made **novel observations** about the following caveats in the existing functions (Sect. 3.2) used to operate on any neighborhood set.

- Ideally, the value of the function at a point $p_{i,j,t}$ should be able to differentiate when the neighborhood values are similar or different than the value of $p_{i,j,t}$. However, *Entropy* function is not able to do so. For example in Fig. 2, entropy values[1] of Fig. 2a(= 0.1514) and 2c(= 0.0) are more closer rather than that of Fig. 2b(= 0.2764) and 2c(= 0.0) or Fig. 2a(= 0.1514) and 2b(= 0.2764).
- If the function directly uses angle magnitude, there will be an erroneous blind spot. Consider for example that values of angle lie in the range [0, 360], then even though magnitude wise 0 and 360 are separate, they actually point to the same direction.
- If the function directly uses angle magnitude, then even zero vectors are treated as vectors in some direction. Exact value depends on how angle is calculated from the $MVY_{i,j,t}$ and $MVX_{i,j,t}$, but even zero vectors are assigned angle values in the range [0, 360]. Extra processing needs to be utilized to make sure that this phenomenon doesn't cause erroneous results, it might even hinder writing optimal code.

---

[1] Red and white pixels go into separate bins while calculating entropy on 3 × 3 spatial Neighborhood.

Both *Entropy* and *ABSDoA* suffers from the above mentioned drawbacks. While, *ABSDoI* doesn't even utilize the orientation information available within the MVs. However, orientation/angle consistency is an important information. For example, the difference between the motion of tree leaves and human movement is that of orientation consistency. Tree leaves will tend to show noisy motion with inconsistent orientation consistency, while, human movement tend to be more smoother.

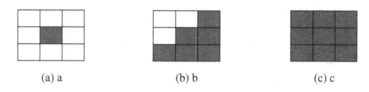

(a) a   (b) b   (c) c

Fig. 2. Various possible values in a spatial neighborhood of size 3×3. Red and white corresponds to different angle values for the pixel MV. (Color figure online)

5   Proposed *RLV* and Pruning Algorithm

5.1   Relative Variance Over Normalized MVs - *RLV*

Given the incapability of existing operating functions to efficiently extract orientation consistency. We propose a new function, *RLV*, to operate on the neighborhood points.

Generally, variance of a given set of values is defined w.r.t. the mean of those values. However, we propose

- use variance w.r.t the point for which neighborhood is defined i.e. relative variance.
- relative variance to be calculated over normalized MV ($normMV$ = unit vector in the direction of MV) rather than MVs themselves.

Given that, we define $RLV_{i,j,t}$ to be the sum of relative variance of $normMVX$ and $normMVY$ values in the $NBH_{i,j,t}$ w.r.t $normMVX_{i,j,t}$ and $normMVY_{i,j,t}$, respectively.

Mathematically, for a point $p_{i,j,t}$, $RLV_{i,j,t}$ is defined as

$$RLV_{i,j,t} = \frac{1}{N} \sum_{k=1}^{k=N} (normMVX_{i,j,t} - normMVX_{NBH_{i,j,t}(k)})^2$$

$$+ \frac{1}{N} \sum_{k=1}^{k=N} (normMVY_{i,j,t} - normMVY_{NBH_{i,j,t}(k)})^2 \quad (7)$$

Assuming the general definition of vector difference, we can re-write it as

$$RLV_{i,j,t} = \frac{1}{N} \sum_{k=1}^{k=N} I(norm(MV_{i,j,t}) - norm(MV_{NBH_{i,j,t}(k)})))^2, \quad (8)$$

where $I(.)$ refers to the Intensity. Equation 8 has a very nice interpretation, because given two unit vectors V1 and V2.

$$\text{Intensity of } (V1 - V2) \propto \text{Angle btw } (V1, V2) \tag{9}$$

From Eq. 8 and 9, it can be deduced that RLV map is a measure of angle consistency between the neighborhood of the pixel and the pixel. Our RLV function is free of all the limitations mentioned in Sect. 4 and still incorporates angle consistency information into the algorithm.

Moreover, our RLV only uses frame level operations as opposed to pixel level operations. Our RLV function uses sum of relative variance w.r.t. MVX and MVY. Consider, just the relative variance for MVX, it can be written as

$$RLV \text{ w.r.t. } MVX = \frac{1}{N} \sum_{k=1}^{k=N} (normMVX_{i,j,t} - normMVX_{NBH_{i,j,t}(k)})^2 \tag{10}$$

which can be rearranged as,

$$RLV \text{ w.r.t. } MVX = \frac{1}{N} \left(\sum_{k=1}^{k=N} normMVX^2_{NBH_{i,j,t}(k)} \right) + normMVX^2_{i,j,t}$$
$$- (2 * normMVX_{i,j,t} * \frac{1}{N} \sum_{k=1}^{k=N} normMVX_{NBH_{i,j,t}(k)}) \tag{11}$$

Equation 11 utilizes neighborhood set mean and squared-mean, and the $MVX_{i,j,t}$ value itself at a pixel $p(i,j,t)$ to calculate RLV w.r.t. MVX. All of these can be easily computed at frame level for each pixel $p_{i,j,t}$ using fixed convolution kernels. This allows code optimization through techniques such as vectorization, which can help reduce execution time significantly. We were able to use these techniques to implement RLV in Halide-C++ (more details in Sect. 6.5).

5.2 Our Pruning Algorithm

Our Pruning Algorithm is based on the template mentioned in Sect. 3.1.

- We first apply a Median filter to the input Motion vector frame/field.
- We use only two maps in our algorithm
  - Map-1: Use RLV function to operate on a temporal neighborhood ($N = 7$).
  - Intensity Map
- To calculate NBH_{th}, we first define an angle θ and then use following formulae, which represent the intensity square of the difference of two unit vectors, θ angle apart.

$$NBH_{th} = \sin^2(\theta) + (1 - \cos(\theta))^2 \tag{12}$$

In Sect. 6, we provide the results and ablation studies to justify our choices for the algorithm. We also show how our RLV method outperforms other prior-art functions.

Table 1. Results by utilizing different operating functions

Method	NBH_{th}	$Frame_{th}$	f1Score	Precision	Recall	Accuracy
$ABSDoA$	30	2	0.734	0.627	0.885	0.641
$ABSDOI$	30	15	0.755	0.634	0.932	0.661
$Entropy$	3.83	0.01	0.749	0.628	0.946	0.65
$Entropy - Norm$	3.83	0.01	0.721	0.561	**0.99**	0.56
RLV	**0.268**	**1e−6**	**0.8536**	**0.843**	0.864	**0.834**

6   Results

6.1   Dataset Details

We use 20 videos that are similar to typical surveillance videos for generating results. In each video, frames containing interesting motion have been identified. By interesting, we subjectively mean movements of humans, cars, pets, etc., while the motion of leaves, water, etc. has been label as uninteresting.

- 16 of the videos are part of dataset2014 from ChangeDetection.net, [5]. However, in dataset2014 the ground truth is only provided for Region of interest(RoI). The provided ground truth also marks static objects. Hence, we re-annotated the dataset at frame-level. Following are the video names, busStation, copyMachine, cubicle, office, peopleInShade, PETS2006, sofa, winterDriveway, abandonedBox, backdoor, blizzard, boats, canoe, fall, streetLight and snowFall.
- 4 videos are taken from video summarization dataset by [11]. However, since they provided dynamic object mask as ground truth, we didn't have to annotate them ourselves. Following are the video names, Building, Cesta4, Transitway1 and Transitway2.

6.2   RLV vs Others

Through these experiments, we want to prove that our RLV function is better than other available approaches. For these set of experiments, we generate two maps for the scoring algorithms. One map uses spatial neighborhood ($N = 5$), while the other uses temporal neighborhood ($N = 5$). But, both maps are operated by the same function. Table 1 summarizes the F1-scores achieved.

For $Entropy$, both [9,19], advocate to normalize the $Entropy$ maps to a range of [0, 1], we believe that it is counter productive, because normalization kills the relative value of maps across frames.

- In Table 1, $Entropy$ method doesn't utilize normalization.
- In Table 1, $Entropy - Norm$ utilizes normalization and suffers f1Score drop.

It can be seen from the Table 1, that our proposed RLV function far exceeds the results generated by other functions used throughout the literature.

Table 2. Results by utilizing different neighborhood definition

Method	$frame_{th}$	f1Score	Precision	Recall	Accuracy
Spatial	1e−4	0.766	0.670	0.895	0.694
Temporal	1e−4	0.862	0.828	0.900	0.84
Temporal-pooling	1e−05	0.851	0.784	0.930	0.818
Spatial & temporal	1e−06	0.853	0.843	0.864	0.834
SpatioTemporal	1e−7	0.859	0.894	0.825	0.848
Fwd & bwd accu.	1e−8	0.745	0.76	0.749	0.727

6.3   Ablation Study: Results Comparing Neighborhood Choices

Through these experiments, we want to justify our choice of using Temporal neighborhood set in the first map of our pruning Algorithm. In this section we provide results for following combination of neighborhood choices. Number of neighborhoods type involved in a choice also determine the number of maps considered in that frame scoring algorithm. We use RLV function to operate on the neighborhood values, with NBH_{th} = 0.267 (corresponds to $\theta = 30°$)

– Spatial: A map of spatial neighborhood($N = 5$) is used.
– Temporal: A map of temporal neighborhood($N = 5$) is used.
– Temporal-pooling: Before any processing, raw MV field is processed by a 4 × 4 average pooling kernel (further explained in Sect. 6.5). A map of temporal neighborhood ($N = 5$) is used.
– Spatial and Temporal: A map of spatial neighborhood ($N = 5$) and map of temporal neighborhood ($N = 5$) is used.
– SpatioTemporal: A map of spatiotemporal neighborhood ($N, M = 5$) is used.
– Forward and Backward Accumulated Temporal Neighborhood: A map of forward and backward accumulated temporal neighborhood ($N = 5$)

Table 2 shows the results for various settings. It can be seen that temporal neighborhood map alone performs better than rest of the approaches. Hence, we have used temporal neighborhood map in our pruning algorithm (Sect. 5.2). A possible reason for spatial neighborhood map's negative effect is that spatial neighborhood map intrinsically applies a morphological erosion operations to all the edges of an object boundary.

A peculiar result is the low score for Forward and Backward Accumulated Temporal Neighborhood. We believe that the main cause is that if distance between the frames is more than 1, then accumulation happens with the sum of MVs between the frames rather than being recursively accumulated.

6.4   Ablation Study: Results by Applying Auxiliary Techniques

In this section we apply several auxiliary techniques that can be used in conjunction with the template described in Sect. 3.1 and present the compiled results. For experiment in this section, we compare results with a baseline method in which we use RLV

function to operate on a spatial neighborhood ($N = 5$) and a temporal neighborhood ($N = 5$) with $NBH_{th} = 0.267$. Results for baseline method are available in Table 2, in the 'Spatial & Temporal' row. Results for following experiments are shown in Table 3.

MV Clipping. MV clipping is a technique in which all the MV with intensity lower than $clipping_{thresh}$ are set to zero. As shown in Table 3, there is a reduction in the f1Score by applying MV clipping w.r.t. baseline model. We have observed that the main reason for this is that MV clipping removes MVs corresponding to human movements, which tend to have lower MV as compared to those of cars, etc. As shown in the Table 3, there is a significant drop in the recall values corresponding to MV clipping.

Median Filter. Median filter has been used throughout the literature and rightly so. As, shown in Table 3, there is slight increase in the f1Score, owing to the increase in the precision score.

Table 3. Results by applying auxiliary techniques

Technique	Variable	Value	$Frame_{th}$	f1Score	Precision	Recall	Accuracy
MV Clipping	$clipping_{thresh}$	1	1e−7	0.781	0.884	0.699	0.78
Median filter	$filter\_size$	5×5	1e−5	0.857	0.878	0.836	0.843

6.5 Execution Time Details

We have realized two possible ways to further reduce the time taken by our algorithm.

- 79.1% of the MBs in a frame are actually 16×16 coded. Thus, we can further reduce the size of the original MV field by 4×4. Hence, by applying a average pooling we can reduce the size of MV field to 16×16 of original frame. Performance metrics are shown in the Table 2.
- As mentioned in the Sect. 5, our RLV can be implemented by frame level codes, which in turn allows us to use batch processing in order to reduce the time of execution at the expense of memory. Optimal batch size can be calculated based on the hardware and memory configurations of the device.

Table 4 shows the execution time for the baseline algorithm and the two alternatives applied independently to the baseline on full HD videos (1920×1080). The time shown in the table is the time taken by our algorithm to process the frame, excluding the time taken for extracting MV from the frame. We are using a python based implementation on an Ubuntu18.04 OS on top of an Intel Core i7-7700 CPU @ 3.60 GHz. We also implemented our algorithm in Halide C++ with optimized vectorized operations, results for same have been presented as well. It can be seen that our Halide implementation is extremely fast and optimal to use in IoT-Edge scenario.

Table 4. Execution time

Method	Language	Time per frame (ms)
Baseline	Python	20
Pooling	Python	16
Batch [Batch size = 50]	Python	11
Baseline	Halide-C++	1.8
Pooling	Halide-C++	0.7

7   Conclusion

In this paper, we made novel observations regarding the limitations of existing approaches to capture orientation consistency information in videos. Based on these observations, we proposed our RLV function to operate on a neighborhood set. We used this function to develop a fast, computationally cheap and efficient frame scoring algorithm. The frame scoring algorithm can be utilized in the IoT-Edge domain to prune uninteresting motion for the task of video summarization. This pruning methodology not only reduces the further processing cost but also the bandwidth cost if the further processing happens on a cloud.

References

1. Babu, R.V., Ramakrishnan, K.R., Srinivasan, S.H.: Video object segmentation: a compressed domain approach. IEEE Trans. Circuits Syst. Video Technol. **14**(4), 462–474 (2004). https://doi.org/10.1109/TCSVT.2004.825536
2. Chen, Y., Bajić, I.V., Saeedi, P.: Moving region segmentation from compressed video using global motion estimation and Markov random fields. IEEE Trans. Multimed. **13**(3), 421–431 (2011). https://doi.org/10.1109/TMM.2011.2127464
3. Dong, P., Xia, Y., Feng, D.D.: Real-time storyboard generation for H.264/AVC compressed videos. In: 2012 IEEE International Conference on Multimedia and Expo, pp. 544–549 (2012). https://doi.org/10.1109/ICME.2012.49
4. Erol, B., Lee, D., Hull, J.: Multimodal summarization of meeting recordings. In: 2003 International Conference on Multimedia and Expo, ICME 2003. Proceedings (Cat. No. 03TH8698), vol. 3, pp. III-25 (2003). https://doi.org/10.1109/ICME.2003.1221239
5. Goyette, N., Jodoin, P., Porikli, F., Konrad, J., Ishwar, P.: Changedetection.net: a new change detection benchmark dataset. In: 2012 IEEE Computer Society Conference on Computer Vision and Pattern Recognition Workshops, pp. 1–8 (2012). https://doi.org/10.1109/CVPRW.2012.6238919
6. Herranz, L., Martinez, J.M.: An efficient summarization algorithm based on clustering and bitstream extraction. In: 2009 IEEE International Conference on Multimedia and Expo, pp. 654–657 (2009). https://doi.org/10.1109/ICME.2009.5202581
7. Herranz, L., Martínez, J.M.: A framework for scalable summarization of video. IEEE Trans. Circuits Syst. Video Technol. **20**(9), 1265–1270 (2010). https://doi.org/10.1109/TCSVT.2010.2057020

8. Eng, H.-L., Ma, K.-K.: Spatiotemporal segmentation of moving video objects over mpeg compressed domain. In: 2000 IEEE International Conference on Multimedia and Expo, ICME 2000. Proceedings. Latest Advances in the Fast Changing World of Multimedia (Cat. No. 00TH8532), vol. 3, pp. 1531–1534 (2000). https://doi.org/10.1109/ICME.2000.871059
9. Lai, J.L., Yi, Y.: Key frame extraction based on visual attention model. J. Vis. Commun. Image Represent. 23(1), 114–125 (2012). https://doi.org/10.1016/j.jvcir.2011.08.005
10. Laumer, M., Amon, P., Hutter, A., Kaup, A.: Compressed domain moving object detection by spatio-temporal analysis of H.264/AVC syntax elements. In: 2015 Picture Coding Symposium (PCS), pp. 282–286 (2015). https://doi.org/10.1109/PCS.2015.7170091
11. Lai, P.K., Décombas, M., Moutet, K., Laganière, R.: Video summarization of surveillance cameras. In: 2016 13th IEEE International Conference on Advanced Video and Signal Based Surveillance (AVSS), pp. 286–294 (2016). https://doi.org/10.1109/AVSS.2016.7738018
12. Pritch, Y., Rav-Acha, A., Peleg, S.: Nonchronological video synopsis and indexing. IEEE Trans. Pattern Anal. Mach. Intell. 30(11), 1971–1984 (2008). https://doi.org/10.1109/TPAMI.2008.29
13. Sugano, M., Nakajima, Y., Yanagihara, H.: Automated mpeg audio-video summarization and description. In: Proceedings of International Conference on Image Processing, vol. 1, pp. I-I (2002). https://doi.org/10.1109/ICIP.2002.1038186
14. Szczerba, K., Forchhammer, S., Stottrup-Andersen, J., Eybye, P.T.: Fast compressed domain motion detection in H.264 video streams for video surveillance applications. In: 2009 Sixth IEEE International Conference on Advanced Video and Signal Based Surveillance, pp. 478–483 (2009). https://doi.org/10.1109/AVSS.2009.78
15. Wang, R., Zhang, H.-J., Zhang, Y.-Q.: A confidence measure based moving object extraction system built for compressed domain. In: 2000 IEEE International Symposium on Circuits and Systems (ISCAS), vol. 5, pp. 21–24 (2000). https://doi.org/10.1109/ISCAS.2000.857353
16. Wang, S.Z., Wang, Z.Y., Hu, R.M.: Surveillance video synopsis in the compressed domain for fast video browsing. J. Vis. Commun. Image Represent. 24(8), 1431–1442 (2013). https://doi.org/10.1016/j.jvcir.2013.10.001, https://www.sciencedirect.com/science/article/pii/S1047320313001818
17. Wiegand, T., Sullivan, G.J., Bjontegaard, G., Luthra, A.: Overview of the H.264/AVC video coding standard. IEEE Trans. Circuits Syst. Video Technol. 13(7), 560–576 (2003). https://doi.org/10.1109/TCSVT.2003.815165
18. Yeo, C., Ahammad, P., Ramchandran, K., Sastry, S.S.: High-speed action recognition and localization in compressed domain videos. IEEE Trans. Circuits Syst. Video Technol. 18(8), 1006–1015 (2008). https://doi.org/10.1109/TCSVT.2008.927112
19. Ma, Y.-F., Zhang, H.-J.: A model of motion attention for video skimming. In: Proceedings of the International Conference on Image Processing, vol. 1, pp. I-I (2002). https://doi.org/10.1109/ICIP.2002.1037976
20. Zen, H., Hasegawa, T., Ozawa, S.: Moving object detection from mpeg coded picture. In: Proceedings 1999 International Conference on Image Processing (Cat. 99CH36348), vol. 4, pp. 25–29 (1999). https://doi.org/10.1109/ICIP.1999.819460

A Data-Driven Approach to Improve 3D Head-Pose Estimation

Nima Aghli$^{(\boxtimes)}$ and Eraldo Ribeiro

Florida Institute of Technology, Melbourne, FL 32904, USA
naghli2014@my.fit.edu, eribeiro@fit.edu

Abstract. Head-pose estimation from images is an important research topic in computer vision. Its many applications include detecting focus of attention, tracking driver behavior, and human-computer interaction. Recent research on head-pose estimation has focused on developing models based on deep convolutional neural networks (CNNs). These models are trained using transfer-learning and image augmentation to achieve better initiation states and robustness against occlusions. However, methods that use transfer-learning networks are usually aimed at general image recognition and offer no in-depth study of transfer learning from more task-related networks. Additionally, for the head-pose estimation, robustness against heavy occlusion, and noise such as motion blur and low-brightness are vital. In this paper, we propose a new image-augmentation approach that significantly improves the estimation accuracy of the head-pose model. We also propose a task-related weight initialization to further improve the estimation accuracy by studying internal activations of models trained for face-related tasks such as face-recognition. We test our head-pose estimation model on three challenging test sets and achieve better results to state-of-the-art methods.

1 Introduction

Determining the pose of a person's head from images is a key computer-vision problem, which has a number of applications. For example, head-pose detection is a main step of some algorithms for gaze detection in human-computer interaction systems. One can use head pose to reject unsuitable face images prior to performing recognition for methods that are sensitive to extreme out-of-plane head rotations.

Traditional methods were proposed to model head-pose estimation. Template Models [13,27] were a common approach that use traditional classifiers such as support vector machines. Training multiple face-detector as a detector array [23,34] for different head-pose angles achieved good accuracy. Manifold learning [1,22] were also a successful approach, which learned a low-dimensional manifold embedding to model nonlinear face appearance for estimating head-pose.

Deep-learning methods for pose estimation are divided into landmark-free and landmark-based methods. Landmark-based methods require facial landmark detection before pose estimation. Zhu *et al.* [35] proposed a deep CNN to extract

© Springer Nature Switzerland AG 2021
G. Bebis et al. (Eds.): ISVC 2021, LNCS 13017, pp. 546–558, 2021.
https://doi.org/10.1007/978-3-030-90439-5_43

facial-landmarks from RGB images followed by fitting 3D face model on the landmarks for head-pose estimation. Gupta *et al.* [9] used a higher-level representation to regress head-pose using CNN. The proposed method first extracts 5 facial keypoints using uncertainty maps in the form of 2-D localization heatmaps. Then, the extracted facial landmarks are fed to a CNN to regress the head-pose. Although deep landmark-based methods achieve significant improvement over traditional methods, they suffer from dependency on accurate landmark detection where invisibility of some landmarks due to occlusion has a significant effect on the accuracy of the estimation.

KEPLER [18] is a multi-task learning framework that proposes a Heatmap-CNN architecture, which captures structured global and local features of facial images for joint prediction of keypoints and pose. HyperFace [21] is also a deep multi-task approach that combines feature maps from different layers of CNNs for multiple tasks including head-pose, facial landmarks, and gender estimation.

Ruiz *et al.* [24] proposed a landmark-free head pose estimation using a multi-loss convolutional neural network. They add a coarse bin classification layer before the regression layer in the backbone network. Wang *et al.* [30] introduced a hybrid coarse-fine classification scheme to improve the result of regression by increasing the number of the classification bins and adding several dense layers to the backbone network in [24].

FSA-NET [31] is the state-of-the-art landmark-free pose estimation that proposes a compact head-pose estimation model based on a soft stage-wise regression scheme [32]. The proposed framework learns a fine-grained structure mapping for grouping spatial features before aggregation.

The majority of pose estimation proposals use a single RGB image as input, but some methods take advantage of 3D depth or temporal information to achieve better accuracy. Fanelli *et al.* [7] used a low-quality depth camera to estimate location and pose of the head from the depth images using discriminative random regression forests. Martin *et al.* [19] combined both RGB and point cloud information from consumer depth cameras to create a 3D head model using iterative closest point algorithm. Gu *et al.* [8] used temporal information from video frames to train a combination of VGG16 [28] and recurrent neural network (RNN) to improve the head pose and tracking accuracy.

Weight initialization in neural networks from pre-trained networks is a common transfer learning technique to reduce the training time as well as providing a better initialization point for optimizers. Ranjan *et al.* [21] initialized the AlexNet [17] backbone network from ImageNet [4] weights. Wang *et al.* [30] used weights from ResNet50 [11] network trained on ImageNet. Ruiz *et al.* [24] achieved better pose estimation accuracy by pre-training ResNet50 on ImageNet and fine-tuning on the head-pose dataset.

Increasing the robustness of the models against various alternations on the images such as occlusion, illumination, and motion blur is a challenging problem in designing a good head-pose estimation model. Drouard *et al.* [5] proposed a mapping method for combining the merits of the unsupervised manifold learning and mixtures of regressors with training a robust head-pose estimate against facial landmark occlusion and change of illumination condition. Ruiz *et al.* [24] applied down-sampling on different rates to increase the robustness of the head-pose estimation model over low-resolution images. FSA-Net [31] applies random cropping and random scaling on the training images.

In this paper, we improve the accuracy of state-of-the-art head-pose estimation models on challenging datasets as follows: 1) We introduce a new transfer-learning approach for better weight initialization of the head-pose estimation network. Additionally, we explain the effectiveness of the new transfer-learning approach by performing activation analysis. 2) We propose a new image-augmentation approach that, when applied to training data, increases the accuracy of the pose-estimation and the robustness of the model against heavy occlusion, brightness, and motion-blur.

2 Method

In this section, we formulate the head-pose estimation problem and train a baseline CNN network to estimate the head-pose in 3D from a single RGB image. Second, we introduce our proposed image-augmentation approach and run experiments with networks trained by augmented training set. Third, We study the activation functions of a model trained for face-recognition purpose and use it as a weight initializer to the model.

2.1 Problem Definition

In this paper, we focus on estimating head-pose in 3D space as yaw, pitch, and roll values from an RGB image which by definition is a regression problem. We define the training images as X where $X = \{X_m | m = 1, ..., M\}$ and M is the total number of the images in the training set. The goal is to minimize the following objective function:

$$F(X) = \frac{1}{M} \sum_{i=1}^{M} ||\hat{y}_i - y_i||, \qquad (1)$$

where y_i is ground truth pose vector as yaw, pitch, and roll of the ith image and $\hat{y}_i$ is the prediction pose vector by the model for the ith image.

2.2 Weight Initialization with Activation Analysis

Estimating head-pose from a facial image is dependent on extracting accurate facial-landmarks. Landmark-free CNN methods do not explicitly extract facial-landmarks, but they learn facial-landmarks in the network's hidden layers. Initializing network weights from a previously trained model for a face-related task can provide a better starting point for the optimizer and lead to a better pose estimation accuracy. In search of better weight initialization other than using models trained for general object recognition such as ImageNet, we propose

Fig. 1. First row shows the original images and the second row shows the applied augmentation to the original image.

using models trained on large datasets similar to ImageNet but for more related tasks. In this work, we propose the initialization of the network weights from a face-recognition network. To show the potential of using a more task-specific pre-trained model, we perform in-depth activation analysis of internal neurons of a ResNet50 [11] network trained on two different datasets: 1) Imagnet [4] for classifying 1000 general objects from 14 million images. 2) VGGFace2 [3] for classifying 8631 identities from total of 3 million facial images. We apply Grad-CAM [26] to all layers of the both networks to show the attention region of each Conv layer and its filters on a sample face image. Given an input image and Conv filter of interest f and its activation value y^f, Grad-Cam computes the gradient of y^f with respect to feature map activation values of previous Conv layer A^k to calculate filter attention weights as follows:

$$\alpha_k^c = \overbrace{\frac{1}{Z} \sum_i \sum_j \underbrace{\frac{\partial y^f}{\partial A_{ij}^k}}_{\text{gradients via backprop}}}^{\text{pooling}}, \tag{2}$$

where the gradients flowing are global average pooling over i and j dimensions. Figure 2 shows attention regions of filters in different layers of two networks.

The visualization results show that while ImageNet and VGGFace2 networks have similar attention maps in the shallow layers, deeper layers of VGGFace2 network learned to capture different facial parts more accurately, which makes it an ideal weight initialization method for our head-pose estimation network.

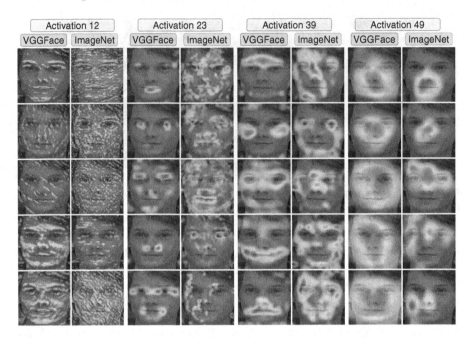

Fig. 2. Grad-Cam on different layers in the face-recognition network and visualizing attention on a sample face image. Shallow layers capture simple features such as edges, deeper layers focus on complex features such as mouth and eyes.

2.3 Augmented Image Duplication

Training images we use in this paper are synthesized or taken in a controlled environment that means faces are mostly centered in the samples with the same lighting condition, but the testing data is gathered from the wild and has large pose variation. It is predictable that the training on such images reduces the possibility of learning spatial transformation between facial features. Hence, the model does not achieve the best accuracy over the test-set. To address this issue and achieve better generalization over training images, we apply duplicated image augmentation on the training set described in method 1.

After augmentation, each sample in the original dataset will have a copy of a randomly augmented version of it. Random zoom and cropping can help the model to be robust against the displacement of the facial features in the image, while random brightness brings robustness against lighting change. Figure 1 shows some examples of augmented images from the training-set. Unlike FSA-Net, we apply the augmented images on top of the training set and shuffle them before training, which increases the size of the dataset from 244, 830 to 489, 660.

Algorithm 1: Image augmentation and duplication on training images

---

   Input: (X, Y): Training data and labels
   Output: (D_x, D_y): Augmented Training data and labels
1 $X_A \leftarrow \mathrm{Copy}(X)$
2 **for** *sample in X_A* **do**
3 | *sample* $\leftarrow$ RandomCrop(sample, height=15, width=15)
4 | *sample* $\leftarrow$ RandomZoom(sample, min=0.7, max=1.3)
5 | *sample* $\leftarrow$ RandomBrightness(sample, maxDelta=0.2)
6 **end**
7 $D_x \leftarrow \mathrm{Concatenate}(X, D_x)$
8 $D_y \leftarrow \mathrm{Concatenate}(Y, Y)$
9 $D_x, D_y \leftarrow \mathrm{Shuffle}(D_x, D_y)$
10 **return** D_x, D_y

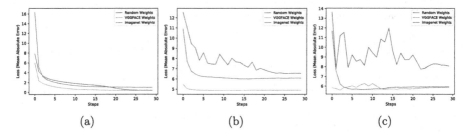

Fig. 3. Training without augmented sample duplication. (a) MAE on 300W-LP train-ing dataset. (b) MAE on AFLW2000 testset. (c) MAE on BIWI testset.

3 Experiments

3.1 Setup

We use Keras[1] for training all the experiments with a batch size of 64 for 30 epoch. The loss function used in training is Mean Absolute Error (MAE) over head-pose angles.

ResNet50 [11] is the backbone architecture for training all scenarios with input image size of 224×224. We add two Dense layers of size 512 and 128 with ReLU activation to the last pooling layer of the ResNet50 network. The last layer of the network is a linear Dense layer of size 3 for Yaw, Pitch, and Roll values. In the case of fine-tuning ImageNet and VGGFace2 networks, we remove the classification layers and replace them with regression layers as described above.

3.2 Datasets

We train head-pose estimation networks on 300W-LP [35] dataset and test on AFLW2000 [35] and BIWI [6]. The 300W-LP is a collection of synthesized facial

---

[1] https://keras.io/.

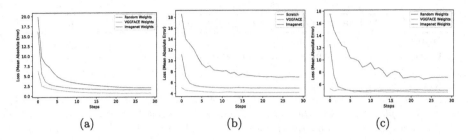

Fig. 4. Training with our augmentation method. (a) MAE on 300W-LP training dataset. (b) MAE on AFLW2000 testset. (c) MAE on BIWI testset.

images created by applying face-profiling with 3D image meshing to the images from the 300W [25] dataset that includes facial images with 68 facial landmarks annotated from various datasets. In total, there are 61,225 images in the dataset, and after applying horizontal flipping to the images, the total images in the dataset reaches 122,450. The AFLW2000 is a challenging test-set for evaluating head-pose estimation models. It includes ground-truth 3D faces as well as 68 facial-landmarks and head-pose values in yaw, pitch, and roll from the first 2000 images in the AFLW [16] dataset. Unlike the synthesized images in the 300W-LP, the images in the AFLW2000 are gathered from the wild and undergo various illumination and transformation.

BIWI dataset is collected from video frames captured in a controlled environment. There are approximately 15,000 frames saved from videos as an RGB image with their head-pose. In addition to RGB images, BIWI provides depth information for each frame.

We adopt evaluation protocols from FSA-Net [31] commonly used in state-of-the-art head-pose-estimation papers. The training and testing protocols that we use to evaluate the effectiveness of our approach are as follows:

- **Protocol 1.** Train on 300W-LP, test on AFLW2000. To be consistent with the latest testing protocols from recent state-of-the-art papers, we remove the samples from the train and test images with any yaw, pitch, or roll values larger than 90 or smaller than −90.
- **Protocol 2.** Train on 300W-LP, test on BIWI. Faces in BIWI are detected using MTCNN [33] and cropped loosely with an enlargement margin of 0.2.
- **Protocol 3.** Train on 70% of BIWI, test on the remaining 30%. We create three different splits of 70/30 randomly following the protocol in [24] and [8]. Reported error on this protocol is averaged over three splits.

3.3 Optimizer

Networks in protocol 1 and 2 are trained using SGD with momentum [29] set to 0.9. We adopt Hyperbolic-Tangent Decay (HTD) [12] as our learning-rate scheduler. HTD is originally applied for training different classification models and achieved better accuracy for large datasets. In this paper, we fine-tune HTD to achieve better results on our regression network since the size of training dataset gets significantly large after applying augmentation as well as the risk of over-fitting. We schedule the learning-rate of the optimizer after each epoch based on the following formula:

$$lr_t = lr_{min}\frac{lr_{max} - lr_{min}}{2}(1 - tanh(L + (U - L)\frac{t}{T})), \qquad (3)$$

where t is the epoch number, L and U defines the lower and upper bound for $tanhx$ function respectively. lr_{max} indicates the starting learning-rate, and lr_{min} defines the stopping learning-rate. When training the network, we set the lr_{max} to 0.01, while for fine-tuning ImageNet and VGGFace2 networks, we set lr_{max} to 0.0001 to avoid overfitting. In all experiments lr_{min} is 0 where L and U are set to -1.5 and 3 respectively.

Experiments based on protocol 3 are trained with Adam [15] optimizer with an initialization learning rate of 0.01 and scheduling learning rate 0.001, 0.0001, and 0.0001 after epoch 5, 15, and 25.

Table 1. Comparisons with state-of-the-art methods on protocol 1.

	Yaw	Pitch	Roll	MAE
Dlib (68 points) [14]	23.1	13.6	10.5	15.8
FAN (12 points) [2]	6.36	12.3	8.71	9.12
Landmarks [24]	5.92	11.86	8.27	8.65
3DDFA [35]	5.40	8.53	8.25	7.39
Hopenet [24]	6.47	6.56	5.44	6.16
SSR-Net-MD [32]	5.14	7.09	5.89	6.01
FSA-Caps [31]	4.50	6.08	4.64	5.07
DDD-Pose (Random) (ours)	8.30	6.64	4.77	6.57
DDD-Pose (ImNet) (ours)	6.53	6.34	5.48	6.11
DDD-Pose (VF2) (ours)	5.43	5.29	3.96	4.89
DDD-Pose (Random-AUG) (ours)	8.34	7.01	5.68	7.01
DDD-Pose (ImNet-AUG) (ours)	4.70	5.73	4.56	4.99
DDD-Pose (VF2-AUG) (ours)	**4.38**	**4.85**	**3.44**	**4.22**

3.4   Results

We have six different training scenarios to evaluate the effectiveness of using a face-recognition network as a weight initializer and augmented training image duplication. We train the ResNet50 network with weights initialized randomly, from ImageNet and VGGFace2 pre-trained networks, as well as training the same networks with and without the duplicated augmented training dataset.

Table 2. Comparisons with state-of-the-art methods on protocol 2.

	Yaw	Pitch	Roll	MAE
3DDFA [35]	36.2	12.3	8.78	19.1
KEPLER [18]	8.80	17.3	16.2	13.9
Dlib (68 points) [14]	16.08	13.8	6.19	12.2
FAN (12 points) [2]	8.53	7.48	7.63	7.89
Hopenet [24]	4.81	6.61	3.27	4.90
SSR-Net-MD [32]	4.49	6.31	3.61	4.65
FSA-Caps [31]	**4.27**	**4.96**	**2.76**	**4.00**
DDD-Pose (Random) (ours)	7.05	12.60	4.63	8.09
DDD-Pose (ImNet) (ours)	6.02	7.21	4.57	5.93
DDD-Pose (VF2) (ours)	6.06	7.99	3.57	5.87
DDD-Pose (Random-AUG) (ours)	5.58	11.41	4.42	7.13
DDD-Pose (ImNet-AUG) (ours)	5.14	6.49	3.49	5.04
DDD-Pose (VF2-AUG) (ours)	4.60	6.02	2.94	4.52

Figure 3 and 4 shows the results in Mean Absolute Error (MAE) on the training and testsets for all scenarios on protocol 1 and 2. Table 1 shows a comparison of validating different scenarios on AFLW2000. The results show that models trained on VGGFace2 achieve better results than initializing the weights randomly or from the ImageNet network. We confirm that fine-tuning VGGFace2 network trained on the augmented 300W-LP dataset outperforms the state-of-the-art models on AFLW2000.

Table 2 shows the validation results on BIWI dataset (protocol 2) where the MAE on networks trained with our proposed method achieves comparable results to the state-of-the-art. Additionally, for both testsets, VGGFace2 converges to a minimum faster although we keep training epochs constant for all experiments.

The BIWI dataset is originally captured as a video with depth information. In this work, we only use RGB images captured from the videos. Some papers take advantage of depth [19] or temporal [8] information as well as RGB images to improve the accuracy of the estimation. Table 4 shows a comparison to RGB based methods and Depth/Time-based method on test protocol 3. The results show that not only our method outperforms the state-of-the-art on RGB based methods but also archives better results than the RGB+Depth method.

3.5 AFLW2000 Occlusion, Motion-Blur, and Brightness Study

In real-world applications of head-pose estimation, images taken by cameras can undergo various transformations such as occluded faces, capturing in low light or motion-blurred images due to objects moving fast. To evaluate the performance of the model trained with our proposed method on such image transformations, we have created three versions of AFLW2000 as follows:

Table 3. AFLW2000 with occlusion, motion-Blur and low brightness.

	Motion Blur			Low Brightness			Random Occlusion		
	FSA-Net [31] Caps-Fusion	DDD-Pose VF2-AUG	DDD-Pose VF2-AUG-DS	FSA-Net [31] Caps-Fusion	DDD-Pose VF2-AUG	DDD-Pose VF2-AUG-DS	FSA-Net [31] Caps-Fusion	DDD-Pose VF2-AUG	DDD-Pose VF2-AUG-DS
Yaw	21.90	**9.60**	**10.68**	7.80	**7.07**	7.93	8.57	**6.79**	**7.79**
Pitch	11.07	**7.34**	**7.78**	7.28	**6.18**	**6.54**	7.87	**6.11**	**6.63**
Roll	11.05	**6.32**	**6.71**	6.11	**4.93**	**5.37**	7.05	**4.92**	**5.43**
MAE	14.67	**7.85**	**8.39**	7.06	**6.06**	**6.61**	7.83	**5.94**	**6.61**

- AFLW2000-MB Convolve images with blur kernel of size 25×25.
- AFLW2000-LB Reduce the brightness of the images in the dataset with a delta value of -0.4.
- AFLW2000-OC Randomly subtract three rectangular patches of size 35×35 pixels from the images.

Figure 5 shows 3 different examples from augmented versions of AFLW2000. We select our best performing model (VF2-AUG) on the AFL2000 and compare it to the latest best-performing work from [31].

Since the model in [31] is trained on images of size 64×64, we also evaluate our model with a down-sampled version of augmented images and name it VF2-AUG-DS. When evaluating on VF2-AUG-DS, we first resize the images to 60×60 and then resize back to 224×224 with nearest-neighbor interpolation. For fair comparison in AFLW2000-OC, since patches are randomly generated, we create three versions of AFLW2000-OC and report the average error. Table 1 shows the comparison of variations of AFLW2000 between our method and the state-of-the-art. The results show that our model outperforms [31] in both original image size and down-sampled versions of AFLW2000.

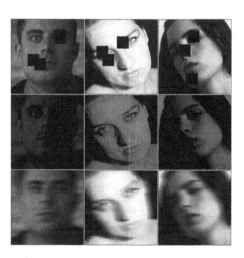

Fig. 5. Random occlusion, brightness and motion-blur applied to AFLW2000.

Table 4. Comparisons with state-of-the-art methods on protocol 3.

	Yaw	Pitch	Roll	MAE
RGB based				
DeepHeadPose [20]	5.67	5.18	–	–
SSR-Net-MD [32]	4.49	6.31	3.61	4.65
VGG-16 [8]	4.24	4.35	4.19	4.26
FSA-Caps [31]	2.89	4.29	3.60	3.60
Gustafsson *et al.* [10]	**2.67**	3.61	2.75	3.01
DDD-Pose (VF2-AUG)(ours)	3.04	**2.94**	**2.43**	**2.80**
RGB + Depth				
Martin [19]	3.6	2.5	2.6	2.9
RGB + Time				
VGG-16+RNN [8]	3.14	3.48	2.6	3.07

4   Conclusion

In this paper, we proposed a data-driven method to improve landmark-free deep head-pose estimation by using better weight initialization and training data manipulation. We showed that the network's initialization from the face-recognition model for the head-pose estimation achieved better accuracy than initialization from general object-recognition networks. Second, our image-augmentation approach improved head-pose estimation accuracy and yielded better robustness against heavy occlusion, motion blur, and brightness changes.

We tested our proposed method on three different test sets and compared them to the state-of-the methods. Our results showed an improvement or comparable results to the state-of-the-art head-pose estimation methods. Additionally, we introduced three new variations of the challenging AFLW2000 test set and showed the robustness of the model trained with our method on heavily occluded and blurred versions of AFLW2000 by comparing to the state-of-the-art.

In future works, we plan to reduce the complexity of the model for real-time estimation in low-power systems with less powerful computing capabilities.

References

1. Balasubramanian, V.N., Ye, J., Panchanathan, S.: Biased manifold embedding: a framework for person-independent head pose estimation. In: 2007 IEEE Conference on Computer Vision and Pattern Recognition, pp. 1–7. IEEE (2007)
2. Bulat, A., Tzimiropoulos, G.: How far are we from solving the 2D & 3D face alignment problem? (And a dataset of 230,000 3D facial landmarks). In: Proceedings of the IEEE International Conference on Computer Vision, pp. 1021–1030 (2017)
3. Cao, Q., Shen, L., Xie, W., Parkhi, O.M., Zisserman, A.: VGGFace2: a dataset for recognising faces across pose and age. In: 2018 13th IEEE International Conference on Automatic Face & Gesture Recognition (FG 2018), pp. 67–74. IEEE (2018)

4. Deng, J., Dong, W., Socher, R., Li, L.J., Li, K., Fei-Fei, L.: ImageNet: a large-scale hierarchical image database. In: 2009 IEEE Conference on Computer Vision and Pattern Recognition, pp. 248–255. IEEE (2009)
5. Drouard, V., Horaud, R., Deleforge, A., Ba, S., Evangelidis, G.: Robust head-pose estimation based on partially-latent mixture of linear regressions. IEEE Trans. Image Process. **26**(3), 1428–1440 (2017)
6. Fanelli, G., Dantone, M., Gall, J., Fossati, A., Van Gool, L.: Random forests for real time 3D face analysis. Int. J. Comput. Vis. **101**(3), 437–458 (2013)
7. Fanelli, G., Weise, T., Gall, J., Van Gool, L.: Real time head pose estimation from consumer depth cameras. In: Mester, R., Felsberg, M. (eds.) DAGM 2011. LNCS, vol. 6835, pp. 101–110. Springer, Heidelberg (2011). https://doi.org/10.1007/978-3-642-23123-0_11
8. Gu, J., Yang, X., De Mello, S., Kautz, J.: Dynamic facial analysis: from Bayesian filtering to recurrent neural network. In: Proceedings of the IEEE Conference on Computer Vision and Pattern Recognition, pp. 1548–1557 (2017)
9. Gupta, A., Thakkar, K., Gandhi, V., Narayanan, P.: Nose, eyes and ears: head pose estimation by locating facial keypoints. In: ICASSP 2019–2019 IEEE International Conference on Acoustics, Speech and Signal Processing (ICASSP), pp. 1977–1981. IEEE (2019)
10. Gustafsson, F.K., Danelljan, M., Timofte, R., Schön, T.B.: How to train your energy-based model for regression. arXiv preprint arXiv:2005.01698 (2020)
11. He, K., Zhang, X., Ren, S., Sun, J.: Deep residual learning for image recognition. In: Proceedings of the IEEE Conference on Computer Vision and Pattern Recognition, pp. 770–778 (2016)
12. Hsueh, B.Y., Li, W., Wu, I.C.: Stochastic gradient descent with hyperbolic-tangent decay on classification. In: 2019 IEEE Winter Conference on Applications of Computer Vision (WACV), pp. 435–442. IEEE (2019)
13. Huang, J., Shao, X., Wechsler, H.: Face pose discrimination using support vector machines (SVM). In: Proceedings. Fourteenth International Conference on Pattern Recognition (Cat. No. 98EX170), vol. 1, pp. 154–156. IEEE (1998)
14. Kazemi, V., Sullivan, J.: One millisecond face alignment with an ensemble of regression trees. In: Proceedings of the IEEE Conference on Computer Vision and Pattern Recognition, pp. 1867–1874 (2014)
15. Kingma, D.P., Ba, J.: Adam: a method for stochastic optimization. arXiv preprint arXiv:1412.6980 (2014)
16. Koestinger, M., Wohlhart, P., Roth, P.M., Bischof, H.: Annotated facial landmarks in the wild: a large-scale, real-world database for facial landmark localization. In: 2011 IEEE International Conference on Computer Vision Workshops (ICCV Workshops), pp. 2144–2151. IEEE (2011)
17. Krizhevsky, A., Sutskever, I., Hinton, G.E.: ImageNet classification with deep convolutional neural networks. In: Advances in Neural Information Processing Systems, pp. 1097–1105 (2012)
18. Kumar, A., Alavi, A., Chellappa, R.: KEPLER: keypoint and pose estimation of unconstrained faces by learning efficient H-CNN regressors. In: 2017 12th IEEE International Conference on Automatic Face & Gesture Recognition (FG 2017), pp. 258–265. IEEE (2017)
19. Martin, M., Van De Camp, F., Stiefelhagen, R.: Real time head model creation and head pose estimation on consumer depth cameras. In: 2014 2nd International Conference on 3D Vision, vol. 1, pp. 641–648. IEEE (2014)
20. Mukherjee, S.S., Robertson, N.M.: Deep head pose: gaze-direction estimation in multimodal video. IEEE Trans. Multimedia **17**(11), 2094–2107 (2015)

21. Ranjan, R., Patel, V.M., Chellappa, R.: Hyperface: a deep multi-task learning framework for face detection, landmark localization, pose estimation, and gender recognition. IEEE Trans. Pattern Anal. Mach. Intell. **41**(1), 121–135 (2017)
22. Raytchev, B., Yoda, I., Sakaue, K.: Head pose estimation by nonlinear manifold learning. In: Proceedings of the 17th International Conference on Pattern Recognition, 2004, ICPR 2004, vol. 4, pp. 462–466. IEEE (2004)
23. Rowley, H.A., Baluja, S., Kanade, T.: Neural network-based face detection. IEEE Trans. Pattern Anal. Mach. Intell. **20**(1), 23–38 (1998)
24. Ruiz, N., Chong, E., Rehg, J.M.: Fine-grained head pose estimation without keypoints. In: Proceedings of the IEEE Conference on Computer Vision and Pattern Recognition Workshops, pp. 2074–2083 (2018)
25. Sagonas, C., Tzimiropoulos, G., Zafeiriou, S., Pantic, M.: 300 faces in-the-wild challenge: the first facial landmark localization challenge. In: Proceedings of the IEEE International Conference on Computer Vision Workshops, pp. 397–403 (2013)
26. Selvaraju, R.R., Cogswell, M., Das, A., Vedantam, R., Parikh, D., Batra, D.: Grad-CAM: visual explanations from deep networks via gradient-based localization. In: Proceedings of the IEEE International Conference on Computer Vision, pp. 618–626 (2017)
27. Sherrah, J., Gong, S., Ong, E.J.: Understanding pose discrimination in similarity space. In: BMVC, pp. 1–10. Citeseer (1999)
28. Simonyan, K., Zisserman, A.: Very deep convolutional networks for large-scale image recognition. arXiv preprint arXiv:1409.1556 (2014)
29. Sutskever, I., Martens, J., Dahl, G., Hinton, G.: On the importance of initialization and momentum in deep learning. In: International Conference on Machine Learning, pp. 1139–1147 (2013)
30. Wang, H., Chen, Z., Zhou, Y.: Hybrid coarse-fine classification for head pose estimation. arXiv preprint arXiv:1901.06778 (2019)
31. Yang, T.Y., Chen, Y.T., Lin, Y.Y., Chuang, Y.Y.: FSA-Net: learning fine-grained structure aggregation for head pose estimation from a single image. In: Proceedings of the IEEE Conference on Computer Vision and Pattern Recognition, pp. 1087–1096 (2019)
32. Yang, T.Y., Huang, Y.H., Lin, Y.Y., Hsiu, P.C., Chuang, Y.Y.: SSR-Net: a compact soft stagewise regression network for age estimation. In: IJCAI, vol. 5, p. 7 (2018)
33. Zhang, K., Zhang, Z., Li, Z., Qiao, Y.: Joint face detection and alignment using multitask cascaded convolutional networks. IEEE Sig. Process. Lett. **23**(10), 1499–1503 (2016)
34. Zhang, Z., Hu, Y., Liu, M., Huang, T.: Head pose estimation in seminar room using multi view face detectors. In: Stiefelhagen, R., Garofolo, J. (eds.) CLEAR 2006. LNCS, vol. 4122, pp. 299–304. Springer, Heidelberg (2007). https://doi.org/10.1007/978-3-540-69568-4_27
35. Zhu, X., Lei, Z., Liu, X., Shi, H., Li, S.Z.: Face alignment across large poses: a 3D solution. In: Proceedings of the IEEE Conference on Computer Vision and Pattern Recognition, pp. 146–155 (2016)

Object Detection and Recognition

Chicken Detection in Occlusion Scenes with Modified Single Shot MultiBox Detector

Yunlong Zhang and Seiji Hotta[✉]

Department of Computer and Information Sciences, Tokyo University of Agriculture and Technology, Koganei, Tokyo 184-8588, Japan
s-hotta@cc.tuat.ac.jp

Abstract. In modern poultry farming, chickens live together densely. Using auto-monitoring will save human power and funds, and all basic tasks such as detection or counting can be finished automatically. However, different from typical object detection tasks, occlusion will happen in chicken detection and decrease the accuracy. Especially, the existence of cages and fences will influence the detection result heavily. In this paper, we propose a series of novel methods based on Single Shot MultiBox Detector (SSD), which can improve performance when used in the scene of chicken detection. Our proposal is composed of two parts: the modified attention module of Convolutional Block Attention Module (CBAM) and a kind of novel data augmentation. In addition, Distance Intersection over Union Non-Maximum Suppression (DIoU-NMS) is used in the post-processing instead of the original Non-Maximum Suppression (NMS). Experiment results show that the novel structure and data augmentation can improve the performance, especially in the scene of cages and fences.

Keywords: Object detection · Animal detection · Convolutional neural network · Computer vision · Occlusion handling

1 Introduction

In modern poultry farming, animals live together densely. Compared with traditional breeding methods, modern methods are more mechanized, automated, and need less manpower. Although the production efficiency has improved, the living environment of animals becomes worse than before. In the breeding of chickens, dense space and poor sanitary conditions make chickens on the edge of diseases, and they become potential factors affecting production efficiency. To provide a good living environment for chickens in modern farming, it is essential to understand the behavior and habits of chickens. However, checking each chicken manually is time-consuming and not practical. Therefore, using new object detection technologies to detect chickens automatically can save manpower, help improve the living environment of chickens and improve the welfare of poultry.

© Springer Nature Switzerland AG 2021
G. Bebis et al. (Eds.): ISVC 2021, LNCS 13017, pp. 561–572, 2021.
https://doi.org/10.1007/978-3-030-90439-5_44

Fig. 1. Occlusion with each other (left) and blocked by cages (right).

In recent years, the speed and accuracy of object detection are increasing with the development of computer vision technologies. Applications of object detectors are largely used in real-world scenes, such as traffic surveillance, industrial production, and science research. Some object detection techniques have already been used in studies of animals. Applications used in Animal detection [3] show that automatic detection can be used in wild animal observation. Basic tasks such as classification, recognition, and counting numbers can be done by the detectors.

However, the detection of animals suffers from crowding and occlusion frequently. Animals may always get together and impede each other or be blocked by something under real-world scenes. This problem will always happen in chicken detection, demonstrated in Fig. 1. The action of chickens, such as walking, running, or eating will impede others. As the example shown in the right of Fig. 2, the occluded chicken may sometimes be lost in the detection or be merged into others, and the accuracy will be influenced. On the chicken farm, chickens may get together behind a vast cage or fence, as shown in Fig. 1. The fences or cages will cut the image of the chicken into pieces, such as the example shown in the left of Fig. 2, this kind of occlusion will make detector difficult to extract the feature of the chicken and get a lower detection score.

Therefore, we propose novel methods for chicken detection based on the SSD detector in this paper. First, the attention module CBAM [15] is modified and merged into the SSD network. This modified attention module will highlight the information of the parts of objects, this is proposed to make the network extract more information of the occluded objects. Second, the DIoU-NMS [17] is adopted in the post-processing. It can remove the redundant results after detection and can keep more results influenced by the occlusion. Third, to deal

Fig. 2. Examples of detection mistakes in particular situations.

with the special scene of cages and fences, a kind of novel data augmentation is proposed to simulate the shape of fences and cages.

2   Related Work

2.1   Object Detection

The deep learning-based methods now dominate the object detection. For instance, single-stage detectors, such as SSD [9] or You Only Look Once (YOLO) [11] directly detect the object based on feature maps extracted from the main network. Two-stage detectors extract the region that may contain the object after the generation of the feature map, then carry out the second detection, such as Faster RCNN [12]. Some up-to-date object detectors have shown better performance but have more complex structures. Combining existing network structures or introducing structures from other fields into object detection is a viable method in the future.

2.2   Non-Maximum Suppression

Non-Maximum Suppression (NMS) is a post-processing algorithm, and it is the last step in most object detection algorithms. The objective of NMS is to remove the redundant detection boxes. Although a large number of redundant detection boxes can be removed by NMS, in the case of occlusion, two detection boxes belonging to two different objects but overlapping each other will face the risk of being removed. To deal with this problem, Soft-NMS [2] decays the detection scores of all detection boxes using a continuous function based on the Intersection over Union (IoU) value, then uses a fixed score threshold to keep the boxes that may be the correct detection results. Softer-NMS [5] uses a bounding box regression loss for learning bounding box transformation and localization variance together, then neighboring bounding boxes are merged during NMS by using the learned localization variance. In addition, DIoU-NMS [17] which uses the distance between detection boxes is applied in this work, it will be introduced later.

2.3   Attention Mechanisms in the CNN

The attention mechanism is first applied in Machine Translation and is largely used in the field of natural language processing. The attention module is a kind of network structure with an assistant mechanism that can highlight the key points of the information. It doesn't require much calculation and can combine with other structures easily. Some attention modules can be adopted to object detection or classification. For instance, SKNet [8] focuses on different reception field sizes and kernel sizes, a dynamic selection mechanism in CNNs is proposed to allow each neuron to adjust the receptive field size based on multiple input scales information. Squeeze-and-Excitation Networks (SENet) [6] is an attention network structure that channel-wise re-weights the feature by learning the interdependencies between channels.

Different from the SENet that only applied to the field of the channel, CBAM [15] uses attention mechanisms to focus on both the channel and spatial fields. Information of "where" and "what" can be highlighted using channel attention and spatial attention. The structure of the attention module in CBAM is shown in Fig. 3.

2.4   Pedestrian Detection

There are many works of handling the problem of occlusion or enhancing robustness against occlusion, many of them are based on pedestrian detection. The scene of pedestrian detection is in a street or town, so pedestrians are often blocked by cars or other obstacles, and pedestrians will also block each other. These occlusions make it difficult to extract features of pedestrians and cause miss detection.

For this problem, Tian et al. [13] present a model that the pedestrian area is segmented into pieces of blocks, different patterns of occlusion are presented as different templates by these blocks. These templates will be used to train a CNN classifier to detect each of them. This kind of part-based method is also presented in Noh et al. [10], the area of pedestrians is divided into several blocks and different templates of occlusion are set up. The detection is based on the single-stage detector, and the detection of each block is merged into the network. Finally, the state of occlusion is detected based on the template and the detection score of each block. Other methods solve the problem in the view of the loss function. Wang et al. [14] inspired by a magnet's characteristics, present the repulsion loss function that includes the attraction term and the repulsion terms. In this function, the attraction term makes the predicted box approach

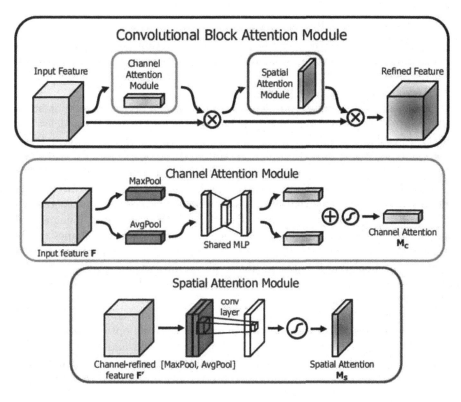

Fig. 3. The attention module in CBAM [15].

the designated targets, the repulsion term makes a predicted box keep away from other surrounding ground truth objects and other predicted boxes with different designated targets. In the work of Zhang et al. [16], the relationship between different body parts of pedestrians and the channels of the feature map is researched. And many channels show a strong correlation with different body parts of pedestrians in the experiment. Based on this finding, different attention modules are applied to generate the guidance of feature maps, and the guidance will highlight the information of visible parts of objects.

3 Modified Convolutional Neural Network

Our approaches include three parts. We build a detection network for chicken detection based on SSD using the modified CBAM structure described in Sect. 3.1. The method of DIoU-NMS is applied in the post-processing, and it comes from Zheng's work [17]. A brief introduction of DIoU-NMS is in Sect. 3.2. The data augmentation method for chicken detection is explained in Sect. 3.3

3.1   Network Structure

It seems that the problems faced in pedestrian detection are similar to chicken detection, both of them need to handle the occlusion. However, some differences exist between them and make the methods used in pedestrian detection hard to be fully adopted in chicken detection.

First, obstacles in pedestrian detection and chicken detection are not in the same type. As demonstrated in Fig. 4, people can be blocked by vehicles, but chickens are blocked by cages or fences with grid shapes. It may be easy to get a complete body part in pedestrian detection, but the obstacles with grid shape can cut the images of chicken into pieces and make the detection more difficult.

Second, chickens can change their shape in front of the camera frequently. Different from pedestrians that always appear in some fixed shape, *e.g.* standing or walking, Fig. 4 shows some shapes of chickens in the real world. Using a fixed template to present the pattern of occlusion is difficult, as many shapes can be shown in the real-world scene. Besides, different from pedestrian detection which can use some benchmark datasets, there are no datasets for chicken detection specifically. Without the support of large numbers of data, build a library of different templates becomes impossible.

Therefore, use an attention module that can be easily combined into other network structures as an assistant mechanism is a viable option. In this work, a new attention module structure modified from CBAM and used for SSD is proposed. We use the channel attention module and spatial attention module demonstrated in Fig. 3, and merge them into the network structure of SSD. The structure of this network is shown in Fig. 5.

We select SSD300 as the basic network of the chicken detector. Because the detection speed of SSD is faster than the two-stage detectors, and SSD has a simpler structure than some up-to-date detectors and the detection accuracy is still acceptable. In the 11 layers of the SSD network, lower layers have a larger resolution, but upper layers have more semantic representation capability. Thus, the characteristic of large resolution is combined with spatial attention, enough semantic meaning is combined with channel attention.

The structures of the spatial attention module and channel attention module are the same as the original CBAM. However, different from the original CBAM, spatial attention is generated from the last feature layers of each stage, start from Conv4_3 to Conv10_2, then used on the last feature layers of later stages, from Conv5_3 to Conv11_2. Channel attention is generated from the last layers of each stage, start from Conv11_2 back to Conv5_3, used on the last feature layers of previous stages, from Conv10_2 back to Conv4_3. Max pooling and full connection layers are used to connect attention maps and other feature maps because the mismatch of resolution and channels exists between each layer.

3.2   DIoU-NMS

DIoU-NMS [17] is used for post-processing in our approach. Distance-IoU is a kind of loss function based on IoU. It has a penalty term in the loss function. The penalty term can be defined as:

Fig. 4. Different shapes of obstacles (left). Different shapes of chickens in the real world (right).

$$\mathcal{R}_{DIOU} = \frac{\rho^2(\mathbf{b}, \mathbf{b}^{gt})}{c^2} \tag{1}$$

where $\mathbf{b}$ and $\mathbf{b}^{gt}$ denote the central points of two boxes, $\rho(.)$ is the Euclidean distance, and c is the diagonal length of the smallest enclosing box covering the two boxes. In DIoU-NMS, this penalty term is used combining with IoU values. The function of DIoUNMS can be defined as:

$$s_i = \begin{cases} s_i, IoU - \mathcal{R}_{DIoU}(\mathcal{M}, B_i) < \epsilon \\ 0, IoU - \mathcal{R}_{DIoU}(\mathcal{M}, B_i) \geq \epsilon \end{cases} \tag{2}$$

where $\mathcal{M}$ is the predicted box with the highest score, B_i are other predicted boxes, s_i is the classification score, and ϵ is the NMS threshold. The DIoU-NMS can keep the predicted boxes that have IoU values higher than the threshold but central points are distant from the highest score box. According to Zheng's work [17], experiment results showed that detectors using DIoU-NMS have better performance than those using the original NMS. The improvement of the average precision value is about from 0.05 to 0.35.

3.3 Data Augmentation

In chicken detection, fences and cages will sometimes divide the chicken images into multiple parts, which makes the extraction of features difficult. Shapes of most cages and fences can be presented as the shape of the grid. Therefore, to enhance the robustness of this scenario, the new data augmentation will simulate the shape of fences and cages. Images of the chickens are occluded by "drawing"

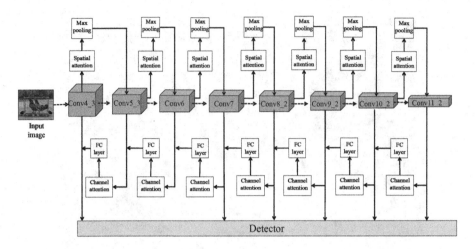

Fig. 5. The structure of the detector with the new attention module.

the grid, that is, adding the mask with grid shape on images. As demonstrated in Fig. 6, two types of grids are used. The first type uses black lines to form the grids and cover whole images. The second type turns the grids from the first type with a 45-degree angle. Five different widths (from 1 pixel to 5 pixels) are used to simulate the width of cages, and six different numbers of lines (from using five lines to using ten lines) are used to simulate the cage's density. The detector will adapt to the scene with fences and cages by combining the new augmented and original data.

4   Experiment

4.1   Datasets

We use the data collected from other datasets because no datasets are used for chicken detection specifically. We use the dataset of Chicken-Photos [4], Animals-10 [1], and the test dataset of chicken from Open Images Dataset V6 [7]. We filter three datasets and select 800 images. 300 images are chosen for training, 100 images for validation, and 400 images for testing. Among these 400 images, 100 images contain cages and fences are used for evaluation in the experiment of data augmentation. The rest 300 images are divided averagely into three different subsets. Three subsets contain three different levels of occlusion: strong, weak, and no occlusion. Three subsets are used for the evaluation of the modified CBAM structure. If chickens in an image are occluded by more than 50%, the image will belong to the "strong" subset. Otherwise, the image will belong to the "weak" subset. If no occlusion shows in the image, the image will belong to the "no occlusion" subset.

Fig. 6. Examples of black lines used in data augmentation.

Table 1. The experiment result of modified CBAM structure.

Method	SSD (baseline)	SSD+ DIoU-NMS	SSD+ original CBAM	SSD+ modified CBAM	SSD+ modified CBAM+ DIoU-NMS (proposed method)
No occlusion	99.4	**99.6**	**99.6**	99.4	**99.6**
Weak occlusion	89.7	90.8	90.6	90.6	**90.9**
Strong occlusion	68.2	67.8	67.5	**68.4**	**68.4**
All images	80.8	81.0	80.8	81.1	**81.3**

4.2 Experiment of Modified CBAM Structure

In this experiment, the original SSD 300 is set as the baseline method. The baseline method, SSD+DIoU-NMS, SSD+original CBAM, SSD+modified CBAM, and SSD+modified CBAM+DIoU-NMS (the proposed method) are trained for the comparison experiment.

We load weights provided by the official [9] and fine-tune the SSD network for the baseline method. The network is trained for 50k iterations, and the batch size is 8. In the training of other networks, the weights trained from the baseline method are used for fine-tuning, and only the attention module is trained. Other settings are the same as the baseline method. In the training of SSD+original CBAM , the connection of two attention modules and the usage of attention maps are the same as the original CBAM.

Average precision (AP) is adopted for the evaluation metrics, and the high AP score reflects high accuracy. The threshold of the classification score is set to 0.01, and the threshold of NMS is 0.45, which is the same as the setting in SSD. The experiment result is shown in Table 1.

Table 2. The experiment result of data augmentation.

Method	Baseline	SSD + Data augmentation
Chicken+fence	54.9	**60.6**

The best results are written in bold. All the methods get lower accuracy along with the occlusion getting stronger, this result shows the influence of occlusion exists indeed.

The method of original CBAM increases the AP score by a little compared to the baseline, and it gets a lower AP score when applied in the strong occlusion scene. The performance of the modified CBAM is improved in the strong occlusion scene, and it can also get the same performance in the weak occlusion scene. This shows the improvement of the new attention module. In addition, compared to the method of baseline+DIoU-NMS, the proposed method can get better performance in the strong occlusion scene due to the existence of the modified attention module. This shows that the enhancement of performance is not simply because of the adoption of DIoU-NMS, it is the result that both DIoU-NMS and modified CBAM work together. Some examples of successful detection using the proposed method are shown in Fig. 7. More results can be kept in the detection and sometimes more accurate results can be generated.

4.3   Experiment of Data Augmentation

The original SSD 300 is trained as the baseline method, and the detector trained by new data augmentation is used for the comparison experiment. The training of the baseline is the same as the experiment of the modified CBAM structure. In the training of the proposed method, newly generated images (800 images with two types of augmentations) are combined with the original dataset (400 images), 1200 images are used for training in total. Other settings are the same as the baseline method. We use the test dataset of 100 images that contain cages and fences for evaluation. The experiment result is shown in Table 2.

The best result is written in bold. The detector trained by the new data augmentation increases the AP score by 5.7. It's obvious that the new method can improve the performance of the detector when applied to the scene of fences and cages. This shows the new data augmentation can improve the robustness against the scene of fences and cages. Some examples of successful detection using the detector trained by augmented data are shown in Fig. 7. The new detector becomes more robust against cages, but still has more room for improvement.

Fig. 7. Examples of successful detection using the proposed method (the second column from left), and compared with the baseline (the first column from left). Examples of successful detection using detector trained by augmented data (the fourth column from left), and compared with original detector (the third column from left).

5   Conclusion

In this paper, we proposed a structure used for chicken detection. This structure contained the modified CBAM designed for the SSD network and DIoU-NMS used for post-processing. To deal with the occluded situation by cages and fences, we proposed a new data augmentation that simulates the shape of cages and fences. Our proposed methods showed their performance in experiments. In the experiment of modified CBAM, the average precision of the new structure was increased by 0.2 to 1.2 compared with the baseline. In the experiment of data augmentation, the average precision of novel data augmentation was 5.7 higher than the baseline. In the next step, the attention module can be established by combining the body parts of the chicken. Using the shape of fences generated randomly as data augmentation and join the training may bring greater robustness. We believe more research is necessary for the future about the application in this special scene.

References

1. Alessio, C.: Animals-10. Website (2019). www.kaggle.com/alessiocorrado99/animals10
2. Bodla, N., Singh, B., Chellappa, R., Davis, L.S.: Improving object detection with one line of code. CoRR abs/1704.04503 (2017). arxiv.org/abs/1704.04503
3. Gómez, A., Salazar, A., Vargas-Bonilla, J.F.: Towards automatic wild animal monitoring: identification of animal species in camera-trap images using very deep convolutional neural networks. CoRR abs/1603.06169 (2016). arxiv.org/abs/1603.06169
4. gunthercox: chicken-photos. Website (2017). github.com/gunthercox/chicken-photos
5. He, Y., Zhang, X., Savvides, M., Kitani, K.: Softer-nms: Rethinking bounding box regression for accurate object detection. CoRR abs/1809.08545 (2018). arxiv.org/abs/1809.08545
6. Hu, J., Shen, L., Sun, G.: Squeeze-and-excitation networks. CoRR abs/1709.01507 (2017). arxiv.org/abs/1709.01507
7. Kuznetsova, A., et al.: The open images dataset v4: unified image classification, object detection, and visual relationship detection at scale. IJCV (2020)
8. Li, X., Wang, W., Hu, X., Yang, J.: Selective kernel networks. CoRR abs/1903.06586 (2019). arxiv.org/abs/1903.06586
9. Liu, W., et al.: SSD: single shot multibox detector. CoRR abs/1512.02325 (2015). arxiv.org/abs/1512.02325
10. Noh, J., Lee, S., Kim, B., Kim, G.: Improving occlusion and hard negative handling for single-stage pedestrian detectors. In: 2018 IEEE/CVF Conference on Computer Vision and Pattern Recognition, pp. 966–974 (2018). https://doi.org/10.1109/CVPR.2018.00107
11. Redmon, J., Divvala, S.K., Girshick, R.B., Farhadi, A.: You only look once: unified, real-time object detection. CoRR abs/1506.02640 (2015). arxiv.org/abs/1506.02640
12. Ren, S., He, K., Girshick, R.B., Sun, J.: Faster R-CNN: towards real-time object detection with region proposal networks. CoRR abs/1506.01497 (2015). arxiv.org/abs/1506.01497
13. Tian, Y., Luo, P., Wang, X., Tang, X.: Deep learning strong parts for pedestrian detection. In: 2015 IEEE International Conference on Computer Vision (ICCV), pp. 1904–1912 (2015). https://doi.org/10.1109/ICCV.2015.221
14. Wang, X., Xiao, T., Jiang, Y., Shao, S., Sun, J., Shen, C.: Repulsion loss: detecting pedestrians in a crowd (2017)
15. Woo, S., Park, J., Lee, J., Kweon, I.S.: CBAM: convolutional block attention module. CoRR abs/1807.06521 (2018). arxiv.org/abs/1807.06521
16. Zhang, S., Yang, J., Schiele, B.: Occluded pedestrian detection through guided attention in cnns. In: 2018 IEEE/CVF Conference on Computer Vision and Pattern Recognition, pp. 6995–7003 (2018). https://doi.org/10.1109/CVPR.2018.00731
17. Zheng, Z., Wang, P., Liu, W., Li, J., Ye, R., Ren, D.: Distance-iou loss: faster and better learning for bounding box regression. CoRR abs/1911.08287 (2019). arxiv.org/abs/1911.08287

PoseTED: A Novel Regression-Based Technique for Recognizing Multiple Pose Instances

Afsana Ahsan Jeny⬛, Masum Shah Junayed⬛, and Md Baharul Islam$^{(\boxtimes)}$⬛

Bahcesehir University, Yıldız, Çırağan Cd., 34349 Beşiktaş/İstanbul, Turkey
mdbaharul.islam@eng.bau.edu.tr

Abstract. Pose estimation for multiple people can be viewed as a hierarchical set predicting challenge. Algorithms are needed to classify all persons according to their physical components appropriately. Pose estimation methods are divided into two categories: (1) heatmap-based, (2) regression-based. Heatmap-based techniques are susceptible to various heuristic designs and are not end-to-end trainable, while regression-based methods involve fewer intermediary non-differentiable stages. This paper presents a novel regression-based multi-instance human pose recognition network called *PoseTED*. It utilizes the well-known object detector YOLOv4 for person detection, and the spatial transformer network (STN) used as a cropping filter. After that, we used a CNN-based backbone that extracts deep features and positional encoding with an encoder-decoder transformer applied for keypoint detection, solving the heuristic design problem before regression-based techniques and increasing overall performance. A prediction-based feed-forward network (FFN) is used to predict several key locations' posture as a group and display the body components as an output. Two available public datasets are tested in this experiment. Experimental results are shown on the COCO and MPII datasets, with an average precision (AP) of 73.7% on the COCO val. dataset, 72.7% on the COCO test dev. dataset, and 89.7% on the MPII datasets, respectively. These results are comparable to the state-of-the-art methods.

Keywords: Keypoints estimation · Pose recognition · Person detection · Transformer encoder-decoder · STN · FFN

1 Introduction

Humans frequently use various forms of gestures framed with different organs to communicate their cognitive and emotional wellness. Correctly recognizing those poses will aid in observing the present mental and physical state of the individual. Thus, human pose recognition is receiving research attention in recent years. The pose evaluation was necessary owing to the difficulty in identifying human joints in photos or films (often known as the essential points - knees, arms, elbows, etc.). In addition to being a challenging area of research, human pose measurement is critical in many practical uses,

This work is supported by the Scientific and Technological Research Council of Turkey (TUBITAK) under 2232 Outstanding Researchers program, Project No. 118C301.

ⓒ Springer Nature Switzerland AG 2021
G. Bebis et al. (Eds.): ISVC 2021, LNCS 13017, pp. 573–585, 2021.
https://doi.org/10.1007/978-3-030-90439-5_45

including action recognition, pedestrian detection, medical imaging, human-computer interaction, animation, health, and sports, and others. However, pose detection is a complicated subject that has remained unsolved. Many factors contribute to the difficulties, including prominent position and size diversity, cross-body connection, considerable visual variance, and background complexity. Several methods for estimating occluded joints involve using statistical and topological approaches to address the difficulties associated with occlusion [19].

To solve this problem, researchers have found solutions to this challenge by breaking it down into smaller tasks, including assessing a single-person stance, assessing multiple-person poses, and determining the pose of a human in a busy environment. To complete these sub-tasks, few methodologies have been tested in prior studies. First, top-down techniques utilize a bounding box as an object detector to identify and focus on a single individual to maximize efficiency [23]. Following that, calculating the posture of a single person, whereas with a bottom-up approach, examine various independent semantics elements and put them together to form a single-person pose [7]. Several heat map-based methods [23,30] are used to implement complex key points identification, which is then followed by subsequent processes for clustering and grouping. Only a few research studies [24,28,32] have focused on regression-based techniques, primarily because regression-based methods often perform worse than heat map-based methods in terms of accuracy and precision. However, heatmaps establish a gap between the overall estimate of the key points cannot make an end-to-end learning framework. On the other hand, regression-based methods are still inefficient because of a significant number of heuristic designs of the architecture, computation efficiency, and it is challenging to detect keypoint in occluded scenes [18,28].

Toshev et al. [26] introduced one of the earliest regression methods named Deep-Pose using AlexNet as a backbone, then extended it to learn essential key points from pictures. Since DeepPose has shown such remarkable results, the human pose estimation (HPE) research community has moved from traditional techniques to convolutional neural networks (CNNs) because of the weak localization. In 2017, a regression-based method, namely LCRNet, was proposed to identify human pose in both 2D and 3D. One disadvantage of this approach is that the restricted number of anchors places a constraint on the network's ability to estimate new positions. Luvizon et al. [15] combine soft-argmax function and soft-plus (which produces vectors with equivalent joint coordinates) to provide an utterly differentiable approach for HPE. However, the convolutional features are misaligned. It also faced typical localization and quantization problems. Then, in [16], a single pose regression-based method based on a transformer and CNN was presented. The model assumes a series of keypoint locations utilizing CNN and transformer simultaneously. This method is inefficient since it causes design issues and is computationally costly. However, the design of all recently advanced model architectures is more complicated since it has many levels of complexity.

Contributions. Motivated by the above observations, a regression-based 2D multi-instance human pose identification technique is proposed to utilize the modified YOLO-v4 for person detection. The keypoints detection transformer is used for pose estimation. For the feature extractor of the image of the bounding boxes, we utilize the CNN-based three networks such as DarkNet-53 [21], ResNet-101 [10], and VGG-19 [22] by eliminating the fully connected layer. As a result, the total number of parameters is minimized from 44.6 million, 143.6 million, and 40.5 million to 8.2 million, 25.8 million, and 5.6 million, respectively. Furthermore, to mitigate the parameters, the computing cost is significantly decreased as well. We compare the proposed architecture to the available regression-based methods to ensure the proposed method is more robust. It shows the competitive performance in posture recognition while eliminating the need for heuristic designs and allowing for quicker and more accurate pose recognition. The following contributions are significant in this paper.

– A novel regression-based multi-instance human pose recognition technique is proposed based on a general-purpose object detector, which is end-to-end trainable with two networks and can solve several limitations using transformers with YOLOv4.
– For faster and more accurate person detection, the modified YOLO-v4 [2] object detection model is used, followed by a cropping filter and passing images through a spatial transformer network (STN) to crop in the original images. The cropped images are fed into a CNN-based backbone that uses to extract covariance features. This feature passes into the transformer encoder-decoder using positional encoding, which involves defining the location of an object relative to its bounding box.
– DarkNet-53 [21], ResNet-101 [10], and VGG-19 [22] are three well-known CNN-based modified backbones are utilized for deep covariance feature extraction and decreased parameters. A prediction-based feed-forward network (FFN) was also employed to forecast the pose of multiple key points as a group and depict the body components as output.
– The efficacy of the PoseTED is experimentally shown on two complex benchmark datasets: the COCO [14] datasets (COCO val set and COCO test dev set), and the MPII [1] Human Pose dataset. It significantly improves the state-of-the-art performance on recent advanced regression-based techniques and is comparable to the heatmap-based methods.

2   Proposed PoseTED

Figure 1 depicts the PoseTED model's architecture. It has four parts: a modified YOLO-v4 well-known object detector is utilized for human detection with the bounding box; STN is used for cropping filter, then a CNN-based backbone network is utilized for feature extraction of the image; then it is connected to the transformer encoder-decoder combinations, and finally, feed-forward networks are used to detect and locate long-range spatial interactions of the linear combination of classes, person keypoint coordinates, and ultimately visible of identifying key points.

Person Detector (YOLO-v4). Our method is used for a regression approach to solve the multi-person pose recognition issue, and we used YOLO-v4 [2], a well-known object detection architecture, as the detection method. It is chosen for this study because of its excellent accuracy and reliability, the speed with which it can be assembled, simplicity of implementation, stability, and promise of acceptable results even in minute details. We studied the impact of various network resolutions, detection accuracy, and transfer learning parameters on detection outcomes while improving the YOLOv4 model. The updated YOLOv4 person detector is shown in Fig. 2.

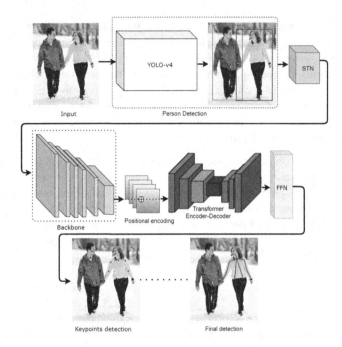

Fig. 1. The PoseTED architecture has been proposed. Here, YOLO-v4 is used for human detection with a bounding box. After detecting the person, the STN was utilized to crop the original image with the predicted boxes. Then, the backbone is used to generated in-depth features. The Transformer encoder-decoder with positional encoding works as keypoint-detection relative to corresponding bounding boxes. Finally, prediction-based FFN has predicted key points and displays vectors of body parts.

There are three main parts of this model: the spine, the neck, and the head. For reducing unwanted highlights, the spine is directly responsible. This CSPDarknet53 connection has been shown out to be an excellent choice. In [2], the yield is split into two portions: one is in the base layer and the other is in the reserved layer. One person heads to the Dense Block, while the other takes the following steps along the path as an exhibit presentation. Thick squares are composed of layers stacked on top of each other, with each subsequent layer beginning with Batch Normalization and ReLU, followed by a convolutional layer. A Dense Block layer is created by using all of the component guides from previous levels. That increases the area of the spinal column that may be accessed and aids in recognition of complicated image features. The concept of spatial pyramid pooling (SPP) [21] is used in neckbands to increase the acquiring field and provide interfaces that permit connections between different levels of the spine. A final portion has two parts; a classification head is placed on the object and assigned to the person or background detection, and a 4-channel regression head is applied for the predict and computed bounding boxes.

STN. After obtaining the detected pictures with bounding boxes, the STN [8] identifies the object as a person and predicts the bounding boxes to crop out the necessary portions

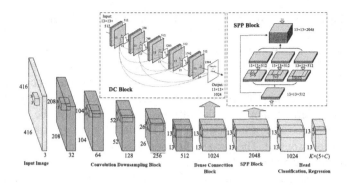

Fig. 2. The architecture of the YOLO-v4 person detector.

of the detected human with the bounding box. In the first step, STN selects the bounding box of the detected feature, rotates the area to normalize the posture, and then scales the cropped region before passing it to the CNN backbone. Feature maps and bounding box coordinates can be used to differentiate this cropping process. The grid $(w \times h)$ of the bounding box $(b = (x_l, x_r, y_t, y_d))$ is generated by,

$$x_i = \frac{w - i}{w} x_l + \frac{i}{w} x_r \tag{1}$$

$$y_j = \frac{h - j}{h} y_t + \frac{j}{h} y_d \tag{2}$$

where b, w and h are the original detected image's bounding box, height and weight of feature map respectively. And, (x_l, x_r, y_t) and y_d are denoted by coordinates of the bounding box in detected image respectively.

Backbone. The CNN architecture is often considered to be a backbone framework. The feature extractor in PoseTED's backbone extracts essential low-level characteristics such as body key points of humans. In order to arrive at more relevant comparisons, we have chosen three representative backbone designs, including ResNet, VGG, and DarkNet. Simplicity is essential when working with complex data sets such as images, and we thus maintain the first, pre-trained portion of the ImageNet CNN model as the initial layers to extract low-level characteristics from the input picture. After tuning these feature extractors, ResNet-101 [10], VGG-19 [22], and DarkNet-53 [21] are given to us as ResNet-P, VGG-P, and DarkNet-P. Compare to the three competitor backbone's parameters count are only 8.2 million, 25.8 million, and 5.6 million, respectively, representing 18.3%, 17.8%, and 13.8% of the original ResNet-101 (44.6 million), VGG-19 (143.6 million), and DarkNet-53 parameters, respectively (40.5 million).

Transformer Encoder Decoder. After getting the low-level feature maps of the CNN backbones, the detection of pose key points is used to the conventional architecture as the basis for the transformer encoder-decoder model with positional encoding [4]. There are six layers and eight attention heads in the encoder and decoder [27]. Reducing the size of the input channels by a 1×1 convolution is done in the encoder. The multi-head method requires sequential input; thus, the tensor is first downsampled and then compressed on the spatial dimension to one dimension. Because the transformer design is permutation-invariant, we encoded the picture as a fixed positional encoding to get the results we want. Instead, the positional encodings used by the decoder are known as object queries, and they correspond to the learned embeddings that we refer to as objects. Without permutation invariance, these queries will have to be changed when using the decoder because of the permutation. The decoder input is formed by adding them to the encoder output. The decoder first converts the queries to input embeddings before converting them to output embeddings. The poses are generated separately, and then the class labels and poses are decoded together to provide the final pose keypoints predictions and class labels. The resulting capability enables a query to find one instance, identify it, and forecast its posture keypoints and location.

Motivated by [5, 12, 34], we instead demand all decoder layers to anticipate the keypoint coordinates. The thing that we specifically allow is for the first decoder layer to guess the destination coordinates directly. Refining the predictions of each subsequent decoder layer helps improve the predictions of each preceding decoder layer. The key points then build on each other by becoming increasingly more nuanced.

FFN. After getting nuanced features from the transformer encoder-decoder, a 2-channel regression map predicts the coordinates of each key point. After that, the 3-layer perceptron with ReLU activation and a linear prediction layer estimates the final posture. The linear layer produces the class label using a softmax function, while the perceptron layer provides the center coordinate of key points. It produces an output consisting of the body component's respective coordinate and displacement values and the scores for every body part. The resulting vector is sent through a softmax classifier, which yields the class label. As a result, we made images normalize around their center and their offset from their origin.

3   Experiments

3.1   Dataset

MPII Dataset. There are around 25,000 photos of annotated body joints in the MPII [1] collection, covering more than 40,000 participants. The images were culled from YouTube videos depicting 410 different types of ordinary human activity. There are frames with 2D and 3D joint labels, head, torso alignments, body component occlusions in the collection, and frames with no labels. Another peculiarity of the MPII dataset is that it comprises frames from the prior and subsequent frames. However, they are not labeled.

COCO Dataset. It is the most broadly utilized enormous scope dataset. In our work, we used the COCO keypoints 2017 dataset. More than 200k pictures of the MS COCO keypoint dataset [14] in public, and more than 250k person instances are tagged with 17 human joints in this dataset. We train our networks using the COCO 2017 training dataset, which contains 57K pictures and 150K tagged human instances without using any additional data. We assess our networks' performance with the val2017 (5k pictures) and the test-dev2017 (20k images) datasets.

3.2 Experimental Setup and Training Details

To estimate human posture, we used a regression-based model. After detecting humans with the bounding box, cropped pictures of a single individual are provided in the training samples. All pictures are resized to a resolution of 384×288 and 256×192 pixels. As with [23], we used the same training methods and person's key detection outcomes. In the [31], they used to coordinate decoding method to minimize quantization error, which decodes detecting features from downsampled data, which is also used in our implementation. ReLU activates the function after training the feed-forward layers with 0.1 dropouts. Due to the ability to handle three backbones and the usage of the parameters, we configured the Transformer encoder hyperparameters in a way to avoid creating an excessive model capacity. To this end, thee stage networks are used throughout all of our studies. When throwing the forward pass, the time to execute is about 0.8–1.0 milliseconds on the Geforce RTX 2080 2080 GPU. When we compared the multi-view regression model's calculation time to the usage of the 2D detector, we can conclude that the computation time of our multi-view regression model is practically significant. For the COCO dataset, the Adam optimizer is used to train this model. To minimize error, first the learning rate at 0.001 is used, then exponentially decreased this rate to 0.0001. To conduct the validation of the MPII dataset, we randomly picked up 350 pictures from the training set to be used for this purpose. For the 300th epoch, all the single-person samples and the remaining training pictures are utilized. For extreme situations when centroids are overlapped, an offset is applied to significantly disrupt the centroids.

3.3 Evaluation Matrics

We utilized the well-accepted approach described in [23] and employed Object Keypoint Similarity (OKS) for the COCO dataset to assess the overall performance. For the MPII dataset, Percentage of Correct Keypoints (PCK) is used to determine the precision with which various keypoints may be located within a certain threshold. For each test image with the head segment length, the threshold is set to 50%, and it is marked as PCKh@0.5. The larger the PCK number, the greater the model's performance can be considered.

4 Results and Discussions

4.1 Performance on COCO Dataset

Table 1 shows the outcomes of several 2D pose detection techniques on the COCO dataset's validation dataset, as well as the description of the test parameters (approaches, backbones in models, input picture size, the size of parameters (PM), the GFLOPs network, and AP values). It is clear from Table 1 that our proposed approach PoseTED achieved more AP score than the popular TFPose (72.3 vs. 71) with the same input size 256×192. When the input size is increased to 384×288, our network outperformed others regression-based methods in terms of AP score (73.7%), particularly from Deep-Pose [26] (58.3%), PointSetNet [28] (65.7%), PointSetNet [28] (69.8%), and even from

Table 1. Comparing performance with other state-of-the-art studies using the COCO val. dataset. We compared the evaluation matrices to the backbones, input size, parameter size, and evaluation matrices.

Approaches	Backbone	Input size	PM	GFLOPs	AP	AP@50	AP@75
	Heatmap based approaches						
CMU-Pose [3]	VGG-19	-	-	-	64.2	86.2	70.1
Hourglass [17]	HourGlass-8	256 × 192	25.1M	14.3	66.9	-	-
CPN [6]	ResNfet-50	256 × 192	27M	6.20	68.6	-	-
SimpleBaseline [30]	ResNet-101	384 × 288	53M	26.7	73.6	89.6	80.3
HRNet [23]	HRNet-W32	384 × 288	28.5M	16.0	75.8	90.6	82.7
	Regression based approaches						
DeepPose [26]	ResNet-152	256 × 192	-	7.69	58.3	-	-
PointSetNet [28]	ResNeXt-101		-		65.7	85.4	71.8
PointSetNet [28]	HourGlass-W48	-	-	-	69.8	88.8	76.3
TFPose [16]	ResNet-50	256 × 192	-	9.2	71	-	-
TFPose [16]	ResNet-50	384 × 288	-	20.4	72.4	-	-
PoseTED	VGG-19	256 × 192	33.6M	13.8	68.2	88.7	78.6
PoseTED	ResNet-101	256 × 192	52.1M	19.0	70.5	89.1	78.9
PoseTED	DarkNet-53	256 × 192	52.8M	17.5	72.3	89.6	78.4
PoseTED	VGG-19	384 × 288	33.6M	17.0	71.4	90.1	80.3
PoseTED	ResNet-101	384 × 288	52.1M	23.2	72.1	90.3	80.5
PoseTED	DarkNet-53	384 × 288	52.8M	21.0	**73.7**	**90.5**	**80.9**

TFPose [16] (72.4%) as well as their backbone networks (ResNet-152, ResNeXt-101, and HourGlass-W48) are significantly larger than ours (DarkNet-53) except TFPose (ResNet-50). Furthermore, the PoseTED obtained higher AP scores than the famous heat map-based SimpleBaseline network (73.7 vs. 73.6) when the input size is the same as the SimpleBaseline network [30]. Moreover, in terms of 50 and 75% AP IoU thresholds, the performance of PoseTED is comparable with others.

Figure 3 depicts various qualitative findings from the COCO datasets, such as in the cases of walking, roller skating, basketball, exercising, inline skating, crossing, sitting, racing cars, and so on. It is seen from these instances that, although twisted postures have been observed among the public pictures, the estimates are still accurate enough. Identifying joints in limbs that are not adequately separated from one another and dislocate one another are examples of challenging circumstances.

Table 2 demonstrates the evaluation of the COCO test-dev set's performance with several regression-based methods such as DeepPose [26], CenterNet [33], Directpose [25], SPM [18], Integral [24], PointSetNet [28] and TFPose [16] are compared to our PoseTED as well as heat map-based approaches. As can be shown in Table 2, our PoseTED outperformed regression-based techniques such as DeepPose, Drictpose, and Integral while using the same backbone network and input size as the other two methods. Furthermore, it is also 3.3% and 0.4% higher than the heatmap-based methods such as G RMI [20] and Personlab [19], respectively, when the backbone network

Fig. 3. Various qualitative results from the COCO datasets e.g. in the case of walking, roller skating, basketball, exercise, inline skatin, crossing, sitting, racing vehicles and so on.

Table 2. Comparing performance with other state-of-the-art studies using the COCO test dev. dataset. We compared the evaluation matrices to the backbones, input size, parameter size, and evaluation matrices.

Approaches	Backbone	Input size	PM	GFLOPs	AP	AP@50	AP@75
Heatmap based approaches							
Mask RCNN [9]	ResNet-50	-	-	-	63.1	87.3	68.7
G RMI [20]	ResNet-101	353 × 256	42.6M	57.0	64.9	85.5	71.3
PifPaf [13]	Dilation ResNet-101	-	-	-	66.7	-	-
Personlab [19]	ResNet-101	-	-	-	67.8	88.6	74.4
Higher-HRNet [7]	HRNet-W48	-	-	-	70.5	89.3	77.2
DARK [31]	HRNet-W48	384 × 288	63.6M	32.9	76.2	92.5	83.6
Regression based approaches							
DeepPose [26]	ResNet-101	256 × 192	-	7.69	57.4	86.5	64.2
CenterNet [33]	Hourglass-2	-	-	-	63.0	86.8	69.6
Directpose [25]	ResNet-101	-	-	-	63.3	86.7	69.4
SPM [18]	HourGlass	-	-	-	66.9	88.5	72.9
Integral [24]	ResNet-101	256 × 256	45.0M	11.0	67.8	88.2	74.8
PointSetNet [28]	HourGlass-W48	-	-	-	68.7	89.9	76.3
TFPose [16]	ResNet-50	256 × 192	-	9.2	70.9	90.5	79
TFPose [16]	ResNet-50	384 × 288	-	20.4	72.2	**90.9**	**80.1**
PoseTED	VGG-19	256 × 192	33.6M	13.8	67.3	88.8	74.7
PoseTED	ResNet-101	256 × 192	52.1M	19.0	68.2	89.4	75.8
PoseTED	DarkNet-53	256 × 192	52.8M	17.5	70.3	89.1	77.7
PoseTED	VGG-19	384 × 288	33.6M	17.0	69.1	90.3	76.5
PoseTED	ResNet-101	384 × 288	52.1M	23.2	69.8	90.6	77.5
PoseTED	DarkNet-53	384 × 288	52.8M	21.0	**72.7**	90.4	79.2

(ResNet-101) is the same. When the input size is extended to 384 × 288 pixels, the suggested PoseTED with the backbones (VGG-16 and ResNet-101) beat all regression-based techniques, except TFPose. However, when the DarkNet-53 is used as a backbone with the input size 384 × 288, the PoseTED obtained higher results even from TFPose (72.7 vs. 72.2). Furthermore, our network has greater GFLOPs than other networks, suggesting that it is also more efficient.

4.2 Performance on MPII Dataset

Our proposed model PoseTED has achieved the highest performance among the regression-based techniques when tested against the MPII dataset in Table 3. When VGG-19, ResNet-101, and DarkNet-53 are used as the backbone in our network, 89.7, 88.2, and 89.5 PCKh@0.5 scores have been obtained through our proposed model PoseTED which is higher than regression-based methods such as Integral [24] and Carreira et al. [5]. The PoseTED with the backbone network VGG-19 is also 2% higher than the heatmap-based method CPM [29] and 7.3% higher than the method presented by Hu et al. [11] (89.7% vs. 87.7% and 89.7% vs. 82.4%). PoseTED is generally comparable to heatmap-based techniques in terms of performance.

Table 3. Comparing performance with other state-of-the-art studies using the MPII dataset. We compared the evaluation matrices to backbones, and other evaluation matrices.

Approaches	Backbone	Head	Sho	Elb	Wri	Hip	Knee	Ank	Mean
Heatmap based approaches									
Hu et al. [11]	VGG-16	95.0	91.6	83.0	76.6	81.9	74.5	69.5	82.4
CPM [29]	CPM	96.2	95.0	87.5	82.2	87.6	82.7	78.4	87.7
SBL [30]	ResNet-152	97.0	95.9	90.3	85.0	89.2	85.3	81.3	89.6
HRNet [23]	HRNet-W32	97.1	95.9	90.3	86.4	89.1	87.1	83.3	90.3
Regression based approaches									
Carreira et al. [5]	-	95.7	91.7	81.7	72.4	82.8	73.2	66.4	81.3
Integral [24]	ResNet-101	-	-	-	-	-	-	-	87.3
PoseTED	VGG-19	96.4	94.9	88.4	82.6	**90.2**	84.1	78.4	**89.7**
PoseTED	ResNet-101	**97.9**	95.6	89.8	82.6	88.6	**85.4**	78.4	88.2
PoseTED	DarkNet-53	97.8	**96.0**	**90.0**	**84.3**	89.8	85.2	**79.7**	89.5

5 Conclusion

In this article, we introduced a new architecture for regression-based multi-instance pose recognition called PoseTED. It eliminates the need for complicated pre-processing and post-processing techniques and employs less heuristic approaches than the prior methods. The PoseTED employs YOLO-v4 well-known object detector for person detection with a bounding box and STN for cropping the original detected picture. Following cropping, three CNN-based backbones (DarkNet-53, VGG-19, and ResNet-101) are used to extract deep covariance low-level features. Then, a transformer encoder-decoder with positional encoding is utilized to match queries of human keypoints included in the loss calculation. The prediction-based FFN is then used to identify pose keypoints and visualize them as a vector between human body joints, resulting in enhanced performance. The experimental results on MS-COCO and MPII datasets are tested and compared to the recent advanced approaches. The PoseTED outperforms all contemporary techniques that are state of the arts. However, when people are highly obscured in situations, it is difficult to estimate these scenarios using our method in certain instances. Therefore, to be implemented in the future, we would like to work on the previously mentioned limitations and try to make more powerful backbone networks to experiment with regression-based person identification and posture recognition to enhance flexibility.

References

1. Andriluka, M., Pishchulin, L., Gehler, P., Schiele, B.: 2D human pose estimation: new benchmark and state of the art analysis. In: Proceedings of the IEEE Conference on computer Vision and Pattern Recognition, pp. 3686–3693 (2014)
2. Bochkovskiy, A., Wang, C.Y., Liao, H.Y.M.: Yolov4: Optimal speed and accuracy of object detection. arXiv preprint arXiv:2004.10934 (2020)
3. Cao, Z., Simon, T., Wei, S.E., Sheikh, Y.: Realtime multi-person 2D pose estimation using part affinity fields. In: Proceedings of the IEEE Conference on Computer Vision and Pattern Recognition, pp. 7291–7299 (2017)
4. Carion, N., Massa, F., Synnaeve, G., Usunier, N., Kirillov, A., Zagoruyko, S.: End-to-End object detection with transformers. In: Vedaldi, A., Bischof, H., Brox, T., Frahm, J.-M. (eds.) ECCV 2020. LNCS, vol. 12346, pp. 213–229. Springer, Cham (2020). https://doi.org/10.1007/978-3-030-58452-8_13
5. Carreira, J., Agrawal, P., Fragkiadaki, K., Malik, J.: Human pose estimation with iterative error feedback. In: Proceedings of the IEEE Conference on Computer Vision and Pattern Recognition, pp. 4733–4742 (2016)
6. Chen, Y., Wang, Z., Peng, Y., Zhang, Z., Yu, G., Sun, J.: Cascaded pyramid network for multi-person pose estimation. In: Proceedings of the IEEE Conference on Computer Vision and Pattern Recognition, pp. 7103–7112 (2018)
7. Cheng, B., Xiao, B., Wang, J., Shi, H., Huang, T.S., Zhang, L.: Higherhrnet: scale-aware representation learning for bottom-up human pose estimation. In: Proceedings of the IEEE/CVF Conference on Computer Vision and Pattern Recognition, pp. 5386–5395 (2020)
8. Fang, Y., Zhan, B., Cai, W., Gao, S., Hu, B.: Locality-constrained spatial transformer network for video crowd counting. In: 2019 IEEE International Conference on Multimedia and Expo (ICME), pp. 814–819. IEEE (2019)
9. He, K., Gkioxari, G., Dollár, P., Girshick, R.: Mask r-cnn. In: Proceedings of the IEEE International Conference on Computer Vision, pp. 2961–2969 (2017)
10. He, K., Zhang, X., Ren, S., Sun, J.: Deep residual learning for image recognition. In: Proceedings of the IEEE Conference on Computer Vision and Pattern Recognition, pp. 770–778 (2016)
11. Hu, P., Ramanan, D.: Bottom-up and top-down reasoning with hierarchical rectified gaussians. In: Proceedings of the IEEE Conference on Computer Vision and Pattern Recognition, pp. 5600–5609 (2016)

12. Hu, T., Qi, H., Xu, J., Huang, Q.: Facial landmarks detection by self-iterative regression based landmarks-attention network. In: Thirty-Second AAAI Conference on Artificial Intelligence (2018)
13. Kreiss, S., Bertoni, L., Alahi, A.: Pifpaf: Composite fields for human pose estimation. In: Proceedings of the IEEE/CVF Conference on Computer Vision and Pattern Recognition, pp. 11977–11986 (2019)
14. Lin, T.Y., et al.: Microsoft COCO: common objects in context. In: Fleet, D., Pajdla, T., Schiele, B., Tuytelaars, T. (eds.) ECCV 2014. LNCS, vol. 8693, pp. 740–755. Springer, Cham (2014). https://doi.org/10.1007/978-3-319-10602-1_48
15. Luvizon, D.C., Tabia, H., Picard, D.: Human pose regression by combining indirect part detection and contextual information. Comput. Graph. **85**, 15–22 (2019)
16. Mao, W., Ge, Y., Shen, C., Tian, Z., Wang, X., Wang, Z.: Tfpose: Direct human pose estimation with transformers. arXiv preprint arXiv:2103.15320 (2021)
17. Newell, A., Yang, K., Deng, J.: Stacked hourglass networks for human pose estimation. In: Leibe, B., Matas, J., Sebe, N., Welling, M. (eds.) ECCV 2016. LNCS, vol. 9912, pp. 483–499. Springer, Cham (2016). https://doi.org/10.1007/978-3-319-46484-8_29
18. Nie, X., Feng, J., Zhang, J., Yan, S.: Single-stage multi-person pose machines. In: Proceedings of the IEEE/CVF International Conference on Computer Vision, pp. 6951–6960 (2019)
19. Papandreou, G., Zhu, T., Chen, L.C., Gidaris, S., Tompson, J., Murphy, K.: Personlab: Person pose estimation and instance segmentation with a bottom-up, part-based, geometric embedding model. In: Proceedings of the European Conference on Computer Vision (ECCV), pp. 269–286 (2018)
20. Papandreou, G., et al.: Towards accurate multi-person pose estimation in the wild. In: Proceedings of the IEEE Conference on Computer Vision and Pattern Recognition, pp. 4903–4911 (2017)
21. Redmon, J., Farhadi, A.: Yolov3: An incremental improvement. arXiv preprint arXiv:1804.02767 (2018)
22. Simonyan, K., Zisserman, A.: Very deep convolutional networks for large-scale image recognition. arXiv preprint arXiv:1409.1556 (2014)
23. Sun, K., Xiao, B., Liu, D., Wang, J.: Deep high-resolution representation learning for human pose estimation. In: Proceedings of the IEEE/CVF Conference on Computer Vision and Pattern Recognition, pp. 5693–5703 (2019)
24. Sun, X., Xiao, B., Wei, F., Liang, S., Wei, Y.: Integral human pose regression. In: Proceedings of the European Conference on Computer Vision (ECCV), pp. 529–545 (2018)
25. Tian, Z., Chen, H., Shen, C.: Directpose: Direct end-to-end multi-person pose estimation. arXiv preprint arXiv:1911.07451 (2019)
26. Toshev, A., Szegedy, C.: Deeppose: Human pose estimation via deep neural networks. In: Proceedings of the IEEE Conference on Computer Vision and Pattern Recognition, pp. 1653–1660 (2014)
27. Vaswani, A., et al.: Attention is all you need. In: Advances in Neural Information Processing Systems, pp. 5998–6008 (2017)
28. Wei, F., Sun, X., Li, H., Wang, J., Lin, S.: Point-set anchors for object detection, instance segmentation and pose estimation. In: Vedaldi, A., Bischof, H., Brox, T., Frahm, J.-M. (eds.) ECCV 2020. LNCS, vol. 12355, pp. 527–544. Springer, Cham (2020). https://doi.org/10.1007/978-3-030-58607-2_31
29. Wei, S.E., Ramakrishna, V., Kanade, T., Sheikh, Y.: Convolutional pose machines. In: Proceedings of the IEEE Conference on Computer Vision and Pattern Recognition, pp. 4724–4732 (2016)
30. Xiao, B., Wu, H., Wei, Y.: Simple baselines for human pose estimation and tracking. In: Proceedings of the European Conference on Computer Vision (ECCV), pp. 466–481 (2018)

31. Zhang, F., Zhu, X., Dai, H., Ye, M., Zhu, C.: Distribution-aware coordinate representation for human pose estimation. In: Proceedings of the IEEE/CVF Conference on Computer Vision and Pattern Recognition, pp. 7093–7102 (2020)
32. Zhou, X., Koltun, V., Krähenbühl, P.: Tracking objects as points. In: Vedaldi, A., Bischof, H., Brox, T., Frahm, J.-M. (eds.) ECCV 2020. LNCS, vol. 12349, pp. 474–490. Springer, Cham (2020). https://doi.org/10.1007/978-3-030-58548-8_28
33. Zhou, X., Wang, D., Krähenbühl, P.: Objects as points. arXiv preprint arXiv:1904.07850 (2019)
34. Zhu, X., Su, W., Lu, L., Li, B., Wang, X., Dai, J.: Deformable detr: Deformable transformers for end-to-end object detection. arXiv preprint arXiv:2010.04159 (2020)

Unsupervised Pixel-Wise Weighted Adversarial Domain Adaptation

Haitao Tian[1,2]([✉]), Shiru Qu[1], and Pierre Payeur[2]

[1] Northwestern Polytechnical University, Xi'an, China
htian026@uottawa.ca
[2] University of Ottawa, Ottawa, Canada

Abstract. Fully convolutional networks have been leveraged extensively in semantic segmentation tasks. While possessing demonstrated competency for dense prediction, such supervised learning networks are restricted to labeled data during training and hence show poor generalization while confronting unseen domains. As a pivotal transfer learning technique, domain adaptation aims to alleviate discrepancies between distinct domain distributions to improve the performance of generalization in unsupervised manners. Although a family of domain adaptation methods have demonstrated significant effectiveness on cross-domain semantic segmentation tasks, the overlook of pixel-wise domain divergences leads to over-adaptation. To deal with this problem, we investigate effective pixel-wise inter-domain discrepancy metrics to regularize the training of adaptation networks at a pixel-wise level. We first leverage generation confidence encoded from the output space as a weighting map to impose more adaptation emphasis on deeply shifted regions. Furthermore, we employ discrimination confidence on the feature space to refine generation confidence into a more reliable weighting map. The formulation of generation and discrimination confidence does not introduce additional computations over the fundamental DA framework. In our experiments, the proposed pixel-wise weighted adaptation approach outperforms state-of-the-art methods on two cross-domain segmentation tasks and demonstrates effective alleviation of over-adaptation.

Keywords: Domain adaptation · Semantic segmentation · Pixel-wise adaptation · Generation confidence · Discrimination confidence

1 Introduction

Even though fully convolutional networks (FCNs) recently dominated the field of semantic segmentation [1–3], such networks are generally trained using a huge number of pixel-wise labeled data, which precludes its application in practical scenarios, such as autonomous driving and robotic navigation, where collecting labeled data in changing scenarios with large appearance gaps is extremely expensive. Recently developed photo-realistic synthetic street-scene datasets [4] offer an appealing workaround by simulating various scenarios for supervised network training. However, an FCN pre-trained on synthetic datasets will generally fail on real-world inference, which is referred to as

© Springer Nature Switzerland AG 2021
G. Bebis et al. (Eds.): ISVC 2021, LNCS 13017, pp. 586–600, 2021.
https://doi.org/10.1007/978-3-030-90439-5_46

the cross-domain shift [5, 6]. This domain shift cannot be eliminated even with a large number of synthetic data.

The domain adaptation (DA) technique is recognized for its capability of transferring learnt semantic patterns from a source domain to a target domain without using labeled data from that target domain. Therefore, DA has been well leveraged into cross-domain semantic segmentation tasks between synthetic datasets (source domain) and real-world datasets (target domain). Early research [7–9] developed a discrimination network (discriminator) on the feature space to align domain distributions. However, feature-level adaptation is limited when decoding high dimensional visual cues that have been suppressed in the feature space [10]. To overcome this issue, alternative approaches [10–12] turned to utilize structural information on the output space and hence obtained promising domain adaptation performance.

Despite such advances, pixel-wise divergence on inter-domain discrepancy is generally overlooked in conventional DA works. For instance, as shown in Fig. 1, while clear domain shift exits in between two domains, the source-trained network still preserves a capability to correctly classify parts of the pixels that are originally exhibiting light domain discrepancy in the target domain. However, conventional domain adaptation methods would have negative effectiveness on such pixels while treating all pixels under a same degree of domain shift, thereby segmenting parts of lightly shifted pixels incorrectly.

In this paper, we propose a pixel-wise weighted DA scheme for semantic segmentation. We align the cross-domain distributions by interpreting pixel-wise inter-domain discrepancy amongst the target domain pixels, so as to deploy weighted adaptation regularization that allows domain adaptation to pay more attention to deeply shifted regions than to lightly shifted ones. As such, each pixel contributes differently and separately to the adaptation loss. Moreover, given the uncertainty associated with generation confidence on discrepancy indication, we introduce discrimination confidence from an auxiliary discriminator to refine the generation confidence with the goal of further improvements.

The main contributions of this work are: 1) a pixel-wise weighted domain adaptation approach, which leverages a synthetic-data-trained segmentation network more effectively when applied on a real-world dataset; and 2) an auxiliary discriminator on the feature space, which is trained to measure the inter-domain discrepancy in a different perspective.

2 Related Work

2.1 Semantic Segmentation

Fully convolutional network [3] based models have outperformed traditional non-CNN models [13, 14] in the field of semantic segmentation. For instance, FCN- based Deeplab v2 [1] and PSPNet [2] show state-of-the-art performance on semantic segmentation tasks. Meanwhile, the development of pixel-wise labeled datasets (e.g., PASCAL VOC 2012 [15] and Cityscapes [16]) made FCNs usage possible in supervised training setting. But when confronting cross-domain segmentation tasks, the domain shift across datasets degrades the performance of many state-of-the-art FCNs. Expanding the volume of datasets is the first attempt to deal with this problem. But collecting datasets with widespread variability that cover various testing scenarios is extremely time-consuming in the real world. As such, provided that the domain shift problem can be properly handled, FCN-based segmentation networks can alternatively be trained on synthetic datasets [4, 17], which are easily generated by graphics engines, and transposed onto real-world datasets and scenarios.

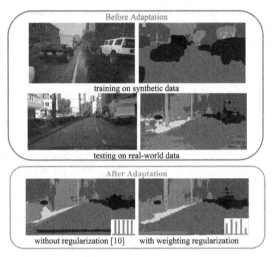

Fig. 1. Illustration of proposed pixel-wise weighting adaptation. **Top 2 rows**: samples from source and target domain (lft), a source-domain pretrained model for semantic segmentation inferred on these samples without adaptation (right). **Bottom row**: prediction results on target domain are improved by output-space domain adaptation method [10], while visible over-adaptation results (negative segmentations) exist (left). The proposed pixel-wise weighting adaptation method obtains comparable improvement while it alleviates over-adaptation (right).

2.2 Adversarial Domain Adaptation

Adversarial domain adaptation [6] has been successfully leveraged in cross-domain image classification [18, 19] and object detection tasks [20, 21]. When applied to semantic segmentation [7–12, 22–25], it embeds a discrimination network (discriminator) into FCN-based segmentation networks as an adaptation component. By imposing the DA operation, the segmentation network not only learns discriminative representations but also invariant encodings from different domains. Specifically, the DA model consists of a generator and a discriminator. During training, as a generator, the segmentation network interacts with the discriminator in an adversarial manner [26] by which the discriminator is trained to upper bound the source and target domains distributions. The generator then minimizes this bound to eliminate the discrepancy between two distinct distributions. With this adversarial training process, the generator manages to produce invariant-discriminative features, such that the segmentation network can be applied on both domains.

3   Preliminaries

In this section, we introduce mathematical preliminaries on supervised segmentation model settings and unsupervised domain adaptation settings, upon which we introduce the pixel-wise weighted adaptation approach in the next section.

The goal of domain adaptation for semantic segmentation is to train an FCN-based segmentation network on the source domain and transpose it to the target domain without supervision. To this end, we set a source domain $\mathcal{D}_S = \{(X_s^{[i]}, Y_s^{[i]})\}_i^{n_S}$, where $X_s^{[i]} \in \mathbb{R}^{W \times H \times 3}$ is the i th of n_S synthetic dataset images with a size of $W \times H \times 3$ in $\mathcal{D}_S$, and $Y_s^{[i]} \in \mathbb{R}^{W \times H \times L}$ is a corresponding pixel-wise annotation label with L categories. We also set a target domain in the same way, i.e., $\mathcal{D}_T = \{(X_t^{[i]})\}_i^{n_T}$, where $X_t^{[i]} \in \mathbb{R}^{W \times H \times 3}$ is a real-world dataset image. Note that there are no available labels in $\mathcal{D}_T$. For clarity, (X_s, Y_s) and X_t correspond to a random sample from $\mathcal{D}_S$ and $\mathcal{D}_T$ respectively in the rest of this paper.

3.1   Supervised Semantic Segmentation

For training a FCN-based segmentation network, a source domain sample (X_s, Y_s) is fed into a feature encoder F, then a dense classifier C takes high-dimensional feature encodings from F and produces a final soft-max probability distribution $P_s = C(F(X_s))$, where the structural prediction likelihood is $P_s^* = \max_l(P_s)$. The objective loss function is formed by the multi-class cross entropy with P_s and Y_s, formulated as:

$$\mathcal{L}_{\text{seg}}(\text{F,C}) = - \mathbb{E}_{(X_s,Y_s)\in\mathcal{D}_S}[\sum_{(w,h)} \sum_l I_{\left[l=y_s^{(w,h)}\right]} \log C\left(F(x_s^{(w,h)})\right)^{(l)}] \quad (1)$$

where $\mathbb{E}[\cdot]$ is the statistical expectation and ground truth label Y_s is correspondingly encoded into one-hot vector.

As for a target sample, $X_t \in \mathcal{D}_T$, the source-trained segmentation network under the parameter distribution of $\mathcal{D}_S$ can also generate a direct probability distribution P_t, while it would hardly reflect the genuine label distribution of $\mathcal{D}_T$ because of the presence of domain shift. Meanwhile the absence of pixel annotation in $\mathcal{D}_T$ does not allow for fine-tuning on the trained segmentation network.

3.2   Unsupervised Output-Space Based Domain Adaptation

Different from feature-space based DA models that embed a discriminative network on the feature space, the output-space adaptation scheme considers the entire FCN-based segmentation model as a generator ($G = C[F(\cdot)]$), and embeds a discriminator D at the end of G in order to take advantage of structural information available on the output space.

During training, the G and D are updated alternatively by adversarial optimization on binary cross entropy loss (2). In detail, the discriminator D is firstly trained to classify each element on the soft-max outputs P_s and P_t into its original domain label (we denote source domain label as 0, and target domain as 1), aiming to best represent inter-domain distribution discrepancy. D is updated with back propagation by minimizing (2), formulated as:

$$
\begin{aligned}
\mathcal{L}_{adv}(G, D) = &-\mathbb{E}_{\mathrm{X}_s \in D_S}[\sum_{(w,h)} \log(1 - D(G(x_s^{(w,h)})))] \\
&-\mathbb{E}_{\mathrm{X}_t \in D_T}[\sum_{(w,h)} \log\left(D\left(G(x_t^{(w,h)})\right)\right)]
\end{aligned}
\tag{2}
$$

During the discriminative network training, G is fixed for just taking part in the forward propagation.

Second, with the supervision from D, the generator G is trained to produce "source-style" soft-max output P_t to eliminate the inter-domain discrepancy. G is trained by maximizing (2), while D is only allowed for forward propagation in this stage.

Combining with supervised training using (1), the segmentation network G manages to generate discriminative and invariant distributions among pixels within the source and target domains.

4 Pixel-Wise Weighted Adaptation Method

In this section, building upon the conventional output-space DA model, the proposed pixel-wise weighted adaptation approach is introduced in two stages. It first investigates the use of the generation confidence to develop a pixel-wise weighting method for output-space based adaptation. Second, it employs an auxiliary discriminator on the feature space to measure the inter-domain discrepancy from a different perspective, which contributes to further improvements.

4.1 Generation Confidence Weighted Adaptation

In Tsai *et al.* [10], although the pixel-wise adaptation process is carried out by an output-space based DA network, each element on the output space is considered under a same inter-domain discrepancy. In other words, such an approach implements a global adaptation for each target domain sample without any consideration on the pixel-wise inter-domain discrepancy. To deal with the problem, the proposed pixel-wise weighted adaptation focuses on emphasizing precise regularization on the adaptation process by using pixel-wise inter-domain discrepancy.

From the perspective of self-supervised adaptation [27, 28], the structural prediction likelihood P_s^* for a source domain sample shows the segmentation confidence of an FCN when classifying pixels into correct categories. It further infers that, for a target domain sample, P_t^* indicates the generation confidence in the context of DA, which tells the confidence of a FCN generating distributions on the target domain that are consistent with the source domain. In other words, a large value in P_t^* corresponds to small inter-domain discrepancy as the generator can segment the target-domain pixel with high generation confidence. As such, pixel-wise inter-domain discrepancy could effectively be estimated by the generation confidence.

Based on the above observation, we introduce a pixel-wise weighted adversarial adaptation framework that minimizes distribution distance across domains on the output space according to the pixel-wise inter-domain discrepancy. We consider the pixel-wise inter-domain discrepancy as a weighting map to drive the adaptation model to pay more attention on deeply shifted pixels. To further protect well aligned regions from over-adaptation, we set the pixel-wise discrepancy to a small value, here empirically set at 0.01, on well aligned regions (where the generation confidence is higher than a threshold, T). As such, the generation-confidence weighting map $d^{(w,h)}$ is formulated as:

$$
d^{(w,h)} = \begin{cases} 0.01 & \text{, if } p_t^{(w,h)*} > T, \\ e^{-p_t(w,h)*} & \text{, otherwise.} \end{cases} \tag{3}
$$

The generation-confidence weighting map (shown on the upper-left of Fig. 2) allows domain adaptation to pay more attention to deeply shifted regions than to lightly shifted ones. Specifically, the weighting map $d^{(w,h)}$ is utilized to pixel-wise weight conventional adversarial adaptation loss (2). As such, each pixel contributes differently and separately to the adaptation loss. Following [11], we also employ a small adaptive weight (see details in Section V.B) to stabilize the adversarial training process. Hence, the proposed pixel-wise weighted adaptation approach can be formulated as:

$$
\mathcal{L}_{advl}(G, D) = -\mathbb{E}_{X_s \in D_S}[\sum_{(w,h)} \log(1 - D(G(x_s^{(w,h)})))]
$$
$$
-\mathbb{E}_{X_t \in D_T}[\sum_{(w,h)} (d^{(w,h)} + \mu) \cdot \log(D(G(x_t^{(w,h)})))] \tag{4}
$$

4.2 Discrimination Confidence Weighted Aadaptation

In this section, we introduce discrimination confidence to integrate with generation confidence for a more reliable adaptation weighting map. It is based on the observation that target domain pixels that are far away from source domain decision boundaries would be hardly interpreted by generation confidence due to the unreliable value of $p_t^{(w,h)*}$ generated by the source FCN on the output space. In this way, a part of the discrepancy-agnostic pixels would be wrongly weighted according to the second condition of (3). This factor influences the generation confidence in the adaptation procedure, which eventually is prone to over-adaptation on the target domain.

To handle the above problem, it is proposed to rather use an auxiliary discriminator D^{aux} on the feature space to estimate domain divergence from a different perspective. As such, a complementary regularization is introduced that aims to further refine the generation-confidence weighting map. Specifically, we first introduce a discriminator on the feature space of the FCN for distinguishing the difference grid of the feature encodings between source and target domain images. Second, we involve the discriminator D^{aux} into an auxiliary adversarial training with feature encoder F using the binary cross entropy loss, as formulated in (5).

$$
\mathcal{L}_{aux}(F, D^{aux}) = -\mathbb{E}_{X_s \in D_S}[\sum_{(w,h)} \log(1 - D^{aux}(F(x_s^{(w,h)})))]
$$
$$
-\mathbb{E}_{X_t \in D_T}[\sum_{(w,h)} \log(D^{aux}(F(x_t^{(w,h)})))] \tag{5}
$$

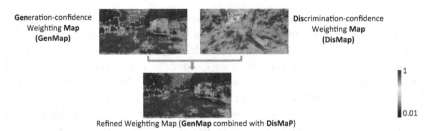

Fig. 2. Illustration of proposed weighting maps. The generation-confidence weighting map is encoded by the segmentation network that is trained on the source domain and tested on a target domain image. The discrimination-confidence weighting map is encoded by the auxiliary discrimination network that is trained on both domains. The two weighting maps interpret the inter-domain discrepancy from different perspectives. The combination of the two maps, Eq. (6), provides a refined weighting map for pixel-wise adaptation regularization.

In the auxiliary adversarial training, D^{aux} allocates a membership of the target domain, $D^{\mathrm{aux}}(F(x^{(h,w)})) \in [0, 1]$, to each feature grid. It further infers that the encodings of D^{aux} represent the confidence of a source-trained feature encoder when generating consistent-with-target distributions. As such, pixel-wise domain discrepancy in the target domain is estimated by the discrimination confidence as $D^{\mathrm{aux}}(F(x_t^{(h,w)}))$, from a different perspective. We also visualize the discrimination-confidence weighting map on the upper-right of Fig. 2. Lastly, the generation-confidence weighting map is refined by the discrimination-confidence weighting map, which is illustrated on the bottom of Fig. 2. The weighted adversarial adaptation loss is therefore updated as in (6):

$$
\begin{aligned}
\mathcal{L}_{advII}(\boldsymbol{G}, \boldsymbol{D}) = & -\mathbb{E}_{X_s \in D_S}\Big[\sum\nolimits_{(w,h)} \log(1 - D(G(x_s^{(w,h)})))\Big] \\
& -\mathbb{E}_{X_t \in D_T}\Big[\sum\nolimits_{(w,h)} (d^{(w,h)} + \mu) \cdot \boldsymbol{D}^{\mathrm{aux}}(\boldsymbol{F}(x_t^{(w,h)})) \cdot \log(D(G(x_t^{(w,h)})))\Big]
\end{aligned}
\tag{6}
$$

4.3 Network Overview and Optimization

The proposed pixel-wise weighted adaptation network is illustrated in Fig. 3, which is formed of three components: a generator $\boldsymbol{G}$, a discriminator $\boldsymbol{D}$ (embedded on the softmax output space) and an auxiliary discriminator $\boldsymbol{D}^{\mathrm{aux}}$(embedded on the final feature layer). The network training is carried out by the interaction between (1), (5) and (6), which are alternatively optimized according to the stages below:

- **Segmenter Updating.** The segmentation network is initially trained in a supervised way utilizing labeled source domain data $(X_s, Y_s) \in \mathcal{D}_S$. Parameters in $\boldsymbol{F}$ and $\boldsymbol{C}$ are updated by minimizing the loss function (1) as follows:

$$
\min_{F,C}[\mathcal{L}_{seg}(\boldsymbol{F}, \boldsymbol{C})]
\tag{7}
$$

- **Generator updating**. At this stage, unlabeled target domain data $X_t \in D_T$ are used to optimize the generator G and feature encoder F. Note that, unlike the previous stage, G and F are updated to confuse the D and D^{aux} by which the target-generated features and soft-max output will be considered as derived more likely from the source domain. The D and D^{aux} are fixed at this step, and G and F are updated by maximizing the loss functions (5) and (6) as in (8), where λ_{adv} is the trade-off weight used to balance the supervised training in (7) and adversarial training in (8).

$$\max_{G,F} \lambda_{\text{adv}} [\mathcal{L}_{advII}(G, D) + \mathcal{L}_{aux}(F, D^{\text{aux}})] \tag{8}$$

- **Discriminator updating**. Data and domain labels in $\mathcal{D}_S$ and $\mathcal{D}_T$ are used to update D and D^{aux} simultaneously to ensure the capability of distinguishing soft-max output and feature encodings respectively. At this stage, the F and C are fixed. The loss functions (5) and (6) are minimized as in (9).

$$\min_{D, D^{aux}} [\mathcal{L}_{advII}(G, D) + \mathcal{L}_{aux}(F, D^{\text{aux}})] \tag{9}$$

5 Experiments

In this section, the proposed method is evaluated on two classical synthetic-to-real semantic segmentation tasks. Meanwhile we analyze the results with qualitative and quantitative comparisons to the state-of-the-art.

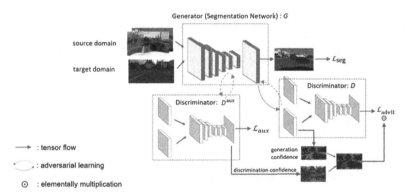

Fig. 3. A conceptual overview of the proposed weighted adaptation network. Entire network is composed of 3 different fully convolutional networks: segmentation (generation) network, G, and 2 discrimination networks, D and D^{aux}. The weighted adaptation is deployed through an adversarial learning with the pixel-wise weighting map.

5.1 Datasets

Cityscapes [16] is a real-world street scene dataset collected by dash cameras mounted on a moving car wandering in European cities. It contains 2,975 training images and 500 validation images, with high resolution (2048 × 1024), and pixel-wise labels in 34 categories of street objects. The training set (without labels) is considered as the target domain. **GTA5** [17] is a synthetic street scene dataset extracted from a realistically rendered computer game: Grand Theft Auto V. As rendered and annotated by a graphics engine, it forms a large dataset with 24,966 images with high resolution (1914 × 1052), and pixel-wise labels in 19 of the 34 categories of Cityscape. The entire image set with ground truth labels are used as the source domain in the task "GTA5 to Cityscapes". **SYNTHIA** [4] contains 9,400 synthetic images with 16 of the 19 categories of GTA5. The resolution of each image is 760 × 1280. While this dataset is also rendered by a graphics engine, it is less realistic than GTA5 and uses different viewing angles. That presents more severe domain shift that will challenge the adaptation capability of the proposed model. This dataset is used as the source domain in the task "SYNTHIA to Cityscapes".

5.2 Implementation Details

The proposed network is deployed using PyTorch on a NVIDIA GTX 1080Ti GPU. Following the settings in MRNet [12], we use ResNet-101 with memory module as the FCN backbone for generator G (the segmentation network). Discriminator D comprises four convolutional layers and a classifier layer with stride 2 and kernel size 4 followed by a leaky ReLU. The auxiliary discriminator D^{aux} comprises three convolution layers with stride 1 and kernel size 1 followed by a leaky ReLU, and a classifier layer with kernel size 1. Before feeding into D and D^{aux}, the encodings from output space and feature space are up-sampled into the input image size of $W \times H$.

The performance of the proposed method is evaluated under the metric of mean Intersection over Union (mIoU) proposed in [15]. During hyper-parameter learning, we first consider threshold T that is used to protect well aligned (high generation confidence) pixels from over-adaptation. Following self-training strategies proposed in [25, 27], we set T to 0.9 to involve sufficient well aligned pixels. In our best model, the adaptive weight μ is set to 0.1. We then consider hyper-parameter λ_{adv} as a trade-off for the supervised training in (7) and the adversarial training in (8). We follow [10] to set it as 0.0005.

5.3 Adaptation from GTA5 to Cityscapes

The overall quantitative experimental results over 19 classes are detailed in Table 1. The "Source-only" model (trained on data from the source domain (GTA5) only and inferred on the target domain (Cityscapes) reaches 36.6% on mean IoU. The proposed method outperforms the "source-only" model by 10.6% on mean IoU after imposing domain adaptation training. We also compare against the method proposed by Tsai *et al.* [10] considered here as a vanilla method for output-space based DA network. The proposed method brings a 5.8% improvement over [10] on mean IoU and demonstrates efficient

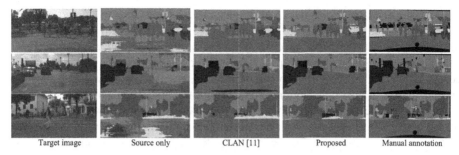

| Target image | Source only | CLAN [11] | Proposed | Manual annotation |

Fig. 4. Qualitative results obtained for semantic segmentation without and with domain adaptation. The third column is the adaptation results shown in CLAN [11]. The fourth column is the proposed pixel-wise weighted adaptation results, and the fifth column is the ground truth manual annotation.

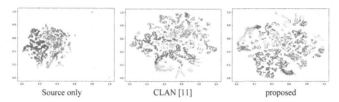

| Source only | CLAN [11] | proposed |

Fig. 5. Feature clusters visualization by t-SNE [34]. Each color represents a different class cluster.

alleviation of over-adaptation on several classes (e.g., "pole" and "bike") as a result of the proposed pixel-wise weighted adaptation regularization.

Besides, we also present experimental comparisons with three state-of-the-art DA models [11, 12], and [29] in Table 1. Luo *et al.* [11] introduce a weighted adaptation method based on a different discrepancy measurement. The proposed method outperforms [11] on mean IoU by a margin of 4%. It shows a more efficient adaptation operation under similar complexity of the model structure (i.e., two discriminators vs. two generators). Zheng and Yang [12] recently proposed an output-space adaptation method that introduces a memory module for semantic segmentation. Conversely, Pan *et al.* [29] utilize entropy information in the intra-domain space for adaptation operation. As shown in Table 1, the proposed method leads to further adaptation improvements for [12] and [29] in general mean IoU, demonstrating the complementary effectiveness of the proposed adaptation method on the conventional methods that were elaborated on different DA strategies. Nevertheless, the proposed method happens to underperform on some classes (e.g., "train" and "truck"). We infer that a possible unbalance may develop in the pixel-wise weighted adaptation when several categories are involved simultaneously, which deserves further investigation.

At last, we illustrate qualitative experimental evaluation of the proposed method. First, in Fig. 4, it can be observed that the "Source only" model experiences a severe drop on segmentation performance when applied on the target domain. Compared to the "Source only" model, the proposed method provides a clear improvement in the segmentation results. Second, in comparison to [11], there are visible improvements on specific classes in the segmentation results, demonstrating the adaptation capability of the proposed model on those classes. Lastly, we visualize the feature space encodings by using t-SNE [30] in Fig. 5. It reveals how the proposed method provides more separable feature clusters for the target domain, which facilitates the domain adaptation process.

5.4   Adaptation from SYNTHIA to Cityscapes

We next demonstrate the efficacy of the proposed method on the task "SYNTHIA to Cityscapes". As detailed in Table 2, the proposed method brings a 12.3% improvement over the "Source only" model compared to a 7.3% improvement obtained in [10]. It is also worth noting that the leading performance of [29] on mean IoU in the task "GTA5 to Cityscapes" is here surpassed by the proposed method and by [12], which indicates that, even though all three methods leverage different underlying principles, the proposed method could obtain a more reliable performance in both cross-domain adaptation tasks. Regarding specific classes, the proposed method outperforms [12] on seven classes, such as "sky", "person" and "moto.", and outperforms [29] on nine classes, such as "side.", "person" and "bike".

5.5   Ablation Studies

Three experimental ablation studies are conducted with respect to the two proposed weighting maps (illustrated in Fig. 2), to evaluate the efficacy of each component introduced in this work. First, we examine the generation-confidence weighting map when disregarding the protection of well aligned pixels by setting $T = 1$ (**GenMap**$^{T=1}$). As shown in Table 3, **GenMap**$^{T=1}$ provides an improvement of 1.0% on mean IoU compared to the DA method developed upon the baseline [12] only. It indicates that while the generation-confidence weighting map might be limited by the implicit uncertainty mentioned in section IV.B, it still remains capable to implement pixel-wise adaptation regularization. The ablation study also conducts domain adaptation based on the generation confidence weighting map with a lower threshold at $T = 0.9$ (**GenMap**$^{T=0.9}$), and on combined generation and discrimination confidence weighting maps (**GenMap**$^{T=0.9}$+ **DisMap**), under the experimental settings detailed in section V.B. As shown in Table 3, the adaptation model with **GenMap**$^{T=0.9}$ reaches mean IoU of 46.8%, which indicates that an improvement can be achieved through applying thresholding ($T = 0.9$). Furthermore, the combined adaptation model **GenMap**$^{T=0.9}$+ **DisMap** reaches 47.2%, demonstrating that **DisMap** is a valid complementary strategy to further refine the generation confidence to reach higher performance.

Table 1. Experimental results of the adaptation task "GTA5 to Cityscapes" under the metric of mean IoU.

GTA5 to Cityscapes-	Road	Side	Build	Wall	Fence	Pole	Light	Sign	Vege	Terrain	Sky	Person	Rider	Car	Truck	Bus	Train	Moto	Bike	mIoU
Source only	75.8	16.8	77.2	12.5	21.0	25.5	30.1	20.1	81.3	24.6	70.3	53.8	26.4	49.9	17.2	25.9	6.5	25.3	36.0	36.6
AdaptSegNet [10]	86.5	25.9	79.8	22.1	20.0	23.0	33.1	21.8	81.8	25.9	75.9	57.3	26.2	76.3	29.8	32.1	**7.2**	29.5	32.5	41.4
CLAN [11]	87.0	27.1	79.6	27.3	**23.3**	28.3	35.5	24.2	83.6	27.4	74.2	58.6	28.0	76.2	33.1	36.7	6.7	31.9	31.4	43.2
MRNet [12]	89.1	23.9	82.2	19.5	20.1	33.5	**42.2**	**39.7**	85.3	33.7	76.4	60.2	**33.7**	86.0	**36.1**	43.3	5.9	22.8	30.8	45.5
IntraDA [29]	90.6	37.1	**82.6**	30.1	19.1	29.5	32.4	20.6	**85.7**	**40.5**	**79.7**	58.7	31.1	**86.3**	31.5	**48.3**	0.0	30.2	35.8	46.3
Proposed	**91.4**	**55.1**	80.3	**30.6**	18.1	**35.0**	35.0	27.9	84.3	29.8	74.6	**60.9**	28.0	83.0	28.2	42.5	0.1	**35.8**	**48.9**	**47.2**

Table 2. Experimental results of the adaptation task "SYNTHIA to Cityscapes" under the metric of mean IoU.

-SYNTHIA to Cityscapes-	road	side	build	light	sign	vege	sky	person	rider	car	bus	moto	bike	mIoU
Source only	55.6	23.8	74.6	6.1	12.1	74.8	79.0	55.3	19.1	39.6	23.3	13.7	25.0	38.6
AdaptSegNet [10]	79.2	37.2	78.8	9.9	10.5	78.2	80.5	53.5	19.6	67.0	29.5	21.6	31.1	45.9
CLAN [11]	81.3	37.0	80.1	16.1	**13.7**	78.2	81.5	53.4	21.1	73.0	32.9	22.6	30.7	47.8
MRNet [12]	82.0	36.5	**80.4**	**18.0**	13.4	**81.1**	80.8	61.3	21.7	**84.4**	32.4	14.8	**45.7**	50.2
IntraDA [29]	84.3	37.7	79.5	9.2	8.4	80.0	84.1	57.2	23.0	78.0	**38.1**	20.3	36.5	48.9
Proposed	**85.1**	**41.2**	79.2	10.1	13.1	79.0	**85.6**	**61.7**	**26.6**	77.4	36.4	**23.4**	42.6	**50.9**

Table 3. Ablation studies in the task "GTA5 to Cityscapes".

Methods	MRNet [12]	GenMap$^{T=1}$	GenMap$^{T=0.9}$	DisMap	mIoU
DA without pixel-wise weighting	✓				45.5
Pixel-wise weighted DA ($T = 1$)	✓	✓			46.5
Pixel-wise weighted DA ($T = 0.9$)	✓		✓		46.8
Pixel-wise weighted DA (refined w/ DisMap)	✓		✓	✓	47.2

6   Conclusion

In this work, we propose a pixel-wise weighted adversarial adaptation framework. We first utilize generation confidence to regularize the output-space adaptation process at a finer level of details. Second, we introduce an auxiliary feature space based discriminator as a complementary discrepancy indicator to refine generation confidence, which contributes additional improvements on adaptation. The experimental results demonstrate that the proposed method is effective for over-adaptation alleviation and outperforms leading state-of-the-art methods for semantic segmentation. Future work will involve designing more efficient domain discrepancy metrics and combining DA schemes to improve the performance of the proposed method for application on cross-domain semantic segmentation.

Acknowledgments. This work was supported by the China Scholarship Council (CSC) under Grant: 201906290105, and by Natural Sciences and Engineering Research Council of Canada under the Discovery grants program.

References

1. Chen, L.C., Papandreou, G., Kokkinos, I., Murphy, K., Yuille, A.L.: Deeplab: Semantic image segmentation with deep convolutional nets, atrous convolution, and fully connected crfs. Trans. Patt. Recog. Mach. Intell. (PAMI) **40**(4), 834–848 (2018)

2. Zhao, H., Shi, J., Qi, X., Wang, X., Jia, J.: Pyramid scene parsing network. In: IEEE Conference on Computer Vision and Pattern Recognition (CVPR), pp. 2881–2890 (2017)
3. Long, J., Shelhamer, E., Darrell, T.: Fully convolutional networks for semantic segmentation. In: IEEE Conference on Computer Vision and Pattern Recognition (CVPR), pp. 3431–3440 (2015)
4. Ros, G., Sellart, L., Materzynska, J., Vazquez, D., Lopez, A.M.: The synthia dataset: a large collection of synthetic images for semantic segmentation of urban scenes. In: IEEE Conference on Computer Vision and Pattern Recognition (CVPR), pp. 3234–3243 (2016)
5. Tommasi, T., Patricia, N., Caputo, B., Tuytelaars, T.: A deeper look at dataset bias. CoRR, vol. arXiv:1505.01257 (2015)
6. Gong, B., Sha, F., Grauman, K.: Overcoming dataset bias: an unsupervised domain adaptation approach. In: NIPS Workshop on Large Scale Visual Recognition and Retrieval (LSVRR) (2012)
7. Hoffman, J., Wang, D., Yu, F., Darrell, T.: FCNS in the wild: Pixel-level adversarial and constraint-based adaptation. CoRR, abs/1612.02649 (2016)
8. Hoffman, J., et al.: Cycada: Cycle-consistent adversarial domain adaptation. In: International Conference on Machine Learning (ICML) (2018)
9. Chen, Y. H., et al.: No more discrimination: cross city adaptation of road scene segmenters. In: IEEE International Conference on Computer Vision (ICCV) (2017)
10. Tsai, Y.H., Hung, W.C., Schulter, S., Sohn, K., Yang, M.H., Chandraker, M.: Learning to adapt structured output space for semantic segmentation. In: IEEE Conference on Computer Vision and Pattern Recognition (CVPR), pp. 7472–7481 (2018)
11. Luo, Y., Zheng, L., Guan, T., Yu, J., Yang, Y.: Taking a closer look at domain shift: category-level adversaries for semantics consistent domain adaptation. In: IEEE Conference on Computer Vision and Pattern Recognition (CVPR), pp. 2507–2516 (2019)
12. Zheng, Z., Yang, Y.: Unsupervised scene adaptation with memory regularization in vivo. In: International Joint Conference on Artificial Intelligence (IJCAI) (2020)
13. Zhang, C., Wang, L., Yang, R.: Semantic segmentation of urban scenes using dense depth maps. In: Daniilidis, K., Maragos, P., Paragios, N. (eds.) ECCV 2010. LNCS, vol. 6314, pp. 708–721. Springer, Heidelberg (2010). https://doi.org/10.1007/978-3-642-15561-1_51
14. Tighe, J., Lazebnik, S.: SuperParsing: scalable nonparametric image parsing with superpixels. In: Daniilidis, K., Maragos, P., Paragios, N. (eds.) ECCV 2010. LNCS, vol. 6315, pp. 352–365. Springer, Heidelberg (2010). https://doi.org/10.1007/978-3-642-15555-0_26
15. Everingham, M., Eslami, S.A., Van Gool, L., Williams, C.K., Winn, J., Zisserman, A.: The pascal visual object classes challenge: a retrospective. Int. J. Comput. Vis. (IJCV) 111(1), 98–136 (2015)
16. Cordts, M., et al.: The cityscapes dataset for semantic urban scene understanding. In: IEEE Conference on Computer Vision and Pattern Recognition (CVPR), pp. 3213–3223 (2016)
17. Richter, S.R., Vineet, V., Roth, S., Koltun, V.: Playing for data: ground truth from computer games. In: Leibe, B., Matas, J., Sebe, N., Welling, M. (eds.) ECCV 2016. LNCS, vol. 9906, pp. 102–118. Springer, Cham (2016). https://doi.org/10.1007/978-3-319-46475-6_7
18. Long, M., Cao, Y., Wang, J., Jordan, M.I.: Learning transferable features with deep adaptation networks. In: International Conference on Machine Learning (ICML) (2015)
19. Saenko, K., Kulis, B., Fritz, M., Darrell, T.: Adapting visual category models to new domains. In: Daniilidis, K., Maragos, P., Paragios, N. (eds.) ECCV 2010. LNCS, vol. 6314, pp. 213–226. Springer, Heidelberg (2010). https://doi.org/10.1007/978-3-642-15561-1_16
20. Sun, B., Saenko, K.: From virtual to reality: fast adaptation of virtual object detectors to real domains. In: BMVA British Machine Vision Conference (BMVC) (2014)
21. Vazquez, D., Lopez, A.M., Marin, J., Ponsa, D., Geronimo, D.: Virtual and real world adaptation for pedestrian detection. Trans. Pattern Recog. Mach. Intell. (PAMI) 36(4), 797–809 (2014)

22. Sankaranarayanan, S., Balaji, Y., Jain, A., Lim, S.N., Chellappa, R.: Learning from synthetic data: addressing domain shift for semantic segmentation. In: IEEE Conference on Computer Vision and Pattern Recognition (CVPR), pp. 3752–3761 (2018)
23. Saito, K., Watanabe, K., Ushiku, Y., Harada, T.: Maximum classifier discrepancy for unsupervised domain adaptation. In: IEEE Conference on Computer Vision and Pattern Recognition (CVPR), pp. 3723–3732 (2018)
24. Li, Y., Yuan, L., Vasconcelos, N.: Bidirectional Learning for Domain Adaptation of Semantic Segmentation," in the IEEE Conference on Computer Vision and Pattern Recognition (CVPR), pp. 6936–6945 (2019)
25. Biasetton, M., Michieli, U., Agresti, G., Zanuttigh, P.: Unsupervised domain adaptation for semantic segmentation of urban scenes. In: IEEE Conference on Computer Vision and Pattern Recognition (CVPR) (2019)
26. Goodfellow, J. et al.: Generative adversarial nets. In: NIPS (2014)
27. Zou, Y., Yu, Z., Vijaya Kumar, B.V.K., Wang, J.: Unsupervised domain adaptation for semantic segmentation via class-balanced self-training. In: Ferrari, V., Hebert, M., Sminchisescu, C., Weiss, Y. (eds.) ECCV 2018. LNCS, vol. 11207, pp. 297–313. Springer, Cham (2018). https://doi.org/10.1007/978-3-030-01219-9_18
28. Zou, Y., Yu, Z., Liu, X., Kumar, B.V., Wang, J.: Confidence regularized self-training. In: IEEE International Conference on Computer Vision (ICCV), pp. 5982–5991 (2019)
29. Pan, F., Shin, I., Rameau, F., Lee, S., Kweon, I.S: Unsupervised intra-domain adaptation for semantic segmentation through self-supervision. In: IEEE Conference on Computer Vision and Pattern Recognition (CVPR) (2020)
30. Maaten, L.V., Hinton, G.: Visualizing data using t-SNE. J. Mach. Learn. Res. **9**(11), 2579–2605 (2008)

A Quantum 3D Convolutional Neural Network with Application in Video Classification

Kostas Blekos$^{(\boxtimes)}$ and Dimitrios Kosmopoulos

University of Patras, University Campus, 26504 Rion, Achaia, Greece
`mplekos@physics.upatras.gr`, `dkosmo@upatras.gr`

Abstract. Quantum computing seeks to exploit the properties of quantum mechanics to perform computations at a fraction of the cost compared to the classical computing methods. Recently, quantum methods for machine learning have attracted the interest of researchers. Those methods aim to exploit, in the context of machine learning, the potential benefits that the quantum computers should be able to offer in the near future. A particularly interesting area of research in this direction, investigates the union of quantum machine learning models with Convolutional Neural Networks. In this paper we develop a quantum counterpart of a 3D Convolutional Neural Network for video classification, dubbed Q3D-CNN. This is the first approach for quantum video classification we are aware of.

Our model is based on previously proposed quantum machine learning models, where manipulation of the input data is performed in such a way that a fully quantum-mechanical neural network layer can be realized and used to form a Quantum Convolutional Neural Network. We augment this approach by introducing quantum-friendly operations during data-loading and appropriately manipulating the quantum network. We demonstrate the applicability of the proposed Q3D-CNN in video classification using videos from a publicly available dataset. We successfully classify the test dataset using two and three classes using the quantum network and its classical counterpart.

1 Introduction

Quantum computing (QC) is using the as-yet-untapped quantum mechanical properties of nature, such as superposition and entanglement, to provide a new toolbox for computational problems. Such a toolbox is expected to provide great theoretical and technological advancements in the near future. A large number of algorithms have been proposed lately and are being investigated, while researchers are still trying to understand the advantages that a quantum computer has to offer.

Image processing algorithms are an important subset of algorithms where quantum computing is developing rapidly. Recently, in the context of image processing and computer vision research in general, there have been many interesting proposals for quantum processing techniques which employ fully-quantum,

© Springer Nature Switzerland AG 2021
G. Bebis et al. (Eds.): ISVC 2021, LNCS 13017, pp. 601–612, 2021.
https://doi.org/10.1007/978-3-030-90439-5_47

quantum-classical hybrids or quantum-inspired models [8,10–12,19,32]. On the other hand, to our best knowledge, the closely related subfield of video processing has not employed QC yet. During the last decade the deep learning methods have revolutionized the field of video classification using CNNs (see, e.g., [6,14,26,30]) or RNNs (e.g., [27,29,31]). The research question we tackle in this paper is how to exploit the benefits of QC using a CNN architecture for video classification. This is a very challenging task but there are already many directions that are being investigated [1,3,5,9,11,13,16,20–22]. A particularly interesting line of investigation is to directly translate neural network layers to quantum devices exploiting the better-understood methods of the classical ML algorithms [2,4,15,23,24,28].

To the best of our knowledge, there has been no work for video processing using quantum machine learning techniques. Here we propose an experimental setup and we investigate the quantum video processing prospects. Thus we test the applicability of a quantum 3D-CNN (dubbed Q3D-CNN) for video classification.

Our main contributions are:

- A quantum machine learning procedure for video classification;
- A comparison of the proposed Q3D-CNN to the classical 3D-CNN with the same structure, and
- An investigation of the scaling properties of the quantum algorithm, thus highlighting the differences in efficiency to known classical algorithms

2   Related Work

Many models have been proposed lately for the extension or enhancement of Neural Networks using quantum computing techniques [13]. Few of the proposed models for quantum neural networks aim to function in a way similar to convolutional neural networks so that they can be useful in computer vision. A non-exhaustive list of these relevant quantum neural network architectures include Quanvolutional Neural Networks [11], Quantum Convolutional Neural Networks [7], Quantum M-P Neural Networks [34], Quantum Competitive Neural Network [33] and more. Variational Circuits represent a very important class of hybrid quantum-classical algorithms [5] that also implements neural networks. A Variational Neural Network (eg [17,25]) is a parametrized quantum circuit, with the parameters been fed to a classical machine learning algorithm.

In [7] Cong et al. proposed a new quantum circuit model dubbed "Quantum Convolutional Neural Network" that could be used in signal processing. Their proposed quantum circuit model shares aspects with a classical CNN but can not reproduce in general the operations of a classical CNN and, therefore, can not be used to "translate" abstract classical CNN architectures to quantum.

At the same time, a more general approach was proposed by Kerenidis et al. [15]. Using the observation that an inner product estimation could replace the matrix convolution process of a CNN, they proposed a "hardware agnostic" method to construct a quantum CNN layer that can be used to build quantum counterparts of any classical CNN architecture. This model is presented in detail in the next section. Our Q3D-CNN builds on top of this model so that it can be used for video classification.

3   Methodology

The main goal of this work is to build a quantum 3D-CNN, in such a way that (a) it can successfully discriminate different classes of video input data and (b) it can do so in a more efficient way than the equivalent classical CNN. To this end we first employ quantum-efficient replacements for the classical components of the 3D-CNN as proposed in [15]. Then, we add a quantum process with no efficient classical analog that further boosts the efficiency of the QCNN.

3.1   Quantum Background

The whole point of "translating" a classical process to quantum is to try and take advantage of efficiency boosts that are offered by some quantum processes. Before describing these boosts and the way we use them, we will first briefly describe what it means to have a quantum version of a classical algorithm.

In a quantum computing process instead of using bits of 0 and 1 to store information we use quantum states of two levels (a *qubit*). These quantum states are 2D vectors of complex parameters and measure 1. A series of n quantum bits (often referred to as a *quantum register*) form a 2^n-dimensional vector of complex parameters and measure 1. The *computational basis*, then, is the one-hot orthonormal basis: $|0\rangle = \left(1, 0, \ldots, 0\right)^T, |1\rangle = \left(0, 1, \ldots, 0\right)^T, |2\rangle = \ldots\ldots$

The quantum states are manipulated by use of quantum gates which act as the quantum analog of the classical logical gates (AND, OR, NOT, etc.); they are represented by complex unitary matrices. By acting the quantum gates on the quantum states, we can rebuild the classical logical circuits. The key differences of the quantum-vs-classical can be derived from this vector-matrices representation and can be summarized as follows:

- We can form and then exploit interference patterns when combining complex vectors in order to get to a result more efficiently than what is classically possible. This inference-pattern-exploitation is what is sometimes referred to as "taking advantage of quantum parallelism".
- Applying unitary matrices on complex vectors is a linear and reversible process, therefore quantum computing is linear and reversible in nature; this forced linearity is a serious obstacle in implementing the many nonlinear processes of neural networks.
- A direct consequence of the previous point is that a quantum register (a series of quantum bits) can not be copied. This is a point that should be emphasized: there can be no physical way of copying a qubit. The exact complex parameters of a qubit are *unknowable*. Therefore, to extract the information from a quantum register one has to repeat the quantum algorithm while sampling the output.

When simulating a quantum computer, the output quantum state vector is obviously known. However, since the actual state is unknowable, when using a real quantum computer we can only approximate the output quantum state vector to an arbitrary degree by repeating the quantum process many times and keeping track of the distribution of the outcomes. This process is called *tomography* and has to be taken into consideration by inserting "noise" parameters into the simulation [15].

Another important issue is the conversion between classical and quantum data. Since the algorithms that we are concerned with deal with both classical and quantum procedures, a way to translate between classical and quantum data is needed. For example, the input image is initially stored in a classical computer but needs to be converted to a quantum state so that can be manipulated by the quantum CPU. A usual practice, and the one that we use in this paper, is to encode a classical vector by mapping its elements to the corresponding amplitudes of the basis vectors. So, if $v = (v_0, v_1, \ldots, v_n)$:

$$|v\rangle = \frac{1}{\|v\|} \sum v_i |i\rangle$$

Using this encoding, one can devise classical data structures (a "quantum RAM" (QRAM)) that provide efficient implementations for the crucial quantum state storing and retrieving procedures.

3.2 Quantum Convolutional Neural Network

We now turn to the implementation of the Q3D-CNN. The crucial parts of a classical CNN are the input matrices, the kernels, the convolution between them and the nonlinear activation function. Ideally, we would have an at-least-as-efficient quantum counterpart for each of these parts. We construct a quantum CNN based on the procedure in [15]. Our key differences are a) we are applying the algorithm to 3D volumes of videos instead of greyscale images and, most importantly, b) we introduce a quantum-efficient preprocessing step based on the observation that video classification heavily depends on differences between successive frames. This is a crucial step that significantly boosts the efficiency of the network as we will show.

The key observation in [15] is that the matrix convolution can be replaced by the quantum-efficient *inner product estimation algorithm*. The inner product estimation algorithm estimates inner products between two quantum vectors with high probability and high efficiency. To use the algorithm, the image and kernel matrices have first to be unraveled so as regions where matrix multiplication was to be applied, are now rows and columns where inner product operation will be applied. More specifically, a region $w \times h$ of the input image is converted to a quantum vector $|A\rangle$ and the corresponding $w \times h$ kernel is converted to a quantum vector $|F\rangle$. The inner product $\langle A|F\rangle$ is then estimated using the efficient quantum routine (Fig. 1). If the matrices are stored in a QRAM, the rows and columns can be directly efficiently extracted.

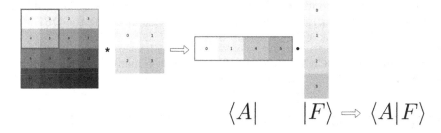

$$\langle A| \qquad |F\rangle \Rightarrow \langle A|F\rangle$$

Fig. 1. Converting matrix convolution to inner product operation.

The difference between successive frames can be calculated quantum-efficiently for vectors that are stored in a QRAM at the expense of using one more qubit (an *ancilla* qubit). For two successive frames f_0, f_1 we can form the following quantum stating using only two QRAM queries

$$|f_0\rangle |0\rangle_a + |f_1\rangle |1\rangle_a$$

Then, by applying only one quantum operation on the ancilla qubit and measuring until we find the ancilla qubit in state $|1\rangle_a$ we are left with the state $|f_0\rangle - |f_1\rangle$ which represents the difference between two successive frames.

To form all difference frames, we can either store the new state as the input frame and repeat the process for the rest of the frames, or, if the number of qubits is a cheaper resource, we can form all difference-frames with just one pass by using one ancilla qubit for each new frame (Fig. 2).

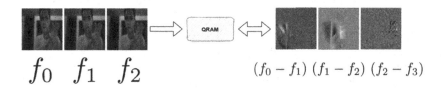

$$f_0 \quad f_1 \quad f_2 \qquad\qquad (f_0 - f_1)\,(f_1 - f_2)\,(f_2 - f_3)$$

Fig. 2. Process of calculating and storing the difference frames

The full algorithm, for a single layer, works as follows (see Algorithm 1; step numbers referred in Fig. 3):

1 Store into QRAM: the classical matrices that represent the input image layers and the kernels are stored in an efficient QRAM structure.
1A "3D" preprocess: Perform the difference operation and update the QRAM.
2 Unravel: from the QRAM we can efficiently extract quantum states that represent regions of the input image layers as rows and the kernels as columns.
3 Inner Product Estimation: Using the inner product estimation algorithm we construct a state that is proportional to the inner product of the rows and columns of the previous step. This represents the convolution of the initial input images and kernels.

4 Activation function and QRAM update: A final step applies a classical non-
linear activation function to the inner product while updating the QRAM by
sampling the output of the previous step.

The next layer of a QCNN loops back from step 2 as many times as there are
layers to the CNN.

Algorithm 1. Q3D-CNN layers

QRAM ← (video, kernels)
Perform difference operation → QRAM
repeat
    Unravel and perform Inner Product Estimation
    Perform the classical operations while updating the QRAM
until no more layers

---

4 Experimental Evaluation

We now describe an implementation of the Q3D-CNN that showcases the network performance and the accuracy advantage that the difference-operation provides. In the following we describe the dataset, the network architectures and
report the respective classification results.

Dataset and Pre-processing. We evaluate our Q3D-CNN using a small subset of the publicly available *20BN-jester Dataset V1*, containing labeled video
clips showing humans performing predefined hand gestures [18]. The full dataset
contains about 150000 video samples split in 27 classes. Each video has a height
of 100 pixels and variable width of the same order. The average duration of each
video sample is around 36 frames at 12 fps. To be able to perform the training
simulations at a reasonable time we used only a small part of the dataset and we
reduced those videos both in dimensions and duration. We cropped and downscaled each image keeping only the Red channel (see Table 1). The rationale for
keeping the Red channel—instead of the more commonly kept Green channel—is
that the skin is usually brightest on the Red channel making it more appropriate
for our target application.

    We perform experiments with two and three of the available classes for train-
ing. Preliminary runs have shown that the method scales well for more classes
in terms of accuracy but greatly increases the simulation times so we opted for
the smaller classes as proof-of-concept work.

Network Architecture. We trained four different networks for two versions
of the dataset as shown in Table 2. For each dataset, comprised by two or three
classes, we run the classical and quantum CNN with or without the 3D pre-
processing step. Different input sizes where tried with similar results. We only
present here the smaller (32×32)-sized datasets, as these better highlight the
accuracy advantage given by the 3D step.

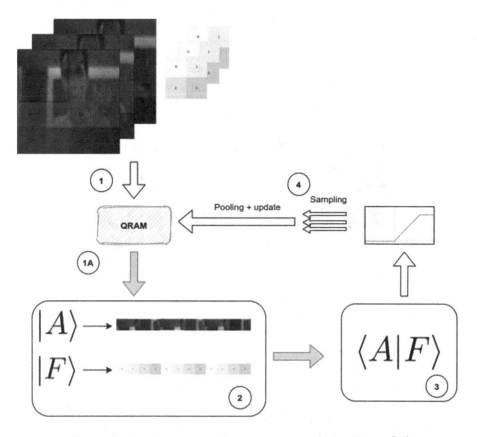

Fig. 3. Graphical summary of a quantum convolutional layer [15]

The network architecture, common among all instances, was kept as simple as possible so as the results can be as comparable as possible though, as already noted, a truly direct comparison cannot be made. We used two convolutional layers with 8×8 kernels followed by two fully connected layers and one output layer. The activation function is a capped ReLu [15] with a cap at 10.

Training. Both the classical and quantum networks were trained for 200 epochs using a simple backpropagation algorithm with learning rate of 0.01. We use the quantum version of the backpropagation algorithm as described by [15].

Simulation and simulation parameters. Since there are as yet no real quantum computer implementations, the quantum processes have to be simulated on a classical computer. The simulation requires sampling of the output of the quantum processes as described in Sect. 3.1. This greatly affects the accuracy of the network and execution speed. It is obvious that until there is a real quantum computing device to run the quantum algorithms on, the evaluation of the algorithms is incomplete at best. For a more complete discussion of the simulation parameters we refer the reader to [15].

Table 1. The reduced 20BN-Jester dataset.

Label	Videos	Image size	Frames
Swipe Left	250	32×32	16
Swipe Right	250	32×32	16
Turning Hand Clockwise	250	32×32	16

Fig. 4. Sample frames for the classes of "Swipe Left" (top row), "Turning Hand CLockwise" (middle row) and "Swipe Down" (bottom row).

Results. We evaluate the performance of the Q3D-CNN in terms of prediction accuracy and run-time efficiency. Since we can not directly compare training efficient and run-times— as quantum devices for tasks like this don't yet exist— we report the calculated complexity of the networks. We compare each of the four networks' performance (CNN, 3D-CNN, QCNN and Q3D-CNN) for each dataset (2 & 3 classes) (Table 2). The corresponding confusion matrices are shown in Table 3.

We see that the best accuracy was achieved by the 3D-CNN at 87% for 2 classes and 72% for three classes. The accuracies for the Q3D-CNN where very similar to the classical with 83% and 67% respectively. The non-3D versions of both networks achieved, as was expected, significantly lower accuracy values, validating the use of the "3D" post-processing for improving the network's performance.

In terms of network complexity, we highlight the difference in efficiency between the classical and quantum "3D" post-processing operation. We notate $\tilde{O}_C$ and $\tilde{O}_Q$ the base classical and quantum network complexities respectively. In general, $\tilde{O}_C$ depends on the kernel and input image sizes quadratically, while $\tilde{O}_Q$ depends on the kernel and input image sizes almost linearly. For a more detailed analysis of $\tilde{O}_Q$ see [15]. The "3D" operation, on the other hand, has a complexity of $O(\text{size})$ for the classical case but a complexity of $O(1)$ for the quantum case, as the depth of the quantum circuit needed to perform the operation is constant.

Table 2. Comparison of accuracy and one-layer-complexity for the various classical and quantum networks.

Network	Classes	Accuracy	Complexity
CNN	2	0.69	$\tilde{O}_C$
	3	0.49	
QCNN	2	0.73	$\tilde{O}_Q$
	3	0.58	
3D-simulated CNN	2	0.87	$O(\text{size}) + \tilde{O}_C$
	3	0.72	
Q3D-CNN	2	0.83	$O(1) + \tilde{O}_Q$
	3	0.67	

Table 3. Confusion matrices for 2- and 3-class datasets and all networks. A = "Swiping Left", B = "Swiping Down", C = "Turning Hand Clockwise"

CNN	Predicted	
	A	C
True A	0.30	0.16
True C	0.15	0.39

CNN	Predicted		
	A	B	C
True A	0.10	0.06	0.15
True B	0.00	0.17	0.15
True C	0.04	0.11	0.22

QCNN	Predicted	
	A	C
True A	0.25	0.23
True C	0.04	0.48

QCNN	Predicted		
	A	B	C
True A	0.17	0.08	0.07
True B	0.02	0.22	0.11
True C	0.07	0.08	0.19

3D-CNN	Predicted	
	A	C
True A	0.43	0.06
True C	0.06	0.44

3D-CNN	Predicted		
	A	B	C
True A	0.23	0.03	0.03
True B	0.02	0.22	0.09
True C	0.03	0.08	0.27

Q3D-CNN	Predicted	
	A	C
True A	0.38	0.11
True C	0.06	0.45

Q3D-CNN	Predicted		
	A	B	C
True A	0.20	0.05	0.04
True B	0.03	0.21	0.10
True C	0.03	0.08	0.26

5 Discussion and Conclusion

We presented a convolutional neural network architecture built using quantum processes that is able to discriminate between different classes of videos with comparable accuracy to the classical counterpart but with higher efficiency. This is the first approach for quantum video classification we are aware of. It is based on quantum-efficiently calculating the difference between successive video frames and then training a quantum convolutional neural network by replacing the convolution operation with a quantum inner product estimation [15].

The classification performance of the Q3D-CNN appears to be lower compared to the classical one. However, the trade-off between accuracy and efficiency that our Q3D-CNN offers, appears to be an option worth considering, especially in the context of time-critical applications. We should note here that the Q3D-CNN becomes more efficient, compared to the 3D-CNN, as the kernel and layer size increase, meaning that it could provide an attractive starting point for quantum video processing.

Furthermore, the process of calculating the difference between the successive video frames provides two advantages. Firstly, it significantly boosts the prediction accuracy in both networks (59% mean to 80% for the classical networks and 66% to 79% for the quantum versions). Secondly it is a very quantum-efficient operation requiring only a constant number of quantum operations to perform—independently of the input size— at the expense of a few more qubits. This capability is only found in the quantum version and has no efficient classical analog.

Acknowledgment. This research has been co-financed by the European Regional Development Fund of the European Union and Greek national funds through the Operational Program "Competitiveness, Entrepreneurship and Innovation", under the call "RESEARCH - CREATE - INNOVATE" (project code:T2EDK-00982).

References

1. Adcock, J.,et al.: Advances in quantum machine learning. arXiv:1512.02900 December 2015
2. Allcock, J., Hsieh, C.Y., Kerenidis, I., Zhang, S.: Quantum Algorithms for Feedforward Neural Networks. ACM Trans. Quant. Comput. **1**(1), 6:1–6:24 (2020). https://doi.org/10.1145/3411466
3. Allcock, J., Zhang, S.: Quantum machine learning. Nat. Sci. Rev. **6**(1), 26–28 (2019). https://doi.org/10.1093/nsr/nwy149
4. Behrman, E.C., Nash, L.R., Steck, J.E., Chandrashekar, V.G., Skinner, S.R.: Simulations of quantum neural networks. Inf. Sci. **128**(3), 257–269 (2000). https://doi.org/10.1016/S0020-0255(00)00056-6
5. Cerezo, M., et al.: Variational quantum algorithms. arXiv:2012.09265 (2020)
6. Chatzis, S.P., Kosmopoulos, D.: A nonparametric bayesian approach toward stacked convolutional independent component analysis. In: Proceedings of the IEEE International Conference on Computer Vision (ICCV), December 2015

7. Cong, I., Choi, S., Lukin, M.D.: Quantum convolutional neural networks. Nat. Phys. **15**(12), 1273–1278 (2019). https://doi.org/10.1038/s41567-019-0648-8
8. Dang, Y., Jiang, N., Hu, H., Ji, Z., Zhang, W.: Image classification based on quantum k-nearest-neighbor algorithm. Quantum Inf. Process. **17**(9), 1–18 (2018). https://doi.org/10.1007/s11128-018-2004-9
9. Garg, S., Ramakrishnan, G.: Advances in quantum deep learning: an overview. arXiv:2005.04316 May 2020
10. Gawron, P., Lewiński, S.: Multi-spectral image classification with quantum neural network. In: IGARSS 2020–2020 IEEE International Geoscience and Remote Sensing Symposium, pp. 3513–3516, September 2020. https://doi.org/10.1109/IGARSS39084.2020.9323065
11. Henderson, M., Shakya, S., Pradhan, S., Cook, T.: Quanvolutional neural networks: powering image recognition with quantum circuits. Quantum Mach. Intell. **2**(1), 1–9 (2020). https://doi.org/10.1007/s42484-020-00012-y
12. Hernández, H.I.G., Ruiz, R.T., Sun, G.H.: Image classification via quantum machine learning. arXiv:2011.02831 December 2020
13. Jeswal, S.K., Chakraverty, S.: Recent developments and applications in quantum neural network: a review. Arch. Comput. Methods Eng. **26**(4), 793–807 (2018). https://doi.org/10.1007/s11831-018-9269-0
14. Karpathy, A., Toderici, G., Shetty, S., Leung, T., Sukthankar, R., Fei-Fei, L.: Large-scale video classification with convolutional neural networks. In: Proceedings of the IEEE Conference on Computer Vision and Pattern Recognition (CVPR), June 2014
15. Kerenidis, I., Landman, J., Prakash, A.: Quantum algorithms for deep convolutional neural networks. In: International Conference on Learning Representations, September 2019
16. Kulkarni, V., Kulkarni, M., Pant, A.: Quantum computing methods for supervised learning. arXiv:2006.12025 June 2020
17. Lockwood, O., Si, M.: Reinforcement learning with quantum variational circuits. arXiv:2008.07524 August 2020
18. Materzynska, J., Berger, G., Bax, I., Memisevic, R.: The jester dataset: A large-scale video dataset of human gestures. In: 2019 IEEE/CVF International Conference on Computer Vision Workshop (ICCVW), pp. 2874–2882. IEEE Computer Society (2019)
19. Nguyen, N.T., Kenyon, G.T.: Image classification using quantum inference on the d-wave 2x. In: 2018 IEEE International Conference on Rebooting Computing (ICRC), pp. 1–7, November 2018. https://doi.org/10.1109/ICRC.2018.8638596
20. Niu, X.F., Ma, W.P.: A novel quantum neural network based on multi- level activation function. Laser Phys. Lett. **18**(2), 025201 (2021). https://doi.org/10.1088/1612-202X/abd23c
21. Oh, S., Choi, J., Kim, J.: A tutorial on quantum convolutional neural networks (QCNN). arXiv:2009.09423 September 2020
22. Perdomo-Ortiz, A., Benedetti, M., Realpe-Gómez, J., Biswas, R.: Opportunities and challenges for quantum-assisted machine learning in near-term quantum computers. Quantum Sci. Technol. **3**(3), 030502 (2018). https://doi.org/10.1088/2058-9565/aab859
23. Schuld, M., Sinayskiy, I., Petruccione, F.: Simulating a perceptron on a quantum computer. Phys. Lett. A **379**(7), 660–663 (2015). https://doi.org/10.1016/j.physleta.2014.11.061

24. Tacchino, F., Barkoutsos, P., Macchiavello, C., Tavernelli, I., Gerace, D., Bajoni, D.: Quantum implementation of an artificial feed-forward neural network. Quantum Sci. Technol. **5**(4), 044010 (2020). https://doi.org/10.1088/2058-9565/abb8e4
25. Tacchino, F., Barkoutsos, P.K., Macchiavello, C., Gerace, D., Tavernelli, I., Bajoni, D.: Variational learning for quantum artificial neural networks. In: 2020 IEEE International Conference on Quantum Computing and Engineering (QCE), pp. 130–136, October 2020. https://doi.org/10.1109/QCE49297.2020.00026
26. Tran, D., Wang, H., Torresani, L., Feiszli, M.: Video classification with channel-separated convolutional networks. In: Proceedings of the IEEE/CVF International Conference on Computer Vision (ICCV), October 2019
27. Ullah, A., Ahmad, J., Muhammad, K., Sajjad, M., Baik, S.W.: Action recognition in video sequences using deep bi-directional LSTM with CNN features. IEEE Access **6**, 1155–1166 (2018). https://doi.org/10.1109/ACCESS.2017.2778011
28. Wan, K.H., Dahlsten, O., Kristjánsson, H., Gardner, R., Kim, M.S.: Quantum generalisation of feedforward neural networks. npj Quantum Inf. **3**(1), 1–8 (2017). https://doi.org/10.1038/s41534-017-0032-4
29. Wu, Z., Wang, X., Jiang, Y.G., Ye, H., Xue, X.: Modeling spatial-temporal clues in a hybrid deep learning framework for video classification. In: Proceedings of the 23rd ACM International Conference on Multimedia, MM 2015, pp. 461–470. Association for Computing Machinery, New York (2015). https://doi.org/10.1145/2733373.2806222
30. Xie, S., Sun, C., Huang, J., Tu, Z., Murphy, K.: Rethinking spatiotemporal feature learning: speed-accuracy trade-offs in video classification. In: Proceedings of the European Conference on Computer Vision (ECCV), September 2018
31. Yue-Hei Ng, J., Hausknecht, M., Vijayanarasimhan, S., Vinyals, O., Monga, R., Toderici, G.: Beyond short snippets: deep networks for video classification. In: Proceedings of the IEEE Conference on Computer Vision and Pattern Recognition (CVPR), June 2015
32. Zhou, N.-R., Liu, X.-X., Chen, Y.-L., Du, N.-S.: Quantum k-nearest-neighbor image classification algorithm based on K-L transform. Int. J. Theoret. Phys. **60**(3), 1209–1224 (2021). https://doi.org/10.1007/s10773-021-04747-7
33. Zhou, R.: Quantum competitive neural network. Int. J. Theoret. Phys. **49**(1), 110 (2009). https://doi.org/10.1007/s10773-009-0183-y
34. Zhou, R., Ding, Q.: Quantum M-P neural network. Int. J. Theoret. Phys. **46**(12), 3209–3215 (2007). https://doi.org/10.1007/s10773-007-9437-8

Author Index

Printed in the United States
by Baker & Taylor Publisher Services